CONGRESS VOLUME

PARIS 1992

SUPPLEMENTS

TO

VETUS TESTAMENTUM

EDITED BY
THE BOARD OF THE QUARTERLY

J.A. EMERTON – PHYLLIS A. BIRD – W.L. HOLLADAY
A. van der KOOIJ – A. LEMAIRE – B. OTZEN – R. SMEND
J.A. SOGGIN – J.C. VANDERKAM – M. WEINFELD
H.G.M. WILLIAMSON

VOLUME LXI

CONGRESS VOLUME

PARIS
1992

EDITED BY

J.A. EMERTON

E.J. BRILL
LEIDEN · NEW YORK · KÖLN
1995

The paper in this book meets the guidelines for permanence and durability of the Committee on Production Guidelines for Book Longevity of the Council on Library Resources.

Library of Congress Cataloging-in-Publication Data

Congress volume : Paris, 1992 / edited by J.A. Emerton.
    p.   cm. — (Supplements to Vetus Testamentum, ISSN 0083-5889 ; v. 61)
    English, French, and German.
    Papers read at the Congress of the International Organization for the Study of the Old Testament, held July 19-24, 1992 in Paris.
    Includes bibliographical references.
    ISBN 9004102590
    1. Bible. O.T.—Criticism, interpretation, etc.—Congresses.
I. Emerton, John Adney. II. International Organization for the Study of the Old Testament. Congress (14th : 1992 : Paris, France)
III. Series.
BS410.V452   vol. 61
[BS1171.2]
221 s—dc20
[221.6]
                                                      95-3906
                                                      CIP

Die Deutsche Bibliothek – CIP-Einheitsaufnahme

[Vetus testamentum / Supplements]
Supplements to Vetus testamentum – Leiden ; New York ; Köln : Brill.
    Früher Schriftenreihe
    Reihe Supplements zu: Vetus Testamentum
    ISSN 0083-5889
NE: HST
Vol. 61. International Organization for the Study of the Old
    Testament: Congress volume .../ [International Organization
    for the Study of the Old Testament].
    1992. Paris. - 1995
International Organization for the Study of the Old Testament:
Congress volume .../ [International Organization for the Study
of the Old Testament]. - Leiden ; New York ; København ;
Köln : Brill.
    (Supplements to Vetus testamentum ; ...)
NE: Congress volume ...
1992, Paris 1992. - 1995
    (Supplements to Vetus testamentum ; Vol. 61)
    ISBN 90-04-10259-0

ISSN   0083-5889
ISBN   90 04 10259 0

PRINTED IN THE NETHERLANDS

CONTENTS

PREFACE

It had been hoped that the present volume would be published much earlier, but unfortunately exceptional pressure of work has caused a delay. The Congress held in Paris 19–24 July 1992 under the Presidency of Professor André Caquot, of the Collège de France, was a memorable meeting of the International Organization for the Study of the Old Testament. I am grateful to Professor André Lemaire, not only for his efficient work as Secretary of the Congress, but also for his help in editing some of the articles in French. I am also grateful to Dr J.L.W. Schaper, Fellow of Clare College, Cambridge, for allowing me to consult him on some questions concerning the German language.

J.A. Emerton

UNE CONTRIBUTION OUGARITIQUE À LA PRÉHISTOIRE DU TITRE DIVIN SHADDAY

par

ANDRÉ CAQUOT
Paris

S'il est une contribution française particulièrement méritoire à une compréhension plus appronfondie de la pensée et de la piété de l'Ancien Testament, c'est d'avoir fait découvrir aux biblistes les richesses littéraires et religieuses d'une mythologie des Sémites de l'ouest qui a jeté sur la Bible hébraïque plus d'un jour nouveau. Un congrès de notre organisation se tenant à Paris ne saurait s'offusquer de rendre hommage aux pionniers de l'ougaritologie: Claude Schaeffer, l'archéologue heureux, Edouard Dhorme et Hans Bauer, les déchiffreurs de génie, Charles Virolleaud, l'infatigable éditeur et premier traducteur, Andrée Herdner, aussi scrupuleuse que modeste dans sa belle réédition des tablettes trouvées avant la guerre, sans oublier René Dussaud qui a tant apporté à la connaissance des antiquités orientales et qui fut l'un des premiers à exposer en un volume pourquoi les découvertes de Ras Shamra intéressaient les spécialistes de l'Ancien Testament. Le thème du livre de René Dussaud paru en 1937 a été repris par des dizaines de monographies, et il est aujourd'hui peu de biblistes ignorant cette problématique. C'est pourquoi je me permets de présenter d'abord devant ce congrès une réflexion d'ordre général sur ce que peut apporter la connaissance d'une mythologie syrienne de l'âge du Bronze à celle de la religion officielle d'Israël que nous entrevoyons dans la Bible.

L'hénothéisme normatif de la Bible n'est peut-être pas postérieur à l'apparition d'Israël sur la scène de l'histoire si on met Israël au nombre de ces Etats-nations qui ont vu le jour en Syrie-Palestine au début de l'âge du Fer et si l'on pense que le culte exclusif du tétragramme est l'indice d'une religion de prime abord nationale. Il n'y a aucune raison de croire l'hénothéisme israélite postérieur à celui des Moabites, car le dieu 'Ashtarkemosh nommé à la ligne 17 de l'inscription de Mesha' n'est autre que Kemosh dont le nom est ici précédé du déterminatif divin 'Ashtar commun à plusieurs langues sémitiques. Quelle que soit l'origine d'Israël et de son Dieu, ceux qui ont parlé de l'un et de l'autre dans la Bible s'adressaient à des hommes imprégnés d'une religiosité qui venait de plus loin. Il ne s'agit pas de ce que Morton Smith a heureusement appelé "the common theology of the Ancient Near East",[1] commandé par un sentiment très général et peut-être universel de dépendance à l'égard du divin. Je parle d'une piété aussi bien collective qu'individuelle que déterminent les conditions de vie et les besoins de l'homme dans un cadre géographique donné. Ces conditions et ces besoins ne sont pas les mêmes en Egypte, en Mésopotamie et en Syrie-Palestine, même si, sur ces trois aires, les hommes ont ressenti leur dépendance à l'égard d'un monde divin multiple et organisé, au Ie millénaire et avant. Dans un système religieux polythéiste, les besoins vitaux sont satisfaits par une multitude de dieux aux fonctions spécialisées constantes et se définissant les uns par rapport aux autres. Les conflits, les contradictions qui forment la trame de l'existence sont expliqués par des rapports que les dieux nouent les uns avec les autres, de manière à garantir la continuité de la nature et de la société humaine.

Les textes de Ras Shamra sont les seuls témoins utilisables du polythéisme syrien parce qu'ils révèlent une mythologie cohérente où chacun des grands dieux et des grandes déesses trouve sa place. Ils nous permettent d'entrevoir une mentalité religieuse qui n'a pas pu ne pas survivre au Ie millénaire, jusque chez les Israélites de l'âge classique. Ils définissent de façon très claire les fonctions des divinités dont le jeu garantit l'équilibre cosmique, et au premier rang de celles-ci les dieux El et Baal. Je crois erronés les essais expliquant la présence de deux grands dieux mâles par une superposition ethnique, El étant "cananéen" et Baal "amorite", ou recourant à la phénoménologie du *deus otiosus* (El supplanté par un rival plus jeune et plus actif). Dans la théologie qu'exprime le mythe ougaritique, il y a moins conflit entre les deux grandes figures du panthéon qu'il n'y a collaboration, par répartition des tâches. Le rôle de chaque dieu se perçoit dans la physionomie qui lui est donnée. El à la chevelure blanche, trônant au milieu de ses "fils", les *bᵉnê 'él,* géniteur des dieux, créateur du monde et des hommes, sage et indulgent, est le portrait idéal du vieillard, Baal le svelte guerrier, à la barbe en pointe, armé de pied en cap et dressé pour se battre, qui combat les puissances

---

[1] Titre d'un célèbre article publié en *JBL* 71 (1952), pp. 135–47.

hostiles de la mer et de la mort ainsi que les ennemis de la cité, qui donne à la terre la pluie et la fécondité, qui pousse l'héroïsme jusqu'au don de soi en faveur des "multitudes humaines", est la perfection de l'homme jeune. Les vertus contrastées qu'incarnent les deux divinités sont nécessaires, ensemble, au bien de l'univers, mais on ne peut penser les trouver réunies en un seul être. La sagesse est en effet le privilège du vieillard comme la force celui du jeune homme. Le polythéisme donne à chacune des fonctions une figure inspirée par l'expérience humaine et la réflexion morale les plus élémentaires.

Survient la révolution hénothéiste, que certains appelleront révélation monothéiste. Le Dieu unique assume à lui seul l'ensemble des fonctions et doit cumuler, en particulier, la sagesse et la force, il est le véritable El et le véritable Baal. On a beaucoup discuté pour savoir si le Dieu unique d'Israël était une divinité du type d'El ou du type de Baal. Vaine dispute, car il en est la synthèse, puisqu'il est unique. Réunissant en lui des fonctions qu'on avait coutume de voir exercer par des âges différents, chez les dieux comme chez les hommes, le Dieu unique échappe à l'imagination visuelle. Sa représentation plastique sous forme humaine devient impossible. Mais si on peut se dispenser de le sculpter ou de le peindre, on ne peut se dispenser d'en parler, pour le prier ou le célébrer. On recourt alors aux représentations mentales imposées par l'accoutumance des esprits au polythéisme. C'est ainsi que la lyrique d'Israël—où se dévoile au mieux l'arrière-fond religieux—donne au Dieu unique les traits et les attributions de l'un ou l'autre des grands dieux du polythéisme: il est El lorsqu'on le chante, en particulier, comme créateur et souverain juge du monde, aux psaumes viii, xxiv, xxxiii, xc, xcv, xcvi, cii, cxxi, cxxxvi, cxlvi, cxlvii, cxlviii; il est Baal, maître de l'orage qui est source de vie et symbole de vaillance, quand on chante ses victoires sur les éléments et les adversaires de la nation, ainsi aux psaumes xviii, xxix, xlvi, lxv, lxxvii, lxxviii, xciii, cvi, cvii, cxliv. Il est rare que les deux images se rencontrent dans un même poème, c'est le cas au Ps. lxxiv. Il est exceptionnel que l'artiste joue sur la dualité El-Baal pour organiser son œuvre. C'est le cas du Ps. lxxxix; il serait facile de montrer que l'"hymne cosmique" des *vv.* 6–15 fait alterner l'image d'El (aux *vv.* 6–8 et 12–13) et celle de Baal (aux *vv.* 9–11 et 14–15). La persistance inévitable de représentations liées à un polythéisme antérieur à l'hénothéisme biblique est un des points qu'éclaire au mieux la comparaison entre les textes de Ras Shamra et l'Ancien Testament.

On s'est interrogé sur la pertinence de cette démarche comparative. Entre Jérusalem et Ras Shamra il y a plus de cent lieues. Entre le temps de gravure des tablettes ougaritiques et l'âge présumé des plus vieux textes bibliques il y a au moins trois siècles et l'un des bouleversements les plus profonds qu'ait connus l'ancien monde, celui qui sépare l'âge du Fer de l'âge du Bronze. A-t-on le droit de franchir ces distances et de privilégier Ras Shamra quand on cherche les racines des idées et des pratiques religieuses de l'ancien Israël? De surcroît, ne serait-il pas *methodisch falsch* de vouloir interpréter la Bible par recours à des textes qui ont été en grande partie déchiffrés grâce à elle? On répondra que ce n'est pas tant l'hébreu de la Bible qui donne les clés de l'ougaritique, c'est le sémitique en général, et que des objections de pure théorie n'invalideront pas les résultats souvent heureux de soixante ans d'efforts, car il y a bien soixante ans que s'est institué entre les ougaritologues et les spécialistes de l'Ancien Testament un échange continu d'informations et de réflexions. Il importe de le poursuivre dès qu'une donnée nouvelle apparaît. C'est le propos que voudrait illustrer la communication que j'ai maintenant l'honneur de vous présenter.

*
* *

En juin dernier, la mission archéologique franco-syrienne de Ras Shamra, que dirige Mme Marguerite Yon a obtenu quelques résultats laissant présager de futures découvertes, en particulier au sud-est du tell. On a retrouvé les traces d'une large voie d'accès qui devait mener de ce côté-là à la grande porte de la ville, et près de cette voie, les restes d'une grande construction aux murs épais. Un fragment de tablette lexicographique annonce qu'il doit y avoir là un gisement de textes. En outre, reprenant l'examen du déblai qui a déjà fourni, en 1973, des tablettes du plus haut intérêt, la mission franco-syrienne en a extrait quelques nouveaux fragments épigraphiques, ougaritiques et accadiens. Parmi les premiers se trouvent une brève conjuration contre les morsures de serpent et de scorpion et le curieux document dont je vais vous entretenir. Il s'agit de la partie droite d'une tablette gravée des deux côtés qui a reçu la cote RS 92.2016. Elle n'est pas encore nettoyée. Cependant, les épigraphistes de la mission, MM. Pierre Bordreuil et Dennis Pardee, en ont procuré une lecture provisoire, certaine sur plus d'un point. On reconnaît l'écriture très fine du maître scribe Ilumilku, le rédacteur des grands textes mythologiques découverts autour de 1930, et c'est certainement de lui que parle le colophon en partie conservé du nouveau document. La tablette est trop mutilée pour qu'on puisse espérer parvenir à une traduction suivie. On reconnaît cependant au début les restes d'un "signalement lyrique", portrait de quelque belle personne, et vers la fin un dialogue entre le dieu Ḥoron et une "reine" au titre mystérieux. On peut imaginer un récit de théogamie à l'analogie de la grande tablette *KTU* 1.100 où intervient aussi le dieu Ḥoron. Vers le haut, après le signalement lyrique, il est question de plusieurs "astres" (*kbkb*) dont on dit, semble-t-il, qu'ils se sont dépêchés, si l'on traduit bien le verbe *aṣ*, nouveau à Ougarit. Le nom *kbkb*, "astre", paraît avoir été suivi chaque fois de noms de divinités groupées deux par deux: on reconnaît ainsi *bʿl wpdry* (Pidray fille de Baal). On se demandera donc si le nom "astre" ne sert pas en ce contexte de déterminatif des théonymes, comme bien souvent le nom *il*, à l'instar peut-être de l'idéogramme DINGIR du cunéiforme accadien. La ligne 11' de la tablette présente un nom divin double jusqu'ici inconnu, *ydd wšd*, précédé de *kbkb*, "astre".

Les noms divins doubles, bien connus dans les religions sémitiques, témoignent soit d'un lien généalogique établi entre les deux divinités composantes, soit d'une affinité fonctionnelle,[2] si bien que le deuxième élément peut passer pour une épithète du premier comme c'est le cas pour *ktr (w)ḥss*. Dans le nom *ydd wšd* le premier élément est connu depuis longtemps en ougaritique. On l'a toujours interprété par l'hébreu *yādîd*, "favori, bien-aimé". C'est un titre donné étrangement au personnage de Mot qui figure la mort dans le grand mythe de Baal, mais ne fait point partie du panthéon ougaritique. Pour l'expliquer ici, on pensera plus volontiers à une représentation divine populaire dans l'antiquité méditerranéenne et proche-orientale, le jeune dieu cher aux femmes qu'on a appelé Tammuz, Adonis et auquel la Bible fait quelques allusions reconnues par Heinrich Ewald[3] et même par Wilhelm von Baudissin[4] si volontiers sceptique: la référence d'Isa. xvii 10 aux *niṭʿé naʿămānîm* et celle de Daniel xi 37 à la *ḥemdat nāšîm*. Le second terme de notre théonyme double, *šd*,

---

[2] Voir P. Xella, "« Divinités doubles » dans le monde phénico-punique", *Semitica* 39 (1990), pp. 167–75.

[3] *Die Propheten*[2] III (Leipzig, 1868), p. 463.

[4] Voir *Adonis und Esmun* (Leipzig, 1911), pp. 87–8, sur Isa, xvii 10.

vient confirmer l'indication d'un fragment de Ras Ibn Hani (77/8 A) où se lit *šd qdš*,[5] Le nom *šd* en ce contexte mutilé présente une équivoque. En effet, *šd* peut être le correspondant ougaritique de l'hébreu *śādeh*, "champ", ainsi quand les rituels font mention d'une *'ṭtrt šd* on ne doit pas hésiter à y reconnaître une "Ashtart de la campagne", équivalent de l'*Ishtar ṣeri* d'une lettre accadienne d'Ougarit.[6] Les éditeurs du fragment de Ras Ibn Hani avaient traduit "*šd* le saint", parce que ces mots paraissent venir en parallèle à des théonymes, mais cette interprétation était des plus hypothétiques. La nouvelle occurrence de *šd*, pour laquelle la traduction "champ" ou "campagne" est exclue, montre que les Ougaritains ont connu un dieu *šd* qui n'a laissé chez les Sémites de l'ouest que des traces sporadiques.

Il est certainement impossible de le séparer du *šedu* des Mésopotamiens connu comme une puissance protectrice, un génie,[7] où Alexandre Oppenheim[8] a voulu voir une forme de l'"âme extérieure". La puissance du *šedu* n'est pas toujours bénéfique. A côté du *šedu damqu*, le "bon" *šd*, on a un *šedu lemmu*, le "mauvais" *šd*, et c'est ce dernier aspect qui a fini par l'emporter en Mésopotamie, par un processus analogue à celui qui a fait du *deva* aryen le *daeva* démoniaque de l'Iran. Si en accadien *šedu* paraît aussi imprécis que *ilu*, l'Egypte aide à cerner les traits du *šd* des Sémites occidentaux. En 1931, l'égyptologue Georges Loukianoff[9] a rassemblé les monuments, remontant jusqu'à la XVIIIe dynastie, d'un dieu-enfant appelé *šd* et accompagné d'animaux dangereux. L'origine sémitique de *šd* est suggérée par le protome de gazelle qui orne son bandeau frontal, ornement attribué aussi par les Egyptiens au dieu sémitique Reshep, ainsi qu'à Ḥoron auquel *šd* a été du reste associé. Le nom *šd* fait sens en égyptien: il signifie "le sauveur" et apparaît comme titre de l'enfant Horus, très populaire à la basse époque, que de nombreuses stèles représentent foulant aux pieds des crocodiles. C'est pourquoi Bernard Bruyère[10] a soutenu que le *šd* des monuments anciens avec son protome de

---

[5] Publiée par P. Bordreuil et A. Caquot, *Syria* 56 (1979), p. 303.

[6] RS 17.352 (*PRU* IV, p. 121).

[7] Voir W. von Soden, "Die Schutzgenien *lamassu* und *schedu* in der babylonisch-assyrischen Literatur", *Bagdader Mitteilungen* 3 (1964), pp. 140–56.

[8] *Ancient Mesopotamia* (Chicago, 1964), pp. 199 sq.

[9] "Le dieu Ched. L'évolution de son culte dans l'ancienne Egypte", *Bulletin de l'Institut d'Egypte* 13 (1930–1), pp. 67–84.

[10] "Sur le dieu Ched. A propos de quelques monuments nouveaux trouvés à Deir

gazelle n'était autre qu'un "Horus sauveur" sémitisé. L'attestation, maintenant confirmée, du dieu *šd* dans la Syrie du IIe millénaire corrobore, me semble-t-il, l'idée de Loukianoff. La jeunesse du dieu égyptien illustre peut-être ce qu'implique l'association du *šd* ougaritique à un "Bien-aimé".

Au Ier millénaire, les traces de *šd* sont un peu plus nettes. Il y a un témoignage onomastique de son culte dans le nom de personne *gršd*—la lecture est assurée—gravé sur un sceau phénicien du VIe siècle.[11] Mais on discerne surtout la popularité de *šd* dans la vaste diffusion du culte de Shadrafa, vocalisation conventionnelle et sûrement erronée d'un syntagme sémitique signifiant "*šd* guérisseur".[12] La graphie phénicienne présente toujours comme lettre finale un *alef* qui ne peut être que la 3e radicale du verbe *rp'*, "guérir", et non une *mater lectionis*. C'est pourquoi on refusera de voir en Shadrapha une transcription sémitique de nom iranien connu en grec sous la forme σατράπης, bien que la version araméenne de la trilingue de Xanthos, faisant correspondre à la désignation d'Apollon le terme iranien *ḫštrpty*, "maître du pouvoir royal", ait remis en honneur cette ancienne hypothèse sur l'origine de Shadrapha.[13] Ce nom n'a rien d'iranien et apparaît bien acclimaté sur des aires encore éloignées de l'influence iranienne. En Phénicie propre, il est attesté dès le VIe siècle par la célèbre stèle d'Amrit qui le montre en maître des lions,[14] on trouve son nom un peu plus tard à Sarepta.[15] Dans les colonies d'occident, les témoignages sur Shadrafa se sont multipliés: à Carthage même (*KAI* 77), en Tripolitaine où une bilingue de Leptis Magna (*KAI* 127) l'assimilant au Liber Pater latin identique à Dionysos suggère une fois de plus une figure divine juvénile, en Sardaigne à Antas,[16]

---

el Medineh en 1939", *Rapports sur les fouilles de Deir el Medineh* III (Le Caire, 1952), pp. 138–70.

[11] Voir P. Bordreuil, *Catalogue des sceaux ouest-sémitiques inscrits de la Bibliothèque Nationale du Musée du Louvre et du Musée biblique de Bible et Terre Sainte* (Paris, 1986), p. 36.

[12] Voir A. Caquot, "Chadrapha. A propos de quelques articles récents", *Syria* 29 (1952), pp. 74–88; P. Xella, "Sulla più antica storia di alcune divinità fenicie", *Atti del I Congresso Internazionale di Studi Fenici e Punici* II (Rome, 1983), pp. 405–7.

[13] L'origine iranienne de "Shadrapha" a été soutenue par A. Dupont-Sommer, "L'énigme du dieu « Satrape » et le dieu Mithra", *CRAI* 1976, pp. 648–60, suivi par J. Teixidor, *Syria* 52 (1975), p. 289, et *The Pantheon of Palmyra* (Leyde, 1979), pp. 101–6.

[14] Voir J. Starcky, "Autour d'une dédicace palmyrénienne à *Šadrafa* et à *Du'anat*", *Syria* 36 (1949), pp. 43–85.

[15] J. Teixidor dans J.B. Pritchard, *Sarepta* (Philadelphie, 1975), p. 100.

[16] M. Fantar, *Ricerche puniche ad Antas* (Rome, 1969), p. 81.

en Sicile parmi les graffiti de la Grotta Regina.[17] En Orient son culte
apparaît dans ce conservatoire des cultes sémitiques que révèle l'épi-
graphie palmyrénienne, grâce à trois inscriptions araméennes et à
une série de tessères.[18] Les attributions de Shadrafa y sont précisées
par une iconographie associant son nom à des serpents et à des scor-
pions, tandis qu'une mention conjointe de Shadrafa et de Du 'Anat—
qui est Aphlad = *Apil Addu*, le fils d'Adad—indique encore une fois
un jeune dieu. L'ultime référence est une conjuration araméenne sur
coupe où *šdrps* est donné comme l'un des "anges qui apportent la
guérison à tous les humains".[19]

Le nom *šdrp'* rend explicite une fonction attribuée au *šd* des Sémites de l'ouest, celle de guérisseur. Cette attribution fait corps avec
les représentations et associations juvéniles car c'est aux dieux jeunes
qu'il appartient d'incarner la vie renaissante qui recrée la santé. Les
inscriptions de Deir 'Alla suggèrent que *šd* a dû avoir un pouvoir
fécondateur. Le dieu y apparaît comme démultiplié en *šdyn*, c'est-à-
dire en êtres appartenant à *šd* ou dépendant de lui, car le *yod* n'est
pas une *mater lectionis* pour la désinence du pluriel, mais un suffixe de
dérivation. La sombre prophétie du Balaam de Deir 'Alla montre les
šdyn ordonnant la fermeture des cieux (Groupement I, lignes 5–6).
La calamité signifiée de la sorte est la sécheresse et la disette. C'est
donc que les *šdyn* ont une autorité sur ce qui assure la fertilité. Le
texte de Deir 'Alla est intéressant à un autre titre. Les interprètes
s'accordent maintenant à penser qu'aux lignes 5–6 du morceau principal, le nom *šdyn* est en parallèle à *'lhn*, "les dieux". On est tenté de
voir en *šdyn* une épithète des "dieux" et on la rend souvent par
"puissants" en vertu de la traduction conventionnelle de l'hébreu
šadday. Une autre solution peut être envisagée: de même que les
gens d'Ougarit distinguaient deux catégories d'êtres divins, les *ilm* et
les *ilnym*, sans que nous saisissions ce qui les séparait, de même l'auteur
des textes de Deir 'Alla reconnaissait l'existence côte à côte de "dieux"
'lhn, et d'entités appartenant à *šd*, de l'ordre de *šd* ou de la nature
de *šd*, les *šdyn*. C'est probablement cette classe d'êtres supérieurs qui
apparaît dans une dédicace palmyrénienne aux *šdy'* qualifiés, semble-t-il, de "bons dieux".[20] On a interprété ce nom comme pluriel

---

[17] G. Coacci-Polselli, M. Guzzo Amadasi, V. Tusa, *Grotta Regina II, Studi Semitici*
52 (Rome, 1979), pp. 25 (n. 1), 64 et 93 sq.
[18] Voir Starcky, art. cité à la n. 14.
[19] J.A. Montgomery, *Aramaic Incantation Texts from Nippur* (Philadelphie, 1913), p. 207.
[20] J. Cantineau, "Tadmorea", *Syria* 12 (1931), pp. 130–2.

araméen, à l'état emphatique, du babylonien *šèdu* dont on connaît l'évolution sémantique vers l'acception "méchant démon". L'association que cette inscription opère entre les *šdyʾ* et le dieu Bolastor, inconnu en dehors de Palmyre et appartenant sûrement à la couche la plus ancienne du panthéon local, suggère bien plutôt que les *šdyʾ* sont des figures anciennes du monde religieux de Palmyre.

La mise en parallèle à Deir ʿAlla des *ʾlhn* et des *šdyn* a été récemment rapprochée par M. Matthias Delcor[21] du verset du "cantique de Moïse" (Dt. xxxii 17) *yizbᵉḥû laššédîm lōʾ ʾĕlōah ʾĕlōhîm lōʾ yᵉdāʿûm*, "ils sacrifiaient à des *šédîm* qui ne sont pas Dieu, à des dieux qu'ils ne connaissaient pas". M. Delcor estime à bon droit que dans ce verset du Deutéronome et en Ps. cvi 37 le nom *šédîm* n'a pas encore la connotation défavorable du français "démon", acception qu'il prend à Qoumran[22] et en hébreu mishnique et que suppose déjà la version grecque de Ps. xci 6 lisant au lieu de *yāšûd ṣohŏrayim* "(qui) sévit à midi" *wešéd ṣohŏrayim* ce qui a donné naissance au fameux "démon de midi". Il n'est pas sûr que l'Ancien Testament ait cru comme le traducteur grec de Ps. xcvi 5 que πάντες οἱ θεοὶ τῶν ἐθνῶν δαιμόνια. Au regard de l'hénothéisme biblique les dieux des nations, les faux dieux ne sont capables de rien, pas même de tourmenter les individus, ce qui est l'exercice habituel des "démons". Si *šédîm* a pris ce sens en hébreu, c'est plutôt sous l'influence du babylonien *šedu* qu'en vertu d'une évolution interne dans le sémitique occidental. Même si c'est pour dénoncer l'inanité de la croyance des gentils le verset du Deutéronome en conserve le souvenir sur un point précis: cette croyance reconnaissait deux classes d'êtres divins, les *ʾĕlōhîm* et les *šédîm*, les derniers ainsi nommés parce qu'ils participent à la nature et aux fonctions du dieu *šd*. L'hébreu *šédîm* est ici soit le pluriel de l'ancien nom divin, soit, comme le pense M. Delcor, la vocalisation tendancieuse d'un nom correspondant aux *šdyn* de Deir ʿAlla qu'on aurait voulu à un moment de la transmission transformer en celui de démons.

Le nom des *šédîm*, et celui du dieu *šd* ne cessent pas de tracasser les étymologistes. Les anciens l'expliquaient par *šōd*, "dévastation": *šédîm šeyāšûdû haddaʿat* écrit Abraham Ibn Ezra sur Ps. cvi 37. Les modernes ont multiplié les conjectures, sur la base de rapprochements

---

[21] "Des inscriptions de Deir ʿAlla aux traditions bibliques. A propos des *šdyn*, des *šedim* et de *šadday*", dans M. Görg, *Die Väter Israels* (Stuttgart, 1989), pp. 33–40.

[22] 1QH, fg. 5, 6 et 9, 3; 11Q Ps Apᵃ 1, 3.4.

aventureux, avec l'arabe *'aswad*, "noir", ou l'arabe *sayyid*, "seigneur",
pour ne point parler d'une explication par *śādeh*, "champ", qui ins-
pirait les "Feldgeister" de Luther et les "agrestes" de Dom Calmet.
Il y a plus de cent ans que von Baudissin[23] a repoussé ces tentatives
et a reconnu dans *šd* un de ces noms primaires qui résistent à l'analyse étymologique tout autant que le nom *'l* désignant un principe
divin. Le même scepticisme s'imposerait à l'égard du nom *šadday*
donné 31 fois comme titre au Dieu d'Israël. Il a découragé lui aussi
les recherches étymologiques. La version qui a prévalu, le "Tout-
Puissant" (procédant de l'*omnipotens* de St Jérôme, du παντοκράτωρ
des Septante), est elle-même difficile à expliquer. Elle ne peut guère
se recommander d'une racine *šdd*, qui en hébreu dénote la violence
et non la puissance. On comprend que le targoum samaritain récent
et, parfois, Sa'adya aient traduit par "puissant", car l'un et l'autre
ont dû avoir à l'esprit l'arabe *šadīd*, "fort" (en bonne part). Mais est-
ce possible pour la Septante et la Vulgate? Je me demande si la traduction "tout puissant" ne procède pas de l'interprétation devenue
classique par le notarikon *ša-dday* paraphrasé dans le midrash "celui
qui suffit",[24] "celui qui se suffit"[25] ou "celui qui dit 'assez'!",[26] interprétation qui sous-tend certainement le ἱκανός d'Aquila ou le *kāfī* de
Sa'adya. Les exégètes ne se sont pas contentés de ce jeu de mots et
ont envisagé diverses explications qui ne sont guère plus probables.
Certains ont pensé à un dérivé de *śādeh*, "champ",[27] rejoignant l'opinion du targoum samaritain de Nb. xxiv 4 et 16, d'autres plus nombreux, suivent Friedrich Delitzsch[28] et voient en *šadday* un dérivé de
l'accadien *šadû* "montagne". L'hypothèse la plus vraisemblable serait
de le rattacher au nom *šd*, ce qu'avait envisagé Theodor Nöldeke,
proposant comme forme originale *šédî* "mon *šd*".[29] Le schème de

---

[23] "Die Anschauung des A.T. von den Göttern des Heidentums", *Studien zur semitischen Religionsgeschichte* (Leipzig, 1876), pp. 130–6.

[24] Bere'shit Rabba XLVI 3: Dieu dit à Abraham: "il te suffit que je sois ton Dieu".

[25] Ibid.: "Je suis celui dont la divinité ne trouve rien digne d'elle en ce monde et tout ce qu'il contient" (dict de R. Eliezer b. Yaqob).

[26] Ibid.: "Je suis celui qui a dit au monde: c'est assez" (pour en fixer les limites), dict de R. Isaac (le Forgeron).

[27] Ainsi M. Weippert "Erwägungen zur Etymologie des Gottesnamens *'Ēl Šaddaj*", *ZDMG* NF 111 (1961), pp. 49–62; W. Wifall, "El Shadday or El of the Fields", *ZAW* 92 (1980), pp. 26–32; O. Loretz, "Die kanaanäische Ursprung des biblischen Gottesnamen El šadday", *UF* 12 (1980), pp. 420–1; E.A. Knauf "El šadday der Gott Abrahams", *BZ* NF 29 (1985), pp. 97–103.

[28] *Prolegomena eines neuen hebräisch-aramäischen Wörterbuchs zum AT* (Leipzig, 1886), p. 95.

[29] D'après W.W. von Baudissin, *Kyrios* II (Leipzig, 1929), p. 42, n. 2. Baudissin

šadday fait de toute manière difficulté. La gémination du *d*, attestée par la Septante d'Ezéch, x 5 provient-elle déjà du notarikon *ša-dday* ou reflète-t-elle une prononciation affective, emphatique, du titre divin conformément à un schème hypocoristique de nom de personne?

Ce qui invite à reprendre l'hypothèse voyant en *šadday* un dérivé de *šd* ou de *šdy*, "ce qui est de la nature de *šd*", c'est moins la spéculation étymologique que les informations données par la Bible elle-même sur *šadday*. Titre divin, il vient naturellement équilibrer l'appellatif *'él* ou un autre titre de Dieu d'un hémistiche parallèle, c'est le cas en Nb. xxiv 4 et 16, en Ps. xci 1 et dans la plupart des occurrences du livre de Job. On ne peut rien en conclure sur la nature et les attributions de *šadday*; on trouvera seulement ici le souvenir de la dualité *'l-šd* qui a signifié, comme nous l'avons vu, la totalité du monde divin. Il est plus instructif de regarder les quelques passages où *šadday*, précédé ou non du déterminatif *'él*, n'a point de parallèle désignant la divinité par l'une de ses appellations habituelles. Comme l'a bien relevé M. Klaus Koch,[30] le *'él šadday* cher à la tradition sacerdotale de la Genèse est le Dieu qui promet la fécondité humaine, la prolifération (Gn. xvii 1–2, xxviii 3, xxxv 11, xlviii 3). C'est déjà le cas de la bénédiction de Jacob sur Joseph en Gn. xlix 25 *we'ét šadday wîbār°kekkā*, "quant à Shadday il te bénira". D'autres passages indiqueraient une autre physionomie de Shadday, une autre activité. Ezéchiel (i 24) compare la voix ou le bruit de Shadday à celui d'une tempête, Isaïe (xiii 6) et Joël (i 15) en font un dévastateur, dans la ligne peut-être de Ps. lxviii 15 qui appelle Shadday celui qui disperse l'ennemi. Rassemblons ces traits. Shadday est une puissance de bénédiction et de vie, il rejoint ainsi ce qu'on peut entrevoir du *šd* des anciens sémites occidentaux. Mais Shadday est aussi un dieu de l'orage et de la guerre, ce que nos informations épigraphiques ne laissent pas entrevoir pour *šd*. On pourrait toutefois tenir compte de l'attitude de vaillance que donne à Shadrafa la stèle d'Amrit et de l'accoutrement militaire qu'il revêt sur un relief palmyrénien. Les détails convergent pour montrer en Shadday et en *šd* son ancêtre une divinité du type de Baal si l'on se rapporte à la grande dichotomie opérée parmi les dieux dans le polythéisme syrien et dont l'Ancien

---

lui-même concluait (*Kyrios* III, p. 132): "Die Bedeutung dieses Namens ist fur uns ganz unklar".

[30] "Šadday. Zum Verhältnis zwischen israelitischer Monolatrie und nordwestsemitischen Polytheismus", *VT* 26 (1976), pp. 299–332.

Testament révèle plus d'une trace quand il évoque les figures du
Dieu unique.[31] Malgré le laconisme de nos informations sur *šd*, les
šdyn et les *šédîm* non encore démonisés, on supposera que les divinités de ce groupe ont été dans une couche ancienne du paganisme
sémitique des puissances de vie, de fécondité, de force et de victoire,
fonctions que les mythes de Ras Shamra font assumer par Baal. En
regard de *šd* et de ses dérivés, l'élément lexicographique *'l* qui fournit le déterminatif le plus employé pour ce qui est divin, est la base
d'un autre théonyme, pour un dieu ou un groupe de dieux présidant
de plus haut à l'ordre du monde, mais non moins nécessaires et non
moins estimés des humains.

En établissant de façon définitive que les Ougaritains ont connu
un dieu *šd*, la tablette Ras Shamra 92.2016 exhumée en juin 1992,
nous a invités à voir sous un aspect particulier et—je crois—nouveau
l'apport des textes ougaritiques à l'étude des religions sémitiques
anciennes, si pauvrement documentées, et à celle de l'Ancien Testament qui en est solidaire. L'étude de l'Ancien Testament que nous
avons charge de promouvoir ne peut se dispenser de veiller à ce qui
sort de la terre syrienne, tout en espérant que le tell de Ras Shamra
et d'autres apporteront un jour des centaines d'informations nouvelles et permettront de mieux pénétrer la pensée des auteurs bibliques.
Car ce qui vient de l'ancien Orient n'est pas affaire de littérature
pure, de rhétorique ou de poétique. Ce que nous recevons et atten-
dons, ce sont des témoignages sur une mentalité religieuse forgée
dans des millénaires de polythéisme et qui a légué au Dieu unique
les composants de sa complexité. En un temps où l'on se préoccupe
beaucoup et avec raison de la "réception" de la Bible, il importe de
demeurer attentif à ces données de l'archéologie qui en éclairent la
production et font découvrir ce que nous devons à des expériences
religieuses venues du fond des âges.

---

[31] Le théonyme *'él šadday* fait qu'on a voulu mettre *šadday* dans la mouvance du
dieu El (ainsi J. Heller, "Die Entmythisierung des ugaritischen Pantheon im AT",
ThLZ 101 [1976], col. 1–10). Mais *'él* est ici un déterminatif de nom divin et non
pas un nom divin de plein exercice.

DU MESSAGE AU MESSAGER.
REMARQUES SUR 1 ROIS XIII

par

J. BRIEND
Paris

Il peut paraître téméraire de revenir une fois de plus sur le texte de 1 Rois xiii qui a fait l'objet de si nombreuses études depuis plusieurs années. A vrai dire, notre but n'est pas de présenter un commentaire exhaustif de ce passage bien connu, mais de proposer quelques remarques sur des points débattus.

La structuration du texte

Les commentateurs de 1 Rois xiii[1] discutent pour savoir si le texte comporte un ou deux récits prophétiques. La lecture du texte dans sa forme actuelle montre qu'il y a deux unités littéraires dont la seconde est en étroite dépendance avec la première si bien qu'on peut parler d'un texte unifié, abstraction faite de l'histoire de la tradition et de la rédaction.

La première unité va du *v.* 1 au *v.* 10. Du point de vue des personnages il est question d'un homme de Dieu (*vv.* 1, 4, 5, 6, 7, 8) et d'un roi (*vv.* 4a, 6, 6, 7, 8). Celui-ci est appelé Jéroboam aux *vv.* 1 et 4aβ. Après le *v.* 10 le roi n'est plus mentionné si ce n'est dans une incise que l'on trouve au *v.* 11 ("toutes les paroles qu'il avait parlées au roi"). C'est là un premier indice de l'indépendance relative du récit.

Du point de vue géographique on observe qu'entre le *v.* 1 et le *v.* 10 le nom de lieu Béthel fait inclusion comme le montre la comparaison entre les deux versets:

---

[1] Les principaux commentaires consultés ont été les suivants: Martin Noth, *Könige. I. Könige 1–16* (Neukirchen-Vluyn, 1968); John Gray, *I and II Kings* (Londres, 1970²); Ernst Würthwein, *Die Bücher der Könige. 1. Könige 1–16* (Göttingen, 1977); Martin Rehm, *Das erste Buch der Könige* (Würzburg, 1979); Georg Hentschel, *1 Könige* (Würzburg, 1984); Burke O. Long, *1 Kings with an Introduction to Historical Literature* (Grand Rapids, 1984); Simon J. De Vries, *1 Kings* (Waco, 1985). Dans la suite de l'article ces commentaires seront cités avec le nom de leur auteur et la page.

- *v.* 1: "et voici qu'un homme de Dieu vint de Juda . . . à BETHEL,"
- *v.* 10: "et il s'en alla par un autre chemin et il ne revint pas par le chemin par lequel il était venu à BETHEL."

Certes le nom de lieu revient au *v.* 4, mais pour préciser que l'homme de Dieu avait parlé "contre l'autel à Béthel". Par ailleurs le *v.* 10 constitue une formule de conclusion narrative et le texte pourrait s'arrêter là.

Enfin le mot-clé des *vv.* 1–10 est le terme "autel" qui revient dix fois alors qu'on ne le rencontre qu'une fois (*v.* 32a) en xiii 11–32.

Dans la seconde partie du texte on retrouve le même fonctionnement du code géographique. En effet le nom de Béthel opère une inclusion entre le *v.* 11 et le *v.* 32a:

- *v.* 11: "Un certain vieux prophète habitait à BETHEL . . ."
- *v.* 32a: "car elle arrivera sûrement la parole qu'il a proclamée . . . contre l'autel qui est à BETHEL".

Cette inclusion, sans doute calquée sur celle de la première partie, pose la question de la fonction des *vv.* 32b–34 sur laquelle il nous faudra revenir.

Du point de vue des personnages la seconde partie en introduit un nouveau, le "vieux prophète" (*vv.* 11, 25, 29) ou, simplement, le prophète (*vv.* 18, 20, 23, 26, 29). Les autres acteurs humains du récit n'ont qu'un rôle accessoire, qu'il s'agisse du ou des fils du prophète (*vv.* 11–13, 31) ou encore des passants (*v.* 25). Plus décisif pour le programme narratif et la nature du passage est la présence d'animaux, le lion et l'âne, qui jouent un rôle important. Observons enfin que toute l'action du vieux prophète est commandée par la présence de l'homme de Dieu:

- dès le *v.* 11 le vieux prophète enquête sur ce qu'a fait et a dit l'homme de Dieu à Béthel;
- cet homme de Dieu qui est venu de Juda (*vv.* 12, 14) le vieux prophète entreprend de le retrouver et de le faire venir chez lui pour manger et pour boire;
- à la suite de ce qui apparaît comme une désobéissance, l'homme de Dieu devient un cadavre gisant sur le chemin (*vv.* 24, 25, 28);
- ce cadavre devient ossements au *v.* 31.

Ainsi les *vv.* 11–32a représentent un élargissement du premier récit prophétique et n'a de sens que par rapport à celui-ci. Un des mot-clés qui relie la seconde partie à la première est celui d'ossements qui se trouve au *v.* 2b et au *v.* 31.

L'interprétation du texte doit tenir compte de ces premières observations pour découvrir la logique narrative de l'ensemble.

Un récit encadré

Le texte de 1 Rois xiii 1–32a se présente comme un récit encadré. En effet en xiii 1 le texte s'ouvre par un *vaw* qui relie le *v.* 1 à ce qui précède, donc à 1 Rois xii 33. Comme l'a montré par exemple Walter Dietrich,[2] xii 33 est la reprise de xii 32 avec modification de l'ordre des propositions et quelques précisions supplémentaires. Les derniers mots du *v.* 33: "et il (= le roi) monta à l'autel pour y faire fumer" ont pour fonction de préparer le récit qui va suivre, car on les retrouve en xiii 1b: "et Jéroboam se tenait (*'md*) sur l'autel pour y faire fumer". Le *v.* 33 permet au lecteur de passer de la fabrication des statues de veau (xii 26–32) à l'autel qu'il avait fait à Béthel, renforçant ainsi la condamnation de Jéroboam. L'insertion du récit de 1 Rois xiii dans le règne de Jéroboam I lève l'anonymat du roi dans le récit primitif. La mention de Jéroboam aux *vv.* 1b et 4a est due au rédacteur qui opère l'insertion. A ce rédacteur on doit donc xii 33 et xiii 1b et la mention de Jéroboam au *v.* 4.

A l'autre bout du texte il faut examiner les *vv.* 32b–34. Le *v.* 32b qui est en dehors de l'inclusion établie entre le *v.* 11 et le *v.* 32a est une reprise, adaptée au contexte, de 2 Rois xxiii 19a par le rédacteur qui a inséré le récit à sa place actuelle. Le texte est ainsi relié au règne de Josias et donc à 2 Rois xxiii 16–20.

Le *v.* 33 est une conclusion généralisante et polémique à l'égard de Jéroboam due au rédacteur du *v.* 32b selon toute probabilité. Le mot *dābār* au début du *v.* 33 désigne l'affaire de l'autel rapportée dans le ch. xiii. L'expression "il ne revint pas de sa mauvaise conduite" est sans doute dtr en se souvenant que dans la suite du livre des Rois Jéroboam est pris comme référence et que les textes évoquent "la conduite (*drk*) de Jéroboam".[3] Le *v.* 33b pour sa part s'inspire de 1 Rois xii 31a avec l'expression "pris parmi des gens de

---

[2] *Prophetie und Geschichte* (Göttingen, 1972), p. 115; Erik Eynikel, "Prophecy and Fulfillment in the deuteronomistic History 1 Kgs 13; 2 Kgs 23, 16–18", dans C. Brekelmans et J. Lust (éd.), *Pentateuchal and Deuteronomistic Studies* (Leuven, 1990), p. 229.

[3] "Le chemin de Jéroboam": 1 Rois xv 34; cf. xv 26, xvi 2, 19, 26, xxii 53.

toutes sortes" et de xii 32b avec la mention des "prêtres des hauts lieux". La suite du *v.* 33b s'en tient à la question du sacerdoce et utilise l'expression technique "remplir la main" (*millé' yād*) pour désigner l'investiture,[4] Autrement dit, le *v.* 33 use du procédé utilisé en 1 Rois xii 33, celui de la reprise. On peut donc attribuer les *vv.* 32b–33 à un même rédacteur.

Le *v.* 34 offre une autre formule de jugement à l'égard de Jéroboam et de sa maison; c'est une sorte de doublet du *v.* 33, mais sa formulation est originale. Nous proposons d'y voir la conclusion du récit sur la fabrication des deux statues, conclusion repoussée lors de l'insertion de 1 Rois xiii 1–33. En effet le mot *dābār*, surtout après le *v.* 33, ne peut désigner l'affaire de l'autel, mais bien l'affaire des statues.[5] D'autres indices vont dans ce sens pour ce verset qu'on peut traduire ainsi: "Cette affaire conduisit au péché la maison de Jéroboam, à ce qu'elle soit détruite et exterminée de dessus la face du sol." Les premiers mots du verset ("et cette affaire fut à péché") se trouvent déjà en 1 Rois xii 30a et y représentent sans doute une glose mal placée à une époque ancienne. La suite du verset comporte une formulation assez rare et ne trouve de véritable parallèle qu'en Ruth iv 15.[6] Même l'expression "de dessus la face du sol" avec un verbe qui annonce un châtiment n'est pas très caractéristique.[7] Par contre le *v.* 34 comporte un jugement relatif à la maison de Jéroboam, expression étonnante comme le notait M. Noth.[8] La relation entre le péché et le jugement est limitée dans le temps, à moins de donner à "maison de Jéroboam" un sens élargi.

En conclusion, le *v.* 34 avec sa formulation originale pourrait bien être la conclusion primitive de 1 Rois xii, mais déplacée lors de l'insertion du ch. xiii.

L'encadrement du récit prophétique semble bien indiquer que le rédacteur insère un récit préexistant qui avait déjà sa structure littéraire propre.

---

[4] "Remplir la main": l'expression se rencontre en Jg. xvii 5, 12 et en dehors de 1 Rois xiii elle est fréquente dans les textes sacerdotaux (Ex. xxviii 41, xxix 9, 29, 33, 35; Lv. viii 33, xvi 32, xxi 10; Nb. iii 3). Le rédacteur a un grand souci de la pureté du sacerdoce israélite, autre indice qui révèle les préoccupations de la période post-exilique. Sur l'expression, voir Rehm, p. 145.

[5] Gottfried Vanoni, *Literarkritik und Grammatik. Untersuchung der Wiederholungen und Spannungen in 1 Kön 11–12* (St Ottilien, 1984), p. 85.

[6] Vanoni (n. 5), p. 122 s.

[7] L'expression se rencontre en Dt. vi 15; 1 Sam xx 15; 1 Rois ix 7, xiii 34; So. i. 3.

[8] Noth, p. 305, observait avec raison que la mention "maison de Jéroboam" dis-

Le contenu de l'oracle

Dans la première partie du récit (xiii 1–10) se rencontrent successivement trois éléments plus ou moins bien reliés l'un à l'autre: un oracle proféré par un homme de Dieu (*v.* 2), un présage (*vv.* 3, 5) et l'intervention d'un roi (*vv.* 4, 6–9). La principale difficulté du texte dont la solution commande l'interprétation de l'ensemble est de savoir ce qui constitue le contenu de l'oracle. Sur ce point les commentateurs récents sont divisés. Ernst Würthwein[9] qui ne retient comme récit primitif que les *vv.* 1, 4, 6 considère que l'oracle ancien était une parole de menace contre le roi et qu'il a été remplacé à une époque tardive par l'actuel *v.* 2. Simon J. De Vries (p. 170) adopte à peu près la même position et tient que le *v.* 2aß–b est un discours dtr. qui a supplanté l'oracle primitif. Allant plus loin, E. Eynikel[10] retient comme oracle le *v.* 3b: "Voici l'autel se fendra et la graisse qui est sur lui se répandra", rejetant la solution la plus souvent retenue[11] qui voit l'oracle au *v.* 2bγ: "on brûlera des ossements d'homme sur toi".

Les arguments présentés par Eynikel sont les suivants:

(1) le *v.* 2a doit être considéré comme rédactionnel, car le prophète s'adresse à l'autel et non au roi;

(2) au *v.* 2 l'homme de Dieu annonce que Josias sacrifiera des prêtres sur l'autel alors qu'au *v.* 3 l'autel est démoli, ne laissant rien sur quoi faire un sacrifice; le *v.* 2 est donc une addition tardive, sans doute dtr;

(3) l'oracle du *v.* 2bγ n'a aucun sens à moins de le lire en lien avec 2 Rois xxiii 16, ce qui contribue à en faire un élément rédactionnel;

---

parut rapidement des textes, ne serait-ce qu'à cause de la brièveté de cette dynastie. Si on attribue le *v.* 34 à Dtr, il faut alors donner à l'expression le sens de royaume d'Israël, ce qui est difficile. James L. Crenshaw, *Prophetic Conflict* (Berlin, 1971), p. 41, rattachait le *v.* 34 à 1 Rois xii 31.

[9] "Die Erzählung vom Gottesmann aus Juda in Bethel. Zu Komposition von 1 Kön 13", dans *Wort und Geschichte. Festschrift für Karl Elliger* (Neukirchen, 1973), p. 184; idem, com., p. 169.

[10] (n. 2), p. 229–31. Pour sa part Hentschel, p. 87, hésite pour le contenu de l'oracle primitif entre le *v.* 2b et le *v.* 3b, mais il se rallie finalement à la première solution. De son côté Dietrich (n. 2), p. 118, estimait que le *v.* 3b était primitivement plus ancien que le *v.* 2bγ.

[11] C'est la solution adoptée par Noth, Gray et Rehm. Voir aussi Uriel Simon, "1 Kings 13: A Prophetic Sign—Denial and Persistence", *HUCA* 47 (1976), p. 85; Walter Gross, "Lying Prophet and Disobedient Man of God in 1 Kings 13: Role Analysis as an Instrument of theological Interpretation of an OT Narrative Text", *Semeia* 15 (1979), p. 102.

(4) enfin le verbe *śrp* au pluriel (*v.* 2bγ), vocalisé au qal par les massorètes, était primitivement un niphal.

Les arguments exigent d'être examinés avec soin, mais ils ne peuvent emporter la conviction.

– Rien n'exige que l'homme de Dieu s'adresse au roi plutôt qu'à l'autel; bien plus, le *v.* 1b qui cite Jéroboam est à attribuer au rédacteur qui insère le récit. Dès lors l'homme de Dieu ne peut s'adresser à un roi dans le récit primitif puisque ce personnage n'intervient qu'au *v.* 4.

– Au *v.* 3 il n'est pas dit que l'autel est démoli, mais qu'il est fendu (*qrʿ*); ce n'est d'ailleurs qu'en 1 Rois xiii 3, 5 qu'un tel verbe est utilisé pour un autel. Si le texte voulait parler de la démolition de l'autel, le verbe *ntṣ* aurait dû être employé.[12] On peut d'ailleurs penser que les *vv.* 3, 5 ont été insérés tardivement dans le récit.

– On ne peut dire que la parole du *v.* 2bγ: "on brûlera des ossements d'homme sur toi" n'a aucun sens. Si l'on accepte que l'homme de Dieu s'adresse à l'autel, l'action annoncée pour un futur indéterminé doit en opérer la désécration. Objet sacré par excellence, l'autel perd sa fonction au contact des ossements humains.

– Le verbe *śrp* au pluriel (TM) est une lectio difficilior;[13] le singulier des versions (LXX, Pesch., Vg.) s'explique parce que le verbe *zbḥ* qui précède est au singulier et qu'elles sont sous l'influence de 2 Rois xxiii 20 (cf. xxiii 16).

L'argument principal pour retenir le *v.* 2bγ comme oracle primitif repose sur une donnée inéluctable, l'action du vieux prophète racontée en xiii 11–32a. Cette action est incompréhensible sans l'oracle puisque le vieux prophète veut que ses ossements soient déposés à côté de ceux de l'homme de Dieu pour être certain qu'ils ne serviront pas à la désécration de l'autel. Le mot "ossements" est un des mot-clés du texte. L'enlever du récit prophétique ne peut avoir que des conséquences pour l'interprétation du texte.

Ceci dit, le *v.* 2bαβ est un vaticinium ex eventu qui sert au rédacteur

---

[12] Le verbe *ntṣ* est bien documenté pour traduire la démolition d'un autel: Ex. xxxiv 13; Dt. vii 5; Jg. ii 2, vi, 30–2, cf. vi 28 (Pual); 2 Rois xxiii 12, 15. A propos des *vv.* 3 et 5, voir les remarques de Hermann Spieckermann, *Juda unter Assur in der Sargonidenzeit* (Göttingen, 1982), p. 115.

[13] Eynikel (n. 2), p. 229, n. 12.

responsable de l'insertion à préparer le lien entre 1 Rois xiii et 2 Rois xxiii 16–20, ce qui est très généralement reconnu (Eynikel [n. 2], p. 229). De même que ce rédacteur a introduit la mention de Jéroboam dès le *v.* 1 (cf. *vv.* 4, 33), de même il annonce la naissance de Josias en pensant à la notice d'accomplissement (2 Rois xxiii 16–20).

Le présage

A moins de considérer le *v.* 3b comme un oracle ancien, ce que nous avons refusé, il convient de prendre les *vv.* 3 et 5 comme allant ensemble. A leur sujet plusieurs remarques s'imposent. Tout d'abord ces versets ne sont pas absolument nécessaires au récit;[14] en second lieu ils sont introduits par l'expression *bayyôm hahû'* qui peut signaler une addition;[15] enfin on assiste à un changement de style entre le *v.* 2 où l'autel est interpellé directement à la 2e personne du singulier et le *v.* 3 où il est question de ce même autel à la 3e personne. Le *v.* 3 et le *v.* 5 sont en rapport d'annonce et d'accomplissement et il vaut mieux les prendre comme formant un tout.

Le mot important est celui de *môpét* qui revient aux *vv.* 3 et 5; il désigne non pas tant un prodige ou un miracle qu'un présage dont la réalisation accrédite la parole prophétique, ce qui suppose une parole antérieure qui ne peut être que celle du *v.* 2bγ. *môpét* avec le sens de "présage" est bien documenté dans la littérature prophétique (Isa. viii 18, xx 3; Ez. xii 6, 11, xxiv 24, 27; Za. iii 8) et c'est son sens en 1 Rois xiii.

Dans le Deutéronome le mot est toujours pris dans un binôme, "signe et prodige", soit au singulier (xiii 2–3), soit au pluriel (iv 34, vi 22, vii 19, xxvi 8, xxix 2, xxxiv 11) et il désigne un miracle. Dans les textes sacerdotaux le mot se rencontre au singulier (Ex. vii 9) mais surtout au pluriel (Ex. iv 21, vii 3, xi 9–10) pour désigner des actions extraordinaires en lien avec l'Exode. Dès lors il est difficile d'attribuer les *vv.* 3, 5 soit à dtr ou DtrP,[16] soit à un rédacteur proche de Ῥ (Hentschel, p. 88).

On doit donc conclure que ces versets sont un trait prophétique

---

[14] Noth, p. 293; Alfred Jepsen, "Gottesmann und Prophet. Anmerkungen zum Kapitel 1 Könige 13", dans H.W. Wolff (éd.), *Probleme biblischer Theologie* (München, 1971), p. 177, n. 12.

[15] Peter A. Munch, *The Expression BAJJOM HAHU' is it an Eschatological Terminus Technicus?* (Oslo, 1936), p. 25 ss.; cf. Dietrich (n. 2), p. 118, n. 35.

[16] Würthwein (n. 1), p. 169; Dietrich (n. 2), p. 118–20.

dont la fonction est de renforcer et de confirmer le message de l'homme de Dieu. Il est beaucoup plus difficile de préciser à quelle étape de la rédaction ces versets ont été introduits. Brisant le fil narratif entre le *v*. 4 et le *v*. 6, ils l'ont été à une époque assez tardive, mais avant l'insertion du récit dans le livre des Rois. Plusieurs indices linguistiques mis en lumière par Würthwein ([n. 9] p. 183) montrent que l'on est à la période post-exilique. Les *vv*. 3 et 5 sont une addition postérieure au fond ancien du *v*. 2.

Apaiser la face de Dieu et prier (v. 6)

Face à la parole proclamée par l'homme de Dieu contre l'autel de Béthel un roi, anonyme à l'origine, mais appelé Jéroboam dans le texte actuel, ordonne que l'on se saisisse de cet homme, mais le roi est immédiatement châtié pour cette action qui visait à travers le messager à tenir pour nul le message. On retrouve ici un autre trait caractéristique des récits prophétiques, l'opposition entre roi et prophète.

Pour obtenir la guérison de sa main le roi doit s'adresser à l'homme de Dieu et lui dit: "Apaise donc la face de Yahvé ton Dieu et prie pour moi . . ." (*v*. 6a). Le *v*. 6b énonce l'exécution de cette demande: "l'homme de Dieu apaisa la face de Yahvé". Il saute aux yeux que les deux verbes du *v*. 6a se réduisent à un seul au *v*. 6b. Si l'on tient compte du fait qu'une partie de la version grecque (LXX[BL]) n'a pas d'équivalent pour le verbe *pll*, "prier", la présence de ce verbe dans le TM peut se comprendre soit comme une glose théologique destinée à tempérer l'expression précédente jugée trop crue (Gray, p. 324, n. d), soit comme une addition pléonastique (De Vries, p. 166).

L'explication que nous voudrions proposer est différente. Si on examine les textes où l'on a l'expression "apaiser la face de Yahvé" pour préciser la forme concrète que peut revêtir cette action, celle-ci prend deux formes, la prière (Ex. xxxii 11; 2 Rois xiii 4; 2 C. xxxiii 12; Ps. cxix 58) ou un acte cultuel sous forme d'un sacrifice (1 Sam. xiii 12, cf. xiii 9–10; Mal. i 9; Dn. ix 13, cf. *vv*. 3, 20–1).[17] L'emploi du verbe *pll* (hithp.) après cette première expression a très probablement pour but de préciser la nature concrète de l'action. Il s'agit d'une prière, non d'un sacrifice, car dans ce dernier cas l'homme

---

[17] Cf. Klaus Seybold, "Reverenz und Gebet. Erwägungen zu der Wendung *ḥillā panîm*", *ZAW* 88 (1976), p. 12 s.

de Dieu aurait utilisé l'autel de Béthel, ce qui était contraire au contexte. La précision "et prie pour moi" est destinée au lecteur et évite toute méprise. On a affaire à une addition nécessairement tardive.

La moralité du récit

La seconde partie du texte (xiii 11–32a) qui met en scène le vieux prophète est-elle chargée de transmettre un message moral et si oui, lequel? A lire le récit on serait tenté de dire avec Alexander Rofé[18] qu'il offre un niveau moral douteux. Mais la première question que l'on doit se poser est de savoir si le récit comporte un jugement d'ordre moral face à une conduite précise. Pour cela l'attention doit se porter successivement sur les deux personnages du récit.

Dans son désir de faire venir l'homme de Dieu chez lui le vieux prophète se heurte d'abord à un refus. En effet comme il l'avait fait avec le roi (v. 7), l'homme de Dieu refuse l'invitation qui lui est faite, quoique en termes moins abrupts que lorsqu'il s'adressait au roi, et il fonde son refus sur un ordre reçu de Dieu (v. 17; cf. v. 9). L'homme de Dieu se montre ainsi obéissant à la parole divine.

Devant cette intransigeance le vieux prophète se sert d'une ruse qui sera d'autant mieux acceptée que lui-même se présente comme prophète. Ayant donc invoqué sa qualité ("Moi aussi je suis prophète comme toi"), le vieillard déclare avoir reçu d'un ange un message qui annulait l'ordre divin (v. 18). Le narrateur précise pour le lecteur: "Il lui mentait".[19] C'est donc à cause d'un mensonge que l'homme de Dieu accède à l'invitation de venir manger et boire.

On pourrait donc penser que le récit manque de moralité. A vrai dire, le mensonge est ici une nécessité dramatique, car il constitue un tournant dans le récit; sans lui la suite ne serait pas possible. Si coupable il y a, c'est le vieux prophète et pourtant on ne voit pas que sa ruse entraîne pour lui quelque conséquence néfaste. Au contraire, grâce à son mensonge le vieux prophète parvient à ses fins; assuré que rien n'arrêtera la malédiction proférée contre l'autel, il se fera enterrer auprès des ossements de l'homme de Dieu. Aucune sanction ne lui est donc infligée. On doit donc distinguer entre la trame narrative et le jugement qui est proposé au lecteur.

---

[18] *The Prophetical Stories* (Jérusalem, 1988), p. 173.

[19] On a parfois contesté l'ancienneté de cette mention, mais rien ne vient appuyer ce soupçon; cf. D.W. Van Winkle, "1 Kings xiii: true and false prophecy", *VT* 39 (1989), p. 35, discute ce point et considère le texte comme primitif.

Si le vieux prophète ne reçoit aucune sanction pour son action, il n'en va pas de même pour l'homme de Dieu qui aux *vv.* 20–2 est accusé de désobéissance à l'égard de Dieu et reçoit comme châtiment de ne pas être enseveli dans le tombeau de ses pères. Comme l'ont reconnu plusieurs auteurs,[20] ce jugement est l'œuvre d'un rédacteur dtr qui insère dans la trame narrative un long discours du vieux prophète. On observera tout d'abord que le début du *v.* 23 reprend la fin du *v.* 19 et que les *vv.* 21–2 sont un élément de parole détachable du récit et introduit par le *v.* 20. De plus le *v.* 21 décalque en partie le *v.* 2 par l'emploi du verbe "crier" (*qr*') et par la formule "ainsi parle Yahvé". Le discours qui suit, ouvert par *ya'an kî*, précise la nature de la faute. Les expressions "être rebelle à la bouche de Yahvé",[21] "garder le commandement",[22] "que Yahvé ton Dieu avait ordonné"[23] sont deutéronomiques. C'est donc un rédacteur dtr tardif qui introduit un jugement à l'égard de la conduite de l'homme de Dieu. Il y a dans le texte actuel un retournement de la situation plein d'ironie, car si au début du texte c'est l'homme de Dieu qui proclame la parole de Dieu, ici c'est le vieux prophète qui proclame le jugement à l'encontre de l'homme de Dieu alors qu'il lui a menti. Bref, les *vv.* 20–2 brisent d'une certaine manière le fil narratif et ceci se manifeste d'autant mieux qu'au *v.* 23 l'homme de Dieu quitte la maison de son hôte sans réagir au jugement qui vient d'être prononcé, ce qui est surprenant.

Si l'on s'en tient au seul niveau narratif qui est le plus ancien, les choses se présentent tout autrement. En ayant fait manger et boire l'homme de Dieu, le vieux prophète peut espérer avoir détourné le message de son but grâce à la désobéissance du messager. En fait, il n'en est rien et le récit se charge de le dévoiler.

Le *v.* 24 constitue un autre tournant dans le récit en faisant inter-

---

[20] Par exemple Frank-Lothar Hossfeld et Ivo Meyer, *Prophet gegen Prophet. Eine Analyse der alttestamentlichen Texte zur Thema: wahre und falsche Propheten* (Fribourg, 1973), p. 24–5; Werner E. Lemke, "The Way of Obedience: I Kings 13 and the Structure of the Deuteronomic History", dans Frank M. Cross, Werner E. Lemke et Patrick D. Miller (éd.), *Magnalia Dei. The Mighty Acts of God* (New York, 1976), p. 308 s. et p. 321, n. 43 ss.

[21] L'expression se rencontre 10 x: Nb. xx 24, xxvii, 14 (P); Dt. i 26, 43, ix 23; 1 Sam. xii 14–15; 1 Rois xiii 21, 26; Lm. i 18.

[22] Dans le Deutéronome le verbe *šmr* est employé 32 x avec comme complément un terme désignant la loi ou les commandements; ici l'expression est adaptée au contexte et le complément est au singulier pour traduire un ordre précis de Dieu.

[23] Avec des variantes l'expression revient plusieurs fois dans le Deutéronome (v 32, vi 1, 20, xiii 6).

venir le monde animal dans l'exécution des desseins divins. Un lion
rencontre l'homme de Dieu et le fait mourir. Qu'un lion fasse mourir l'homme de Dieu, cela n'a en soi rien d'extraordinaire comme le
montrent 1 Rois xx 36; 2 Rois xvii 25–6 où cet animal est l'instrument du châtiment divin. Ce qui l'est bien davantage, c'est qu'après
avoir fait mourir l'homme de Dieu le lion se tient d'un côté du
cadavre, l'âne se tenant de l'autre côté. Les animaux obéissent à un
ordre mystérieux; ils montent la garde autour du cadavre de l'homme
de Dieu et manifestent ainsi le caractère sacré de cet homme en
dépit de sa désobéissance objective.

Apprenant cela, le vieux prophète ne s'y trompe pas et déclare:
"C'est l'homme de Dieu... Yahvé l'a livré au lion qui l'a brisé et
l'a fait mourir..." (v. 26).[24] Il ne s'agit pas là d'une simple déclaration
d'identité, mais de la reconnaissance de la qualité de cet homme. La
désobéissance provoquée par le vieux prophète n'est pas parvenue à
changer le cours des choses; l'oracle de malédiction contre l'autel se
réalisera. Le vieux prophète n'a donc plus qu'un seul souci, se faire
ensevelir auprès de l'homme de Dieu pour éviter que ses ossements
ne servent à réaliser la désécration de l'autel qui est à Béthel.

Le but du récit n'est donc pas de savoir si l'homme de Dieu est
ou non un vrai prophète.[25] Mais de montrer que l'oracle prophétique se réalisera malgré tous les obstacles. Même la faute du messager ne parvient pas à empêcher la réalisation du message.

Légende, parabole ou conte

Lorsqu'on cherche à caractériser la forme littéraire de 1 Rois xiii
11–32a, on se heurte à de multiples propositions entre lesquelles il
faut choisir.

On qualifie souvent 1 Rois xiii de légende en y distinguant même
deux légendes.[26] Cette désignation a été récusée avec raison par Rofé

---

[24] Le v. 26 a reçu deux précisions au cours du temps; la première qualifie l'homme
de Dieu "celui qui a été rebelle à la bouche de Yahvé" et dépend du v. 21; la
seconde, absente de la LXX, achève le verset par ces mots: "selon la parole de
Yahvé qu'il lui avait parlé" et se trouve mal adaptée au contexte.

[25] Plusieurs auteurs centrent l'interprétation du texte sur l'opposition entre vraie
et fausse prophétie, par exemple Hossfeld et Meyer (n. 20); Thomas B. Dozeman,
"The Way of the Man of God from Judah: True and False Prophecy in the Pre-
Deuteronomistic Legend of 1 Kings 13", *CBQ* 44 (1982), p. 379–93; Van Winkle
(n. 19).

[26] Voir par exemple Eynikel (n. 2), p. 228–37.

([n. 18] p. 173), car si la légende cherche à exalter un personnage, ici l'homme de Dieu reste anonyme et il est puni pour avoir désobéi à Dieu. Si on devait parler de légende, cela serait à la rigueur possible pour 1 Rois xiii 1–10.

Rofé propose donc de voir dans le récit sur le vieux prophète une sorte de parabole, mais il est difficile d'accepter cette proposition. En effet la parabole est avant tout une comparaison développée qui peut prendre la forme d'un récit, mais qui est destinée à éclairer une situation ou un débat.[27] La parabole renvoie à autre chose qu'elle-même.

1 Rois xiii 11 ss. se présente davantage comme un conte prophétique. Pour reprendre la définition d'André Jolles.[28] Le conte "s'efforce de raconter un fait ou un incident frappants de manière qu'on ait l'impression d'un événement réel et que cet incident nous semble lui-même plus important que les personnages qui le vivent". Ce n'est donc pas uniquement l'anonymat des personnages qui fait le conte, mais le fait que le récit gravite autour du messager d'un oracle de malédiction pour savoir si celui-ci s'accomplira. Toute l'action du vieux prophète a pour but de mettre à l'épreuve le messager pour voir si l'oracle peut ne pas se réaliser et lorsqu'il sait que sa réalisation est inéluctable, d'échapper à ses conséquences. Enfin il faut tenir compte de la place du merveilleux avec l'intervention d'animaux qui obéissent à la divinité et se comportent mieux que l'homme. Le comportement du lion qui n'a pas mangé juge celui de l'homme de Dieu qui a mangé et a désobéi à l'ordre de Dieu. L'univers du conte n'est pas loin de celui de la fable, mais il ne s'y réduit pas.[29]

---

[27] François Marty, "Parabole, symbole, concept", dans Jean Delorme (éd), *Les Paraboles évangéliques* (Paris, 1989), p. 171–92.
[28] *Einfache Formen* (Tübingen, 1968), p. 231 (trad. française, Paris, 1972, p. 183).
[29] Hermann Gunkel, *Das Märchen im Alten Testament* (Tübingen, 1921), p. 32–3.

THE ORIGIN OF EVIL IN APOCALYPTIC LITERATURE AND THE DEAD SEA SCROLLS

by

JOHN J. COLLINS
Chicago

One of the more novel approaches to the study of apocalypticism in recent years has been that of the Italian scholar Paolo Sacchi. Sacchi has argued in a series of articles, recently collected in his book *L'Apocalittica Giudaica e la sua Storia*, (Brescia, 1990),[1] that apocalypticism should be understood primarily as an ideology. He distinguishes this ideology from the literary genre apocalypse, but remains vague on what if any relationship there is between them. He looks for the essence of the tradition in its origin, which he finds in the Enochic Book of the Watchers. Here, he claims, the generative idea lies in the notion that sin is not of human origin but is antecedent to human choice. The fall of the Watchers is the primordial sin. The apocalyptic tradition that unfolds in 1 Enoch addresses this generative idea in various ways. The tradition is not static. The book of Jubilees marks a significant development along the same lines as the Book of the Watchers. Mastema, or Satan, now emerges as the personalized embodiment of evil. The Epistle of Enoch even records a contradiction of the original conception: "I swear to you, you sinners, that as a mountain has not, and will not, become a slave, nor a hill a woman's maid, so sin was not sent upon the earth, but man of himself created it" (1 Enoch xcviii 4). The Doctrine of the two Spirits at Qumran (which Sacchi attributes to the Teacher of Righteousness) is alleged to be completely in line with the Book of the Watchers, although it does not share the eschatology of the Enochic book (Sacchi, p. 76). The continuity lies in the fact that evil is attributed to a supernatural source.

Sacchi's view of apocalypticism has now been taken up by Florentino García Martínez, and used as one of the pillars of the so-called

---

[1] See the endorsement of Sacchi's approach by F. García Martínez, "Encore l'Apocalyptique", *JSJ* 17 (1987), p. 231.

"Groningen hypothesis" of the origin of the Qumran sect.[2] This hypothesis assumes, with most scholars, that the major rule books and such crucial documents as 4QMMT and the Pesharim pertain to the same sect. It also assumes, in accordance with the long-standing consensus, that the sect is Essene, or at least an offshoot of the Essene movement. It locates the origin of this movement in Palestine, specifically "in the Palestinian apocalyptic tradition before the antiochian crisis".[3] The understanding of this apocalyptic tradition is taken from Sacchi. García Martínez claims that the dualism of Qumran was a modification of the tradition found in 1 Enoch and Jubilees, and that the *yḥd* can be seen as development of the same movement.[4] My objective here is to examine the coherence of this movement and more specifically its relevance to the dualism of the two spirits, as we find it in the Qumran Community Rule.

Sacchi is certainly correct that the problem of evil has a generative role in the apocalyptic literature, and that the typical apocalyptic explanation of evil posits a supernatural source. Whether this idea can be treated as the essence of apocalypticism is another matter. The problem of evil is as central in wisdom as in apocalyptic literature. What is distinctive is the kind of explanation and resolution of the problem that is provided. Like most scholars, I would argue that the apocalyptic explanation of evil lies in its eschatology, at least as much as in its protology. The Book of the Watchers does not stop with the fall of the Watchers. It also describes their judgement and punishment, and fully two thirds of the work are taken up with Enoch's tour of the cosmos, where he sees such marvels as the chambers of the dead and the place prepared for the final judgement. These motifs are not incidental. They are fully as important to the structure of apocalyptic thought as the primordial sin. Sacchi's focus on the origin of evil is too narrow to comprehend the phenomenon of apocalyp-

---

[2] F. García Martínez, "Qumran Origins and Early History: A Groningen Hypothesis", *Folia Orientalia* 25 (1989), pp. 113–36; García Martínez and A.S. van der Woude, "A 'Groningen' Hypothesis of Qumran Origins and Early History", *Revue de Qumrân* 14 (1990), pp. 521–41.

[3] García Martínez, "Qumran Origins", p. 113. The hypothesis also attaches great importance to the formative period before withdrawal to Qumran and embraces van der Woude's theory of multiple Wicked Priests (van der Woude, "Wicked Priest or Wicked Priests? Reflections on the Identification of the Wicked Priest in the Habakkuk Commentary", *JJS* 33 1982, pp. 349–59).

[4] García Martínez, "Orígenes apocalípticos del movimiento esenio y orígenes de la secta qumránica", *Communio* 18 (1985) p. 358.

ticism. That said, however, the origin of evil is also important, and it provides one good testing ground for the hypothesis that the Community Rule stands in a continuous tradition with the apocalypses.

Here, however, we encounter a second problematic dimension in Sacchi's work: it is unclear whether the continuity of the tradition is supposed to lie in phenomenological similarity or in adherence to specific traditions. Phenomenological similarity can be found on a relatively high level of abstraction, and does not require direct influence. The proposition that the origin of evil is antecedent to human decisions is as true of Persian dualism as it is of the Book of the Watchers. It does not follow that the Enochic book is in any way dependent on Persian sources, and it scarcely makes sense to say that it stands in the same tradition as the Gathas. It is not entirely clear to me whether this is the kind of continuity Sacchi has in mind, but I think not. García Martínez, at least, has been explicit in rejecting this kind of broader phenomenological similarity as the basis for apocalyptic tradition ([n. 1] p. 228). If we look for a narrower kind of continuity, however, based on specific traditions, then the relationship between the myth of the Watchers and Qumran dualism is not so simple.

The myth of the Watchers

The fundamental myth used by the Book of the Watchers has been aptly characterized by Paul Hanson as "Rebellion in Heaven".[5] The creation itself is good, just as it is in Gen. i. The Watchers, led by Aśael and Šemihazah, revolt; they are not evil from the beginning. The origin of this myth is unclear. Gen. vi, which provides the starting point for the story with its enigmatic reference to *bny h'lhym* who have intercourse with human women, does not posit rebellion in heaven.[6] The "sons of God" are not accused of any sin in Genesis. The Nephilim or "mighty men of old", who were on the earth in those days and are usually taken to be the offspring of these unions,[7] are described as "men of renown", surely a positive reference. The

---

[5] "Rebellion in Heaven, Azazel and Euhemeristic heroes in 1 Enoch 6–11", *JBL* 96 (1977), pp. 195–233.

[6] D.L. Petersen, "Genesis 6:1–4, Yahweh and the Organization of the Cosmos", *JSOT* 13 (1979) pp. 52–4; R.S. Hendel, "Of Demigods and the Deluge: Toward an Interpretation of Genesis 6:1–4", *JBL* 106 (1987), p. 16.

[7] C. Westermann, *Genesis 1–11* (Minneapolis, 1984), p. 368 = *Genesis 1* (Neukirchen-Vluyn, 1974), p. 497.

flood is brought on by the wickedness of humankind, and the inclination of the thoughts of their hearts. The Yahwist may be giving a
moralising adaptation of an older myth, but the prototype is more
likely to conform to the Atrahasis epic, where the Flood is brought
about by the increase of humanity, than to a story such as we find
in 1 Enoch.[8] J.T. Milik's suggestion, that the Enochic myth is presupposed in Genesis, is without foundation.[9] On the other hand, the
Enochic Book of the Watchers clearly embodies sources, which vari-
ously ascribe leadership of the revolt to Šemihazah or Aśael, and which
can have originated no later than the 3rd century BCE.[10]

In the Book of the Watchers, the union with human women is
assumed to be sinful, probably because it involves the transgression
of divinely appointed boundaries. The sin is compounded by the il-
licit revelation which the Watchers impart, and by the violence of
the giants whom they beget. It is reasonable to infer that this sin is
paradigmatic. Various allegorical applications have been suggested,
to the spread of Hellenism[11] or to the corruption of the priesthood.[12]
In 1 Enoch xii–xvi, a secondary expansion of the story of the Watchers,[13] the spirits of the giants become evil spirits on earth (1 Enoch
xv 8–10). In this way the revolt of the Watchers becomes the ultimate cause of the existence of evil spirits and, by implication, of
human sin.

The author of the book of Jubilees knew and used the Book of the
Watchers, but adapted it in several respects.[14] Jubilees is basically a
re-telling of Genesis, and unlike the Book of the Watchers it includes
the story of Adam and Eve (ch. iii). Sin does not originate in heaven,
but on earth. The angels initially come down "to teach men to do

---

[8] On the relevance of Atrahasis to Genesis see B. Batto, *Slaying the Dragon:
Mythmaking in the Biblical Tradition* (Louisville, 1992), ch. 2. See also the comments of
Hanson (n. 6), pp. 213–15, and Hendel (n. 6), pp. 22–3.

[9] *The Books of Enoch* (Oxford, 1976), p. 31.

[10] There is no reason to push the date back to the 5th century, *pace* Sacchi,
L'Apocalittica, p. 67.

[11] So G.W. Nickelsburg, "Apocalyptic and Myth in 1 Enoch 6–11", *JBL* 96 (1977),
pp. 383–405.

[12] So D.W. Suter, "Fallen Angel, Fallen Priest. The Problem of Family Purity in
1 Enoch 6–16", *HUCA* 50 (1979), pp. 115–35.

[13] G.W. Nickelsburg, *Jewish Literature Between the Bible and the Mishnah* (Philadelphia, 1981), pp. 52–4.

[14] J.C. VanderKam, "Enoch Traditions in Jubilees and Other Second-Century
Sources", in Paul J. Achtemeier (ed.), *Society of Biblical Literature 1978 Seminar Papers*
(Missoula, 1978) 1, pp. 229–51.

what is just and right on earth" (iv 15), and are subsequently attracted to human women. As in Enoch, the spirits of the giants become evil spirits on earth, and after the Flood, "the unclean demons began to lead the children of Noah's sons astray and to mislead them and destroy them" (Jub. x 1). They were created for the purpose of destroying (Jub. x 5–6), although they were not part of the original creation. These spirits now have a leader, Mastema, who is described as a prince, and who bears a strong resemblance to the Satan of Hebrew Scriptures.[15] Only one tenth of the spirits are allowed to remain with him, for the purpose of destroying and misleading mankind. These spirits operate by divine permission, but they are not ultimately responsible for human sin, since Adam fell long before they came on the scene.

The story of the Watchers continues to provide a major frame of reference in Jubilees, even though it is altered, and placed in a new context. We may, then, speak of a common tradition, at least with regard to the origin of evil. It does not necessarily follow that Jubilees and the Enoch books came from the same community or that the continuity was sociological in nature. The ideological differences between Enoch and Jubilees are considerable, and would also have to be taken into account. What the "common tradition" involves here is simply that the author of Jubilees continues to frame the discussion of evil in terms of the myth of the Watchers.

The Qumran Sect

That there is some relationship between the Qumran sect and the books of Enoch and Jubilees is beyond doubt. Some eleven manuscripts preserve portions of the Enochic literature (Milik [n. 9], p. 6). Jubilees, is also preserved in multiple copies,[16] and is cited as authoritative in the Damascus Document (CD XVI 3). Perhaps the most important point of affinity between Enoch and Jubilees and Qumran lies in the common tradition of a solar calendar, which is

---

[15] Mastema first appears in Jub. x, and is presumably one of the spirits of the giants. In later tradition Satan was identified with the serpent of the Garden of Eden (e.g. Rev. xii 9). This identification is not made, at least explicitly, in Jubilees. The account of creation in Jub. ii has no place for an evil spirit. On Satan in the Hebrew Scriptures, see Peggy L. Day, *An Adversary in Heaven. Satan in the Hebrew Bible* (Atlanta, 1988).

[16] J.C. Vander Kam and J.T. Milik, "The First *Jubilees* Manuscript from Qumran Cave 4: A Preliminary Publication", *JBL* 110 (1991), pp. 243–70.

highlighted as a major factor in the dispute between the Qumran
sect and the Jerusalem Temple, especially in the Damascus Document and 4QMMT.[17] One may also speak of a phenomenological
similarity between the world view expressed in several sectarian documents and that of the apocalypses, in so far as major importance is
attached to the influence of the supernatural world on human affairs
and the expectation of eschatological judgement.[18]

To speak of shared traditions and phenomenological similarity,
however, is not necessarily to speak of a unified tradition or a single
movement. The Groningen hypothesis shares with the older Hasidic
hypothesis (which saw the Hasidim of the Maccabean period as the
matrix of all sorts of sectarian developments) a tendency to over-
simplify sectarian Judaism. Since some of the Enochic compositions
and Jubilees refer to the emergence of a distinct (sectarian?) group
about this time, there is a powerful temptation to lump all sectarian
movements together and obliterate their differences.[19] This tendency
is to be resisted.

We find remarkably little appeal to the Enoch tradition in the
major sectarian documents of Qumran. The Damascus Document
cites the story of the Watchers in the course of an admonition to
"walk perfectly in all His ways and not follow after thoughts of the
guilty inclination and after eyes of lust". The Watchers provide the
first negative example in a review of human conduct: "because they
walked in the stubbornness of their heart, the Heavenly watchers
fell; they were caught because they did not keep the commandments
of God". The fall of the Watchers is paradigmatic for human sinful-

---

[17] E. Qimron and J. Strugnell, "An Unpublished Halakhic Letter from Qumran",
*Biblical Archaeology Today. Proceedings of the International Congress on Biblical Archaeology
Jerusalem, April, 1984* (Jerusalem, 1985), pp. 400–7; "An Unpublished Halakhic Let-
ter from Qumran", *The Israel Museum Journal* 4 (1985), pp. 9–12; J.J. Collins, "The
Origin of the Qumran Community, A Review of the Evidence", in P. Kobelski and
M. Horgan (ed.), *To Touch the Text. Biblical and Related Studies in Honor of Joseph
A. Fitzmyer, S. J.* (New York, 1989), pp. 160–1.

[18] See my essay "Was the Dead Sea Sect an Apocalyptic Movement?", in L.H.
Schiffman (ed.), *Archaeology and History in the Dead Sea Scrolls* (Sheffield, 1990), pp. 25–
51. See also the somewhat random survey of apocalyptic influence on the Scrolls by
F. García Martínez, "Les Traditions Apocalyptiques a Qumrân", in C. Kappler
(ed.), *Apocalypses et Voyages dans l'Au-Dela* (Paris, 1987), pp. 201–35.

[19] 1 Enoch xc 6–9, xciii 10; Jub. xxiii 26. See also P.R. Davies, *Behind the Essenes*
(Atlanta, 1987), pp. 107–34. D. Dimant, "Qumran Sectarian Literature", in M.E.
Stone (ed.), *Jewish Writings from the Second Temple Period* (Assen and Philadelphia, 1984),
p. 544, regards the Animal Apocalypse (1 Enoch lxxxv–xc) as a work of the Dead
Sea sect.

ness, in so far as it illustrates a pattern that is repeated through history. It is not causative, however, and it is not understood as the origin or source of human sinfulness.[20]

A much more elaborate explanation of the origin of evil is found in the Community Rule. Here we read:

> From the god of Knowledge comes all that is and shall be. Before ever they existed He established their whole design, and when, as ordained for them, they come into being, it is in accord with His glorious design that they accomplish their task without change . . . He has created man to govern the world, and has appointed for him two spirits in which to walk until the time of His visitation: the spirits of truth and falsehood . . ."[21]

This explanation of the origin of evil is not only different from what we find in Enoch and Jubilees. It bears scarcely any relation to the myth of the Watchers. The Epistle of Enoch, with its explicit denial that sin was sent on earth, stands in the Enochic tradition, even though it contradicts the Book of the Watchers. It still operates with reference to the same myth. This is not the case with the Community Rule. There is, perhaps, a reminiscence of Jubilees at 1QS III 23–4, which refers to the dominion of the Spirit of Darkness as *mmšlt mštmtw* and refers to the spirits of his lot who cause the sons of light to stumble. But the Rule makes no mention of the Watchers, or of any angelic rebellion. Instead, the demonic spirits are subsumed into a new system and given a new origin. Dualism was instituted by God as part of creation itself.[22] There is a different underlying myth here, and it was recognized almost as soon as the Scroll was published. It is the myth of Persian dualism.[23]

---

[20] The "pesher on Azazel and the angels" in the "Pesher on the Periods" (4Q180), published by J.T. Milik, "Milkî-ṣedeq et Milkî-reša' dans les anciens écrits juifs et chrétiens", *JJS* 23 (1972), p. 112, attributes a more causative role to Azazel and his cohorts in misleading Israel, but the text is very fragmentary. Milik reconstructs the text to say that God established the activity of the angels before creation.

[21] Trans. G. Vermes, *The Dead Sea Scrolls in English* (Harmondsworth, 1975), p. 75.

[22] Compare 1QM XIII 10–12, which says that Belial, *ml'k mstmh*, was created to destroy. The difference between the Book of the Watchers and the Community Rule at this point is noted by M.J. Davidson, *Angels at Qumran. A Comparative Study of 1 Enoch 1–36, 72–108 and Sectarian Writings from Qumran* (Sheffield, 1992), p. 297.

[23] A. Dupont-Sommer, *Aperçus préliminaires sur les manuscrits de la Mer Morte* (Paris, 1950), pp. 107, 113, 119, and *Nouveaux aperçus sur les manuscrits de la Mer Morte* (Paris, 1953), pp. 157–72; K.G. Kuhn, "Die Sektenschrift und die iranische Religion", *ZTK* 49 (1952), pp. 296–316. For the debate on this issue see P.J. Kobelski, *Melchizedek and Melchireša'* (Washington, 1981), pp. 84–98.

In the Gathas, the oldest part of the Avesta, which are generally considered to be the work of Zoroaster himself, humanity and even the supreme God has to choose between two Spirits, one of whom is holy and the other a destroyer. The two Spirits are the twin children of Ahura Mazdah, the Wise Lord,[24] although later the holy Spirit is identified with Ahura Mazdah, and the spirit of destruction is primordial.[25] These spirits were associated with light and darkness from an early time, as evidenced by Plutarch, who cites Theopompus (about 300 BCE) as his source.[26] There is, of course, some adaptation of the Persian myth in the Jewish context. God creates rather than begets the two Spirits. As creator, God is clearly transcendent, above both light and darkness. This doctrine was already affirmed by Second Isaiah, who claimed for his God the sovereignty Zoroaster attributed to Ahura Mazda: "I form light and create darkness, I make weal and create woe; I the Lord do all these things" (Isa. xlv 7).[27] This affirmation of the creator, however, has the consequence of making responsibility for evil rest with God. In the Persian myth, the evil spirit still becomes evil by choice. In the Jewish treatise, it is created evil by God. There are, of course, several precedents in biblical tradition for the notion that evil comes from the Lord (cf. 2 Sam. xix 9; Amos iii 6; Sir. xxxiii 14–15). Such a monistic view is typical of the Deuteronomic tradition, with its negative attitude towards mythology. There is a sharp difference, however, between Deuteronomic monism and the dualism under God that we find in the Scroll. There is an equally sharp difference between the Scroll and earlier apocalyptic tradition on this point.

It has been argued that the dualistic myth of the Two Spirits is a secondary development at Qumran, introduced into the Community Rule by interpolation.[28] It should be noted, however, that this is not the only evocation of Persian dualism in the Scrolls. In the Gathas,

---

[24] R.C. Zaehner, *Dawn and Twilight of Zoroastrianism* (London, 1961), pp. 50–1.

[25] This development is attested as early as the 4th century BCE by Eudemus of Rhodes, a pupil of Aristotle. See Kobelski (n. 23), p. 92.

[26] Plutarch, *Isis and Osiris*, 46–7. See J. Gwyn Griffiths, Plutarch, *De Iside et Osiride* (Cardiff, 1970), p. 471, J. Hani, "Plutarque en face du dualisme iranien", *REG* 77 (1964), pp. 489–525.

[27] Morton Smith, "II Isaiah and the Persians", *JAOS* 83–4 (1963), pp. 415–21; D. Winston, "The Iranian Component in the Bible, Apocrypha and Qumran", *History of Religions* 5 (1965–6), p. 189.

[28] See J.L. Duhaime, "Dualistic Reworking in the Scrolls from Qumran", *CBQ* 49 (1987), pp. 32–56.

the opponents of Zoroaster are "the followers of the Lie", and the evil spirit is "He who is of the Lie".[29] In the Damascus Document, the opponent of the Teacher is "the man of the Lie".[30] The occurrence of this designation in a document which lacks the explicit contrast of the two Spirits, and which is largely concerned with the early history of the sect, suggests that the Persian influence cannot be limited to the obviously dualistic passages. It should also be noted that one of the most explicitly dualistic texts, the Testament of Amram, appears on palaeographic grounds to be one of the earliest of the non-biblical scrolls.[31] This too weighs against the hypothesis that the dualism was a secondary development in the Qumran sect.[32]

García Martínez claims that Sacchi "has clearly demonstrated that the determinism characteristic of the Essene movement according to the classical sources and so prominent in the sectarian writings comes from the idea of an original sin which antedates history" ("Qumran Origins" [n. 2]. p. 278). This is far from true. In fact, Sacchi has clearly recognized the contradiction between the myth of the Watchers and the myth of the Two Spirits. He also acknowledges that the myth of the fallen angels is not used in the major writings of the Qumran sect (p. 290). But if that myth is crucial to the apocalyptic tradition, how then can the Qumran community be regarded as part of that tradition? or how can the treatise of the Two Spirits be said to be perfectly in line with the Book of the Watchers? (p. 76). There is no doubt that the Book of the Watchers was known, and preserved in multiple copies at Qumran. The fact that the Community Rule departs from the Enochic tradition, or rather ignores it, is therefore all the more remarkable.

---

[29] Yasna 30.3–6; 32.3–5; Zaehner (n. 24), pp. 42–3.

[30] CD III 13, XIX 26, XX 15; see also 1QpHab II 1–2, V 9–12, X 9; 4QpPs XXXVII i 18, iv 14. See G. Jeremias, *Der Lehrer der Gerechtigkeit* (Göttingen, 1963), pp. 79–126, H. Stegemann, *Die Entstehung der Qumrangemeinde* (Bonn, 1971), pp. 41–53; Collins (n. 17). pp. 172–7.

[31] J.T. Milik, "4Q Visions de Amram et une citation d'Origène", *RB* 79 (1972), pp. 77–79. Milik suggests a date in the first half of the 2nd century BCE. He also claimed that Jub xlvi. 6–xlvii. 9 was dependent on Test. Amram, but his argument rests on speculation about a passage that is not actually extant in Test. Amram.

[32] The date of the War Scroll, the other great dualistic document from Qumran, is disputed. Y. Yadin, *The Scroll of the War of the Sons of Light against the Sons of Darkness* (Oxford, 1962), p. 246, argued for a Roman date. An early date for the dualistic framework of the scroll was defended by L. Rost, "Zum Buch der Kriege der Söhne des Lichts gegen die Söhne der Finsternis", *TLZ* 80 (1955), col. 206, and P. von der Osten-Sacken, *Gott und Belial. Traditionsgeschichtliche Untersuchungen zum Dualismus in den Texten aus Qumran* (Göttingen, 1969), pp. 28–30.

In fact, the whole notion of "the apocalyptic tradition" which García Martínez derives from Sacchi is too simple. While the Book of the Watchers may be the earliest extant apocalypse, it is not for that reason normative. A different strand of apocalyptic tradition, prior to the Qumran Community, can be found in the book of Daniel. Sacchi's student, Gabriele Boccaccini, has quite correctly pointed out[33] that Daniel does not belong to the same ideological tradition as Enoch, by Sacchi's own criteria. Boccaccini's inference that Daniel is not an apocalyptic text only confuses the discussion by changing the accepted reference of words. Better to say that apocalypticism should not be identified with the Enochic tradition. Moreover, Daniel was at least as influential as 1 Enoch on the major sectarian texts. It is preserved in six manuscripts at Qumran, and is cited as authoritative prophecy in 4Q Florilegium and 11QMelchizedek. The influence of Daniel is also evident both in previously unknown "pseudo-Danielic" literature, and in literary borrowings in sectarian compositions, notably in the War Scroll.[34]

Other myths of the origin of evil

Several different myths of the origin of evil, or mythic paradigms for human sinfulness, can be found in apocalyptic literature. We have seen two of them in 1 Enoch and the Community Rule. While the book of Daniel does not address the subject directly, it uses a familiar mythic pattern as a paradigm for the eruption of evil in the Maccabean era. The myth of the sea and its monsters, which provides the imagery for Daniel's dream in ch. vii, can be traced back to Ugarit.[35] Several allusions to it can be found in the Hebrew Bible.[36]

---

[33] *Middle Judaism* (Minneapolis, 1991), pp. 159–60. I do not accept Boccaccini's characterization of Daniel, but he is correct that it is different from Enoch.

[34] See the survey of A. Mertens, *Das Buch Daniel im Lichte der texte vom Toten Meer* (Würzburg, 1971). This study needs to be brought up to date, at least to take account of the "Son of God" text (4Q246). See my study, "The Son of God Text from Qumran", in M. de Boer (ed.), *From Jesus to John. Essays on Jesus and Christology in Honour of M. de Jonge* (Sheffield, 1993), pp. 65–82. See now also F. García Martínez, *Qumran and Apocalyptic. Studies on the Aramaic Texts from Qumran* (Leiden, 1992), pp. 137–79.

[35] See my article "Stirring Up the Great Sea. The Religio-Historical Background of Daniel 7", in A.S. van der Woude (ed.), *The Book of Daniel* (Leuven, 1993), pp. 121–36. On the contrast between this myth and the dualism of Qumran see Collins, "The mythology of Holy War in Daniel and the Qumran War Scroll", *VT* 25 (1975), pp. 596–612.

[36] See J. Day, *God's Battle with the Dragon and the Sea* (Cambridge, 1985). On the

In this tradition, evil or chaos is primordial, not created, but it does not have a pre-determined sphere of influence in human affairs, such as we find in the myth of the two Spirits.

Yet another explanation of evil in the apocalyptic literature emerges in 4 Ezra and 2 Baruch, at the end of the first century of the common era. These apocalypses witness to a dispute about responsibility for evil. In one of the most poignant passages in the apocalyptic literature 4 Ezra complains, "O Adam what have you done? For though it was you who sinned, the fall was not yours alone, but ours also who are your descendants."[37] The question is repeated in 2 Baruch: "O Adam, What was it that you did to all your posterity? And what should be said to Eve who first listened to the serpent?" (xlviii 42). This time, however, Baruch answers his own question: "For though Adam first sinned and brought untimely death upon all men, yet each one of those who were born from him has either prepared for his own soul its future torment or chosen for himself the glories that are to be . . . Adam was responsible for himself only: each one of us is his own Adam."[38]

4 Ezra and 2 Baruch evidently belong to a common tradition: their disagreement is formulated with reference to the same myth. The myth in question, however, is not the myth of the Watchers, but the story of Adam and Eve, the myth which eventually dominated the western tradition. Here the responsibility for sin lies unequivocally on the human level. The dispute concerns the degree of Adam's responsibility, but there is no role for fallen angels. In fact, 2 Baruch attributes responsibility for the fall of the angels to humanity, rather than *vice versa*: "For the man who was a danger to himself became a danger even to the angels. For at the time he was created they enjoyed freedom. And some of them came down to earth and had intercourse with women. And those who did so then were tormented in chains. But the rest of the innumerable host of angels restrained themselves. And those who lived on earth perished all

---

importance of this myth in Israelite religion see also J.D. Levenson, *Creation and the Persistence of Evil. The Jewish Drama of Divine Omnipotence* (San Francisco, 1988), pp. 1–50.

[37] 4 Ezra vii 1. On the whole issue see A.L. Thompson, *Responsibility for Evil in the Theodicy of IV Ezra* (Missoula, Montana, 1977), and the excursus on Adam's sin in M.E. Stone, *Fourth Ezra* (Minneapolis, 1990), pp. 63–7.

[38] 2 Baruch liv 15–19, trans. of R.H. Charles revised by L.H. Brockington in *The Apocryphal Old Testament* (Oxford, 1984) pp. 874–75.

together through the waters of the flood" (2 Bar. lvi 10–15). This summary of the story of the fallen angels goes beyond what we find in Genesis, and presupposes the tradition as found in the Book of the Watchers, but it does not use that tradition to frame the discussion of the origin of evil.

It is not clear that the author of 4 Ezra even knew the Enoch literature. It may be that there is a tacit polemic against Enochic revelation in 4 Ezra: Ezra insists that he did not wish to inquire about the ways above, but about those things that we daily experience (iv 23). It would be grossly misleading, however, to say that 4 Ezra stands in the same tradition as 1 Enoch in its approach to the origin of evil. Equally, I find no basis for the claim of García Martínez that 4 Ezra deliberately rejects the dualistic explanation of evil found in the Community Rule and that the rejection is still within a common tradition.[39] The fact is that 4 Ezra never refers to the two spirits. His own explanation of the origin of evil does not point outside of history, but to its beginning. The source of evil lies within the human heart, the *cor malignum*, not in the sin of angels or in the Spirit of Darkness. The divergence of 4 Ezra from both 1 Enoch and Qumran on this point is not a disagreement within a common framework, such as we find between the Book of the Watchers and the Epistle of Enoch, or between 4 Ezra and 2 Baruch. It is a divergence that arises from radically different premises.

In some later apocalyptic texts the myth of the Watchers is integrated with other explanations of the origin of evil, as indeed is already the case in Jubilees. So in 2 Enoch xviii 3 (long recension) Satanail becomes the leader of the Watchers, and in the Books of Adam and Eve there is a unique combination of the fall of Satan, the fall of the angels and the fall of Adam.[40] The Testaments of the Twelve Patriarchs draw on both the dualism of the Two Spirits (T. Judah xx, T. Asher) and the myth of the Watchers (T. Reuben v 6–7, T. Naphtali iii 5), but in the Testaments the women seduce

---

[39] F. García Martínez, "Traditions Communes dans le IV^c Esdras et dans les MSS de Qumrân", *Revue de Qumrân* 15 (1991), p. 297. His attempt to trace common traditions in 4 Ezra and Qumran also suffers from the failure to distinguish between properly sectarian documents and other texts found at Qumran.

[40] M. Delcor, "Le myth de la chute des anges et de l'origine des géants comme explication du mal dans le monde dans l'apocalyptique juive; Histoire des traditions" *RHR* 190 (1976), p. 48; G. Stroumsa, *Another Seed: Studies in Gnostic Mythology* (Leiden, 1984), p. 24.

the angels rather than *vice versa*. This is also the case in Baruch. This kind of conflation becomes common in texts that may plausibly be dated to the 1st century CE, but not in 4 Ezra, and only to a very limited degree in 2 Baruch, in the passage cited above (lvi 10–15). Later the myth of the Watchers is integrated with a dualism of Light and Darkness in the system of Mani.[41]

One conclusion that follows from this brief overview concerns the coherence of the apocalyptic corpus. I agree with Sacchi, against J. Carmignac,[42] and H. Stegemann,[43] that apocalypticism cannot be reduced to a literary genre. There is a genre apocalypse, but the apocalypses share enough common patterns to enable us to extrapolate a world view, and this world view can also come to expression in works that are not formally revelations.[44] I do not agree, however, that apocalypticism can be reduced to a single stream of tradition, or a single socially continuous movement. The nature of the coherence is phenomenological, and apocalypticism can not be confined to Judaism and Christianity in the Hellenistic and Roman periods. It is because of the phenomenological similarity that a conservative, almost xenophobic community such as we find in the Qumran Community Rule could adapt the dualistic structure of Zoroastrianism for its purposes. Within this phenomenological complex, however, we find a number of distinct apocalyptic movements, each with its own theological premises. There are of course common motifs, shared by different movements, but our overview of the diverse myths of the origin of evil shows that there is real diversity too.

Communities are founded by people, not by traditions, and people may be informed and influenced by more than one strand of tradition. This was surely the case at Qumran. It is now universally acknowledged that all the documents found at Qumran are not ideologically consistent. If we accept the hypothesis that the scrolls represent the library of the sect, then the sectarians were quite widely read.

---

[41] J.C. Reeves, *Jewish Lore in Manichaean Cosmogony. Studies in the Book of Giants Traditions* (Cincinnati, 1992), p. 207.

[42] "Quest-ce que l'Apocalyptique? Son emploi à Qumrân", *Revue de Qumrân* 10 (1979–81), pp. 3–33.

[43] "Die Bedeutung der Qumranfunde für die Erforschung der Apokalyptik", in D. Hellholm, *Apocalypticism in the Mediterranean World and the Near East* (Tübingen, 1983), pp. 495–530.

[44] See further my essay "Genre, Ideology and Social Movements in Jewish Apocalypticism", in J.J. Collins and J.H. Charlesworth (ed.), *Mysteries and Revelations. Apocalyptic Studies since the Uppsala Colloquium* (Sheffield, 1991), pp. 11–25.

The books of Enoch and Jubilees were still preserved and read. The ideology of the sect, however, as formulated in the Community Rule, was a *novum* over against the apocalyptic tradition as found in either Daniel or Enoch. Part of the novelty lay in its heavy reliance on Deuteronomic tradition, in its conception of a new covenant. This covenant was put in a new context, that was phenomenologically akin to the apocalypses, but owed more to Persian traditions than to 1 Enoch for the structure of its teaching. How these traditions found their way into the Qumran community remains enigmatic. The sharp antithesis of light and darkness was certainly congenial to a sectarian view of the world, but the myth of the Watchers could surely have been adapted for that purpose too. One suspects that the choice of myth was related to the pre-history of the Qumran group, and that the authors of the Community Rule and the War Scroll came from different circles than those that produced the Enoch material, even though they had some things in common. The Qumran community cannot be traced to a single root, and the apocalyptic literature cannot all be attributed to a single tradition.

WOMEN IN THE WISDOM OF BEN SIRA AND THE BOOK OF JUDITH: A STUDY IN CONTRASTS AND REVERSALS

by

ALEXANDER A. DI LELLA

Washington

Introduction

Ben Sira's attitude toward women is, to say the least, uncongenial to most contemporary Western readers. Even in his laudatory remarks he views women primarily in relationship to men. Ben Sira's highest acclaim appears in xxxvi 29:

> He who possesses a wife possesses his principal possession,
> a help like himself, a strong support.[1]

Ben Sira derived the Hebrew phrase *rē'šît qinyān*, "principal possession", from the middle two words of Prov. viii 22a, in which personified Wisdom is the speaker: *yhwh qānānî rē'šît děrākāw*,[2] "Yahweh took possession of me as the principle of his ways".[3] The noun *qinyān* (root *qnh*) has the same consonants as the verb form *qānānî* (with *yod* and second *nun* reversed). By describing the wife as a husband's *rē'šît qinyān*, Ben Sira clearly suggests that she is like Lady Wisdom in the majestic poem of Prov. viii 22–36—high praise indeed even though, to be sure, the wife is still viewed as a husband's possession.

Ben Sira makes other favorable comments about women, but the emphasis is chiefly on the value a woman can have for a man. Regarding marriage, Ben Sira writes:

---

[1] My literal translation of MS B *v.* 29a, *qnh 'iššâ rē'šît qinyān,* to bring out the word play in Hebrew; I read *qnh* as a participle, *qōneh,* a reading supported by MS B^mg *qwnh* and the Greek; the Syriac, however, read *qnh* as imperative. The phrase, "a helper like himself", comes from the Greek and Syriac (in *v.* 29b, MS B is corrupt). Unless noted otherwise, translations from the Wisdom of Ben Sira are taken from P.W. Skehan and A.A. Di Lella, *The Wisdom of Ben Sira* (Garden City, New York, 1987). All other biblical quotations, unless otherwise noted, are taken from the *NAB* (*New American Bible*).

[2] So LXX, Symmachus, and Vulgate; the MT has *darkô*.

[3] Translation based upon B. Vawter's convincing article, "Prov 8:22: Wisdom and Creation", *JBL* 99 (1980), pp. 205–16.

Happy the husband of a good wife,
  twice lengthened are his days;
A worthy wife brings joy to her husband,
  peaceful and full is his life.
A good wife is a generous gift
  bestowed upon him who fears the Lord;
Be he rich or poor, his heart is content
  and a smile is ever on his face (xxvi 1–4).

Ben Sira also defends a mother's rights over her children; what he says in iii 2 is typical:

... the Lord sets a father in honor over his children;
  a mother's right he confirms over her sons.

See also iii 4, 6–7, 9, 16. Nonetheless, most of what Ben Sira writes about woman as wife, daughter, adulteress, or prostitute is sexist, patronizing, and objectionable.[4] To be sure, Ben Sira was not alone among the wisdom writers to have such attitudes toward women (see, e.g., Prov. v 3–14, vii 10–27; Qoh. vii 26–8). Like others in his society, he viewed women primarily, if not exclusively, in terms of their sociologically validated and religiously legitimated roles, i.e., in their relationships to the significant males of their family—father, husband, brother(s), son(s)—and not as autonomous and independent persons or as the equals of men.[5]

The book of Judith provides a sharp contrast to many of the statements Ben Sira makes about women and their roles in society. In describing the life, actions, and speeches of Judith, the book reverses a number of stereotypes and biases the Jewish community of Ben Sira's day held about men and women. These contrasts and reversals

---

[4] Skehan and Di Lella (n. 1), pp. 90–2. See also W.C. Trenchard, *Ben Sira's View of Women: A Literary Analysis* (Chico, California, 1982), and the critical reviews of Trenchard by A.A. Di Lella, *CBQ* 46 (1984), pp. 332–4, and C. Meyers, *BSOAS* 47/2 (1984), pp. 339–40. Regarding the status of Jewish women, see L.J. Archer, *Her Price Is Beyond Rubies: The Jewish Woman in Graeco-Roman Palestine* (Sheffield, 1990). For texts about women in the classical period, see M.R. Lefkowitz and M.B. Fant, *Women's Life in Greece and Rome* (Baltimore, 1982).

[5] Skehan and Di Lella (n. 1), p. 91. C.V. Camp ("Understanding a Patriarchy: Women in Second Century Jerusalem Through the Eyes of Ben Sira", in A.-J. Levine [ed], *"Women Like This:" New Perspectives on Jewish Women in the Greco-Roman World* [Atlanta, 1991], pp. 1–39) examines Ben Sira's views about women through the lens of the honor-shame complex, suggesting that "social identity is construed with particular attention to sexual relationships, such that male 'honor'—the highest, and a highly contested good—is determined essentially by the control men exercise over women's 'shame,' that is their sexuality" (p. 2).

are the basis of my study of the intertextuality[6] between the book of Judith and the Wisdom of Ben Sira as well as other books of the O.T.

That at least the person responsible for the Greek of the book of Judith knew the Greek forms of the Wisdom of Ben Sira can be shown from a comparison of Sir. i 6–7a and Jdt. xi 8.

ῥίζα σοΦίας τίνι ἀπεκαλύΦθη;
καὶ τὰ πανουργεύματα αὐτῆς τίς ἔγνω;
ἐπιστήμη σοΦίας τίνι ἐΦανερώθη;[7]

To whom has *wisdom's* root been revealed?
Who knows her *subtleties?*
An *understanding* of wisdom—to whom has this been disclosed? (Sir. i 6–7a)

In Jdt. xi 8 we read:

ἠκούσαμεν γάρ τὴν σοΦίαν σου καὶ τά πανουργεύματα τῆς ψυχῆς σου, καὶ ἀνηγγέλη πάσῃ τῇ γῇ ὅτι σὺ μόνος ἀγαθὸς ἐν πάσῃ βασιλείᾳ καὶ δυνατὸς ἐν ἐπιστήμῃ καὶ θαυμαστὸς ἐν στρατεύμασιν τολέμου,[8] "Indeed we heard of your *wisdom* and of *the subtleties* of your soul, and it was revealed to all the world that you alone are the good man in the entire kingdom and powerful in *understanding* and marvelous in strategies of war" (my literal translation of Judith's ironic words to Holofernes). ΣοΦία, πανουργεύματα,[9] and ἐπιστήμη occur in exactly that sequence both in Ben Sira and in Judith. Πανουργεύματα, moreover, is rare, occurring in the Greek O.T. only in Sir. i 6, xlii 18; and Jdt. xi 8.

---

[6] On the importance of intertextuality see R. Alter, *The World of Biblical Literature* (New York, 1992), pp. 107–30. He quotes (on p. 108) from the French literary theorist Laurent Jenny ("The Strategy of Form", in T. Todorov [ed], *French Literary Theory Today* [Cambridge, 1982], p. 34), who argues that "without intertextuality, a literary work would simply be unintelligible, like speech in a language one has not yet learned".

[7] The Greek of Ben Sira is taken from J. Ziegler's critical edition, *Sapientia Iesu Filii Sirach* (*Septuaginta* 12/2; Göttingen, 1965). V. 7a comes from Greek II. Since the translator of Judith apparently knew this colon, we have here another indication of the early date of Greek II; see P.W. Skehan, "Didache 1,6 and Sirach 12,1", *Bib* 44 (1963), pp. 533–6. Regarding Hebrew I and II, the *Vorlagen* of Greek I and II, respectively, see Skekan and Di Lella (n. 1), pp. 55–9.

[8] The Greek of Judith is taken from R. Hanhart's critical edition, *Iudith* (*Septuaginta* 8/4; Göttingen, 1979).

[9] Variant in Ben Sira and Judith, πανουργήματα.

1. *Daughter Viewed as a Loss*

The Jewish male in antiquity viewed the birth of a daughter with less than joyful enthusiasm. Ben Sira writes:

> Being the father of an undisciplined son brings shame,
>   but the birth of a daughter[10] is a loss (xxii 3 my translation).

V. 3b reflects accurately the ancient Jewish male bias against women. B. Menachoth 43b urges a man to bless God daily for not having made him a woman or a slave. In the daily morning prayer the pious Jew (male of course) is to pray: "Blessed are you, O Lord our God, King of the Universe, who have not made me a woman". In xlii 9–10, Ben Sira provides a longer and more dreary litany of anxieties:

> A daughter is a treasure that keeps her father wakeful,
>   and worry over her drives away sleep:
> Lest in her youth she remain unmarried,
>   or when she is married, lest she be childless;
> While unmarried, lest she be defiled,
>   or lest she prove unfaithful to her husband;
> Lest she become pregnant in her father's house,
>   or be sterile in that of her husband.[11]

The perspective in all these statements is male-centered. The life, well-being, and interests of the daughter seem of little account. Ben Sira concludes this passage with a theologically absurd comment: "Better a man's wickedness than a woman's goodness" (xlii 14a). As will be noted below, Ben Sira has more admonitions to offer a father regarding the dangers to the virtue of his daughter. There is no mistaking Ben Sira's sexist views that doubtless were shared by other men in that society. A daughter was considered a source of anguish and worry; she was hardly ever thought of as a source of happiness.

In the patriarchal, patrilineal, patrilocal, and patrimonial[12] society of Ben Sira's day, the birth of a son, however, was quite another matter, for economic control and leadership in government and re-

---

[10] The text is not extant in Hebrew. A few minor Greek MSS and other witnesses read "foolish [or wicked] daughter", apparently in an attempt to soften the force of Ben Sira's words.

[11] The order of cola 10acbd, as given here, is found in the Masada MS and MS B from the Geniza.

[12] I borrowed these adjectives from C.V. Camp, who explains that these four

ligion, tribe and family were in the hands of men and were passed
along to their sons. Men shared in all aspects of Jewish life, while
women were severely restricted by social constraints and law (Archer
[n. 4], pp. 21–2). To insure that male children fulfill what is expected of them, Ben Sira urges strict discipline:

> If you have sons, chastise them;
>   cure their stubbornness in their early youth (vii 23).
> Whoever loves his son chastises him often,
>   that he may be a joy to him when he grows up.
> Whoever disciplines his son will benefit from him,
>   and boast of him among his intimates (xxx 1–2).

A pampered son, however, brings his father shame and untold grief
(xxx 7–13). A good son is a boon to his father even in death, for the
son insures surrogate immortality to his father.

> At the father's death, he will not seem dead,
>   since he leaves after him one like himself,
> Whom he looks upon through life with joy,
>   and even in death, without regret (xxx 4–5).

In contradistinction to these statements about the value of a disci-
plined son, Ben Sira has virtually nothing to say about a well-
behaved daughter and the delight she can bring to her father, her
husband, and her family. The short comment in xxii 4a is the closest
Ben Sira comes to saying something agreeable about a daughter: "A
sensible daughter obtains (κληρονομήσει) a husband of her own" (*NRSV*
= *New Revised Standard Version*).[13] Daughters were of little account in
the social and power structures of that day, nor could they carry on
the family name.

In sharp contrast to what Ben Sira writes about daughters, the
book of Judith extols a woman named Judith, "the daughter of Merari"
(viii 1),[14] a woman who will be depicted as superior to every Judahite
and Gentile male in the book. The irony implied in God's choice of
a woman to save the nation from mortal peril could not have been

---

terms "specify the degree to which Israelite society was controlled by men" (*Wisdom
and the Feminine in the Book of Proverbs* [Sheffield, 1985], pp. 79 and 304n.).

[13] But it is interesting to note that for κληρονομήσει, MS 443 has τιμήσει, "A
sensible daughter *fears* her husband", and the Latin witnesses have *hereditas*, "A sensible daughter is *the inheritance* of her husband." The Hebrew is not extant.

[14] The phrase "the daughter of Merari" also occurs in xvi 6 by way of *inclusio* at
the beginning and near the end of the story about her.

missed by the males in the ancient audience.[15] It is significant that in response to the Assyrian patrol that asks Judith what people she belongs to, she says, "I am a daughter of the Hebrews" (x 12). The phrase "a daughter of the Hebrews" occurs nowhere else in the O.T. Perhaps the author uses this expression to reflect the name Judith, in Hebrew yĕhûdît,[16] which means "a woman of Judah". Judith is indeed one daughter who is no loss or worry to her father or anybody else. In fact, Achior[17] says to her, "Blessed are you in every tent of Judah" (xiv 7). Judith became, in the words of the high priest and the elders of the Judahites, "the glory of Jerusalem, the surpassing joy of Israel . . . the splendid boast of our people" (xv 9). No male heroes in the O.T. receive that kind of praise.

The reason for Judith's exaltation is clear: she performed in an outstanding way the role and functions normally assumed by males, who alone held the positions of authority and control in matters of state. Under divine guidance, Judith outwitted the enemy by means of feminine beauty and alluring charm.[18] It is these very things that prompted Ben Sira to write many unsavory maxims to which we now turn.

2. Woman Viewed as Seductress

In many passages Ben Sira warns against the dangers attractive women can pose to the male audience he addresses. He also gives the impression that men should be extremely circumspect when associating with women, for "In a woman was sin's beginning: on her account

---

[15] The irony of the book has rightly been emphasized by scholars: e.g., L. Soubigou, "Judith", in L. Pirot and A. Clamer (ed.), La Sainte Bible 4 (Paris, 1952), pp. 550–1; J.C. Dancy, The Shorter Books of the Apocrypha (Cambridge, 1972), p. 110; L. Alonso Schökel, Narrative Structures in the Book of Judith (Berkeley, 1975), p. 8; J. Craghan, Esther, Judith, Tobit, Jonah, Ruth (Wilmington, 1982), p. 100; A. Lacocque, The Feminine Unconventional: Four Subversive Figures in Israel's Tradition (Minneapolis, 1990), pp. 33–4, 38. C.A. Moore (Judith [Garden City, New York, 1985], p. 86) writes, "Irony, of various shapes and shades, is the pervasive technique in Judith, which is a fact too frequently overlooked". In a section entitled "Irony: the Key to the Book" (pp. 78–85) Moore analyses many of the ironic scenes and elements in Judith.

[16] The name of the Hittite wife of Esau (Gen. xxvi 34).

[17] On the role of Achior in the book see A.D. Roitman, "Achior in the Book of Judith: His Role and Significance", in J.C. VanderKam (ed.), "No One Spoke Ill of Her": Essays on Judith (Atlanta, 1992), pp. 31–45.

[18] As J.G. Williams remarks (Women Recounted: Narrative Thinking and the God of Israel [Sheffield, 1982], p. 79), "Beauty, piety and wisdom may sometimes have to take the form of seduction, aggressiveness and cunning for God's Israel to be maintained in the world."

we all die" (Sir. xxv 24; see also 2 Cor. xi 3 and 1 Tim. ii 14). What Ben Sira has to say is, for the most part, unfair and repugnant, but without question it reflects the sexist mentality of that day.

> Worst of all wounds is that of the heart,
>> worst of all evils is that of a woman (xxv 13).
> No poison worse than that of a serpent,
>> no venom[19] greater than that of a woman.
> With a dragon or a lion I would rather dwell
>> than live with an evil woman.
> Wickedness changes a woman's looks,
>> and makes her sullen as a female bear (xxv 15–7).
> There is scarce any evil like that in a woman;
>> may she fall to the lot of the sinner!
> Like a sandy hill to aged feet
>> is a railing wife to a quiet man.
> Stumble not through a woman's beauty,
>> nor be greedy for her wealth[20] (xxv 19–21).

Ben Sira makes little mention of the fact that most of the disasters and misfortunes Israel experienced in its history were caused by wicked men rather than by women.

Ben Sira is explicit about the caution a father should exercise regarding his daughter:

> My son, keep a close watch on your daughter,
>> lest she make you the sport of your enemies,
> A byword in the city and the assembly of the people,
>> an object of derision in public gatherings.
> See that there is no lattice in her room,
>> no spot that overlooks the approaches to the house.
> Let her not reveal her beauty to any male,
>> or spend her time among married women;
> For just as moths come from garments,
>> so a woman's wickedness comes from a woman (xlii 11–13).

Judith fits into none of these biased and odious characterizations of women. The narrative tells us that Judith "was beautiful in appearance, and very lovely to behold" (viii 7 *NRSV*), ἦν καλὴ τῷ εἴδει καὶ ὡραία τῇ ὄψει σφόδρα (the same expressions are used in the LXX to

---

[19] Only the Greek has this text. For "poison" and "venom" the grandson has κεφαλή and θυμός, respectively; but he obviously misunderstood his Hebrew original that would have been *rō'š* which means "poison" (see Deut. xxix 17, xxxii 32; Jer. ix 14, xxiii 15) as well as "head", and *ḥēmâ*, which means "venom" (see Deut. xxxii 24, 33; Pss. lviii 5, cxl 4; Job vi 4) as well as "anger".

[20] So the Hebrew and Syriac; the Greek has "beauty".

describe Rachel [Gen. xxix 17²¹] and Joseph, with of course a change
in the gender of the adjectives [Gen. xxxix 6]). Though the reader
is often reminded of Judith's attractiveness (x 4, 7, 14, 19, 23, xi 21,
23, xii 13), there is not the slightest hint that she ever exploited her
beauty to captivate any one other than the enemy. Rather, Judith
employs her physical endowments and alluring speech in order to
entice the *pagan* general Holofernes to invite her into his tent so that
she may achieve her divinely appointed goal of destroying him and
thus saving her people. Holofernes' attempted seduction of Judith
and his subsequent death by her hand (xii 11–xiii 10; see also xvi
7–9) call to mind Ben Sira's warning:

> Avert your eyes from a comely woman;
>   gaze not upon beauty that is not for you—
> Through woman's beauty many have perished,
>   and love for it burns like fire.
> With a married woman recline not at table
>   nor drink intoxicants with her,
> Lest your heart incline toward her
>   and you decline in blood to the grave (ix 8–9).

In the book of Judith, however, a woman is not the cause of sin for
any male Jew. Rather a woman, Judith, becomes the Lord's instrument of salvation and deliverance of the nation. To be sure, there
have been other heroines in Israel's history—Miriam, who led the
Israelite women in a song of thanksgiving after the decisive event of
the Exodus (Exod. xv 20–1); Deborah, prophetess and judge, who
rallied the people to fight against the Canaanite king Jabin (Judg. iv
4–9); Jael, who drove a tent peg through Sisera's temple (Judg. iv
17–22);²² and Esther, who dressed herself in royal attire in order to
win the favor of the king so that he would spare the lives of her
people (Esth. v 1–viii 12). Deborah, Jael, and Esther also were involved in saving the nation.

No one of these women, however, is described as having the kind
of piety and wisdom we see in Judith. The narrative makes it clear
that Judith was not only strikingly beautiful but also eminently virtu-
ous and wise. Judith "feared God with great devotion" (viii 8 *NRSV*;
see also viii 31, xi 17). The elder Uzziah says to her, "Not today

---

²¹ Though σφόδρα is well attested here, many witnesses omit it.
²² As regards Deborah and Jael, see M. O'Connor, "The Women in the Book of
Judges", *HAR* 10 (1986), pp. 281–6; and S.A. White, "In the Steps of Jael and
Deborah: Judith as Heroine", in VanderKam (n. 17), pp. 5–16.

only is your wisdom made evident, but from your earliest years all
the people have recognized your prudence, which corresponds to the
worthy dispositions of your heart" (viii 29). Even the pagans "mar-
veled at her wisdom and exclaimed, 'No other woman from one end
of the world to the other looks so beautiful and speaks so wisely'" (xi
20–1). Judith fasted all the days of her widowhood except on the
religious festivals and the eves of the sabbath and new moon (viii 6).
She wore sackcloth around her waist (viii 5). She deplored the community's violation of the laws concerning forbidden foods, first-fruits,
and tithes of wine and oil (xi 12–5). She prayed to the Lord to give
her the strong hand and the guile of her lips to crush the pride of
the Assyrians by the hand of a woman (ix 1–14), and at the decisive
moment she prayed for strength to carry out the execution of
Holofernes (xiii 4–5, 7). She fully observed the laws of kašrût, eating
only permissible foods and refusing to eat pagan delicacies (x 5, xii
1–2, 9, 19).

Though Holofernes is consumed with lust and passion, the narrator makes it clear that the Assyrian general never touched Judith
(see xii 16–xiii 2). In fact, Judith herself clearly affirms her sexual
integrity: "As the Lord lives, who has protected me in the path I
have followed, I swear that it was my face that seduced Holofernes
to his ruin, and that he did not sin with me to my defilement or
disgrace" (xiii 16). At the end of the story (xvi 22) the narrator states
explicitly that after her husband's death Judith remained celibate,
having no sexual relations with anyone. In sum, Judith, "a woman
of Judah", was the beautiful, faithful, and wise Judahite *par excellence*.
In contrast, the men of Judah are found wanting in courage, faith,
and imagination.

In this carefully constructed narrative,[23] the contest is between the
pagan Holofernes with his armed might and the devout Judith with
her strong belief in the God of Israel and his power to save.
Holofernes, burning with carnal desire, makes elaborate plans to seduce
the gorgeous Judith. The narrator depicts Judith as fully aware of
the sexual weaknesses of men—a dramatic and ironic reversal of Ben
Sira's statements about wayward women and lusting daughters as
causes of concern for the Jewish male. Under divine inspiration Judith
exploits these weaknesses in her contest with Holofernes. As in other

---

[23] See T. Craven, *Artistry and Faith in the Book of Judith* (Chico, California, 1983),
pp. 47–112.

parts of the O.T., God allows even human wickedness to play a part in the ultimate salvation of his people (see, e.g., Gen. xlv 4–8). Since the situation of her people was desperate, Judith shows herself resourceful in beating Holofernes at his own game: the seducer becomes the seduced, the deceiver is deceived, the conqueror is conquered, by of all people a woman![24] The final judgement of Judith's behavior in slaying Holofernes is given by the high priest Joakim, the elders, and the people: "With your own hand you have done all this; you have done good to Israel, and God is pleased with what you have wrought. May you be blessed by the Lord Almighty forever and ever" (xv 10).

3. Male Elders Viewed as Wise and Virtuous

There is no question that in Ben Sira's vocabulary "elder" meant an older male, never a female. The elders possessed religious, social, and political authority. Like other wisdom writers (e.g., Job xii 12), Ben Sira assumes that elders possess wisdom. Thus he writes for the benefit of his male students:

> Frequent the company of the elders:
>   whoever is wise, stay close to him (vi 34).
> Reject not the tradition of the elders
>   which they have learned from their fathers;
> From it you will obtain the knowledge
>   how to answer when the need arises (viii 9).

In the book of Judith, however, it is precisely the elders who lack the wisdom and political willpower to act when they are confronted by the Assyrian menace. After the disheartened Judahites come to Uzziah and the other elders of Bethulia (vii 23) and propose that they should surrender to the Assyrians and become their slaves (vii 27), Uzziah has little to say to them except that they should wait five more days and then the Lord will have mercy on them. But if no help comes to them after five days, then Uzziah will do as the people say (vii 30–1). When Judith hears about all this, she sends her maid to summon the elders Uzziah, Chabris, and Charmis (viii 9–11). That a woman should take the initiative and exercise a leadership role in the Jewish community by summoning the elders to herself must have struck the ancient audience as daring and unusual.

---

[24] See Judg. ix 53–4 regarding the disgrace of a ruler being slain by a woman.

In his praise of the gracious wife who delights her husband, Ben Sira states:

> A silent wife is a gift from the Lord,
> and nothing is so precious as her self-discipline (xxvi 14 *NRSV*).

In another ironic reversal of Ben Sira, Judith not only is not silent, but proceeds to chastise the elders for *their* rash words, reminding them that they have no right to test the Lord (see Deut. vi 16; Ps. cvi 14; Wis. i 2; Sir. xviii 23). She tells them, in words reminiscent of the Yahweh speeches in the book of Job, that since they do not understand the human heart or mind, they cannot possibly understand God's mind and plan (see Job xxxviii 2–3, xl 2, 7–8; also xlii 3). She then lectures the elders about the religious history of the nation, telling them that they should be grateful that the Lord is putting them to the test, as he did their ancestors (viii 11–27).[25] Uzziah responds to Judith: "All that you have said was spoken with good sense, and no one can gainsay your words" (viii 28). These are startling words for an elder to say to a woman in a patriarchal society. Judith then tells the elders that she is about to do something that will go down from generation to generation among the people. She promises that within five days the Lord will rescue the nation by her hand. She adds that she will not tell them her plan until it has been accomplished. This is another astounding statement for a woman to make to those who have responsibility for the affairs of the state and its survival.

4. *The Widow Viewed as* persona misera

The Law and the rest of the O.T. are explicit regarding the community's responsibility for the orphan and the widow, *personae miserae*. The legislation of Exod. xxii 21–3 is typical: "You shall not wrong any widow or orphan. If ever you wrong them and they cry out to me, I will surely hear their cry. My wrath will flare up, and I will kill you with the sword; then your own wives will be widows, and your children orphans."[26] Ben Sira also teaches that the orphan and widow receive special care from God:

---

[25] Dancy writes ([n. 15] p. 99): "Judith's long speech shows a deep understanding of two theological problems, those of faith and suffering. These are the two themes of the book of Job, and in this passage the author of Judith can stand comparison with the author of Job".

[26] See also Deut. x 18, xxiv 17–18, xxvii 19; Zech. vii 10; Ps. lxviii 6; Prov. xxiii 10–1.

[God] does not reject the cry of the orphan,
　　nor the widow when she pours out her complaint;
Do not the tears that stream down her cheek
　　cry out against the one that causes them to fall? (xxxv 17–9)

Since the orphan and widow usually had no one to plead their cause
or to defend their rights,[27] Ben Sira gives this counsel to his male
audience:

To the fatherless be as a father,
　　help the widows in their husbands' stead (iv 10ab).

It is noteworthy that Judith's widowhood is mentioned seven times
in the book (χηρεύω in viii 4; χήρευσις in viii 5, 6, x 3, xvi 7; χήρα
in ix 4, 9).[28] But rather than being a *persona misera*, Judith is a wealthy
and self-sufficient person in charge of her own life and fortune. At
her husband's death she was left with "gold and silver and male and
female slaves and livestock[29] and fields, which she was maintaining"
(viii 7, my translation).

She puts her faithful maid (ἄβρα), and not a man, in charge of all
her possessions (viii 10). What Judith does seems directly to contra-
vene the exhortation of Ben Sira:

Let neither son nor wife, neither kindred nor friend,
　　have power over you as long as you live.
Yield what you have to no one else,
　　lest then you must plead for support yourself (xxxiii 20).

After the Lord delivered the nation "by the hand of a woman" (xvi
5),[30] Judith, an eminently marriageable woman, turns down the many
men who want to marry her. Before her death she herself distributes

---

[27] Regarding the widow, see P. Hiebert, "'Whence Shall Help Come to Me?'
The Biblical Widow", in P.L. Day (ed), *Gender and Difference in Ancient Israel* (Minneapolis, 1989), pp. 125–41.

[28] Since seven as a symbolic number denotes perfection (see, e.g., Zech. iv 10;
Rev. v 6), the narrator may be suggesting by these seven references to her widowhood that Judith was the perfect widow.

[29] χρυσίον καὶ ἀργύριον καὶ παῖδας καὶ παιδίσκας καὶ κτήνη. It seems certain that the
author borrowed the first four nouns and adapted the last from Gen. xxiv 35 where
Abraham is described in the LXX as having πρόβατα καὶ μόσχους καὶ ἀργύριον καί
χρυσίον, παῖδας καὶ παιδίσκας. The last four nouns occur together in the Greek O.T.
only in Gen. xxiv 35 and in Jdt. viii 7. In Gen. xiii 2 LXX, Abram is said to be
very wealthy κτήνεσι καὶ ἀργυρίῳ καὶ χρυσίῳ. Note that in Judith these same three
nouns are found, but in reverse order. In the O.T., Judith alone is depicted as
possessing the kind of wealth Abraham had.

[30] Note the irony of this expression when we compare it with the similar phrase

her enormous wealth to her husband's relatives as well as to her own family (xvi 24); her final goodwill gesture is to set free her faithful maid (xvi 23,[31] ἄβρα, as in viii 10).

5. Reversals and Contrasts with Other O.T. Books

Giving the genealogy of a woman is not common in the patrilineal society reflected in the Bible. Yet Judith receives not simply a genealogy but the longest genealogy of any woman in the O.T. (Dancy [n. 15], p. 95). She is at the end of sixteen generations that go back to Israel himself (viii 1).[32] Her husband's name, Manasseh, is not even mentioned till after her genealogy is completed. Not only is no genealogy given for her husband, but the narrator explicitly mentions that Manasseh belonged to *her* tribe and *her* family (viii 2); it is not said that Judith belonged to *his* tribe and *his* family. The irony here can hardly be missed. By way of contrast, Tobit tells us that he married a woman of *his* own lineage (i 9; see Num. xxxvi 6). In his famous speech to his son Tobiah, Tobit urges the boy to marry a woman of the lineage of their ancestors (iv 12).

In the book of Judith, there is no mention that Judith ever gave birth to a child (see viii 2–8, xvi 24). Yet in a society that viewed childlessness as a reproach or a disgrace (see, e.g., Gen. xxx 23; Sir. xlii 10; Luke i 25), the narrator never speaks of Judith as being disgraced for not having had children.[33] Quite the contrary, because of what she had done she was honored by all the people, the high priest Joakim, and the elders of the Judahites (xv 8–13). For the rest of her days Judith was famous throughout the land (xvi 21). She lived to the ripe old age of one hundred and five years.[34] After she

---

in the mouth of boasting Nebuchadnezzar in ii 12. In the MT, the phrase *bĕyad 'iššâ*, "by the hand of a woman", LXX ἐν χειρὶ γυναικὸς, occurs only once; the words are spoken by Deborah (Judg. iv 9). In Judith, the phrase is ἐν χειρὶ θηλείας, which occurs three times: ix 10, xiii 15; xvi 5. These are the only four occurrences of such a phrase in the entire O.T. Judith speaks of her own hand in viii 33, ix 9, xii 4, and xiii 14.

[31] The *NAB*, following one Greek MS (58), most Latin MSS, and the Syriac, puts the clause in which Judith grants freedom to her maid after *v.* 24, a position that seems more logical.

[32] For the text-critical problems regarding the names in that genealogy, see Hanhart (n. 8), p. 94; and Moore (n. 15), pp. 176, 179–80.

[33] The Wisdom of Solomon (iii 13, iv 1) reverses the generally held biblical view about the barren wife.

[34] S. Zeitlin (*The Book of Judith* [Leiden, 1972], p. 181) notes that the Maccabean period (168–63 B.C.) also was one hundred and five years in length. I would add

died she was mourned by the house of Israel for seven days (xvi 23–4), the customary period according to Israelite practice (see Gen. l 10; Sir. xxii 12).

Conclusion

The book of Judith was written of course primarily as a good story of the Lord's rescue of Israel "by the hand of a woman". Nonetheless, it appears beyond doubt that the author also intended to challenge, among other things, many of Ben Sira's sexist biases against women and to provide sometimes startling and ironic narrative details that reverse much of what Ben Sira has written about women.

The author of Judith is not the first (or last) person to correct an earlier biblical tradition. One of the purposes of the book of Jonah, for example, was to counteract the extreme nationalism, self-righteousness, and exclusivism of many Israelites (see, e.g., Jer. vii 1–15; Ezra x 9–12, 44; Neh. xiii 1–3, 23–7).[35] It is generally recognized that in the N.T. Jas. ii 14–26 was composed to correct an erroneous understanding of Paul's teaching on justification by faith (see Rom. i 17, iii 20–8, 30, iv 2–5, 16–24; Gal. ii 16, iii 6–12, 24).[36]

In view of the evidence presented above, it seems reasonable to conclude that the author of Judith intended many of the narrative details, including the dialogue, to serve as a corrective to the sexist mind-set of that day. From this point of view, the book of Judith must be judged a notable achievement.

---

that the only other reference in the O.T. to "one hundred and five years" is Gen. v 6: "When Seth was one hundred and five years old, he became the father: of Enosh". Ben Sira writes: "The sum of a person's days is great if it reaches a hundred years" (xviii 9). Perhaps the author of Judith had this text in mind and thus supplied another ironic twist by giving the number "one hundred *and five* years" as the length of Judith's life.

[35] See J. Magonet, *Form and Meaning: Studies in Literary Techniques in the Book of Jonah* (Sheffield, 1983), pp. 94–9.

[36] See T.W. Leahy, "The Epistle of James", *New Jerome Biblical Commentary* (Englewood Cliffs, New Jersey, 1990), pp. 912–13.

LES ARAMÉENS DU MOYEN-EUPHRATE AU VIIIe SIÈCLE À LA LUMIÈRE DES INSCRIPTIONS DES MAÎTRES DE SUHU ET MARI[1]

par

PAUL-EUGÈNE DION

Toronto

I. *Introduction*

A. Présentation générale

N'appartenant clairement ni aux terres classiques de Syrie-Palestine, ni à celles de la Mésopotamie, le cours moyen de l'Euphrate à l'est du Habur échappe aisément à l'attention des historiens. Heureusement, les archéologues viennent de tirer de l'oubli une nouvelle portion de son histoire. Les découvertes éclatantes qui se sont succédé à Mari depuis 1933 avaient mis au jour les couches les plus anciennes et la brillante civilisation du XVIIIe siècle av. J.-C.; depuis 1975 les fouilles de Terqa avaient donné une dimension plus concrète à la survie de cette culture au XVIIe siècle.[2] Les fouilles de sauvetage nécessitées par le barrage d'Al-Qadissiya, en amont de Haditha, nous ouvrent de nouveaux aperçus sur la région avant la stabilisation de l'empire assyrien par Téglath-Phalazar III.[3]

Ces sources nous font voir un monde renouvelé, où les Araméens jouent un rôle crucial. Aucun progrès sérieux de nos connaissances ne saurait laisser les biblistes indifférents, lorsqu'il s'agit d'un groupe aussi proche d'Israël que les Araméens. Nous verrons d'ailleurs que

---

[1] Nous tenons à remercier le Professeur A.K. Grayston, qui a bien voulu lire notre manuscrit. Seules les ressources du Royal Inscriptions of Mesopotamia Project (Université de Toronto, Near Eastern Studies) et le soutien offert par ses membres ont rendu possibles les recherches sur lesquelles repose cet article.

[2] Cf. G. Buccellati, "The Kingdom and Period of Khana", *BASOR* 270 (1988), pp. 43–61. L'importance de Tell 'Ashara et les noms de plusieurs rois de Hana après la grande époque de Mari étaient déjà connus par des travaux de Thureau-Dangin et d'autres assyriologues, remontant jusqu'à 1897.

[3] Cf. A. Cavigneaux et B. Kh. Ismail, "Die Statthalter von Suhu und Mari im 8. Jh. v. Chr. anhand neuer Texte aus den irakischen Grabungen im Staugebiet des Qadisija-Damms (Taf. 35–38)", *Baghdader Mitteilungen* 21 (1990), pp. 321–456.

les hommes, les événements et les structures qui transparaissent dans les nouveaux documents peuvent affecter l'interprétation de l'Ecriture sur plusieurs points tels que la patrie d'Abraham, l'origine ethnique de Balaam, et l'univers de Job.

B. Ce qu'on savait déjà sur le Moyen-Euphrate au Fer I–II

Les inscriptions araméennes de Syrie contemporaines des rois d'Israël et les démêlés avec Damas racontés dans la Bible ont toujours attiré l'attention, et les Araméens de Syrie faisaient récemment l'objet de plusieurs monographies.[4] Il n'en va pas de même pour les états de Haute-Mésopotamie, et en particulier pour les principautés du Moyen-Euphrate en aval du Bît-Adini. Ici, les annales militaires des rois d'Assur[5] forment le gros de la documentation,[6] et la nature des entités géopolitiques qu'elles nous révèlent est souvent difficile à définir.[7] Avant d'évaluer l'apport des nouveaux documents, nous rappellerons brièvement ce qui était connu avant leur publication.

On savait depuis longtemps que les efforts de Téglath-Phalazar Ier au tournant du XIe siècle n'avaient pu endiguer l'expansion araméenne; l'Assyrie avait perdu l'empire bâti par Salmanazar et Tukulti-Ninurta en Haute-Mésopotamie à la fin du Récent Bronze, et s'était vue appauvrie et resserrée dans son foyer national.[8] Les sources écrites se taisent à peu près complètement sur cette période, et ce que nous savons de la carte du Moyen-Euphrate durant ces siècles obscurs dépend essentiellement de la nouvelle expansion assyrienne qui allait avoir lieu au IXe siècle.

Dès avant la publication des documents que nous analyserons, nos

---

[4] Cf. W.T. Pitard, *Ancient Damascus* (Winona Lake, 1987); H. Sader, *Les Etats araméens de Syrie depuis leur fondation jusqu'à leur transformation en provinces assyriennes* (Wiesbaden, 1987); G.G.G. Reinhold, *Die Beziehungen Altisraels zu den aramäischen Staaten in der israelitisch-judäischen Königszeit* (Francfort, 1989).

[5] Les textes qui nous intéressent le plus précèdent les conquêtes définitives de Téglath-Phalazar III. Nous citerons ceux qui furent écrits de Téglath-Phalazar I à Aššurnaṣirpal II d'après l'édition critique d'A.K. Grayson, *Assyrian Rulers of the Early First Millennium BC I (1114–859 BC)* (Toronto, 1991).

[6] La seule exception d'importance est la grande inscription babylonienne de Shamash-resh-uṣur, publiée par F.H. Weissbach, *Babylonische Miszellen* (Leipzig, 1903), pp. 9–15.

[7] A partir du IXe siècle les Assyriens ne précisent souvent plus s'ils ont affaire à des Araméens.

[8] Cf. P. Garelli et V. Nikiprowetzky, *Le Proche-Orient Asiatique. Les Empires mésopotamiens et Israël* (Paris, 1974), pp. 46, 58–61, 218, 226–8; A.K. Grayson, pp. 24–9 dans la *Cambridge Ancient History* III/1 (2e éd., 1982).

connaissances sur cette période avaient beaucoup profité de la pros-
pection qui s'intensifia dans les années soixante-dix en vue de la
compilation du *Tübinger Atlas des Vorderen Orients*[9] et à l'approche du
harnachement de l'Euphrate. On parvint à identifier plusieurs sites
nommés dans les itinéraires assyriens[10] et mieux situer les états soumis par les rois d'Assur.[11] Il s'agit principalement de deux "pays"
(KUR) appelés Laqu et Suhu. Le Laqu englobait le Bas-Habur et
débordait sur l'Euphrate de chaque côté de leur confluent.[12] Le Suhu,
lui, s'étendait sur l'Euphrate en aval du Laqu, en direction de la
Babylonie. La cité-état de Hindanu, qui séparait le Suhu du Laqu,[13]
était sise près d'Abou Kemal et de l'actuelle frontière syro-irakienne.[14]

Hindanu et le Suhu figuraient déjà dans les archives royales de
Mari,[15] et le Suhu avait appartenu au royaume de Babylone,[16] mais

---

[9] Cf. W. Röllig et H. Kühne, "A Preliminary Report on a Survey Conducted by
the Tübingen Atlas des Vorderen Orients in 1975", *AAAS* 27–8 (1977–8), pp. 115–
40; H. Kühne, "Zur historischen Geographie am Unteren Habur. Vorläufiger Bericht
über eine archäologische Geländebegehung", *AfO* 25 (1975–7) pp. 249–55; 26 (1978–
9), pp. 181–95.

[10] Campagnes d'Adad-nirari II (894), cf. Grayson (n. 5), pp. 153–4; Tukulti-Ninurta
II (885), cf. Grayson, pp. 174–6; Aššurnaṣirpal II (878), cf. Grayson, pp. 212–15; cf.
pp. 198–200, 221.

[11] Cf. spécialement H. Kühne, "Zur Rekonstruktion der Feldzüge Adad-Nirari
II., Tukulti-Ninurta II. und Aššurnaṣirpal II. im Habur Gebiet", *Baghdader Mitteilungen*
11 (1980), pp. 44–70; H.F. Russell, "The Historical Geography of the Euphrates
and Habur according to the Middle and Neo-Assyrian Sources", *Iraq* 47 (1985),
pp. 57–74. Cf. aussi Kh. Nashef, *Die Orts- und Gewässernamen der mittelbabylonischen und
mittelassyrischen Zeit* (Wiesbaden, 1982); R. Zadok, *Geographical Names According to New-
and Late-Babylonian Texts* (Wiesbaden, 1985); au moment où nous écrivons le volume
sur les sources néo-assyriennes n'a pas encore paru.

[12] Au temps d'Adad-nirari II, le pays se divisait en "Haut et Bas-Laqu"; cf. Grayson
(n. 5), p. 154, texte A.O.99.2, lignes 118–19, Adad-nirari II divisait de même en
"Haut" et "Bas" le Hanigalbat, situé plus au nord (même inscription; Grayson,
p. 153, lignes 98–9), Ces divisions rappellent le "Haut et Bas-Aram" des inscriptions
de Sfiré (I A 6).

[13] Habituellement la cité de Hindanu fait nombre avec Laqu et Suhu, mais des
textes plus sommaires semblent l'inclure dans l'un de ces blocs. Dans un passage de
Téglath-Phalazar Ier Hindanu fait partie du Suhu (Grayson [n. 5], p. 43); et un
texte d'Aššurnaṣirpal II divise le Moyen-Euphrate en Laqu et Suhu p. 221).

[14] E. Lipiński, "Apladad", *Or* N.S. 45 (1976), pp. 53–74, localise Hindanu plus
précisément à 'Anqa, "à une quinzaine de kilomètres en aval d'Abou Kemal"
(p. 61, n. 78). Nashef (n. 11), s.v. Hindanu, s'en tient plutôt à Ash-Sheich-Jaber,
déjà proposé par A. Musil, *The Middle Euphrates. A Topographical Itinerary* (New York,
1927), pp. 203, 206–7.

[15] Pour Hindanu, cf. J.N. Postgate, "Hindanu", *Reallexikon der Assyriologie* IV (1972–
5), p. 415. Pour Suhu, cf. N. Háklár, "Die Stellung Suhis in der Geschichte, eine
Zwischenbilanz", *AO* 22 (1983), pp. 25–36, spécialement p. 28.

[16] A Khirbet ed-Diniyeh, la Délégation Archéologique Française en Irak a pu

le Laqu est une entité nouvelle, dont la formation marque un change-ment majeur dans la carte politique de l'Euphrate. C'est au début du IXe siècle que son nom apparaît pour la première fois.[17] Il rem-place le royaume de Hana, qu'on ne trouve plus dans les textes à compter d'environ 1050.[18] Au premier millénaire, Mari n'est prati-quement plus qu'une nécropole,[19] et Terqa, qui s'appelle maintenant Sirqu,[20] fait partie du Laqu avec d'autres petits états.[21] Cette nou-velle puissance est une fédération araméenne; la principauté la plus septentrionale s'appelle *Bît-Halupe*,[22] et les princes du Laqu portent des noms ouest-sémitiques ou typiquement araméens.[23]

---

vérifier le caractère babylonien de Haradu, la principale ville de l'ouest suhéen (fouilles de 1981–4 et 1988). Cf. F. Joannès, C. Képinski et O. Lecomte, "Présence babylo-nienne dans le pays de Suhu, au XVIIe siècle av. J.-C.: l'exemple de Khirbet ed Diniye (Irak)", *RA* 77 (1983), pp. 119–42, spéc. p. 140. Sommaires des campagnes dans *Iraq* 45 (1983), pp. 209–10; 47 (1985), pp. 219–20; 51 (1989), p. 254.

[17] Ceci dans les annales d'Adad-nirari II (Grayson [n. 5], p. 153, texte A.O.99.2, lignes 113 ss.).

[18] Dans une dédicace trouvée à Sippar (Grayson, [n. 5], p. 111, texte A.O.89.2001) un Tukulti-Mer se présente comme roi du pays de Hana, et fils d'un autre roi de Hana; ce même personnage figure comme roi de Mari dans les inscriptions d'Aššur-bêl-kala (1073–1056), qui fit deux fois campagne contre lui; cf. Grayson, p. 89, texte A.O.89.1, lignes 14–16; p. 92, texte A.O.89.2, ii, ligne 5. Au siècle précédent, un autre "roi de Mari" avait été défait et son pays soumis par Babylone, suivant une chronique fragmentaire; cf. C. Walker, "Babylonian Chronicle 25: A Chronicle of the Kassite and Isin II Dynasties", dans G. van Driel et al., *Zikir shumim. Assyriological Studies Presented to F.R. Kraus on the Occasion of His Seventieth Birthday* (Leiden, 1982), pp. 398–417, spéc. pp. 400–1.

[19] Cf. J. Mallet, "Mari: une nouvelle coutume funéraire assyrienne", *Syria* 52 (1975), pp. 23–36; plus brièvement, J.-M. Aynard, "Mari. B. Archäologisch", *RLA* 7 1987–90), pp. 390–418, spéc. pp. 392, 403–4.

[20] L'identification de Sirqu avec Terqa, aujourd'hui acceptée des experts, re-monte à E. Herzfeld, "Hana et Mari", *RA* 11 (1914), pp. 131–9, spéc. p. 138. Outre la consonance des deux noms et les données topographiques, cette opinion s'appuie sur l'orthographe *Sir-qa* déjà utilisée par un roi de Hana vers la fin du XVIIe siècle; cf. F.J. Stephens, "A Cuneiform Tablet from Dura-Europas" (sic), *RA* 34 (1937), pp. 183–90.

[21] Dans les annales d'Adad-nirari II Sirqu peut sembler dominer le Laqu (cf. Grayson [n. 5], p. 153, à la fin), et dans les principales inscriptions d'Aššurnaṣirpal sur la fondation de Calah (Grayson, textes A.O.101.26; A.O.101.28; A.O.101.29; A.O.101.30), Sirqu fait nombre avec Suhu et Laqu; mais la prépondérance de Sirqu n'est pas évidente dans les récits détaillés sur la conquête du Moyen-Euphrate, et Suru de Bît-Halupe paraît même plus importante. Ainsi, chez Tukulti-Ninurta II, le prince laqéen Haran paie un tribut comparable à celui de Sirqu, et le tribut de Suru est encore plus considérable (Grayson, pp. 175–6). Voir aussi les annales d'Aššurnaṣirpal (pp. 198–200, col. i, lignes 74–99; pp. 212–15, col. iii, lignes 1–48).

[22] Grayson (n. 5) p. 153, ligne 114, etc.

[23] Ces noms sont Bar-'Atar (cf. Grayson [n. 5], p. 153); *Mawdad (ibid. et pp. 175–6); "Le Hamatéen" (pp. 176 et 198 [voir ici n. 85]); Ahi-yabab (pp. 198–9

Au temps d'Aššurnaṣirpal, même le prince de Hindanu est un Ara-méen.[24] Quant au Suhu, les noms de ses dynastes et la nature de son terroir[25] orientent plutôt vers la Babylonie; mais différents facteurs, tels que l'attestation d'une présence araméenne dès le XIIIe siècle,[26] la fréquente solidarité avec Hindanu et le Laqu au IXe siècle, le nom araméen d'un défenseur de la capitale au temps d'Aššurnaṣirpal,[27] l'existence d'une région appelée *Bît-Shabi*,[28] et l'onomastique des temps gréco-romains[29] ont fait croire à plusieurs que ce pays aussi avait pris un caractère araméen.[30] Quoi qu'il en soit de l'ethnie domi-nante, les bouleversements politiques de la fin du deuxième millé-naire avaient sûrement valu une longue période d'autonomie à tous

---

Ahi-yabab ["mon Frère exulte"] a la même base que l'hébreu Yôbab. Un exemple de ce nom se trouve en Gen. xxxvi 33–4, dans une liste royale [*vv.* 31–9] sans doute araméenne plutôt qu'édomite; voir A. Lemaire, "Bala'am/Bela' fils de Be'ôr", *ZAW* 102 [1990], pp. 180–7); 'Azi-el (cf. Grayson, pp. 199 et 214 s.); Ilah (p. 215).— Deux autres noms qui apparaissent dans les mêmes contextes, Haran et Hen/mti-el, sont plus opaques que ceux que nous avons mentionnés, mais ne s'expliquent pas par l'akkadien.

[24] En akkadien son nom s'écrit *Ha-ia-u-nu*; c'est la forme que donne Salmanazar III au nom de Haya de Bît-Gabbari, le prédécesseur de Kilamuwa à Zencirli (mo-nolithe de Kurk, i 42, 53; ii 24, 83). Une génération plus tôt, le prince de Hindanu s'appelait *'Ammi-'alab (Am-me-a-la-ba; annales de Tukulti-Ninurta II, voir Grayson [n. 5], p. 175). Ce nom rappelle à la fois Su-mu-a-la-ab, un nom amorite attesté à Alalakh, et Abî-'albôn de 2 Sam. xxiii 31, qu'on a peut-être tort de corriger à l'aide du grec et des Chroniques.

[25] Le Suhu ne se prêtait pas à un système de canaux comme ceux qui irriguaient la partie basse du Laqu; sauf rares élargissements comme à 'Ana, où les terres basses étaient irriguées et intensément cultivées, la vallée de l'Euphrate était étroitement encaissée (cf. Buccellati [n. 2], p. 46). Le Suhu produisait un vin réputé (cf. déjà Weissbach [n. 6], p. 14), et la culture du palmier dattier, si importante en Babylonie, florissait pour la dernière fois autour de 'Ana; cf. S.H. Horn, "Zur Geographie Mesopotamiens", *ZA* 34 (1922), pp. 123–53, spéc. p. 136. Pour une courte descrip-tion du Suhu, voir Háklár (n. 15), pp. 25–6.

[26] Déjà au XIIIe siècle les Hiranu fréquentait ces parages, cf. O.R. Gurney, "Texts from Dur-Kurigalzu", *Iraq* 11 (1949), texte n° 10, pp. 139–40, 148. Vers la même époque, une lettre d'Emar (Tell Meskéné) cite les dires de deux Ahlamu (l'éditeur traduit: "deux Araméens") venus du pays de Suhu; cf. D. Arnaud, *Recher-ches au pays d'Aštata, Emar VI.3* (Paris, 1986), p. 260, n° 263 lignes 18–19. Dans Grayson (n. 5), p. 43, texte A.O.87.4, lignes 34–6, Téglath-Phalazar Ier signale des Araméens à 'Anat en Suhu (cf. p. 23, texte A.O.87.1, lignes 48–50).

[27] Le "frère" du roi de Babylone, envoyé par lui au secours du dynaste Kudurru, s'appelait Zabdanu; cf. Grayson (n. 5), p. 213, texte A.O.101.1, col. iii, ligne 20.

[28] Grayson (n. 5), p. 213, texte A.O.101.1, col. iii, lignes 14–15.

[29] Cf. Lipiński (n. 14), spéc. p. 70.

[30] Cf. S. Schiffer, *Die Aramäer, Historisch-geographische Untersuchungen* (Leipzig, 1911), pp. 36, 54; A. Dupont-Sommer, *Les Araméens* (Paris, 1949), p. 22; J.A. Brinkman, *A Political History of Post-Cassite Babylonia, 1158–722 B.C.* (Rome, 1968), p. 279; Lipiński (n. 14), pp. 73–4 (voir aussi *Acta Orientalia* 27 [1979], p. 73).

les états du Moyen-Euphrate, et vers 900 av. J.-C., le Suhu n'appartenait ni à la Babylonie,[31] ni à l'Assyrie.[32]

C. Les découvertes de 'Ana et de Sur Jar'a[33]

Dès 1899, on avait découvert à Babylone la grande inscription d'un Shamash-resh-uṣur, qui s'intitulait curieusement gouverneur (šaknu) de Suhu et Mari et comptait ses années de règne en prince indépendant.[34] Comme contexte historique on pouvait songer à un recul passager de l'Assyrie, peut-être durant la première partie du VIIIe siècle,[35] et ce monument isolé soulevait la question du sort du Moyen-Euphrate au siècle qui suivit Aššurnaṣirpal; la réponse allait venir des découvertes de 1978–9.[36]

Une vingtaine de tablettes cunéiformes et trois inscriptions lapidaires furent d'abord mises au jour par des chercheurs irakiens à Sur Jar'a, et des fouilles britanniques y ajoutèrent une autre tablette.[37] Les Irakiens découvrirent encore quatre stèles dans l'île de 'Ana[38] et trouvèrent ailleurs des fragments moins importants. Stèles et tablettes appartiennent aux mêmes types d'inscriptions royales, dédicaces et surtout inscriptions historiques à un ou plusieurs sujets.[39]

Au moins trois documents, une tablette de Sur Jar'a (n° 5), une

---

[31] Au Moyen Bronze, le Suhu avait été babylonien, mais le raid hittite de Murshili semble avoir mis fin à cette situation; cf. Háklár (n. 15), spéc. pp. 31–2. Par la suite, des armées de Babylone avaient encore pu traverser le Suhu (cf. Walker [n. 18], A.K. Grayson, *Babylonian Historical-Literary Texts* [Toronto, 1975], p. 77); mais les "gouverneurs" du Suhu étaient capables d'audacieuses initiatives, tel un raid à Qatna du Habur au XIIIe siècle; cf. Arnaud (n. 26), p. 260, n° 263, lignes 22–9. Au temps de Tukulti-Ninurta II le protectorat babylonien ne s'exerçait décidément plus; le roi d'Assur se garde de rien réclamer lorsqu'il traverse un pan de territoire babylonien, mais il se met à lever tribut dès qu'il arrive à 'Anat, ville principale du Suhu; cf. Brinkman (n. 30), p. 183.

[32] Aššurnaṣirpal remarque que les dynastes du Suhu n'avaient pas coutume de se présenter devant ses prédécesseurs. Cf. Grayson (n. 5), p. 200, texte A.O.101.1, ligne 100.

[33] Pour l'historique et la description des découvertes nous dépendons plus étroitement que jamais de Cavigneaux et Ismail (n. 3), spéc. pp. 321–40.

[34] Cf. Weissbach (n. 6).

[35] Ainsi Weissbach (n. 6), p. 14; le déclin final de l'empire lui paraissait une autre possibilité, mais la plupart des auteurs récents favorisent le VIIIe siècle.

[36] Encore en 1980, K. Kessler considérait la date de Shamash-resh-uṣur comme inconnue (*Untersuchungen zur historischen Topographique Nordmesopotamiens nach keilschriftlichen Quellen des 1.Jahrtausends v. Chr.* [Wiesbaden, 1980], p. 229, n. 840).

[37] N° 16 dans l'édition de Cavigneaux et Ismail (n. 3).

[38] N°s 17, 18, 20 et 27.

[39] Excepté n° 28, une tablette de Sur Jar'a à contenu magique.

tablette (n° 16) et une stèle (n° 20) de ʿAna, remontent à Shamash-resh-uṣur et nous livrent sa généalogie; mais les textes les plus nombreux et les mieux conservés appartiennent à son fils Ninurta-kudurri-uṣur. Parmi ceux-ci, l'inscription n° 2[40] est fondamentale; cette tablette contient la présentation la plus complète de Ninurta-kudurri-uṣur et de presque tous ses actes. On retiendra surtout la défaite d'un rezzou araméen, l'aménagement de puits et d'un poste fortifié dans la steppe, le récit modèle d'une fondation de ville sur l'Euphrate, et la capture d'une caravane d'Arabie. Il faut compléter cette source par la stèle n° 18,[41] qui raconte la mise au rancart de la déesse ʿAnat[42] par les Assyriens et la restauration de son culte par les dynastes locaux. L'un et l'autre documents abondent en doublets et parallèles.[43]

II. *Esquisse historique*

A. Les auteurs et leur temps

La mention d'un dignitaire déjà connu, Sîn-shallimanni, place décidément les tablettes d'ʿAna et Sur Jarʿa au deuxième quart du VIIIe siècle.[44] A cette époque plusieurs officiers supérieurs du roi d'Aššur, tels que Shamshi-ilu, Nergal-eresh et Bêl-Harran-bêli-uṣur s'arrogeaient

---

[40] Voir Cavigneaux et Ismail (n. 3), pp. 342–57, 412–17.

[41] pp. 383–8, 437–9.

[42] On remarquera la survie de la déesse ʿAnat. Cette divinité sera encore attestée beaucoup plus tard sous la forme araméenne ʿth, qui recevra le préfixe ʿtr (déterminatif divin plutôt que modification d'ʿštrt comme le voulait Albright), pour devenir ʿtrʿth, Atargatis. L'identité ʿth=ʿtrʿth apparaît au IVe s. av. J.-C. dans les monnaies de Hiérapolis; cf. S. Ronzevalle, "Les monnaies de la dynastie de ʿAbd-Hadad et les cultes de Hiérapolis Bambycé", *MUSJ* 23 (1940), pp. 3–82. Les attestations abondent en syriaque et en palmyrénien; noter spécialement Dura-Europos à mi-chemin entre Mari et Terqa; cf. C.B. Welles et al., *The Excavations at Dura-Europos. Final Report V, Part I, The Parchments and Papyri* (New Haven, Conn., 1959), pp. 61–3. Aux exemples déjà connus on ajoutera un Brʿth d'environ A.D. 240 et un Brʿt; cf. J. Teixidor, "Deux documents syriaques du IIIe siècle après J.-C. provenant du Moyen-Euphrate", *CRAI* 1990, pp. 144–66, spéc. pp. 148, 157. Cette longue survie de la déesse en Syrie permet de nuancer la constatation de R. Oden comme quoi, après les pointes de flèche d'el-Khadr "ʿAnat then fades from sight on the continent" (*Studies in Lucian's De Syria Dea* [Missoula, Montana, 1977], p. 87; à ses exemples de survie plus à l'ouest, en Chypre, et dans l'Occident punique, on ajoutera *RES* 453). Nous verrons qu'il ne faut pas séparer l'est et l'ouest à un tel point.

[43] Cf. surtout l'inscription n° 17, qui traite du même sujet que le n° 18 sous un angle différent.

[44] Sin-shallimanni (2 i 33) allait être éponyme en 747. Au temps visé par l'inscription, l'année d'accession de Ninurta-kudurri-uṣur, il n'était pas encore au sommet de sa carrière.

des pouvoirs qui allaient devenir impensables après 744.[45] Pour leur part, sans porter le titre de roi,[46] les "gouverneurs", ou plutôt, les dynastes,[47] de Suhu et Mari agissaient et s'exprimaient comme de véritables souverains héréditaires.[48]

Leur modèle n'est autre qu'Hammurapi, roi de Babylone. Ils le mettent en tête de leur généalogie,[49] ils ont soin d'imiter ses ordonnances rituelles,[50] et quand Ninurta-kudurri-uṣur bâtit un temple à Adad, il lui donne le nom sumérien d'un temple de la première dynastie de Babylone.[51] De fait, le dialecte et la graphie des inscriptions locales sont plutôt babyloniens qu'assyriens.[52] Cet horizon babylonien ne doit pas surprendre.[53] Le Suhu avait appartenu à Babylone, les éléments Marduk et *kudurru* se répètent dans les noms princiers du Ier millénaire,[54] et un siècle avant Shamash-resh-uṣur, un corps expéditionnaire babylonien avait soutenu le dynaste local contre les Assy-

[45] Sur ces dignitaires assyriens semi-autonomes, voir Háklár (n. 15), pp. 25, 30–1; A. Lemaire et J.-M. Durand, *Les inscriptions araméennes de Sfiré et l'Assyrie de Shamshi-ilu* (Genève, 1984), spéc. pp. 38–44.

[46] Ninurta-kudurri-uṣur passe plus proche de se faire roi que Cavigneaux et Ismail (n. 3), pp. 325 et 351, ne veulent l'avouer. Les dieux lui ont donné la royauté (2 i 6); l'ont fait asseoir sur un trône (ligne 8; cf. la grande inscription de son père, éd. Weissbach, ii 40); et l'ont placé au-dessus de puissants rois et dynastes (4, 29–31, cf. 10 i 2–3). Dans la dédicace à la déesse 'Anat (n° 17), il la loue d'éclairer "le roi son adorateur" (ligne 6), et appelle Hammurapi "un roi son prédécesseur" (ligne 32).

[47] Cf. Weissbach (n. 6), p. 14.

[48] Ninurta-kudurri-uṣur fonde en son propre nom la ville de Dur-Ninurta-kudurri-uṣur (2 iii 16); pour Shamas-resh-uṣur, voir le texte mal conservé de 5, 12–21. Le cliché d'avoir surpassé tous ses pères apparaît plusieurs fois dans ces textes du Suhu: 2 ii 27–8 (= 4, 43–5); iii 11–12; iv 4–6; 5 recto 7; Shamash-resh-uṣur, éd. Weissbach, iv 13–16. Un autre cliché significatif est l'évocation d'une nation lointaine qui n'avait jamais envoyé d'ambassadeur (2 iv 28–9); cf., p. ex., Sargon II sur Midas de Phrygie (D.D. Luckenbill, *Ancient Records of Assyria and Babylonia* II [Chicago 1927], p. 22 43) ou sur la Nubie (p. 32 § 63).

[49] Pour Shamash-resh-uṣur, voir les n°s 5 et 16; pour Ninurta-kudurri-uṣur, voir les n°s 1, 2, 4, 17, 18. Cavigneaux et Ismail (n. 3), pp. 326–9, étudient ces généalogies.

[50] 17, 30–2; 18 ii 9–12 et par.

[51] É-nam-he; 1, 8.

[52] Cf. Cavigneaux et Ismail (n. 3), p. 340. Ces auteurs notent en même temps plusieurs particularités locales et quelques aramaïsmes sur lesquels nous reviendrons.

[53] Dans son chapitre sur le Suhu (pp. 100–14), S. Schiffer soulignait déjà l'allure babylonienne de ce pays.

[54] Marduk-apal-uṣur payait tribut à Salmanazar III (cf. D.D. Luckenbill, *Ancient Records of Assyria and Babylonia* I [Chicago, 1926], p. 592); Iqisha-Marduk était l'un des prédécesseurs immédiats de Shamash-resh-uṣur selon les passages généalogiques énumérés plus haut; Kudurru, le nom du dynaste attaqué par Aššurnaṣirpal en 878 (Grayson [n. 5], p. 213) est un caritatif babylonien; et le nom de Ninurta-kudurri-uṣur avait été porté par deux rois babyloniens du Xe siècle.

riens.[55] L'élément cassite jouait un rôle dans ces rapports avec Babylone. Aššurnaṣirpal parle de forces cassites au service de son adversaire,[56] et les dynastes du VIIIe siècle se rattachent à Hammurapi à travers l'ancien chef cassite Tunamissah.[57]

Au début du règne de Ninurta-kudurri-uṣur, les rapports avec l'Assyrie paraissent bons. Devant le raid araméen, ce dynaste fait cause commune avec les gouverneurs assyriens du Laqu et de Ruṣapu.[58] Sans doute avec le consentement de l'Assyrie, Ninurta-kudurri-uṣur semble même exercer un certain protectorat[59] sur ses voisins immédiats,[60] le Laqu et la ville de Hindanu.[61] Rien n'indique que la composition ethnique de ces provinces ait changé, mais, par contraste avec les pillards de la steppe, elles représentent un monde araméen domestiqué, inféodé aux vieilles civilisations et envié pour sa prospérité. Hindanu, un important nœud caravanier,[62] joue peut-être le rôle de

---

[55] Cf. Grayson (n. 5), p. 213, texte A.O.101.1, col. iii, lignes 16–20.

[56] Brinkman (n. 30), p. 185, n. 1131, identifiait ces troupes cassites au contingent babylonien. On ne peut écarter complètement cette possibilité, mais l'ordre du récit fait plutôt penser à une armée locale, et la survie d'un élément cassite au pays de Suhu n'a rien d'invraisemblable. En Babylonie même, les Cassites jouaient encore un rôle important au Xe siècle, et le premier roi Ninurta-kudurri-uṣur appartenait à une dynastie néo-cassite, dite de Bazi; cf. Brinkman, *Cambridge Ancient History* III/1 (2e éd., 1982), pp. 295–7.

[57] L'élément cassite avait également joué un rôle au pays voisin sous les rois de Hana. Cf. Cavigneaux et Ismail (n. 3), p. 326.

[58] 2 i 30–5 et parallèles, spéc. le verso mal conservé du n° 4.

[59] L'hostilité du dynaste de Suhu est censée avoir fait hésiter les Araméens à pénétrer dans le Laqu (2 i 14–16), alors que pourtant ils allaient y entrer directement, avant d'avoir affaire aux forces de Ninurta-kudurri-uṣur.

[60] Sur Hindanu et le Laqu comme formant l'horizon immédiat du Suhu cf. 2 iii 7.

[61] Si vraiment la région de Mari, située au Laqu tout près de Hindanu, n'échappait pas entièrement à la juridiction suhéenne, le titre de "*šaknu* de Suhu et Mari" pourrait représenter quelque chose de plus qu'un effort pour se parer d'un passé glorieux; ceci, malgré Cavaignac et Ismail (n. 3), p. 327. La position de ces auteurs vient toutefois d'être renforcée par l'exemple d'un certain Aššur-ketti-lēšer, "roi du pays de Mari" et vassal de Téglath-Phalazar Ier, qui ne régnait en fait que sur un petit district du Habur au nord de Shadikannu; cf. Stefan M. Maul, *Dis Inschriften von Tall Bderi* (Berlin, 1992), pp. 52–4.

[62] Hindanu bénéficiait entre autres du commerce arabe. Comme le notait R. Zadok, "Notes on the Historical Geography of Mesopotamia and Northern Syria", *Abr-Nahrain* 27 (1989), pp. 154–69, spéc. p. 160, seules les cités de Hindanu et Sirqu livraient de la myrrhe aux Assyriens. Nos sources sur Hindanu laissent voir le passage du chameau de Bactriane au dromadaire venu d'Arabie. Au début du IXe siècle, Tukulti-Ninurta II (voir Grayson [n. 5], p. 175, texte A.O.100.5, ligne 78) et Aššurnaṣirpal II (p. 200, texte A.O.101.1, ligne 97) avaient prélevé des *udrāte* à Hindanu. Ce mot désigne le chameau de Bactriane; cf. A. Salonen, *Hippologica accadica* (Helsinki, 1955), pp. 85–7. Mais un siècle plus tard, les dromadaires prenaient le dessus.

centre régional que Mari et Terqa avaient tenu plus anciennement.[63]

Avant de recouvrer son indépendance, le Suhu aussi avait connu une période de vassalité assyrienne. La stèle n° 18 commence son récit à une époque où les princes locaux payaient tribut à l'Assyrie (i 6–8). Cette inscription et la stèle n° 17, trouvée elle aussi dans l'île de ʿAna, font suivre une période de cinquante ans,[64] où, par la faute des citoyens, la ville de ʿAnat était tombée sous la domination directe d'un certain Assyrien.[65] Plus tard, la ville avait fait retour au dynaste de Suhu et Mari, Shamash-resh-uṣur, on ne sait dans quelles circonstances. On en conclura que les conquêtes du IXe siècle avaient mis en place une réelle suzeraineté assyrienne;[66] vers la fin du IXe siècle, celle-ci s'appesantit encore davantage sur ʿAnat, le principal centre du Suhu, mais elle finit par s'évanouir au profit d'une dynastie locale de tradition babylonienne.

B. Les Araméens

L'histoire que nous avons rappelée est essentiellement celle des établissements sédentaires qui formaient l'épine dorsale du Suhu. Mais ce chapelet de petits bourgs égrenés au fond de la vallée était entouré de hautes-terres semi-arides trop élevées pour l'irrigation.[67] A l'instar de Mari et Terqa mille ans plus tôt,[68] les dynastes du Suhu avaient mis la steppe au service de l'élevage et du transit caravanier[69] grâce à un réseau de points d'eau. Les annales de Ninurta-

---

Sur Jarʿa 2 iv 35 parle de la capture des deux cents dromadaires d'une caravane; un quart de siècle plus tard, des dromadaires seront mentionnés dans la correspondance commerciale de Nippur, étudiée par Steven W. Cole "Nippur in Late Assyrian Times, 750–612" thèse inédite de l'Université de Chicago, 1991 (lettres 12N114 p. 111; 12N141 p. 117), et les marchands de Nippur étaient en relation avec Hindanu (12N37, p. 116; 12N188, p. 123). A la même époque une lettre assyrienne mentionne 60 dromadaires (*ibīlē*, un emprunt arabe) prélevés dans le Suhu; cf. H.W.F. Saggs, "The Nimrud Letters, 1952—Part II", *Iraq* 17 [1955], pp. 126–54, et pls xxx–xxxv, voir p. 136, lettre n° 17, verso, ligne 17.

[63] Selon Buccellati (n. 2), p. 44, le Moyen-Euphrate ne pouvait servir de bassin qu'à un seul grand centre urbain à la fois.

[64] 18 i 24.

[65] On peut l'identifier avec Nergal-eresh; cf. Cavigneaux et Ismail (n. 3), pp. 324–6, Avant de se voir assigner des gouverneurs séparés, le Laqu et Hindanu avaient fait partie du vaste domaine de ce même Nergal-eresh.

[66] Avant les découvertes d'ʿAna et Sur Jarʿa, on pouvait croire que les rois d'Assur avaient exagéré leur succès, et que leurs expéditions du IXe siècle avaient laissé la région essentiellement autonome; cf. Brinkman (n. 30), pp. 185–7.

[67] Désignées dans nos textes par le sumérogramme EDIN (2 i 14, 26; ii 5).

[68] Cf. Buccellati (n. 2), pp. 45–6. Au moment où nous écrivons la démonstration détaillée à laquelle l'auteur renvoie dans cet article n'a pas encore paru.

[69] Chose curieuse, dans les inscriptions qui ont été retrouvées le dynaste ne s'in-

kudurri-uṣur nomment sept puits différents,[70] qui servent de repère à ses opérations contre la horde araméenne et les contrebandiers arabes. Un autre passage raconte fièrement la découverte et l'aménagement de l'un de ces puits.[71]

Les aramaïsmes des documents[72] et certains indices déjà mentionnés laissent entrevoir un élément ouest-sémitique dans la population du Suhu, spécialement dans la steppe.[73] Mais les textes ne donnent le nom d'Araméens qu'à des forces hostiles, d'abord le grand rezzou au début du règne de Ninurta-kudurri-uṣur,[74] puis une bande de vingt hommes qui tenteront de s'emparer d'un poste militaire (2 iii 14–16). C'est le premier de ces épisodes qui retiendra notre attention. Selon les deux premières colonnes de l'inscription n° 2 et leurs parallèles,[75] deux mille Araméens s'étaient jetés sur le Laqu trois mois après l'intronisation du dynaste,[76] Avec des effectifs assyriens et sa propre armée, Ninurta-kudurri-uṣur attaqua les pillards et en fit un horrible carnage.

---

téresse à la steppe qu'au sujet des voyageurs et maraudeurs qui peuvent la traverser; cf. 2 iii 9–11 (voyageurs); 2 iii 20–1 (ennemis).

[70] Liste dans Cavigneaux et Ismail (n. 3), pp. 409–10.

[71] 2 iii 2–11.

[72] Sans enquête systématique nous avons glané dans l'inscription n° 2 quelques exemples d'emprunt ou d'influence ouest-sémitique qui demanderaient évidemment de plus longues discussions: *gepen "arbre fruitier" (2 i 26, dans un passage mis sur les lèvres des Araméens; comparer iii 28, qui représente indiscutablement la langue littéraire du dynaste, et utilise kirû, "verger", commun en akkadien). Les noms de puits *makir (rare en akkadien), et *surib (de l'araméen "aspirer, sucer"?) (2 ii 9–10). L'emploi inusité du verbe naṭālu (2 ii 15; cf. Cavigneaux et Ismail [n. 3], p. 355]; ce passage contient les meilleurs parallèles de certaines expressions de Gen. xv 11a. Le nom de ville URU gab-ba-ri-KAK (2 ii 26 et souvent; cf. Cavigneaux et Ismail, pp. 355–6). ni-iq-bu-u2-nû (2 iii 11); le sens semble être "[les eaux que] nous avons collectées", et Cavigneaux et Ismail, p. 356, renvoient au syriaque qbo. *kneśśet (2 iii 13). *gedûd (2 iii 14), hapax legomenon en akkadien, semble apparenté à l'hébreu 'ēzôr; cf. Cavigneaux et Ismail, p. 357.

[73] Lorsque Ninurta-kudurri-uṣur fonde un poste militaire pour surveiller le steppe (2 iii 11–22), les travailleurs enrégimentés pour le bâtir sont appelés "les gens de la *kneśśet" (kinaltu dans l'adaptation babylonienne, ligne 13).

[74] Entre amis et ennemis du dynaste l'opposition est moins ethnique que socio-économique. Les Araméens du Laqu se trouvent ici du côté assyro-babylonien, face à leurs frères de race. On peut comprendre dans le même sens un passage du plan des envahisseurs: "nous nous dresserons contre les maisons du Suhu" (2 i 25). "Maison" (É, bîtu) désigne sans doute ici la même structure sociale araméenne que dans le nom de la Bît-Shabi, intégrée au Suhu; aux lignes 26–7, les maraudeurs ne parlent d'attaquer que les villages de la steppe, où pourtant d'autres Araméens doivent prédominer; les vrais centres urbains paraissent hors de leur portée.

[75] Enumérés par Cavigneaux et Ismail (n. 3), p. 334; les documents 3–4 donnent une version condensée du récit. Les deux parties du texte principal sont séparées par une longue lacune, que les parallèles ne permettent pas de combler entièrement.

[76] Ces pillards s'inscrivaient dans une longue tradition. La lettre n° 23 de la

Les maraudeurs araméens étaient des archers,[77] sans doute comparables aux guerriers barbus des portes de Balawat[78] et des bas-reliefs de Tell Halaf,[79] Ils s'étaient recrutés dans la tribu des Hatallu,[80] et ils comptaient faire boule de neige en cours de route (2 i 24). Leur concentration paraît s'être effectuée "dans la steppe" (2 i 14) à l'est du Habur et de l'Euphrate, puisqu'ils intimidèrent le gouverneur de Ruṣappu (dans le Sindjar) avant de rencontrer le dynaste de Suhu et Mari. Les douars des Hatallu jalonnaient peut-être toute la Djéziré jusqu'au Tigre, en passant par le Suhu;[81] mais des éléments décisifs du rezzou étaient issus du nord-ouest. Le chef suprême[82] et l'une des bandes[83] venaient de la région de Sarug, 40 km au nord-est de Karkémish,[84] et un autre chef se rattachait en quelque façon à Hamath en Syrie.[85]

Correspondance de Iasmah-Addu, éd. G. Dossin (ARMT 5, Paris, 1952), parle d'un rezzou de deux mille Sutéens en marche vers Qatna; ce récit ressemble sur plusieurs points à celui de Ninurta-kudurri-uṣur. Le père de ce dernier avait lui-même stoppé un raid de quatre cents Tu'manu (éd. Weissbach, col. ii, lignes 17–26), une tribu qui se retrouvera en Babylonie un demi-siècle plus tard.

[77] 2 i 10, ii 2; 4, 34; 7 i 16.

[78] Cf. L.W. King *Bronze Reliefs from the Gates of Shalmaneser King of Assyria B.C. 860–825* (Londres, 1915) pls LXXIX–LXXX.

[79] Cf. M. Freiherr von Oppenheim, *Tell Halaf* 3, *Die Bildwerke*, ed. A. Moortgat (Berlin, 1955), pls 11a; 18a.

[80] 2 i 9–10; 17, 22; 4, 20; 9 recto 7.

[81] Une lettre probablement écrite entre 734 et 728 nomme côte-à-côte le pays de Suhu et le pays des Hatallu; cf. J.N. Postgate, *The Governor's Palace Archive* (Londres, 1973), pp. 187–8, n° 188, lignes 7 s.; Postgate établit la date à la p. 11. La tablette n° 4 de Sur Jar'a ligne 20, nomme les Minu'u parmi les segments des Hatallu impliqués dans le raid; or la ville de Minu, à laquelle les Minu'u se rattachent vraisemblablement, apparaît ailleurs dans le même contexte que Dur-Kurigalzu ('Aqar Quf); cf. S. Parpola, *Neo-Assyrian Toponyms* (Kevelaer-Neukirchen-Vluyn, 1970), p. 248. Dans la longue liste des lignes 5–10 d'une tablette éditée par P. Rost, *Die Keilschrifttexte Tiglat-pilesers III.* (Leipzig, 1893), p. 54, Téglath-Phalazar III nomme les Hatallu parmi beaucoup d'autres tribus araméennes de l'est de la Babylonie.

[82] 2 i 12–13; ii 23–4.

[83] 2 i 9; 4, 20. Le texte parle des Sarugu comme d'un groupe ethnique (LU2 *Sarugu*), mais les noms de plusieurs tribus araméennes de Babylonie coïncident pareillement avec des noms de lieux. Sur ces tribus, cf. Brinkman (n. 30), pp. 267ff.; R. Zadok, "Zur Geographie Babyloniens während des sargonidischen chaldäischen, achämenidischen und hellenistischen Zeitalters", *WO* 16 (1985), pp. 19–79, spéc. pp. 63–70(–74).

[84] Le nom de Sarug survit dans celui de Sürüc en Turquie, dont les coordonnées répondent aux implications générales des quelques attestations néo-assyriennes; mais son site exact est inconnu. Cf. Kessler (n. 36), pp. 197–200.

[85] Iaé le fils de Balaam est décrit comme un a-mat-a-a (2 i 17; 21 i 8). Les textes de Salmanazar III emploient souvent cette orthographe avec -mat- pour les gens de Hamath (Parpola [n. 81], p. 14), et celle-ci n'est apparemment pas utilisée lorsqu'il s'agit d'Amatu sur la rivière Uqnu à l'est du Tigre (pp. 14–15). Les frontières de

Cette "grande compagnie" ne représentait aucun des états araméens ou néo-hittites qui survivaient encore, et le titre de ses chefs, *rēš karaši*,[86] ne correspond à aucun rang déterminé dans les armées de l'époque. L'homme de Hamath pouvait être un simple *condottiere* ou le chef d'un clan Hatallu sujet du roi de Hamath. L'homme de Sarug, le pivot de toute l'expédition, venait de l'ancien royaume de Bît-Adini, conquis et annexé par Salmanazar III près d'un siècle auparavant.

Ninurta-kudurri-uṣur en fait un serviteur félon du Suhu comme de l'Assyrie (2 ii 24), et c'est sur lui qu'il concentre son ressentiment. Avec une certaine ironie, il lui donne plusieurs fois le titre akkadien de *nāgiru* (NIMGIR; 2 i 12 et par.). Ce titre, porté par des personnages de haut rang[87] aussi bien que par des magistrats subalternes, était connu en dehors de la Mésopotamie. Dans le royaume d'Arpad, entre Hamat et l'ancien Bît-Adini, un *nāgiru* figure juste après les membres de la famille royale sur la troisième stèle de Sfiré.[88] On ne peut préciser ce que cette charge signifiait dans la carrière du chef des Hatallu, mais l'étiquette semble s'être collée à lui comme un mémorial de sa trahison des pouvoirs établis.[89]

Les textes de Sur Jar'a nous révèlent ainsi un autre monde araméen que celui des principautés reconnues: un monde mouvant de tribus dont les segments s'éparpillent à travers l'empire assyrien et les états périphériques, et dont le terrain d'action est la steppe plutôt que la ville. Ces groupes forment entre eux des structures aussi instables que leurs ententes avec les rois et les cités; ainsi, le récit de

---

Hamath s'étaient rapprochées jusqu'à environ 70 km de l'Euphrate et des provinces assyriennes, depuis que l'Araméen Zakkur avait uni Hamath et Lu'ash au début du VIIIe siècle. Au début du IXe siècle un dynaste de Suru en Bît-Halupe qui collabora avec l'Assyrie s'appelait "Hamathéen" (KUR Ha-ma-ta-a-ia, cf. Grayson [n. 5], p. 176, texte A.O.100.5, lignes 87, 101; ᵐHa-ma-ta-a-ia, p. 198, texte A.O.101.1, ligne 75); mais on ne peut rien bâtir sur cette donnée, où la désignation ethnique est devenue un nom propre comme François ou Germain.

[86] SAG KALxBAD (2 i 10, 18). L'expression ne se retrouve que dans une lettre néo babylonienne, avec un sens ("commencement de la campagne" selon *CAD* K, p. 212) qui ne convient pas ici.

[87] Shamshi-ilu était *nāgiru rabû*; cf. F. Thureau-Dangin et M. Dunand, *Til-Barsib* (Paris, 1936), p. 145, ligne 9. Bêl-Harran-bêl-usur était *nāgir ekalli*; cf. V. Scheil "Stèle de Bêl-Harrân-bêl-utsur", *Recueil de Travaux* 16 (1894), pp. 176–82, spéc. p. 179, ligne 9.

[88] Cf. A. Lemaire et J.-M. Durand, *Les inscriptions araméennes de Sfiré et l'Assyrie de Shamshi-ilu* (Genève-Paris, 1984), p. 145, commentaire de la ligne 10.

[89] Bien qu'avortée, l'aventure de ce *nāgiru* qui fomenta le pillage du Laqu et tenta de s'emparer du Suhu rappelle les initiatives couronnées de succès de David, le vassal des Philistins qui s'empara d'Hébron (2 Sam. ii 1–4), et de l'officier d'Hadadézer qui entra dans Damas après la défaite de son maître (1 Rois xi 23–5).

Ninurta-kudurri-uṣur présente les Luhuaï comme un segment des Hatallu; mais quelques années plus tard, les listes de Téglath-Phalazar III mettront les deux groupes sur le même pied.[90] Tenu en respect ou apprivoisé par les conquérants et les centres urbains, cet univers tribal devient plus remuant aux époques d'incertitude et de faiblesse du pouvoir central, et les aventuriers tentés par les circonstances y trouvent des partisans.

III. *Intérêt pour les études bibliques*

A. Structures

L'activité des bandes araméennes sur l'Euphrate en plein VIIIe siècle est chronologiquement toute proche des *gĕdûdîm* araméens et moabites mentionnés dans le cycle d'Elisée.[91] Cette remarque nous amène pour de bon aux lumières que les études bibliques peuvent tirer des inscriptions d'ʿAnat et Sur Jarʿa. Nous pourrions nous arrêter aux dimensions sociales et culturelles éclairées par ces textes: la manière de fonder une ville,[92] les faibles effectifs des armées,[93] la menace de rébellion, pro-assyrienne[94] ou autre,[95] l'importance et les

---

[90] Il est plus que tentant d'identifier les Luhuaï (Lu-hu-ú-a-a) de Sur Jarʿa avec les Luhuatu (Lu-hu-u-a-tu) des textes déjà connus. Téglath-Phalazar III nomme les Luhuatu juste avant les Hatallu dans une liste de tribus araméennes aux lignes 5–10 d'une tablette éd. par Rost (n. 81), p. 54, et ceux-ci apparaissent de nouveau dans le même contexte que les Hatallu dans la lettre ABL 1175.

[91] Les bandes araméennes de 2 Rois v 2, vi 23 (cf. J. Gray, *I & II Kings* [2e éd., Londres], 1970, p. 517); la bande moabite de xiii 20. En Cilicie, Azitiwadda de Karatepe se vante d'être venu à bout des chefs de bande de l'arrière-pays (*KAI* 26 A i 15). Tous ces exemples emploient des mots apparentés à *gĕdûd*; cf. le *gudūdu* de Sur Jarʿa 2 iii 14. Sous Sargon II il est souvent question de pillards. La tribu araméenne des Hamranu s'attaque aux caravanes babyloniennes (cf. A.G. Lie, *The Inscriptions of Sargon II King of Assyria, Part I The Annals* [Paris, 1929], lignes 379–81); des Arabes s'en prennent au Laqu et au Hinzanu (sic; lettre ABL 547, dans I. Ephʿal, *The Ancient Arabs* [Jérusalem, 1984], p. 116, n. 393, d'après une collation de K. Deller); les gens de Nippur se plaignent des bandes chaldéennes (encore *gudūdu*) du Dur-Iakin (lettres nᵒˢ 12N164–5, dans Cole (n. 62), pp. 121–2; cf. lettre 167, p. 122). Les déprédations de ces bandes chaldéennes rappellent l'enlèvement des chameaux en Job i 17, auquel on n'avait pas encore trouvé de parallèle précis.

[92] 2 iii 22–32.

[93] Selon 4, 32, Ninurta-kudurri-uṣur mit en campagne cent cinq chars, deux cent vingt cavaliers et trois mille fantassins contre les deux mille Araméens, sans faire appel à toutes les forces du Suhu. Selon 10 recto i 10 il avait aussi mobilisé sa garde palatine.

[94] 17, 15–18; 18, col. i.

[95] 2 iv 15–21. Avec les éditeurs (p. 357), on remarquera le sous-titre donné à cet épisode (ligne 15). Malgré la différence de style, la fin de ce passage rappelle le testament de revanche de David, 1 Rois ii 5–9.

détours du commerce arabe,[96] les dimensions et la décoration des palais,[97] la restauration des cultes légitimes et la fascination des rites anciens.[98] La combinaison de l'écrit avec la tradition orale.[99] Nous pourrions ajouter des exemples de motifs littéraires attestés aussi dans l'Ancien Testament, tels que l'hommage de la victoire à la divinité seule,[100] ou le schéma question-réponse attribué aux générations à venir,[101] Nous préférons cependant signaler quelques points de contact plus précis, suivant un ordre diachronique.

B. Traditions patriarcales

Commençons par la Genèse. La mention du segment de tribu des Sarugu peut affecter l'interprétation de Gen. xi 20–6. Ce passage donne à Abraham trois ancêtres immédiats: Serug, Nahor, Térah. Ces noms répondent à ceux de trois villes situées dans le bassin du Balikh. Tout comme Harran, ces villes sont bien attestées au VIIe siècle; mais jusqu'à présent au moins deux d'entre elles, Sarugi et Til sha Turahi, n'étaient pas aussi bien représentées aux époques plus anciennes.[102] Les tablettes de Sur Jar'a nous apportent une nouvelle attestation de Sarug avant le VIIe siècle,[103] et renforcent les attaches araméennes de la région.[104] On doit verser cette pièce au dossier de l'"Araméen errant" (Deut. xxvi 5) qu'un courant de tradition mettait à l'origine d'Israël.

---

[96] En 2 iv, une caravane de Têma et de Saba essaie d'échapper au contrôle du Suhu.

[97] A 'Anat: 18 ii 22–5; 21 iv 18–27. A Ra'il: 2 iv 9–15; 3–4, 10–14.

[98] 17, 19–32; 18 ii 7–12. Cf. 2 Rois xxiii 21–2.

[99] 2 ii 29–34; 4, 43–8; 5, verso; cf. Shamash-resh-uṣur (éd. Weissbach), col. v.

[100] 2 ii 31–4; 4, 45–6; cf. Ps. xliv 4.

[101] 2 ii 29–31, iii 9–11; 4, 43–50; 5, 5–7; 16 verso 9–10. Cf. Deut. xxix 21–7.

[102] Cf. R. de Vaux, *Histoire ancienne d'Israël des origines à l'installation en Canaan* (Paris, 1971), pp. 189–90. La seule attestation plus ancienne de Sarug était à la ligne 35 du monolithe de Kurkh de Salmanazar III, dont le texte mutilé est maintenant complété et confirmé par un parallèle que le Professeur A.K. Grayson a bien voulu nous signaler: M. Mahmud et J. Black, "Recent Work in the Nabu Temple, Nimrud", *Sumer* 44 (1985–6), pp. 135–55 (voir p. 140, ligne 52).

[103] A la rigueur on pourrait supposer que les Sarugu donnèrent leur nom à la ville et non l'inverse, et imaginer qu'ils nomadisaient ailleurs au temps des inscriptions de Sur Jar'a; mais comme le mouvement général des Araméens de Mésopotamie se portait plutôt vers le sud-est (cf. Brinkman (n. 30), pp. 283–4; mais Zadok (n. 83), spéc. pp. 65–6, pensait à une descente des Araméens du nord de la Babylonie vers le sud) on ne voit pas pourquoi ils auraient fini par fonder Sarug dans le bassin du Balikh s'ils n'avaient déjà été attachés à la Syrie septentrionale.

[104] Le caractère araméen de la population transparaissait déjà dans C.H.W.

Il faut aussi remarquer la nécessité vitale des puits dans la steppe. Dans les textes de Ninurta-kudurri-uṣur comme dans les légendes patriarcales, on notera le souci de donner des noms aux puits et d'en conserver un souvenir précis.[105] Les conditions écologiques et les efforts d'adaptation reflétés dans les légendes d'Abraham et d'Isaac au pays d'Abimélek (Gen. xxi 22–32, xxvi 12–22) avaient donc encore leur équivalent sur le Moyen-Euphrate longtemps après la grande époque de Mari.

C. Balaam

Les inscriptions de Sur Jar'a éclairent un autre épisode des origines israélites, le cycle de Balaam; en effet, le chef de bande "hamathéen" dont nous avons parlé s'appelait Iaé fils de Balaam.[106] Son patronyme correspond à celui du devin du livre des Nombres et nous livre la première attestation cunéiforme de ce nom biblique.[107] Pour trouver Balaam en dehors de l'Ecriture, il faut en effet descendre jusqu'au VIIIe siècle; c'est alors qu'il apparaît à peu près en même temps sur les tablettes de Ninurta-kudurri-uṣur et dans le "groupement I" de Deir 'Alla sur le Yabboq.[108] Ce dernier texte représente sûrement une composition plus ancienne que sa mise par écrit, et le père du brigand hamathéen doit être né vers la fin du IXe siècle.

Johns (éd.) *Assyrian Doomsday Book* (Leipzig, 1901); il est reconnu par F.M. Fales dans sa nouvelle édition de ce cadastre, *Censimenti e catasti di epoca neo-assira* (Rome, 1973).

[105] Trait relevé par V. Matthews, "The Wells of Gerar", *BA* 49 (1986), pp. 118–26, spéc. 123–4.

[106] ᵐBa-la-am-mu en 2 i 17; ᵐBa-li-am-mu en 21 i 8.

[107] Ce que l'on répète sur Balaam comme forme tardive de Yabil-'Ammu dérive finalement de W.F. Albright, "The Name of Bildad the Shuhite", *AJSL* 44 (1927–8), pp. 31–6; or Yabil-'Ammu n'est pas une forme directement attestée, mais une reconstruction basée sur Bil'am, Yabil-Wirra et le nom de lieu Yible'am (p. 32). Comme attestations cunéiformes de Balaam, on cite parfois aussi le Bêl-amma (EN-am-ma) d'une inscription de Merodach-Baladan II (cf. E. Schrader et al., *Keilinschriftliche Bibliothek* III/1 [Berlin, 1892], p. 190, iv 29); mais, tout comme le Am-me-ba-a'-li rencontré par Tukulti-Ninurta II (Grayson [n. 5], p. 172, texte A.O.100.5, ligne 23), ce Bêl-Amma est basé sur le nom de Ba'al, et ne peut correspondre aux consonnes ouest-sémitiques de *bl'm*.

[108] Editio princeps: J. Hoftijzer et G. van der Kooij, *Aramaic Texts from 'Alla* (Leiden, 1977). Sur l'état actuel de l'interprétation, cf. *The Balaam Text from Deir 'Alla Re-evaluated. Proceedings of the International Symposium held at Leiden 21–24 August 1989* (Leiden, 1991; mêmes éditeurs). Parmi les experts réunis à Leiden A. Lemaire et D. Pardee soutenaient le caractère araméen des textes, et M. Weippert penchait pour un état de langue plus ancien mais en marche vers l'araméen (cf. pp. 159–63). P.K. McCarter et J. Huehnergard, qui refusaient de choisir entre cananéen et araméen, représentent mieux la majorité des congressistes. Tous soulignaient l'archaisme de la langue.

Une partie des textes bibliques (Num. xxii 5; Deut. xxiii 5) fait venir Balaam de Pethor sur l'Euphrate (non loin de Til Barsip[109]), en terre araméenne (Num. xxii 5, surtout xxiii 7); et les commentateurs citent souvent le texte où Salmanazar III admet la conquête de Pethor par un roi d'Aram autour de l'an mille.[110] Certains passages de l'Ancien Testament pourraient suggérer un enracinement moabite ou madianite pour ce devin dont les activités se déroulent au pays de Moab,[111] mais les nouveaux documents du Moyen-Euphrate donnent plus de réalisme que jamais à un Balaam araméen, et leur histoire de rezzou montre que le nom de Balaam était connu non loin de Pethor.[112]

D. Contacts Syrie-Palestine/Moyen-Euphrate. "Bildad"

Dans le cas de Balaam comme dans celui des ancêtres immédiats d'Abraham, la vision israélite des origines s'est donc efforcée de faire une place aux Araméens du nord. S'ajoutant à d'autres données encore peu exploitées, les textes nouvellement découverts permettent d'élargir la scène encore davantage. Dès avant les conquêtes de Téglath-Phalazar III, les contacts, militaires et autres, entre Syrie-Palestine et Moyen-Euphrate ne se limitaient pas aux incursions assyriennes.

On remarquera d'abord la symétrie qui existe entre l'aventure d'un chef de bande issu de Hamath et marchant sur le Suhu—principale ville: 'Anat—, et celle de Zakkur, "l'homme de 'Ana(t)", qui avait pris le pouvoir au royaume de Hamath un quart de siècle plus tôt.[113] Nous savons maintenant par des inscriptions trouvées dans le monde grec que, quelques décennies plus tôt, Hazaël avait réussi à contre-

---

H.-P. Müller, "Die Sprache der Texte von Tell Deir 'Alla im Kontext der nordwestsemitischen Sprachen", *Zeitschrift für Althebraistik* 4 (1991), pp. 1–31, penchait de même vers un état archaïque du sémitique du nord-ouest, où l'araméen ne s'était pas encore vraiment séparé du cananéen.

[109] Pethor (akk. Pitru) était sur la rive droite de l'Euphrate au confluent de la rivière Saghur, mais le cours du fleuve a changé et le site exact ne sera peut-être jamais retrouvé. Cf. Kessler (n. 36), pp. 191–4.

[110] Monolithe de Kurkh, ii 36–8; traduction dans Luckenbill (n. 54), p. 218 ¶ 603.

[111] Cf. M. Noth, *Überlieferungsgeschichte des Pentateuch* (Stuttgart, 1948), pp. 82–3.

[112] Ces textes favorisent du même coup la vieille hypothèse qui rapprochait Balaam du Bela' fils de Be'or de Gen. xxxvi 32–3, pour peu qu'on remplace "Edom" par "Aram", paléographiquement semblable et sujet à fréquente confusion. Cf. Lemaire (n. 23).

[113] Les textes de Ninurta-kudurri-uṣur apportent un nouveau soutien à cette interprétation du fameux 'š 'nh 'nh, défendue récemment par A.R. Millard, "The Homeland of Zakkur", *Semitica* 39 (1990), pp. 47–52. Millard a eu le mérite de montrer que

attaquer au-delà du Fleuve, en sens inverse de ces traversées de l'Euphrate dont se vantaient les rois d'Aššur.[114] Ces textes devraient peut-être susciter un nouvel examen de l'inscription monumentale d'un roi de Hamath, en hiéroglyphes louvites, qui fut découverte en 1934 à Hines, dans le nord de l'Assyrie;[115] on sait que Hamath avait été avec Damas l'âme de la résistance à Salmanazar III, et ce en un temps où son roi utilisait le louvite dans ses inscriptions.[116] Le va-et-vient peut avoir été encore plus actif aux XIe et Xe siècles, avant la renaissance de l'Assyrie, et on ne doit pas douter de la possibilité des contacts transeuphratains attribués à Hadadézer roi de Ṣoba dans le livre de Samuel (2 Sam. viii 3, x 16).

Les Araméens jouaient aussi un rôle crucial dans le commerce transeuphratain. En se basant sur les listes de tribut assyriennes, on avait relevé la part du Laqu et de Hindanu dans la distribution des étoffes pourprées apportées de la côte méditerranéenne à Karkémish.[117] L'histoire de caravane arraisonnée de Sur Jarʿa (2 iv 26–38) vient confirmer cette perception. La laine pourprée tient la première place dans la cargaison saisie par Ninurta-kudurri-uṣur (ligne 36). La mauvaise conservation du début du récit ne permet pas de déterminer par quels chemins la caravane était parvenue à Hindanu; mais il est

---

l'orthographe akkadienne *Hanat*, avec un *t* final, peut recouvrir une prononciation où *t* est déjà quiescent comme dans l'inscription de Zakkur (pp. 49–50). On peut différer d'avis avec Millard sur quelques points secondaires. Ainsi, en montrant l'importance du culte d'ʿAnat dans la ville du même nom, les nouveaux documents suggèrent plus que jamais que la cité devait son nom à la déesse (comp. Millard, p. 49); le nom de Tukulti-Mer, le dernier roi connu de Hana/Mari (vers 1050), donne plus de poids au dieu Mer/Wer comme lien entre Zakkur et le "Suhu et Mari" que Millard ne voulait l'admettre (p. 51).

[114] Bibliographie dans J.A. Fitzmyer et S.A. Kaufman, *An Aramaic Bibliography, Part I, Old, Official and Biblical Aramaic* (Baltimore, 1992), pp. 22–3, n° B.1.17.

[115] Hines est à 1 km de Bavian, un point crucial du système d'aqueducs de Sennachérib; voir la carte dans T. Jacobsen et S. Lloyd, *Sennacherib's Aqueduct at Jerwan* (Chicago, 1935), p. 32, fig. 9—Editio princeps du monument par T. Jacobsen dans H. Frankfort et T. Jacobsen, *Oriental Institute Discoveries in Iraq, 1933/34* (Chicago, 1935), pp. 101–3. Le texte est reproduit dans des corpus tels que P. Meriggi, *Manuale di Eteo Geroglifico, Parte II: Testi—2ª e 3ª Serie* (Rome, 1975), p. 254, et pl. xlvi, mais il est à peu près complètement oublié des historiens. Seul B. Landsberger, *Samʾal. Studien zur der Entdeckung der Ruinenstätte Karatepe* (Ankara, 1948), p. 33, n. 66, écrivait qu'il fallait bien admettre l'avance d'un roi de Hamath jusqu'en pleine Assyrie quelque temps avant 800, tout difficile qu'il soit d'en comprendre la portée historique.

[116] Selon Jacobsen (n. 17), p. 102, l'inscription de Hines était du même style que celles d'Urhilina, c.-à-d, d'Irhuleni, l'associé d'Adad-idri à Qarqar.

[117] Cf. N.B. Jankowska, "Some Problems of the Economy of the Assyrian Empire", dans I.M. Diakonoff (éd.), *Ancient Mesopotamia, Socio-Economic History* (Moscou, 1969), pp. 259–60 (l'original russe était de 1947).

clair qu'elle avait quitté cet emporium chargée de produits syriens.

Le trafic allait aussi en sens inverse, et les archéologues de l'Université de Tel Aviv trouvèrent à Bersabée un sceau votif[118] dédié au dieu Apladad[119] par un Rimut-ilani, fils d'Adad-idri, c.-à-d., Hadadézer, manifestement un prince araméen. Le sceau ne peut être daté, mais la graphie est néo-babylonienne comme celle des documents d'ʿAnat et Sur Jarʿa.

L'inscription de Shamash-resh-uṣur éditée par Weissbach fournissait la première attestation d'Apladad (iii 2), et les exemples se multipliaient à partir du VIIe siècle av. J.-C., spécialement à l'intérieur des noms théophores; ils ne s'espaçaient définitivement qu'à partir du IIIe siècle de notre ère. On savait déjà qu'Apladad était le dieu d' ʿAnat aux temps gréco-romains,[120] et les nouveaux documents de Shamash-resh-uṣur et de son fils nous le montrent en passe d'accaparer ce privilège.

Dans ces textes Apladad apparaît au moins vingt-sept fois,[121] souvent associé à son père Adad.[122] Dans l'inscription n° 1, Ninurta-kudurri-uṣur dédie un même temple à Adad et Apladad; les appelle ensemble, au singulier, Seigneur de la ville d'ʿAnat; leur fait hommage des épithètes cultuelles d'Adad; et, grammaticalement, les traite comme une seule et même personne.[123] Dans la stèle sur l'histoire d'ʿAnat, Adad et Apladad sont censés avoir déterminé le sort de la ville et ce

---

[118] Cf. A.F. Rainey, "The Cuneiform Inscription on a Votive Cylinder from Beer-Sheba", dans Y. Aharoni (éd.), *Beer-Sheba I. Excavations at Tel Beer-Sheba, 1969–1971 Seasons* (Tel Aviv, 1973), pp. 61–70 et p. xxvi.

[119] DINGIR A DINGIR IM, "le fils d'Adad". Les lectures sémitiques—et grecques—du nom divin se présentent en plusieurs variantes sur lesquelles cf. Lipiński (n. 14), pp. 53–74.

[120] Rainey et Lipiński l'ont montré indépendamment dans les articles cités. Cruciale est une inscription grecque de Dura-Europos, qui appelle Aphlad (sic) "le dieu du bourg d'ʿAnath sur l'Euphrate"; cf. C. Hopkins, dans M.I. Rostovtzeff (éd.), *The Excavations at Dura Europos. Preliminary Report of the Fifth Season of Work: October 1931–March 1932* (New Haven, Conn., 1934), pp. 112–13, n° 416.

[121] Les listes qui suivent ne tiennent compte ni de l'inscription publiée par Weissbach, ni du n° 3, simple doublet du n° 4: Apladad apparaît en 1, 1.15.20; 2 i 4, [32], iii 25, 28, 29 iv 31; 4, 29.31.32.45.48.49; 7 i 3, 9, iv [11]; 9 verso 1.7.10.11.12; 10 recto i 4, iii 1, 11; 18 ii 3, tranche droite 14. Aux endroits suivants, on lit "Adad et Apladad": 1, 1.15.20; 2 i 4, [32]; 4, 2.9.45; 7 i 9, iv [11]; 9 verso 10.11; 10 recto iii [11]; 18 ii 3, tranche droite 14.

[122] On se souviendra que dans l'inscription éditée par Weissbach, Apladad suivait immédiatement Adad, avant Shala sa parèdre (iii 2).

[123] Lignes 1–11.—Les textes qui parlent des dieux Adad et Mishar au lieu d'Adad et Apladad ne vont pas aussi loin. Cf. 2 iv 2–9; 4, 4–9; 9 iii 13–20; 12, 3–8; 19 iii 3–12; 21 iii 1–4.

sont eux, plutôt que la déesse 'Anat, qui font figure de divinité tuté-
laire.[124]

D'autres passages, où Apladad seul est nommé, montrent l'importance toute spéciale qu'il avait déjà prise au Suhu. Ninurta-kudurri-
uṣur donne le nom de Kar-Apladad à la ville qu'il fonde sur l'Euphrate,[125] il appelle Apladad "mon seigneur",[126] et lui attribue sa victoire
sur les Araméens.[127]

Apladad et le Suhu rappellent forcément le deuxième ami de Job,
Bildad le shuhite (Job ii 11, viii 1, xviii 1, xxv 1, xlii 9). Déjà en
1881, Friedrich Delitzsch avait expliqué le Shuah biblique par Suhu
et s'était approché d'une explication de Bildad par Apladad,[128] mais
le nom d'Apladad était encore mal compris, et en 1902 l'association
de Shuah et des tribus arabes issues de Qeturah (Gen. xxv 1–4) amena
Delitzsch à rétracter son identification avec le Suhu;[129] sans être
oubliée, celle-ci ne prit pas pied fermement dans notre tradition
exégétique.

Pourtant, Gen. xxv ne posait pas un vrai problème. Israël Eph'al
trouvait déjà aux "fils de Qeturah" un dénominateur commun non
dans la nationalité arabe mais dans le commerce international, et
cette solution est renforcée par ce que de nouvelles sources nous ont
appris sur le rôle-clé du Moyen-Euphrate et sa fréquentation par les
caravaniers arabes. Les mêmes sources ayant remis à l'honneur le
rôle joué par Apladad dans cette région dès le VIIIe siècle, nous
pouvons revenir avec confiance à l'ancienne intuition de Delitzsch.[130]

IV. *Conclusion*

Concluons brièvement. A notre avis, le principal profit que les études bibliques peuvent tirer des nouveaux documents du Moyen-
Euphrate réside dans la lumière qu'ils jettent sur des nations histori-
quement contemporaines de la monarchie israélite, et comparables à

---

[124] 18 ii 3–5; tranche droite 14–15. Cf. 2 iii 29, où Apladad (nommé seul) est
appelé "celui qui réside à 'Anat".

[125] Cf. 2 iii 25, iv 31.

[126] Cf. 4, 31.32.48.49; 9 verso 7, 12; 10 recto i 7

[127] Il a consulté ce dieu avant la bataille: 4, 31–32; 10 recto i 4.7; et c'est à lui
qu'il doit sa victoire: 4, 48–50; 9, 12.

[128] Cf. F. Delitzsch, *Wo lag das Paradies?* (Leipzig, 1881), pp. 297–8.

[129] Cf. *Das Buch Hiob neu übersetzt und kurzerklärt* (Leipzig, 1902), p. 139.

[130] Lipiński (n. 14), pp. 64–5, défendait cette identification et dissipait les problèmes de détail posés par la chute du /a/ initial d'Apladad, et le remplacement du
/p/ par un /b/.

celle-ci par leurs dimensions et leurs origines ethniques.

Ces nouvelles sources nous auront aussi fait voir, sur trois sujets distincts, à quel point les Israélites étaient conscients du monde araméen et soucieux de l'intégrer à leur vision historique et à leurs compositions littéraires. La tradition d'Israël place les noms auxquels nous nous sommes arrêtés à des siècles de distance les uns des autres, mais toujours en des temps très anciens: Abraham et Job d'une part, et Balaam d'autre part. Les points de référence que nous leur avons trouvés ne permettent aucune datation précise, mais ils nous orientent vers les premiers siècles du premier millénaire, et ils appuient modestement une formule de Yohanan Aharoni, "Nothing early and nothing late".

THE CITY OF WOMEN: WOMEN'S PLACES IN ANCIENT ISRAELITE CITIES

by

C.H.J. DE GEUS
Groningen

If one tries to visualize life in a biblical city, one is still compelled to use parallels from the modern Near East, preferably from old drawings and the first photographs taken by travellers of the last century.[1] There are still many questions as to details of architecture, of clothing or even of the physiognomy of the people that archaeology cannot answer.

For modern men in Western Europe or the USA women in the Near East are immediately associated with veils and *hareems*. Both of these are aspects of a deeply-felt need to seclude women from public life and to keep them away as much as possible from agressive looks, remarks and gestures, or even pawing of strangers.

This need to protect the privacy of women has always found spatial expression in the architecture of palaces and of simple private dwellings. Many modern visitors have seen the splendour of the *haremliks* of Istanbul or Teheran. But even in the tents of the bedouin there is a division in space for men and women (plus children). In Eastern Turkey and Northern Syria the simple one-room house of poor farmers is often surrounded by a wall and the courtyard thus formed around the house is again divided—formerly by another wall—into a *haremlik* and a *selamlik*. But whenever possible the second storey of the house is reserved for the women. A modern traveller who is in the company of a woman or children today will still be led to a "family room" on the second floor of a restaurant, even if they would prefer to remain downstairs where many more customers (all men) are sitting.

---

[1] During the 19th century many hundreds of accounts of journeys to the East were published in Europe and in the USA, several of them by women. As they had access to the *haremliks*—some of them even lived there for many years—these books are the most relevant for our subject. See, for instance, Lucy M.J. Garnett, *The Women of Turkey and their Folk-Lore* (London, 1891). At this time Palestine was still "Turkey".

As far as we can tell the system of seclusion is very old and has always been a matter of social prestige. The higher in the social hierarchy, the more secluded are the women. It was always more strict in the urban culture than on the fringes of the desert.[2]

Female seclusion was already a general rule in classical times. This also applied to the Jews of Palestine. In Greek texts there are several words to denote the rooms for women: γυναικών, γύναιον, γυναικεῖοσ, γυναικεῖα. The equivalent of *hareem*, γυναικωνῖτις, is used by Flavius Josephus to denote the area for women in the Temple of Jerusalem (*De Bell. Jud.* V 199). Léonie J. Archer describes the very strict rules of seclusion for Jewish women, especially for the unmarried girls, during the Greek and Roman periods, "Without doubt, therefore, seclusion was the only acceptable standard of modesty for young girls in Graeco-Roman Palestine".[3]

There is an interesting remark in 2 Macc. iii 19, that in the panic that broke out in Jerusalem, when Heliodorus threatened to loot the Temple, young girls and women were seen who normally lived in seclusion.

Hareems existed already at the courts of ancient Egypt and Assyria.[4] More familiar to us are the *hareems* of David and Solomon, or the *bēt hannāšīm* that is mentioned four times in the book of Esther (ii 9, 11, 13, 14).

If at the courts of Jerusalem and Samaria the royal women were held in seclusion, there is reason to assume that the lower echelons of Israelite and Judean society did likewise. The governors of the cities and all the great men would have tried to imitate the royal life-style as much as possible. From this starting point my question arises: if we may assume that there was some spatial division between men and women in the ancient Israelite cities, is it possible to identify them?

---

[2] The custom of seclusion is typical of Near Eastern urban culture: *Encyclopaedia of Islam* III (Leiden and London, 1971), p. 209. There seems to be only one comprehensive study of the *hareem* and *pardah* system: a Dutch dissertation from 1954: J. Wattel, *Harem- en Pardahsysteem* (Meppel, 1954).

[3] *Her Price is Beyond Rubies. The Jewish Woman in Graeco-Roman Palestine* (Sheffield, 1990). The quotation is from p. 118.

[4] Many texts have been preserved pertaining to *hareem*-ladies: E. Weidner, "Hof- und Haremserlasse assyrischer Könige aus dem 2. Jahrtausend v. Chr.", *AFO* 14 (1956), pp. 257–93; B.F. Batto, *Studies on Women at Mari* (Baltimore, 1974). Letters from ladies of the royal *hareem* at the Neo-Assyrian court are now available in Th. Kwasman and S. Parpola, *Legal Transactions of the Royal Court of Nineve, Part I. Tiglath*

It is remarkable that the Israelite city of biblical times is always described as a city of men, even by modern female authors.[5] If one wanted to have a word with somebody, the meeting place for men was at the city-gate, or the gates if there were more than one.[6] Alternatively, men could meet at the local sanctuary or a private house. Women also passed through the gates, but apparently it was not considered proper to address them there. The meeting place of women was at the spring or at the pool or whatever water-system a city had.[7] There is a certain ambivalence about the biblical spring-stories: it was considered risky for girls to go out of the city and descend to the spring. They might have unwanted meetings with men or they could even be harassed by shepherds or strangers. Among the 104 new settlements of Iron Age I, I. Finkelstein[8] found only 7 that were situated more than 3 km. from a spring. In such cases much time and energy would have been lost fetching water, not to speak of all the dangers mentioned above. In the course of Iron Age II most of the Israelite villages and cities built waterworks to make access to water safer and quicker. They built pools to collect rainwater, and canals to conduct it to the city and the fields.

Tunnels were hewn out through hills to bring spring-water to the other side of the hill, as was the case with the famous Siloam tunnel in Jerusalem.[9] The impressive water-systems in cities like Megiddo, Hazor and Beer-sheba and also the Warren shaft in the City of David are now dated by archaeologists in Iron Age I or II. These works are called by A. Mazar "unparalleled in contemporary neighbouring countries".[10] The purpose of such water-systems was first of all to facilitate access to the spring-water from inside the city. For

Pileser III through Esarhaddon (Helsinki, 1991). For the veil in ancient Assyria: H.W. Saggs, *The Greatness that was Babylon* (London, 1962), p. 214.

[5] Sh. Geva, *Hazor, Israel. An Urban Community of the 8th Century B.C.E.* (Oxford, 1989), p. 30: "(Hazor) was a city in the full sense of the term, with a lively community attuned to the latest in the arts, commerce, agriculture and industry; through its gates passed farmers, merchants and wayfarers, administrators and rulers from the surrounding areas."

[6] L. Köhler, *Der hebräische Mensch* (Tübingen, 1953). Z. Herzog, *Das Stadttor in Israel und in den Nachbarländern* (Mainz, 1986), pp. 157–65, speaks briefly about the military, political, juridical, economic and cultic functions of the city-gate, but does not enter into its social functions as the meeting place *par excellence*.

[7] Gen. xxiv 13–21, xxix 1–12; Ex. ii 16–20; 1 Sam. ix 11–14.

[8] *The Archaeology of the Israelite Settlement* (Jerusalem, 1988) p. 195.

[9] Z.Y.D. Ron, "Development and Management of Irrigation Systems in Mountain Regions of the Holy Land", *Trans. Inst. Br. Geogr.* N.S. 10 (1985), pp. 149–269.

[10] *Archaeology of the Land of the Bible* (New York and Toronto, 1990), pp. 478–85.

years we have been used to a purely defensive interpretation of the water-systems. Nowadays, one tends more and more to interpret these gigantic enterprises as primarily constructed for the benefit of the women, to make their daily trip to the spring easier and safer. The usual military explanation is founded on the combination of 2 Kings xx 20 with 2 Chron. xxxii 2–5. But it is not at all sure that the Gihon spring was also included in "the springs that were outside the city". Along the Eastern slope of the Ophel Hill there existed a built-up area outside or under the city-wall. At the foot of the city-wall there ran an extra-mural street.[11] The text of 2 Kings xx 20 speaks only of peace, and also the famous Siloam-inscription gives not the faintest impression of the impending dangers of war. This function of supplying water in peacetime for everyday needs is also stressed by Mazar.

A convincing case might be the covered stairway at Tell es-Saʻidiyeh in the Jordan-valley (fig. 1). At this site steps were found constructed over the surface of the mound, leading from a point inside the walls and passing under the city-wall—probably by means of a postern gate (now lost)—over the tell to the spring north of the tell. The excavator estimates that this stairway originally consisted of 120 steps. On both sides of the steps there ran a stone wall, and a third wall of clay and stones was erected over the middle of the steps. In this way the covered corridor was divided into one side for the girls descending and another for those climbing the steps with their heavy jars of water.[12] The covering of the stairway consisted of a roof of branches with clay. This would surely have given good protection against the sun but not against an armed and trained enemy.[13] From the viewpoint of the seclusion of women, however, it makes excellent sense. At the same time, single files of ascending and descending women and girls might give the impression of great efficiency but not of many opportunities for social contact.

In the northern Israelite town of Hazor we face a similar situation. There too the water-drawing was a well-organized affair (fig. 2). Here too the entrance to the great shaft was strictly organized. In no way was the area around the water-shaft conducive to social contact. In

---

[11] M.L. Steiner, "A Note on the Iron Age Defence Wall on the Ophel Hill of Jerusalem", *PEQ* 118 (1986), pp. 27–32.

[12] J.B. Pritchard, *Tell es-Saʻidiyeh. Excavations on the Tell. 1964–1966* (Philadelphia, 1985), pp. 57–9.

[13] Helga Weippert, *Palästina in vorhellenistischer Zeit.* (München, 1988), p. 550.

this there is a marked difference from the city-gates where in several cities benches have been found. Especially in the small plaza between the outer and inner gate of Dan one can imagine the men sitting and talking and watching the days go by. No such thing for women.[14]

The waterworks seem to be the only clear case of gender differentiation in ancient Israelite cities that was exclusively for women, and maybe an occasional slave.

If we turn now to the private dwellings, the situation is still unclear and confused, especially with regard to the basic living conditions of ancient Israelite women. In a way this is astonishing. During the last decades so many studies have been written on biblical women, most of them by women. Practically all of them are purely literary or sociological investigations. There is hardly any interest in the archaeological, material context of women in biblical antiquity, although at the same time so many women have held leading positions in Palestinian archaeology. As will be made clear below, the archaeological material available is indeed meagre and elusive. But one should at least try to squeeze some relevant data from it. The only exception is Carol Meyers who is herself involved in practical archaeology. But pertaining to her women-studies the use of archaeological data is disappointing.[15]

Analysis of biblical texts informs us that the traditional place of the women was at home and in the family. But it is still impossible to describe the daily routine and living conditions of the women. The situation is complicated further because of the social hierarchy in which women lived.[16] The rule is: the higher the social status of

---

[14] "The other missing link relates to activities around the water source. In studying Hazor's water-systems, we saw how its structure, shape, access roads, and internal design indicate that its sole function was to supply water. The activities usually associated with the water source — watering animals, resting, a quick dip to freshen up, social intercourse, etc.—took place . . . outside the walls and some distance away" (Geva [n. 5], p. 109).

[15] In the volume edited by P.L. Day, *Gender and Difference in Ancient Israel* (Minneapolis, 1989), the questions of spatial difference and seclusion are not even mentioned.

[16] One of the reasons for Meyers, in her search for the Israelite woman, to restrict herself to the highland villages of the Iron I period is that at this stage the social structure of the Israelites was still simple. Social and economic diversity was also limited or absent in these small settlements: C. Meyers, "Roots of Restriction: Male-Female Balance in Early Israel", *Journ. American Academy of Religion* 51 (1983), pp. 569–93: *Discovering Eve: Ancient Israelite Women in Context* (New York and Oxford, 1988).

women, the more secluded and restricted to their quarters they lived. "Ordinary" women worked with the men in the fields. Thus Samson's mother (Judg. xiii 9), and the girl in the Song of Songs acquired a deep tan from her work in the vineyards (i 5–6). The book of Ruth and many passages from the Prophets attest this working together of families and sexes. Unfortunately, it is no longer accepted that a greater role in the family economy resulted in a more equal position with men.[17] The female hierarchy in an average household could consist of wife(s), concubine(s), daughter(s), daughters(s)-in-law, maid-servant(s) and slave-girl(s), not to speak of grandmother(s), aunt(s), sister(s) etc.[18]

A second complication is that we are still unable to offer a reconstruction of the Israelite house of the Iron Age. What we have are just ground-plans. About the actual construction we know very little. There is, however, a growing consensus that such houses had at least two storeys.[19] Analysis of finds made on the ground-level has led to the conclusion that this level was in the first place the production-area of the household, in combination with the courtyard if there was one. What we find are all kinds of tools: mill-stones, oil-presses, ovens, hearths, loom-weights, pottery for cooking and eating, pottery for storage. Most of these objects would surely have been handled by women in antiquity. When we find smaller pottery-forms and more expensive wares, bone instruments and other objects, it is often hard to tell what belonged on the ground-floor and what fell from above. At Hazor sherds of the beautiful "Samaria-ware" (probably a Phoenician import) were also found in courtyards and around buildings, obviously having fallen from an upper storey.[20]

It seems to me that we must look at the upper storeys for the women's quarters, as was the case in ancient Greece. But we find no equivalents of the men's room—ἀνδρών—of the Greeks in the ground plan. The richer houses would have had at least two storeys and an

---

[17] M.K. Whyte, *The Status of Women in Preindustrial Societies* (Princetown, 1978), p. 172.

[18] K. Engelken, *Frauen im Alten Israel. Eine begriffsgeschichtliche und sozialgeschichtliche Studie zur Stellung der Frau im Alten Testament* (Stuttgart, 1990).

[19] F. Braemer, *L'Architecture domestique du Levant à l'age de fer* (Paris, 1982). Braemer leaves the question of an upper storey open. Outspoken are C.H.J. de Geus, "On the Profile of a Biblical City", *BA* 49 (1986), pp. 224–8: L.E. Stager, "The Archaeology of the Family in Ancient Israel", *BASOR* 260 (1985), pp. 1–36.

[20] Y. Yadin, *The James A. de Rothschild Expedition at Hazor I–IV* (III/IV ed. by A. Ben-Tor) (Jerusalem, 1958 and 1960, 1989). Also Geva (n. 5), pp. 35, 43, 47.

"upper room": *'ăliyyā*. This *'ăliyyā* was a social meeting-room and guest-room for men. Compare the *'ăliyyat hamm^eqērā* of Judg. iii 20. Such a room would probably have taken up only part of the roof of a house.[21] That the broad room on the ground-floor in the rear of the Four-Room Houses was in any way an equivalent of the Greek ἀνδρών seems unlikely to me. Analysis of the finds does not point in that direction. In that case, male visitors had to pass through the central room with all its activities.[22]

Besides the identification of objects that may have fallen down from upstairs including fragments of roofing—there is the evidence of stairways. Stairs are well known in ancient Israelite cities. Stone stairways consist of about 10 steps but are presumed to have continued with brick steps or wooden ones. Maybe the higher steps were simply robbed later on. There are stairs outside the houses and inside. When outside a building, they usually run parallel to the wall; when inside, then usually in one of the front rooms of the house.[23] I know of only a few cases where stairs were built in the central room ("courtyard").[24] Besides the stone steps, wooden ladders would have been used. Stairs and ladders inside the house undoubtly led to the upper storeys and the roof. The position of the stairs indicates that (male?) visitors were led straight to the guest-room on the roof. The production area and family area were passed by (fig. 3).

Outside stairs had the same function but also a more public one. They were necessary in those parts of a city that were built on a slope. They gave access to the upper storeys of a building, but also

---

[21] About the technical building details little can be said as yet. I presume that the ground-level of most houses, including the so-called Four-Room Houses was completely covered. Light could come in and smoke get out through small openings/windows high on the walls. This can still be seen in the high houses of Yemen. Real windows were only present in the walls of the upper floors.

[22] It is not possible to draw conclusions as to gender differentiation from the ground plan of the Israelite house. Cf. for Greece: S. Walker, "Women and Housing in Classical Greece. The Archaeological Evidence", in A. Cameron and A. Kuhrt, *Images of women in Antiquity* (London, 1983), pp. 81–91 (see fig. 6). In Palestinian Iron Age domestic architecture there existed no men's room comparable to those of Persian and Hellenistic Babylon or Dura Europos. At least not on the ground-floor. Maybe the function of the *'ăliyyā* resembled that of the Yemenite *mafrağ*. It is of interest to point out here that among classical archaeologists the introduction of the ἀνδρών is considered to be an Eastern influence. W. Hoepfner and E.L. Schwandner, *Haus und Stadt im klassischen Griechenland. Wohnen in der Polis* I (München, 1986), pp. 236–9.

[23] This was often the case at Beersheba. But cf. also Tell en-Nasbeh 685, TBM SE 1 13/16 and TBM SE 50/3 (quoted according to Braemer [n. 19]).

[24] Horvat Ritma A; TBM SE 1 2/3.

to other roofs or storeys and to a street on a higher or lower level. Several excavators have observed that such outside steps gave access to other roofs too.[25] An example of such a more public stairway is the one next to Ahiel's house in the City of David. In the citadel of Hazor a beautiful stairway led up to the main building/palace in area B, but probably also to the roofs or upper floors of the adjacent buildings 3103, 3100 and 3235/3067 (figs 4 and 5). There are no indications that the inner or outer stairs were meant especially for women. But it is clear that their location aimed at avoiding any sort of "traffic" through the inner parts of the buildings.

The word *hallōn* "window" is often used in the Hebrew Bible in connection with palaces and women: Judg. v 28; 1 Sam. xix 12; 2 Sam. vi 16; 2 Kings xiii 17; Jer. ix 20; Joel ii 9. In the story of Jezebel mention is made of an Egyptian-style "Window of Appearance": this was large enough to show at least three persons and low enough to push the queen over. I think that such a big "window" is indicated by the large opening on the second floor of the cult-stand from Taänach (10th century). Important is also the use of the root *šqp* N and H for verbs meaning looking out of the window from a high position.

From the military viewpoint of defenders, stairways to city walls are logical. But also in peacetime they were used intensively. Those stretches of the walls that were not built over or incorporated into houses (Josh. ii 15; 1 Sam. xix 12) could be used as streets. It was often the quickest way for people on foot to move from one part of a city to another, over the wall and also using the roofs of houses and other buildings. In Mizpah (Tell en-Nasbeh) there was a large cistern in the north-eastern corner of the city, just inside the city wall. Next to this pool, stairs were built leading up to the wall. These stairs were built to facilitate the "traffic" to and from this water-source via the wall. Possibly, the enigmatic text Neh. xii 37 describes a similar situation in post-exilic Jerusalem.

If my conclusion is right that the "city of women" had at least two poles; the family-house and the source of water, then the connecting area was also important. This consisted of the streets and "squares", and, for ladies of some status, the roofs and the city-wall. We do not know to what extent women were involved in shopping

---

[25] This was already observed by C.C. McCown, *Tell en-Nasbeh* I (Berkeley and New Haven, Conn., 1947), pp. 213–15.

and selling. In an Israelite city there was no such thing as a market place.[26] Trade took place outside and in front of the city-gates. In my opinion, so far insufficient attention has been devoted to the roofs as an area in the city that was widely used for socializing, for storage, but also for moving about.

Men received guests on the roof (1 Sam. ix 25–6). There was a prescription necessary to assure the safety of the roof (Deut. xxii 8). In Isa. xv 3, xxii 1, and Jer. xlviii 33 gag is used parallel with $r^eh\bar{o}b$ and $h\bar{u}s$. Women had their activities on the roofs too. Three times they are condemned for unlawful offerings "on the roofs" (Zeph. i 5; Jer. xix 13, xxxii 29).

It is not difficult to imagine the situation in the narrow, crowded, muddy (Micah vii 10) and slippery streets and alleys of an Iron Age city. Anyone who wanted to avoid this jumble of men and animals stayed as much as possible on the higher level of roofs and walls: the $m^er\bar{o}m\bar{e}$ $q\bar{a}ret$ (Prov. ix 3 and 14). As an analogy, and no more than that, I recall the situation that existed in North Africa where the flat roofs of the cities used to be the exclusive terrain of women.[27]

If this hypothesis should hold true, then the three basic activities of the community,[28] "subsistence", "living/procreation" and "defence/gouvernment", corresponded also with separate vertical levels in the Israelite city.

---

[26] C.H.J. de Geus, *De Israëlitische Stad* (Kampen, 1984).

[27] J. et J. Tharaud, *Rabat ou les heures marocaines* (Paris, 1918), p. 18. E.F. Gauthier, *Le passé de l'Afrique du Nord* (Paris, 1937), p. 243: "Les terrasses d'une ville musulmane sont tout autre chose que la couverture des maisons: ils communiquent d'une bout à l'autre de la vie féminine, rançon de la claustration... La terrasse est le domaine de la femme, à qui la rue est interdite."

[28] Cf. Meyers's publications in n. 16.

1. Drawing of the stairs at Tell es-Sa'idiyeh (from C.H.J. de Geus, *De Israelitische Stad* [Kampen, 1984])

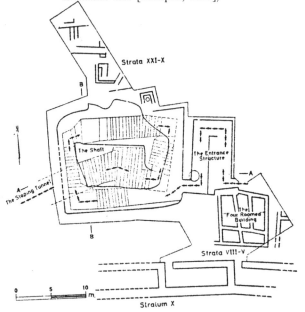

2. The Water-System and the adjacent buildings at Hazor (from Y. Yadin, *Hazor* The Schweich Lectures for 1970 [London, 1972], fig. 46).

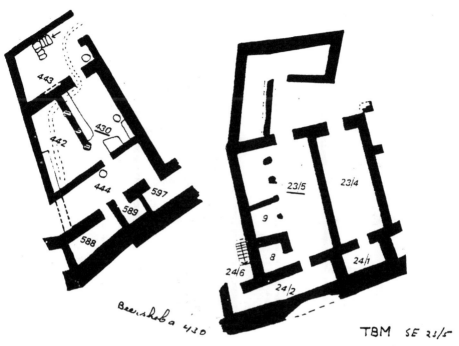

3. Hazor, the Citadel of Stratum Vb
(from Yadin, *Hazor*, fig. 51)

4. House plan with a stairway along
the exterior wall at Tell Beit Mirsim.
(House SE 23/5). The house is again
connected with the city-wall of the
casemate-type (from Braemer, p. 194).

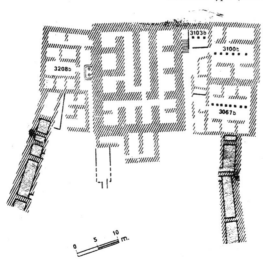

5. House 430 at Beer-sheba. A stairway is built in the first room, or a small
courtyard, from the street. This house is also built into the city wall (from
F. Braemer, *L'architecture domestique du Levant à l'age du fer* [Paris, 1982], p. 179).

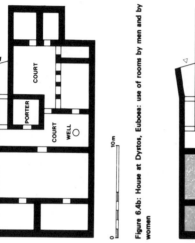

Figure 6.4a: House at Dystos, Euboea: probable functions of rooms

COURT

PORTER

COURT
WELL

10 m

0

Figure 6.4b: House at Dystos, Euboea: use of rooms by men and by women

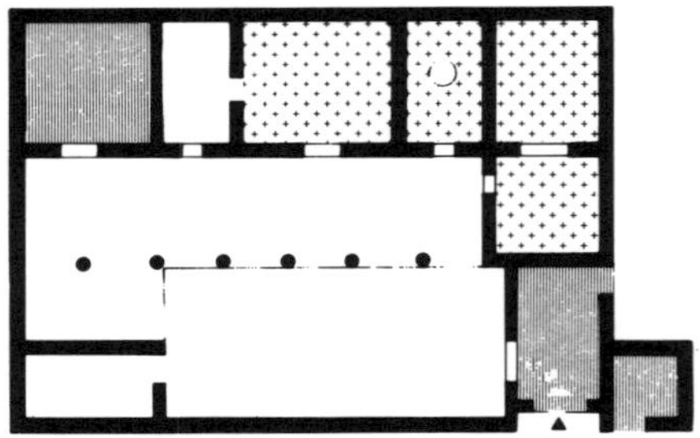

Areas used by women are marked +; those used by men are shaded. Entrances to houses from the street are marked with arrows.

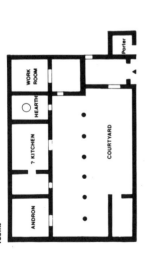

Figure 6.3a: The Dema House at Ano Liossia: probable functions of rooms

ANDRON | ? KITCHEN | HEARTH | WORK ROOM

COURTYARD

Porter

10 m

0

Figure 6.3b: The Dema House at Ano Liossia: use of rooms by men and by women

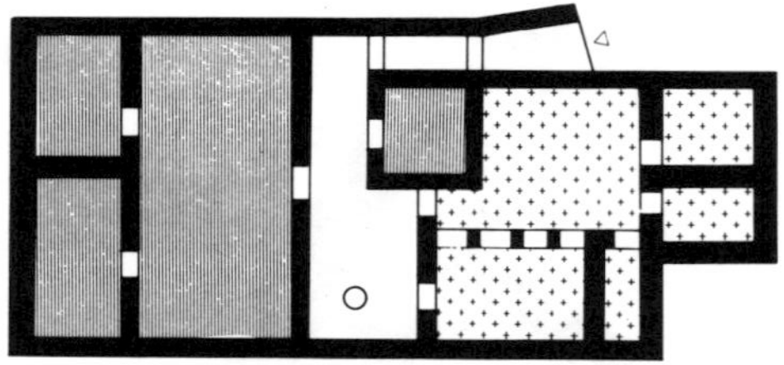

Areas used by women are marked +; those used by men are shaded. Entrances to houses from the street are marked with arrows.

6. Division of areas in use by men or women in two ancient Greek houses according to Susan Walker, "Women and Housing in Classical Greece", figs 6, 3, the "Dema House" at Ano Liossia; and 6, 4, a house at Dystos, Euboea

DIE ANFÄNGE DES DODEKAPROPHETON:
HOSEA UND AMOS

von

JÖRG JEREMIAS
Marburg

In jüngster Zeit sind verstärkt Beobachtungen mitgeteilt worden, die darauf hindeuten, daß das Dodekapropheton weit mehr ist als eine zufällige Zusammenstellung zuvor je selbständiger Bücher. Ganz neu ist diese Erkenntnis nicht. Manche literarische Beziehungen wie etwa diejenigen zwischen Joel iv 16, 18 und Am. i 2 bzw. ix 13 oder diejenigen zwischen Am. ix 12 und Ob. 19 waren seit langer Zeit im Bewußtsein der Ausleger. Nur wurden sie bisher üblicherweise allein dazu genutzt, die Reihenfolge der Zwölf Propheten, die anerkanntermaßen grundsätzlich nach chronologischen Gesichtspunkten erfolgt ist, im Einzelfall zu erklären.[1] Jedoch sind die literarischen Bezüge und Querverweise zwischen den einzelnen Büchern des Dodekapropheton zu zahlreich und zu auffällig, als daß diese Erklärung zureichen könnte. Sie verlangen vielmehr nach einer redaktionsgeschichtlichen Deutung. Am konsequentesten hat sie jüngst—nach mancherlei verschiedenartigen Vorarbeiten anderer[2]—O.H. Steck durchzuführen versucht mit der These, die letzten redaktionellen Wachstumsstufen des Jesajabuches und des Zwölfprophetenbuches seien aufeinander bezogen erfolgt.[3] Mit einer solchen Annahme tritt ein Zwölfprophetenbuch in den Gesichtskreis der Forschung, das, ungleich mehr als bislang vermutet, als ein eigenständiges Buch wahrgenommen werden will und nicht nur als eine lockere Sammlung von separat auszulegenden kleineren Einzelbüchern.

---

[1] Vgl. z. B. U. Cassuto, "The Sequence and Arrangement of the Biblical Sections", in ders., *Biblical and Oriental Studies* I (Jerusalem, 1973), S. 1–6; 5–6.

[2] Ich nenne nur E. Bosshard, "Beobachtungen zum Zwölfprophetenbuch", *BN* 40 (1987), S. 30–62; J.D. Nogalski, *The Use of Stichwörter as a Redactional Unification Technique in the Book of the Twelve*, Master's Thesis, Faculty of the Baptist Theological Seminary (Rüschlikon/Schweiz, 1987) [masch.], *Literary Precursors to the Book of the Twelve*, BZAW 217 (Berlin, 1993), *Redactional Processes in the Book of the Twelve*, BZAW 218 (Berlin, 1993). P.R. House, *The Unity of the Twelve* (Sheffield, 1990).

[3] *Der Abschluß der Prophetie im Alten Testament. Ein Versuch zur Frage der Vorgeschichte des Kanons* (Neukirchen, 1991).

Die folgenden Überlegungen sind der Frage gewidmet, wann und
unter welchen Umständen der Prozeß begonnen hat, daß ehedem
eigenständige Prophetenbücher aufeinander bezogen gelesen wurden
und auf diese Weise einen neuen, übergreifenden hermeneutischen
Kontext erhielten. Sie beschränken sich auf Beobachtungen an den
Büchern der beiden ältesten Propheten im Dodekapropheton, Amos
und Hosea. Auszugehen ist dabei von gegenseitigen Bezugnahmen
zwischen beiden Prophetenbüchern, die nur als literarische gedeutet
werden können.

I

Es versteht sich von selbst, daß derartige literarische Bezüge streng
zu trennen sind von Gemeinsamkeiten, wie sie zwischen zwei Propheten, die nahezu Zeitgenossen waren und beide im Nordreich
auftraten, von vornherein zu erwarten sind. Entsprechendes gilt von
den Bezugnahmen, die am ehesten aus der Kenntnis der Botschaft
des älteren Propheten, Amos, durch den etwas jüngeren, Hosea,
herzuleiten sind.

Bei näherem Zusehen sind die zuletzt genannten Gemeinsamkeiten zwischen beiden Propheten aber erstaunlich gering.[4] Zwar sprechen Amos und Hosea ihre Unheilsbotschaft gegen Israel mit der
gleichen uneingeschränkten Schärfe aus—man denke nur etwa an
die 4. Vision des Amos ("das Ende ist gekommen zu meinem Volk
Israel" Am. viii 2) und an den Namen des jüngsten Hoseakindes
("Nicht-mein-Volk" Hos. i 9)—; zwar haben sie manche Themen
gemeinsam—man denke etwa an die jeweilige Polemik gegen Wallfahrten (Am. iv 4, v 5; Hos. x 5, xii 5, 13–14)—; aber die Differenzen zwischen den Worten beider Propheten überwiegen deutlich, selbst
bei gemeinsamer Thematik. Diese Differenzen sind so tiefgreifend, daß
sie m. E. nur damit erklärt werden können, daß Amos im Südreich
aufwuchs, Hosea aber im Nordreich. Ich nenne einige Beispiele:

(1) Immer aufgefallen ist, wie verschieden beide Propheten das von
    ihnen gemeinsam erwartete nahende Ende Israels begründen. Im
    Mittelpunkt der Anklagen des Amos gegen Israel steht das Zusam-
    menbrechen der gesellschaftlichen Ordnungen Israels und damit
    die Sozialkritik—nicht zufällig belegt er gerade mit ihr, wieviel

---

[4] Ein bekanntes Beispiel ist die Verballhornung des Namens Bet-El in Bet-Awen
in Am. iv 5 und Hos. v 8 sowie x 5. Auf Hos. iv 15 ist noch zurückzukommen.

schuldiger das biblische Gottesvolk ist als alle noch so grausamen Nachbarvölker (Am. ii 6ff.). Bei Hosea fehlt diese für Amos so zentrale Thematik nahezu völlig, wenn man von den summarischen Bezugnahmen in Hos. vi 7–vii 2 und xii 8–9 absieht.

(2) Urteilt man aus der Perspektive des Amosbuches, so müßte als nächstgewichtiger Anklagepunkt die Rechtskritik genannt werden, die besonders in Kap. v entfaltet wird. Das Recht im Tor wird dort betont als Gabe Gottes in den Blick genommen (Am. v 7, vi 12).[5] Es hätte im Falle der Zerrüttung der Gemeinschaft die Funktion der Kontrolle und Streitbeseitigung einnehmen sollen, wurde aber durch massive Bestechung am Ausfüllen dieser Funktion gehindert (v 10, 12). Wiederum gilt: Bei Hosea begegnet dieses Thema allenfalls am Rande; wo es einmal angesprochen wird, wird auf diesem Feld die Schuld des Königtums hervorgehoben wie nie bei Amos (Hos. x 4) bzw. wird auf den Rechtsbruch an bestimmten Kultorten verwiesen (Hos. v 1).

(3) Scheinbar ist damit ein Stichwort für eine wesentliche Übereinstimmung zwischen beiden Propheten gefallen: die Kultkritik. Sie spielt unbestreitbar in der Verkündigung beider Propheten eine tragende Rolle. Aber bei näherem Zusehen ist diese Rolle hier und dort je verschieden zu charakterisieren. Hosea übt inhaltliche Kritik am Gottesdienst seiner Zeit, wenn er die Vermehrung von Altären und Priestern als Zeichen kanaanäischer Überfremdung des Kults anprangert (iv 7, viii 11–13, x 1–2, u.ö.); er rügt damit, daß eine ritualisierte Opfermentalität an die Stelle dessen getreten ist, was er mit dem Stichwort "Gotteserkenntnis" (*da'at 'aelohîm*) als wahren Gottesdienst bezeichnet: Orientierung an der Geschichte Gottes mit Israel und am überlieferten Gotteswillen.[6] Demgegenüber konzentriert sich Amos ganz auf den Gegensatz zwischen einem Kult, der ein intaktes Gottesverhältnis vorspiegelt, und dem faktischen Unrecht in Gestalt der Unterdrückung der Armen im Alltag. Für Amos dient der Kult in seiner Gegenwart zur Gewissensberuhigung; er verhindert Schulderkenntnis und fördert damit "Verbrechen" (Am. iv 4–5). Wo er praktiziert wird,

---

[5] Diesen Aspekt hat insbesondere K. Koch, "Die Entstehung der sozialen Kritik bei den Profeten", in H.W. Wolff (Hg.), *Probleme biblischer Theologie. Festschrift G. von Rad* (München, 1971), S. 236–57; 250ff., hervorgehoben.

[6] Die beste Analyse bietet noch immer der vorzügliche Aufsatz von H.W. Wolff, "'Wissen um Gott' bei Hosea als Urform von Theologie", *EvTh* 12 (1952/3), S. 533–54, wieder abgedruckt in *Ges. St. z. AT* (²München, 1973), S. 182–205.

obwohl Gottes Gaben in Gestalt von "Recht und Gerechtigkeit" mit Füßen getreten werden, hat sich Gott diesem Treiben längst entzogen, und die Feste sind von Jahwes Festen zu Israels eigenen Festen pervertiert worden (v 21–4).

(4) Wollte man die Differenzen zwischen Amos und Hosea von letzterem aus entwerfen, müßte man etwa darauf verweisen, daß Hosea nirgends leidenschaftlichere und gefühlsbetontere Entrüstung über die Zustände seiner Zeit äußert als im Fall des Stierbildes von Bet-El, das er mit einem Abstraktplural als "Kalbszeug" (Hos. x 5) beschimpft und das ihm zum Symbol tödlicher Verirrung in der Gottesvorstellung Israels geworden ist (viii 5, xiii 2). Immer aufgefallen ist demgegenüber, daß Amos zwar wie Hosea die Wallfahrten nach Bet-El verwirft, das Stierbild von Bet-El aber mit keiner einzigen Silbe erwähnt.

(5) Man müßte weiter daran erinnern, wie bei Hosea ganze Kapitel geprägt sind von intensiven Rückblicken in die Geschichte Israels, wie sie in der gesamten Prophetie singulär sind—letztlich ist Hosea von der Überzeugung geprägt, daß sich an der Beschäftigung mit seiner von Gott bestimmten Geschichte das Gottesverhältnis Israels entscheidet. Wiederum muß demgegenüber auffallen, daß bei Amos dieses Thema so gut wie keinerlei Rolle spielt; die wenigen Ausnahmen[7] bestätigen nur diese Differenz.

Über solchen Unterschieden zwischen der Verkündigung des Amos und der des Hosea, die sich erheblich vermehren ließen, wird erkennbar, was es heißt, daß Hosea aus dem Nordreich stammt, Amos aber aus dem Südreich. In der Auswahl seiner Themen hat Amos viel gemeinsam mit Jesaja, dem Jerusalemer, auf den er zudem nachweislich eingewirkt hat.[8] Hoseas Einfluß ist ungleich stärker als auf Jesaja ein Jahrhundert später beim jungen Jeremia und—indirekter—beim Deuteronomium wahrzunehmen, was wiederum für Amos weit weniger gilt. Kurz: Man würde beide Propheten kaum für Zeitgenossen, die dazu noch im gleichen geographischen Raum aufgetreten sind, halten, verfügte man nicht über die Überschriften ihrer Bücher und vor allem über die zeitgeschichtlichen Anspielungen in ihren Worten.

---

[7] ii 9 (stark umstritten) und ix 7. Zu iii 2 vgl. unten Abschnitt III.

[8] Vgl. einstweilen R. Fey, *Amos und Jesaja. Abhängigkeit und Eigenständigkeit des Jesaja* (Neukirchen, 1963). Das Thema bedarf einer neuen Behandlung.

Jedoch sind es auffälligerweise nicht die soeben beschriebenen
gewichtigen Unterschiede zwischen Amos und Hosea gewesen, die
sich den Auslegern durch die Jahrhunderte bis zur Aufklärung ein-
geprägt haben. Diese Ausleger gingen vielmehr nahezu ausnahmslos
von dem Bewußtsein aus, die Propheten des Alten Testaments seien
durch eine gesamtprophetische, d.h. sie untereinander verbindende
Botschaft geprägt. Erst die historisch-kritische Forschung auf ihrem
Höhepunkt[9] hat überzeugend nachgewiesen, daß die Vereinheitlichung
der großen Propheten—sei es im Sinne der deuteronomistischen
Theologie oder sei es später im Sinne der beginnenden Apokalyptik—
erst das Werk Späterer war.

Kann man dann formulieren, die Vereinheitlichung der Propheten untereinander habe im Exil eingesetzt, als die klassischen Propheten, die zu ihrer eigenen Zeit von ihren Hörern weitestgehend
abgelehnt worden waren, als "wahre Propheten" erkannt wurden und
den Menschen in der Katastrophe Orientierung boten? Diese These
wäre plausibel, wenn die Vereinheitlichung der Propheten im Sinne
der deuteronomistischen Theologie die älteste wäre. Es ist der Grund-
gedanke der folgenden Ausführungen, daß eine solche Vereinheitlichung—zumindest partiell—schon erheblich früher begann, freilich
auch im Zusammenhang mit einer Katastrophe und ihrer Bewälti-
gung: dem Fall Samarias 722. Ich beschränke meine Beobachtungen
dabei auf Beispieltexte aus den Büchern Amos und Hosea, die ge-
genseitige literarische Bezugnahmen bieten.

II

Die Ausführungen zum Buch Hosea können kürzer ausfallen, weil
die Fragestellung für dieses Prophetenbuch weniger austrägt als für
das Amosbuch. Es ist seit längerer Zeit aufgefallen, daß sich im
Hoseabuch einzelne Worte finden, die terminologisch klingen, als
stünden sie im Amosbuch. Ich wähle zwei Beispiele.[10]

1. Hos. iv 15. Im Kap. iv beschreibt der Prophet Hosea den von ihm
verabscheuten Gottesdienst auf den Höhen Israels so präzise wie sonst
nie. Zusätzlich zu dem häufigeren Vorwurf, daß die Kultstätten, die
Priester und die Opfer vermehrt werden und für Hosea damit der
Sinn des Gottesdienstes auf die Sicherung des Wohlstandes reduziert

---

[9] Als repräsentativ kann B. Duhm, *Israels Propheten* (Tübingen, 1916), gelten.
[10] Ein drittes, hier nicht behandeltes Beispiel bietet Hos. xi 10.

wird (V. 7–8),[11] nennt er diejenigen Elemente dieses Gottesdienstes, die ihm besonders fremd sind:

(a) den Alkoholkonsum, der für den Propheten das "Herz meines Volkes", d. h. seine Fähigkeit zu abgewogener rationaler Entscheidung raubt (V. 11);

(b) die Rhabdomantie, die für ihn besonders abwegig ist, da Israel doch Propheten besitzt (V. 12);

(c) am Höhepunkt (V. 13–14) die Sexualriten, die die Fruchtbarkeit des Mutterschoßes sichern und mehren sollen, für den Propheten aber primär die Familienbande zerstören (V. 14a).

Mit dem letztgenannten Vorwurf rundet sich der Gedanke, der in V. 11 mit der Klage über den Verlust der Urteilsfähigkeit des Volkes eingesetzt hatte; er endet in V. 14b wiederum mit einer Klage darüber, daß durch das Vorbild der Priester das unverständige Volk in die Irre geführt wird und zu Fall kommt.

Auf diesen durch die genannte Inklusion abgeschlossenen Gedankengang folgt ein Vers, der eindeutig Amossprache widerspiegelt:

> Wenn du, Israel, schon Unzucht treibst,
> so soll sich doch Juda nicht versündigen:
> Kommt nicht nach Gilgal,
> zieht nicht hinauf nach Bet-Awen,
> schwört nicht (in Beerscheba):[12] "So wahr Jahwe lebt"!

V. 15a fällt sogleich auf durch den plötzlichen und unvorbereiteten Wechsel von der Schilderung der vorangehenden Verse zunächst zur singularischen Anrede und dann über den Jussiv zur pluralischen Anrede, durch den sehr künstlich der Übergang der Adressaten vom Nordreich zum Südreich markiert wird. Die verneinten Imperative V. 15b ihrerseits bieten ein leicht erkennbares Mischzitat aus Am. iv 4, V 5 und viii 14. Alle drei Verse des Amosbuches haben gemeinsam, daß sie die Nutz-und Sinnlosigkeit von Wallfahrten zu den berühmten Heiligtümern des Nordreichs (Bet-El und Gilgal) sowie zu dem tief im Süden gelegenen Heiligtum von Beerscheba darlegen wollen. Was ist dann der Sinn des Verses Hos. iv 15? Offensichtlich soll späteren judäischen Lesern unmöglich gemacht werden, die vor-

---

[11] Wie sehr für Hosea Vermehrung von Kultstätten, Opfern und Priestern zusammengehören, zeigen in Verbindung mit iv 7–8 etwa viii 11–12, x 1–2 und xiii 4–6.

[12] Der unlösliche Zusammenhang zwischen dem kultischen "Schwur" mit dem Namen Beerscheba ergibt sich sowohl aus Gen. xxvi wie aus Am. viii 14.

anstehenden Hoseaworte "historisch" zu lesen. Von Höhengottes-
diensten, die wie in Hos. iv von Rhabdomantie und Sexualriten
geprägt gewesen wären, hören wir andernorts in Juda nichts.[13] Wohl
aber muß es in Juda zur Zeit von Hos. iv 15 den Wunsch nach
Wallfahrten nach Bet-El und Gilgal gegeben haben, den berühmten
Orten der Jakob-und Landnahmetradition, beide nur ca. zwanzig
Kilometer von Jerusalem entfernt. Für Beerscheba, den Ort der
Abraham- und Isaaktradition, in Juda selbst gelegen, ist Analoges
noch evidenter.

M. E. läßt sich die genannte Beobachtung zu Hos. iv 15 genera-
lisieren: Je konkreter einzelne Prophetenbücher Sachverhalte benennen, die an bestimmte lokale Traditionen und zeitliche Umstände
gebunden waren, desto schwieriger war die Aktualisierung solcher
Worte für spätere Tradenten, insbesondere dann, wenn sie wie im
Falle von Hos. iv 15 nicht nur in anderen Lebensumständen, sondern auch an anderem Ort (d. h. im Südreich statt im Nordreich)
vollzogen werden mußte. Überkommene Prophetenworte wurden im
Zuge der Überlieferung daher immer stärker auf das in ihnen ent-
haltene Grundsätzliche hin (im vorliegenden Falle im Blick auf grundsätzliche Verfehlungen im Gottesdienst) gehört und formuliert, um
eben in solcher wachsenden Abstraktion Lebenshilfe auch für Menschen in anderen Lebensumständen bieten zu können.

2. Hos. viii 14. Das Kapitel viii im Hoseabuch ist sehr kunstvoll gestaltet, insofern in ihm die Hauptthemen der Kritik Hoseas zusammengestellt sind, die sich steigernd aneinander fügen,[14] als Belege des
Satzes: "Israel hat das Gute verworfen" (V. 3):

(a) anfangs die Kritik am Staat (die von Gottes Urteil und Willen
    gelöste Wahl von Königen im Zuge der wechselnden Revolutio-
    nen wird mit Götzendienst parallelisiert und gleichgestellt: V. 4),
    dann

(b) die Kritik am Staatskult (das Stierbild in Bet-El ist "dein Kalb,
    Samaria", mit dem Jahwe nichts zu schaffen hat: V. 5–6), weiter

(c) die Kritik an der Außenpolitik (Hilfesuche bei Assur impliziert
    die Verwerfung Jahwes mit tödlichen Folgen: V. 8–10) und zuletzt

---

[13] Bei den vielfältigen Anspielungen an hoseanische Sprache im Jeremiabuch,
besonders in Jer. ii, ist durchgehend mit übertragenem Sprachgebrauch zu rechnen.

[14] Die kunstvolle Fügung der Worte tritt erst dann voll zutage, wenn man beachtet, daß Kap. viii eine abgekürzte Parallel-Komposition zu v 8–vii 16 darstellt; vgl.
J. Jeremias, *Der Prophet Hosea* (Göttingen, 1983), S. 103–4.

(d) als Höhepunkt die Kritik am Gottesdienst (die Vermehrung der Opfergottesdienste statt des Achtens auf die vielfältigen Willenskundgebungen Jahwes: V. 11–13). Diese vielfache Anklage führt zu der ungeheuer harten Folgerung, daß Jahwe die gesamte Heilsgeschichte revoziert und Israel in jene Unterdrückung "Ägyptens" zurückkehren muß, aus der es einst von Jahwe befreit worden war (V. 13b).

Sachlich post festum und in auffällig anders gehaltenem Stil (Narrative) folgt ein abschließender V. 14, der in der Strafansage voller Anspielungen an die Völkerworte des Amosbuches ist:

> Israel vergaß seinen Schöpfer und erbaute Paläste,
> und Juda vermehrte befestigte Städte.
> Doch ich sende Feuer in seine Städte,
> daß es deren Palastfestungen verzehrt.

Erneut wird wie zuvor in Hos. iv 15 vom Nordreich als Adressaten übergegangen zum Südreich, offensichtlich wieder in der Befürchtung, Juda könnte sich von den in Hos. viii genannten Schuldmerkmalen nicht betroffen fühlen. In der Tat ist keiner der vier Vorwürfe ohne weiteres und in gleicher Weise auf Juda anwendbar. Mit den nun in viii 14 zusätzlich genannten neuen Schuldgründen des Luxus und des Sicherungsbedürfnisses in den Palästen der Hauptstadt wird noch eindeutiger als in iv 15 ein Amosthema aufgegriffen (vgl. etwa Am. iii 9–11, vi 8) und damit zugleich ein neues Strafgericht mit Hilfe von Zitaten der Völkersprüche des Amos angefügt. Hier wird in der veränderten Strafankündigung gleichzeitig der zeitliche Abstand von V. 14 zum Rest des Kapitels Hos. viii erkennbar. Hosea kündigt *vor* dem Fall Samarias das Ende der Geschichte Gottes mit seinem Volk an; V. 14 verdeutlicht judäischen Lesern *nach* dem Fall Samarias, daß ihnen selber das Ende allen Luxus in der Stadt und das Ende allen Sicherungsstrebens in Gestalt des Baus von Palästen und Burgen noch bevorsteht.

Aus den genannten Beobachtungen geht deutlich hervor, daß die Worte im Hoseabuch, die von Amos beeinflußt sind, Nachtragscharakter besitzen. Sie sind leicht mit literarkritischen Mitteln aus ihrem Kontext ablösbar und setzen die schon abgeschlossene Komposition der Hoseakapitel voraus, also das schriftliche Hoseabuch oder doch zumindest Teile davon. Ihr Ziel besteht darin, die Judäer, die das Hoseabuch lesen, daran zu hindern, es mit einem historischen Bewußtsein als vergangenes Buch zu lesen und sie stattdessen zu nötigen, es auf sich selber zu beziehen. Aus solchem Gebrauch von Amoszitaten geht zugleich hervor, daß den judäischen Lesern der Prophet Amos, obwohl er im Nordreich verkündete, sachlich näher stand als der Nordreichsprophet Hosea. Dabei setzen die judäischen Aktualisierungen den Fall Samarias voraus. Für eine genauere zeitliche Einordnung ergibt sich aus dem Vorwurf gegen den Luxus der Paläste (viii 14) und noch deutlicher aus der Warnung vor einer Wallfahrt nach Bet-El (iv 15), daß sie noch vor den Vollzug der Kultreform Josias anzusetzen sind. Grob gesprochen gehören sie in das Jahrhundert zwischen 720 und 620 v. Chr.

III

Einen ganz anderen Sachverhalt findet man vor, wenn man nach literarischen Bezugnahmen des Amosbuches auf Hoseaworte fragt. Der Einfluß von Hoseaworten auf Formulierungen im Amosbuch ist viel breiter belegt, ja nahezu auf Schritt und Tritt zu spüren. Vor allem aber findet er sich nicht erst in aktualisierenden Zusätzen, die sich mit literarkritischen Mitteln isolieren lassen, sondern schon im ursprünglichen schriftlichen Textbestand. Obwohl die mündlichen Worte des Amos noch nicht von Hosea beeinflußt sein können, da Amos früher als Hosea auftrat, hat es m.E. ein schriftliches Amosbuch ohne diesen Einfluß nie gegeben. Seit man die Amosworte systematisch gesammelt hat, hat man sie offensichtlich sogleich auf die überlieferten Worte Hoseas hin gelesen, d. h. mit den Worten Hoseas im Ohr. Diese Beobachtung führt zu der Folgerung, daß das schriftliche Hoseabuch—bzw. ein Teil von ihm—älter ist als das Amosbuch, obwohl Amos der ältere Prophet von beiden war.[15]

Auch im Falle des Amosbuches beschränke ich mich auf zwei Beispiele und wähle sie bewußt aus verschiedenen Teilen des Buches. Wie ich andernorts in Weiterführung von Beobachtungen H.W. Wolffs zu zeigen versucht habe,[16] war das älteste für uns erkennbare Amosbuch aus zwei verschiedenen Teilen zusammengesetzt: a. einer

---

[15] Vielleicht ist die ungewöhnliche Wortfügung in Hos. iv–xiv mit ihrem weitgehenden Verzicht auf Ein- und Ausleitungsformeln aus einer solchen relativ frühen Niederschrift erklärbar, während die Komposition der Kapitel i–iii mit ihren zahlreichen späten Heilsworten erheblich jünger sein könnte.

[16] J. Jeremias, "Amos 3–6. Beobachtungen zur Entstehungsgeschichte eines Prophetenbuches", ZAW 100 (1988), Suppl., S. 123–38; ders., "Völkersprüche und Visionsberichte im Amosbuch", in V. Fritz—K.-F. Pohlmann—H.C. Schmitt (Hg.), Prophet und Prophetenbuch, BZAW 185 (Berlin, 1989), S. 82–97.

Wortsammlung (Kap. iii–vi), die jetzt den Mittelteil des Buches aus-
macht, und b. zwei parallel gebildeten, strophenartigen Kompositio-
nen, dem Völkerspruchzyklus (Kap. i–ii) und dem Visionenzyklus (Kap.
vii–ix), die sich wie ein Rahmen um diese Wortsammlung legen, aber
von vornherein aufeinander zu komponiert waren. Dabei ist der Mittelteil des Amosbuches, der zuerst betrachtet werden soll, in sich
zweigeteilt; beide Teile werden durch eine ganz analoge Überschrift
eingeleitet, wobei gerade aufgrund der Analogie die Differenzen deutlich ins Auge fallen:[17]

> iii 1: Hört dieses Wort, das *Jahwe* über euch redet, ihr *Israeliten!*
> v 1: Hört dieses Wort, das *ich* über euch als Leichenklage anhebe,
> *Haus Israel!*

Beide Überschriften zeigen, daß die Kap. iii–iv und v–vi aufeinander
bezogen und doch voneinander unterschieden gelesen und verstanden werden sollen. Kap. iii–iv enthalten der Überschrift zufolge
wesenhaft Jahwewort, Kap. v–vi dagegen wesenhaft Prophetenwort;
Kap. iii–iv betreffen Israel als Gottesvolk, Kap. v–vi dagegen Israel
als Staat.[18] Zusammengenommen besagen die beiden Überschriften,
daß der Prophet den (damals bevorstehenden) Untergang des Nordreichs als Staat beklagen mußte, weil das Gottesvolk restlos am Gotteswillen versagt hatte. Die Reihenfolge der Kapitel ist unumkehrbar.
So geht allein schon aus der überlegten Formulierung der Teilüber-
schriften hervor, daß die Tradenten mehr wollten, als nur Amosworte in relativ beliebiger Reihenfolge zusammenzustellen.

1. Am. iii 2. Wenden wir uns im folgenden dem Eingang des Gotteswortes Kap. iii zu, so ist sogleich erkennbar, daß ab V. 9 typische
Einzelworte gegen bestimmte Gruppen in Israel beginnen; näherhin
handelt es sich in iii 9–iv 3 um eine Sammlung von Worten gegen
die Einwohner der Hauptstadt Samaria, die im Block Am. v–vi ihre

---

[17] Im Unterschied zu iii 1 und v 1 ist der Aufmerksamkeitsaufruf in Am. iv
1 dem sowohl der Relativsatz als auch die nota accusativi fehlen, nur als Einleitung
der Untereinheit iv 1–3 zu verstehen, wie schon K. Koch und Mitarbeiter, *Amos.
Untersucht mit den Methoden einer strukturalen Formgeschichte* (Kevelaer-Neukirchen, 1976),
II, S. 107–8, erkannt haben.

[18] Auf den ersten Blick könnte man diese Differenz in der Charakterisierung der
Adressaten für Zufall halten. Das ist jedoch unmöglich, wenn man beachtet, daß
Am. iii–iv konsequent "ihr Israeliten" (iii 1, 12, iv 5), Am. v–vi noch konsequenter
"Haus Israel" (v 1, 3, 4, 25, vi 1, 14) verwenden, der jeweils andere Begriff aber nie
begegnet. Zu "Haus Israel" als Begriff für den Staat vgl. H.W. Wolff, *Dodekapropheton
2. Joel. Amos* (²Neukirchen, 1975), S. 199–200.

Entsprechung in Kap. vi findet. Voraus gehen dieser Sammlung zwei Worte ungleicher Länge, die aber beide von übergeordneten Gesichtspunkten bestimmt sind:

(a) Unmittelbar auf die Überschrift folgt ein kurzes Wort programmatischen Charakters, das eine Art Zusammenfassung der nachfolgenden Einzelworte bildet (V. 2).

(b) Danach folgt eine lange Kette von Fragen, die jeweils Ursache und Wirkung miteinander verbinden (V. 3–8). Ihr Sinn geht aus den letzten Versen hervor, die am Höhepunkt Gott als Subjekt nennen (V. 6, 8).[19] V. 8 zielt auf den Zwangscharakter der prophetischen Botschaft ab:

Der Löwe brüllt—
wer muß sich nicht fürchten?
(Der Herr) Jahwe redet—
wer muß nicht als Prophet auftreten?

Der voranstehende V. 6 zeigt aber, daß nicht prophetisches Verkünden allgemein im Blick ist, sondern speziell prophetische Unheilsbotschaft:

Stößt man ins Horn in einer Stadt,
ohne daß die Leute aufschrecken?
Trifft ein Unglück eine Stadt,
ohne daß Jahwe am Werk war?

Zusammen legen V. 6 und V. 8 dar, daß Amos nicht freiwillig Bote des strafenden und richtenden Gottes geworden ist.

Die beiden zitierten Abschlußverse der Fragenreihe verdeutlichen somit, daß die Fragen in Am. iii 3–8 im Kontext Legitimationsfunktion ausüben. Das Wort Jahwes, das die Überschrift V. 1 thematisch einführt, wird durch die Kette der Fragen in V. 3–8 mit dem Wort identifiziert, das dem Propheten aufgenötigt ist (V. 8) und das inhaltlich ein Unheilswort ist (V. 6). Bevor es aber in den Versen 9ff. in Gestalt von Einzelsprüchen des Amos näher ausgeführt wird, wird dieses Gotteswort zuvor in V. 2 zusammenfassend charakterisiert. Für das Verständnis von V. 2 ist seine Position wesentlich. Da der Vers unmittelbar auf die Überschrift folgt und noch vor der Legitimationsperikope V. 3–8 steht, ist deutlich, daß dieser Vers mehr sein will als

---

[19] Der Vers iii 7, der die Fragen mit einer These unterbricht, ist dtr. Zusatz; vgl. W.H. Schmidt, "Die deuteronomistische Redaktion des Amosbuches", *ZAW* 77 (1965), S. 168–93; 185–8.

ein beliebiges Einzelwort des Amos. Vielmehr bietet er die Quintessenz all jener Einzelworte, die in iii 9–iv 3 genannt und zuvor in iii 3–8 als dem Amos aufgenötigtes Gotteswort ausgewiesen werden.

V. 2 lautet:

> Euch allein habe ich erkannt
> aus allen Sippen der Erde;
> daher ahnde ich an euch
> alle eure Vergehen.

Bemerkenswert an V. 2 ist aber nun nicht nur, daß er so betont in seiner Zwischenstellung zwischen Überschrift und Legitimationsperikope als zentrales Gotteswort des Amos hervorgehoben wird, sondern ebenso, daß für dieses programmatische Wort eine Sprache gewählt ist, die völlig untypisch für Amos ist. Das gilt (1) für das Verb "erkennen" (*yd*ᶜ) als Bezeichnung für Gottes erwählendes Handeln, das keine Parallele im Amosbuch findet, und darüber hinaus für das Erwählungsthema generell, das im Buch Amos nur noch in ix 7 begegnet, dort aber in ganz anderer Funktion, insofern in ix 7 mit ihm gerade ein Vorrecht Israels vor seinen Nachbarvölkern bestritten wird.[20] Es gilt (2) für die Bezeichnung der Strafe mit dem Verb *pqd* "ahnden, heimsuchen", das im Amosbuch nur noch in iii 14 begegnet, dort aber literarisch von iii 2 abhängig ist.[21] Es gilt vor allem aber (3) für die Bezeichnung der Schuld mit dem Begriff ʿāwôn. Der Begriff begegnet auffälligerweise nirgends sonst im Amosbuch, obwohl in ihm nicht gerade selten von Israels Schuld die Rede ist. Aber das Amosbuch gebraucht zur Benennung der Schuld Israels und der Völker zumeist konsequent den von Haus aus politischen Begriff *pæšaʿ* und nur gelegentlich Substantive der allgemeineren Wurzel *ḥṭ*ʾ.

Wenn Am. iii 2 aber in einer für Amos ganz untypischen Terminologie fomuliert ist, woher stammt dann diese Sprache? M.E. kann die Antwort nur lauten: Sie verdankt sich im wesentlichen dem Hoseabuch. Zwar wird der Begriff des "Erkennens" (*yd*ᶜ) für Gottes Erwählungshandeln auch im Hoseabuch nur einmal (Hos. xiii 5 MT)

---

[20] Von den anerkannt dtr. Stellen (ii 10–12, iii 1b; vgl. Schmidt, *ebd.* S. 172ff.) kann hier abgesehen werden.

[21] Daß Am. iii 13–14 insgesamt einer nachexilischen Redaktion zuzuschreiben sind, hoffe ich an anderem Ort zeigen zu können; vgl. einstweilen S. Mittmann, "Amos 3, 12–15 und das Bett der Samarier", *ZDPV* 92 (1976), S. 149–67; 150–2, sowie R.F. Melugin, "The Formation of Amos. An Analysis of Exegetical Method", *SBL 1978 Seminar Papers* I (1979), S. 369–91, 382.

verwendet—er ist dort trotz der anders nuancierenden Deutung von LXX und Pesch. durch das Wortspiel mit dem gleichen Verb in V. 4 fest verankert[22]—, aber der Begriff *pqd* für Jahwes Strafe begegnet in breiter Streuung an zentralen Stellen (Hos. i 4, ii 15, iv 9, 14, viii 13, ix 9, xii 3) und Entsprechendes gilt für die Bezeichnung der Schuld Israels mit dem Begriff *ʿāwôn*.[23]

Wird für die Zusammenfassung des Gotteswortes des Amos in seiner programmatischen Gestalt in Am. iii 2 somit eine Sprache gewählt, die stark von hoseanischer Theologie her geprägt ist, kann das kaum etwas anderes heißen, als daß die Leser des Amosbuches aufgefordert werden, das Gotteswort des Amos nicht "historisch" zu begreifen, also nicht als das unverwechselbare und singuläre Wort des Amos, sondern es vielmehr von Hosea her zu verstehen und auf Hoseas Worte hin zu lesen. Mit dieser hermeneutischen Vorgabe wird den Lesern insbesondere eingeschärft, die im folgenden Amosbuch dargelegte Schuld des Gottesvolkes (und auch die je eigene Schuld) am Maßstab der unvergleichlichen Erfahrungen Israels mit Gott in seiner Geschichte zu messen, wie sie Amos voraussetzt (vgl. Am. ii 9), Hosea sie aber breit dargelegt hat. Die Tradenten der Amosworte sind erkennbar der Meinung, daß das Gotteswort des Amos und dasjenige des Hosea in einem letzten Sinne miteinander identisch sind, sich jedenfalls gegenseitig interpretieren.

IV

2. Am. viii 9 (10–17). Das zweite Beispiel für die Beeinflussung eines Wortes aus dem Amosbuch durch Hoseasprache wähle ich aus dem Visionenzyklus. Wahrscheinlich haben die Visionsberichte des Amos einmal eine separate Sammlung gebildet. Zumindest gilt das für die ersten vier Visionen,[24] da sie betont paarweise gestaltet sind und die

---

[22] In der kleinen Einheit Hos. xiii 4–6 bildet V. 5 einen Brückenvers, der durch Wortspiele mit V. 4 und V. 6 verbunden ist. Während MT (*ydʿ*) das Wortspiel mit V. 4 verstärkt, legen LXX und Pesch. (*rʿh*) den Ton auf die Verbindung mit V. 6.— Im übrigen ist die Erwählungsthematik im Buch Hosea reich belegt; vgl. etwa Hos. i 9, ii 16–17, ix 10, x 11, xi 1.

[23] Weder vom Amos- noch vom Hoseabuch aus erklärlich bleibt die Wendung "Sippen der Erde". Will man zur Deutung nicht auf Gen. xii 3, xxviii 14 rekurrieren, müßte man am ehesten an die Vorgeschichte des Sprachgebrauchs denken, der im Jeremiabuch (Jer. i 15, ii 4, xxv 9; vgl. Ez. xx 32) bzw. später in den Psalmen (Ps. xcvi 7, xxii 28) belegt ist.

[24] Daß die fünfte Vision fest zu dieser Sammlung hinzugehört, habe ich an anderer Stelle zu zeigen versucht ("Das unzugängliche Heiligtum. Zur letzten Vision

beiden Visionenpaare im Kontrast zueinander gelesen werden wollen. In den ersten beiden Visionen sieht Amos jeweils ein für Israel tödliches Unheil zum Zeitpunkt seiner Entstehung; in der ersten Vision ist es die Bildung eines Heuschreckenschwarms durch Jahwe, in der zweiten Vision steigernd eine kosmische Dürre. Beide Male bricht Amos in eine spontane Fürbitte aus, die nahezu wörtlich gleich formuliert ist und auf Gottes Mitleid mit dem "kleinen Jakob" zielt, der den Schlag Jahwes nicht überleben könnte. Jeweils erreicht Amos mit seiner Fürbitte, worum er bat: Jahwe nimmt das Unheil zurück, und zwar trotz Israels großer Schuld, die der Prophet kennt, der daher Jahwe anfangs um Vergebung bittet. Wollte man dieses Visionenpaar separat lesen—was vom Kontext nicht gestattet ist—, so müßte man formulieren: Israel überlebt nur, weil es Propheten hat, die wie Amos in letzter Stunde Gottes strafendem Willen in den Arm gefallen sind.

Auch die dritte und vierte Vision sind paarweise formuliert, aber sie haben einen völlig anderen Sinn. Jetzt sieht Amos nicht mehr ein bevorstehendes Unheilsgeschehen, sondern ein statisches Bild: eine "Mauer aus Zinn", auf der Jahwe mit Zinn in seiner Hand steht,[25] bzw. einen Korb mit Sommerobst. Jeweils wird Amos aufgefordert, das Geschaute zu benennen ("Was siehst du, Amos?"), und erst nachdem der Prophet das Bild präzise auf den Begriff gebracht hat, wird das Symbol ihm von Gott gedeutet: "Ich bin dabei, Zinn (vermutlich Sinnbild für Waffen) mitten in mein Volk Israel zu legen" bzw. "Das Ende ist gekommen zu meinem Volk Israel". Beide Deutungen der Visionen führen eine Konsequenz herauf, die wörtlich gleich formuliert ist: "Ich kann nicht mehr (schonend) an ihm (gemeint ist Israel) vorübergehen" (Am. vii 8, viii 2). Dieser letzte Satz zeigt eindeutig, wie eng die beiden Visionenpaare aufeinander bezogen gelesen werden sollen: Was Amos in den ersten beiden Visionen gelang—die Rücknahme des geplanten Unheils durch Jahwe—, wird in der dritten und vierten Vision gerade als unmöglich ausgeschlossen. Diese letzteren Visionen schärfen dem Leser ein, daß es eine Grenze der

---

des Amos", in R. Bartelmus—Th. Krüger—H. Utzschneider (Hg.), *Konsequente Traditionsgeschichte. Festschrift K. Baltzer* (Freiburg-Göttingen, 1993), S. 155–67.

[25] Daß *an(n)āku* im Akkadischen und sein Lehnwort *'ānāk* im Hebräischen "Zinn" und nicht "Blei" bedeuten, haben in jüngster Zeit viele Arbeiten gezeigt; vgl. grundlegend B. Landsberger, "Tin and Lead", *JNES* 24 (1965), S. 285–96, sowie stellvertretend für andere W. Beyerlin, *Bleilot, Brecheisen oder was sonst?* (Freiburg-Göttingen, 1988), S. 18ff.

göttlichen Geduld gibt; wenn sie erreicht ist, muß die Fürbitte des Propheten verstummen.

Die beiden Visionenpaare wollen also einen Weg aufzeigen, den der Prophet Amos von Gott geführt worden ist. Hat er anfangs mit der Macht seiner Fürbitte erreicht, daß Gott seinen Unheilsplan zugunsten Israels fallen ließ, so muß der Prophet danach erkennen, daß am Ende des Weges kein Raum mehr für eine solche Fürbitte ist. Amos muß sozusagen ganz auf die Seite des strafenden Gottes treten. Er darf ihn nicht mehr am vernichtenden Handeln gegenüber Israel hindern. Mit der Niederschrift dieses Weges will Amos offensichtlich seine Unheilsverkündigung im Namen Jahwes vor seinen Hörern rechtfertigen. Er selber hat nie verkündigen wollen, was er jetzt verkündigen muß; aber als Bote seines Gottes hat er keine andere Wahl, als das Gotteswort zu sagen, das ihm aufgetragen ist.

Auffällig ist nun, daß sich zwischen die dritte und vierte Vision, die so deutlich als ein Visionenpaar zusammengehören, die berühmte Erzählung von dem Zusammentreffen des Amos mit dem Priester Amazja in Am. vii 10–17 schiebt. Sie ist literarisch vielfältig mit der dritten Vision verknüft,[26] ist also bewußt auf diese Vision hin gestaltet worden, um sie zu erläutern. Ihre Funktion im Kontext ist unschwer zu bestimmen. Sie will an der Nahtstelle der Visionsberichte, d. h. nach der ersten Erwähnung des Endes der göttlichen Geduld und des Endes der Möglichkeit des Propheten, Gott zu beeinflussen, erläutern, *warum* die Geduld Gottes am Ende war. Die Visionsberichte selber konstatieren ja nur das Faktum, daß Gottes Bereitschaft zur Strafrücknahme mit der dritten Vision aufhört, sie begründen es aber nicht. Sie setzen schwere Schuld Israels voraus—Amos bittet schon in der ersten Vision um Vergebung—, benennen diese Schuld aber nicht. Auch aus dieser Beobachtung geht hervor, wie stark die Visionsberichte ursprünglich auf die Verkündigung des Amos bezogen waren, sie voraussetzten und sie legitimieren wollten. Eine spätere Generation aber, die schon den Untergang des Nordreichs erlebt hatte, fühlte das Bedürfnis, die Grenzlinie genau bestimmt zu erhalten, an der Gottes Bereitschaft zur Verschonung Israels endet. Die Erzählung von Am. vii definiert im Kontext der Visionen diese Grenze, indem sie die Interessenbereiche des Staates, repräsentiert durch den treuen Staatsbeamten Amazja, und denjenigen Jahwes, repräsentiert

---

[26] Vgl. den Nachweis von H. Utzschneider, "Die Amazjaerzählung (Am 7, 10–17) zwischen Literatur und Historie", *BN* 41 (1988), S. 76–101.

durch den Propheten Amos, in einer Konfliktsituation gegeneinander abgrenzt.[27] Auf ihren Kontext hin interpretiert, besagt die Erzählung, daß noch nicht Israels Schuld im sozialen Bereich Gottes Willen zur Bewahrung Israels vor der Vernichtung unmöglich macht, wohl aber die Anmaßung des Staates, Gott das Reden durch seinen Propheten zu verbieten, der solche Schuld aufdeckt. Wo die Staatsräson, d. h. die Sorge des Staates um die von ihm definierte Ordnung am Reichsheiligtum, vor das Reden Gottes tritt, ist Gottes Unheil nicht mehr aufhaltbar (vgl. V. 16–17: "*Du* sagst . . .; darum hat *Jahwe* so gesprochen . . .").

Wesentlich für unsere Fragestellung ist nun, daß sich die genannte Erzählung nicht unmittelbar an die dritte Vision anschließt, sondern durch einen Verbindungsvers (Am. vii 9) von der dritten Vision getrennt ist. Dieser Verbindungsvers hat Brückenfunktion: Er ist einerseits terminologisch stark auf die Erzählung vii 10–17 bezogen und insofern deutlich als deren Einleitung formuliert; er ist andererseits aber poetisch gestaltet und insofern deutlich von der Erzählung abgehoben.

> Dann werden die Höhen Isaaks verwüstet
> und die Heiligtümer Israels verödet;
> dann stehe ich gegen das Haus Jerobeams mit dem Schwerte auf.

Der Bezug des Brückenverses auf die Erzählung von Amos und Amazja ist mit Händen zu greifen:

(a) Er redet von "Heiligtümern", die zerstört werden—wie Am. vii 13 von Bet-El als Reichs- "Heiligtum".

(b) Er redet vom "Schwert", dem das Haus Jerobeams anheimfällt—wie Amos in V. 11 Jerobeam im Namen Gottes mit dem "Schwert" bedroht.

(c) Er redet von "Isaaks Höhen", die verwüstet werden—wie V. 16 vom "Haus Isaaks". Diese Übereinstimmung ist die evidenteste und auffälligste, da beide Begriffe nie andernorts in der vorexilischen Prophetie begegnen und der Name "Isaak" jeweils anders als in der Regel geschrieben ist.

---

[27] Wie sehr Amos und Amazja als Repräsentanten ihrer Institution im Blick sind, geht schon daraus hervor, daß sie sich jeweils explizit auf die Autorität berufen, in deren Dienst sie stehen (V. 13 bzw. V. 14–15). Dennoch mag die Erzählung als Einzeltext, d. h. bevor sie in den Kontext der Visionen gestellt wurde, viel stärker als ein Standeskonflikt (Priester und Prophet) gestaltet worden sein. Auf ein solches älteres Stadium könnte insbesondere das ausführliche Strafwort gegen den Priester in V. 17 deuten.

Genauso deutlich wie die Gemeinsamkeiten mit vii 10–17 sind aber auch die Unterschiede. vii 9 redet eben (a) von "Heiligtümern" im Plural; (b) weiter vom "Königshaus", gegen das sich das Schwert richtet, und nicht mehr nur vom König persönlich; (c) schließlich von den "Höhen" Isaaks statt vom "Haus" Isaaks. Die Differenzen ergeben zusammengenommen, daß V. 9 die Aussagen der Verse 10–17 ausweitet ("Haus Jerobeams"), generalisiert ("Heiligtümer") und ihr Zentrum auf das kultische Gebiet verschiebt ("Höhen Isaaks"). Diese offensichtlich bewußte Veränderung der Aussagen der Erzählung durch den ihr vorangestellten Brückenvers will deren Bedeutung für den Kontext im voraus festlegen. Sie wird aber erst voll erklärlich, wenn erkannt ist, daß Am. vii 9 nicht von der Sprache des Amos geprägt ist, sondern von der Sprache Hoseas:

(a) Die "Höhen" Isaaks bezeichnen eine Thematik, die Amos nirgends sonst berührt, die aber ganz geläufig im Buch Hosea ist.

(b) Die "Heiligtümer" in ihrer Vielzahl haben andernorts nie Amos erregt, wohl aber auf Schritt und Tritt Hosea (vgl. oben Abschnitt I und II).

(c) Am bemerkenswertesten aber ist die in Am. vii 9 betont herausgestellte Verbindung von kultischer und staatlicher Schuld. Diese Verbindung betrifft eine *der* charakteristischen Merkmale der Botschaft Hoseas.

Es ergeben sich folgende Möglichkeiten der Entwicklung:

1. Wahrscheinlich haben die Visionsberichte einmal eine eigenständige Sammlung für sich gebildet, da die paarweise Gestaltung der ersten vier Visionen ihr Hauptmerkmal ist. Sie hätten dann zur Legitimation der harten Botschaft des Propheten gedient.

2. Als Teil des Amosbuches haben die Visionsberichte kaum je ohne die Erzählung von Amos und Amazja in vii 10–17 bestanden, die literarisch vielfach mit ihnen verknüpft ist, vermutlich aber auch nicht ohne den eng mit V. 10–17 verzahnten Brückenvers vii 9. So wohl vii 9 als auch vii 10–17 wollen in ihrer Stellung unmittelbar nach der dritten Vision für Leser nach dem Fall Samarias die Schuldkategorie benennen, jenseits derer ein Verschonen Israels durch Jahwe—wie in den ersten beiden Visionen—nicht mehr möglich ist. Sie stehen damit wie Am. iii 2 an entscheidender hermeneutischer Position innerhalb des Amosbuches. Wie Am. iii 2 beziehen sie die Verkündigung des Amos und des Hosea aufeinander, die als zwei Boten Gottes mit einer gemeinsamen Botschaft vorgestellt werden: Gottes

Wille, Schuld in Israel zu ertragen, ist dort zu Ende, wo der Staat ihn am Reden hindert und der Gottesdienst einem baalisierten Jahwe gilt, der nicht mehr der Jahwe der Anfänge ist (vii 9).

3. Aber auch wenn der poetische Brückenvers vii 9 spätere Interpretation der Verse 10–17 in ihrem Kontext sein sollte,[28] so gilt doch auch schon von dieser Erzählung, daß sie zumindest in Kenntnis der Theologie Hoseas gestaltet ist. Weder die vorausgesetzte (aber nicht ausgeführte) Schuld des Königs noch die mit dem Begriff "Heiligtum" verbundenen Assoziationen noch gar die Verbindung von König/Staat und Heiligtum finden im älteren Amosbuch eine Parallele (vgl. später Am. ix 8); wohl aber begegnen diese Merkmale vielfach im Hoseabuch. Auch die vorausgesetzte Funktion des Propheten als Jahwes letztes Mittel, Israel zu retten, kennt das Hoseabuch (Hos. vi 5–6).[29] Unter dieser Voraussetzung hätte der dann jüngere V. 9 die Bezüge zur hoseanischen Theologie, besonders zu Hoseas Kultpolemik, die schon in vii 10–17 vorhanden waren, kräftig verstärkt und ausgeweitet.

V

Versuchen wir die Ergebnisse zusammenzufassen:

1. Historisch sind Amos und Hosea sehr verschiedene Propheten gewesen mit im einzelnen sehr unterschiedlichen Thematiken in ihrer Verkündigung. In diesen Differenzen spiegelt sich am ehesten wider, daß Amos und Hosea zwar beide in den Zentren des Nordreichs, Samaria und Bet-El, verkündeten, aber Hosea aus dem Nordreich, Amos dagegen aus dem Südreich stammte.

2. Jedoch beziehen die Tradenten, und zwar offensichtlich schon in vorexilischer Zeit, die Verkündigung beider Propheten aufeinander. Sie verbieten ihren Lesern damit die theologische Isolierung eines der beiden Propheten. Diese Intention der Überlieferung kann auch dem modernen Ausleger nicht gleichgültig sein. So sehr für ihn

---

[28] Die stilistische Nähe von vii 9 zum Brückenvers viii 3, der die 4. Vision mit einer jüngeren, neuen Zusammenfassung der Amosbotschaft in viii 4–14 verbindet (Wolff [Anm. 18], S. 132: jeweils perf. cons.), könnte dafür sprechen, daß vii 9 und viii 3 gleichzeitig dem Amosbuch zugefügt wurden.

[29] Sie gehört ins Vorfeld der geläufigen dtr. Sicht, daß Jahwe "früh und spät" Propheten gesendet habe, die Israel abwies. Vgl. dazu O.H. Steck, *Israel und das gewaltsame Geschick der Propheten* (Neukirchen, 1967), sowie im Amosbuch die späteren Worte viii 11–12 und ix 8 zusammen mit 9–10.—Auch die Gestalt der Verbannungsankündigung ("fort von seinem Land": V. 11 und 17) klingt mit der Betonung des Landes hoseanisch (vgl. bes. Hos. ix 1–4), während Amos üblicherweise die Richtung der Verbannung anzeigt (Am. iv. 3, v 27).

nach der Aufklärung die Frage nach dem jeweilig Spezifischen der Verkündigung eines einzelnen Propheten notwendig und unumgänglich ist, so sehr muß er sich bei dieser Fragestellung im klaren sein, daß er an der theologischen Zielsetzung der Überlieferer der Prophetenbücher—zumindest im Fall der Bücher des Amos und Hosea—vorbeifragt, da dieses Ziel gerade darin bestand, das Gemeinsame der beiden Prophetenbücher herauszustellen. Daran wird deutlich, daß die nachgeborenen Generationen zu alttestamentlicher Zeit die Verkündigung des Amos und Hosea nicht mit dem Interesse eines Historikers gelesen und weitergereicht haben, also nicht mit der Frage nach einem vergangenen Damals, sondern vielmehr mit aktuellem Interesse, d. h. mit der Frage nach der Bedeutung der Botschaft der beiden Propheten für ihre eigene Zeit und damit implizit mit der Frage nach dem Wesen des Wortes Gottes durch *die* Propheten schlechthin. Sie waren freilich weit davon entfernt, eine Propheten-Harmonie im Sinne Tatians anzustreben.

3. Allerdings ist nun bemerkenswert, daß dieser Prozeß bei beiden Prophetenbüchern verschieden eingesetzt hat.

(a) Beim Buch des Propheten Hosea ist die Frage nach dem Gemeinsamen mit der Botschaft des Amos erst gestellt worden, als dieses Buch (in wesentlichen Teilen) schon fertig vorlag; die Berührungen mit dem Amosbuch sind als literarische Zusätze ablösbar. Offensichtlich ist das Hoseabuch aufgrund der frühen Bewahrheitung der Prophetenworte im Untergang des Nordreichs besonders früh niedergeschrieben worden. Der Prozeß der Annäherung der beiden Propheten ist im Falle des Hoseabuches vermutlich erst erfolgt, als man das Buch nach dem Fall Samarias in den Süden brachte, wo es bekanntlich auch (den jungen) Jeremia beeinflußte. Die literarisch zugefügten Anspielungen an Amosworte wollen primär vermeiden, daß die Judäer das ihnen fremde Buch aus dem Nordreich mit einer Zuschauerhaltung zur Kenntnis nehmen, statt es auf ihre eigenen Zustände in Jerusalem und im Land Juda zu beziehen.

(b) Im Gegensatz zu diesem Befund haben Hoseaworte anscheinend von allem Anfang an auf die Formulierung der schriftlichen Worte des Amosbuches eingewirkt, und zwar gerade an literarisch zentralen Stellen, d. h. an den hermeneutischen Weichenstellungen.[30] Aus diesem Vergleich ergibt sich mit großer Wahrscheinlichkeit,

---

[30] Analoges gilt etwa auch für Am. v 25 (eine Frage, die auf Erkenntnis der Leser

daß das Amosbuch später als das Hoseabuch niedergeschrieben
wurde, zu einer Zeit, als das Hoseabuch in prophetischen Kreisen Judas schon Autorität gewonnen hatte. Insofern setzt das
Dodekapropheton zu Recht mit dem Hoseabuch ein, obwohl Amos
geschichtlich früher als Hosea gewirkt hat.

4. Der theologische Wille, zwei Prophetenbücher aufeinander zu
beziehen, der offensichtlich im 7. Jh. v. Chr. einsetzte, hat eine lange Entwicklung eingeleitet. Am Ende dieser Entwicklung—knapp ein
halbes Jahrtausend später—steht das fertige Zwölfprophetenbuch. Daß
die zwölf Propheten in *einem* Buch versammelt sind, daß nun am
Ende der Entwicklung eine Fülle literarischer Querverbindungen,
teilweise früher, teilweise späterer Herkunft, zwischen den Büchern
besteht, macht deutlich, daß im Sinne derer, die alle zwölf Bücher
auf eine Prophetenrolle schrieben, nicht zwölf verschiedene Botschaf-
ten Gottes vereinigt werden sollten, sondern die *eine* prophetische
Botschaft im Mund von zwölf verschiedenen Zeugen zu verschiedenen Zeiten. Wenn O.H. Steck Recht hat mit seiner eingangs genannten Vermutung, daß die späteren Tradenten auch bei dieser
Intention nicht stehenblieben, sondern im Prozeß des Abschlusses des
Prophetenkanons die vielstimmige Botschaft des Buches Jesaja auf
die vielstimmige Botschaft des Buches der Zwölf bezogen (vgl. o. Anm.
3), müßte man diese Aussage auf den gesamten Prophetenkanon
ausweiten. Wir stehen heute erst ganz am Anfang der Aufgabe, den
Prozeß des Werdens des Prophetenkanons nachzuzeichnen. Das eine
aber ist schon sicher: Die mit einer "Theologie des Alten Testaments"
gestellte Aufgabe, das *eine* Wort der Propheten hinter den vielen
Wörtern der Einzeltexte in den Prophetenbüchern herauszustellen,
ist ein Vorhaben, das schon seit dem 7. Jh. v. Chr. von den Tradenten
der Prophetenworte als ihre wesentlichste Pflicht erkannt wurde.

---

aus ist) sowie später für viii 11–12, 14 (wie vii 9–17 ebenfalls in den Visionenzyklus
eingeschoben) und für ix 8, 9–10.

THE EXPLICIT AND IMPLICIT IN BIBLICAL NARRATIVE

by

ZECHARIA KALLAI
Jerusalem

I

The study of biblical texts for historiographical research is bound to attend to the reliability of sources and will examine the data available accordingly. The literary techniques of the ancient authors and redactors, as well as the rules of composition, must therefore be scrutinized from that point of view. This is in effect a literary problem, but the application of historical and historical-geographical criteria may enhance this investigation, as it introduces tangible tests and perceptions. The perfection of literary criteria as a result of such investigation benefits not only historiography but literary research in general.[1]

When verifying the testimony of a given text in respect of its historical or ideological notions, a cardinal question generally posed is what is the cognizance of the text. Awareness of certain aspects, or lack thereof, is noted, as well as differences of detail and formulation compared to other texts that refer to the same subject. It is in this sphere of the testimony of texts that the question of explicit and implicit expression arises.

Explicit and implicit modes of expression in biblical texts, narrative or poetical, are known. The object of this study is a programmatic review of some of the more prominent phenomena that may assist in classifying and defining literary ways and means of the ancient authors in this respect. Closer attention to the scribal tradition and technique may lead to better understanding of the art of composition. It may furthermore facilitate the perception of literary complexes

---

[1] The subjects dealt with in this study touch upon many basic problems of the historical, literary and textual research of the biblical canon. The relevant literature is both comprehensive and basic, and comprises the commentaries on the individual books and the standard studies devoted to the various issues and textual problems raised. It therefore seems superfluous to itemize the extensive literature, and only a few specific or summarizing references will be given.

underlying the compositions known, and contribute to a reappraisal of literary relativity and history.

Whereas implicit rendering is always an abbreviated expression that refers in different ways to features otherwise known, and thus patently constitutes a citation, explicit writing may be a primary or a quoted formulation. Beyond that distinction another aspect of quoted formulation, common to both explicit and implicit writing, should be noted. Besides factual plain formulation, normative and stylized representative expressions may be used. Furthermore, a composition may be straightforward and informative relating events, or be designed to express ideas and concepts, in which case the details and motifs adduced may not be basically integral but chosen for illustration and redactional requirements only. All these aspects intimated here emphasize some of the more obvious marks of the intricate literary development that has to be considered when analyzing ways and features of composition.

Considering the complexity of the texts a cardinal requirement of any analysis must be reliance on the internal evidence as to the import of the composition and its objects. The questions to be posed must be aimed at differentiating the components and their place in the final product, and the manner of their integration must be elicited from the circumstances of their incorporation in the text. No imposition of extraneous criteria may be substituted for the presumable rationale of the text as it stands. An integral part of this attitude is to seek the message of the text as formulated. It is in this spirit that the scribal art, its rules and technique, must be studied.

II

As intimated already, the literary phenomena under discussion, centred on the explicit and implicit modes of expression, may best be scrutinized, when reviewing the question of cognizance of textual complexes. The diverse aspects involved will become apparent when various examples of such textual problems will be examined in detail.

In Num. xxxiii the story of the wandering of the Israelites from Egypt to the land of Canaan is summarized by listing the stations of their itinerary. The theophany at Mount Sinai is not even hinted at in this account. A few of the other occurrences, known from the detailed narrative are briefly alluded to, namely the strife due to lack of water at Rephidim in *v.* 14, Aaron's death in *vv.* 38–9, and the encounter with the Canaanites in *v.* 40. All other events along the Israelites' trek and during their sojourn in the desert, including the pre-eminent revelation of Sinai, are completely ignored. Is this text unaware of those episodes, or should they be regarded as implicitly referred to? For some reason the occurrences intimated were deemed to be particularly worthy of recalling. The question is whether a given detailed reference, as against the lack of it, reflects cognizance or selective emphasis.

Before turning to further instances some of the manifestations in this passage should be defined and classified.

This summarizing description is specified as a list of stations. Therefore, whatever is known from the detailed account of the itinerary may be deemed to be known to the compiler of this list and to be referred to implicitly by the very recording of the stations. All events related to the wandering and what they entail are thus represented, and if some of them are singled out the question arises what prompted that choice. The revelation of Sinai is not less important than the particular events recalled. Therefore, the catalogue of stations conveys the complete story of the exodus and wandering with all its ramifications, and stands for this focal event as a whole, whereas the episodes alluded to emphasize within that complex a particular aspect. The common denominator of these references is the rebellious behaviour of the people and the resulting punishments, a feature that markedly shaped the tradition of the wandering towards the land of Canaan.

All these allusions are most succinct, but even the full stories in the detailed account referred to are stylized formulations of motifs that signify an advanced stage of the literary process. These episodes express concepts which are incorporated into the composition. In this manner the brief references may be regarded as signals of an intricate literary structure.

The first of these references is in *v.* 14: "And they journeyed from Alush, and encamped at Rephidim and there was no water there for the people to drink." The full story referred to is in Exod. xvii 1–7. It is centred on the element of discontent of the people due to hardships of the wandering. The aspect of disbelief is rather loosely related to the event, without any apparent result, and there is even a disconnected link to Horeb (*v.* 6). The same motif of discontent is applied in a much more profound manner in the episode of producing water for the thirsty people at Kadesh (Num. xx 2–11, 12–13), also in a contrived combination with further elements which this passage emphasizes. The epithet "Waters of Strife" given to the spring of Kadesh is similar to the name of "Trial and Strife" related to Rephidim in Exod. xvii. At Kadesh, however, the event is linked to the punishment meted out to Moses and Aaron not to enter the Promised Land.

The second specific reference in *vv.* 38–9 describes the death of Aaron on Mount Hor, related in detail in Num. xx 22–9. There the reason for Aaron's death is specified as being punishment for the people's disbelief demonstrated at Kadesh (*vv.* 12, 24). In this setting the punitive aspect is clearly shown, and the brief allusion in Num. xxxiii 38–9 undoubtedly indicates this episode, as evinced by the reference to Mount Hor. In another formulation the death of Aaron and the succession of his son is not related to any particular circumstance, and also the place of death is in a different location (Deut. x 6). It is possible that either the punitive cause of Aaron's death was taken for granted in this reference, or that in this formulation Aaron's death was not related to this motif. According to Deut. ix 20, for instance, Aaron's punishment may be related to his involvement with the Golden Calf.

The third implicit remark in this passage refers to the encounter with the Canaanites in the south of the country (*v.* 40). This is the most intricate of the implicit remarks in this summary of the story of the wandering. Not only is it very abbreviated, but it is also elliptical. Moreover, the episode referred to is an obviously stylized anecdote that has already undergone a process of patterned formulation of a historical concept.

The wording "And the Canaanite, the king of Arad who dwells in the Negeb, in the land of Canaan, heard of the coming of the sons of Israel" is an abbreviated quotation of the story as told in Num. xxi 1, which states that the Canaanites fought against Israel and took captives of them. The sequel there, in *vv.* 2–3, which tells of the ultimate prevailing of Israel over the Canaanites in the south of the country, is a parallel of the story in Judg. i 16–17. This represents a conquest tradition, reflected also in Josh. xii 14 in the catalogue of conquered Canaanite city-kings. All these passages display a combination of stylized, patterned anecdotes related to the conquest and settlement in the land of the Negeb. The names and terms that figure in this complex within the wanderings narrative serve to illustrate the motif of the unsuccessful attempt of Israel to penetrate the country from the south. Alternatively, these descriptions may be phrased to explain the punitive reason for not choosing the route from the south, just as Exod. xiii 17 gives a reason for not following the nearest approach from Egypt along the coastal road, "the road of the land of the Philistines".

To appreciate the variegated application of the implicit expressions that figure in this complex, all relevant passages must be considered in conjunction. The texts concerned are related to the episode of the spies in the wilderness of Paran (Num. xiii 29, xiv 25a, 40–2, 43–5), then to the Israelites' leaving Kadesh (Num. xxi 1, 2–3, paralleled in xxxiii 40 and similarly in Deut. i 41–3, 44), and finally to accounts depicting the conquest (Josh. xii 14; Judg. i 16–17). The representative names and terms used may be found in various combinations. They are: Canaanite/Amorite and Amalek, Canaan and the Negeb, Arad and Hormah. The place-names Arad and Hormah represent the Negeb and particularly the northern, sedentary part, the Canaanite/Amorite stands for the country as a whole and Amalek for the Negeb in particular, similar to the terms Canaan and Negeb. Except for the conquest traditions, in which the place-names figure in their natural setting, each representing a different area of the northern Negeb, east and west, with Hormah probably chosen for its aetiological connotation, all other passages compound more or fewer of these names and terms, and use them figuratively. Consequently, Arad and Hormah are applied in their representative nature and not according to precise topographical considerations. Similarly, Canaan/Canaanite/Amorite and Negeb, as well as Amalek are used throughout for the whole region of the southern part of the country which the Israelites, coming from the Sinai Peninsula, encounter.

The literary manner in which this complex of names and terms is applied shows that reference to any or several of them implies the issue as a whole. The hindrance of Israel's entry into the country from the south is presented in conjunction with varying reasons according to the requirements of the composition in every case. Similarly, also the place at which this punitive hindrance is ordained changes in the different formulations. The summary in Num. xxxiii 40, quoting Num. xxi 1, paralleled by Deut. i 44, places the episode after the sojourn at Kadesh, whereas in Num. xiv it is located in the wilderness of Paran. Kadesh, mentioned in Num. xiii 26 together with the wilderness of Paran, must be a harmonizing interpolation, as according to the sequence of the narrative the two are quite distinct localities.[2] In one instance, in Deut. i 44, an additional name appears in this context, namely, that the Israelites were beaten in Seir. This designation fits in with the episode being related to the approaches of the land, as Seir is regularly referred to as beyond the southern, or rather south-eastern, border of Canaan.[3] The special allusive character of these references is most conspicuous in those texts that mention the names of the peoples with or without any further detail. In Num. xiii 29 Amalek who dwells in the Negeb is specifically added to the standard enumeration of the pre-Israelite nations.[4] From then on Amalek together with the Canaanite/Amorite or sometimes the Canaanite/Amorite alone serve as an indicator of the regional circumstances related to this motif, either with descriptive details added, or alone. So it is in Num. xiv 25a, 43, 45, xxi 1, xxxiii 40; Deut. i 44. The implicit expression is thus reduced to the barest minimum. For completeness' sake it should be mentioned, that this combination of the Amalekite and the Canaanite/Amorite, as representing this concept of the south of the country encountered by Israel, is expressed also in the narrative of the campaign of Chedorlaomer (Gen. xiv 7), which provides the proto-historical prelude to Israel's activity, and is fully dependent on the wandering description and its terminology.[5]

Another passage that may well illustrate the question of cognizance and implicit references employed from yet another angle is to be found in the recapitulation of the wanderings narrative in Deut. i–iii. The opening of the discourse of Moses in Deut. i 6 starts the description of the wandering at Horeb. The brief preface to this discourse in *vv.* 1–5 does not go back beyond Horeb either. The

---

[2] Cf. M. Noth, *Das vierte Buch Mose* (Goettingen, 1966), p. 94.

[3] Z. Kallai, "The southern border of the Land of Israel—pattern and application", *VT* 37 (1987), pp. 438–45.

[4] About the problem in general see T. Ishida, "The Structure and Historical Implications of the Lists of Pre-Israelite Nations", *Biblica* 60 (1979), pp. 461–90. It is obvious that the object of listing the pre-Israelite nations, be it in full or part, is to indicate the land of Canaan. It is likewise clear that certain partial listings may be formulated to emphasize a given area, in this case the Negeb. For comparison it may be appropriate to cite the example of the special position of the Perizzite in connection with the centre of the country in Gen. xiii 7, xxxiv 30; Judg. i 4–5 and in a variation in Josh. xvii 15.

[5] Cf. Z. Kallai, "The Campaign of Chedorlaomer and Biblical Historiography", *Shnaton, An Annual for Biblical and Ancient Near Eastern Studies* 10 (Jerusalem, 1986–1989, Tel-Aviv), pp. 153–68 (Hebrew), XXII–XXIII (English summary).

emphasis in this passage is on the command to proceed to the promised land. This passage, however, is obviously not ignorant of the exodus from Egypt and of the revelation of Sinai. These unspecified events are implicitly referred to, though in a different manner from that observed previously. The literary form here is an elliptical formulation that clearly implies the missing details. The mentioning of Horeb recalls the whole tradition in which the events at Horeb figure.

The problem of cognizance of events and the veracity of the information found in texts pertains also to the sphere of explicit expression. Within the framework of this discussion it is of particular interest to establish whether such formulation is factual and informative or stylized and schematic, with the sole object of conveying a concept.

This issue may best be examined in the book of Joshua. The book is composed of several sections. A descriptive part deals with the entry into the country and its conquest. The next section relates the allotment of the conquered land to the tribes and the allocation of the cities of Refuge and Levitical cities. The book winds up with concluding chapters that deal with the relationship of Cis- and Transjordanian tribes and summarizing discourses. For this study the descriptive part and the summarizing historical oration are pertinent.

The description of the conquest with the summarizing list of vanquished city-kings, though very stylized and schematic, is quite explicit in its formulation. The historical review at the end of the book is similarly phrased. Still their historicity has been justly questioned. Within the framework of this investigation the problem to be addressed is in what way the testimony of explicit texts can be assessed to establish their historical veracity, and what are the literary criteria involved. It is obvious that the explicit, factual formulation alone is not the touchstone of historicity. The solution is to be sought in a combination of the historical-critical and literary analysis.

Archaeological-historical research leaves no doubt that the historical narrative of the book of Joshua cannot be upheld. The most extreme approach, therefore, is to invalidate the historicity of the book of Joshua entirely. This then is based on the literal sense of the explicit text, confronting it with the verifiable facts without considering the intricacy of the composition. However, in relation to the historical data that can be established by independent means, i.e. through archaeological and historical investigation, the questions that must be posed are as follows. What is the intrinsic information presented, and in what way is this information expressed? If, as it seems to me, the essential historical process is indeed expressed in a schematic and stylized manner, this testimony must be judged historically by its abstraction only, whereas the explicit details belong to the realm of literary technique. The extant formulation, even if explicit, is thus but a patterned presentation of a concept which is historically compatible, and the illustrating details adduced need not be historically precise, as they are chosen for their representative purpose only.

This schematic stylized formulation describes the basic historical phenomena. The land of Canaan is characterized as consisting of city-kingdoms, and the fundamental demographic change achieved in a variety of ways, including armed conflict, in a measurable period, is the conquest. Roaming the land in the preparatory stages, especially in the Patriarchal stories, and conducting warfare in the conquest tradition are the instruments of possession of the land. The historical concept expressed in this manner rests on historical experience and is therefore conclusive as far as historiography is concerned. The explicit, even if in part unhistorical, details are narrated in a manner prescribed by scribal tradition. Being representative, their essential message is important and not their literal import. Differing details do not necessarily constitute conflicting testimony, as long as they are complementary and not incompatible with the concept they are meant to convey.

The description of the conquest relates a number of episodes which are summarized in the list of vanquished kings. Additional details in that catalogue attest further episodes which were not rendered or preserved in the detailed narrative. This is a variation in the degree of detail only. In the same manner the historical oration in Josh. xxiv must be judged by its general tenor and according to the meaning of the patterned terms used. Some data seem not to tally with the known narratives. The revelation of Sinai is not mentioned, the encounter with Balak, the king of Moab, is defined as belligerent, and the notables of Jericho are cited as having fought Israel. The events not mentioned, however, are clearly implied by the elliptical formulation, and the belligerence of Balak and the masters of Jericho, not attested elsewhere, is due to the paradigmatic character of the descriptions. In this respect the function of every act in the patterned historiography must be considered. The encounter between Israel and its adversaries is defined as warfare. The reference to Balak and Jericho, as representing the general circumstance in this summary, is therefore in line with the stereotyped description of the events. Moreover, Jericho is listed as a detail opening the generalized reference to the whole country, represented by the enumeration of the pre-Israelite nations.[6] The detailed descriptions, however, present each of these episodes in the particular setting required by the overall concept governing these narratives. The encounter with Moab is obscured, obviously because of the doctrine that forbids the Israelites to fight the Moabites,[7] whereas the fall of Jericho is presented as a miraculous event.

These explicit references are thus representative and patterned, and not necessarily a testimony to be regarded literally.

In the discussion of the literary phenomena reviewed so far, diverse observations were made regarding the cognizance of texts and different aspects of explicit and implicit expression. Bearing them in mind we may turn our attention to yet another literary complex that abounds in problems in this respect, the books of Chronicles.

It is generally recognized that compared to their parallels the books of Chronicles not only contain additional material, but on various issues display a distinct approach and particular emphasis. Within the more limited sphere of the specific attitude of Chronicles there are features that are directly linked to this study. It has been contended that the books of Chronicles are apparently unaware of certain basic elements of Israelite proto-history and related concepts. These problems have been studied extensively and arguments to the contrary have been offered.[8] Therefore, it is not intended to

---

[6] For a different opinion see J.A. Soggin, "The Conquest of Jericho Through Battle (Note on a Lost Biblical Tradition)", *Eretz-Israel* 12 (Jerusalem, 1982), pp. 215*–17*.

[7] Regarding the doctrine that regulates the relationship of Israel and the kindred peoples of Transjordan who are inviolable cf. Z. Kallai, "The Wandering-Traditions from Kadesh-Barnea to Canaan: A Study in Biblical Historiography", *JJS* 33 (1982), pp. 175–84. In a subsequent, as yet unpublished study I show the gradual metamorphosis of the descriptions related to the encounter with the Moabites. It starts with Balak's efforts to secure his prevalence over Israel (Num. xxii 2–3, xxv 1–3), in conjunction with the Midianites (Num. xxii 4, xxv 6, 10–15). Further on, the emphasis is shifted to the Midianites alone (Num. xxv 16–18, xxxi 1–12), ending with coupling the Midianites with Sihon the Amorite, who is not inviolable and may be fought, and whose territory may be conquered (Josh. 21aβ–22).

[8] As examples of the discussion in this field it may be advisable to cite two studies of differing attitudes with ample literature. S. Japhet, "Conquest and Settlement in Chronicles", *JBL* 98 (1979), pp. 205–18, underlines the different stand of Chronicles on the proto-history of Israel. G. Galil, "The Pre-Davidic Period in Chronicles",

examine whether Chronicles is cognizant of the exodus, the revelation of Sinai, the conquest of Canaan and related issues, but rather how these phenomena are expressed in Chronicles and the literary means involved.

Chronicles opens the orderly narration of historical events in the middle of the concluding episode of Saul's life. This abrupt introduction to David's story is indicative of the conspicuous characteristic of Chronicles' treatment of the early history of Israel, which is presented in an elliptical manner. This abridgement is part of the manner of composition which displays the special interest, emphasis and inclination of the Chronicler. The main subject is detailed, and in respect of other features he shows his awareness through a system of allusive remarks. These may refer briefly to episodes of the proto-history not detailed in Chronicles, as for instance the avoidance of warfare against the kindred nations in Transjordan (2 Chron. xx 10), or even briefer allusions. A different manifestation is the expression of a geographical concept regarding the scope of the Transjordanian tribal territories in 1 Chron. v, which is obviously based on that of Josh. xiii. Many of these remarks figure in the narration, and others are inserted into the genealogical prolegomenon of the composition. Some examples of these will be reviewed.

It must be borne in mind that genealogies are an instrument that expresses formal relationships and are not necessarily an ethnographical-biological record. Many apparent internal conflicts and quandaries are due to this primary object of the lists. In relating the structure of families and tribes, individuals personify a public body, and when various segments of that entity are integrated, the interlocking may create peculiar constructions. Moreover, as the *pater eponymus* of the tribe or family represents that corporate unit, the activities attributed to that figure must be evaluated accordingly and not as those of the individual depicted otherwise.

Notable examples of the mechanism of the genealogies are, for instance, the following. References to Salma in the lineage of Judah, in 1 Chron. ii 11, 51, 54, are obviously aimed at showing the connection of David's family to the prominent clan of his residential base. Another facet may be seen in the involvement of Ephraim, representing the tribe and not the individual, in the settlement tradi-

---

Ẓion 55 (1989/90), pp. 1–26 (Hebrew), I–II (English summary), assembles the evidence for the Chronicler's awareness of the proto-history of Israel.

tion in 1 Chron. vii 23. No conclusion regarding the proto-history of Israel may be drawn from this presence of Ephraim, as the individual, in the land.

As far as this study is concerned, however, particular attention is due to the patently individual figures in the genealogies. They are clearly distinct from the rest of the lists. These individuals represent specific traditions or stories which are related about them elsewhere, or in which they figure.[9] Their listing, even without further details, or with scant intimation of the circumstances, implies that unspecified tradition. Such are the following, all in 1 Chronicles. Achar (or Achan) son of Carmi (ii 7), Nahshon son of Amminadab, prince of the sons of Judah (ii 10), Hur (ii 19), Bezaleel son of Uri, son of Hur (ii 20), Caleb son of Jephunneh (iv 15) and Joshua son of Nun (vii 27).

III

In conclusion of this review it is appropriate to summarize some of the more significant inferences.

The phenomena observed in the compositions examined, reveal a multitiered development of an elaborate literary history. Concepts and motifs evolved at one stage are used again in different ways, partly in the form of signals and coded, patterned expressions. This is evidence of an intensive literary activity in which importance attaches to the background involved at all stages. The question whether such concepts had been formalized in writing or not is immaterial and hard to prove; their very existence, however, must be assumed. The focal interest as far as historiography is concerned, is in the realm of the reality that produced these concepts and motifs, and pertains to the historical consciousness that employs them as an instrument of expression. Any study in this field is bound to examine the essential elements involved in the components used in a given composition. Because of this complex nature of composition, which is based on selectively adduced material, the import of the final product is most significant. At the same time this relativity of quoted and quoting formulations attests the dimension of depth of the literary history involved.

---

[9] This does not preclude the possibility that ultimately these individual figures personify clans or similar corporate units.

CONCEPTIONS RELIGIEUSES DOMINANTES EN PALESTINE/ISRAËL ENTRE 1750 ET 900

par

OTHMAR KEEL

Fribourg, Suisse

Quelques caractéristiques de la recherche récente sur les origines d'Israël

La recherche de ces dernières années sur les origines d'Israël aux 12ème et 11ème siècles se caractérise au moins en bonne partie par les traits suivants:

- Défiance à l'égard de la valeur historique des textes bibliques rapportant les événements de cette période.[1] Néanmoins tout le monde, aussi critique qu'on soit, fait appel à *certains* textes bibliques pour la reconstruction de l'histoire et de l'histoire religieuse d'Israël dans la mesure où ils cadrent avec ce que l'on connaît ou croit connaître par d'autres sources.[2] Par là on reconnaît donc que les textes de la Bible hébraïque contiennent du matériel ancien ce qui nous fait revenir au vieux problème, mais qui reste toujours actuel,[3] de savoir par quel procédé le matériel plus ancien peut être extrait du matériel plus récent.
- Confiance dans l'applicabilité des modèles sociologiques. Cette confiance caractérise déjà la théorie de la transhumance d'A. Alt,[4] mais également la théorie des révolutions motivées par la religion de N.K. Gottwald[5] et la théorie des émigrations à motif économique

---

[1] Cf. par exemple N.P. Lemche, *Early Israel. Anthropological and Historical Studies in the Israelite Society Before the Monarchy*, SVT 37 1985), pp. 306–85; la méfiance est explicitement adaptée à l'histoire de la religion dans: Id., "The Development of the Israelite Religion in the Light of Recent Studies on the Early History of Israel", *SVT* 42 (Leiden, 1991), pp. 103–5. Une position contradictoire est tenue entre autres par S. Herrmann, "Israels Frühgeschichte im Spannungsfeld neuer Hypothesen", *Studien zur Ethnogenese* 2 (Opladen, 1988), 43–95.

[2] Cf. par exemple Lemche, "Development", pp. 109–10.

[3] Comme le montre dans ce volume la contribution de Mr M. Weippert.

[4] *Die Landnahme der Israeliten in Palästina* (Leipzig, 1925).

[5] *The Tribes of Yahweh. A Sociology of the Religion of Liberated Israel 1250–1050 B.C.E.* (Maryknoll, New York, 1979).

de N.P. Lemche.[6] Mais ce qui, en ces théories, fait problème, c'est que, tout en étant indispensables pour l'interprétation des sources et des témoignages de ce temps-là, de tels témoignages et sources sont encore bien plus indispensables parce que sans eux, il n'y aurait rien à interpréter.

– Ce dilemme exige de manière impérative une prise en compte systématique des résultats des fouilles. De ces résultats s'étaient déjà servis W.F. Albright,[7] R. de Vaux[8] et d'autres pour soutenir leurs hypothèses sur une conquête plus ou moins mitigée par des infiltrations pacifiques.[9] Les fouilles en Palestine se sont limitées jusqu'à ces dernières années aux tells des grandes villes connues ou supposées telles. Mais étant donné que les Proto-Israélites n'étaient pas des citadins on ne pouvait espérer, de cette manière, entrer en possession de leurs reliquats.

– Une utilisation nouvelle et conséquente de la méthode d'exploration de surface et de ses résultats, inspirée par les travaux d'A. Alt fut introduite par Y. Aharoni dans les années cinquante.[10] Des explorations de surface étendues qui avaient eu lieu après la guerre des Six Jours dans le pays montagneux au centre et au sud de la Palestine furent exploitées dans une synthèse impressionnante par I. Finkelstein.[11]

De ces procédés résulte une écriture de l'histoire qui utilise davantage les découvertes archéologiques que la tradition scripturaire et qui, de ce fait, s'intéresse plus à une histoire de durée moyenne et une histoire de longue durée qu'à une histoire événementielle.

Surprenante dans ce contexte est la concentration presque exclusive sur les aspects économique, sociologique et politique et le manque d'intérêt porté au système symbolique religieux,[12] alors que celui-ci

---

[6] *Early Israel*, pp. 95–305.

[7] Pour sa position et celle de ses disciples cf. Lemche, *Early Israel*, pp. 56–7.

[8] R. de Vaux, *Histoire ancienne d'Israël. Des origines à l'installation en Canaan* (Paris, 1971), spéc. pp. 441–620.

[9] Surtout R. de Vaux attache, à côté de la conquête, une grande importance à l'infiltration pacifique et ne ramène pas non plus toutes les couches de destruction à la fin du Bronze Récent aux Proto-Israélites.

[10] Pratiquée la première fois dans sa thèse de doctorat à Jérusalem en 1955, où il décrit l'histoire des implantations de la Haute Galilée sur la base d'explorations de surfaces et de fouilles complémentaires ciblées.

[11] *The Archaeology of the Israelite Settlement* (Jérusalem, 1988); à comparer W.G. Dever, "Archaeological Data on the Israelite Settlement: A Review of Two Recent Works", *BASOR* 284 (1991), pp. 77–88.

[12] Cela vaut aussi bien pour Lemche, *Early Israel*, que pour Finkelstein, mais

est un facteur typique de la durée moyenne sinon de la longue durée. Lorsque des chercheurs s'expriment néanmoins à ce sujet, ils mettent généralement l'accent sur le fait que la religion du Proto-Israël était la religion en usage dans l'aire nordouest sémitique en général.[13] Ils illustrent alors le système symbolique religieux de la Palestine du 12ème au 10ème siècle avec des représentations provenant de la lointaine Ougarit et datant du 16ème au 13ème siècle,[14] ou bien avec la polémique d'Osée et de ses successeurs du 8ème au 6ème siècle. Aucune de ces deux données ne peut servir de sources premières et authentiques pour l'histoire religieuse de la Palestine du 12ème au 10ème siècle. H. Seebass, dans une courte critique à Lemche, renvoie aux nouveaux rites d'ensevelissement à l'époque du Fer I qui témoigneraient non seulement d'un changement de population mais également de religion.[15] H. Weippert, auquel Seebass se réfère, nomme comme nouvelles mœurs l'ensevelissement dans des sarcophages anthropoïdes, l'orientation vers l'ouest de beaucoup de tombes de terre et de sarcophages et la situation de beaucoup de cimetières à l'ouest des agglomérations.[16] Elle interprète ces faits correctement comme expression de l'influence égyptienne sur la Palestine, influence spécialement forte au 13ème siècle mais durant encore bien au-delà de ce temps. Le changement de la population et de la religion, présent à l'esprit de Seebass, ne peut être prouvé par cela.

Les sources pour la reconstruction du système symbolique religieux

Le problème chez Dever, Lemche et d'autres n'est pas la continuité unissant la culture de l'époque du Bronze Récent à celle du Fer I, mais la fausseté des sources utilisées pour la reconstruction et le manque d'un développement du système symbolique religieux qui

---

également, en grande partie, pour le recueil publié par E.M. Lapperrousaz intitulé *La protohistoire d'Israël. De l'exode à la monarchie* (Paris, 1990).

[13] W.G. Dever, "The Contribution of Archaeology to the Study of Canaanite and Early Israelite Religion", dans P.D. Miller, P.D. Hanson et S. Dean McBride (éd), *Ancient Israelite Religion. Essays in Honor of Frank Moore Cross* (Philadelphia, 1987), pp. 209–47; N.P. Lemche, "Development".

[14] Des cinq images de divinités par lesquelles Dever (n. 13), p. 227, illustre sa représentation des divinités de la Palestine du 13e au 11e s., trois proviennent d'Ougarit, voire de son port Minet el-Beida, une de Byblos et une de Gezer.

[15] "Dialog über Israels Anfänge", J. Hausmann et H.J. Zobel (éd.), *Alttestamentlicher Glaube und Biblische Theologie. Festschrift für H.-D. Preuss zum 65. Geburtstag* (Stuttgart, 1992), pp. 15 et 18.

[16] *Palästina in vorhellenistischer Zeit* (Munich, 1988), pp. 366–73 et 413–15.

résulte de l'appel fait à ces sources. Continuité ne veut pas dire stag-
nation. Certaines représentations de l'histoire religieuse d'Israël qui
se basent essentiellement sur les textes (et les images) de la lointaine
Ougarit essaient de suggérer que rien d'important n'a changé dans
le panthéon de la Palestine entre 1750 et 700. Ceci est déjà invraisemblable du simple fait que pendant ce temps des modifications importantes du système symbolique socio-politique ont eu lieu en Palestine. Il est impensable que le passage des villes-états florissantes à
un statut de colonies égyptiennes et le passage de l'effondrement de
celles-ci à la naissance d'états territoriaux n'ait pas influencé le système
symbolique religieux. Les développements parallèles peuvent s'appuyer
sur des sources de première main.

Mais pour être disposé à admettre le témoignage de ces sources,
il faut d'abord avoir compris que les images sont des témoins d'un
système symbolique culturel tout aussi importants que les textes. Il
n'est guère admissible de vouloir reconstituer un système symbolique
culturel uniquement à partir de la philologie. Les documents visuels
doivent être pris au sérieux comme témoignages autonomes. Il ne
s'agit pas de l'histoire de l'art mais de l'histoire des images en tant
que partie de l'anthropologie culturelle.[17] Les images, en tant que
témoins d'une certaine manière de voir, d'un système d'orientation
ou d'une mentalité sont indispensables à la reconstruction de n'importe
quelle culture. Pour la Palestine du 12ème au 10ème siècle c'est tout
particulièrement vrai parce que des textes d'une stratigraphie assurée
font presque entièrement défaut. En utilisant des images comme
documents pour la reconstruction d'une culture il faut distinguer entre
la phase créative où les images venaient d'être créées ou introduites
et les époques où elles ne sont plus que transmises. Par "créées" je
comprends également les modifications importantes. L'image d'un dieu
ou d'une déesse peut être si profondément modifiée que la forme
antérieure et la forme suivante n'ont plus guère que le nom en commun.

Lorsqu'on feuillette les rapports de fouilles, on a souvent l'impression
que le matériel iconographique qui s'y trouve est un pêle-mêle sans
valeur signifiante. Des scarabées de différentes époques se trouvent à
côté des cylindres-sceaux et des amulettes égyptiennes et on a tendance
à les considérer comme ayant été importés en Palestine par le hasard
pur et simple. Mais, quand on les groupe par ordre chronologique et

---

[17] D. Freedberg, *The Power of Images. Studies in the History and Theory of Response*
(Chicago, 1989), p. 23.

thématique, on découvre souvent des tendances claires. Ce n'est pas du tout par hasard qu'on trouve le croissant sur hampe entre deux arbres stylisés surtout à la fin du 8ème et au 7ème siècle. Ce sujet marque une influence assyro-araméenne prononcée. Ce n'est pas non plus par hasard que le prophète Zacharie au 6ème siècle voit le Seigneur comme lampe entre deux arbres.[18]

Quand on a trouvé un moule pour fabriquer des statuettes d'une déesse nue (*fig. 1*) dans un sanctuaire du Bronze Moyen au bord de la mer près de Naharia, on a conclu que ce sanctuaire appartenait à une déesse. Et la présence des figurines d'un lion (*fig. 2*) et d'un vautour (*fig. 3*) a été considérée comme pur hasard. Mais il faut chercher les relations dans lesquelles se trouvent déesse, vautour et lion sur des monuments contemporains et on découvre qu'ils entourent la déesse comme maîtresse d'animaux (*fig. 4*) et que la présence de ces animaux dans le sanctuaire n'a rien d'un hasard. Ainsi on découvrira, au lieu d'un pêle-mêle, une texture bien dense et bien structurée.

Dans un livre qui vient de paraître,[19] Christoph Uehlinger et l'auteur de cette contribution ont essayé de présenter pour la première fois,[20] par ordre chronologique et géographique, le système des symboles iconographiques de la Palestine depuis le Bronze Moyen IIB jusqu'à l'époque perse. Je me bornerai ici à présenter et à commenter quelques résultats de ce livre, pour autant qu'ils concernent le 2ème et le début du premier millénaire.

Bronze Moyen IIB: Des divinités masculines et féminines en interaction[21]

Selon le DtrG une des raisons de la chute d'Israël en 721 fut l'érection de Massébas et d'Ashéras à la manière des peuples que YHWH avait chassés devant Israël (2 R. xvii 10–11). Le Dt défend déjà de planter

---

[18] Cf. O. Keel, *Jahwe-Visionen und Siegelkunst. Eine neue Deutung der Majestätsschilderungen in Jes 6, Ez 1 und 10 und Sach 4* (Stuttgart, 1977), pp. 274–320.

[19] O. Keel et Ch. Uehlinger, *Göttinnen, Götter und Gottessymbole. Neue Erkenntnisse zur Religionsgeschichte Kanaans und Israels aufgrund bislang unerschlossener ikonographischer Quellen* (Freiburg i.Br., 1992, ³1995); des traductions en anglais et en français sont en préparation.

[20] On peut considérer comme précurseur de cette entreprise le livre de St. A. Cook, *The Religion of Ancient Palestine in the Light of Archaeology. The Schweich Lectures of the British Academy 1925* (Londres, 1930). Mais comme chez H. Gressmann ou J.B. Pritchard, l'approche est là aussi avant tout phénoménologique. Chronologiquement il ne distingue que deux périodes, "The Old Oriental Period" et "The Graeco-Roman Age".

[21] Les documents mentionnés dans cette partie—pour autant que rien d'autre ne

à côté d'un autel pour YHWH une Ashéra ou d'ériger une Masséba (xvi 21–2). Dans le sanctuaire de YHWH d'Arad, on a établi une Masséba encore à la fin du 8e ou au début du 7e siècle.[22] Mais l'apogée des pierres sacrales n'était pas l'époque de la naissance d'Israël, ni l'époque royale tardive, mais le Bronze Moyen comme la fameuse série des stèles de Gezer, celle moins connue de Tel Kittan et d'autres en témoignent. Une Masséba pouvait, comme le montre l'exemple de Tel Kittan, représenter une divinité féminine (*fig. 5*). Les idoles féminines de ce temps-là sont souvent caractérisées par la mise en valeur de leurs parties sexuelles. Un certain nombre de pendentifs en or de Tell el-ʿAǧǧul, fabriqués tout à la fin du Bronze Moyen IIB ou au début du Bronze Récent I, réduit la déesse nue à sa vulve, son nombril, deux petits seins et sa tête. De la vulve ou du nombril de ces idoles-pendentifs sort parfois un petit rameau (*fig. 6*). Il symbolise l'étroite relation entre la déesse et la végétation. On le voit également chez les déesses nues des scarabées, par ex. dans un exemple trouvé à Gezer (*fig. 7*) et dans un autre trouvé à Afeq (*fig. 8*). La déesse se dresse sous forme tout à fait humaine entre deux branches et des branches sortent de sa vulve. De même que le culte des Massébas, celui des arbres sacrés, entre lesquels ou dans lesquels la déesse apparaît, était à son apogée au Bronze Moyen IIB. Il est représenté tout aussi bien sur les scarabées typiquement égyptiens de la Palestine, comme par ex. sur un scarabée trouvé à Sichem (*fig. 9*), que sur les cylindres-sceaux typiques de la Syrie du Nord et du Proche Orient en général, comme par ex. sur une pièce trouvée à Tell el-ʿAǧǧul (*fig. 10*).

A cette époque, le dieu de l'orage a une relation tout aussi étroite avec la végétation que la déesse. Sur des scarabées de Lakhish, de Gezer ou de Jérusalem (*fig. 11*), il tient dans une main un sceptre fait de branches ou de fleurs (*fig. 12a*). L'autre main est levée de manière triomphante. Au verso d'une plaque ovale achetée à Jérusalem, on voit ses adorateurs qui saluent avec enthousiasme son retour dans la pluie d'automne (*fig. 12b*). L'appropriation active et pleinement consciente des représentations égyptiennes se manifeste dans le fait qu'on a identifié le dieu égyptien du ciel, Horus, avec le dieu de l'orage cananéen à qui on a, ce qui est contraire à l'habitude

---

soit mentionné—sont publiés et discutés dans Keel et Uehlinger (n. 19), pp. 21–54.

[22] Pour cette datation cf. D. Ussishkin, "The Date of the Judaean Shrine at Arad", *IEJ* 38 (1988), p. 151.

égyptienne, mis le sceptre de branches ou de fleurs en main (*fig. 13*). On a même combiné le faucon d'Horus, symbole de la royauté égyptienne, avec des symboles de la végétation (*fig. 14*).[23] Mais la composition la plus typique pour le Bronze Moyen II montre la déesse qui tire de côté sa robe pour s'offrir au dieu de l'orage, comme on le voit sur un cylindre-sceau trouvé à Megiddo (*fig. 15*). Sur un cylindre-sceau cassé de Hazor, elle la retrousse devant le même dieu. Dans l'art de cour, c'est la composante érotique de cette rencontre qui a été relevée alors que chez les paysans on a plutôt insisté sur ses conséquences pour la fertilité du pays.

La rencontre des deux sexes joue un rôle décisif non seulement sur le plan divin mais également sur le plan humain. Ainsi nous voyons—ce qui ne sera plus jamais le cas dans les périodes ultérieures—homme et femme assis ensemble pour boire comme sur un cylindre-sceau de Tell el-ʿAǧǧul (*fig. 16*) ou s'étreignant comme sur un scarabée de Megiddo (*fig. 17*).

Bronze Récent: la prédominance égyptienne conduit à la politisation du système symbolique[24]

Comme toutes les périodes de transition, celle qui va du Bronze Moyen au Bronze Récent n'a pas lieu soudainement ni simultanément dans les différentes parties du pays. Alors que le Sud était fortement marqué par les événements politiques en Égypte (expulsion des Hyksos), le Nord était plus ou moins à l'abri des répercussions de ce changement. Ainsi, le temple H à Hazor, construit pendant la dernière phase du Bronze Moyen IIB, fut restauré trois fois tout au long de la période du Bronze Récent et cela sur une base plus ou moins identique et avec un mobilier provenant en partie du Bronze Moyen.[25] Des fragments d'une figurine en basalte montrent le dieu de l'orage debout sur un taureau à la manière anatolienne ancienne comme nous le connaissons aussi par une figurine en bronze du Bronze Moyen provenant de Byblos.[26] Elle représente le taureau marchant tranquillement,

---

[23] O. Keel, H. Keel-Leu et S. Schroer, *Studien zu den Stempelsiegeln aus Palästina/Israel II* (Freiburg/Schweiz-Göttingen, 1989), pp. 232–9 et 243–80.

[24] Les documents mentionnés dans cette partie—pour autant que rien d'autre ne soit mentionné—sont publiés et discutés dans Keel et Uehlinger (n. 19), pp. 55–122.

[25] Y. Yadin, Hazor, *The Head of all those Kingdoms* (Londres, 1972), pp. 75–95.

[26] H. Seeden, *The Standing Armed Figurines in the Levant* (Munich, 1980), p. 42 no. 196 et pl. 32, 196.

comme c'est aussi le cas pour le taureau plaqué d'argent d'Ascalon, qui, datant du Bronze Moyen et découvert en 1990, est devenu très vite célèbre.[27] Cependant un taureau du Bronze tardif de Hazor a une attitude quelque peu différente. Son avant-train est raide, comme s'il se préparait à l'attaque.

Un taureau qui doit être associé moins à la fertilité qu'à l'agression est le taureau comme métaphore du pharaon qui piétine ses ennemis comme par exemple sur un scarabée d'Aménophis II de Tell el-'Aǧǧul.[28] Les nouveaux thèmes typiques du système des symboles iconographiques du Bronze Récent palestinien sont: le pharaon qui part au combat dans son char de guerre (*fig. 18*), qui lie ses ennemis, qui les ramène en Égypte (*fig. 19*) et qui les abat devant Amon. Par analogie avec des ennemis humains, le pharaon anéantit aussi les bêtes sauvages, surtout les lions, comme cela se voit sur un scarabée récemment trouvé par la mission dirigée par L.E. Stager à Ascalon. Pendant que le pharaon menace deux lions avec son arc, un haut fonctionnaire vêtu d'un habit long lève la main en signe de vénération (*fig. 20*).

Les princes locaux se comportent comme des petits pharaons. Eux aussi, comme le montre un dessin d'ivoire de Megiddo (*fig. 21*), partent au combat sur des chars de guerre et ramènent leurs ennemis liés à la maison—dans ce cas probablement des nomades Shasu.

L'image du pharaon triomphant et abattant ses ennemis caractérise aussi l'image de la divinité du Bronze Récent. Le métal, matériel précieux, ne sert plus que rarement à fabriquer des figures féminines. Parmi les figures masculines on préfère le type du dieu qui a un bras levé pour frapper, dont le prototype est le pharaon triomphant (*fig. 22*). Dans certains cas on ne peut même pas dire avec certitude s'il s'agit du pharaon ou d'un dieu, comme le montre une figure en bronze de Megiddo (*fig. 22a*). W.G. Dever voit dans ces figures un "warlike Baal, often brandishing in his upraised arm a bundle of thunderbolts, recalling Baal's storm-god imagery ('Cloud Rider') at Ugarit".[29] En réalité, aucun de ces personnages ne tient un éclair ou un faisceau d'éclairs. Dever a ajouté librement cet attribut peut-être à partir de

---

[27] L.E. Stager, "When Canaanites and Philistines ruled Ashkelon", *BAR* 17/2 (1991), p. 25.
[28] A. Rowe, *A Catalogue of Egyptian Scarabs, Scaraboids, Seals and Amulets in the Palestine Archaeological Museum* (Le Caire, 1936), no. 527.
[29] "Contribution" (n. 13) (v.s. n. 11), p. 226. Pour la réfutation de cette interprétation cf. O. Keel, M. Shuval et Ch. Uehlinger, *Studien zu den Stempelsiegeln aus Palästina/Israel III. Die Frühe Eisenzeit. Ein Workshop* (Freiburg/Schweiz-Göttingen 1990), pp. 400–3.

quelques cylindres-sceaux du Bronze Moyen. Les personnages du Bronze Récent ont perdu ce qu'ils tenaient en main et quand ce n'est pas le cas, il tiennent des armes comme un bronze de Megiddo (*fig. 23*). Avec celles-ci le dieu guerrier menace un lion ou un serpent cornu, comme le montrent des cylindres-sceaux d'Acco, de Bet-Shéan, de Tell eṣ-Ṣafi (*fig. 24*) et de Tell el-'Aǧǧul. Le dieu est parfois identifié par un haut bonnet et une longue mèche comme le dieu de l'orage asiatique, parfois par une tête d'animal avec de longues oreilles comme le Seth égyptien. Dans des textes égyptiens du Nouvel Empire "Baal" est régulièrement déterminé par l'animal Seth. Mais Baal-Seth ne combat pas seulement le lion, comme l'a déjà montré le cylindre-sceau de la *fig. 24*, mais aussi un serpent cornu, qu'on voit sur le même cylindre et sur des scarabées provenant de Lakhish, de Tell el-Fara'-Sud (*fig. 25*) et de Tell Deir-'Alla. Le Baal-Seth qui combat le serpent est l'héritier de deux traditions: d'une part, du Seth égyptien, qui, à la proue de la barque du soleil, lutte contre le serpent-Apophis qui incarne le danger que représente la nuit pour le cours du soleil; d'autre part, de la tradition syrienne où le serpent représente les eaux qui inondent la terre fertile et la dévastent. La réunion de ces deux traditions en Baal-Seth vainqueur du serpent a occasionné l'estompement des connotations cosmiques et la mise en valeur de l'élément guerrier.[30]

Quant aux divinités féminines, la déesse aux rameaux est remplacée par une déesse égyptisante avec des cheveux bouclés jusqu'aux épaules qui, à la place des rameaux, tient des fleurs de lotus ou des tiges de papyrus (cf. *fig. 28*). A côté de cette figure traditionnelle, il y a une déesse égyptisante habillée, comme on la voit sur un cylindre-sceau de Bet-El (*fig. 26*). Elle se tient en face du Baal caractérisé par des cornes de taureaux et est probablement Anat. Le mot "Astarté" entre les deux n'est pas une explication mais renvoie à une troisième figure. La lance dans la main de Baal et d'Anat donne aux deux un aspect guerrier. Cet aspect est encore plus marquant chez une Astarte à cheval qui passe au-dessus d'un ennemi (*fig. 27*). Mais, à l'époque du Bronze Récent même la déesse aux rameaux ou aux fleurs peut, elle aussi, être représentée à cheval, comme sur une plaque d'or de Lakhish (*fig. 28*) et un moule des environs de Beth-Shan. Et, parce

---

[30] Cf. pour toute la chaîne de tradition O. Keel, *Das Recht der Bilder gesehen zu werden. Drei Fallstudien zur Methode der Interpretation altorientalischer Bilder* (Freiburg/Schweiz-Göttingen, 1992), pp. 209–216 et figs. 222–40.

que le cheval à cet époque possédait exclusivement des connotations guerrières, elle obtenait ainsi un aspect guerrier.

Une autre tendance, à part l'intégration en des contextes guerriers, est celle qui consiste à remplacer la déesse par son symbole, la branche voire l'arbre. Une terre cuite, dont on a trouvé des exemplaires à Afeq et à Revadim montre à côté de sa vulve des arbres avec des capridés (*fig. 29*). Souvent au Bronze Récent on remplace totalement la déesse par l'arbre flanqué de capridés. De temps en temps, celui-ci a été influencé en outre par la déesse de l'arbre égyptienne, qui dispense de l'eau (*fig. 30*). On ne peut guère expliquer autrement le motif étrange que constitue l'eau avec les poissons qui part de l'arbre avec les capridés (*fig. 31*).

Dans un contexte de guerre, la déesse n'a pas subsisté à côté des divinités masculines. Réduite à un simple symbole, elle a pu être interprétée facilement comme bénédiction des divinités masculines.

Outre les thèmes de victoire et de domination du pharaon qui ont influencé fortement l'iconographie de la Palestine au Bronze Récent, la relation étroite du pharaon avec la divinité jouait un rôle central. Sa filiation divine garantissait au roi, déjà comme enfant, la victoire sur les neuf "Arcs", les ennemis traditionnels de l'Égypte. Amon et Rê conduisent le roi (*fig. 32*). Le roi les vénère (*fig. 33*) et, en même temps, il se montre par ce service filial comme leur héritier légitime. Sur une grande stèle égyptienne, trouvée à Bet-Shéan (*fig. 34*), nous voyons Amon remettre à son fils, Ramsès II, l'épée de la victoire. Celui-ci lui consacre le butin de la guerre en signe de reconnaissance. Le début et la fin de la campagne la retracent toute entière. Les hauts fonctionnaires de Ramsès II et de Ramsès III imitent la piété à l'égard d'Amon de leurs seigneurs comme le montrent bon nombre de monuments de ce temps-là (*fig. 35*).

L'âge du Fer I: Le dieu caché, les dieux triomphants et la bénédiction de la fertilité[31]

Le Fer I est marqué par l'arrivée de nouvelles forces politiques dans le cadre de la Palestine. Dans les montagnes nous voyons s'établir à partir de 1250 tout un réseau de petites et très petites implantations. Les villes cananéennes sont menacées. Les Égyptiens sont en train de se retirer; cependant à Lakhish et à Megiddo ils occupent encore les

---

[31] Les documents mentionnés dans cette partie—pour autant que rien d'autre ne soit mentionné—sont publiés et discutés dans Keel et Uehlinger (n. 19), pp. 123–48.

lieux au moins jusqu'au milieu du 12ème siècle et à Bet-Shéan et dans la plaine côtière du sud plus longtemps encore. A la fin du 13ème siècle la plaine côtière du milieu et plus tard également celle du sud sont tombées sous le contrôle des Philistins. Le temple d'Amon à Gaza semble avoir été repris, au moins au début, par les Philistins. La gravure à la base d'un scarabée trouvé à Tell el-Faraʿ-Sud peut être interprétée comme un souverain philistin devant Amon (*fig. 36*). C'est d'autant plus vraisemblable, que la tête de bélier semble être le seul symbole iconographique d'Amon, qui a survécu du Bronze Récent au Fer I (*fig. 37*).[32] Un témoignage sûr de la vénération d'Amon par les Philistins est la décoration des sceaux en forme de pyramides tronquées. Ce type de sceaux surgit au 12ème–11ème siècle dans la région des Philistins. On les a trouvés par ex. à Tell Qasile (*fig. 38*) et à Tell Djerishe (*fig. 39*). Sur le sceau est gravé le nom d'Amon-Rê, parfois de manière tout à fait traditionnelle, parfois de telle façon que le *m* dans *Jmn* est écrit cryptographiquement à l'aide d'un lion (*m3j*). Le lion est en même temps une métaphore pour la supériorité et la royauté d'Amon. Pendant le Fer I on trouve des amulettes avec le nom d'Amon partout dans le pays (*fig. 40*).

A côté du nom d'Amon nous trouvons sur les sceaux en pyramide tronquée et sur les scarabées de l'époque encore deux dieux: le Baal-Seth avec des ailes, qui est parfois debout sur un lion (*fig. 41*), et un dieu qui se trouve régulièrement debout sur une bête à cornes. Sur des pièces exécutées avec soin, l'animal est clairement une gazelle (*fig. 42*).[33] De temps en temps, on trouve ces deux dieux l'un à côté de l'autre (*fig. 43*). L'attribution de Baal-Seth à Rê, voire Amon-Rê, qui existait déjà à l'âge du Bronze Récent, est sauvegardée sur les pyramides tronquées. Étant donné que Baal-Seth a déjà été représenté comme vainqueur du lion au Bronze Récent (cf. *fig. 24*), le fait d'être debout sur un lion doit signifier le triomphe de Baal-Seth sur le lion. Le taureau par contre est l'animal-attribut, dans et sur lequel Baal-Seth se manifeste. Il s'agit là non plus en première ligne de la fertilité mais de l'agressivité du taureau. Sur des sceaux du Fer I ou IIA le taureau est représenté vainqueur d'un lion ou d'une lionne (*fig. 44*).

---

[32] J. Weinstein, "Review of R. Giveon, Egyptian Scarabs from Western Asia from the Collections of the British Museum, Freiburg/Schweiz-Göttingen 1985", *BASOR* 281 (1991), p. 82.

[33] Pour l'identification de ces dieux voir maintenant I. Cornelius, *The Iconography of the Canaanite Gods Reshef and Baʿal. Late Bronze and Iron Age I Periods (c. 1500–1000 BCE)* (Freiburg/Schweiz-Göttingen, 1994), pp. 112–24 et 181–208.

Cette victoire plutôt inhabituelle est interprétée sur une empreinte d'un sceau d'Ini-Teshub de Karkemish (*fig. 45*) comme victoire du dieu de l'orage sur le lion du dieu Môt. Lors de la dédicace de l'image du taureau de Bet-El, Jéroboam Iᵉʳ l'interprète lui aussi non pas comme symbole de la fertilité mais comme métaphore du dieu guerrier qui a fait sortir Israël d'Égypte (1 R. xii 28b). Nous avons ici un bel exemple de l'interprétation historico-politique des puissances qui commence à la fin du Bronze Récent et au Fer I alors que celles-ci avaient, au Bronze Moyen, une connotation cosmique de fertilité.

Au Fer I, les déesses ne sont plus guère représentées de manière anthropomorphe. Seules quelques terres cuites montrent des femmes nues. Sur les nouveaux types de sceaux-amulettes conoïdes nous voyons des mères animales qui allaitent (*fig. 46–7*). Elles seront encore dans le Dtn mentionnées comme ʿštrwt ḥṣʾn, comme "Astartés du petit bétail" (vii 13, xxviii 4, 18, 51). De même, des arbres flanqués de capridés et des arbres seuls peuvent être compris comme représentations des déesses.

De l'âge du Bronze Récent, où était si présente l'iconographie égyptienne du roi, seule l'image du roi qui abat ses ennemis s'est maintenue jusque dans le Fer I. Le pharaon qui tient en échec des hommes et des animaux à partir de son char de combat ou de son trône avec un arc ou le roi à la chasse des lions (cf. *fig. 20*) a été transformé à l'âge du Fer I en une image qui montre un tireur d'arc qui, sans les attributs pharaoniques, maîtrise avec son arc hommes et bêtes (*fig. 48*).

Fer IIA: Le temple de Salomon[34]

L'événement marquant l'histoire religieuse d'Israël au 10ème siècle est la construction ou plutôt la rénovation[35] du temple de Jérusalem par Salomon. Comment comprendre, à partir de l'archéologie et de l'iconographie, ce qui est dit en 1 R. vi et vii à la lumière de l'évolution esquissée ici? Nous ne pouvons en aborder ici que quelques aspects. Le temple était orienté est-ouest, ce qui surprend eu égard à la tradition de la plupart des temples du Bronze Récent qui étaient orientés

---

[34] Les documents mentionnés dans cette partie—pour autant que rien d'autre ne soit mentionné—sont publiés et discutés dans Keel et Uehlinger (n. 19), p. 186–96.

[35] K. Rupprecht dans *Der Tempel von Jerusalem. Gründung Salomos oder jebusitisches Erbe?* (Berlin, 1977) a démontré de façon convaincante qu'il faut plutôt compter avec une rénovation et un élargissement du Temple qu'avec une fondation toute nouvelle.

nord-sud.[36] Des modèles en terre cuite de sanctuaires palestiniens des 11ème-10ème siècles montrent que deux figurines féminines nues, qui flanquent l'entrée, peuvent être remplacées par des arbres stylisés.[37] Mais comme les deux noms Yakin et Boaz sont masculins, il ne faut pas y voir des symboles de substitution de déesses. Deux arbres peuvent aussi, particulièrement à cause de l'orientation est-ouest du temple, symboliser la porte céleste par laquelle le dieu-soleil, selon la tradition non seulement du Proche Orient mais également de l'Égypte, apparaît le matin.[38] On parle de chérubins et de palmes sur les battants de la porte et à d'autres endroits à l'intérieur du temple. Il faut probablement se représenter chaque fois une palme entourée de deux chérubins (cf. Ez. xli 18). Un symbole très ancien de la déesse est l'arbre flanqué par des capridés, comme nous l'avons vu (cf. *fig. 29* et *31*). Par contre l'arbre flanqué par des chérubins aux têtes d'hommes (*fig. 49–50*) ou de faucons (*fig. 51*) est un symbole de l'ordre garanti et protégé par le roi voire le dieu-roi.[39]

C'est encore un symbole royal d'origine égyptienne que constitue le trône aux chérubins dont témoignent d'abord—et déjà deux fois— les ivoires de Megiddo aux environs de 1250 et 1150 (cf. *fig. 21*), puis le relief du sarcophage d'Ahiram de Byblos vers l'an 1000 (*fig. 52*). B. Janowski a souligné dernièrement, avec raison, qu'un tel objet était présupposé à l'apparition du titre de "siégeant sur les chérubins" et de la titulature royale portée par YHWH.[40] Il me semble cependant difficilement imaginable que le trône géant ait été placé dans le Saint des Saints, sans que les représentations qui ont été suggérées par lui n'aient trouvé une expression dans les paroles, les titres et les chants; bref, qu'on ait dû attendre 200 ans (Isa. vi) pour que ce que l'on voyait soit entré dans le *langage*.

Dans le Ps. xviii les chérubins ou le chérub exercent une fonction de porteurs en liaison avec YHWH présenté comme Dieu de l'orage (vs. 11). Au verset précédant (10) on parle d'une "sombre nuée" ('rpl),

---

[36] Par ex. le temple de Baal à Ougarit, le temple H à Hazor, le "Festungstempel" à Megiddo, le "Grabentempel" à Lakhish, etc.

[37] Cf. J. Bretschneider, *Architekturmodelle in Vorderasien und der östlichen Ägäis vom Neolithikum bis in das 1.Jahrtausend* (Neukirchen-Vluyn, 1991), Catalogue No. 77 et 78 femmes; Catalogue No. 86 et 87 arbres.

[38] Vgl. Keel (n. 18), pp. 296–303.

[39] Keel et Uehlinger (n. 19), pp. 264–7.

[40] B. Janowski, "Keruben und Zion. Thesen zur Entstehung der Zionstradition", D.R. Daniels, U. Glessmer, M. Rösel (Hrsg.), *Ernten, was man sät. Festschrift für Klaus Koch zu seinem 65. Geburtstag* (Neukirchen-Vluyn, 1991), pp. 231–64.

au verset suivant (12) des "ténèbres" (*ḥšk*). Cette constatation est importante en vue des paroles de Salomon à l'occasion de la dédicace du temple dans 1 R. vii 12–13. Ces paroles constituent selon le Grec une citation du "livre des chants" ou du "brave" et sont considérées en général, avec raison, comme très anciennes.[41] La sentence commence avec l'affirmation étonnante:

> La divinité solaire a fait savoir partir du ciel:
> YHWH a décidé d'habiter la nuée obscure ('*rpl*).[42]

Ces paroles évoquent le remplacement d'une divinité solaire hors du temple et son remplacement par YHWH qui veut comme un dieu de l'orage ou de la tempête vivre dans l'obscurité. Des noms de lieux dans la région de Jérusalem renvoient à un ancien culte du soleil, par ex. En-Shemesh, Beth-Shemesh. Le récit de Sodome parlait originellement d'un jugement porté par le dieu-soleil[43] sur une ville criminelle au bord de la Mer Morte, qui a maltraité ses deux serviteurs, peut-être Zedeq et Mishpat ou Zedeq et Mishor. E. Otto a renvoyé à plusieurs reprises à l'importance de la tradition de Zedeq pour l'éthos de la bible hébraïque.[44] Isaïe mentionne encore l'histoire de Sodome ainsi que Zedeq comme une divinité de Jérusalem (i 10, ii 26).[45]

Une divinité solaire comme habitante originelle du temple de Jérusalem pourrait aussi expliquer l'absence d'une image cultuelle ainsi que le trône vide. L'explication socio-culturelle, que j'ai donnée, il y a 15 ans, suivant laquelle les régions périphériques n'auraient pas possédé de sculptures et le refus de représenter la divinité serait issu d'une tendance conservatrice,[46] ne me semble maintenant plus tout à fait convaincante étant donné la sculpture monumentale des chérubins. Par contre le culte, en grande partie aniconique, d'Amon-Rê pendant le Fer I en Palestine aurait pu favoriser un culte aniconique. Pour un culte aniconique du soleil au Proche Orient nous avons des témoignages du 14ème jusqu'au 10ème siècle. Sur un gobelet d'or

---

[41] En dernier lieu V. Hurowitz, *I have built you an Exalted House. Temple Building in the Bible in Light of Mesopotamian and Northwest Semitic Writings* (Sheffield, 1992), pp. 107–8 et 294.

[42] A propos du texte voir O. Keel, "Eine Kurzbiographie der Frühzeit des Gottes Israels", *Bulletin. Europäische Gesellschaft für Kath. Theologie* 5 (1994), S. 168 n. 30.

[43] O. Keel, "Wer zerstörte Sodom?", *Theologische Zeitschrift* 35 (1979), pp. 10–17.

[44] Par ex. E. Otto, "Die Bedeutung der altorientalischen Rechtsgeschichte für das Verständnis des Alten Testaments", *ZThK* 88 (1991), p. 166 avec n. 127.

[45] En ce qui concerne la tradition du soleil dans la Bible hébraïque cf. de manière générale H.P. Stähli, *Solare Elemente im Jahweglauben des Alten Testaments* (Freiburg/ Schweiz Göttingen, 1985).

[46] Keel (n. 18), pp. 37–45.

de Hasanlu dans l'Iran du nord-ouest, daté du 12ème/11ème siècle on voit un adorateur versant une libation devant un trône vide (*fig. 53*). P. Calmeyer a fait remarquer que des escabeaux sur des sceaux médio-assyriens sont stylisés d'une manière semblable. Ces escabeaux sont élevés par des êtres mixtes. Au-dessus d'eux on voit en général un soleil ailé ou sans ailes (*fig. 54*). Celui-ci peut aussi manquer.[47] On peut interpréter cet état de choses en disant que le trône vide rend présent le soleil qui, lui, peut figurer ou non sur l'image.[48] Le trône géant aux chérubins aurait remplacé le trône vide lorsque la divinité solaire eût été transférée au ciel et avant l'intronisation de YHWH.

Fer IIB: l'influence exercée sur YHWH par la divinité solaire bannie[49]

Dans les ivoires gravés et dans la glyptique de la Samarie des 9ème et 8ème siècles, des motifs solaires d'inspiration égyptienne dominent de manière claire: des disques solaires ailés, des scarabées et autres. Au 8ème siècle nous trouvons deux soleils ailés sur le sceau d'un ministre du roi judéen Uzziya ou Uzziyahu (*fig. 55*). Mais le scarabée à quatre ailes se trouve également en Juda au 8e siècle (*fig. 56*). Des Uréus à quatre ailes sont particulièrement appréciés (*fig. 57–9*). Sur le sceau d'un ministre du roi judéen Achaz ils flanquent un disque solaire couronné (*fig. 60*). Les Uréus qui, dans la vision d'Isaïe vi, flanquent le trône de YHWH confèrent à celui-ci quelque chose de solaire. Sous le successeur d'Achaz, Ézéchias, les symboles solaires, le scarabée à quatre ailes (*fig. 61*) et le disque solaire ailé (*fig. 62*), deviennent les emblèmes officiels de la royauté voire de l'état de Juda. On peut difficilement s'imaginer que ces emblèmes, même s'ils étaient au début ceux de la royauté de Juda, n'aient pas eu d'importance pour la représentation du Dieu national et du Dieu protecteur de Juda.

---

[47] P. Calmeyer, "Zur Genese altiranischer Motive. II. Der leere Wagen", *Archäologische Mitteilungen aus Iran* 7 (1974), p. 72; D.M. Matthews, *Principles of Composition in Near Eastern Glyptic of the Later Second Millennium B.C.* (Freiburg/Schweiz-Göttingen, 1990), fig. 452–67; A. Moortgat, *Tell Halaf III. Die Bildwerke* (Berlin, 1955), Taf. 98 et 104.

[48] Dans l'écrit attribué à Lucien "De Dea Syria", on parle du temple à Membiǧ dans la Syrie du Nord: "Dans le temple même, à droite en entrant, est établi d'abord le trône du dieu Soleil, mais de lui, il n'y a pas d'image. Le dieu Soleil (Hélios) et la déesse Lune (Séléné) sont les seuls dont on ne montre pas d'images... On dit qu'il sied de faire des images des autres divinités, car elles ne tombent pas sous les yeux, alors que Hélios et Séléné se montrent à tous." (Paragraphe 34; C. Iacobitz, *Lucianus III* [repr. Hildesheim 1963], p. 531.)

[49] Les documents mentionnés dans cette partie—pour autant que rien d'autre ne soit mentionné—sont publiés et discutés dans Keel, Uehlinger (n. 19), pp. 282–317.

En tout cas dans le texte postexilique d'Isa. lx 1–2, YHWH est présenté comme le dieu-soleil quand on s'adresse à Jérusalem:

> Debout! Resplendis! car voici ta lumière,
> et sur toi se lève (*zrḥ*) la gloire de YHWH.
> Tandis que les ténèbres s'étendent sur la terre
> et l'obscurité ('*rpl*) sur les peuples,
> sur toi se lève (*yzrḥ*) YHWH,
> et sa gloire sur toi paraît.

Là non plus, YHWH n'est pas le soleil et il ne se manifeste pas dans le soleil, mais le soleil ici et dans beaucoup d'autres textes est devenu une métaphore décisive pour YHWH. D'autres et de plus anciennes métaphores ne sont pas dépassées pour autant. Ainsi, dans la sagesse qui plaisante dans Prov. viii 30–1 (cf. 2 S. vi 5, 20–1),[50] resurgit la représentation typique du Bronze Moyen de la divinité qui par sa plaisanterie à nuances érotiques anime le dieu de la tempête à procréer (cf. *fig. 15*). Aux métaphores anciennes, réutilisées dans une naïveté post-critique, s'ajoutent de nouvelles comme celle du dieu-lune en Zach. iv. A travers ces acculturations toujours nouvelles le Dieu d'Israël reste vivant et maître de l'histoire.

Indications des sources des figures

Fig. 1 H. Seeden, *The Standing Armed Figures in the Levant* (Munich, 1980), pl. 22c; *fig. 2–3* M. Dothan, "The Excavations at Nahariya", *IEJ* 6 (1956), pl. 4A et C; *fig. 13–14* O. Keel, H. Keel-Leu, S. Schroer, *Studien zu den Stempelsiegeln aus Palästina/Israel* II (Freiburg/Schweiz-Göttingen, 1989), p. 261 fig. 43 et p. 225 fig. 27; *fig. 20* Scarabée de stéatite, 19, 5 x 14, 75 x 8, 8 mm, trouvé à Ascalon par la mission archéologique dirigée par le prof. L.E. Stager, publié avec sa permission; *fig. 22a–23* H. Seeden, *The Standing Armed Figures*, pl. 104, 1735 et 1737; *fig. 30* N. de G. Davies, A.H. Gardiner, *Seven Private Tombs at Ḳurnah* (London, 1948), pl. 35 [top]; *fig. 41* B. Buchanan, P.R.S. Moorey, *Catalogue of Ancient Near Eastern Seals in the Ashmolean Museum III. The Iron Age Stamp Seals* (Oxford, 1988), pl. 4, 113; *fig. 45* C.F.A. Schaeffer, *Mission de Ras Shamra VIII. Ugaritica III* (Paris, 1956), p. 24, fig. 32; *fig. 52* R. Muyldermans, "Two Banquet Scenes in the Levant",

---

[50] U. Winter, *Frau und Göttin. Exegetische und ikonographische Studien zum weiblichen Gottesbild im Alten Israel und in dessen Umwelt* (Freiburg/Schweiz-Göttingen, ²1987) pp. 516–23.

L. de Meyer, E. Haerinck (éd.), *Archaeologia Iranica et Orientalis I. Miscellanea in Honorem Louis Vanden Berghe* (Gent, 1989), p. 407, fig. A; *fig. 53* O. Keel, *Jahwe-Visionen und Siegelkunst. Eine neue Deutung der Majestätsschilderungen in Jes 6, Ez 1 und 10 und Sach 4* (Stuttgart, 1977), p. 41, Abb. 20; *fig. 54* D.M. Matthews, *Principles of Composition in Near Eastern Glyptic of the Later Second Millennium B.C.* (Freiburg/Schweiz-Göttingen, 1990), Fig. 461; *fig. 60* E.L. Sukenik, "A Note on the Seal of the Servant of Ahaz", *BASOR* 84 (1941) p. 17; toutes les autres illustrations sont tirées de l'ouvrage d'O. Keel et de Ch. Uehlinger, *Göttinnen, Götter und Gottessymbole. Neue Erkenntnisse zur Religionsgeschichte Kanaans und Israels aufgrund bislang unerschlossener ikonographischer Quellen* (Freiburg i. Br., 1992, ³1995).

1

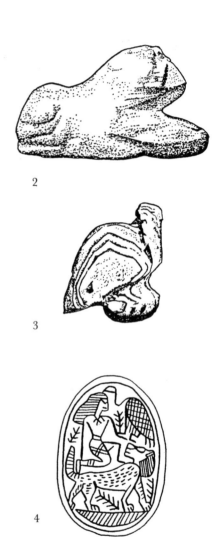

2

3

4

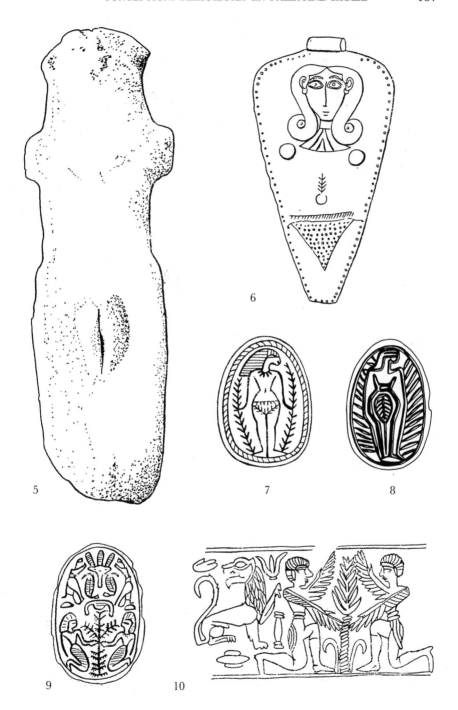

11

12a

12b

13   14

15

16

17

18   19   20

21

22   22a   23

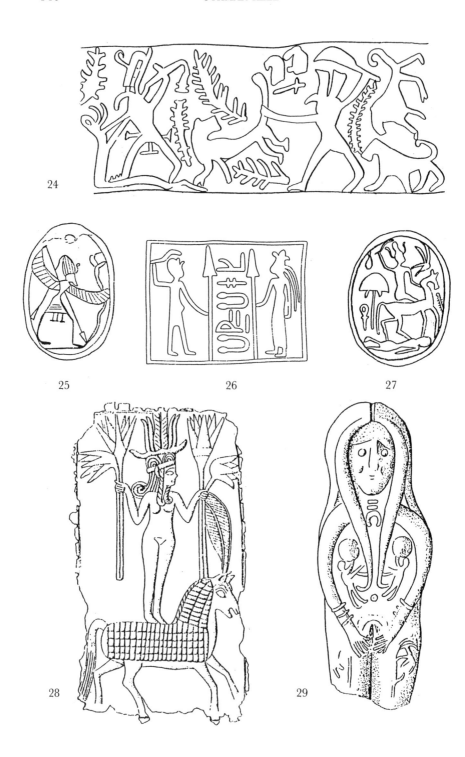

24

25 26 27

28 29

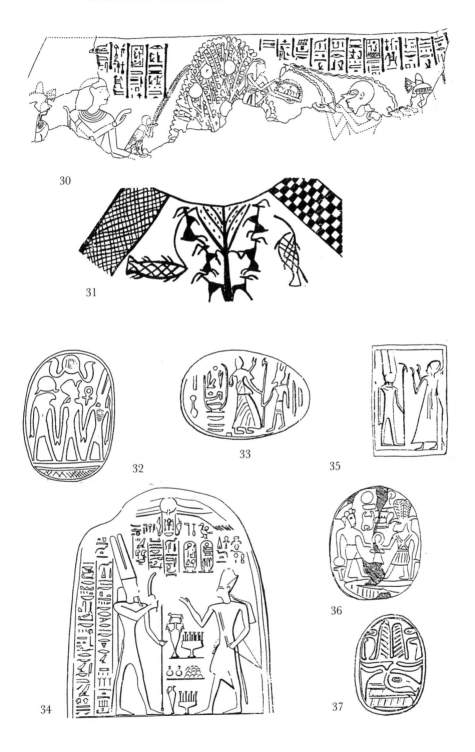

30

31

32

33

34

35

36

37

38

39

40   41   42   43

44

45

46   47   48

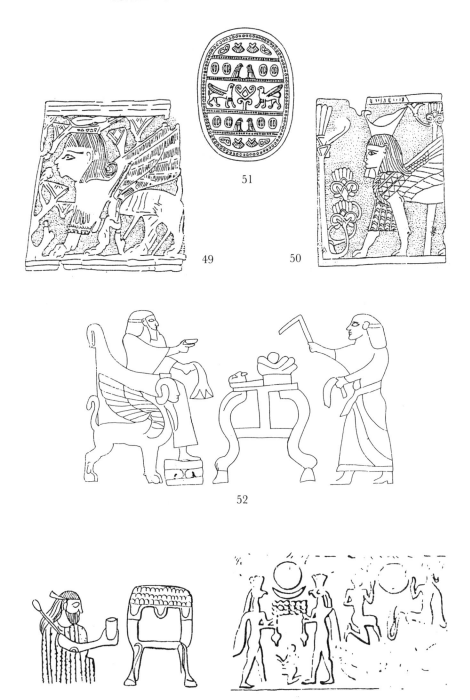

51

49   50

52

53   54

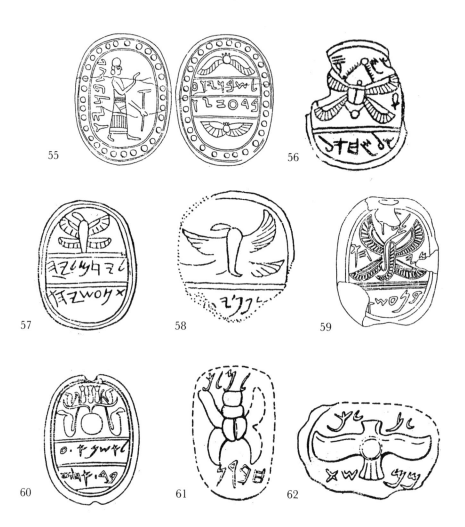

DIE VERBINDUNG VON GOTTESHERRSCHAFT UND KÖNIGTUM GOTTES IM ALTEN TESTAMENT

von

SIEGFRIED KREUZER
Wuppertal

Das Thema der Gottesherrschaft wird in der alttestamentlichen Forschung unter verschiedenen Vorzeichen diskutiert. Zum einen ist es ein nicht unbedeutendes Thema des Alten Testaments selber und damit ein Thema der Darstellungen der alttestamentlichen Theologien. Weiter ist das Kommen der Gottesherrschaft ein wichtiges Thema des frühen Judentums ebenso wie der neutestamentlichen Botschaft. Schließlich hat das Thema seine Bedeutung im Zusammenhang der ethischen Diskussion des 20.Jh. ebenso wie in der sozialgeschichtlichen Erforschung des Alten Testaments in den letzten Jahren.[1] Dabei werden, je nachdem, sowohl die stabilisierende als auch die kritische Funktion der Rede von Gottesherrschaft thematisiert[2]—Diese kurzen Bemerkungen mögen das Umfeld und den Hintergrund des Themas bewußt machen. Das Wissen um diese Aspekte kann den Blick schärfen, soll aber andrerseits nicht die exegetische Wahrnehmung trüben.

Wenn in der alttestamentlichen Forschung nach der Vorstellung von der Gottesherrschaft gefragt wird, so geschieht dies in der Regel und fast ausschließlich durch eine Untersuchung des Verbums *mlk* und des Nomens *mælæk*. Das ist besonders deutlich bei den entsprechenden Lexikonartikeln,[3] findet sich aber auch dort, wo auf bestimmte sozial- und ideologiekritische Aspekte abgehoben wird.[4] Durch die

---

[1] Siehe dazu die verschiedenen Teile des Artikels "Herrschaft Gottes/Reich Gottes" in *TRE* 15 (Berlin/New York, 1986).

[2] Als Beispiele für die Problematisierung sei genannt A.H.J. Gunneweg– W. Schmithals, *Herrschaft* (Stuttgart u.a., 1980), und W. Dietrich, "Gott als König. Zur Frage nach der theologischen und politischen Legitimät religiöser Begriffsbildung", *ZThK* 77 (1980), S. 251–65.

[3] Z.B.E. Zenger, "Herrschaft Gottes/Reich Gottes, II. Altes Testament", *TRE* 15 (1986), S. 176–89, oder M.-T. Wacker, "Reich Gottes", *Neues Handbuch theologischer Grundbegriffe* 4 (München, 1991), 38–41.

[4] N. Lohfink, "Der Begriff des Gottesreichs vom Alten Testament her gesehen", in J. Schreiner (Hg.), *Unterwegs zur Kirche* 1987 (Freiburg, 1987), S. 33–86, der allerdings

Begrenzung auf das Königtum entsteht eine weitere Ambivalenz. Einerseits wird das Thema der Gottesherrschaft als ein für das Alte Testament sehr wichtiges betrachtet, andrerseits sind die Belege gar nicht so zahlreich und vor allem fast durchwegs spät. Darüber hinaus wurde vor allem durch die Arbeit von Werner H. Schmidt deutlich, daß das Thema "Königtum Gottes" ein keineswegs problemloses kanaanäisches Erbe darstellt.

Mit den folgenden Ausführungen soll gezeigt werden, daß zwischen Gottesherrschaft und Königtum Gottes zu unterscheiden ist, daß für eine adäquate Erfassung neben den Aussagen vom Königtum Jahwes weitere Wortfelder und Traditionen zu beachten sind und daß sich dadurch nicht nur eine wesentlich breitere Textbasis ergibt, sondern auch schon inneralttestamentlich interessante kritische Differenzierungen zu beobachten sind.

I. *Das Königtum Gottes im Alten Testament*

1. Als Belege für die Aussage vom Königtum Gottes sind die Vorkommen des Verbums *mlk* und des Nomens *mælæk*, König, heranzuziehen. 13x ist Jahwe Subjekt von *mlk* Q., davon 7x in Psalmen einschließlich des Schilfmeerliedes (Ps. xlvii 9, xciii 1, xcvi 10, xcvii 1, xcix 1, cxlvi 10; Ex. xv 18); darüber hinaus je einmal in 1 Sam. viii 7; Jes. xxiv 23, lii 7; Ez. xx 33; Mi. iv 7; 1 Chr. xvi 31 (= Ps. xcvi 10).

Als *mælæk*, König, wird Jahwe benannt in Num. xxiii 21; Dtn. xxxiii 5; Jes. vi 5; weiters 3x bei DtJes. (xli 21, xliii 15, xliv 6); je 2x in Jer. (x 7, xlvi 18), Micha (ii 13) und Zeph. (iii 15) und im aramäischen Teil von Dan. (iv 34), wieder am häufigsten sind die Belege in den Psalmen, nämlich 18 (v 3, x 16, xxiv 7–10, xxix 10, xliv 5, xlvii 3, 7, xlviii 3, lxviii 25, lxxiv 12, lxxxiv 4, lxxxix 19, xcv 3, xcviii 6, xcix 4, cxlv 1, cxlix 2).

Dazu kommen noch die Nomina *malkût*, *melûkâ* und *mamlākâ*, die jeweils nur 1 oder 2x und in durchwegs späten Texten vorkommen.[5]

Die Belege haben einen auffallenden Schwerpunkt in den Psalmen und in der prophetischen Literatur der Exilszeit (einschließlich Mi. ii

---

an einigen Stellen über die geläufigen Grenzen hinausgeht und auch einige der modernen Vorurteile thematisiert. Ähnlich J.G. Oesch, "Königtum und Heil. Eine Skizze", in J. Niewiadomsky, *Verweigerte Mündigkeit? Politische Kultur und die Kirche, theol. trends* 2 (Thaur, 1989).

[5] Zu den Belegen s. J.A. Soggin, "*mælæk*", *THAT* I, Sp. 915–16.

13 und iv 7). Eher spät sind auch die 3 Belege im Pentateuch: Ex. xv 18 gehört in die exilisch-nachexilische Zeit; Num. xxiii 21 gehört bestenfalls in den Zusammenhang der elohistischen Version der Bileamgeschichte, und Dtn. xxxiii 5 aus der Umrahmung des Mosesegens ist sowohl vom Verständnis wie von der Datierung her umstritten.[6]

So bleibt als Fixpunkt für die Bezeichnung Jahwes als König nur die bekannte Stelle Jes. vi 5 im Rahmen des Berufungsberichtes Jesajas.[7] Dort wird der dem Propheten im Jerusalemer Tempel erscheinende Gott zunächst in V. 1 *ʾadonāy yošeb ʿal-kisseʾ rām wᵉnissāʾ*, als der Herr, sitzend auf einem hohen und erhabenen Thron, bezeichnet. Es ist dabei wohl mehr als eine bloße Datumsangabe, wenn die Vision einleitend in das Jahr des Todes des Königs Usia datiert wird. Angesichts der überwältigenden Erscheinung dieses Herrn, vor dessen Majestät sich sogar die Seraphen schützen müssen, bleibt Jesaja nur die erschrockene Reaktion:

Wehe mir, ich vergehe,
denn den König, Jahwe Zebaoth, haben meine Augen gesehen!
. . . *kî ʾæt-hammælæk yhwh ṣᵉbāʾôt rāʾû ʿênāy* (V. 5).

Es ist merkwürdig, daß der Königtitel im Unterschied zu anderen Leitbegriffen der Berufungsvision sonst in den Worten Jesajas jedenfalls nicht explizit vorkommt. V. 5 mit dem Königstitel für Jahwe ist dabei durchaus als Kulmination der Beschreibung Jahwes in den vorangehenden Versen zu betrachten. Die Verwendung des Königtitels für Jahwe ist wahrscheinlich keine Erfindung Jesajas, sondern Jesaja übernimmt den Titel wohl aus dem Tempelkult.[8] Die pointierte Verwendung im Kontext prophetischer Verkündigung ist aber doch neu. Der Hinweis auf Jahwe als König steht dabei in einer

---

[6] Zur Diskussion des Alters dieser Belege u.a. K. Seybold, "*mælæk*", *ThWAT* IV, Sp. 948, und Lohfink (Anm. 4), S. 45–6 A. 20.

[7] Aus der fast uferlosen Diskussion sei lediglich genannt. H. Wildberger, *Jesaja 1–12* (Neukirchen, ²1980), S. 230–61; O.H. Steck, "Bemerkungen zu Jesaja 6", *BZ* NF 16 (1972), S. 188–206; jetzt in ders., "Wahrnehmungen Gottes im Alten Testament", *ThB* 70 (1982), S. 149–70; O. Keel, *Jahwe-Visionen und Siegelkunst. Eine neue Deutung der Majestätsschilderungen in Jes 6, Ez 1 und 10 und Sach 4* (Stuttgart, 1977); H. Irsigler, "Gott als König in Berufung und Verkündigung Jesajas", in *Festschrift für Notker Füglister* (Würzburg, 1991), S. 127–54; dort jeweils weitere Literatur.

[8] Siehe dazu W.H. Schmidt, *Königtum Gottes in Ugarit und Israel*, *BZAW* 80 (Berlin/ New York, ²1966); ders., *Alttestamentlicher Glaube in seiner Geschichte* (Neukirchen, ⁷1990), S. 170–8; J. Jeremias, *Das Königtum Gottes in den Psalmen. Israels Begegnung mit dem kanaanäischen Mythos in den Jahwe-König-Psalmen* (Göttingen, 1987); M.Z. Brettler, *God as King. Understanding an Israelite Metaphor* (Sheffield, 1989).

Frontstellung, die aus dem Kontext genauer bestimmt werden kann. Jahwe ist der, der die Geschichte lenkt, und zwar nicht nur die Geschichte Israels, sondern auch die Geschichte der umliegenden Königreiche (Nordreich und Aram) bis hin zu den Assyrern. Das Königsein Jahwes wird damit auf die Geschichte bezogen und in Gegensatz zu den Ansprüchen der irdischen Könige gesehen. Insofern wäre zu übersetzen: "Wehe mir, ich vergehe, denn den *wahren* König, Jahwe Zebaoth, haben meine Augen gesehen." Die Verwendung des Königtitels erfolgt hier offensichtlich als Hinweis auf die universale Dimension des Wirkens Jahwes auch in der Völkerwelt.

2. Für die Bedeutung der Bezeichnung Jahwes als König ist die Erhellung des religionsgeschichtlichen Hintergrundes wichtig, wie sie besonders von W.H. Schmidt geleistet wurde. Die Vorstellung vom Königtum Gottes ist nicht auf dem Hintergrund oder in Konkurrenz zur Regierung eines irdischen Königs über Israel[9] entwickelt worden. Vielmehr geht es beim Königtum eines Gottes zunächst um das Königtum über die Götter. Das Königtum Gottes steht in Analogie zum irdischen Königtum, aber es bezieht sich nicht auf Menschen, sondern auf die Götter. So wie der König über sein Volk herrscht, so der König der Götter über die Götter.

Die Herrschaft des Götterkönigs bezieht sich auf Schöpfung und Natur. Er ist Schöpfergott und Herr der Naturmächte. Während für Ugarit eine Funktionsunterscheidung zwischen dem zum deus otiosus werdenden El und dem aktiveren Baal zu beobachten ist, ist dies für Jerusalem weniger gesichert. Während in der früheren Forschung die Annahme vorherrschte, Jahwe habe bei der Übernahme des Königtitels El-Aspekte und Baal-Aspekte assimiliert, stellte sich später die Frage, ob eine solche Unterscheidung für Jerusalem überhaupt anzunehmen sei,[10] was jedoch für unsere Frage wenig Unterschied macht.

Für unseren Zusammenhang wichtiger ist die Beobachtung, daß das Königtum Gottes es zunächst mit der außermenschlichen Welt zu tun hat. Erst im Lauf der Jahwesierung erfolgt auch eine Israelitisierung und Historisierung des Königtums Gottes.

Die Israelitisierung der Vorstellung vom Königtum Gottes läßt sich

---

[9] Anders verhält es sich wohl mit der Entstehung dieses Gottestitels im Alten Orient überhaupt. Hier ist zwischen der seinerzeitigen Entstehung und der Übernahme eines entfalteten Vorstellungskomplexes zu unterscheiden.

[10] Besonders vertreten von P.D. Miller, *The Divine Warrior in Early Israel* (Cambridge, Mass., 1973).

sehr schön an Ps. xxix verfolgen. In diesem auf (alte) kanaanäische Vorlage zurückgehenden Psalm[11] ist es jetzt natürlich Jahwe, dem die Huldigung gilt. Aber seine Macht zeigt sich nicht nur an der Natur, sondern ebenso in der Geschichte Israels; und es sind nicht mehr nur die Himmlischen, die ihm huldigen, sondern auch die Israeliten:

> Die Stimme Jahwes zerbricht die Zedern des Libanon . . .,
> die Stimme Jahwes sprüht Feuerflammen;
> die Stimme Jahwes läßt die Wüste Kadesch erbeben;
> erbeben läßt Jahwe die Wüste Kadesch;
> in seinem Tempel ruft alles kabod, Ehre!
> Jahwe hat seinen Thron über der Flut;
> Jahwe bleibt König in Ewigkeit;
> er gibt seinem Volk Kraft. (Ps. xxix 5–11)

Das Volk ist hier zweifellos Israel; der Tempel, in dem Jahwe gehuldigt wird, muß der Tempel von Jerusalem sein, und daß neben den Zedern des Libanon die Wüste Kadesch[12] weit im Süden, genannt wird, drückt jedenfalls für die nunmehrige israelitische Fassung des Psalms den Gedanken an die Frühzeit Israels und die Sinaitheophanie aus.

3. Wie alt ist nun diese Vorstellung von Jahwe als König in Israel? Auch wenn vor allem Ps. xlvii und xciii wahrscheinlich doch in die vorexilische Zeit zurückreichen, so bleibt Jes. vi 5 der älteste sichere Beleg. Vom Königtum Jahwes wurde somit in Jerusalem jedenfalls ab dem 8.Jh. gesprochen. Ob ältere Belege existierten, muß offen bleiben.

Die Spärlichkeit der Belege ist auffallend, denn in der engeren und weiteren Umgebung Israels war die Vorstellung vom Königtum eines Gottes sehr wohl bekannt. Als Belege können theophore Eigennamen genannt werden, die in die vor-bzw. frühisraelitische Zeit zurückreichen: Der Priesterkönig von Salem bzw. Jerusalem (Gen. xiv; Ps cxxxii) trägt den Namen Melkiṣedeq; Gen. xx und xxvi nennen

---

[11] Die kanaanäische Grundlage des Psalms ist—insbesondere seit Entdeckung der ugaritischen Texte—sehr häufig diskutiert worden, z.B. G. Sauer, "Erwägungen zum Alter der Psalmendichtung in Israel", *ThZ* 22 (1966), S. 81–95; H. Strauß, "Zur Auslegung von Psalm 29 auf dem Hintergrund seiner kanaanäischen Bezüge", *ZAW* 82 (1970), S. 91–102; H.J. Kraus, *Psalmen* (Neukirchen, ⁵1978), z.St. (Lit.); O. Loretz, *Psalm 29. Kanaanäische El- und Baaltraditionen in jüdischer Sicht* (Soest, 1984); Jeremias (Anm. 8), S. 29–45.—Ob der Psalm noch in die vorexilische Zeit gehört, ist jedoch keineswegs sicher.

[12] In *UT* 52 (*CTA* 23). 65 ist die Wüste *qdš* erwähnt. Über diese Heilige Wüste ist kaum Näheres zu sagen. Wenn man die Angabe geographisch verstehen kann, so ist sie wohl für ugaritische Gegebenheiten als die syrische Wüste anzusehen; so etwa, Jeremias, S. 42, " 'heilige' syrische Wüste".

einen Philisterkönig Abimelek; nach dem Buch Ruth lebt im Bethlehem der Richterzeit der Bauer Elimelek. Ein anderer Abimelek wiederum versucht zur Unzeit ein kanaanäisch-israelitisches Königtum in Sichem zu errichten (Ri. ix), und einer der Söhne Sauls, des ersten israelitischen Königs, heißt *malkišûaʿ* (1 Sam. xiv 49, xxxi 2), wobei *malk* zweifellos ein theophores Element darstellt. Dieser *malkišûaʿ* ist der Erste, von dem wir mit ziemlicher Sicherheit sagen können, daß es Jahwe ist, der hier als König angesprochen wird. Der nächste entsprechende und eindeutige Name, nämlich *malkiyahu*, findet sich erst gut 300 Jahre später wieder in Israel, und zwar in Jer. xxi 1 und xxxviii 1, 6 und auf je einem Stempelsiegel aus Arad von 701 bzw. um 600.[13]

Wir haben somit das Vorhandensein der Vorstellung vom Königtum Gottes im kanaanäischen Raum der vorisraelitischen Zeit, wir haben vor- und frühisraelitische Namen mit dem theophoren Element *mælæk*, aber wir haben den ersten sicheren Beleg für das Königtum Jahwes erst bei Jesaja und damit für die Mitte des 8.Jh.s.— So eindrucksvoll das Thema des Königtums Gottes ist, so ist der Traditionsstrang doch eher schmal und war vielleicht zudem auf Jerusalem beschränkt.[14]

Zur Erklärung dieses Sachverhalts ist die Funktion des Themas zu bedenken: Die Vorstellung vom Königtum eines Gottes hat im kanaanäischen Raum zwei Funktionen: Einerseits wird dadurch das Pantheon geordnet, andererseits legitimiert der himmlische König den irdischen König und das himmlische Königtum das irdische Königtum. Beides ist für das israelitische Jerusalem durchaus günstig: Das erbliche davidische Königtum war für eine religiöse Legitimation gewiß empfänglich. Zweitens waren ab dem davidisch-salomonischen Groß-

---

[13] Y. Aharoni, "Three Hebrew Ostraca from Arad", *Eretz-Israel* 16 (1969), S. 11 und 15 (hebr. sect.); zu dem ins 8./7.Jh. zu datierenden Jhwmlk-Siegel siehe G.R. Driver, "Brief Notes", *PEQ* 77 (1945), S. 5. Vgl. K. Seybold, "*mlk*", *ThWAT* IV, Sp. 949, und J.D. Fowler, *Theophoric Personal Names in Ancient Hebrew. A Comparative Study* (Sheffield, 1988), S. 50–3.

[14] Z.B. Schmidt (*Glaube*, Anm. 8), S. 170: "Schon der lexikalische Überblick zeigt, daß dem Begriff des göttlichen Königtums im Alten Testament keine entsprechend große Bedeutung zukommt. Die insgesamt relativ geringen Belegstellen sind recht ungleichmäßig verteilt, häufen sich nur in hymnischen Abschnitten des Psalters."— Von den über 2500 Belegen der Wurzel *mlk* sind nur ca. 50 auf Jahwe bezogen; vgl. Soggin (Anm. 5), Sp. 909, 915–6—T.N.D. Mettinger, *In Search of God. The Meaning and Message of the Everlasting Names*, (Philadelphia, 1988), S. 92–122, kommt zu seiner ganz anderen Einschätzung der Bedeutung und des Alters der Vorstellung nur dadurch, daß er weit über die expliziten Belege für Gott als König hinausgreift, vgl. S. 116–17.

reich auch die nicht-israelitischen Bevölkerungsgruppen und deren Götter zu berücksichtigen. Ein Pantheon mit Jahwe als Götterkönig bot hier ein gutes Ordnungsmodell. Diese Aspekte trugen wesentlich dazu bei, daß die wahrscheinlich schon im jebusitischen Jerusalem vorhandene Anschauung vom Königtum Gottes in Israel aufgenommen und im salomonischen Tempel auf Jahwe übertragen wurde.— Allerdings sind die Vorgänge keineswegs einlinig und unkritisch verlaufen: Zwar zeigen die Königpsalmen sehr deutlich die religiöse Legitimation des israelitischen Königs, aber zugleich fällt auf, daß dort, wo der israelitische König vorkommt, Jahwe nicht als König bezeichnet wird und umgekehrt.[15] Darüber hinaus zeigen etwa Ps. xxix, Jes. vi und DtJes, daß die Vorstellung mit der Zeit wesentlich modifiziert wurde.

II. *Alternative Traditionen von der Gottesherrschaft*

Zum Vorstellungsbereich Herrscher und Herrschaft gehören nicht nur die Termini *mælæk* und *mlk*, sondern eine Reihe weiterer Begriffe. Zu nennen wären die Vorstellungen vom Thron und vom Thronen des Herrschers, dazu auch die Vorstellung vom Thronrat. Für die Gottesvorstellung des Alten Testaments wären dementsprechend die Bedeutung der Lade und des Titels *yōšeb hakk^erubîm* und die Vorstellung vom himmlischen Thronrat anzusprechen. Diese Traditionen werden hier zunächst ausgeklammert, nicht nur, weil sie in der Forschung sehr kontrovers sind,[16] sondern vor allem, weil ihre Zuordnung erst auf dem Hintergrund des Gesamtbildes, das hier entwickelt werden soll, neu zu bedenken wäre.

Weitere Begriffe zum Vorstellungsbereich Herrscher und Herrschaft beziehen sich auf den Vorgang der Huldigung und der Akklamation. Das Wichtige an diesen Begriffen ist, daß sie auch bezüglich Jahwe verwendet werden, und zwar in Zusammenhängen, wo der Königtitel für Jahwe nicht vorkommt. Die Begriffe als solche aber gehören zum Vorstellungsbereich Herrscher und Herrschaft und signalisieren insofern die Vorstellung von Jahwe als Herrscher. Die hier zu nennenden Begriffe sind *hištah^awâ*, huldigen, *mšl*, herrschen und die

---

[15] D.h. in den Königpsalmen kommt Jahwe nicht als König vor und in den Jahwe-König-Psalmen kommt der König nicht vor.

[16] Hier ist insbesondere die Diskrepanz zwischen den mit der Lade verbundenen Thronvorstellungen und andrerseits der geringen Zahl und der späten zeitlichen Einordnung der Belege über Jahwe als König zu nennen.

Schwurformel *ḥay yhwh*. Schließlich ist die Frage nach einem eventuellen alternativen Titel Jahwes in diesen Zusammenhängen zu stellen.

1. *hištaḥᵃwâ*[17] kommt im Alten Testament 170x vor, außerhalb des Alten Testaments ist es nur in Ugarit belegt. Die 12 ugaritischen Belege stehen in den mythologischen und epischen Texten. Die Huldigung bezieht sich dort siebenmal auf den Götterkönig El, je zweimal auf die Göttin Anat und den Handwerkergott Koschar (wa Chasis) und einmal auf den Meeresgott Yam.

Das Wort bezeichnet die Huldigung an den Herrscher. Für die Etymologie braucht man nicht nach einer arabischen oder ägyptischen Wurzel Ausschau zu halten, sondern das Wort ist Št-Stamm von *ḥwh*, leben, ganz im Sinn der Huldigungsformel *yᵉḥî hammælæk*. D.h. das Wort beschreibt nicht den Vorgang der Proskynese, sondern deren ideelle Bedeutung, eben die Huldigung an den Herrscher.[18]

Das mit 170 Belegen im Alten Testament relativ häufige Wort bezieht sich sowohl auf Jahwe als auch auf menschliche Autoritäten, vor allem auf den König. So huldigt etwa David seinem König Saul (1 Sam. xxiv 9); Abigail huldigt dem künftigen König David (1 Sam. xxv 23); Mefi-Boschet, der Sohn Jonatans, huldigt David, der nun König in Jerusalem ist (2 Sam. ix 6); die Frau aus Tekoa fällt vor David nieder und huldigt ihm, bevor sie ihm ihre Bitte um einen Rechtsentscheid vorträgt, und selbst der General Joab wirft sich nieder, huldigt dem König und dankt ihm für die Entscheidung (2 Sam. xiv 4, 22); auch Batseba huldigt David, wo sie an ihn als König herantritt (1 Kön. i 16, 31), während später dann Salomo sich vor ihr als der Königinmutter beugt und ihr huldigt (1 Kön. ii 19). Im Rahmen der Königsideologie und des Hofstils wird dem König zugesagt, daß alle Könige der Welt ihm huldigen werden (Ps. lxxii 11).

Die Huldigung ist nicht ausschließlich auf den König bezogen. Abraham verneigt sich vor den Hethitern von Hebron (Gen. xxiii 7). Mose begrüßt und huldigt Jitro, der nicht nur sein Schwiegervater, sondern der Priester der Midianiter ist, der dann für Jahwe das Dankopfer für die Errettung aus Ägypten darbringt (Ex. xviii 7).

---

[17] H.P. Stähli, "*ḥwh*", *THAT* I, Sp. 530–3; H.D. Preuß, "*ḥwh*", *ThWAT* II, Sp. 784–94; Ugaritische Belege nach R.E. Whitacker, *A Concordance of the Ugaritic Literature* (Cambridge, Mass., 1972), S. 257, und der Ergänzung in *Newsletter for Ugaritic Studies* 22, 1980.

[18] S. Kreuzer, "Zur Bedeutung und Etymologie von *hištaḥᵃwāh/yštḥwy*", *VT* 35 (1985), S. 39–60; zur Forschungsgeschichte und Diskussion der älteren Positionen: J.A. Emerton, "The Etymology of *hištaḥᵃwāh*", *OTS* 20 (1977), S. 41–55.

Die Josefsgeschichte ist durchzogen vom Problem der Herrschaft. Die Frage "Darf es in Israel einen König geben?" wird abgehandelt unter der Frage "Darf ein Bruder über Brüder herrschen?" Dieses Thema wird signalisiert durch den Traum, in dem sich die Garben der Brüder vor der des Josef verneigen (Gen. xxxvii 7–11). Die Brüder jedenfalls wissen, worum es geht, und reagieren entsprechend empört: "Willst du etwa König sein über uns oder willst du über uns herrschen?" (Beide Begriffe, *mālak* und *māšal*, werden hier verwendet; ihre Differenzierung wird uns noch beschäftigen.)—Dem Traum am Anfang entspricht die Szene gegen Ende der Josefsgeschichte, wo sich die Brüder vor ihm als dem zweitmächtigsten Mann in Ägypten niederwerfen wie vor einem König.

Nicht einem König, sondern einem Propheten gilt die Huldigung der Prophetenschüler um Elisa (2 Kön. ii). Sie erkennen ihn damit als den legitimen Nachfolger Elijas und als den Repräsentanten Jahwes gegenüber Israel an. Damit zeigt sich ein gewisser königskritischer Ansatz, wie wir ihn etwa auch bei Hosea im Nordreich finden.

Dieses für das Thema der Herrschaft so häufige und wichtige Wort ist im Alten Testament für den religiösen Bereich etwa gleich oft belegt wie für den profanen (*ca.* 80 von 170). *Ca.* 45x geht es dabei um die Huldigung an Jahwe, *ca.* 35x um das Verbot der Hinwendung zu anderen Göttern (z.B. im Dekalog) bzw. um die Kritik, daß die Israeliten das getan hätten (so vor allem in deuteronomistischen und exilischen Texten).

Die positiven Aussagen über die Huldigung an Jahwe finden sich vor allem in vorexilischen Texten, in den Psalmen und in spätnachexilischen Texten. Dagegen kommt das Wort im dtn./dtr. Kontext fast nur negativ vor, d.h. im Sinn der Ablehnung der Verehrung fremder Götter. Es seien kurz einige Belege genannt, wo dieses Wort im Blick auf Jahwe verwendet wird, und die mit einiger Wahrscheinlichkeit als vorexilisch und vordtn. gelten können.[19]

Schon in Gen. xviii 2 und xix 1 wirft sich Abraham vor seinen Gästen nieder, wobei klar ist, daß diese Huldigung letztlich Jahwe gilt. In Gen. xxii 5 erklärt Abraham den Knechten, daß er und der Knabe gehen wollen, um Jahwe anzubeten (*wᵉništaḥᵃwê*). In Ex. xxxiv

---

[19] Zu Einzelfragen vgl. die Kommentare. Die Belege erscheinen nach Zahl und Alter den Belegen der *mælæk*-Tradition mindestens gleich. Das Entscheidende ist aber nicht die vergleichende Datierung, sondern die Existenz des Wortfeldes und der entsprechenden Tradition.

8 neigt sich Mose zur Erde und huldigt Jahwe. Beim Herabkommen der Wolke zum Zelt der Begegnung erhebt sich das Volk, so wie eben der Niedrigere vor dem Herrn aufsteht, und huldigt Jahwe (Ex. xxxiii 10). In der Opfervorschrift von Dtn. xxvi 10, einer vordeuteronomistischen Formulierung,[20] huldigt der israelitische Bauer Jahwe, indem er die Opfergabe darbringt und Jahwe anbetet. In 1 Sam. xv 25, 30–1 will Saul Jahwe durch Darbringung eines Opfers huldigen, und in 1 Kön. i 47 reagiert David auf den Bericht über die Inthronisation Salomos mit dankbarer Verneigung und Anbetung Jahwes.

Diese Belege zeigen, daß zur Bezeichnung verschiedener Akte der Verehrung Jahwes, von der Opferdarbringung bis zur Proskynese, jenes Wort *hištaḥᵃwâ* verwendet wird, das im profanen Bereich die Huldigung an den Herrscher bezeichnet. Jahwe wurde somit, jedenfalls ab der Königszeit, als Herrscher gedacht und verehrt, wobei die offensichtliche Vermeidung des Königtitels bzw. des Verbums *mālak* wohl nicht zufällig ist.

2. Die Vermeidung des Königtitels ist auch beim Gideonspruch Ri. viii 22–3 zu bemerken. Dort wird dem Richter Gideon auf Grund seiner Rettungstaten die dauernde Herrschaft für ihn und seine Nachkommen angeboten. Dieses Angebot lehnt er mit folgenden Worten ab:

> Ich will nicht über euch herrschen,
> und mein Sohn soll auch nicht über euch herrschen,
> sondern Jahwe soll über euch herrschen
> *loʾ ʾæmšōl ᵃᵃnî bākæm wᵉloʾ yimšōl bᵉnî bākæm*
> *yhwh yimšōl bākæm* (V. 23).

An diesen bekannten Sätzen fällt nicht nur die konsequente Gegenüberstellung von menschlicher Herrschaft und Gottesherrschaft auf, sondern ebensosehr die konsequente Vermeidung der Worte *mœlæk* oder *mālak*. Die angebotene Würde und Funktion ist ja nichts anderes als das erbliche Königtum.

Was ist der Hintergrund des Gideonspruches? Gegenüber Datierungen in die vorstaatliche Zeit oder in die deuteronomistische Zeit lassen sich gewichtige Argumente für die Datierung in die frühe bis mittlere Königszeit vorbringen. Eine prinzipielle Ablehnung des Königtums wird im deuteronomischen Bereich nicht vertreten, und

---

[20] Zur Analyse von Dtn xxvi s. S. Kreuzer, *Die Frühgeschichte Israels in Bekenntnis und Verkündigung des Alten Testaments*, BZAW 178 (1989), S. 149–82.

dort, wo der Wunsch nach einem König im dtrG als Abfall von Jahwe verstanden wird (1 Sam. viii 7, xii 12), wird Jahwe—anders als in Ri. viii 23—als König bezeichnet.[21] Andrerseits setzen das Angebot und die Ablehnung des erblichen Königtums doch wohl innerisraelitische Erfahrungen mit diesem voraus. Solche gibt es in Jerusalem seit dem Übergang des Königtums von David auf Salomo. Im Gegenbild dazu wird Gideon zu einem Anti-David, und die Gideonerzählung wird zu einer Anti-Dynastieerzählung.[22]

Umso auffälliger ist die Verwendung von *māšal* anstelle von *mālak*. Diese erklärt sich noch nicht allein aus der politischen Frontstellung gegen das Königtum. Mit *mālak* wäre der Gegensatz zwischen dem irdischen Königtum und dem Königtum Gottes noch deutlicher geworden (vgl. 1 Sam. viii 7, xii 12). Die Erklärung liegt darin, daß die Gottesherrschaft, um die es hier geht, die Herrschaft über die Volksgemeinschaft ist, während die Vorstellung vom Königtum Gottes sich jedenfalls zu dieser Zeit noch auf die Herrschaft über die Götter und über die Natur- und Chaosmächte bezog. Sie war daher noch nicht geeignet für das Anliegen des Gideonspruches. Der Gideonspruch bezeugt damit nicht nur die Kritik am israelitischen Königtum vom Konzept der unmittelbaren Gottesherrschaft her, sondern auch die Vorstellung der Gottesherrschaft in ihrer Selbständigkeit gegenüber der Vorstellung vom Königtum Gottes.

3. Mit dem Gideonspruch waren wir in der Nähe der älteren Belege

---

[21] T. Veijola, *Das Königtum in der Beurteilung der deuteronomistischen Historiographie. Eine redaktionsgeschichtliche Untersuchung* (Helsinki, 1977), sieht bei dtrG eine "durchaus positive Einstellung zur Monarchie" (S. 115) während dtrN jenen "königtumsfreundlichen Ton ... durch eine tiefgreifende Revision fast unkenntlich gemacht hat" (S. 119), "Freilich geschieht die Abwertung Sauls in 1 Sam 13, 13.14 zugunsten Davids, der auch für DtrN eine ideale Gestalt verkörpert. Dies verträgt sich natürlich nicht gut mit seiner grundsätzlichen antimonarchischen Einstellung, aber man kann es doch als eine Ausnahme von der Regel verstehen ..." (ebd.)—Während die Verwendung des Königtitels für Jhwh in 1 Sam. viii und xii für eine exilische Einordnung dieser Stellen spricht, ist gerade die Vermeidung dieses Titels in Ri. viii umso mehr von Bedeutung.

[22] Vgl. dazu W. Richter, *Traditionsgeschichtliche Untersuchungen zum Richterbuch* (Bonn, ²1966), S. 236–40; F. Crüsemann, *Der Widerstand gegen das Königtum. Die antiköniglichen Texte des Alten Testamentes und der Kampf um den frühen israelitischen Staat,* (Neukirchen, 1978), S. 50–4. Die neuerdings von U. Becker, *Richterzeit und Königtum, BZAW* 192 (Berlin/New York, 1990), S. 176–80, vorgetragene Zuordnung des Gideonspruchs zu dtrH hängt wesentlich daran, ob die "völlig unterschiedlichen und z.T. einander ausschließenden Konzeptionen der vorstaatlichen Zeit" (S. 305), wirklich sämtlich auf verschiedene dtr Schichten zurückgeführt werden können, während es davor bloß "anekdotische und sagenhafte Heldenerzählungen sowie andere Überlieferungsfragment(en)" (S. 301), aber keine theologische Reflexion gegeben hätte.

eines weiteren Begriffs, der zur Gottesherrschaft gehört, nämlich der Schwurformel, meistens *ḥay yhwh*, "so wahr Jahwe lebt". Die Schwurformel bekräftigt verschiedenste Aussagen durch Hinweis auf die Autorität Jahwes und sein Eingreifen. Sie ist ein wichtiges Element der Redeformen des Rechtslebens im Alten Testament, sie dient aber auch zur Bekräftigung von Aussagen und Handlungsabsichten. Ihre Verwendung an entscheidenden Punkten des Verlaufs von Ereignissen zeigt, daß sie—jedenfalls auf der Ebene des Textes—meistens sehr bewußt gebraucht wurde.

Die Schwurformel *ḥay yhwh* verweist auf Jahwe als den Herrn und Herrscher der Gemeinschaft. Das ergibt sich aus ihrer Funktion im Rechtsleben, aus der Nähe zum Huldigungsruf *yᵉḥî hammœlœk*, es lebe der König, und aus der gelegentlichen Erweiterung zu *ḥay yhwh wᵉḥê napšᵉkā*, so wahr Jahwe lebt und so wahr du lebst, in der Gott und König gemeinsam in ihrer Funktion als Herrscher angesprochen werden.

Es ist auffallend, daß die Schwurformel außer in einigen Einzelbelegen vor allem in zwei deutlich abgegrenzten Textkomplexen auftritt, nämlich in der Davidgeschichte und bei Elia und Elisa. Die Vorkommen in der Davidgeschichte decken sich ziemlich genau mit den Texten, die von Fritz Stolz als Dynastie-Erzählung abgegrenzt und charakterisiert wurden.[23] In dieser Dynastieerzählung wird an markanten Punkten mit der Schwurformel auf die Autorität Jahwes verwiesen. Er ist der, der die Ereignisse lenkt und der die von den Menschen getroffenen und mit der Schwurformel bekräftigten Entscheidungen zu seinem Ziel, der Herrschaft Davids und der Festigung der Herrschaft Salomos führt. So etwa am Ende in 1 Reg. ii 24:

> So wahr Jahwe lebt, der mich bestätigt hat und
> gesetzt auf den Thron meines Vaters David . . .

Die Schwurformeln in der Daviddynastieerzählung stehen dabei zum Teil im Kontext von Rechtsentscheiden, z.T. verweisen sie auf das über dem Lauf der Ereignisse waltende Wirken Jahwes.[24]

Charakteristisch für die Einbindung des Königs in die Gottesherrschaft sind auch die inhaltlichen und formalen Erweiterungen

---

[23] *Das erste und zweite Buch Samuel* (Zürich, 1981). Unabhängig davon bereits auch S. Kreuzer, *Der lebendige Gott. Bedeutung, Herkunft und Entwicklung einer alttestamentlichen Gottesbezeichnung* (Stuttgart u.a., 1983), S. 38–83 ("Die Saul—Jonatan—David—Erzählungen").

[24] Für die Einzelinterpretation der Belege s. Kreuzer ebd.

der Schwurformel. *Inhaltlich* werden die alten israelitischen Retter-traditionen aufgegriffen und aktualisiert, z.B. 1 Sam. xiv 39: *kî hay-yhwh hammôšiaʿ ʾæt-yiśrāʾel*. Damit wird die Verbindung zwischen dem bisherigen Handeln Jahwes für und mit Israel und den neuen Gege-benheiten des Königtums hergestellt.

Als *formale* Erweiterung fällt die bereits erwähnte Beiordnung des Königs zu Jahwe auf: "*hay yhwh wᵉhê napšᵉkā*—so wahr Jahwe lebt und so wahr du lebst". Immerhin an 4 markanten Stellen (1 Sam. xx 3, xxv 26; 2 Sam. xi 11, xv 21)! Mit dieser Einbeziehung des Königs in die Schwurformel wird eine prägnante Form der Verhältnisbestimmung zwischen Gott und König geschaffen. Die Art der Beiordnung des davidischen Königs zu Gott wird hier noch nicht näher definiert. Aber es ist wohl kein sehr weiter Weg zu den Vorstellungen in den Königspsalmen, etwa Ps. ii 7: "Mein Sohn bist du . . ." Jedenfalls wird in diesen Erweiterungen der Schwurformel ein gewaltiger Anspruch erhoben und wird der König zum Mittler der Gottesherrschaft.[25]

Diesen Anspruch kann man auch bestreiten: Entweder prinzipiell wie im Gideonspruch: Nicht irgendein Mensch soll herrschen, son-dern Jahwe selbst und unmittelbar, oder dadurch, daß eine andere Instanz für die Vermittlung der Gottesherrschaft benannt wird. Das geschieht in den Elia- und Elisa-Erzählungen. Dort wird nicht nur durch die markante Verwendung der Schwurformel auf Jahwe als Herrn aber auch Richter Israels hingewiesen, sondern es wird das-selbe formale Mittel wie in der David-Dynastie-Erzählung verwen-det, nämlich die Erweiterung der Schwurformel: "So wahr Jahwe lebt und so wahr du lebst". Nur ist hier nicht der König der Mittler der Gottesherrschaft, sondern der Prophet (2 Kön. ii 2, 4, 6, iv 30). Damit stehen wir inmitten des spannungsvollen Verhältnisses von Prophetie und Königtum, das hier nicht weiter verfolgt werden kann.

Die bisherigen Beobachtungen zu *hištaḥᵃwâ* zu *māšal* und zur Schwurformel zeigen, daß die Vorstellung von der Gottesherrschaft im Israel der Königszeit sehr wohl eine Rolle spielte und daß sie auch ohne Verwendung des Königtitels für Jahwe thematisiert wer-den konnte. Während es beim Königtum Gottes ursprünglich um

---

[25] Siehe dazu auch G. Sauer, "Die Bedeutung des Königtums für den Glauben Israels" *ThZ* 27 (1971) S. 1–15, bes. 9–10; K. Seybold, "*mlk*", *ThWAT* IV, Sp. (1984), 935–47; J.J.M. Roberts, "In Defense of the Monarchy: The Contribution of Israelite Kingship to Biblical Theology", in P.D. Miller-P.D. Hanson-S. Dean McBride (ed.), *Ancient Israelite Religion. Essays in Honor of Frank Moore Cross* (Philadelphia, 1987), S. 377–96.

die Herrschaft über die Götter und über die Naturmächte geht, geht es bei den dargestellten Aussagen zur Herrschaft Jahwes um sein Wirken an Israel. Das entspricht der Tatsache, daß für den Jahweglauben die Beziehung zwischen Gott und Volk jedenfalls sachlich und wahrscheinlich auch chronologisch den Vorrang hat.

4. Es bleibt die Frage, welchen *Titel* Jahwe im Zusamenhang dieser Vorstellungen von der Gottesherrschaft trägt. Es liegt nahe, in Analogie zu dem hier nicht benützten Königtitel einen anderen Titel zu erwarten. Diese Annahme ist jedoch nicht zwingend. Die dargestellten Formulierungen zeigen, daß sie sowohl gegenüber dem irdischen Herrscher als auch gegenüber Jahwe ohne einen Titel verwendet werden können. Das ist sowohl für die Schwurformel als auch für *hištaḥ^awâ* und den Gideonspruch evident.[26] Das heißt, der Jahwename ersetzt den Titel bzw. Jahwe bedarf keines weiteren Titels.[27]

Nun gibt es aber doch einen Titel, der für die Vorstellung von der Gottesherrschaft bestens geeignet ist und der mindestens so früh und so häufig belegt ist, wie der Königtitel für Jahwe. Es ist der Titel *'ādôn* bzw. *'^adōnāy*, Herr. Dieses *'ādôn* wird schon um 1000 v.Chr. als Titel für Jahwe verwendet, wie der Name des Davidsohnes Adonija zeigt. Ein noch älteres Vorkommen des Titels bietet der Name des vorisraelitischen Jerusalemer Königs *Adoniṣedeq* (Jos. x 1, 3; Ri. i 5ff.*). Nach Martin Noth charakterisiert *'ādôn* "die Gottheit in ihrem Verhältnis zu einer Menschengruppe".[28] Andere alte Belege sind wahrscheinlich Ex. xxiii 17 und xxxiv 23, wo jeweils im Rahmen der Kultkalender aufgefordert wird: "Dreimal im Jahr soll alles, was männlich ist, erscheinen vor dem Angesicht des *hā'ādôn yhwh*."

In den Belegen bei Jesaja ist der Titel *'ādôn* in iii 1 so wie in i 24 und x 16, 33 zusammen mit dem Namen Jahwe Zebaoth verwendet, während in vi 1 und 8 *'^adōnāy* absolut gebraucht wird. Da wie dort ist das Handeln des *'ādôn* bzw. *'adōnāy* auf Israel, konkret auf Jerusalem und Juda bezogen. Daß *'ādôn* nicht einfach eine ehrenvolle

---

[26] So wird bei *hištaḥ^awâ* schon für den irdischen Herrscher nicht immer der Königtitel ausgesprochen, sondern oft nur der Name genannt. Gegenüber Jahwe wird *hištaḥ^awâ* einfach mit dem Namen gebraucht; Jahwe wird gehuldigt bzw. Jahwe wird angebetet. Beim Gideonspruch heißt es schlicht: *yahwæh yimšōl bākœm*, Jahwe soll über euch herrschen. Hier wird jeder Anklang an einen Titel vermieden.

[27] Dasselbe zeigt auch ein Vergleich zwischen 1 Kön. xxii und Jes. vi. Bei aller Ähnlichkeit der beiden Visionen kommt 1 Kön. xxii ohne einen Titel aus—der Jahwename allein genügt.

[28] *Die israelitischen Personennamen im Rahmen der gemeinsemitischen Namengebung* (Stuttgart, 1928), S. 114. Dort auch Hinweis auf Adoniṣædæq. Vgl. Melkiṣædæq!

Anrede ist, sondern die konkrete Vorstellung als Herrscher impliziert, ergibt sich aus dem Hinweis auf seinen Thron in vi 1: *wā'ær'æh 'æt-'ᵃdōnāy yošeb 'al-kisse' rām wᵉnissā'*.—Die weitere Entfaltung des Gebrauchs dieses Gottestitels kann hier nicht dargestellt werden.[29] Zu Jesaja s.u.

III. *Die Verbindung von Gottesherrschaft und Königtum Gottes*

1. Mit Gottesherrschaft und Königtum Gottes liegen somit zwei urprünglich verschiedene und getrennte Vorstellungskreise vor. Der wesentliche Unterschied liegt im jeweils angesprochenen Herrschaftsbereich: Beim Königtum Gottes geht es um die Herrschaft im Pantheon und über die Natur. Bei der Gottesherrschaft geht es um die Herrschaft Gottes über eine bestimmte Gemeinschaft. Natürlich stehen beide Vorstellungskreise in einer gewissen Korrelation zu soziologischen Gegebenheiten. Dabei geht es auch nicht darum, eine kanaanäische von einer genuin israelitischen Vorstellung zu unterscheiden. Die Vorstellung von Gott als Herrn über ein Volk ist ja auch in der Umwelt Israels zu finden. Sondern es geht um die möglichst adäquate Erfassung der Vorstellungen und ihrer jeweiligen Bedeutung und Funktion.

2. Diese beiden Vorstellungen wurden allerdings später verbunden und haben einander dabei in charakteristischer Weise ergänzt. Bezüglich des Königtums Gottes ist festzustellen, daß Jahwe dann als König über Israel verstanden wurde. Allerdings sind die Jahwe-König-Psalmen mit entsprechenden Aussagen großteils eindeutig nachexilisch, und bei den vielleicht älteren Jahwe-König-Psalmen sind die auf Israel und seine Geschichte bezogenen Aussagen als Nachinterpretation erkennbar. Die Bezeichnung Jahwes als König Israels oder Jakobs oder Jerusalems findet sich erst ab der exilischen Zeit, besonders bei Deuterojesaja (Jes. xli 21, xliii 15, xliv 6, lii 7), aber auch in deuteronomistischen Texten. Dabei bleibt der kämpferische Aspekt, wie er aus den Jahwe-König-Psalmen bekannt ist, erhalten, und ebenso der universale Aspekt und Anspruch.

3. Wenn auch die Verbindung des Königtums Gottes mit Israel bei Deuterojesaja voll ausgeprägt und geradezu selbstverständlich erscheint,

---

[29] Siehe dazu die Wörterbücher: E. Jenni, "'ādôn", *THAT* I, Sp. 31–8, und O. Eißfeldt, "'ādôn", *ThWAT* I, Sp. 62–78. Allerdings bedürfte der Begriff dringend einer eingehenden neueren Untersuchung. Zur Etymologie und zur älteren Verwendung s. J. Sanmartín "Semantisches über ug. adn", *UF* 9 (1977), S. 269–72.

ist es sinnvoll, nach einer *Vorgeschichte dieser Verbindung* zu fragen. Der Königtitel für Jahwe war in Jes. vi 5 vorgekommen. Er stand dort eingerahmt von der zweimaligen Verwendung von *ʾadōnāy* (V. 1, 8). Der Auftrag Jesajas ist deutlich und massiv auf Israel bezogen, und *ʾadōnāy* kann nur Jahwe als den *Herrn Israels* bezeichnen. D.h. aber, der Königtitel für Jahwe steht hier in einem Kontext, der für diesen Titel zunächst fremd und wohl auch neu ist. In der Situation der Berufung Jesajas und in der Parallele zu *ʾadōnāy* erhielt der Königtitel eine neue Bedeutung, bzw. zunächst zumindest einen neuen Akzent.[30]

Nach der anderen Seite hin ist zu fragen, welche zusätzliche Dimension der Königtitel Jahwes für das Gottesverständnis Jesajas und für seinen Auftrag bringt. Für die Vorstellung vom Königtum Gottes charakteristisch ist die universale Dimension. Als König ist Jahwe König über die ganze Erde. Nach Werner H. Schmidt (*Glaube* [Anm. 8], S. 173–4) ist der Anpruch "Jahwe ist König über die Völker" (Ps. xlvii 9) vielleicht schon eine spezifisch israelitische Weiterführung dieser universalen Dimension. Jedenfalls paßt die Bezugnahme auf Jahwe als König in der Berufung Jesajas bestens dazu, daß zwar Jesajas Verkündigung auf Israel gerichtet ist, daß aber das angekündigte Handeln Jahwes weit über Israel hinausgreift und er nicht nur die Geschicke der benachbarten Königreiche lenkt, sondern sogar die Großmächte Assur und Ägypten herbeipfeift (vii 18–20). So ist *Jahwe der wahre König*, nicht zuletzt gegenüber dem König, nach dessen Todesjahr die Vision datiert wird und gegenüber jenen Königen, vor denen sich Ahas fürchtet.—Somit sah Jesaja bei seiner Vision nicht nur, was er bis dahin geglaubt hatte,[31] sondern noch mehr, und er verstand auch dessen Bedeutung für die konkrete historische Situation.

4. Was bei Jesaja erstmals verbunden ist, bildet offensichtlich die

---

[30] Das bedeutet, um nur diese eine Konsequenz herauszustellen: Jedenfalls nach Jes 6 wäre der Titel "Kerubenthroner" ursprünglich mit dem ʾadôn-Titel und nicht mit dem mælæk-Titel zu verbinden.—Das würde andrerseits gut zu der besonders von Keel (Anm. 7) vorgetragenen Unterscheidung der Serafen von den Keruben und zur Beziehung der Serafen zur Uräusschlange als pharaonischem und damit königlichem Schutzsymbol passen: Das neue Element der Serafen würde zum neuen Element des Königtitels gehören. Nach Keel, S. 108–10, erfreute sich das Bildmotiv des Uräus im Palästina des 8.Jh.'s großer Beliebtheit, was mit den intensiven ägyptischen Kontakten jener Zeit zusammenhängen dürfte. Auf diesem zeitgeschichtlichen Hintergrund hat die Beschreibung Jahwes als des *wahren* Königs (s.o. unter I.1.) ihre besondere Relevanz, etwa im Blick auf die von Jesaja kritisierte Bündnispolitik.

[31] A. Alt, "Gedanken über das Königtum Jahwes" (1945), jetzt in ders., *KS* I (München, ²1963), S. 345–57. ". . . sein jetziges Erlebnis bestand darin, daß er mit Augen sehen durfte, was er bis dahin nur geglaubt hatte" (S. 350).

Grundlage für die Aussagen bei Deuterojesaja, der auch sonst Protojesaja und dessen Berufungsgeschichte kennt. Bei DtJes stellt sich die Frage nach den Objekten des Königtums noch zusätzlich auf Grund der prinzipiellen Bestreitung der Existenz anderer Götter, d.h. bei DtJes ist der Königtitel für Jahwe nur sinnvoll auf dem Hintergrund der Beziehung zu den Völkern und zu Israel.

Auf eben dieser Basis der erfolgten Verbindung von Gottesherrschaft und Königtum Gottes wurde die Herrschaft Jahwes als König sowohl in der prophetischen Literatur und ihrer Nachbearbeitung als auch in den Psalmen aufgenommen und weiter entfaltet. In Ez. xx 3–4 findet sich Schwurformel, Königsherrschaft Jahwes und aktualisierte Exodustraditition zusammen: "So wahr ich lebe, spricht *'ªdōnāy yhwh*, ich will König sein über euch . . . . und will euch herausführen aus den Völkern und Ländern, in die ich euch zerstreut habe." Im großen Hymnus von Jer. x wird Jahwe gepriesen als "der wahre Gott, der lebendige Gott, der ewige König" (V. 10). Die weitere Entfaltung, sowohl in die universale Dimension wie auch in die individuelle Dimension, kann hier nicht mehr darstellt werden. Zu nennen wären Ex. xv 18; Ps. cxlv 1, cxlvi 10, cxlix 2, x 16, v 3, bis hin zu den eschatologischen Erwartungen von Jes. xxiv 21–3 und des Danielbuches.

IV. *Ergebnis*

1. Gottesherrschaft und Königtum Gottes sind ursprünglich zweierlei. Die Gottesherrschaft bezieht sich auf eine Menschengruppe. Das Königtum Gottes bezieht sich auf die Götter eines Pantheons.

2. Die für Israel grundlegende und breiter bezeugte Vorstellung ist die Vorstellung von der Gottesherrschaft. Sie ist durch ein breiteres Wortfeld und insbesondere durch die 'ādôn-Tradition bezeugt.

3. Das Verhältnis von Herrschaft Jahwes und Herrschaft eines irdischen Königs kann sowohl positiv als auch antagonistisch bestimmt werden. Aber auch dort, wo im Alten Testament Gott und König eng verbunden werden, wird Jahwe nicht als König bezeichnet, sondern als 'adôn (Ps. ii 4).

4. Der in der Namengebung und in den Hymnen am Jerusalemer Tempel verwendete Königtitel für Jahwe wurde von Jesaja in die Vorstellung von der Gottesherrschaft über Israel integriert.

5. Die Verschmelzung und die wechselseitige Durchdringung und Ergänzung von Gottesherrschaft und Königtum Gottes erfolgte im wesentlichen erst nach dem Ende des Königtums in Israel.

DAS SYSTEM DER ZWÖLF STÄMME ISRAELS

von

CHRISTOPH LEVIN
Göttingen

Eine historische Hypothese ist so gegründet wie die Quellen, auf welchen sie beruht. Keiner wußte das besser als Martin Noth. Seine Untersuchung *Das System der zwölf Stämme Israels* (Stuttgart, 1930) folgt dem erklärten Ziel, "einem im Alten Testament vorhandenen Überlieferungselement den Platz anzuweisen, auf den es einen Anspruch erheben kann" (p. 2). Folgerichtig setzt Noth ein mit einer überlieferungsgeschichtlichen Untersuchung der alttestamentlichen Nachrichten von den zwölf Stämmen. Erst nachdem er zu dem Ergebnis gelangt ist, daß in den Stämmelisten Gen. xlix; Num. i 5–15 und Num. xxvi 5–51 alte Überlieferung vorliegt, ist die Grundlage gegeben für den—heute viel kritisierten—Vergleich mit den außerisraelitischen Stämmebünden. Erst nachdem auch dieser Vergleich die Existenz einer israelitischen Amphiktyonie als möglich erwiesen hat, fragt Noth nach den Lebensformen und Institutionen sowie der Geschichte der "altisraelitischen Amphiktyonie".

Die Kritik, die Noths Hypothese erfahren hat, hat dieser Abfolge, zumal der exegetischen Grundlegung, nicht immer die Bedeutung beigemessen, die ihr für Noth selbst zukam. Indessen, "really relevant criticism must ... begin with Noth's own argumentation",[1] das heißt wie Noth mit der Kritik der alttestamentlichen Quellen. Wenn die Zeugnisse, auf die Noth sich gestützt hat, nicht als alte Überlieferung wahrscheinlich zu machen sind, endet die Debatte, ob die außerisraelitischen Analogien auf einen hypothetischen altisraelitischen Stämmebund anwendbar sind oder nicht, bevor sie begonnen hat.[2] Dieselbe Einschränkung gilt für die Frage nach den Institutionen des Stämmebundes unter sozialgeschichtlichem Gesichtspunkt.

---

[1] C.H.J. de Geus, *The Tribes of Israel. An Investigation into some of the Presuppositions of Martin Noth's Amphictyony Hypothesis* (Assen, 1976), p. 70.

[2] Cf. O. Bächli, *Amphiktyonie im Alten Testament. Forschungsgeschichtliche Studie zur Hypothese von Martin Noth* (Basel, 1977), p. 182: "Die Sicherung kann nur vom analogatum her erfolgen, dh aus den Quellen des ATs selbst."

Schließlich, ohne die Kritik der alttestamentlichen Überlieferung laufen auch die zum Ersatz vorgeschlagenen Theorien Gefahr, ohne Grundlage zu sein. Nicht umsonst haben Noth wie sein Lehrer Albrecht Alt der Abwägung der Quellen die größte Aufmerksamkeit zugewandt. Die Faszination, die von ihren Thesen ausging, beruhte zu einem guten Teil auf der geradezu künstlerischen Meisterschaft, zu der die Kritik der Überlieferung hier geführt ist. Wer ihnen gerecht werden will, kann das nur, wenn er diesen Maßstab auch seinerseits anerkennt.

I

Das maßgebende Überlieferungselement ist die Liste der Stämme. Noth kommt auf zweiundzwanzig Belege zu sprechen.[3] Die breite Bezeugung stellt nicht ohne weiteres den mehrfachen Niederschlag eines historischen Sachverhalts dar; denn die Listen hängen vielfältig voneinander ab. Sie wurden immer neu zitiert und fortentwickelt. Wer als Historiker die Texte verwenden will, muß diese Entwicklung nachvollziehen und die Ursprünge aufdecken, aus denen sie sich gespeist hat.

Wir lehnen uns dazu an Noths Untersuchung an. Es bedarf keiner Begründung, daß die Listen der Chronik neben ihren Vorlagen im Pentateuch keinen eigenen Quellenwert haben (pp. 13, 20-1). Offensichtlich konstruiert sind die beiden Listen im Anhang des Ezechielbuches Ez. xlviii 1-29, 31-5 (pp. 13, 19). Auch die Einrichtung des geographischen Materials des Josuabuches nach den Stämmen ist künstlich. "Denn weder die Grenzbeschreibungen (. . .) noch die Ortslisten (. . .) sind auf dem Zwölfstämmesystem aufgebaut" (p. 18 n. 3).[4] Die Aufstellung der Stämme "bei Gelegenheit des Befehls Moses über die große Segen-Fluchzeremonie auf Garizim und Ebal" Dtn. xxvii 11-13 ist ein sekundärer Einschub (pp. 11-12, 144-5). Auch der Mosesegen Dtn. xxxiii als ein Beispiel später "Verwilderung" des

---

[3] Gen. xxix 31-xxx 24 + xxxv 16-20, xxxv 23-6, xlvi 8-25, xlix 1-27; Ex. i 2-4; Num. i 5-15, 20-43, ii 3-31, vii 12-83, x 14-28, xiii 4-15, xxvi 5-51, xxxiv 16-29; Dtn. xxvii 12-3, xxxiii; Jos. xiii-xix; Ez. xlviii 1-29, 31-5; 1 Chr. ii 1-2; ii-viii, xii 25-8, xxvii 16-22. Sieht man ab von der Vollzähligkeit, die für Noths Beweisführung wesentlich war, kann man bis achtundzwanzig Belege zählen, cf. H. Weippert, "Das geographische System der Stämme Israels", *VT* 23 (1973), p. 76 n. 1, die Jos. xxi 4-8, 9-42; Jdc. i 1-35, v 14-18; 1 Chr. vi 40-8, 49-66 hinzunimmt.

[4] Noth konnte dazu auf A. Alt, "Judas Gaue unter Josia" (1925), *Kleine Schriften* II (München, 1953), pp. 276-88, sowie ders., "Das System der Stammesgrenzen im Buche Josua" (1927), *Kleine Schriften* I (München, 1953), pp. 193-202, verweisen.

Systems kommt für Noth nicht als alte Überlieferung in Betracht (pp. 21–3).

Die acht Stämmelisten des Buches Numeri führt Noth als Fortschreibungen auf i 5–15 und xxvi 5–51 zurück. Von seinem Urteil über i 5–15 abgesehen, ist ihm zuzustimmen, wenn auch die Herleitung im Einzelfall korrigiert werden muß. Die *Musterung des Heerbanns* Num. i 20–43 erweist sich an ihrer Einleitung in Num. i 2–3 par. xxvi 2 als Nachahmung von Num. xxvi.[5] Der dortige Aufbau wird wiederholt, nur daß die Söhne Josefs in die übliche Folge "Efraim und Manasse" gebracht sind. "Dass bei der zweiten Zählung auf die erste gar keine Rücksicht genommen ist",[6] zeigt, daß diese später hinzukam. Die *Lagerordnung* Num. ii 3–31 nimmt die Zahlen aus Num. i auf.[7] Auch die Reihenfolge erklärt sich von dort: Gemäß den Himmelsrichtungen ist die Liste in vier mal drei Stämme gegliedert, die ersten beiden Gruppen aber sind vertauscht, damit Juda an die Spitze des Heerbanns zu stehen kommt. Num. vii 12–83, die *Liste der Gaben der Stammeshäupter an die Stiftshütte,* beruht auf Num. ii. "Die Reihenfolge ist genau dieselbe, nur hat sie in Num. 2 einen verständlichen Sinn, in Num. 7 dagegen nicht" (pp. 15–16). Auch die *Zuordnung* Num. x 14–28 wiederholt diese Einteilung, die "bei der Marschordnung (. . .) nur dann zu verstehen ist, wenn die Lagerordnung als schon bekannt vorausgesetzt werden darf" (p. 15).

Die *Liste der Kundschafter* Num. xiii 4–15, "wahrscheinlich ein sekundärer Zuwachs zur P-Erzählung",[8] stimmt in der Abfolge "Ruben, Simeon, Juda, Issachar" mit der Liste der Stammeshäupter Num. i 5–15 überein. Da diese Abfolge in Num. i leichter erklärlich ist, ist Abhängigkeit wahrscheinlich.[9] Die Wendung *'lh šmwt h'nšym,* die beide Listen einführt, überschreibt auch Num. xxxiv 16–29, die *Liste der Fürsten, die den westjordanischen Stämmen das Land verteilen sollen.* In ihr ist Kaleb ben Jefunne als *nśy'* Judas wörtlich gleich wie in Num. xiii 6 aufgeführt. Die übrigen Namen folgen derselben Art wie in Num. xiii, so daß man Abhängigkeit unterstellen kann. Noth verweist darauf, daß sowohl in Num. xiii als auch in Num. xxxiv je ein persischer Name vorkommt. Beide Listen stammen "aus *sehr* später Zeit" (p. 19). Num. i 5–15 dürfte von den drei Listen *'lh šmwt h'nšym* die älteste sein.

---

[5] Nach Noth, p. 18, beruht Num. i 20–43 auf i 5–15.

[6] J. Wellhausen, *Die Composition des Hexateuchs* (Berlin, ⁴1963), p. 183. Cf. B. Baentsch, *Exodus-Leviticus-Numeri* (Göttingen, 1903), p. 628.

[7] Noth, p. 16–7, leitet Num. ii von Num. xxvi her.

[8] Noth, *Numeri* (Göttingen, 1966), p. 92.

[9] Noth, *System*, pp. 19–20, leitet Num. xiii von Num. xxvi her. Aber ders. (Anm. 8),

Für Noth nun ist Num. i 5–15 sogar "ein sehr altes Stück . . . aus der zweiten Hälfte der Richterzeit", das hohen Quellenwert besitzt. Den Ausschlag gibt, daß "die hier genannten Namen der Stammeshäupter . . . das Gepräge einer sehr frühen Zeit" tragen (p. 17), wie Noth schon zuvor in seiner Untersuchung *Die israelitischen Personennamen* (Stuttgart, 1928), p. 107, gesehen hat: "In der Liste . . . finden sich 6 Verwandtschaftswörternamen und 9 *'l*-Namen, aber noch keine Zusammensetzung mit *yhwh*". Für hohes Alter spricht insbesondere die Ähnlichkeit mit den westsemitischen Personennamen in Mari.[10] Gleichwohl ist die Frühdatierung nicht zwingend. Der Unterschied zwischen Num. i einerseits und Num. xiii und xxxiv andererseits ist so gering, daß schwerlich zwischen ihnen mehr als ein halbes Jahrtausend liegt. Man darf sich durch die außeralttestamentlichen Parallelen nicht täuschen lassen. "Die Dutzendnamen in Num. 1.8.14 sind fast alle nach der selben Schablone gemacht und haben gar keine Ähnlichkeit mit den echten alten Eigennamen. Daß der Name Jahve nicht in ihrer Komposition vorkommt, beweist nur, daß der Komponist seiner religionsgeschichtlichen Theorie wol eingedenk war."[11] "Man hat hier Namen vor sich, die in ihrer Art an die Vornamen der Mitglieder des Bareboneparlaments erinnern."[12]

Gegen die Frühdatierung von Num. i 5–15 gibt es darüber hinaus einen literargeschichtlichen Grund: Die Namen wiederholen sich in Num. ii, vii und x. Noth entschied, daß Num. i die älteste dieser Listen sei. Sie habe im Unterschied zu Num. ii "die einzige Aufgabe, die zwölf Stammeshäupter mit Namen zu verzeichnen" (p. 16), während sonst jeweils weitere Gesichtspunkte hinzuträten. Doch auch Num. i 5–15 folgt einem weiteren Gesichtspunkt: dem Gedanken, daß Mose und Aaron die 603.550 Israeliten aus Num. i 20–43 nicht ohne Hilfe gemustert haben können. Dazu können die Namen ohne weiteres aus der Heerbannordnung Num. ii exzerpiert worden sein, wo die Heerführer notwendiger Bestandteil sind. Das würde die eigentümliche Reihenfolge von Num. i 5–15 erklären: Die Umstellung der Gruppe "Juda Issachar Sebulon" mußte mit Rücksicht auf Num. i

p. 92: "Die Stämmeaufzählung folgt im wesentlichen dem Vorbild von 1, 5–15".

[10] Cf. Noth, "Mari und Israel. Eine Personennamenstudie" (1953), *Aufsätze zur biblischen Landes- und Altertumskunde* II (Neukirchen-Vluyn, 1971), pp. 213–33, bes. pp. 229–31.

[11] J. Wellhausen, *Prolegomena zur Geschichte Israels* (Berlin, ⁶1905), p. 348. Ebenso äußert sich Noth (Anm. 8), p. 92, über Num. xiii 4–15.

[12] H. Holzinger, *Numeri* (Tübingen, Leipzig, 1903), p. 4.

20–43 rückrevidiert werden, und dabei gewann die genealogische Ordnung die Oberhand. Der Magd-Sohn Gad wurde zu seinem Bruder
Ascher versetzt, so daß jetzt die fünf Lea-Söhne ohne Levi am Anfang stehen. Ist aber Num. i 5–15 abhängig von Num. ii, so führen
alle Stämmelisten des Buches Numeri auf Num. xxvi 5–51 zurück.

II

Das *große Geschlechterverzeichnis* Num. xxvi 5–51 glaubt Noth, "mit voller
Sicherheit der zweiten Hälfte der sogen. Richterzeit... zuweisen zu
können" (p. 14). Wieder wandelt er die relative Frühdatierung in
eine absolute. Bereits angesichts des literarischen Zusammenhangs
überrascht dies: Num. xxvi findet sich im Rahmen der Priesterschrift,
gehört indessen nicht zur Grundschrift, sondern wird zu den Nach-
trägen gerechnet. Es könnte sogar, wie viele Nachträge des Buches
Numeri, die Verbindung der Pentateuchquellen, die sogenannte "Endredaktion", schon voraussetzen.

Überdies hat Num. xxvi in Gen. xlvi 8–25, dem Verzeichnis der
Israeliten, die nach Ägypten zogen, eine enge Parallele. Die Einzelheiten stimmen in einem Maße überein, daß literarische Abhängigkeit unbestreitbar ist. Nur die Richtung ist fraglich. Baentsch und
Procksch vertraten die Auffassung, Gen. xlvi sei Vorlage für Num.
xxvi gewesen.[13] Sollten sie im Recht sein, würde Num. xxvi als selb-
ständige Überlieferung entfallen. Noths Hypothese verlöre ihre wich-
tigste Stütze.[14]

Gen. xlvi vertritt bei der Reihenfolge der Stämme, wie alle Listen
der Genesis, das System mit Levi und Josef, Num. xxvi, wie alle
Listen in Num. und Jos., das System ohne Levi und mit Efraim und
Manasse. Das System mit Levi ist gewiß das ältere. Der Stamm ohne
Land wurde nicht nachträglich eingefügt, sondern unter dem Ge-
sichtspunkt der Landnahme ausgeschlossen. Noch im Anhang von
Num. xxvi werden auch die Nachkommen Levis gezählt (*v.* 57–62),
und es ist paradox, daß sie in der Summe nicht mitzählen sollen.[15]
Die Enkel-Stämme Efraim und Manasse aber sind nur eingefügt, um
Levis Ausscheiden zu kompensieren. In fünf der acht Numeri-Listen
erinnert die Erwähnung Josefs an die Priorität des Genesis-Systems.
Da Num. xxvi der älteste Beleg des Numeri-Systems ist und zugleich

---

[13] Baentsch (Anm. 6), pp. 629–30; O. Procksch, *Die Genesis* (Leipzig, 1913), p. 501.
[14] Daher der ausführliche Exkurs I bei Noth, pp. 122–32.
[15] Num. i 49 läßt deshalb die Zählung des Stammes Levi verbieten.

in unmittelbarer Beziehung zu Gen. xlvi steht, entscheidet sich zwischen diesen beiden Listen das Verhältnis der beiden Systeme. Gen. xlvi bietet eine von mehreren Möglichkeiten, die Söhne nach den Müttern einzuteilen: Die Söhne der Mägde sind jeweils an die Söhne ihrer Herrinnen angeschlossen. Genau diese Anordnung erklärt den Aufbau des Numeri-Systems: Obgleich Levi ausscheidet, wird die Gruppe der sechs Leasöhne beibehalten. Gad, der erste Magd-Sohn nach Lea, rückt an die Stelle. Sein Bruder Ascher aber, der nun allein steht, wird den Söhnen Bilhas am Ende der Liste zugeschlagen, und zwar mitten unter sie eingestellt. Es ergeben sich drei Kategorien: Sechs Lea-Stämme, drei Rahel-Stämme (mit Efraim und Manasse für Josef), drei Mägde-Stämme. Die stehende Abfolge "Dan Ascher Naftali" des geographischen Systems ist auf diese Weise zustandegekommen.

Der größte Unterschied zwischen Gen. xlvi und Num. xxvi betrifft die Nachkommen Manasses und Efraims, die in Gen. xlvi fehlen. Sind sie ausgelassen oder in Num. xxvi hinzugefügt? Für die Zufügung gibt es einen Grund: Sobald die Söhne Josefs in die Rolle vollbürtiger Stämme aufgerückt sind, wendet sich ihrer Genealogie dieselbe Aufmerksamkeit zu wie den übrigen Stämmen.[16] Tatsächlich ist für den Manasse-Abschnitt Num. xxvi 29–34 besondere Herkunft nachweisbar. Nicht weniger als sechs seiner vierzehn Namen sind auf den Ostraka von Samaria belegt. Es ist erwiesen, daß sie "auf tatsächlichen Gegebenheiten beruhen" (Noth, p. 125), nämlich auf den Namen der Krongüter des Nordreichs im achten Jahrhundert.[17] Da Noth voraussetzt, daß Num. xxvi eine im Kern einheitliche Quelle ist, sieht er sich berechtigt, die ganze Stämmeliste in die Bestätigung durch den Inschriftenfund einzubeziehen.[18] Teilt man diese Voraussetzung nicht, kehrt das Argument sich um: Der Manasse-Abschnitt,

---

[16] Eine Auslassung in Gen. xlvi könnte damit begründet sein, daß das Verzeichnis die runde Zahl von siebzig Nachkommen Jakobs geben wollte, wie ja auch unter den Namen einzelne Überschüsse gegenüber Num. xxvi bestehen. Wellhausen sah sich deshalb veranlaßt, Num. xxvi für ursprünglich zu halten (Anm. 6, p. 183). Doch aus der unterschiedlichen Zählweise in Gen. xlvi 26, 27 geht hervor, daß die Zählung auf nachträglichen Bearbeitungen beruht. Die Zwischensummen *v.* 15b, 18b, 22b, 25b lassen sich schadlos ausscheiden. Auch in dem etwas anders zählenden Verzeichnis Ex. i 1–5 ist die Summe ergänzt (*v.* 1bβ, 5a).

[17] Cf. Noth, "Das Krongut der israelitischen Könige und seine Verwaltung" (1927), *Aufsätze zur biblischen Landes- und Altertumskunde* I (Neukirchen-Vluyn, 1971), pp. 159–82.

[18] Die Ostraka lassen sich recht genau im 8.Jh. datieren (cf. A. Lemaire, *Inscriptions Hébraïques* I [Paris, 1977], pp. 21–81). Das muß den Spielraum für die Entstehung

dessen Angaben sich in Jos. xvii 1–3 etwas anderer Zuordnung wiederholen, geht offenbar auf eine eigene, historisch ungleich zuverlässige-
re Überlieferung zürück. Die übrige Liste kann auf Gen. xlvi beruhen.

Der offenkundige Unterschied zwischen Gen. xlvi und Num. xxvi
besteht darin, daß die Genesis-Liste ein Personenverzeichnis ist, die
Numeri-Liste ein Geschlechterverzeichnis. Unbestreitbar ist die Per-
sonifikation von Geschlechtern überlieferungsgeschichtlich sekundär.
Doch fragt sich, ob das auch für Gen. xlvi im Verhältnis zu Num.
xxvi gelten muß. Es ist nämlich sicher, daß Num. xxvi auf Stilisierung
beruht: Für die Nachkommen Dans ist ein einziges Geschlecht genannt, und dennoch ist das Schema starr beibehalten (cf. *v.* 42–3 mit
Gen. xlvi 23).

Gleichwohl gibt es im Ablauf nicht wenige Abweichungen. Be-
zeichnenderweise stimmt der Wortlaut an diesen Stellen mit Gen.
xlvi mehr oder minder überein; und zwar so, daß der Numeri-Text
als bewußte Abwandlung gelten muß.[19] Das deutlichste Beispiel ist
der Abschnitt über Juda. Gen. xlvi 12 nennt fünf Söhne Judas, beginnend mit Er und Onan, bemerkt aber am Ende, daß Er und
Onan im Lande Kanaan gestorben seien. Wie zum Ausgleich werden danach aus der Enkelgeneration zwei Söhne des Perez hinzugefügt. Num. xxvi 19–21 schleppt diese Nachrichten mit, obwohl aus
Er und Onan keine Geschlechter hervorgingen. Die Unstimmigkeit
ist aber bemerkt worden: Die Notiz von ihrem Tode folgt unmittelbar, sobald Er und Onan genannt sind, und darauf beginnt das
Verzeichnis von neuem. Die Sekundarität gegenüber Gen. xlvi ist
offensichtlich.

Dasselbe gilt für den Anfang der Reihe. Die Überschrift *wbny yśr'l
hyṣ'ym m'rṣ mṣrym* "Und die Israeliten, die aus Ägyptenland zogen"
(Num. xxvi 4b*) ist auf die Überschrift Gen. xlvi 8a* bezogen: *w'lh
šmwt bny yśr'l hb'ym mṣrymh* "Und dies sind die Namen der Israeliten,
die nach Ägypten kamen". Die Änderung berücksichtigt, daß Num.
xxvi kein Namensverzeichnis mehr ist. Die Betonung *r'wbn bkwr yśr'l*
"Ruben war der Erstgeborene Israels" (Num. xxvi 5a), die aus dem
Schema fällt, erklärt sich aus Gen. xlvi 8b (dort aus Gen. xxxv 23aβ).
Die Vorlage dominiert am Anfang so stark, daß sie das Schema

---

von Num. xxvi nicht einengen. "Bei der bekanntlich oft großen Konstanz siedlungs-
geographischer Ordnungen kann die Liste ebensogut wesentlich jünger wie wesentlich älter sein als die Ostraka" (Noth, p. 126).

[19] Noth, pp. 123–4, hält die Abweichungen für sekundär, folgt indessen allzu
deutlich seiner Vorausnahme.

überwiegt. Statt der üblichen Phrase: *bny r'wbn lmšphtm lhnwk mšpht hhnky*, beginnt die Reihe wie die Genesis-Parallele: *wbny r'wbn hnwk*, und schwenkt erst dann auf das Schema ein. Alle Beobachtungen erweisen, daß Num. xxvi keine originale Überlieferung, vielmehr ein abgeleiteter Text ist, der Noths Hypothese nicht stützen kann.

III

Der *Jakobsegen* Gen. xlix, Noths dritter Beleg, ist in seiner heutigen Form ebenfalls keine alte Quelle. Die neuere Urkundenhypothese pflegt ihn dem Jahwisten zuzuschreiben. Dagegen spricht, daß die Reihe der Stammessprüche in den Textzusammenhang der Priesterschrift eingeschaltet ist.[20] Die Reihenfolge erklärt sich als Rückübertragung des Genesis-Systems auf das Numeri-System: Den Mägde-Stämmen liegt die Abfolge "Dan Ascher Naftali" zugrunde. Gad, der Levi wieder weichen mußte, wurde an zweiter Stelle unter sie eingestellt. Josef und Benjamin stehen wieder am Schluß.

Wo die Stammessprüche sich mit den Erzählungen der Genesis berühren, zeigt auch der Inhalt die späte Entstehung. Der Ruben-spruch beruht auf der Episode vom Beischlaf mit Bilha Gen. xxxv 22a, die "offenbar ein späteres Einschiebsel (Glosse)" ist,[21] veranlaßt durch die Stämmeliste xxxv 22b–26. Sie will den Widerspruch erklä-ren zwischen Rubens Vorrang als Erstgeborener der zwölf Stämme und seiner historischen Bedeutungslosigkeit. Der Grund, den sie ge-funden hat, ist anhand von Lev. xviii 8 aus der Konstellation der Personen ersonnen.

Für Simeon und Levi, die mit einem gemeinsamen Stammesspruch bedacht werden, ist die Dina-Sage Gen. xxxiv vorausgesetzt. Ihr älte-ster Kern erzählt, wie die Schönheit der Tochter Jakobs den Sohn des Fürsten des Landes bewogen hat, die Beschneidung anzuneh-men. Dazu ist in *v.* 15 das Beschneidungsgebot aus Gen. xvii 10, 12 P wörtlich wiedergegeben. In Überarbeitungen gewann das Konnubi-umsverbot aus Dtn. vii 3 die Oberhand (in *v.* 9 zitiert). Um es durch-zusetzen, wurden Simeon und Levi aufgeboten—und erst so konnte der Eindruck aufkommen, es seien stammesgeschichtliche Hintergründe im Spiel. In Wahrheit ist die Erzählung ein Beispiel später Haggada.

---

[20] Der P-Faden findet sich in *v.* 1a, 28bα (nur *wybrk 'wtm*), 29 (cf. xxviii 1). *V.* 1b und 28* sind redaktionelle Klammern.

[21] H. Hupfeld, *Die Quellen der Genesis und die Art ihrer Zusammensetzung* (Berlin, 1853), p. 74.

Das Urteil über die ersten beiden Stammessprüche muß nicht bedeuten, daß unter den weiteren Sprüchen von Gen. xlix keine alte Überlieferung zu finden ist. In jedem Falle entscheidet es über das Zwölfersystem. Ohne Ruben, Simeon und Levi ist es nicht vollzählig, das heißt nicht vorhanden.

IV

Nachdem alle drei Stämmelisten, auf die Noth seine Hypothese begründet hat, als sekundär erwiesen sind, muß der Versuch, "die Organisation des israelitischen Volkes in der äußeren Form eines Bundes von zwölf Stämmen mit einem kultischen Mittelpunkt, die man einst gern für das Ergebnis einer späten künstlichen Geschichtskonstruktion hielt", als historisch zu erweisen,[22] als gescheitert gelten. Es gibt keinen alten Beleg für sie.

Indessen läßt die Überlieferung von den zwölf Stämmen sich erst beurteilen, wenn über ihre Herkunft entschieden ist. "Wie man auch über den Charakter des Zwölfstämmesystems urteilen mag, die Frage nach der Geschichte des . . . Überlieferungselements kann erst dann als gelöst gelten, wenn es gelungen ist, einen geschichtlichen Ort und eine geschichtliche Zeit zu bezeichnen, aus denen heraus die Entstehung . . . im ganzen und im einzelnen befriedigend zu erklären ist" (Noth, p. 2).

Die Frage ist zunächst an Gen. xlvi als Vorlage von Num. xxvi zu richten. Wie allgemein gesehen wird, ist das *Verzeichnis der Israeliten, die nach Ägypten zogen*, eine späte Kompilation.[23] Die Einzelheiten sind aus beiden Pentateuchquellen zusammengesucht.[24] Die Endredaktion ist also vorausgesetzt. Auch spätere Nachträge sind bereits bekannt. Die Liste der Söhne Jakobs aus Gen. xxxv 22b–26 bildet das Grundgerüst. Sie ist in *v.* 8b, 19 und den (Zwischen-)Unterschriften *v.* 15a, 22a auch wörtlich aufgenommen. Bei Ruben, Simeon und Levi stimmen die Namen mit Ex. vi 14–16 überein, einem Einschub innerhalb priesterschriftlichen Textes. Die Söhne Judas stammen aus Gen. xxxviii. Für die Söhne Issachars und Sebulons ist auf die "kleinen Richter" in Jdc. x 1, xii 11 zurückgegriffen. Die Söhne Josefs sind

---

[22] Noth, "Von der Knechtsgestalt des Alten Testaments" (1943), *Gesammelte Studien zum Alten Testament* II (München, 1969), p. 64.

[23] Der Nachtrag wurde von A. Kayser, *Das vorexilische Buch der Urgeschichte Israels* (Straßburg, 1874), pp. 30–2, erkannt.

[24] Cf. Procksch (Anm. 13), p. 500.

der Geburtsnotiz Gen. xli 50–2 entlehnt, aus der wörtlich zitiert ist.
Von dort erklärt sich die Vorordnung Manasses, die noch in Num.
xxvi nachwirkt. Für die Mägde ist auf Gen. xxix 24, 29 verwiesen.

Die Überschrift: "Dies sind die Namen der Israeliten, die nach
Ägypten kamen, Jakob und seine Söhne", gibt Gen. xlvi als Vorwegnahme und jüngere Ausgestaltung von Ex. i 1–5 zu erkennen, die
eingefügt ist, sobald Jakob mit seinen Söhnen ägyptischen Boden
betritt. Der *Prolog des Buches Exodus* Ex. i 1–5 seinerseits ist eine
Wiederholung von Gen. xxxv 22b–26. Die Reihenfolge ist dieselbe,
nur daß Josef um der Umstände willen an den Schluß gestellt ist.
Gewöhnlich werden die Verse der Priesterschrift zugeschrieben. In
deren Zusammenhang aber hat die Dublette keine Funktion.[25] Ihr
Anlaß ist vielmehr die Büchertrennung gewesen—ein sehr später
Schritt in der Geschichte der Pentateuchredaktion. Die Liste soll dem
Buche Exodus den gebührenden Anfang verschaffen.[26]

Die Vorlage Gen. xxxv 22b–26, die *Aufzählung der zwölf Söhne Ja-*
kobs, wird ebenfalls der Priesterschrift zugewiesen. Die stilistische
Verwandtschaft ist offensichtlich. Jedoch, nach der Anordnung der
Priesterschrift gehören die Söhne Jakobs unter die Toledot Jakobs,
stehen also vor xxxvii 2 an falscher Stelle.[27] Mißt man hingegen am
vorliegenden Zusammenhang, folgt die Liste genau am richtigen Ort:
Unmittelbar nach der Geburt Benjamins xxxv 16–20 JE zieht sie
unter der Feststellung *"Die Söhne Jakobs waren zwölf"* die Summe. Die
Anordnung nach den Müttern bezieht sich unmittelbar auf die Er-
zählung Gen. xxix 31–xxx 24. Mit der Synthese von priesterschrift-
lichem Stil und jehowistischem Stoff setzt auch dieser Beleg die
Endredaktion voraus.[28] Nota bene: Er ist der älteste, der die zwölf
Söhne Jakobs im Sinne eines Systems begreift.

V

Für die Grundlage von Gen. xxxv 22b–26 muß sich das Augenmerk
auf den *Bericht von der Geburt der Söhne Jakobs* in Gen. xxix–xxx richten. Noth hat sich mit Bedacht nicht auf diese Quelle gestützt. Sie
widerspricht zwei Bedingungen seiner Hypothese von vornherein: "daß

[25] Cf. B.D. Eerdmans, *Alttestamentliche Studien* III (Gießen, 1910), p. 8.
[26] Cf. G. Fohrer, *Überlieferung und Geschichte des Exodus* (Berlin, 1964), p. 9.
[27] Procksch stellt die Liste um.
[28] Man überzeugt sich leicht, daß die Geschichtsdarstellung der Priesterschrift das
Zwölfstämmevolk nicht gekannt hat.

dieses System der zwölf Israelsöhne einerseits ein durchaus selbständiges, andrerseits ein in der alttestamentlichen Überlieferung von vornherein fertig und abgeschlossen vorliegendes Traditionselement ist" (p. 4). Gen. xxix 31–xxx 24 ist weder selbständig, vielmehr fester Bestandteil der Jakoberzählungen, noch von vornherein fertig: Der Text ist offensichtlich nicht einheitlich. Er zeigt mannigfache Spuren literarischen Wachstums.

Die neuere Urkundenhypothese weist ihn dem Jahwisten und dem Elohisten zu. Die Aufteilung nimmt in Kauf, daß keine der beiden Quellen das vollständige Zwölfstämmesystem im erhaltenen Text überliefert. Man erklärt, jener Text, der in der einen Quelle fehle, sei aus der anderen geboten, und umgekehrt. Das ist der Inbegriff eines Zirkelschlusses.[29] Der triftigste Grund für eine Quellenscheidung sind die doppelten Etymologien bei Issachar, Sebulon und Josef.[30] Sie führen indessen nicht auf eine zweite Quelle, sondern erklären sich mit einer unselbständigen Bearbeitung (xxx laβ–2, 17a, 18a, 20 [*zbdny* bis *ṭwb*], 22bα, 23b).

Das Schema von Beischlaf, Schwangerschaft, Geburt, Namengebung und Etymologie variiert in einem Maße, das auf sukzessives literarisches Wachstum führt. Es ist hier nicht möglich, die Analyse mit allen Gründen vorzustellen.[31] *Die vorjahwistische Erzählung* handelte von Ruben und Simeon als Söhnen Leas sowie von Josef als Sohn Rahels. Im Rahmen der Ätiologie für Ramat Rahel xxxv 16–20 gehörte die Geburt des Ben-Oni noch hinzu. Der Ablauf ist durch das Motiv der vertauschten Braut vorgegeben. Jakob erhält zuerst die Lea und verbringt mit ihr die Brautwoche. Die Fortsetzung: "Sie wurde schwanger und gebar" kann aber nicht folgen. Denn Jakob erhält sogleich auch die Rahel, mit der er ebenfalls schläft. Die Verwickelung der Geburtsnotizen wird verhindert, indem Rahel zuerst unfruchtbar bleibt. Erst als Lea geboren hat, öffnen die Alraunen, die Ruben gefunden hat, Rahel den Mutterschoß. Jetzt kann auch bei ihr die Geburtsnotiz folgen (xxix 32a, 33a [bis *ḥn*], b, xxx 14, 23a, 24a [bis *ywsp*]).

Der Horizont der Jakobgeschichten wird überschritten, sobald die Etymologien hinzutreten. Bei Ruben und Simeon haben sie enge

---

[29] Kein anderer als der "Vater" des Elohisten in seiner modernen Form, Hupfeld (Anm. 21), pp. 43–4, hat dafür plädiert, die literarische Beschaffenheit von Gen. xxix–xxx mit der Ergänzungshypothese zu deuten.

[30] Cf. Wellhausen (Anm. 6), p. 36.

[31] Cf. dazu meine Untersuchung *Der Jahwist* (Göttingen, 1993), pp. 221–31.

Parallelen in Gen. xvi 11 und Ex. iii 7. Da sie sich leicht ausscheiden lassen, ist redaktionelle Herkunft wahrscheinlich. Der Gottesname
yhwh und die Verbindung von Vätergeschichte und Exodusgeschichte
weisen sie dem *Jahwisten* zu, der sich hier wie andernorts als Redaktor von seinen Quellen unterscheidet (xxix 31, 32b, 33a [ab *wt'mr*]).
Von genau derselben Art sind die Etymologien bei Levi und Juda.
Diesmal freilich steht die Namengebung nicht neben der Etymologie,
sondern geht aus ihr hervor. Der Text ist aus einem Guß. Daraus
folgt: Der Jahwist hat Levi und Juda als Söhne Jakobs hinzugefügt
(xxix 34–5). Bei der Geburt des Josef schließlich ist die Jahwe-Ety-
mologie wiederum nachgetragen (xxx 24 [ab *l'mr*]). Sie weist voraus
auf die Geburt des Benjamin (xxxv 17, 18b). In der jahwistischen
Pentateuchquelle hatte Jakob/Israel sechs Söhne. Drei fanden sich in
den Vorlagen: Ruben, Simeon, Josef; drei sind hinzugefügt: Levi,
Juda und Benjamin.

Von den *weiteren Söhnen* wurde als erster Issachar ergänzt—im
Widerspruch zu der Bemerkung: "Und Lea hörte auf zu gebären"
(xxix 35b). Er ist als "Jakobs fünfter Sohn" eingeführt: Dan, Naftali,
Gad und Ascher waren noch nicht vorhanden (xxx 15–6, 17b, 18b).
Nachträglich wurde ihm Sebulon an die Seite gestellt—ungeachtet
daß das Beilager, das Lea für die Alraunen erkauft hat, nur *eine*
Schwangerschaft zur Folge gehabt haben kann (xxx 19, 20 [ohne
zbdny bis *ṭwb*]). Anschließend scheint die Geburt der Dina eingetra-
gen zu sein, mit der Lea auf sieben Kinder kommt (xxx 21).

Zuletzt kamen *die Mägde und ihre Söhne* hinzu. Das Vorbild war
Abrahams Ehe mit der Hagar, auf die der Text sich indirekt auch
bezieht (cf. xxx 3–5 mit xvi 2–4, 15). Ursprünglich hatte Bilha nur
einen Sohn, nämlich Dan (xxx 1aα, 3–6). Wieder griff das Gesetz der
Verdoppelung: Mit Naftali kam ein zweiter Magd-Sohn hinzu (xxx
7–8). Er brachte die Zahl der Söhne Jakobs auf zehn. Mit einer
zweiten Magd und ihren zwei Söhnen, Gad und Ascher, wurde im
letzten Schritt die Zwölfzahl erreicht (xxx 9–13).

Dabei blieb es. Die Zwölfzahl ist als die Zahl der Monate des Jah-
reskreises das Symbol der abgeschlossenen Gesamtheit. Seither reprä-
sentieren die zwölf Söhne Jakobs das Gottesvolk in seiner gottgewoll-
ten Vollzähligkeit. "Aus der Zwölfzahl der israelitischen Stämme in den
wechselnden Formen läßt sich nichts anderes ersehen, als daß die
angeführten Stämme jeweils die Gesamtheit Israels darstellen sollen."[32]

---

[32] G. Fohrer, "Altes Testament—'Amphiktyonie' und 'Bund'?", *ThLZ* 91 (1966),

VI

Es bestätigt die Analyse von Gen. xxix–xxx, daß die Überlieferung der Genesis bis in späteste Zeit nur sechs Söhne Jakobs gekannt hat: Ruben, Simeon, Levi, Juda, Benjamin und Josef.[33] Nicht von ungefähr nimmt die Haggada Gen. xxxiv Levi und Simeon zu Protagonisten, wird das Paradigma für die Leviratsehe Gen. xxxviii von Juda erzählt, wetteifern Juda und Ruben um die Rettung Josefs (Gen. xxxvii 21–2, 26–9) und sind wechselweise die Sprecher der Brüder (Gen. xlii 22, 37, xliii 3, 8, xliv 14–34, xlvi 28), wird Simeon zur Geisel in Ägypten (xlii 24, 36, xliii 23), ist Benjamin die zweite Hauptperson der Josefsgeschichte (xlii 4, 36, xliii 14–6, 29, 34, xliv 12, xlv 12, 14, 22). All diese Erzählungen und Erzählzüge sind der Genesis erst spät zugewachsen. Doch sie konnten von den übrigen Söhnen Jakobs nicht erzählt werden. Es gab sie nicht.

In bemerkenswertem Unterschied zu den sechs nachgetragenen Söhnen, von denen außerhalb der Listen jede Spur fehlt, spielen Manasse und Efraim eine bedeutende Rolle (Gen. xli 50–2, xlviii). Nächst Israel, Juda und Benjamin sind sie die wichtigsten nationalen Größen, die die Genesis nennt. Indessen sind sie genealogisch dem Josef zugeordnet. Das wäre unverfänglich, hätte die weitere Überlieferung es bei sechs Söhnen Jakobs belassen. Im Zwölfstämmesystem bedeutet es eine irritierende Inkonsequenz, daß ihnen vergleichsweise unwichtige Größen wie Dan, Naftali, Gad, Ascher, Issachar und Sebulon als Söhne Israels den Rang streitig machen. Die weitere Überlieferung hat das nach Kräften zu korrigieren gesucht.

VII

Die Künstlichkeit des Systems der zwölf Stämme erweist sich nicht zuletzt daran, daß es Größen sehr verschiedener Art und verschiedenen Ranges unter ein und derselben Kategorie vereint.

Die sechs nachgetragenen "Stämme" sind durchweg historisch faßbar, aber von geringer Bedeutung. *Issachar* ist in alten Quellen zweimal genannt: Ein "Mann von Issachar" war Tola ben Puwa, der erste der sogenannten "kleinen Richter", wohnhaft auf dem Gebirge

---

p. 814. Cf. F. Heiler, *Erscheinungsformen und Wesen der Religion* (Stuttgart, Berlin, Köln, Mainz, ²1979), pp. 171–2.

[33] Belege wie Gen. xxxii 23a (ab *wyqḥ*), 24a, xxxiii 1b–3a, 5–7, xxxvii 2aβ, 9, xlii 13*, 32* sind spät.

Efraim (Jdc. x 1). Aus dem Hause (*byt*) Issachar stammte Bascha ben Ahija, der das Haus Jerobeams I. gestürzt hat (1 Reg. xv 27).[34] Issachar war danach eine maßgebende Sippe oder ein Sippenverband des Nordreichs. Dazu stimmt, daß der Name, wie immer man ihn deutet, ein Personenname ist.[35] *Sebulon* ist Name eines Landes (*'rṣ*) im südwestlichen Galiläa (Jdc. xii 12), als solches noch in späten Quellen belegt (Jes. viii 23). In Sebulon und Naftali handelt die alte Debora-Überlieferung Jdc. iv. *Dan* bezeichnet in alten Quellen zwei verschiedene Größen: den Ort samt Heiligtum an der Nordgrenze (Dtn. xxxiv 1; 1 Reg. v 5, xv 20; Jer. iv 15, viii 16), identifiziert mit dem heutigen Tell el-Qadi, und eine am Westrand des judäischen Gebirges ansässige Sippe (*mšpḥh*), der Simson entstammt sein soll (Jdc. xiii 2, 25). Beide werden in der Wanderungs-Erzählung Jdc. xviii nachträglich in Verbindung gebracht. *Naftali* ist neben Sebulon die zweite große Landschaft (*'rṣ*) Galiläas (Dtn. xxxiv 2; Jdc. iv 6, 10; 1 Reg. xv 20; 2 Reg. xv 29; Jes. viii 23). Als "Mann von *Gad*" (*'š gd*) wird in der Mescha-Inschrift, Zeile 10, die israelitische Bevölkerung des südlichen Ostjordanlands bezeichnet. An der Historizität des Namens ist daher nicht zu zweifeln, wenngleich frühe Belege im Alten Testament fehlen.[36] In den Listen Jdc. v 14–18 und 1 Reg. iv 8–19 steht Gilead an seiner Stelle. Für *Ascher* findet sich ein alter Beleg neben 1 Reg. iv 16 möglicherweise in 2 Sam. ii 9 (cj.), wo das Herrschaftsgebiet von Sauls Sohn Ischbaal beschrieben ist: Gilead, Ascher, Jesreel, Efraim, Benjamin, ganz Israel. Wie die meisten dieser Namen bezeichnet auch Ascher eine Landschaft.

Von ungleich größerem Rang sind jene "Stämme", die der Jahwist in die Genesis eingeführt hat: *Juda* ist das Südreich, *Benjamin* das historisch bedeutende Land zwischen Nord und Süd. Ihnen zur Seite steht *Israel*. Die Gleichsetzung Jakobs mit dem Nordreich bzw. mit dem Stammvater des Gottesvolkes ist ebenfalls durch die Hand des Jahwisten geschehen, durch einen redaktionellen Einschub in der Jabbokperikope (Gen. xxxii 28–30a). Vom Jahwisten stammt schließlich *Levi* als dritter Sohn Leas, um eine genealogische Brücke zwischen der Vätergeschichte und der Exodusgeschichte zu schlagen;

---

[34] Nicht von gleicher Zuverlässigkeit ist der Anhang der Gauliste Salomos, nach der Joschafat ben Paruach in Issachar als Vogt residierte (1 Reg. iv 17).

[35] Cf. KBL³ 422b.

[36] Die LXX-Lesart von 1 Reg. iv 19 mag hier außer Betracht bleiben. 1 Sam. xiii 7; 2 Sam. xxiii 36, xxiv 5; 2 Reg. x 33; Jer. xlix 1 sind spät.

denn Mose wird nach der Quelle in Ex. ii 1–10 als Sohn eines Mannes aus dem Hause Levi und einer Tochter Levis eingeführt. Auch Levi ist kein Stamm gewesen, sondern eine Priesterklasse. Der Widerspruch, der zwischen Levi als Teil des Zwölfstämmesystems einerseits und der Rolle des Leviten im Deuteronomium anderseits besteht, ist bemerkenswert.

Die merkwürdigsten "Stämme" sind indessen jene, die aus der vorjahwistischen Überlieferung in den Kreis ihrer späteren "Brüder" geraten sind: Ruben, Simeon und Josef. Bekanntlich kann der Historiker die Stämme Ruben und Simeon in der Geschichte Israels mit der Lupe suchen—es gibt sie nicht. Wie schon die Personennamen zeigen, sind Ruben, Simeon und Josef von Hause aus Erzählungsfiguren gewesen, nicht anders als Jakob, Esau, Laban, Lea und Rahel. Die stammesgeschichtliche Deutung der Vätererzählungen ist, gemessen an den Ursprüngen der Überlieferung, falsch. Der deutlichste Beleg ist die Josefsgeschichte, die in ihrer heutigen Gestalt eine Novelle, in ihrem Kern aber das israelitische Brüdermärchen ist. Stammesgeschichtliche Hintergründe sind mit der Gattung schlechterdings unvereinbar.[37] Das "Haus Josef" ist ein fiktiver Begriff, der erst spät belegt ist.[38]

VIII

Von der Spätdatierung des Zwölfstämmesystems wird das Bild der alttestamentlichen Heilsgeschichte kaum berührt. Einzig die Darstellung der Landnahme ist auf die Stämme ausgerichtet, genau besehen nur die Siedlungsgeographie samt der Überlieferung von der Landnahme der zweieinhalb Stämme (Num. xxxii; Dtn. iii; Jos. xxii). Es sagt genug, daß an den wenigen Stellen, die den Zwölfer-Symbolismus in die Geschichtsdarstellung nachtragen, die Zahl erläutert werden muß: "nach der Zahl der Stämme Israels" (Ex. xxiv 4b; Dtn. i 23; 1 Reg. xviii 31–32a; Jos. iv). Noch in einer späten Prophetie wie der Zeichenhandlung mit den zwei Stäben Ez. xxxvii 15–28 wird die Einteilung nach Nordreich und Südreich erst nachträglich von den Stämmen überlagert.

Das bedeutet nicht, die Bedeutung regionaler Einheiten für die

---

[37] Aufgewiesen bereits von H. Gunkel, "Die Komposition der Joseph-Geschichten", *ZDMG* 76 (1922), pp. 55–71.

[38] Auch Am. v 6, 15, vi 6 und Ob. 18 sind spät. "Amos hat das Nordreich nie 'Joseph' genannt" (H.W. Wolff, *Dodekapropheton 2* [Neukirchen-Vluyn, 1969], p. 295).

Geschichte Israels und Judas zu leugnen. Schon die Landschaft Palä-
stinas erzwang eine beträchtliche lokale Eigenständigkeit, die sich auch
unter den Bedingungen des Königtums hielt. Indessen fragt sich sehr,
ob "Stamm" für diesen Sachverhalt die zutreffende Kategorie ist.
Daß es vor dem Aufkommen des Königtums so etwas wie ein ver-
faßtes Israel gegeben hat, davon fehlt in den alten Quellen jede Spur.[39]

Das System der zwölf Stämme Israels ist Fiktion. Es gehört "in
das große Unternehmen . . ., dem exilisch-nachexilischen Judentum
eine für seinen Bestand und sein Wesen maßgebende israelitische
Vergangenheit zu geben".[40] Es spiegelt eine Zeitlage, in der die fa-
miliäre Herkunft an die Stelle von Staat und Gesellschaft getreten
ist: Jahwe, der Gott Israels, ist zum Gott der Väter geworden. Unter
diesen Umständen erhielt die Genealogie für das Selbstverständnis
des Gottesvolkes eine Bedeutung, die sie zuvor nicht besaß. Das System
der zwölf Stämme Israels gehört ziemlich von Anfang an in die "genealogische Vorhalle" der Chronik.

---

[39] Das Debora-Lied Jdc. v, das als Gegenargument angeführt werden könnte (cf.
aber Noth, p. 5: "Dieses Lied kann mit der Tradition von einem Stämmesystem
überhaupt nicht in Zusammenhang gebracht werden"), ist eines der spätesten
Stücke der vorderen Propheten. Es ist nachträglich in das Richterbuch eingeschoben; denn es wird von dem deuteronomistischen Rahmen nicht eingeschlossen, sondern unterbricht ihn zwischen iv 24 und v 31b. Ps. lxviii, der zu Anfang zitiert ist,
bildet das unentbehrliche poetische Gerüst. Daß die Marginalglosse *zh syny* aus Ps.
lxviii 9 mit übernommen ist, beweist die literarische Abhängigkeit. Die Sprache ist
spät, wie die Aramaismen belegen.

[40] R. Smend, *Zur ältesten Geschichte Israels* (München, 1987), p. 10.

GENÈSE XVIII–XIX: PRÉSENCE OU REPRÉSENTATION DE YAHVÉ? ESSAI SUR LA CRITIQUE LITTÉRAIRE ET LA SIGNIFICATION DU RÉCIT

par

JOSÉ LOZA
Jérusalem

Gen. xviii–xix est un texte fascinant: les interprétations de l'exégèse, juive ou chrétienne, ancienne, médiévale et moderne, en sont la preuve. Le récit forme bien un ensemble: pas de division dans le TM, et le texte compte exactement mille mots.

Néanmoins, des surprises attendent ici le lecteur. Un seul exemple en guise d'introduction: si c'est Yhwh qui apparaît à Abraham (xviii 1a), quel rapport a-t-il avec les "trois hommes" qu'Abraham aperçoit près de lui (v. 2)? Yhwh est-il l'un des trois? On le croirait, car Abraham, au v. 3, s'adresse à un seul, et, après le repas, ce sont ses visiteurs, puis l'un d'eux, enfin explicitement Yhwh, qui lui parlent; *wy'mrw* (v. 9), *wy'mr* (v. 10), *wy'mr yhwh* (v. 13; cf. 17). Au moment du départ, il s'agit encore des "hommes" (v. 16). Peu après il est clair que deux sont partis vers Sodome (v. 22a). On dira plus loin qu'ils sont des *ml'kym* (xix 1, 15). Yhwh était resté auprès d'Abraham (xviii 22b) avant de partir à son tour (v. 33a).

Que Yhwh soit l'un des trois est la perspective du texte actuel, mais elle ne fait qu'estomper les problèmes. Certains d'entre eux sont importants: pourquoi Yhwh ne va-t-il pas à Sodome, comme il en avait l'intention (xviii 21)? À qui donc Lot va-t-il présenter sa requête? Pourquoi son interlocuteur, qui répond comme s'il était seul, a-t-il ou s'arroge-t-il tout pouvoir (xix 18–22)? On le voit, la présence directe de Yhwh parmi les "trois hommes" ne prouve pas l'homogénéité du récit. Souvent discuté par la critique moderne, le problème littéraire subsiste: ce sera notre premier point. Le second point proposera un bref *essai de solution*.

I. Le problème littéraire[1]

(a) *Doublets*

Si les doublets précis, les redites inutiles, sont le premier et le plus important des critères d'analyse, il est pratiquement absent de Gen. xviii–xix. Je signalerai pourtant: (1) le double *wy'mrw* en xix 9; (2) deux appositions en xix 4 et 9; (3) une répétition presque littérale en xix 20; (4) xix 29 comme résumé de l'ensemble précédent;[2] (5) le double *wyšb* de xix 30, où l'alternance *bhr* et *bm'rh* pourrait refléter une double tradition.

(b) *Tensions et oppositions*

Richter énumère trois éléments d'analyse 1° données contradictoires, qui par conséquent s'excluent; 2° noms de personnes ou de lieux entre lesquels il existe une tension, inexplicable si l'auteur est unique; 3° ruptures de syntaxe, surtout changement du nombre, passage du sg. au pl. ou vice-versa, si le contexte n'explique le phénomène. Mais, note Richter, "À lui seul, ... s'il n'est pas accompagné par d'autres critères, cet indice ne suffit pas pour donner une base solide au travail de la critique littéraire ([n. 1] p. 59).

Retenons cette mise en garde, mais constatons aussi que le changement du nombre, *en apparence*[3] non motivé, apparaît tout au long du récit. Peut-on l'expliquer autrement qu'en supposant deux versions artificiellement unifiées au stade rédactionnel? Avant de répondre à cette question, vérifions le phénomène, critère secondaire peut-être, mais qui nous fournit l'occasion de lire rapidement le texte.

1. Changement de nombre

Situons le problème du changement de nombre. La première phrase du récit (xviii 1) est une déclaration solennelle sur une apparition de Yhwh. Le lecteur attend la suite. Au *v.* 2 il est déjà dérouté: quel rapport y a-t-il entre l'apparition de Yhwh et la rencontre de "trois

---

[1] Je m'inspire pour la première partie de W. Richter, *Exegese als Literaturwissenschaft* (Göttingen, 1971), pp. 51–72, mais j'y renvoie uniquement quand je le cite textuellement.

[2] Mais ici il y a un point de vue différent; c'est un texte plus récent inséré dans un contexte littéraire antérieur.

[3] Je souligne "en apparence" parce que le fait peut être expliqué différemment. Nous ne pouvons pas supposer d'avance qu'il n'est pas motivé.

hommes"? Il poursuit sa lecture et en vient à formuler l'explication: les discours au pluriel, qu'Abraham adresse aux "hommes" ou leur attribue, vont de pair avec la narration de la rencontre avec les "trois"; les discours au singulier, qu'Abraham adresse à son interlocuteur (cf. *v.* 3) ou que celui-ci lui adresse, sont en relation avec YHWH. Je simplifie: ce que je dis vaut surtout pour xviii 1–15. La réalité est plus complexe et cette complexité est à la source des positions diffé-rentes.[4] Supposer deux apparitions distinctes et simultanées (exégèse rabbinique) n'est certes pas la seule solution possible, mais celle-ci a le mérite de souligner où est le problème. Le texte actuel ferait pen-ser que YHWH se trouve parmi les "trois". Les indications de xviii 22b et 33, en relation avec xix 1, 15 où les "deux" sont des *ml'kym*, sont claires à cet égard. Cette perspective est-elle la seule? N'y eut-il pas des étapes antérieures dont la perspective était différente? Com-mençons par la présentation des données:[5]

Singulier: xviii 1, 3, 10, 13–15, 17, 19–21, 22b–33, xix 17b, 18b (?), 19, 21, 22, 24, 25, (29)

Pluriel: xviii 2, 4, 5, 8, 9, 16, 22a; xix 1–5, 8–13, 15–17a, 18a, 18b(?)

Le problème principal est de déterminer quelle est la relation entre YHWH et les "hommes". J'énumère les questions importantes: 1° YHWH est-il toujours le sujet implicite des verbes au singulier (cf. xviii 10, xix 17b, 18b (?), 19, 21–2)? 2° Les "hommes" sont "trois" en xviii 2 et dans tout le chapitre; en xix 1 ils ne sont plus que "deux". YHWH est bien resté avec Abraham (xviii 22b–33a), mais ne se proposait-il pas d'aller voir ce qu'il en était du péché de Sodome (xviii 21)? 3° Les "deux" sont *ml'kym* en xix 1, 15, titre de fonction qui n'apparaît pas auparavant; au ch. xix, d'ordinaire, on les nomme simplement "hommes". Ce *ml'kym* ne serait-il pas l'indice d'une harmonisation rédactionnelle présupposant qu'on avait déjà identifié YHWH à l'un des "trois"? Si YHWH ne descend pas à Sodome, comment expliquer le singulier en xix 17 22?

2. Tensions et oppositions

La critique littéraire doit considérer les faits suivants:

1° Rappelons le problème de la relation: YHWH/"hommes"/*ml'kym*;

---

[4] L'histoire de la recherche sera esquissée plus loin.

[5] Je mets entre parenthèses xix 29 pour des raisons que j'expliquerai par la suite.

ces derniers peuvent être trois ou deux. Quelle relation conservent-ils avec Yhwh ou celui-ci est-il l'un des "trois"?

2° Pourquoi Yhwh parle-t-il (xviii 13) de lui à la troisième personne (v. 14a)? Plus loin on lui attribue un discours (cf. 17a) dans lequel, contrairement à 17b–19a, 19b parle de l'action de Yhwh à la 3e personne. Notre logique n'est peut-être pas celle du texte, mais la question doit être posée.

3° Le châtiment de Sodome est une décision arrêtée à cause du péché des habitants (xviii 17b, 22b–32). Ailleurs, on en est encore au stade de l'enquête préliminaire: Yhwh veut établir si la "rumeur" du péché des villes (Sodome et Gomorrhe), arrivée jusqu'à lui, est fondée (vv. 20–1). S'il faut enquêter, xix 4–11 serait la constatation positive de la faute (xiii 13 en était l'anticipation narrative). Mais il y a une divergence importante entre xviii 20–1 et xix 4–11: dans le premier cas Yhwh se proposait de mener personnellement l'enquête (v. 21), dans le second ce sont les "deux envoyés" qui se rendront compte de la méchanceté des habitants de Sodome. Pourquoi ce changement? Si l'on souligne que ce sont seulement les deux qui sont allés à Sodome, ne serait-ce pas parce que Yhwh est resté avec Abraham?

La conséquence de la constatation du péché serait le discours des deux à Lot (xix 12–13). Notons ici une autre différence: au v. 13 les deux s'attribuent la future destruction. Or, la suite du récit ne dit pas qu'elle est leur œuvre. Elle est l'œuvre de Yhwh (xix 14, 24–5, cf. 21–2, mais ici le sujet, au sg., n'est pas exprimé). C'est encore le point de vue du v. 29, qui attribue la destruction à Elohîm (pour ne rien dire des échos de la destruction dans l'AT et le NT).

4° Il y a dans le récit une différence sensible de représentation: ici (v.g. xviii 1–16, sauf la et 14a), des traits concrets et anthropomorphiques, là (22b–33a), un passage théologiquement très développé. Si Yhwh est l'un des trois (v. 1a), il a participé au repas offert par Abraham (v. 8)[6] aux "trois hommes" (v. 2). Aux vv. 20–1 Yhwh "descend" pour voir si la "rumeur" qui est lui parvenue est fondée (cf. Gen. iii 9–10 et xi 5, 7).

D'autres indications vont en sens différent. Yhwh, à qui Abraham adresse sa prière pour Sodome (vv. 23–32) n'est rien de moins que

---

Pour Gen. xix 18b, je mets un point d'interrogation parce que l'on peut hésiter pour savoir où le classer.

[6] Le scrupule de la tradition juive ancienne (cf. targumîm), est fort compréhensible. D'où "ils faisaient comme s'ils mangeaient" pour "ils mangèrent".

"le juge de toute la terre" (*v.* 25). Devant lui un homme, fût-il Abraham, l'"ami de Dieu",[7] n'est que "poussière et cendre" (*v.* 27). Abraham ne lui parle qu'avec crainte et tremblement (cf. *vv.* 27, 30a, 31a, 32a). Bref, parfois le style est concret, pittoresque, anecdotique, parfois nettement abstrait et théologique.

5° Certains commentateurs[8] s'étonnent que le texte ne mentionne pas la femme de Lot avant xix 26. Pourtant, la mention, même générale (15b–16a), l'emporte sur l'absence jugée inexplicable. La femme de Lot n'est pas un personnage de l'action, sauf au *v.* 26. S'il existe ici un problème, c'est celui de savoir si l'épisode du *v.* 26 faisait partie du récit principal transmis par la tradition, ou s'il s'agit d'une tradition particulière, ce qui n'est pas impensable.

6° Certains auteurs[9] découvrent en xix 17–23 (ou 18–23) des indices d'un développement tardif de la tradition voire d'une addition littéraire récente. Énumérons-les, même s'ils sont de valeur inégale:

* L'ordre de chercher refuge dans la montagne vient trop tard: il est donné à Lot pendant qu'on le fait sortir (xix 17a), alors que 16 présentait cette action comme achevée.

* Lot doit chercher refuge dans la montagne (*v.* 17). Auparavant, la consigne était vague: sortir (*v.* 12b et 14a).

* En xix, ce n'est qu'ici que nous retrouvons le changement pluriel-singulier. Mais une question se pose: ne serait-ce pas que, avant l'insertion de l'intercession d'Abraham (xviii 22b–33a, avec 17–19), les trois allaient à Sodome, comme Yhwh avait manifesté l'intention, tandis que les "deux envoyés" (xix 1, 15) émaneraient d'un remaniement postérieur? Nous ne pouvons pas encore écarter la possibilité d'un récit ancien qui aurait parlé d'une manière homogène de "trois hommes", quoi qu'il en soit de leur relation avec Yhwh.

* Lot ira finalement à la montagne (*v.* 30). Les répétitions de ce verset viendraient du rapiéçement nécessaire après le détour par Soar.

* La fille aînée de Lot parle d'impossibilité d'avoir une descendance (*v.* 31). Qu'est devenue la ville épargnée pour que Lot puisse s'y sauver? Par ailleurs, le comportement de Lot est contradictoire: d'abord il ne veut pas aller à la montagne; quand ses souhaits se réalisent et que Soar est sauvée, il abandonne Soar et part à la montagne.

---

[7] Voir Isa. xli 8 avec note de la *TOB*.
[8] Cf. H. Gunkel, *Genesis* (Göttingen, 1910³), p. 206.
[9] Cf. récemment W. Zimmerli, *1. Mose 12–25* (Zürich, 1976), p. 86.

xix 17–23 est-il un ajout? On l'a pensé moins fréquemment que pour xviii 17–19, 22b–33a. Ne peut-on pas expliquer les choses autrement, par exemple par l'histoire de la tradition?

3. Problèmes mineurs de cohérence

xix 24 Après Yhwh comme sujet, on ne s'attend guère à *m't yhwh*. Et ce complément semble inséparable de *mn-hšmym*, d'où la tendance à considérer l'ensemble de 24b comme secondaire.

xix 25 Le verbe est suivi d'une série de 4 compléments qui énumèrent les effets de la catastrophe, avec *'t* les trois premiers cas, sans *'t*. le 4e. Par ailleurs, *kl* qualifie le 2e et le 3e, mais non le 1er et le 4e.

Ce verset parle aussi de Gomorrhe (cf. *vv.* 24 et 28). Nous devons regarder de près les données concernant les villes détruites: 1° La narration parle normalement de Sodome seule. Cela vaut pour le départ (xviii 16, 22a) et pour l'intercession d'Abraham (*vv.* 24–32) où un simple *šm* reprend *'yr/mqwm*. Cela vaut aussi pour xix 1, 4, 12–17. Mais on ne parle pas directement de la destruction. 2° Outre xix 24–5, 28, Gomorrhe apparaît seulement en xviii 20–1. Mais là le *v.* 21 n'a plus en vue qu'une seule ville: *hkṣ'qth* fait penser que c'est le péché de Sodome qui préoccupe. 3° En sens contraire, les échos de l'anéantissement en dehors de notre récit mentionnent plusieurs villes, surtout Sodome et Gomorrhe.[10]

Comment expliquer ces faits? La tradition est complexe. La mention explicite de Sodome tient au fait que Lot y résidait. Les témoignages extérieurs au récit portent à croire que Gomorrhe a pu être ajoutée en fonction de la tradition. Mais ce n'est pas la seule explication possible. Le problème est d'histoire de la tradition plutôt que de critique littéraire. À celle-ci, en Gen. xviii–xix, la mention des villes n'apporte guère de lumière.

xix 27–8 Les remarques faites (ou encore à faire) pour considérer xviii 22b–33a comme ajout au récit primitif montrent que le passage a été remanié: il suppose le ch. xviii sous sa forme finale. La référence de 27b est particulièrement claire. Mais tout n'y est pas secondaire.

---

[10] Cf. note de la Bible de Jérusalem à Gen. xix 1 qui cite tous les textes bibliques.

(c) *Remarques stylistiques*

"Un signe de la non-unité d'un texte est la prédominance dans l'une de ses parties de lexèmes abstraits, à la différence d'une autre qui ne contient que des lexèmes concrets." Richter ajoute qu'il faut rester dans le domaine purement littéraire pour ce type d'observations ([n. 1] pp. 60–1). Je précise les observations déjà faites.

xviii 1–16 Le style est concret, pittoresque, anecdotique, même pour la promesse d'un fils (*vv.* 10a, 14b). Nous sommes loin des promesses d'une descendance nombreuse (cf. 18), même si l'on passe logiquement de l'une à l'autre. Deux expressions feraient exception 1° le début du récit (*v.* 1a); 2° le *v.* 14a.

Gunkel ([n. 8] p. 193) considérait la première expression comme une clé d'interprétation théologique comparable à xxii 1a^b. Récemment W.H. Schmidt[11] la compare à Ex iii 2a: il y a réinterprétation du récit du buisson par le *ml'k* (2a) et de la visite des "trois" par la. Il reste à déterminer si cette réinterprétation faisait partie du premier texte écrit. Dans ce cas elle échapperait à la critique littéraire.

Le *v.* 14a est-il une addition? Le doute de Sara explique la réaction de Yhwh. Néanmoins les parallèles (surtout Jer. xxxii 17) permettent de supposer que l'expression a été ajoutée tardivement.

xviii 22a, 33b Les notices sur le départ sont semblables à 1–16. Elles ont été dédoublées à cause de l'addition de 22b–33a. Mais les verbes ont été soigneusement choisis pour éviter la répétition littérale: *wyqmw-wyšqpw* (*v.* 16) / *wypnw-wylkw* (*v.* 22a). Le seul signe rédactionnel en 16, 22a et 33 serait l'indication de la direction (*'l-pny-sdm*, *v.* 16a, et *sdmh*, *v.* 22a) et le dédoublement entre *wylkw* (*v.* 22a) et *wylk yhwh* (*v.* 33a). En toute hypothèse 33b complète les indications de 16 et 22a.

xviii 17–19 Le style est abstrait avec prédominance des formules, surtout "peuple grand et nombreux" (*v.* 18a); "en lui se béniront tous les peuples de la terre" (*v.* 18b); "je l'ai connu" ("distingué"; *v.* 19a); "pour qu'il commande" (*v.* 19a); "pour qu'ils gardent le chemin de Yhwh" (*v.* 19a); "en faisant justice et droit" (*v.* 19a); "pour que Yhwh fasse venir sur Abraham ce qu'il lui a promis" (*v.* 19b).

Ces formules ont une forte saveur théologique. Et l'introduction solennelle souligne aussi l'importance du discours divin. Le *v.* 17b est très proche d'une conception prophétique du rôle d'Abraham. Le

---

[11] *Exodus* (Neukirchen, 1988), pp. 112–13 et 120–1.

texte le plus significatif est Amos iii 3–8, surtout *v.* 7. Ce verset est probablement un ajout deutéronomiste. En Gen. xviii 17–19 la promesse à Abraham est conditionnée. Le monologue divin est donc récent. Avec l'intercession d'Abraham, il relève d'un courant théologique proche des deutéronomistes.

xviii 20–1 Si "rumeur" et "péché" sont des termes abstraits, théologiques, deux indices favorisent l'attribution au récit traditionnel: 1° le châtiment n'est pas encore décidé, à la différence des *vv.* 17b et 22b–33a (surtout 23b–25); 2° on en est encore au stade d'un projet divin (*v.* 21), d'une enquête que Yhwh se propose de faire. Nous en avons signalé le caractère très concret, anthropomorphique même.

xviii 22b–33a La première intervention d'Abraham situe le débat sur un plan juridique quant au langage, théologique quant au contenu. Le fond du problème est la légitimité de la manière d'agir de Yhwh dans l'anéantissement de *la* ville (Sodome; cf. *mqwm* avec une signification ordinaire) où habite Lot. La phraséologie le montre clairement: "faire périr ("mourir") le juste avec le méchant" (*vv.* 23b, 25a) et "le sort du juste sera comme celui du méchant" (*v.* 25a). Elle est renforcée par une série d'expressions: la question "est-ce que tu feras périr?" (*v.* 24b), les mentions des "justes", dont le nombre varie à chaque reprise, "pardonner" (*vv.* 24b et 26b, ensuite sous-entendu), *ḥllh lk* adressé à Yhwh (*v.* 25), "juge de toute la terre (*v.* 25b), "faire justice" (*v.* 25b).

Le problème ainsi posé fonde les *vv.* 25–32, mais d'autres aspects sont à souligner, surtout la forte opposition entre celui qui se déclare "poussière et cendre" (*v.* 27b) et celui qu'il nomme *ʾadōnāy* (*vv.* 27b, 30a, 31a, 32a). Les demandes successives d'Abraham sont faites "avec crainte et tremblement" (*vv.* 27b, [29a], 30a, 31a, 32a).

Sauf 22a et 33, il n'y a aucun développement narratif. Les verbes au wayyiqtôl n'ont d'autre fonction que d'introduire les discours (*wyʾmr*). L'"action" est dans le dialogue.

xix 1–28, 30–8 Ce chapitre est une unité, le *v.* 29 mis à part. Stylistiquement parlant, le récit est concret et pittoresque, comme en xviii 1–16, 22a, 33b. La part respective de la narration et du discours direct semble proportionnée. Il y a de petites touches théologiques, comme: *mlʾkym* (*vv.* 1 et 15) avec le verbe *šlḥ* (*v.* 13b), méchanceté ou péché des habitants de Sodome (surtout *v.* 7), "rumeur" (*v.* 13b; cf. xviii 20–1) avec l'idée d'une destruction de Sodome (et Gomorrhe) à cause de la méchanceté des habitants, requête de Lot pour Soar. Ces touches clairsemées n'infirment pas notre jugement d'ensemble. Dans un récit neutre déjà constitué, la présence d'ajouts rédactionnels est difficilement concevable.[12] La manière dont les éléments traditionnels[13] ont pu être intégrés dans le récit a peut-être été faite différente: les *vv.* 4–11 contiennent un jugement de valeur très sévère, mais rien n'est directement dit des filles de Lot (30–8).[14]

xix 29 Ce résumé n'est pas nécessaire. C'est en considération d'Abraham que Lot et les siens sont sauvés de la catastrophe, idée nouvelle dans le récit. Le nom divin *ʾelōhîm* n'apparaît qu'ici, indice insuffisant en soi, mais qui vient en confirmer d'autres: que ce résumé soit de P ou d'un rédacteur (P[s] ou R[p]), le vocabulaire et les perspectives théologiques y sont sacerdotales.

(d) *Les petites unités*

L'analyse devrait permettre d'isoler les "petites unités" et d'établir leur relation. Pour cela on doit déterminer ce qui va et ce qui ne peut pas aller ensemble.

Une remarque préalable s'impose: le changement du nombre ne peut pas être utilisé ici; il doit être expliqué autrement que par l'origine littéraire différente.

1° Les "petites unités" semblent être les suivantes: xviii 1–13,[15] 14a,[16] 14b–16, 17–19, 20–22a,[17] 22b–3a,[18] 33b; xix 1–24a,[19] 24b, 25–6,[20] 27a, 27b, 28;[21] 29, 30–8.[22]

2° Lesquelles de ces petites unités vont ensemble? Je proposerais:

---

[12] Je ne reviens pas sur le problème de 17–23.

[13] Je suppose sans prouver, mais je garde l'expression malgré tout.

[14] Mais ce que l'on raconte de peu glorieux sur l'origine de ses voisins peut joindre jugement moral et raillerie.

[15] Nous avons dit que la ne peut pas être considéré comme ajout.

[16] Ici il y a réinterprétation rédactionnelle.

[17] La portée théologique n'est pas une raison suffisante pour séparer 20–1 du contexte narratif (16, 22a, 33b).

[18] 33a fait partie de l'intercession d'Abraham. Si 22b–32 oblige à séparer les hommes qui partent (22a) de YHWH qui reste (22b), son départ doit être relaté.

[19] Nous avons posé la question de savoir si 17–23 (ou 18–23) pourrait être secondaire (avec un remaniement du *v.* 30). Les indices semblent insuffisants. Par contre, 24b est un ajout.

[20] Je ne vois pas de raison suffisante pour séparer la notice de 26 du contexte littéraire actuel.

[21] Ce verset fait partie du récit ancien. Si 27 est considéré comme ajout, il manque un sujet, Abraham (après le premier *wayyiqṭôl*). C'est l'addition totale ou partielle de 27 qui a rendu sa mention inutile.

[22] Y a-t-il des éléments rédactionnels au *v.* 30? Voir n. 19.

Récit de base: xviii 1–13, 14b–16, 20–22a, 33b, xix 1–24a, 25–6, 27a, 28, 30–8.

Intercession d'Abraham: xviii 17–19, 22b–33a, xix 27b.

Résumé tardif: xix 29.

Additions: xviii 14a, xix 24b.[23]

II. Essai de solution

Je résume les points de vue exprimés et je donne un aperçu de ma solution.

1. *Solutions proposées*

1° Le plus simple est de prendre la narration comme elle se présente. Si l'on admet la critique littéraire (et l'hypothèse documentaire comme solution aux problèmes du Pentateuque), on dira qu'un seul verset (xix 29) a été ajouté par P à un récit unitaire. Les différences s'expliqueraient par le décalage entre tradition reçue et formulation écrite.[24]

Solution de facilité, elle n'explique pas les problèmes du texte. Elle part d'une idée préconçue sur la nature et les caractéristiques littéraires et théologiques de la source Yahviste à laquelle le récit est attribué. On propose la date la plus haute possible.

2° D'autres prêtent une attention primordiale au changement de nombre. Le texte serait le résultat de la fusion rédactionnelle de deux versions autonomes; l'une d'elles était rédigée systématiquement au pluriel, l'autre au singulier. Proposée d'abord par R. Kraetzschmar,[25] cette solution est suivie par les auteurs qui maintiennent l'existence de deux sources autonomes dans les textes yahvistes.[26]

La solution a le défaut de séparer des éléments qui ne forment pas un récit complet. Parfois on opère de nombreux changements ou l'on élimine des expressions pour chercher la cohérence. La logique qu'on veut imposer aux textes est-elle bien celle des auteurs bibliques?

---

[23] Il faut y ajouter *hml'kym* en xix 1, 15, avec la précision du *v.* 1 (ils ne sont plus que "deux").

[24] G. von Rad, *Genesis* (Göttingen, 1971⁹), pp. 160, 175, parmi d'autres.

[25] "Der Mythos von Sodoms Ende", *ZAW* 17 (1897), pp. 81–92; cf. M.-J. Lagrange, "L'ange de Iahve", *RB* 12 (1903), pp. 212–25 (p. 220).

[26] R. Smend, *Die Erzählung des Hexateuch auf ihre Quellen untersucht* (Berlin, 1912); O. Eissfeldt, *Hexateuch-Synopse* (Leipzig, 1922/Darmstadt, 1962); R.H. Pfeiffer, "A Non-Israelitic Source of the Book of Genesis", *ZAW*, 48 (1930), pp. 66–73; *Introduction to the Old Testament* (Londres, 1953/1948²); (E. Sellin-) G. Fohrer, *Einleitung in das Alte Testament* (Heidelberg, 1965¹⁰).

3° Les solutions de R. Kilian et E. Haag font intervenir J, tout en essayant de répondre aux problèmes spécifiques. Pour Kilian,[27] il y a eu un récit pré-J très ample. J en a repris l'essentiel et l'a complété. Les pluriels correspondraient au récit pré-J et les singuliers à J. Il y a une différence importante par rapport aux auteurs du n° 2: Kilian ne propose pas deux versions autonomes. Il y a une source, J, mais l'auteur disposait d'un récit antérieur. Il ne change pas la formulation au pluriel, mais il ajoute des compléments au singulier.

Haag[28] présente une solution similaire. À l'exception d'un verset de P (xix 29) et des ajouts tardifs, les deux chapitres ont été composés en deux étapes. La première comprend deux brefs récits (Abraham à Mamré; Sodome); sans relation entre eux, ils faisaient partie de l'œuvre de J. R^je les reprend et les amplifie notablement.

L'analyse de Kilian et de Haag a des aperçus valables, mais le découpage atomisant n'est pas justifié.

4° La meilleure explication du texte écrit est d'admettre *un récit de base avec des compléments et des additions*. Plusieurs orientations sont possibles:

(a) E.I. Fripp[29] propose un *récit au singulier*. Il obtient la cohérence par de nombreux changements (cf. Kraetzschmar [n. 5], pp. 81–2). Il n'explique pas pourquoi un rédacteur se serait amusé à introduire les "hommes" et à changer, incomplètement, le nombre des verbes.

(b) Pour Gunkel il y aurait un *récit au pluriel* ([n. 8] in loc.). La formulation primitive a été altérée par des changements du pluriel au singulier et par des additions.

La solution de Gunkel a l'avantage de la cohérence et peut s'expliquer à partir du texte actuel, mais la reconstruction du texte primitif est conjecturale. Ici nous n'avons pas affaire à un pieux israélite qui aurait essayé de cacher YHWH derrière les "trois hommes", mais à un texte qui a une histoire; elle explique l'identification de plus en plus claire de YHWH avec l'un des trois. La séparation des deux, qui vont à Sodome, et de YHWH, qui reste avec Abraham, fait partie du processus. Gunkel a bien vu les problèmes et la direction que doit prendre l'essai de solution. Mais sa solution n'est pas la bonne. On peut expliquer les choses autrement.

---

[27] *Die vorpriesterliche Abrahamsüberlieferungen* (Bonn, 1966).

[28] "Abraham und Lot in Genesis xviii–xix", *Mélanges Bibliques et Orientaux H. Cazelles* (Kevelaer-Neukirchen, 1981), pp. 173–99.

[29] "A Note on Genesis xviii–xix, *ZAW* 12 (1892), pp. 23–9.

(c) Il reste à supposer un *récit non homogène*. Le texte primitif contenait
le changement de nombre. Avec des différences, c'était la position des principaux représentants de l'hypothèse documentaire à
ses débuts.[30] Les auteurs qui l'adoptent par la suite sont nombreux:[31] c'était la solution majoritaire jusqu'à récemment. Le
changement du nombre n'est pas un indice de critique littéraire.
C'est un problème qui doit avoir une solution: ou le pluriel est
un fait de tradition, mais l'auteur du récit primitif identifie YHWH
avec l'un des trois, ce qui explique le changement, ou il n'y a pas
d'identification de YHWH avec l'un des trois et ce sont les additions qui font l'identification. Il reste la question de la relation
des "trois" avec YHWH.

Les différences de nombre et celles entre un récit assez neutre
et des passages où le processus de théologisation est plus évident
s'expliqueraient par la dualité entre tradition reçue et perspective
de l'auteur littéraire. Le récit serait de J.

5° La critique récente, dans la mesure où des positions différentes de
celles de la "critique classique" se manifestent, s'est peu occupée de
Gen. xviii–xix. L'analyse de Haag est symptomatique; la part de J
est considérablement diminuée et le récit serait l'œuvre d'un auteur-
rédacteur postérieur, R^{je}.

L'analyse de E. Blum est la plus significative.[32] Ses résultats sont
similaires à ceux de la critique classique. Mais il simplifie l'hypothèse
documentaire et tente une datation différente des étapes de la composition de Gen. xii–l.

---

[30] J. Wellhausen, *Die Composition des Hexateuchs und der Historischen Bücher des Alten
Testaments* (Berlin, 1899³ / 1963⁶); A. Kuenen, *Historisch-kritisch Onderzoek*... (1885²;
traduction allemande 1886, anglaise 1887) I; H. Holzinger, *Einleitung in den Hexateuch*
(Freiburg-Leipzig, 1893); *Genesis* (Tübingen, 1922⁴); W.E. Addis, *The Documents of the
Hexateuch* I–II (Londres, 1892–8); J.E. Carpenter-G. Harford-Battersby, *The Hexateuch
Arranged in Its Constituent Documents* I–II (Londres, 1900); J. Skinner, *Genesis* (Edinburgh,
1910); C. Steuernagel, *Lehrbuch der Einleitung in das Alte Testament* (Tübingen, 1912);
cf. déja *Deuteronomium/Josua/Allgemeine Einleitung in den Hexateuch* (Göttingen, 1900).
Pour les auteurs antérieurs les résumés de Holzinger sont très pratiques.
[31] M. Noth, *Überlieferungsgeschichte des Pentateuch* (Stuttgart, 1948); H. Cazelles, "Pentateuque", *DBS* VII (1966) ou *Il Pentateuco* (Brescia, 1968); "La Torâh ou Pentateuque", dans *Introduction critique à l'Ancien Testament (Introduction à la Bible)* (éd. nouvelle,
Paris, 1973); H. Schulte, ... *bis auf diesen Tag. Der Text des Jahwisten* (Hambourg,
1967); *Die Entstehung der Geschichtsschreibung im Alten Israel* (BZAW 128; Berlin, 1972);
Zimmerli, (n. 9): C. Westermann, *Genesis 2* (Neukirchen, 1981); W.H. Schmidt,
Einführung in das Alte Testament (Berlin-New York, 1982²); O. Kaiser, *Einleitung in das
Alte Testament* (Gütersloh, 1984⁵); J. Scharbert, *Genesis 12–50* (Würzburg, 1986).
[32] *Die Komposition der Vätergeschichte* (Neukirchen, 1984).

On doit renoncer aux sources classiques. Il y a seulement deux étapes. La première est antérieure au Deutéronome (*Vätergeschichte* 1); la deuxième subit déjà l'influence deutéronomique (sa *Vätergeschichte* 2) et se situe vers l'époque de l'exil ou après. Ces étapes sont complexes. La *Vätergeschichte* 1 comprend une "période israélite" (Royaume du Nord), antérieure à 721 av. J.-C., et une "période judéenne," de peu postérieure. Au deuxième stade, on aurait ajouté au vieux fonds narratif judéen, pour Gen. xii–xxv essentiellement l'histoire d'Abraham et Lot (Gen. xiii* et xviii*–xix*). S'il y avait un "Yahviste", mais Blum refuse le nom même, il se situerait à la fin du VIIIᵉ s. ou dans la première moitié du VIIᵉ av. J.C.

2. *Mon point de vue*

Je ne fais que quelques remarques à propos des questions les plus importantes, mais elles signalent l'orientation; elles doivent être développées.

1º Le récit de base identifie-t-il Yhwh avec l'un des "trois" ou les trois ensemble représentent-ils Yhwh? Les commentateurs modernes sont partagés: s'ils sont nombreux à maintenir la deuxième possibilité, beaucoup, pour différentes raisons,[33] identifient Yhwh avec l'un des trois.

2º Y a-t-il une autre explication? On peut en imaginer beaucoup. Outre un vieux fonds polythéiste, la tradition juive tentait de résoudre les problèmes en distinguant entre une apparition divine et l'envoi de trois anges. Le va-et-vient entre les deux explique le changement de nombre.

3º Peut-on montrer avec des arguments que le récit primitif parlait partout de "trois hommes" et qu'il n'y avait pas identification, mais représentation corporative de Yhwh? Je le crois. Qu'ils soient trois dépend d'une ancienne tradition narrative méditerranéenne.[34] Ce type de représentation est connu dans le cas du *ml'k yhwh/'lhym*. Certes, le titre de *ml'kym* en xix 1, 15 est tardif: les "trois hommes" de xviii 2[35] sont devenus deux *ml'kym*, mais une conception analogue permet de

---

[33] Deux sont importantes: le poids de la tradition et l'attribution à J de xviii 17–19, 22b–33a.
[34] Nous ne pouvons développer ce point.
[35] Nous savons que l'ajout de xviii 17–19, 22b–23a est à la source de cet ajustement.

parler d'une pluralité agissant et parlant au nom de YHWH. Le narrateur simplifie la relation des "trois" avec YHWH: il donne au préalable une clé de lecture (xviii 1a), il présente le geste d'Abraham et le début de son discours (xviii 3) comme si YHWH était présent et non représenté[36] et dans certains discours il est dit en toutes lettres que YHWH parle (xviii [10,] 13, 20). Mais le propre d'un envoyé (ml'k ou même sans ce titre) est de parler au nom d'un autre.[37] Dès lors on peut supposer que YHWH n'est pas présent, qu'il n'est pas l'un des trois, mais qu'il parle par ses représentants.

4° La tradition ne s'est pas arrêtée là. Gen. xviii a grandi, surtout avec le monologue divin (*vv.* 17–19) et l'intercession d'Abraham (*vv.* 22b–33a). Ces ajouts réinterprètent le récit dans le sens d'une identification précise de YHWH avec l'un des trois. Cela exige la distinction: YHWH reste avec Abraham, les deux "hommes", devenus "messagers" (ml'kym; xix 1, 15), vont à Sodome (xviii 22).

---

[36] Il se peut aussi qu'il y ait un ajustement rédactionnel: il suffit de mettre dans la bouche d'Abraham un *ᵃdônây* (*nomen sacrum* pour les massorètes) avec les verbes au singulier. L'hypothèse n'est pas indispensable," ce "Monseigneur, ne passe pas outre . . ." pouvait être adressé à celui des "trois" qui, aux yeux d'Abraham, était le plus important.

[37] Les données sur la pratique humaine où repose la conception du rôle du prophète sont connues. Le rôle du ml'k yhwh/'lhym est similaire. Gen. xix 13 semble être suffisant pour l'affirmer.

BACK TO THE IRON BED: OG'S OR PROCRUSTES'?

by

A.R. MILLARD
Liverpool

The purpose of this article is to consider three matters of material culture, principally in the book of Joshua, and the implications that may follow from our conclusions. The book of Joshua sets the events which it relates at a period commonly placed about 1200 B.C., near to the time when the famous stele of pharaoh Merneptah attests the presence of an entity called Israel in Canaan (c. 1210 B.C). It is the ancient Near East towards the end of the Late Bronze Age, therefore, which gives the primary context.

The archaeologists divide antiquity into ages according to the principal technology for tool-making: Stone, Bronze and Iron. In charts of human history the divisions are often sharp, as if, at a given moment, everyone threw away their stone axes and bought bronze ones, or replaced their bronze knives universally with iron ones. Obviously, that was not the case; stone tools continued long after metal became common, bronze served beside iron for centuries. Contrariwise, there is evidence for some use of metals within the Stone Age, and of iron within the Bronze Age. The latter is our concern here. At the Twelfth Congress, in Jerusalem, I discussed the question of King Og's iron bed and the iron chariots of the Canaanites, arguing that the biblical references could reflect unusual artefacts of the Late Bronze Age.[1] Hardly had that article appeared when Robert Drews proposed an entirely opposite view about the iron chariots: they could only be conceived in terms of 8th-century B.C. Assyrian or even later Persian models.[2] The purpose of the present article is to reinforce the case made in 1986, to consider two other matters of material culture in the book of Joshua, and to explore implications for treatment of the biblical text.

---

[1] "King Og's Bed and Other Ancient Ironmongery", in L. Eslinger and G. Taylor (ed.), *Ascribe to the Lord. Biblical and Other Studies in memory of Peter C. Craigie* (Sheffield, 1988), pp. 481–92.

[2] "The 'Chariots of Iron' of Joshua and Judges", *JSOT* 45 (1989), pp. 15–23.

The iron chariots

Chariots wholly of iron are unlikely; a form of iron plating is the commonly accepted understanding of the Hebrew words in Joshua and Judges (Josh. xvii 16,18; Judg. i 19, iv 3,13). After noting the very lightweight construction of Late Bronze Age chariots found in Egypt, Drews asserted, "iron plating would have immediately collapsed the fragile and flimsy frame" and "an 'iron plated' chariot is thus technological nonsense". Moreover, "nowhere in the ancient world, at any period, are iron plated chariots attested" ([n. 2], p. 18). Initially, the impracticality of iron-plated chariots seems a major objection, but it depends upon the amounts and the application of the iron. Small-scale fittings, holding the axles or hubs, would be insufficient to give a distinctive name to the chariots, so a visible covering of some sort is best envisaged. That it was wholesale plating is not so certain, or necessary. In the Late Bronze Age bronze scales were commonly sewn on to cloth or leather garments to protect men and horses, they even covered helmets, and there are administrative accounts of "hides for the storehouses for the coats of mail (to equip) 20 war chariots".[3] Although iron scale armour is not attested until much later, in neo-Assyrian times,[4] the possibility of an experiment with iron in the 13th or 12th centuries B.C. cannot be ruled out. Whether in plates or scales, the iron would add greatly to the weight of the chariots, as Drews emphasized, yet only in proportion to the amount applied. Three or four thin plates hung over the front to protect the charioteer's legs, which his hauberk did not cover, might have been thought worth the extra load. Once the heavier chariots were moving, they would be hard for opponents, especially foot-soldiers, to withstand. In the relatively rough and uneven terrain of much of Canaan, even in the plains where the iron chariots were stationed, the opportunity for long, fast runs would be limited, unlike Egypt and parts of Syria. Thus iron chariots become intelligible in the contexts where Joshua and Judges place them, and the threat they would pose to the Israelites is seen to be great. The term itself

---

[3] Y. Yadin, *The Art of Warfare in Biblical Lands* (London, 1963), pp. 196–7; T. Kendall, "*gurpišu ša awēli*: The helmets of the Warriors at Nuzi"), in M.A. Morrison and D.I. Owen. (ed), *Studies on the Civilization and Culture of Nuzi and the Hurrians* (Winona Lake, 1981), pp. 201–31. A.T. Clay, *Documents from the temple archives of Nippur dated in the reigns of Cassite rulers* (Philadelphia, 1912), no. 140.25, cited with other cases in *The Assyrian Dictionary* S (Chicago, 1984), p. 314.

[4] M.E.L. Mallowan, *Nimrud and its Remains* (London, 1966), pp. 409–11.

involved a new technology which Israel did not possess. The significance of Deborah luring Sisera with his nine hundred iron chariots
to the Kishon river becomes clearer, for their weight would increase
the difficulty in manoeuvering them on the poorly drained ground.

The amount of iron needed for nine hundred chariots brings another problem. We are told "in the days of Joshua and Deborah—
if we make them historical figures and assign a thirteenth-century
date to the former and a twelfth-century date to the latter—iron was
not yet available in sufficient quantity to have been used for the
plating of chariots" (Drews [n. 2], p. 17). Evidence in support of the
verdict is found in the ratio of 3:147 for iron to bronze weapons and
armour recovered from 12th-century B.C. sites in Palestine, a ratio
which is similar throughout the eastern Mediterranean. Yet the physical
remains have to be set beside the voice of the documents, the textual
references to iron in cuneiform and Egyptian sources. These reveal
a far greater presence of iron objects throughout the Near East in
the Late Bronze Age than the excavated examples indicate, even if
the proportion of iron to bronze remains the same.[5] The majority of
the written records come from the Hittite kingdom, which was the
major source of the metal and iron-working, but there are sufficient
texts from other realms to prove the products, at least, circulated
widely. That they could also circulate in some quantity is plain from
Hittite notes of "56 iron dagger blades" and of an iron tub weighing
ninety minas (about 45 kg.).[6] Hittite power stretched as far as northern Lebanon through most of the 13th century B.C., embracing
Damascus briefly, so its new technology could easily enter the Egyptian province of Canaan. Iron chariots, therefore, whether they carried iron plates or lesser iron reinforcements, cannot be dismissed as
anachronistic for the end of the Late Bronze Age in Canaan.

Flint knives

As iron chariots are out of place in the Late Bronze Age, according
to some scholars, so are the flint blades used for circumcising the
Israelites at Gilgal according to others (Josh. v 2, 3; cf. Ex. iv 25).
"By the time of Joshua, flint tools had been replaced by metal

---

[5] See the material cited in my article (n. 1).
[6] Listed by S. Košak, "The Gospel of Iron", in H.A. Hoffner and G.A. Beckman
(ed.), *Kaniššuwar. A tribute to Hans G. Güterbock on his Seventy-fifth Birthday* (Chicago,
1986), pp. 125–35.

instruments except for such special occasions as the one described
here", said recent commentators, while another observed, "the
Neolithic tool must be used for the archaic operation".[7] Alternatively,
some assume a preference "for materials in the raw state; one might
say as they left the hands of the Creator".[8] The mention of flint
blades in the Late Bronze Age setting Joshua implies, when bronze
was common, easily leads one to suppose they were distinguished
specially. The explanation from religious conservatism is encouraged
by a well-known Egyptian relief carved in the Sixth Dynasty (about
2300 B.C.). Operators are depicted in the act of cutting the foreskins
of youths with carefully made flint knives.[9] That was in the Early
Bronze Age. Although physicians wielded bronze lancets in Hammurabi's day (c. 1792–1750 B.C.; see Hammurabi's Laws paragraphs
215, 218–20), flints were also among their instruments in the first
millennium B.C. An Assyrian medical text prescribes, "you make an
incision in his temple with an obsidian blade and draw blood". Other
Assyrian texts mention flint knives as if they were usual for the slashings
mourners made to display their grief.[10] Here flints were being used
in a less specifically ritual situation, which suggests more mundane
reasons may exist for the Gilgal occasion. At a mass ceremony clean-
liness would be important, to avoid transfer of infection, a principle
recognized in the biblical laws (e.g. Lev. xv) and in some ancient
documents, most famously a letter from Mari of the 18th century
B.C.[11] What simpler means could be conceived than striking sharp
stone flakes which could be used once, then discarded? Indeed, a
freshly broken stone might have a keener edge than an often-used
bronze knife. Flint and other stone tools continued to be made long
after the introduction of copper, bronze, and even iron. They occur

---

[7] J.M. Miller and G.M. Tucker, *The Book of Joshua* (Cambridge, 1974), p. 46; J.P. Brown, "Literary Contexts of Hebrew-Greek Vocabulary", *JSS* 13 (1968), pp. 163–91, see p. 181.

[8] J.A. Soggin, *Joshua. Old Testament Library* (London, 1972), p. 71, following H.W. Hertzberg.

[9] J. Yoyotte in G. Posener (ed.), *Dictionary of Ancient Egyptian Civilization* (London, 1959), pp. 45, 46; for pictures of flints in use in the Middle Kingdom, see F.Ll. Griffith, *Beni Hasan* III, *Archaeological Survey of Egypt*, 5th *Memoir* (London, 1896), pp. 33–38, pls. VII–X; for flint blades from the New Kingdom, see B. Bruyère, *Rapport sur les Fouilles de Deir el Médineh, III, Le Village, Fouilles de l'Institut français du Caire*, XVI (Cairo, 1939), p. 339, pl. XLII, reference supplied by K.A. Kitchen.

[10] See *The Assyrian Dictionary* Ṣ (Chicago, 1962), pp. 257–9, 261, ṣurru and ṣurtu.

[11] G. Dossin and A. Finet, *Correspondance féminine, Archives royales de Mari, textes transcrits et traduits* X, (Paris, 1978), nos 129, 130.

in archaeological strata of the Middle and Late Bronze Ages in Palestine and adjacent lands.[12] In modern times travellers have noted flint blades serving as razors for human beings (in Algeria in the last century[13]) and for shearing sheep. Sir Leonard Woolley recorded an incident when he was working in north Syria in 1912: a sheep-shearer "picked up a couple of large flints, knocked them together and chipped out for himself a perfectly good long flint knife" which was said to be better for the job than iron scissors.[14] Such examples may explain the mention of the stone blades as instruments of circumcision in Joshua and Exodus on a purely practical level.

A Babylonian cloak

Achan's loot from Jericho included "one good *'adderet šin'ār*", usually translated "a beautiful mantle from Shinar" (Josh. vii 21 *Revised Standard Version*). Shinar is certainly a name for Babylonia, a name current in Upper Mesopotamia and Anatolia in the second millennium B.C., continuing in Hebrew as an alternative for Babel, the name originally denoting the town, then by extension the country.[15] In the light of recent remarks about a lack of associations of such a garment with Shinar in other sources,[16] we should give attention to current knowledge of the Babylonian textile business.

Woollen cloth and garments were a staple of Babylonian trade from early times. "The textile industry . . . was probably the largest in the land and the most important from the point of view of commerce" wrote one authority, of the period just after 2000 B.C.[17] In

---

[12] E.g. R. Miller, *Flintknapping and Arrowhead Manufacture at Tell Hadidi, Syria* (Milwaukee, 1985); A.N. Goring-Morris in E. Stern, *Excavations at Tell Mevorakh, Qedem* 9 (Jerusalem, 1978), p. 64; M. Lamdan in Z. Herzog, *Beer-Sheba* II (Tel Aviv, 1984), pp. 122-4, ". . . *débitage* of nine blades and four bladelets; due to their sharp edges, these pieces could be used as knives as they were"; J. Waechter in O. Tufnell, *Lachish* IV: *The Bronze Age* (London, 1958), pp. 325-7.

[13] Cited by A.J. Wensinck in *Encyclopaedia of Islam* (new edn, Leiden, 1979) V, p. 21a.

[14] *As I seem to remember* (London, 1962), pp. 70, 71.

[15] See R. Zadok, "The Origin of the Name Shinar", *Zeitschrift für Assyriologie* 74 (1984), pp. 240-4, where the author proposes a Kassite tribal name as the origin of Shinar.

[16] D.M. Stec, "The mantle hidden by Achan", *VT* 41.3 (1991), pp. 356-9.

[17] S.N. Kramer, *The Sumerians* (Chicago, 1963), p. 104; see also T. Jacobsen, "On the Textile Industry at Ur under Ibbi-Sin", in *Studia Orientalia Ioannes Pedersen dedicata* (Copenhagen, 1953), pp. 172-87, reprinted in *Towards the Image of Tammuz* (Cambridge, Mass., 1970), pp. 216-29.

the 19th century B.C. Assyrian merchants transported fabrics and tin to Anatolia on a regular large-scale basis. Their activities were shared to some extent by traders from Babylonia, too, although records of their activities are rare by comparison.[18] (Indeed, the Assyrian trade is known entirely from documents discovered far from Assyria in the Anatolian emporia.) Among the cloth and clothes carried were some described by their place of origin, or perhaps as in the style of a certain place. There are many qualified as "of Babylonian (work)", while others are accompanied by gentilics, the commonest being *abarnium*, "of Abarnum". In the following century the Mari tablets yield a variety of gentilics applied to textiles or clothing, such as *yamḫādum*, "Aleppine", *gublaītum*, "Byblite", *tutubātum*, "Tuttubite" (Veenhof [n. 18], pp. 189–91). Five hundred years later a considerable industry in preparing and dyeing cloth is recorded by the Nuzi tablets in north eastern Babylonia, and in the following centuries, tablets from Nippur deal with clothes.[19] A letter from Ashur at this time mentions "a Babylonian" garment (TÚG *akkadīte*), and an administrative note records textiles given to an official "for business in Canaan" (*a-na ḫarrān^{mat} ki-na-ḫi*) about 1250 B.C.[20] Ugarit offers documents listing "clothes of Ashdod" (*ṣubātu^{MEŠ al}ašdudi*) and of Tyre (*ktn d ṣr*).[21] At this period exchange of gifts was a major element in international diplomacy, and the El Amarna archive includes lists of gifts sent from Egypt to Mitanni and from Mitanni to Egypt. The pharaoh gave large quantities of linen garments to his ally, and received in return a variety of textiles and clothes. Among those are listed "a shirt of Tukrish type" (a place in western Iran), a garment of Hazor type, and another dress of Tukrish style also described as multicoloured.[22] Even without textual evidence from Canaan itself—and

---

[18] K.R. Veenhof, *Aspects of Old Assyrian Trade and its Terminology* (Leiden 1972), deals with the garment trade in detail; C.B.F. Walker, "Some Assyrians at Sippar in the Old Babylonian Period", *Anatolian Studies* 30 (1980), pp. 15–22, adds sources from the south.

[19] C. Zaccagnini, "A Note on Nuzi Textiles", in Owen (n. 3), pp. 349–61. J. Aro, *Mittelbabylonische Kleidertexte, Sitzungsberichte Sachs. Akad. Wiss. zu Leipzig, Phil.-Hist. Kl.* 115.2 (1970).

[20] E. Ebeling, *Urkunden des Archivs von Assur aus mittelassyrischer Zeit, Mitteilungen der Altorientalischen Gesellschaft* 7 1/2 (Leipzig, 1933), p. 13; E.F. Weidner, "Der Kanzler Salmanassars I", *Archiv für Orientforschung* 19 (1959–60), Taf. 7 Ass. 14410p, VAT 8009.

[21] See M. Heltzer, *Goods, Prices and the Organization of Trade in Ugarit* (Wiesbaden, 1978), p. 70, n. 442, p. 82.

[22] Translations in W.L. Moran, *The Amarna Letters* (Baltimore, 1992), pp. 53, 80.

any such evidence is regrettably rare—this abundant material from other regions, some of it from the Late Bronze Age, surely proves there would be nothing exceptional in finding a Babylonian cloak in Late Bronze Age Jericho.

The Hebrew expression *'adderet šinʿār* is called into question because it shows "an unusual use of a proper name as a *nomen rectum*", therefore the suspicion arises "that the MT is not correct at this point" (Stec. [n. 16], p. 357). This "unusual use" may not occur elsewhere in Biblical Hebrew with articles of dress, but there is a clear analogy in the phrase "gold of Ophir". In 1 Kings ix 28, the parallel 2 Chron. viii 18, and in 1 Kings xxii 48, Ophir is a place, the destination of Hiram's ships (*'ôpîrâ*). The ships returned bringing "gold from Ophir" (*zāhāb mēʾôpîr*, 2 Chron. ix 10). When gold is governed by the proper name Ophir as the *nomen rectum* in the phrases "gold of Ophir" (*zᵉhab ʾôpîr*, 1 Chron. xxix 4, Tell Qasile Ostracon, 8th century B.C.) and *ketem ʾôpîr* (Isa. xiii 12; Ps. xlv 10; Job xxviii 16), Ophir may well indicate the place of origin. At the same time, it could have become a generic term for the type, quality or colour of gold (as damask has for cloth and steel in English), but that does not alter the fact that it began as a proper name. The expression *'adderet šinʿār* may be syntactically unusual, but that is insufficient evidence for emending it to a term occurring elsewhere, *'adderet śaʿar*, reducing the Babylonian cloak to a "cloak of hair" (cf. Gen. xxi 25; Zech. xiii 4), as recently proposed.

There is an adjective attached to the cloak, the cloak is "a good one" (*tôbâ*), and if Shinar pointed to "the costly nature" of the robe, that adjective is thought to "be superfluous", so Shinar could be erroneous (Stec [n. 16], p. 359). Here again, cuneiform texts give the wider context. Scribes serving the Assyrian merchants already mentioned qualified clothing with both a term denoting type (style or origin) and with an adjective of quality, such as "good" (*damqum*), and even "outstanding quality" (*damqum watrum*) (Veenhof [n. 18], pp. 194ff.). Texts concerning textiles found at Mari show the same; Egyptian and other sources could no doubt be added.[23] The eyes of Achan, a man brought up in the Spartan camp-life of the Israelite tribes, the narrator is indicating, were drawn to the cloak for two

---

[23] M. Birot, *Archives royales de Mari* IX, *Textes administratifs de la salle 5 du Palais* (Paris 1960), pp. 303–8.

reasons: it was a garment of fine quality and it had an exotic origin or fashion.[24]

Back to the iron bed

In the three examples given, the value of contextual study is obvious. If the biblical texts are read against the historical era they presuppose, the elements of material culture they mention take their places harmoniously. Complications and problems arise if they are isolated from the culture of that context, the Late Bronze Age, or if modern, western ideas are brought to the study from the start. The immediate assumptions "iron chariots are anachronistic", flint blades are a sign of "conservative religious ritual", or the inability to explore ancient cloth trade, all resulted in mistaken conclusions. In reading any ancient text, the historian accepts its testimony unless there is strong reason to be suspicious of it. Should such reason exist, he cannot reject that testimony out of hand unless it is totally unacceptable when judged by all legitimate criteria, above all, by the sum of the evidence available from the appropriate historical period. Thus the cuneiform inscription on a dagger hilt of the Akkadian period (c. 2200 B.C.) which states the blade was of iron, and the letter written a couple of centuries later which reports the loss of an iron dagger may take their place among the oldest occurrences of iron, even although they date from the Early Bronze Age.[25] They are not susceptible to the charge of anachronism, nor are Assyrian physicians using flint blades in the Iron Age thought strange, nor is there anything peculiar about a king of Upper Mesopotamia (Mitanni) presenting a garment from western Iran to a pharaoh of Egypt.

No one raises objections to those statements because they stand in contemporary documents, although both the use of flint blades by Assyrian physicians and the despatch of garments from a distant place not otherwise known for producing clothes could attract the same criticisms as the biblical passages. The danger of discarding the unusual or unexpected attends every case of this type. Two or more

---

[24] The LXX reading ποικίλην, multi-coloured" or "embroidered", is as likely to be a guess at the type of garment *šin'ār* denoted as a sign that the translators did not find a place name present, as Stec supposes.

[25] E. Sollberger, *Business and Administrative Correspondence under the Kings of Ur* (New York, 1966), pp. 99, 100.

witnesses are essential for proving an accusation, according to Deut. xvii 6, but that does not mean that the testimony of a single witness has no weight; it may be true, only the second or third witness will confirm or disprove it. Failure to believe the single witness at all may result in the discounting or even the loss of genuine evidence about the past, evidence which later research or discovery may corroborate. Archaeology illustrates this repeatedly; isolated finds or written statements eventually gain credibility as we learn more about ancient times. For example, small cube-shaped incense burners of stone or clay occur across the Near East from Arabia to Assyria in the first millennium B.C. In a study of them published in 1983, it was asserted that they belong exclusively to the first millennium B.C. Three isolated specimens from Ur which Sir Leonard Woolley maintained came from deposits of the 18th century B.C. were set aside as anomalous and their dating doubted.[26] Now there are grounds for questioning the dates of two of these pieces, but more recent discoveries prove that incense burners of the same design were made in the Late Bronze Age in Upper Mesopotamia and even earlier.[27] The analogy is clear: whether dealing with ancient artefacts or ancient texts, discounting or discrediting the unusual evidence they give may be to discard valuable information about the past. This does not mean that everything is to be taken at face value, each statement deserves to be assessed critically from every angle, but its evidence can only be rejected when the case against it is well-supported by ancient sources.

Finding that the context of the Late Bronze Age is appropriate for some features in the book of Joshua does not reveal anything about the date of the book. The age of the literary compositions alluding to material culture, or the age of the sources of the books, is a separate topic. What is important to recognise is that those texts could convey accurate reminiscences of the times they describe, whether their composition be placed close to those times, or shortly after, or long after. The study of Babylonian, Egyptian, Hittite, Greek and other texts reporting events in bygone eras shows that they can preserve reliable information about past ages, their customs and their

---

[26] M. O'Dwyer-Shea, "The Small Cuboid Incense Burner of the Ancient near East", *Levant* 15 (1983), pp. 76–109.

[27] A.R. Millard, "The Small Cuboid Incense-Burners: A Note on their Age", *Levant* 16 (1984), pp. 172–3. See now W. Zwickel, *Räucherkult und Räuchergeräte* (Freiburg, 1990), Teil. A.

cultures. Even when their written forms have come down to us in the traditional literature of scribal schools, wandering bards, or religion, those texts can inform us correctly about periods long before they finally took their shape in writing. The assumption from the last century that such narratives only reflect the time when modern scholarship believes they arose is to be rejected. Literary fashions may have formed the text we read, and analysis of those currents is a necessary part of biblical studies, however, there is no reason why literary considerations should dominate those studies to the extent of making every other aspect subject to them. If literary studies indicate the type or period of a text, they do not automatically force the whole content of that text to conform precisely with other texts of the same type, nor do they demand that all in the text was created only at the time of composition. Babylonian epics about Sargon of Akkad, the great emperor of the 23rd century B.C., seem to be products of poets working five hundred years later. When it is possible to check assertions in those epics with information recovered from the time of Sargon, the details they give often prove to be correct recollections of the period half a millennium before the poets wove their tales. Here authors took events of the past to create 'nationalistic" poems for purposes still unknown to us. The historical value of many statements in these texts is now accepted; scepticism is seen to be ill-founded. Other examples of this sort could be cited. There are no grounds for treating a composition such as Joshua differently. Its references to material culture deserve to be assessed against the age the book presupposes first of all. Biblical studies need to give as much weight to the contextual analysis of the Hebrew Scriptures as to the literary. In the light of the examples discussed here, Joshua and Judges appear as reliable records of Late Bronze Age Canaan.

The article of 1986 aimed to show the iron chariots and King Og's iron bed were exceptional, and so noteworthy, objects in that Late Bronze Age world. King Og's bed was long and wide—for reasons we do not know—giving its occupant(s) ample space. Biblical scholarship should recognize the need to give the biblical text and its statements the space they deserve in the ancient world. All too often the tendency is to treat them glibly from modern perspectives, based on generalizations, whether material or conceptual. Consequently, these ancient accounts are forced into a bed of that less comfortable and quite unbiblical style owned by the Greek brigand Procrustes. There they lie, trimmed or stretched to fit shapes for which they were not formed. Only when we read the Old Testament as an ancient Near Eastern book can we begin to appreciate its literary and historical shapes truly.

UGARIT AND ISRAELITE ORIGINS

by

JOHANNES C. DE MOOR
Kampen

1. *Introduction*

The secretary of this congress, André Lemaire, concludes his well-documented review article on the origins of Israel in *La protohistoire d'Israël*, published in 1990, with the statement that the time has come to abandon the fashionable negative attitude towards the feasibility of tracing the outlines of the history of Israel in the premonarchical period.[1] There is no need to alert this audience to the audacity of such a statement. However, in my opinion Lemaire's conclusion was fully justified and in this paper I want to present some further corroboration of his view.

From the very moment of their discovery the relevance of the Ugaritic tablets for the study of the Old Testament has been recognized by all scholars who occupied themselves seriously with these texts.[2] However, it is not uncommon to sound a warning in connection with such comparative studies. To indicate that no direct link between the two cultures may be assumed, the geographic distance between Ugarit and Israel is invoked, as is the fact that most of the biblical testimony is many centuries younger than the texts of Ugarit.[3]

I do not want to dispute the validity of such warnings. In a sense every culture and religion of the ancient Near East is unique, and therefore superficial likeness may never be interpreted in a simplifying way as complete identity. However, both archaeological and linguistic data are nowadays converging to the conclusion that, broadly

---

[1] A. Lemaire, "Aux origines d'Israël: La montagne d'Éphraïm et le territoire de Manassé (XIII–XIᵉ siècle av. J.-C.)", in E.-M. Laperrousaz (ed.), *La protohistoire d'Israël* (Paris, 1990), pp. 291–2.

[2] For an excellent survey see now O. Loretz, *Ugarit und die Bibel: Kanaanäische Götter und Religion im Alten Testament* (Darmstadt, 1990). See now also the contribution of A. Caquot, President of IOSOT 1989–92, elsewhere in this volume.

[3] E.g. D. Kinet, *Ugarit—Geschichte und Kultur einer Stadt in der Umwelt des Alten Testamentes* (Stuttgart, 1981), p. 157; P.C. Craigie, *Ugarit and the Old Testament* (Grand

speaking, the ancient Israelites may be regarded as Canaanites in every respect, including their religion.[4] As Marjo C.A. Korpel has demonstrated recently, about fifty per cent of all terms describing the gods and their world in the Ugaritic literature is also used to describe YHWH and his entourage in the Old Testament. The nature of the differences she found led her to the conclusion that these differences do not point to a non-Canaanite origin of Israel's religion, but rather to a schism within the religion of Canaan itself.[5] In other words, despite the all-important differences, the religion of Israel should still be regarded as an offshoot of the religion of Canaan, just as the Ugaritic religion was such an offshoot.

If the Proto-Israelites were Canaanites, and if we must assume that they were present somewhere in southern Canaan at the very same time when the Ugaritic tablets were written, the possibility of a direct link between Ugarit and the Proto-Israelites cannot be dismissed out of hand. It is an established and indisputable fact that the kingdom of Ugarit maintained close relations with many cities in the south, such as Ashdod, Ashkelon, Acco, Aphek, Tyre and Sidon.[6] Especially interesting are the links between Ugarit and certain places in Galilee and Bashan. An Ugaritic myth mentions the shores of Shamku which in all probability is Lake Huleh.[7] Other Ugaritic texts mention the cities of Haddura'iyu and 'Athtartu, the biblical Edrei and Ashtaroth, as Canaanite centres of the cult of the dead,[8] as does the

---

Rapids, 1983), p. 68; O. Keel and C. Uehlinger, *Göttinnen, Götter und Gottessymbole: Neue Erkenntnisse zur Religionsgeschichte Kanaans und Israels aufgrund bislang unerschlossener ikonogaphischer Quellen* (Freiburg, 1992), pp. 456–7.

[4] See for example M.S. Smith, *The Early History of God: Yahweh and the Other Deities in Ancient Israel* (San Francisco, 1990).

[5] *A Rift in the Clouds: Ugaritic and Hebrew Descriptions of the Divine* (Münster, 1990), esp. pp. 621–35. See also F.M. Cross, *Canaanite Myth and Hebrew Epic: Essays in the History of the Religion of Israel* (Cambridge, Mass., 1973), p. 71: "the god Yahweh split off from 'Ēl in the radical differentiation of his cultus in the Proto-Israelite league".

[6] See e.g. M.C. Astour, "Place Names", in L.R. Fisher (ed.), *Ras Shamra Parallels* 2 (Roma, 1975), pp. 251–369; idem, "Ugarit and the Great Powers", in G.D. Young (ed.), *Ugarit in Retrospect: Fifty Years of Ugarit and Ugaritic* (Winona Lake, 1981), pp. 25–6; D.I. Owen, "Ugarit, Canaan and Egypt: Some New Epigraphic Evidence from Tel Aphek in Israel", ibid., pp. 49–53.

[7] *KTU* 1.10: II.12. Cf. R. Dussaud, "Cultes cananéens aux sources du Jourdain, d'après les textes de Ras Shamra", *Syria* 17 (1936), pp. 283–95; R. de Langhe, *Les textes de Ras Shamra-Ugarit et leurs rapports avec le milieu biblique de l'Ancien Testament* 2 (Gembloux, 1945), pp. 207–17; E. Lipiński, "El's Abode: Mythological Traditions Related to Mount Hermon and to the Mountains of Armenia", *OLP* 2 (1971), pp. 16–17.

[8] This is certain because not only the names of the cities coincide with the Og-tradition, but also other elements, like *ytb b* || *yšb b*, *rp'u* || *rp'ym*. M. Dietrich and

Israelite tradition about Og, king of Bashan.[9] In my opinion it would be begging the question to deny this positive identification. The city of Ashtaroth is mentioned in several other Ugaritic tablets as a famous centre of the cult of the chthonic god Milku.[10] All this would seem to prove that at the end of the Late Bronze Age there existed close connections between Ugarit and the Galilee/Bashan area, connections that included certain religious traditions.

However, if we want to establish whether the texts of Ugarit also have anything definite to say about the Proto-Israelites, we have to know first what we are looking for. For it should be obvious that we cannot expect to find historical confirmation of the picture the Bible draws of the Israelite conquest of the Holy Land. Critical scholarship has long demonstrated the legendary nature of such accounts

---

O. Loretz, "Rāpi'u und Milku aus Ugarit: Neuere historisch-geographische Thesen zu *rpu mlk ʿlm* (*KTU* 1.108:1) und *mt rpi* (*KTU* 1.17 I 1)", *UF* 21 (1989), p. 126, are able to deny the identification of *gtr wyqr*, the founders of the Ugaritic dynasty, with the god who dwells in Ashtaroth and Edrei only by inserting an explicative "(Und es trinke)" in their translation. But why would the scribe have repeated the verb *yšt* in the preceding colon if he could just as well have omitted it? See K. Spronk, *Beatific Afterlife in Ancient Israel and in the Ancient Near East* (Neukirchen–Vluyn, 1986), pp. 177–83; J.C. de Moor, *An Anthology of Religious Texts from Ugarit* (Leiden, 1987), p. 170 n. 15, pp. 187–8 [hereafter: *ARTU*]: idem, *The Rise of Yahwism: The Roots of Israelite Monotheism* (Leuven, 1990) [hereafter: *RoY*], pp. 240–7; K. van der Toorn, "Funerary Rituals and Beatific Afterlife in Ugaritic Texts and the Bible", *BiOr* 48 (1991), col. 57.

[9] Cf. J.C. de Moor, "Rāpi'ūma-Rephaim", *ZAW* 88 (1976), pp. 323–45. The identification with the biblical Edrei, modern Derʿa, is absolutely certain. Cf. M. Görg, *Untersuchungen zur hieroglyphischen Wiedergabe palästinischer Ortsnamen* (Bonn, 1974), pp. 11–18; D.B. Redford, "Contact between Egypt and Jordan in the New Kingdom: Some Comments on Sources", in A. Hadidi (ed.), *Studies in the History and Archaeology of Jordan* 1 (Amman, 1982), p. 119; idem, "A Bronze Age Itinerary in Transjordan", *JSSEA* 12 (1982), pp. 60–1, 74; S. Ahituv, *Canaanite Toponyms in Ancient Egyptian Documents* (Leiden, 1984), pp. 90–1; G.C. Heider, *The Cult of Molek: A Reassessment* (Sheffield, 1985), pp. 119–20; D. Pardee, *Les textes paramythologiques de la 24ᵉ campagne (1961)* (Paris, 1988), p. 96. For a possible occurrence in Emar, see Smith (n. 4), p. 140, n. 14. On the identification of ʿAthtartu see J.G. Wetzstein, *Reisebericht über Hauran und die Trachonen* (Berlin, 1860), pp. 109–11; Görg, pp. 11–18; Astour, in Fisher (n. 6), pp. 313–14; D. Kellermann, "'Aštārōt—'Aštᵉrōt Qarnayim—Qarnayim", *ZDPV* 97 (1981), pp. 45–61; Ahituv, pp. 72–3, 90–1; Heider, pp. 119–20; Pardee, pp. 94–6; idem, "A New Datum for the Meaning of the Divine Name Milkashtart", in L. Eslinger and G. Taylor (ed.), *Ascribe to the Lord: Biblical and Other Studies in Memory of Peter C. Craigie* (Sheffield, 1988), pp. 62–5; B.A. Levine and J.-M. de Tarragon, "'Shapshu Cries out in Heaven': Dealing with Snake-Bites at Ugarit (*KTU* 1.100, 1.107)", *RB* 95 (1988), pp. 497–8; N. Naʾaman, "Biryawaza of Damascus and the Date of the Kāmid el-Lōz 'Apiru Letters", *UF* 20 (1988), p. 183.

[10] *KTU* 1.100: 41; 1.107: 17; RS 86.2235:17; cf. M. Dietrich and O. Loretz, "Die Ortsnamen *gt ʿttrt* und *ʿttrt* || *hdrʿy*", *UF* 22 (1990), pp. 55–6.

as the fall of Jericho. Therefore, it is necessary first to look at the archaeological evidence we now have with regard to the social groups to which the ancestors of Israel may have belonged.

2. *Archaeology*

We know that in the 14th and 13th centuries B.C. impoverished vagrants called ʿApiru or Shosu were sometimes employed as mercenaries, manual labourers and small cattle breeders by the Canaanite city states of Cisjordan. Some of them were allowed to settle there, especially in the neighbourhood of Kumidi and Shechem, whereas others remained on the move.[11] However, the spectacular rise of the number of small farming settlements between the Canaanite cities in the 12th century B.C.[12] can be explained in a satisfactory way only if it is assumed that groups that had been living elsewhere began to settle in Cisjordan when Egyptian control began to dwindle *c.* 1150 B.C. The theory that the newcomers migrated to the hill country from the lowlands and coastal region *west* of the hill country[13] can be rejected as a general explanation because it is based on evidence that could be connected with any part of Canaan, including Transjordan. What seems fairly certain is that *some* Philistines moved from

---

[11] See e.g. L.M. Muntingh, "Syro-Palestinian Problems in the Light of the Amarna Letters", in T. Mikasa (ed.), *Essays on Ancient Anatolian and Syrian Studies in the Second and First Millennium B.C.* (Wiesbaden, 1991), pp. 180–7; De Moor, *RoY*, pp. 108–97; R. Gonen, *Burial Patterns and Cultural Diversity in Late Bronze Age Canaan* (Winona Lake, 1992).

[12] From the vast literature on this subject I can cite only a selection here. Cf. A. Kempinski, "The Overlap of Cultures at the End of the Late Bronze Age and the Beginning of the Iron Age" (Hebr.), *Eretz-Israel* 18 (1985), pp. 394–407; K.-H. Hecke, *Juda und Israel. Untersuchungen zur Geschichte Israels in vor- und frühstaatlicher Zeit* (Würzburg, 1985); G.W. Ahlström, *Who Were the Israelites?* (Winona Lake, 1986), pp. 25–36; R.B. Coote and K.W. Whitelam, *The Emergence of Early Israel in Historical Perspective* (Sheffield, 1987), pp. 117ff.; V. Fritz, "Conquest or Settlement? The Early Iron Age in Palestine", *BiAr* 50 (1987), pp. 84–100; idem, "Die Landnahme der israelitischen Stämme in Kanaan", *ZDPV* 106 (1990) [1991], pp. 63–77; I. Finkelstein, *The Archaeology of the Israelite Settlement* (Jerusalem, 1988); idem, "Searching for Israelite Origins", *BAR* 14 (1988), pp. 34–45; W.G. Dever, *Recent Archaeological Discoveries and Biblical Research* (Seattle, 1990), pp. 39–84; Lemaire (n. 1), pp. 183–292; C.H.J. de Geus, "Nieuwe gegevens over het oudste Israël", *Phoenix* 37 (1991), pp. 32–41; M. and H. Weippert, "Die Vorgeschichte Israels in neuem Licht" *ThR* 56 (1991), pp. 341–90; A. Mazar, "The Iron Age I", in A. Ben-Tor (ed.), *The Archaeology of Ancient Israel* (New Haven, Conn., 1992), pp. 258–301.

[13] J.A. Callaway, "A New Perspective on the Hill Country Settlement of Canaan in Iron Age I", in J.N. Tubb (ed.), *Palestine in the Bronze and Iron Ages: Papers in Honour of Olga Tufnell* (London, 1985), pp. 31–49.

the coast into the hill country,[14] but that is not the massive pattern we are looking for. As a matter of fact, in the turbulent climate of the time, refugees can and will have come from anywhere. But the point at issue is where the population pressure among poor farmers and pastoral nomadists was greatest. In that respect Transjordan is the only viable candidate. This cannot be proved directly from archaeological records because during the Late Bronze Age the pastoral nomadists in Transjordan seem to be just as elusive as in Cisjordan.

It is certain, however, that on both sides of the Jordan a spectacular growth of the number of Iron I settlements can be observed.[15] Since this phenomenon can hardly be attributed to a sudden increase in fertility, the only plausible explanation is that the Egyptians and their Canaanite vassals succeeded in keeping most of these refugees and pastoral nomadists on the move until the end of the Late Bronze Age.

At first sight the facts from Transjordan may seem to support the theory that on both sides of the river the new settlers of the Iron I period were indigenous people who finally got a chance to settle when they felt no longer prosecuted. However, this does not tally with the observation that in Cisjordan the Iron I settlements expand in a westward direction from a point where we find one of the easiest fords in the river Jordan, the crossing between Succoth (Deir ʿAlla) and Shechem. Had the new settlements been distributed evenly all over the hill country, one could have thought of indigenous settlers. Or if the population pressure had come from the west, south or north, one would expect a different pattern of expansion. Now, however, we can only conclude that a considerable number of the Iron I settlers must have crossed the Jordan.

---

[14] Gonen (n. 11), pp. 124ff.; E. Bloch-Smith, *Judahite Burial Practices and Beliefs about the Dead* (Sheffield, 1992).

[15] See for the Transjordan, S. Mittmann, *Beiträge zur Siedlungs und Territorialgeschichte des nördlichen Ostjordanlandes* (Wiesbaden, 1970), p. 225; however, he also found a number of Late Bronze settlements, p. 225, n. 43, p. 228, n. 52; R.H. Dornemann, "The Beginning of the Iron Age in Transjordan", in Hadidi (n. 9), pp. 135–40; M. Weippert, "Remarks on the History of Settlement in southern Jordan during the Early Iron Age", ibid., pp. 153–62; M. Hartal, *Northern Golan Heights: The Archaeological Survey as a Source of Regional History* (Qazrin, 1989), pp. 122–3; J. Mabry and G. Palumbo, "Wadi Yabis Survey", in D. Homès-Fredericq and J.B. Hennessy (ed.), *The Archaeology of Jordan* 2/1 (Leuven, 1989), 96; A.B. Knapp, "Complexity and Collapse in the North Jordan Valley: Archaeometry and Society in the Middle-Late Bronze Ages", *IEJ* 39 (1989), pp. 129–48; W. Zwickel, *Eisenzeitliche Ortslagen im Ostjordanland* (Wiesbaden, 1991), Karten 5–7; Mazar (n. 12), pp. 297–8.

Fortunately we know for certain that Transjordan was a haven for many of these people who rarely got a chance to settle down towards the end of the Late Bronze Age. Egyptian sources and the El-Amarna archive clearly indicate this. Already in the 14th century the number of unruly refugees in northern Transjordan had become so large that the Egyptians decided to deport a number of them to Nubia.[16] Therefore it is not unlikely that many of these 'Apiru and Shosu, among them also Proto-Israelites, crossed the river Jordan when the conditions became more favourable to settlement. The very name "Hebrew" (*'bry*) may well indicate that the Proto-Israelite settlers came from Transjordan (*'br hyrdn*).[17] Num. xxiii 9–10 preserves an old oracle of Balaam[18] testifying to the fact that the Proto-Israelites in Transjordan had indeed become numerous,

ky-mr'š ṣrym 'r'nw	When I see him from the top of the mountains,
wmgbʿwt 'šwrnw	and espy him from the hills,
hn-ʿm lbdd yškn	behold, a people dwelling on its own,
wbgwym l' ythšb	and not reckoning itself among the nations!
my mnh ʿpr y ʿqb	Who can count Jacob's dust,
wm<y> spr 't-rbʿ yśr'l	and who can number Israel's powder?[19]
tmt npšy mwt yšrym	My soul may die the death of the righteous,
wthy 'hryt(y) kmhw	if only my posterity[20] were like his!

Apparently, the Israelites in Transjordan were not only numerous, they also kept themselves more or less apart from cities of the ruling class in northern Transjordan.[21] This tallies with their presumed occupation as pastoral nomadists whose *mšptym* "sheepfolds",[22] attested

---

[16] KL No. 1–2; cf. D.O. Edzard et al., *Kāmid el-lōz—Kumidi* (Bonn, 1970), pp. 50ff. On this kind of "population control" during the New Kingdom see D.B. Redford, *Egypt and Canaan in the New Kingdom* (Beer–Sheva, 1990), pp. 37–9.

[17] De Moor, *RoY*, pp. 113, 177–8.

[18] Balaam was a polytheistic Aramean diviner who had installed himself at Sukkoth/Deir ʿAlla, by the river Jabbok, the boundary of the land of the Ammonites. Cf. S.C. Layton, "Whence Comes Balaam? Num 22,5 Revisited", *Biblica* 73 (1992), pp. 32–61.

[19] Cf. Arab. *rabġ*. Exactly the circumstance that the standard comparison with sand (Gen. xxii 17, xxxii 12, xli 49; Josh. xi 4; Judg. vii 12; 1 Sam. xiii 5; etc.) is missing here points to the originality of this verse.

[20] Cf. Ps. xxxvii 37–8; Akkad. *aḥrâtu, aḥrûtu*.

[21] Cf. A. Malamat, "'*amm lᵉbādād yiškōn*: A Report from Mari and an Oracle of Balaam", *JQR*, NS 76 (1985), pp. 47–50.

[22] It is certain that *mšptym* corresponds to Ugaritic *mtpdm* and primarily means "donkey-pack". Cf. J.C. de Moor, "Donkey-Packs and Geology", *UF* 13 (1982), pp. 303–4; idem, "Ugaritic Smalltalk", *UF* 17 (1986), p. 221. However, because the

in archaic texts like Gen. xlix 14; Ps. lxviii 14 and Judg. v 16, are a typical feature of the grazing grounds of Bashan.[23]

Although the archaeological records for northern Transjordan and the Hauran are too sparse to allow any definite conclusion, it seems that at the end of the Late Bronze we have a similar pattern there as that found in Cisjordan: small farming settlements in symbiosis with the Canaanite cities.[24] Here too the end of the Late Bronze Age is marked by massive destruction patterns, but as in Cisjordan there is clear evidence of a cultural continuity between the Late Bronze and Early Iron Ages.[25]

The model of small settlements of cattle breeders dependent on the strong Canaanite cities reconciles the seemingly contradictory

---

V-shape of the sheepfold resembled the shape of a donkey-pack, it was designated by the same word.

[23] Cf. O. Eissfeldt, *Kleine Schriften* 3 (Tübingen, 1966), pp. 61–70.

[24] G. Barkay et al., "Archaeological Survey in the Northern Bashan (Preliminary Report)", *IEJ* 24 (1974), pp. 173–84; M. Weippert, "The Israelite 'Conquest' and the Evidence from Transjordan", in F.M. Cross (ed.), *Symposia: Celebrating the Seventy-fifth Anniversary of the Founding of the American Schools of Oriental Research (1900–1975)* (Cambridge, Mass., 1979), pp. 15–34; F. Braemer, "Prospections archéologiques dans le Ḥawrān (Syrie)", *Syria* 61 (1984), pp. 219– 50; I. Finkelstein (ed.), *'Izbet Ṣarṭah: An Early Iron Age Site Near Rosh Haʿayin, Israel* (Oxford, 1986), p. 79; Hartal (n. 15.), pp. 121, 138; M. Kochavi, "The Land of Geshur Project: Regional Archaeology of the Southern Golan (1987–1988 Seasons)" *IEJ* 39 (1989), pp. 1–17; K.N. Schoville, "Bashan in Historical Perspective", in *Proceedings of the Tenth World Congress of Jewish Studies*, Division A: The Bible and its World (Jerusalem, 1990), p. 148; D. Homès-Fredericq and J.B. Hennessy (ed.), *Archaeology of Jordan* 1 (Leuven, 1986); 2/1 and 2/2 (Leuven, 1989); Mazar (n. 12), p. 297; Y. Mizrachi, "Mystery Circles", *BAR* 18 (1992), p. 57; O. Negbi, "Metalworking in the Central Jordan Valley at the Transition from the Bronze Age to the Iron Age", *EI* 21 (1990), pp. 212–25.

[25] See especially J.A. Sauer, "Transjordan in the Bronze and Iron Ages: A Critique of Glueck's Synthesis", *BASOR* 263 (1986), pp. 1–26; J.N. Tubb, "Tell es-Saʿidiyeh: Preliminary Report on the First Three Seasons of Renewed Excavations", *Levant* 20 (1988), pp. 23–88; idem, "Preliminary Report on the Fourth Season of Excavations at Tell es-Saʿidiyyeh in the Jordan Valley", *Levant* 22 (1990), pp. 21–46, and the observations of P.E. McGovern on the Baqʿah Valley north of ʿAmmān: *The Late Bronze and Early Iron Ages of Central Transjordan: The Baqʿah Valley Project, 1977–1981* (Philadelphia, 1986); idem, in Homès–Fredericq and Hennessy, (n. 24) 2/1, pp. 25–44. See also B. Hennessy et al. on the transition Late Bronze II—Iron Age I at Pella, ibid., 2/2, p. 422; M.M. Ibrahim, "Saḥāb and its Foreign Relations", in A. Hadidi (ed.), *Studies in the History and Archaeology of Jordan* 3 (Amman, 1987), pp. 76–7; P.E. McGovern, "Central Transjordan in the Late Bronze and Early Iron Ages", ibid., pp. 267–73; J. Mabry and G. Palumbo, "Environmental, Economic and Political Constraints on Ancient Settlement Patterns in the Wadi al-Yabis Region", in M. Zaghoul et al. (ed.), *Studies in the History and Archaeology of Jordan* 4 (Amman, 1992), pp. 69–70; F. Braemer, "Occupation du sol dans la région de Jérash aux périodes de Bronze Récent et du Fer", ibid., pp. 191–8; M. Ottosson, "The Iron Age of Northern Jordan", *SVT* 50 (1993), pp. 98–9.

archaeological and textual evidence in favour of a prolonged contact with the Canaanite culture on the one hand, and Israel's traditions about its nomadic origins on the other. This type of symbiosis
is what also emerges from T. Staubli's impressive review of the iconographic evidence.[26]

Kempinski, Finkelstein and others have argued convincingly that
both the oval courtyard settlement of the late 13th to early 11th
century and the pillared four-room courtyard houses of the late 11th
century were developed out of a pastoral nomadic background.[27] It
has rightly been stressed that this does not provide us with unequivocal
evidence of a migration of any ethnic group we might call "Israelites". On the contrary, the same architecture and earthenware is found
at sites that are undoubtedly "Canaanite".[28] On the whole, Finkelstein
tends to overemphasize the differences between Canaanite and Israelite settlements. He also minimizes the agricultural potential of the
new rural communities.[29] But the whole controversy looses some of
its relevance as soon as it is realized that

a. the Proto-Israelites themselves were in many respects still undiffer-
entiated from their Canaanite background;
b. for pastoral nomadists it was not uncommon to keep moving
between the Canaanite cities[30] as seems to be attested by burial
customs in the Late Bronze Age.[31]

The destruction of the Canaanite cities in the 12th century B.C.
shows a highly complex pattern and cannot be ascribed to any com-

[26] *Das Image der Nomaden im Alten Israel und in der Ikonographie seiner sesshaften Nachbarn* (Freiburg and Göttingen, 1991).
[27] A. Kempinski, "From Tent to House", in V. Fritz, and A. Kempinski, *Ergebnisse der Ausgrabungen auf der Hirbet el-Mšāš (Tēl Māšôš)* I (Wiesbaden, 1983), pp. 31–4; Finkelstein (n. 24), pp. 106–34, 198–217.
[28] W.G. Dever, "Archaeological Data on the Israelite Settlement", *BASOR* 284 (1991), p. 79, with bibliography; Fritz, "Die Landnahme" (n. 12), p. 73.; De Geus (n. 12), p. 41, referring to work of M. Steiner on Kenyon's pottery from pre-Davidic (Canaanite) Jerusalem.
[29] See especially L.E. Stager, "The Archaeology of the Family in Early Israel", *BASOR* 260 (1985), pp. 1–35.
[30] It should not be forgotten that during certain periods of the year the cattle were allowed to graze in the farming land itself, cf. Code of Hammurapi, § 57–58, and the literature mentioned by J.C. de Moor, *The Seasonal Pattern in the Ugaritic Myth of Ba'lu According to the Version of Ilimilku* (Kevelaer and Neukirchen, 1971), pp. 122, 147.
[31] R. Gonen, "Urban Canaan in the Late Bronze Period", *BASOR* 253 (1984), pp. 61–73; idem (n. 11).

mon cause. According to written sources successive waves of Sea Peoples must have been an important factor,[32] but also wars fought by the city states themselves and attacks by ʿApiru who felt themselves strong enough to overthrow their former masters are possible causes for the downfall of the Canaanite cities.[33] In any case, all these events would have been unthinkable if the power of Egypt had not started to diminish rapidly from the beginning of the 12th century onwards.

Now it is interesting that a Shosu-land which the Egyptians called "Yahwe" is attested in a topographical list of Amenophis III (c. 1395–1358). According to M.C. Astour it would have been situated somewhere in northern Canaan and not in the south, as many a wishful thinker assumed.[34] I myself have proposed to interpret the name [ᵐ] Ia-we in the El-Amarna letter No. 154: 6–7 as another designation of the people of YHWH.[35] If this hypothesis proves to be correct, the people of YHWH were probably ʿApiru in the service of prince Aziru of Amurru in the middle of the 14th. As we shall see, this early connection between the Amorites and the Proto-Israelites is far from unlikely.

3. El, the High God

It is certain that the cities of northern Transjordan had been in the hands of Canaanite polytheists for a long time already before the end of the second millennium. The names of cities like hdrʿy ("Haddu-the-Shepherd") and ʿttrt ("Ashtarte"), attested in Ugaritic and Egyptian sources, prove this beyond doubt. But we have fairly impressive evidence that towards the end of the Late Bronze Age El started to

---

[32] See De Moor, RoY, pp. 128, n. 125, 136, 146–7, 151, 153–4, 159, 181, 212, 217–18, 219, 228, to which may be added several articles in M. Heltzer and E. Lipiński (ed.), Society and Economy in the Eastern Mediterranean (c. 1500–1000 B.C.) (Leuven, 1900), and especially J. and E. Lagarce, "The Intrusion of the Sea Peoples and their Acculturation: A Parallel between Palestinian and Ras Ibn Hani Data", in S. Shaath (ed.), Studies in the History and Archaeology of Palestine 3 (Aleppo, 1988), pp. 137–69.

[33] Fritz, "Die Landnahme" (n. 12), pp. 64–8; M. Liverani, Prestige and Interest: International Relations in the Near East ca. 1600–1100 B.C. (Padova, 1990), p. 149.

[34] "Yahweh in Egyptian Topographic Lists", in M. Görg (ed.), Festschrift Elmar Edel (Bamberg, 1979), pp. 17–34.

[35] RoY, pp. 112–13. Of course, it is possible to interpret the signs IA-PI differently, as emphasized by R.S. Hess, "The Divine Name Yahweh in Late Bronze Age sources?", UF 23 (1991), pp. 183–6, but in the light of Al.T. No. 196:12 ᵐIA-PI-e the interpretation I advanced cannot be ruled out.

eclipse all other gods in Bashan, the plain of Hazor and the region north of Shechem.

At Hazor a bronze bull figurine has been found which strongly resembles the Ugaritic bronze statuette of the "Bull" El.[36] The identification of these bull figurines with El is now ascertained by a text from Emar.[37]

In my opinion the basalt statue of a deity standing on a powerful bull which was also found at Hazor represents El simultaneously in anthropomorphic and theriomorphic form.[38] Yadin thinks that it represents Hadad,[39] and indeed the god on a bull is often associated with the weather-god.[40] However, as Keel and Uehlinger have remarked recently, it is highly interesting that this so-called "weather-god" bears a four-pointed star on a disk, the Anatolian–Syrian emblem of the sun, on his breast (Keel and Uehlinger [n. 3], p. 57). This would seem to mean that this god has *combined* the functions of various gods, in other words: he is a high god.[41] The very same four-pointed star on a disk is also depicted on a clay bull's head from Hazor and therefore would seem to be the symbol of the Canaanite bull-god (Yadin [n. 39], Pl XIXc). It may be compared to the six-pointed winged star on a disk depicted on a stele from Ugarit which undoubtedly represents El.[42] This scene in turn is very similar to that depicted on a cylinder seal from the same sanctuary H at Hazor where the winged disk has the four-pointed star (Yadin [n. 39], Pl. XXd). For these reasons I believe that the Hazorite god on a bull is

---

[36] Y. Yadin et al., *The James A. de Rothschild Expedition at Hazor: Hazor III–IV: An Account of the Third and Fourth Seasons of Excavations, 1957–1958* (Jerusalem, 1961), Pl. CCCXLI. Cf. A. Caquot and M. Sznycer, *Ugaritic Religion* (Leiden, 1980), pp. 22–3, Pl. VI. For a similar bull from Megiddo, see H.G. May, "An Inscribed Jar from Megiddo", *AJSL* 50 (1934–5), Pl. 34.

[37] Cf. D. Arnaud, *Emar VI.3* (Paris, 1986), No. 282:16–18.

[38] Cf. Yadin (n. 36), Pl. CCCXXIV–CCCXXV. See also Korpel (n. 5), pp. 523–43, 611.

[39] Y. Yadin, *Hazor; The Head of All Those Kingdoms: Joshua 11:10* (London, 1972), p. 95.

[40] See e.g. D. Collon, *Catalogue of the Western Asiatic Seals in the British Museum: Cylinder Seals III, Isin-Larsa and Old Babylonian Periods* (London, 1986), Nos 449, 450, 452, 453, 455, 456, 458, 460. I am indebted to Mrs. Iziko de Moor–Ozaki, Oxford, for help with the iconographical material.

[41] At Kanesh, for example, the symbol could be connected with various gods; cf. N. Özgüz, *The Anatolian Group of Cylinder Seal Impressions from Kültepe* (Ankara, 1965). The same would seem to hold for Mesopotamia; cf. Collon (n. 40), p. 48.

[42] Caquot and Sznycer (n. 36), Pl. VII. The pendants in Caquot and Sznycer, Pl. XVIIa, show that no difference may be assumed between four-pointed and six-pointed stars.

El. This means that also the emblem on the incense altar from area H[43] may be interpreted as an aniconic representation of El. And again it is remarkable that a similar stele has been excavated at Ugarit, where El was still the head of the pantheon (Caquot and Snycer [n. 36], Pl. XXVI).

The symbolism of the emblem of the star on a disk, sometimes combined with a crescent, is important. It shows that El was seen as lord of sun, moon and the stars, like other universal gods of the time such as Amun-Re and Marduk.[44]

Another mutilated basalt statue from Hazor is perhaps a sitting El comparable to those found at Ugarit.[45] Also the lion orthostats of Hazor could well be interpreted as theriomorphic representations of El.[46]

Finally, Hazor has yielded a bronze statuette of a seated god with

---

[43] Yadin (n. 36), Pl. CXXI, CXXII, CXXIII: 1; idem, (n. 39), Pl. XIXa–b.

[44] The circumstance that in the first millennium the storm-god Hadad is represented standing on a bull and is associated with the same symbol (cf. *ANEP*, Nos 500–1) is only to be expected in the areas where Baal–Hadad took over the role of El as the creator of heaven and earth. See *RoY*, p. 105. However, this combination too has ancient Mesopotamian antecedents; cf. E. Porada, *Corpus of Ancient Near Eastern Seals in North American Collections* 1 (New York, 1948), No. 508; Collon (n. 40), 3, Nos. 453, 456.

[45] Cf. Y. Yadin, *Hazor I: An Account of the First Season of Excavations, 1955* (Jerusalem, 1958), Pl. XXXI.1; idem, (n. 36), Pl. CCCXXX, and compare Caquot and Sznycer (n. 36), Pl. VIIIa; M. Yon and J. Gachet, "Une statuette du dieu El à Ougarit", *Syria* 66 (1989), p. 349; M. Yon et al., "Fouilles de la 48ᵉ campagne (1988) à Ras Shamra-Ougarit", *Syria* 67 (1990), pp. 4–5; idem, "El, le père des dieux", *Monuments et Mémoires de la Fondation Eugène Piot* 71 (1991), 1–19. See also below on the Job stele as well as Smith (n. 4), p. 31, n. 44.

Yadin proposes an identification with the moon-god Sin on the basis of what he describes as an "inverted crescent pendant": (n. 45), p. 88; idem (n. 39) p. 73. Yadin refers to the Bar-rakib stele but the symbol depicted there does not resemble the symbol on the breast of the seated figure (cf. *ANEP*, No. 281.) Moreover, like the Ugaritic El statues, the god wears a long robe and the heavily eroded "pendant" may well be a remnant of the same four-pointed emblem that is depicted on the breast of the statue I discussed earlier. Compare the photographs in Yadin (n. 39), Pl. XXa and XXIa. Moreover, like El at Ugarit the god has a cup in his right hand.

There is no reason at all why El should always be represented as a bearded god. According to the Ugaritic myth he shaved occasionally, *KTU* 1.5: VI. 17–20. Moreover, the beard could have been made of perishable material. The argument that the statue is not in the centre does not speak in favour of an ancestral god, as suggested by Keel Uehlinger (n. 3), p. 60. One might just as well argue that the statue represents the most important god because of his size and his position at the head of the line of steles. As a matter of fact, El was the god who presided over the ancestor cult of the Canaanites. Cf. J.C. de Moor, "El, the Creator", in G. Rendsburg et al. (ed.), *The Bible World: Essays in Honor of Cyrus H. Gordon* (New York, 1980), pp. 184–5; idem, *RoY*, pp. 229–52.

[46] Yadin (n. 45), Pl. XXX.2; idem (n. 36), Pl. CXX. Compare Korpel (n. 5), p. 535, on Num. xxiv 8–9 and xxiii 24.

a cup(?) in one hand while the other is blessing.[47] The attitude and even the facial expression closely resemble a bronze statuette of El at Ugarit.[48]

In a 12th century sanctuary at Dhahrat et-Tawileh, between Dothan and Tirzah north of Shechem, another bronze figurine of a bull was excavated.[49]

According to the Papyrus Anastasi I of the late l9th dynasty an imposing statue of a bull marked the southern border of the country of Upe, the capital of which was Damascus.[50]

All this points to a highly prominent place of the "bull" El in the areas where, if we are not mistaken, many Proto-Israelites must have lived at the end of the Late Bronze Age. This prominence is confirmed by the Ugaritic Legend of Kirtu. It is of considerable interest to observe that according to this Ugaritic text Pubala, the king of Udumu, expressly called himself a servant of El (*KTU* 1.14: III. 31 par.), like Kirtu himself.[51] He regards his country as a gift of none other than El himself.[52]

The Udumu of the Legend of Kirtu is identical with the Udumu

---

[47] Yadin (n. 36), Pl. CCV:2 and CCCXLVI.

[48] Caquot and Sznycer (n. 36), Pl. VIIIa. For similar statuettes from Megiddo see Keel and Uehlinger (n. 3), p. 66. For a possible specimen from Tell Safut, Jordan: D.H. Wimmer, "The Excavations at Tell Safut", in Hadidi (n. 25), p. 280.

[49] A. Mazar, "The 'Bull Site': An Iron Age I Open Cult Place", *BASOR* 247 (1982), pp. 27–42; R. Wenning and E. Zenger, "Ein bäuerliches Baal-Heiligtum im samarischen Gebirge aus der Zeit der Anfänge Israels", *ZDPV* 102 (1986), pp. 75–86; B. Rosen, "Early Israelite cultic centres in the hill country", *VT* 38 (1988), pp. 114–17; H. Shanks, "Two Early Israelite Cult Sites now Questioned", *BAR* 14 (1988), pp. 48–52; G.W. Ahlström, "The Bull Figurine from Dhahrat et-Tawileh", *BASOR* 280 (1990), pp. 77–83. In view of the parallels cited above it is an unlikely hypothesis that this figurine represented Baal rather than El. Ahlström overemphasizes the differences from the "Canaanite" bulls.

[50] H.-W. Fischer–Elfert, *Die satirischen Streitschrift des Papyrus Anastasi I: Übersetzung und Kommentar* (Wiesbaden, 1986), p. 184.

[51] *KTU* 1.14: III. 49, 51; VI. 34–5. Cf. D.J. O'Connor, "The Keret Legend and the Prologue-Epilogue of Job", *Irish Theological Quarterly* 55 (1989), pp. 1–6, 240–2. Note the following statement by S.B. Parker, "The Historical Composition of *KRT* and the Cult of EL", *ZAW* 89 (1977), p. 174, "I insist that Krt is saved from his successive predicaments not just by the gods, but emphatically by El alone. His salvation establishes . . . the virtues of El as the incomparable saviour." Kirtu himself may have lived in the Beqa' if his city *Ḥbr* is equated with *ḥi-bu-ra*-(. . .) in an Egyptian topographical list; cf. W. Helck, *Die Beziehungen Ägyptens zu Vorderasien im 3.und 2.Jahrtausend v. Chr.* (2.Aufl., Wiesbaden, 1971), p. 211. This would tally with the fact that after three days marching Kirtu reached a sanctuary of Athiratu of Tyre and Sidon, whereas four days later he arrived at Udumu. Thus he came from the north.

[52] *KTU* 1.14: III. 31–2, par., cf. De Moor, *ARTU*, p. 197; *RoY*, p. 231.

of the El-Amarna letter No. 256 which letter testifies to the intimate connections between Udumu and the Bashan region.[53] Probably it is identical with Adumim (*itmm*) in a topographical list of Thutmoses III, to Adam in Ps. lxviii 19 and Adamah in Josh. xix 36; it was probably situated north of the Sea of Galilee.[54]

4. The Occupation of Zaphon

4.1 Extra-Biblical Evidence

The most impressive evidence for the prominence of El is furnished by the so-called Job-stele from Sheikh Sa'd, dating from the reign of Ramses II (*c.* 1279–1212 B.C.). It provides us with written proof that El had prevailed over Baal at that time and that place.[55] The inscription runs *i-r3-k3-n-i d3-p3-n* and should be interpreted as *'il qny spn* "El the Creator of the Zaphon", so that El had become the master of the mountain of Baal here.[56] The god who is represented on the left side of the stele is without any doubt El. His headdress is identical with that of El in Ugarit.[57]

The Job-stele implies that according to the local mythology El had dispossessed Baal of his mountain Zaphon. Accordingly, the Bashan

---

[53] For the previous discussion about the identification of Udumu, see A.F. Rainey, "The Ugaritic Texts in Ugaritica 5", *JAOS* 94 (1974) p. 187. For other opinions consult Astour (n. 6), pp. 313–14; 267–9; B. Margalit, "The Geographical Setting of the *Aqht* Story and its Ramifications", in Young (n. 6), pp. 131–58, 158, n. 113. The administrative list *KTU* 4.693 does not contain a reference to Udumu; cf. S. Ribichini, "'*Udm e Šmk*: Due Toponimi 'Mitici'", in *Materiali Lessicali ed Epigrafici—I* (Roma, 1982), pp. 51–2.

[54] Cf. Y. Aharoni, "The Land of 'Amqi", *IEJ* 3 (1953), p. 157, n. 22; idem, "Some Geographical Remarks Concerning the Campaigns of Amenhotep II", *JNES* 19 (1960), pp. 177–81; N. Na'aman, *Borders and Districts in Biblical Historiography* (Jerusalem, 1986), p. 133; Fischer–Elfert (n. 50), p. 181.

[55] See for this stele and its remarkable adventures G. Schumacher, *Across the Jordan* (London, 1889), p. 191; idem, "Der Hiobstein, Sachrat Eijub im Hauran", *ZDPV* 14 (1891), pp. 142–7; A. Erman, "Der Hiobstein", *ZDPV* 15 (1892), pp. 205–11; idem, "Das Denkmal Ramses' II. im Ostjordanland", *Zeitschrift für Ägyptische Sprache und Altertumskunde* 31 (1893), pp. 100–1; A. Alt, "Das Institut im Jahre 1932", *Palästinajahrbuch* 29 (1933), pp. 19–20; B. Porter R.L.B. Moss, *Topographical Bibliography of Ancient Egyptian Hieroglyphic Texts, Reliefs and Paintings* (Oxford, 1952), p. 383; R. Giveon, "Two Egyptian Documents Concerning Bashan from the Time of Ramses II, I. the Job-Stone", *RSO* 40 (1965), pp. 197–200; S.I.L. Norin, *Er spaltete das Meer: Die Auszugsüberlieferung in Psalmen und Kult des alten Israel* (Lund, 1977), pp. 49–51; K.A. Kitchen, *Ramesside Inscriptions: Historical and Biographical* 2 (Oxford, 1979), II, 223 (No. 61).

[56] See for philological details *RoY*, p. 126, n. 118.

[57] See n. 45 above. Incidentally, EA No. 55: 53–60 indicates that it was not unusual for an Egyptian king to erect a statue of a foreign deity.

where the stone was erected had apparently been re-named "Zaphon". Wandering of geographic names is a common phenomenon. To give a few examples from the Old Testament itself, the name of Mt Moriah (Gen. xxii 2) was claimed for Zion (2 Chr. iii 1); the name of Mt Zalmon, probably Ğebel ed-Druz,[58] was transferred to a mountain in the neighbourhood of Shechem (Judg. ix 48); and finally the name of Zaphon itself was claimed both for Mt Zion (Ps. xlviii 3)[59] and for a promontory in the sea near Lake Serbonis.[60]

This usurpation of Baal's mountain would seem to be an extremely important new datum. It means that the El of the Job-stele is not the weak, old god who is on the verge of surrendering his position to Baal of Zaphon. That is the El we meet in the contemporaneous texts of Ugarit. Here in Bashan, however, El appears to have taken over the mountain of Baal, Mt Zaphon. So he is an intolerant kind of El, an El who sought to oust Baal.

We meet the same kind of intolerance in the El-Amarna letter No. 147. It has long been recognized that the sender of this letter, Abi-Milku of Tyre, wanted to make a good impression on the pharaoh by showing his interest in Akhenaten's monotheistic religion.[61] What is remarkable, however, is his explicit claim that the Egyptian Sun-god has taken over Baal's functions as the thunder-god,

> (The Sun) who gives his thunder in heaven like Baal,
> so that the whole country fears for his thunder.[62]

Not Baal, but the Sun-god is the sole dispenser of the north wind (ṣapānu).[63] In other words, we have a second definite proof here of a tendency to eliminate Baal as a contender for the position of supreme god. In Egypt itself there is evidence of a conscious campaign under the Ramessides against a movement for the exclusive worship

---

[58] O. Keel, *Vögel als Boten* (Freiburg and Göttingen 1977), p. 16; Schoville (n. 24), pp. 145–6.

[59] Cf. M.S. Smith, "God and Zion: Form and Meaning in Psalm 48", *SEL* 6 (1989), pp. 70, 75, n. 24; M. Dietrich and O. Loretz, "Ugaritisch ṣrrt ṣpn, ṣrry und hebräisch jrktj ṣpwn", *UF* 22 (1990), pp. 79–86. See also below.

[60] Biblical *bʿl ṣpwn*, Ex. xiv 2, 9; Num. xxxiii 7. See W. Fauth, "Das Kasion-Gebirge und Zeus Kasios", *UF* 22 (1990), pp. 110–18.

[61] Literature *RoY*, p. 66, n. 132.

[62] EA No. 147: 13–15. Cf. W.L. Moran, *Les lettres d'El Amarna: Correspondence diplomatique du pharaon* (Paris, 1987), p. 379, n. 4. See also EA No. 108.

[63] EA 147:10. Cf. C. Grave, "The Etymology of Northwest Semitic ṣapānu", *UF* 12 (1980), pp. 221–9.

of Baal which was seen as incompatible with absolute reliance on the national god Amun-Re.[64]

Apparently, it was the result of the crisis of polytheism in Egypt towards the end of the Late Bronze Age which led to such a widespread concentration of divine functions in the one god Amun-Re (cf. *RoY*, pp. 42ff.). If Goedicke's interpretation of Wen Amun 2.19 is right, the king of Byblos would still have recognized Amun-Re's superiority over Baal as the thunder-god two centuries later.[65]

In my book *The Rise of Yahwism* I have tried to demonstrate that the agressively propagated cult of Amun-Re has had a profound influence on the cult of El and YHWH in southern Palestine towards the end of the second millennium.[66] It is important to note that here we have additional extra-biblical evidence of intolerance towards the young god Baal, an intolerance that has remained so characteristic of Yahwism.

Now the remarkable thing is that the texts of Ugarit appear to know all about El's appropriation of Baal's mountain Zaphon which is attested in the Job-stele. In *KTU* 1.1: IV[67] it is narrated how a

---

[64] *RoY*, pp. 73–4, with bibliography.

[65] *The Report of Wenamun* (Baltimore, 1975), pp. 76, 82–3.

[66] The first to note some striking similarities between the cult of Amun-Re and that of YHWH was K. Sethe, *Amun und die acht Urgötter von Hermopolis: Eine Untersuchung über Ursprung und Wesen des ägyptischen Götterkönigs* (Abh. d. preussischen Akad. d. Wiss. 1929, Phil.-hist. Kl., Nr. 4), (Berlin, 1929), pp. 119–22. To the evidence presented in *RoY*, pp. 44–68, the impressive iconographic testimony collected by Keel and Uehlinger (n. 3), pp. 104–6, 124–8 should be added.
There are several indications that YHWH-El was identified with Amun. In my opinion the original text of Deut. xxxii 4 ran *'l 'mwn hw'* || *ṣdq wyšr hw'* "He is El-Amun" || "He is Ṣedeq-and-Yašar" (Ugaritic *ṣdq wmšr*). The present text of Deut. xxxii 4 is syntactically awkward. The identification formula may be compared to Ex. xxxiv 14 *'l qn' hw'* "He is El-the-Jealous", to the original text of Hos. xiv 8 *'ny 'ntw w'šrtw* "I am his 'Anath and his Asherah", and to toponyms identifying YHWH/El with other deities (*RoY*, pp. 202–3). The *'yn 'wl* is a later gloss rendering the interpretation as proper names of foreign deities impossible. The identification of El and YHWH with Amun is attested epigraphically by the Phoenician and possibly Aramaic PNN *'l'mn* and the epigraphic Hebrew PN *yw'mn*. Cf. F.L. Benz, *Personal Names in the Phoenician and Punic Inscriptions* (Rome, 1972), pp. 61, 269–70; B. Otzen, "The Aramaic Inscription", in P.J. Riis and M.-L. Buhl (ed.), *Hama: Fouilles et Recherches de la Fondation Carlsberg 1931–1938* II/2: *Les objets de la période dite syro-hittite (Âge du Fer)* (København, 1990), p. 279; G.I. Davies, *Ancient Hebrew Inscriptions: Corpus and Concordance* (Cambridge, 1990), p. 370. The element *'mn* must be the name of Amun, because the Phoenician PN *'bd'mn* can only be translated "Servant-of-Amun", as seen by E. Lipiński, *BiOr* 32 (1975), p. 77. The cult of Amun is attested unequivocally in a Punic votive inscription (*KAI* No. 118).

[67] Cf. De Moor (n. 30), pp. 116–20; idem, *ARTU*, pp. 24–5.

goddess, probably Asherah, complains about the nuisance caused by
Baal's building activities on Mt Zaphon. She wants El to appoint a
new viceroy instead of Baal. The god she has in mind is a son of El
called *Yw*. El agrees and renames *Yw* into Yam (Sea). He allows Yam
to take over Baal's palace on Mt Zaphon, with all its gold and silver.

In the next column of the same tablet (*KTU* 1.1: V; cf. *ARTU*, pp.
27–8). Baal suspects that a plot has been laid against him. Specifically he accuses El of coveting his mountain Zaphon,[68]

KTU 1.1: V.24–7	
ʿrb l [bty . ʾat . š̓il .]	You are requesting the right to enter my house,
[wġ]r . mtny ʾat zd l	and you are coveting the mountain I have been given,
[tptq . prq . gbh .]	you want to take over the cella on its crest.
tʿrb[69] . bš̓il[lk .]	Can comply with your request
[kl . tġr . mtnh .]	anyone who protects what has been given to him?
l tzd . l tptq /	Surely you covet it! Surely you want to take it over![70]

The verb *z(y)d* used in this passage describes a strong desire.[71] The
verb *p(w)q* in the Gt-stem means "to appropriate".

Who is this god *Yw* who would take over Baal's mountain with
the help of his father El? In my opinion he is none other than YHWH.
Formerly, I rejected this identification, like most of my esteemed
colleagues. But in view of a number of new data I have revised my
opinion on this issue. From a philological point of view nothing
prevents the identification. According to the rules of Ugaritic pho-
nology the form *yahwê* or *yahwî* would regularly become *yawê* or *yawî*,
in the consonantal alphabet *yw*. It is attested in this form outside
Ugarit[72] and in 9th-century Hebrew epigraphic PNN, where the /w/
cannot be a *mater lectionis*.

In the Ugaritic myth El and Yawê are differentiated but they share
a common goal: to oust Baal and to occupy his mountain. There is

---

[68] Korpel (n. 5), pp. 582–3, was the first to connect this passage with the Job-stele.

[69] The imperfects *tʿrb* and *tġr* are 3rd person masculine singulars. Cf. M. Dijkstra
and J.C. de Moor, "Problematical Passages in the Legend of Aqhâtu", UF 7 (1975),
p. 201. For a particularly convincing example see *KTU* 2.33: 25 ʿly ṯḥ "his tribute
is coming up" next to 2.33: 37 tʿl ṯḥ "let his tribute come up".

[70] Restorations after J.C. de Moor and K. Spronk, *A Cuneiform Anthology of Religious Texts from Ugarit* (Leiden, 1987), p. 12. The restorations are based on a comparison with the traces of the identical passage in *KTU* 1.1: V. 12–14.

[71] Sexual desire in *KTU* 1.24: 8.

[72] See above on Yawê as a name of the people of YHWH. For more etymologi-
cal details and parallels see *RoY*, pp. 237–9.

a number of other peculiarities supporting the view that Yawê/Yam is a deliberate Ugaritic caricature of YHWH:

1. The envoys of Yam have the nerve not to bow (*šḥy* tL) to other gods (*KTU* 1.2: I.14–15, 30–1; *ARTU*, pp. 30ff.). Could this be a reflection of the strange behaviour of actual messengers of the people of YHWH? There is every reason to believe that the biblical injunction not to bow (*šḥh* tL) to other gods is older than some would have it. It occurs in the decalogue, of course (Ex. xx 5; Deut. v 9), as well as in a number of typically North-Israelite traditions. I do not have the time to elaborate this point here (see *RoY*, p. 116). For the moment it is enough to point out that in a polytheistic world the determination not to bow to other gods must have caused quite a stir, especially in the aftermath of Akhenaten's shocking monotheistic revolution. It is, therefore, possible that Ilimilku, the author of the Ugaritic Myth of Baal, was hinting at this odd behaviour when he described the messengers of Yawê/Yam.

2. Yawê/Yam becomes King of the Gods instead of Baal (*KTU* 1.1: IV.24–5; 1.2: III.12, 18, 22; *ARTU*, pp. 26, 6–7). YHWH too became a King ruling over all other gods.

3. Yawê/Yam assumes Hadad's most cherished title, that of *b'l* (*KTU* 1.2: I.17–18; *ARTU*, p. 31), as did YHWH originally (see *RoY*, p. 202, n. 410; Smith [n. 4], pp. 13–15).

4. Yawê/Yam is called *'adn*, "Master", the title which the Ugaritic Myth of Ba'lu accords only to Ilu and to the only other serious contender for the highest position in the pantheon, Baal (*RoY*, p. 105). It is also the standard epithet of YHWH.

5. Yawê/Yam is called *ṭpṭ* "Judge", also a common epithet of both Baal and YHWH.

6. Yawê/Yam wants to appropriate the gold and silver of Ba'lu, the master of the plough-land.[73] According to some tribal characterizations in Gen. xlix[74] and the first part of Ps. lxviii, which I will discuss later on, it was the frankly admitted goal of the people of YHWH to rob the Canaanites of their silver and gold.

---

[73] Cf. *ARTU*, p. 92. The delivery of a large tribute of gold, silver and gems to the sea was also a major theme in "Astarte and the Insatiable Sea", a Canaanite myth that was translated into Egyptian. For an English translation see E.F. Wente, in W.K. Simpson (ed.), *The Literature of Ancient Egypt: An Anthology of Stories, Instructions, and Poetry* (New Haven, Conn., 1972), pp. 133–6.

[74] See provisionally *RoY*, pp. 109–10; my student R. de Hoop will write a dissertation on Gen. xlix.

7. 'Athtar ridicules Yawê/Yam because he has neither a wife nor a son (*KTU* 1.2: III.14, 22–3; *ARTU*. pp. 36–7). Although there have always been attempts to provide YHWH with a consort,[75] there was no legitimate place for a goddess in early Yahwism. The crude nature of the representations of the deities depicted in Kuntillet 'Ajrud (Korpel [n. 5], p. 218), the unpolished idiom of these inscriptions,[76] the gradual disappearance of anthropomorphic goddesses from the iconography of Canaan since the Late Bronze Age,[77] and especially the repression of the Astarte plaques in ancient Israel[78] and the quasi-total absence of Israelite personal names containing the name of Asherah or any other goddess[79] all lead up to the conclusion that the place of goddesses was in unofficial circuits of popular religion which only occasionally found official recognition, as under king Manasseh. A god without a wife must have looked very odd in the polytheistic world and may well have given rise to jests like those in the Ugaritic myth.

All taken together there would seem to be sufficient evidence to assume that the El who was the creator of Baal's mountain Zaphon according to the Job-stele was none other than the jealous El who was also called YHWH.

With regard to the question why the people of Ugarit equated Yawê with Yam, the sea-god, we can only offer hypotheses. It is possible that this equation was merely a ploy to indicate that in the end Baal would be able to defeat this god. However, it is also possible that it points to a historical association of the Proto-Israelites with certain Sea peoples. The theses of C.H. Gordon,[80] M.C. Astour,[81]

---

[75] From the vast literature on this subject I cite only J.A. Emerton, "New Light on Israelite Religion: The Implications of the Inscriptions from Kuntillet 'Ajrud", *ZAW* 94 (1982), pp. 2–20; S.M. Olyan, *Asherah and the Cult of Yahweh in Israel* (Atlanta, 1988); Smith (n. 4), pp. 15–21, 80–114; M. Dietrich and O. Loretz, "*Jahwe und seine Aschera*": *Anthropomorphes Kultbild in Mesopotamien, Ugarit und Israel: Das biblische Bilderverbot* (Münster, 1992).

[76] H.-P. Müller, "Kolloquialsprache und Volksreligion in den Inschriften von *Kuntillet 'Aǧrūd und Ḥirbet el-Qôm*", *Zeitschrift für Althebraistik* 5 (1992), pp. 15–51.

[77] Keel and Uehlinger (n. 3), *passim*, esp. their conclusions, pp. 459–65.

[78] Bibliography *RoY*, p. 170.

[79] J.H. Tigay, *You Shall Have no Other Gods: Israelite Religion in the Light of Hebrew Inscriptions* (Atlanta, 1986); J.H. Fowler, *Theophoric Personal Names in Ancient Hebrew: A Comparative Study* (Sheffield, 1988), pp. 189, 225, 235, 255–6, 298.

[80] "The Mediterranean Factor in the Old Testament", *SVT* 9 (1963), pp. 19–31.

[81] *Hellenosemitica: An Ethnic and Cultural Study in West Semitic Impact on Mycenaean Greek* (Leiden, 1967), pp. 1–112.

and Y. Yadin[82] with regard to a possible connection between the Sea people called Danites and the Israelite tribe of Dan have been all but abandoned.[83] However, now that we know that just like the ʿApiru and Shosu themselves the Sea peoples were sometimes employed as mercenaries or labourers by the Canaanite and Egyptian rulers while at the same time other Sea peoples were regarded as dangerous enemies,[84] the situation may have been more complicated than we had anticipated.[85] In view of the Ugaritic equation of Yawê and Yam the whole matter should perhaps be re-evaluated.[86] The basic possibility of such a friendly connection between early Israel and certain Sea Peoples, whereas others remained enemies, would seem to be demonstrated by the fact that king David employed Cretans and even Aramaic-speaking Philistines as his bodyguard.[87]

I think that the cumulative weight of the evidence presented in favour of the hypothesis that El was elevated to the position of the most high God in northern Transjordan and Galilee towards the end of the Late Bronze Age is impressive. It seems that the people of Ugarit were well informed about El's appropriation of the Zaphon and assumed that El wanted this mountain of Baal for his "son" Yawê.

Finally, it may be added that it is remarkable that in the first millennium El has remained the highest, though not the only god in northern Transjordan, as is attested by the Balaam texts as well as Ammonite and Nabataean inscriptions.[88] This is so different from

---

[82] "And Dan, Why Did He Remain in Ships" (Judges V,17)", *Australian Journal of Biblical Archaeology* 1 (1968), pp. 9–23.

[83] See the critical review by H.M. Niemann, *Die Daniten: Studien zur Geschichte eines altisraelitischen Stammes* (Göttingen, 1985), pp. 273–91.

[84] Cf. R. Stadelmann, *LÄ* 5, cols 814–22.

[85] Also certain aspects in the Israelite concept of God might perhaps be explained in assuming a link with Indogermanic settlers, cf. G. Schmitt, "El Berit—Mitra", *ZAW* 76 (1964), pp. 325–7; P.C. Craigie, "EL BRT. EL DN (RS 24.278, 14–15)", *UF* 5 (1973), pp. 278–9.

[86] See for a first attempt in this direction G.W. Ahlström, "Another Moses Tradition", *JNES* 39 (1980), pp. 65–6; idem, (n. 12) pp. 1–83.

[87] The designation *plṭ* is an Aramaic form of the name of the Philistines. Because of the pun in Mic. i 10 (cf. my remarks in W. van der Meer and J.C. de Moor [ed.], *The Structural Analysis of Biblical and Canaanite Poetry* [Sheffield, 1988], p. 178, n. 12) it is likely that, rightly or wrongly, the name of the Philistines was connected with the Semitic root *plṭ* which became *plš* in Hebrew, but *plṭ* in Aramaic. So we have to postulate the development *plṭty* > Hebr. *plšty* and Aram. *plṭty* > *plṭy*.

[88] K. Jackson, "Ammonite Personal Names in the Context of the West Semitic Onomasticon", in C.L. Meyers and M. O'Connor (ed.), *The Word of the Lord Shall Go Forth: Essays in Honor of D.N. Freedman* (Winona Lake, 1983), pp. 507–21; and the literature cited in *RoY*, p. 75, n. 188. Some Ammonite seals inscribed with theophoric

the situation in other parts of Canaan in the first millennium, where El had to yield his position to Baal, that it may be regarded as an indication of El's long-established supremacy in Transjordan.

In a paper read at a conference in Manchester in September 1992[89] I suggest that the historical Job was a Canaanite city ruler in Bashan towards the end of the Late Bronze Age. His Transjordanian origin explains a number of problems in the book of Job as well as his association with the Ugaritic hero Daniel in Ezek. xiv 14, 20, xxviii 3. As I said before, we now have evidence of direct contacts between Ugarit and the area where the Proto-Israelites probably lived.[90]

4.2 Biblical Evidence

It is most significant that the extra-biblical tradition about the appropriation of the Zaphon by El is confirmed by inner-biblical evidence. The oldest testimony is furnished by Ps. lxviii 2–25. I have dealt extensively with these verses elsewhere,[91] and so I shall confine myself now to some additional comments on this Psalm which describes how YHWH-El took possession of Bashan.

4.3 The Date of Ps. lxviii

First, I want to make some remarks on the date of the Psalm. There have always been scholars who advocated a fairly early date for this Psalm or, to put it more precisely, for the bulk of this Psalm. Many scholars assume that in any case the Psalm must be later than the Song of Deborah because vs. 14 would contain a quotation from Judg. v 16. Actually the number of parallels between the two songs is even greater.[92] It is always difficult to assess the value of this kind

---

El-names are adorned with pictures of a bull, cf. P. Bordreuil, *Catalogue des sceaux ouest-sémitiques inscrits* (Paris, 1986), Nos 69, 75.

[89] "Ugarit and the Origin of Job" in G.J. Brooke, A.H.W. Curtis and J.F. Healey (ed.), *Ugarit and the Bible* (Münster, 1994), pp. 225–57.

[90] Contra H. Niehr, *Der höchste Gott: Alttestamentlicher JHWH-Glaube im Kontext syrisch-kanaanäischer Religion des 1. Jahrtausends v. Chr.* (Berlin, 1990), pp. 11–12.

[91] *RoY*, pp. 118–28. To my philological comments I would add that in contrast to Mic. vii 19 I have translated *'šyb bmṣlwt ym* in vs. 23 as "I will make Yam turn back into the depths", because in Ex. xv 19 *my ym* is the object of *šwb* Hiphil whereas in Ex. xiv 26 *ym* is the subject of *šwb* Qal. See for the syntax C. Brockelmann, *Hebräische Syntax* (Neukirchen, 1956), § 122d, and Ugaritic examples like *KTU* 1.3: II. 30–1; iv. 22–3, 23–4, 29; 1.2: I. 38; 1.5: VI. 20–1, par.; 1.6: I. 10.

[92] Ps. lxviii 5,33 || Judg. v 3; Ps. lxviii 13 || Judg. v 22, 30; Ps. lxviii 14 || Judg. v 16; Ps. lxviii 19 || Judg. v 12; Ps. lxviii 22, 24 || Judg. v 26.

of argument. Which of the two came first? Could not both be dependent on a third source? It is difficult to answer such questions in a really reliable way. However, in my opinion it is much more likely that Ps. lxviii has the older rights, for it appears to have been an extremely famous song which influenced not only the Song of Deborah, but also a number of other archaic traditions, such as Deut. xxxiii and Hab. iii.

Among those advocating an early date, especially the reign of Solomon was favoured, for example in an influential article by John Gray in 1977.[93] The reasons for this are the prominent place of Judah in vs. 28, as well as the kings from Ethiopia and Egypt bringing tribute to the temple in Jerusalem (vss 30, 32).[94] However, all these arguments are derived from the second half of the Psalm.

It is remarkable that this second half, which starts in vs. 26, seems to correct some statements made in the first half of the Psalm. In verse 5 we have the well-known epithet *rkb b'rbwt* which is either a corrupt form of Baal's epithet *rkb 'rpt*, so that it should be translated "the Rider on the Clouds", or a deliberate pun on that Baalistic epithet in which case we should translate "he who rides in the plains". Whatever the correct interpretation may be, it is obvious that vs. 34 of the same Psalm pretends to give the correct interpretation: "he who rides in heavens". So vs. 34 is a later comment on vs. 5. Whereas the first part of the Psalm speaks unabashedly of the "kings" of the armies—in my opinion: the Israelite armies—verses 26 and 28 pointedly correct this into *śrym* "officers". And finally, whereas the first half of the Psalm seems to presuppose that the God of Israel has a holy habitation on Mt Bashan (see especially *m'wn qdšw* in vs. 6, *hytk* "your habitations" in vs. 11), the second part of the Psalm emphasizes the unique position of the temple in Jerusalem (vss 30, 36).

All this leads to the conclusion that the verses 26–36 are a later addition.[95] In this respect my position is fairly close to that of Jeremias

---

[93] "A Cantata of the Autumn Festival: Ps. LXVIII", *JSS* 22 (1977), pp. 2–26. For other dating proposals see Keel (n. 58), pp. 12–13, n. 2; J. Jeremias, *Das Königtum Gottes in den Psalmen* (Göttingen, 1987), pp. 69–82; De Moor, *RoY*, p. 118, n. 88.

[94] Mowinckel and others attach much weight to the fact that Benjamin is mentioned first in vs. 28. For them this indicates that the earliest kernel of the Psalm dates from the reign of Saul. But it should not be overlooked that Benjamin is explicitly called the smallest of the rulers and therefore is no serious rival to Judah.

[95] So I cannot agree with Fokkelman's recent plea for the unity of Ps. lxviii Cf. J.P. Fokelman, "The Structure of Psalm LXVIII", *OTS* 26 (1990), pp. 72–83. He invokes the inclusion between vs. 5 and vss 33–4 in favour of the presumed unity

(n. 93) who also discerns two major levels in this Psalm.[96] However, because this later addition must be fairly old itself (one might refer for example to the use of the relative *zw* in vs. 29), the date *ante quem* for the first half of Ps. lxviii would seem to be the reign of Solomon. Is such a high date possible? I want to present 5 arguments in favour of a positive answer.

1. It has long been recognized that the first half of Ps. lxviii betrays the traditional wording of a number of archaic theophany descriptions which are otherwise found in Judg. v; Hab. iii, Deut. xxxiii.

2. A number of philological peculiarities points to a very high date for this part of the Psalm. Most of these cannot be explained as later archaizing style, because the words and idioms involved simply disappeared from standard Biblical Hebrew, but are still found in Ugaritic (e.g. the consistent mixing of perfect and imperfect as narrative tenses; the imagery of vs. 3; *zh syny* in vs. 9; the verb *l'h* "to vanquish" in vs. 10; *hytk* "your habitations" in vs. 11, the yellow gold of v. 14; *šnn* "elite soldier" in vs. 18; the use of the article as a demonstrative pronoun in vs. 20; several times separative *b*, vss. 6, 18, 25).

3. Ps. lxviii contains a number of archaic metaphors which are either unique in the Old Testament or attested only in a few equally old passages. In all these cases it is possible to cite comparative evidence from Ugarit proving that the imagery involved was used to describe Canaanite gods (Korpel [n. 5], p. 624). For example, according to vs. 6 God is a *dayyān*. This epithet is attested in Ugarit as well as in the equally archaic Hebrew oath formula of 1 Sam. xxiv 16. In vs. 8 God is said to "stride" (*s'd*). This is attested only in the equally archaic passages Judg. v 4, Hab. iii 12 and perhaps Gen. xlix 22 (Korpel, p. 532, n. 59). It derives from the Canaanite picture of El as a striding Bull. According to

---

of the Psalm. However, he overlooks the difference in meaning between the two passages. Morever, he does not take into account the remarkable fact that there are many other poems in the Hebrew Bible the composite nature of which is generally recognized, but which yet exhibit a regular structure in their final form. In other words, the later editors were also accomplished poets who knew how to compose a balanced whole out of the fragments they took over from other sources.

[96] Jeremias distinguishes a North-Israelite hymn which, according to him, dates from the early royal period from the later additions made in the Jerusalemite cult (vss 17, 19, 28–32).

vs. 10 God has a geographic locality on earth as his *nḥlh*. This
idea recurs in Ex. xv 17 only and is apparently derived from
Canaanite religion. In vs. 17 it is said that God desires something
(*ḥmd*)—this is unique in the Old Testament, but not uncommon
in Ugarit. In vs. 20 God is said to carry a load (*'ms*)—again a
unique anthropomorphism that has its parallels in Ugarit. In short,
the concept of God presented in the first part of Ps. lxviii fits a
time close to the texts of Ugarit, but would be extremely difficult
to reconcile with a much later date.

4. A number of divine names used in Ps. lxviii is unique and can
   best be explained by assuming a fairly high date. I refer specifically to the peculiar designation of God in vs. 19 (*yh 'lhym*) (cf.
   RoY, pp. 245–6).

5. In vs. 7 the Kosharoth, Canaanite goddesses of matrimonial happiness occurring in the texts of Ugarit and Emar, are still mentioned quite innocently, which proves that the first part of Ps.
   lxviii dates from an era when official Israelite religion did not yet
   eliminate female beings completely from the entourage of YHWH.[97]
   We know practically for certain that this must have happened
   before the early royal period, probably in the 12th century B.C.
   (see Korpel [n. 5], p. 218, and n. 77 above).

These indications of the very high date of Ps. lxviii 2–25 can be
supplemented by other arguments suggesting a date as early as the
second half of the 13th century. Especially noteworthy is the reference to a battle in the plain of Hazor during which Adam and Merom
were raided by the Israelites (vs. 19 in my reading; cf. *RoY*, p. 121).
Thus success was later on attributed to both Joshua and Deborah,[98]
but was probably an exploit by the Israelite "kings" in Bashan (vs. 12).

We also note the prominence of the notion of settlement in the
first half of Ps. lxviii. Elohim has his own habitation (*m'wn*, vs. 6). He
gives the lonely a home (*yšb* H *byth*, vs. 7), only the recalcitrant
prefer to dwell in the desert (*škn* vs. 7). Elohim vanquishes an inheritance which he creates or establishes (*kwn* L, vs. 10). He founds (*kwn*

---

[97] Of course it is important to note here that goddesses in a subservient role are
not the same as a divine wife.

[98] Josh. xi, see also xii 20 LXX; Judg. iv; cf. V. Fritz, "Das Ende der spät-
bronzezeitlichen Stadt Hazor Stratum XIII und die biblische Überlieferung in Josua
11 und Richter 4", *UF* 5 (1973), pp. 123–39; H. Rösel, "Studien zur Topographie
der Kriege in den Büchern Josua und Richter", *ZDPV 91* (1975), pp. 171–83.

Hiphil) habitations (*ḥyt*) which are situated (*yšb*) in Bashan (vs. 11). God wants to stay (*yšb*) on Mt Bashan; he wants to dwell (*škn*) there for ever (vs. 17). YH wants to settle (*škn*) there (vs. 19).

The warriors of YHWH are predatory bands that go out for a loot of gold and silver in spring when the thunder resounds over the mountains (vss 13–14). But at the same time they appear to have settled more or less. They have sheepfolds (vs. 14) where their wives stay behind, and apparently they have shelter for the winter. So they possess more or less permanent habitations which God had founded for them (vs. 11). They had long been poor, but now they live in houses and are on their way to becoming rich. Their chiefs even dare to call themselves "kings of the armies" (vs. 12). Comparable are the sheikhs of the Bini-Yamina tribes and of Amurru in the Mari texts. They too called themselves "kings".[99] These "kings" even possessed chariots and lifeguards (vs. 18), and therefore it must be assumed that they had progressed to a fairly high level of integration into the culture of Canaan. All this accords extremely well with what we know about the ʿApiru and Shosu who were fully integrated into the culture of Canaan and possessed gold, silver and precious stones, as is attested epigraphically as early as Seti I (*c.* 1294–1279 B.C.).[100]

Because we know that under Merenptah (*c.* 1212–1203 B.C.) "Israel" was an ethnic reality in northern Palestine or the Bashan area[101] there is no reason to doubt that "Israel" in vs. 9 belongs to the original text. But then the circumstance that it had several "kings of the armies" at that time (vs. 12) becomes highly interesting because it means that this "Israel" was a confederation of several tribes already.[102]

---

[99] See G. Dossin, "Kengen, pays de Canaan", *RSO* 32 (1957), pp. 37–8; L.M. Muntingh, "Israelite-Amorite Political Relations During the Second Millennium B.C.", in P. Fronzaroli (ed.), *Atti del Secondo Congresso Internazionale di Linguistica Camito-Semitica, Firenze, 16–19 aprile 1974* (Firenze, 1978), pp. 217–21; M. Anbar, "The Kings of the Beni-Yamina Tribes in the Mari Texts", *Proceedings of the Ninth World Congress of Jewish Studies, Jerusalem, August 4–12, 1985* (Jerusalem, 1986), pp. 13–17. See also the Shasu king depicted on the Baluʿa relief, W.A. Ward and M.F. Martin, "The Baluʿa Stele: A New Transcription with Palaeographical and Historical Notes", *Annual of the Department of Antiquities of Jordan* 8/9 (1964), pp. 5–29 and Pl. III.

[100] K.R. Weeks et al. (ed.), *The Epigraphic Survey: Reliefs and Inscriptions at Karnak* 4: *The Battle Reliefs of King Sety I* (Chicago, 1986), pp. 25, 42.

[101] J. Yoyote, "La campagne palestinienne du pharaon Merneptah: données anciennes et récentes", in Laperrousaz (n. 1), p. 117.

[102] For the early date of this confederation see also my contribution "The Twelve Tribes in the Song of Deborah" *VT* 43 (1993), pp. 483–93.

4.4 Bashan as the Mountain of God in Ps. lxviii

Obviously, the Solomonic appendix to Ps lxviii did not interpret vs. 17 as a reference to Bashan as a mountain of God. Possibly '*lhym* was interpreted as "gods", as a designation of the spirits of the dead that were supposed to roam in this particular area, which played an important part in the Canaanite cult of dead ancestors.[103] Or '*lhym* was understood as an expression of the superlative, "mighty mountain", as it is translated even nowadays in the *Revised Standard Version*. However, against such an interpretation argues the circumstance that in all seven other occurrences of *hr'lhym* or *hr h'lhym* in the Bible the expression must be rendered as "mountain of God".[104] Moreover, it necessitates a different meaning of '*lhym* in vs. 16 and vs. 17, which must be deemed improbable.

Those who nevertheless favoured such a forced interpretation further take the verb *rṣd* in vs. 17 to mean "to envy", so that the following rendering becomes possible: "Mighty Mt Bashan . . . why did you envy the mountain on which Elohim wanted to stay?" The mountain on which Elohim wanted to stay is then Mt Zion. This interpretation is found already in Aquila, Symmachus, the Peshiṭta and Jerome.[105] However, the verb *rṣd* recurs in Ben Sira xiv 22 and surely means "to watch intently, to peep" there.[106] Moreover, both the Akkadian and Arabic cognates of Hebrew *rṣd* simply mean "to lie in wait, to watch intently". In Arabic it is used specifically for serpents lying in wait for passers-by (Lane, p. 1092). When we connect this with the fact that in early Canaanite Bashan means "serpent",[107] it is obvious that a pun was intended. It is for this reason that I reject the Zionistic interpretation of v. 17.[108]

However, two other solutions should shortly be discussed. Some

---

[103] *RoY*, p. 121, n. 96. Cf. 1 Sam. xxviii.

[104] Ex. iii 1, iv 27, xviii 5, xxiv 13; 1 Kgs xix 8; Ezek. xxviii 14, 16.

[105] Aquila ἐρίζετε; Symmachus περισπουδάζετε; Peshiṭta *ṣbyn*; Vulgate *suspicamini*; Versio iuxta Hebraeos *contenditis*. Differently: LXX ὑπολαμβάνετε, Theodotion δικάζεσθε, Targum *ṭpzyn*.

[106] LXX ἐνεδρεύειν, Syriac *kmn*.

[107] This etymology for Bashan was proposed most recently by G. del Olmo Lete, "Bašan o el 'infierno' cananeo", *SEL* 5 (1988), p. 56. See for similar proposals A. Goetze, "Is Ugaritic a Canaanite Dialect?", *Language* 17 (1941); p. 131; S. Mowinckel, *Der achtundsechzigste Psalm* (Oslo, 1953), p. 44.

[108] As stated above, the later editor of the Psalm probably found a way to interpret Ps. lxviii 16 in this manner. See for a judicious discussion of various possibilities, J.A. Emerton, "The 'Mountain of God' in Psalm 68:16", *SVT* (50) 1993, pp. 24–37.

scholars have proposed to take "Bashan" as an alternative name of
Mt Zion here, just as Zion is identified with Mt Zaphon in Ps. xlviii
3. Still others see it as a designation of Mt Tabor. Both proposals
must be rejected because in contrast to Ps. xlviii the context of Ps.
lxviii does not make any such identification explicit. Moreover, neither Zion nor Tabor is ever called a "mountain of God",[109] and this
too argues against a transfer of the name of Bashan to either of
these mountains.

So the most natural interpretation of the text of Ps. lxviii is to
take Bashan simply as the well-known mountain range of that name.
As a consequence Bashan is one of the mountains called "mountain
of God" (vs. 16), next to Sinai and Horeb. This is in accordance
with vss. 6, 11 and 17 according to which YHWH-El, the God
of Israel, has had a sanctuary there. This may have been a semi-
permanent dwelling, because in Ps. lxxvi 3 *m'wn* is balanced by *skh*
"tabernacle".

4.5 Bashan = Zaphon

The anti-Baalistic tone of Ps. lxviii (especially vss 5, 9–10, 12, 21)
suggests that YHWH-El's occupation of Mt Bashan is the Israelite
account of the occupation of Baal's mountain Zaphon as testified by
the stele from Sheikh el-Sa'd located in Bashan and by the Ugaritic
myth. However, in the present text of Ps. lxviii Bashan is not called
Zaphon.[110]

Yet we know that there existed a city and/or a region called
"Zaphon" north of Succoth/Deir 'Alla.[111] Its exact location is uncer-
tain,[112] but it has lent its name to the Transjordanian Gadite tribe
called the Zaphonites (Gen. xlvi 16; Num. xxvi 15).

---

[109] A few times Zion is called "mountain of YHWH". Cf. Isa ii 3 par., xxx 14;
Zech. viii 3; Ps. xxiv 3; cf. Gen. xxii 14.

[110] Korpel (n. 5), p. 582, n. 418, mentions the possibility of emending *slmwn* in vs.
15 into *spwn*, but this would seem too speculative.

[111] Josh. xiii 27; Judg. xii 1. Because Mizpah was Jephthah's home-town (Judg.
xi 34) it is not entirely certain that Zaphon in Judg. xii 1 is a city.

[112] For identification with Tell es-Sa'idiyeh e.g. W.F. Albright, "The Jordan Valley in the Bronze Age", *AASOR* 6 (1926), pp. 45–6; F.-M. Abel, *Géographie de la
Palestine* 2 (Paris, 1938), p. 70; Y. Aharoni, *The Land of the Bible: A Historical Geography*
(transl. A.F. Rainey, 2nd ed. London, 1967), pp. 31, 91, 115, 190; Mittmann
(n. 15), pp. 219–20. For Tell El-Qōs, N. Glueck, *The River Jordan* (London;
Lutterworth, 1946), pp. 109–10; idem, "Explorations in Eastern Palestine IV", *AASOR*
25–8 (1951), pp. 347–53; J. Simons, *The Geographical and Topographical Texts of the Old*

In Ezek. xlvii 17 the north-eastern border of the "ideal" Israel is described as *gbwl dmśq wṣpwn ṣpwnh wgbwl ḥmt* "the territory[113] of Damascus and Zaphon[114] in the north and the territory of Hamath". This description corresponds to *gbwl dmśq . . . gbwl ḥmt . . . gbwl ḥwrn* in Ezek. xlvii 16. The conclusion would seem inevitable that here *ṣpwn* is an alternative name of the Ǧebel Ḥauran, or an area close to it.

Most scholars agree that the geographical list of Ezek. xlvii goes back on a fairly old tradition about the borders of "the land of Canaan" which is preserved in a slightly different form in Num. xxxiv where, unfortunately, the name of Zaphon has dropped out.[115]

The unintelligible *ky šm ḥlqt mḥqq ṣpwn* in the blessing of Gad in Deut. xxxiii 21 may perhaps be translated as "for there was the portion of the ruler of Zaphon"[116] as a reference to the legendary Amorite king Sihon whose territory was allotted to Gad (Josh. xiii 8–11, 24–8). Even the stele of Mesha of the 9th century B.C. acknowledges that the men of Gad had dwelt in northern Transjordan "from time immemorial" (*mꜥlm*, line 10).

The tradition that YHWH founded a sanctuary on a mountain in Transjordan is also preserved in Ps. lxxviii 54. This verse is strikingly close to the wording of the Job-stele: *hr zh qnth ymynw* "the mountain which his hand created". This again should be compared to Ps. lxxxix 13 according to which God has created (*brʾ*) Zaphon and other holy mountains. When we compare Ps. lxxviii 54 to Ex. xv 13–18 it is likely that both accounts were later understood to refer to Mt Zion. But because in both cases the statement about the creation of the holy mountain is placed in the context of Transjordanian victories, I venture the hypothesis that originally both passages referred to Bashan as the first mountain God chose to dwell on.

Also in Isa. xiv 13–14 El appears to have taken over Baal's mountain Zaphon:

Testament (Leiden, 1959), § 598. But see Mittmann, pp. 219–20, n. 31. Contrary to what some scholars have asserted a city Ṣapuna does not occur in the Amarna letters. Cf. Moran (n. 62), p. 498.

[113] On the problem of the translation of the word *gbwl* see Z. Kallai, *Historical Geography of the Bible: The Tribal Territories of Israel* (Jerusalem and Leiden, 1986), pp. 100–1, n. 5.

[114] Often *wṣpwn* is emended without proper justification. Next to the locative *ṣpwnh* it can only have been understood as a geographic name.

[115] See e.g. Aharoni (n. 112), pp. 62–8; Naʾaman (n. 54), pp. 31, 39, 244.

[116] For the occasional exchange of *ṣ* for *s* see Hebr. *ṣmḥ* = Arab. *smḫ*; Hebr. *ꜥlṣ* = Hebr. *ꜥls*; Arab. *ṣfq* = Arab. *sfq*; Hebr. *prṣ* = Hebr. *prs*; Hebr. *qrṣ* = Hebr. *qrs*; Hebr. *ṣpn* = Hebr. *spn*; Ugar. *qlṣ* = Hebr. *qls*.

wʾth ʾmrt blbbk	And you said in your heart:
hšmym ʾʿlh	I will ascend to heaven.
mmʿl lkwkby ʾl	Above the stars of El
ʾrym ksʾy	I will set up my throne.
wʾšb bhr-mwʿd	And I will sit on the mount of the assembly,
byrkty ṣpwn	on the crests of the Zaphon,
ʾʿlh ʿl-bmty ʿb	I will ascend above the heights of the clouds
ʾdmh lʿlywn	and make myself like Elyon.

Apparently, Zaphon is the mountain of El here. The Canaanite background of this passage has long been recognized,[117] but it always remained a problem that the mountain of Baal seemed to be occupied by El. Now we understand that this is in line with the testimony of the Job-stele and the Ugaritic myth.

According to Job xxvi 7, El the Creator stretched Zaphon[118] over the abyss, whereas the next verse uses the verb *ṣrr* which may be an allusion to the function of Baal as the weather-god.[119] Job xxxvii 22 states that gold comes from the Zaphon to cover God with splendour. In other words, the book of Job also appears to support the claim that it was not Baal, but El who was the Master of Zaphon and its gold.

According to Mic. vii 14, there was a time when YHWH lived alone (*škny lbbd*) in the forests of Bashan where he pastured Israel as his flock. The prophet places this episode in the days of old, so that a considerable amount of time must have elapsed between the date of this passage and the actual event to which it refers. It is a tradition that agrees with Deut. xxxiii 22, according to which Bashan would have been the homeland of the tribe of Dan, apparently before the tribe settled in Cisjordan. And it agrees with Deut. xxxii 12, where it is stated that YHWH alone (*bdd*) has led Israel to an area in Bashan (vs. 14) where it became very prosperous. Obviously, such passages recall the oracle of Balaam who described Israel as living alone (*bdd*) in Transjordan.[120]

It appears that YHWH-El's occupation of Zaphon was an important theologoumenon in early Israel and among its immediate

---

[117] Spronk, (n. 8), pp. 213–27; Niehr (n. 90), pp. 102–5.

[118] The real mountain, cf. J.J.M. Roberts, "ṢĀPÔN in Job 26, 7", *Bibl* 56 (1975), pp. 554–7.

[119] Cf. J.C. Greenfield, *Maarav* 5/6 (1990), p. 160, n. 5. Also W.G.E. Watson in a paper read at Kampen, 24 March 1992.

[120] See my treatment of Num. xxiii 9–10 above.

neighbours in northern Transjordan. Is it to be wondered at, then, that the name of Zaphon had to move once more when the temple in Jerusalem had been built? Ps. xlviii 3 identifies Mt Zion with the crests of Zaphon (*yrkty ṣpwn*) and maintains that this was the mountain God had created (vs. 9). The same identification of Zaphon and Zion seems to be presupposed in the "Canaanite" version of Ps. xx 3 found in the Papyrus Amherst No. 63 (col. XII, 13).[121] It is not unlikely that in Ezekiel's description of the theophany *mn-hṣpwn* (i 4) Zion reappears in the guise of Mt Zaphon.

All this accords well with my thesis that YHWH was a manifestation of El and that early Israel worshipped El as the highest God who had dwarfed all other deities, including Baal. As I have tried to show, this intolerant type of religion was *en vogue* at the end of the Late Bronze Age.

5. *What Was the Link?*

If the people of Ugarit knew of YHWH-El's appropriation of Bashan under the name of Baal's mountain Zaphon, and if it is true that they were informed fairly accurately about the peculiarities of this religious concentration on only one God, whereas on the other hand there are strong indications that the same traditions about Jahwe-El's appropriation of Bashan under the name of Zaphon were known in Israel, it remains to establish how this direct link between Ugarit and the Proto-Israelites must be envisaged.

In my opinion the Amorites constituted the link. If I am right in understanding the Yawê of El-Amarna letter No. 154: 6–7 as a designation of the people of YHWH, they seem to have been serving the Amorite ruler Aziru in the 14th century B.C. (see n. 35 above). It is likely that northern Transjordan had fallen prey to the expansionist policies of Amurru towards the end of the Late Bronze Age.[122]

---

[121] S.P. Vleeming and J.W. Wesselius, *Studies in Papyrus Amherst 63* 1 (Amsterdam, 1985), pp. 51, 55; Smith (n. 4), pp. 53–4.

[122] H. Klengel, "Aziru von Amurru und seine Rolle in der Geschichte der Amarnazeit", *MIO* 10 (1964), pp. 57–83; A. Altman, "The Revolutions in Byblos and Amurru during the Amarna Period and their Social Background", in P. Artzi (ed.), *Bar-Ilan Studies in History* (Ramat Gan, 1978), pp. 3–24; M. Liverani, "Aziru, serviteur di due padroni", in O. Carruba et al., *Studi Orientalistici in ricordo di Franco Pintore* (Pavia, 1983), pp. 93–121; idem (n. 33), pp. 71, 85, 149; G. Buccellati, "From Khana to Laqê: The End of Syro-Mesopotamia", in Ö. Tunca (ed.), *De la Babylonie à la Syrie, en passant par Mari: Mélanges offerts à Monsieur J.-R, Kupper* (Liège, 1990), pp. 229–53.

The kingdom of Ugarit maintained close, though not always friendly, relations with Amurru.[123] In any case, the Ugaritic dynasty traced its origins back to Amurru.[124] The righteous Dani'ilu, who was also known in Israel, was king of Amurru, and apparently his kingdom comprised cities in the upper north of Canaan as well as at least part of the Lebanon.[125] Ugarit imported fine vessels from Amurru (*KTU* 1.4: I. 41).

The cult-myth of Tadmor (Palmyra), one of the main cities of Amurru at that time, was probably recited during the Ugaritic New Year festival. Bedouin warriors (*'rbm*) from this country seem to have attended the festivities (*ARTU*, pp. 117–28). A treaty between the two countries stipulates that Amurru will provide Ugarit with armed support if necessary.[126]

A number of characteristics of the Proto-Israelites accords well with their close contacts with the Amorites:

1. Biblical tradition indicates that the ancestors of ancient Israel came from an Aramaic milieu.[127] Especially noteworthy is the so-called "Historical Credo", *'rmy 'bd 'by* "my father was a wandering Aramaean".[128] Gerhard von Rad and others are right in insisting that this tradition must be old.[129] Mostly it is assumed that Ur of

---

[123] M. Liverani, *Storia di Ugarit nell'eta' degli archivi politici* (Roma, 1962), pp. 32–6; idem (n. 33), pp. 192, 200; I. Singer, in S. Izre'el, *Amurru Akkadian: A Linguistic Study* (Atlanta, 1992), pp. 175–6.

[124] B. Levine J.-M. de Tarragon, "Dead Kings and Rephaim: The Patrons of the Ugaritic Dynasty", *JAOS* 104 (1984), pp. 654–5; Spronk (n. 8), pp. 191–6; Smith (n. 4), pp. 76–7, n. 120.

[125] De Moor, *ARTU*, pp. 225, 268, 270, 272–3.

[126] RS 19.86, J. Nougayrol, *La palais royal d'Ugarit IV* (Mission de Ras Shamra 9) (Paris, 1956), pp. 281–6, with the improvements proposed by C. Kühne, "Zum Text RS 19.68", *UF* 3 (1971), pp. 369–71.

[127] See e.g. R.T. O'Callaghan, *Aram Naharaim: A Contribution to the History of Upper Mesopotamia in the Second Millennium B.C.* (Roma, 1948), pp. 29–30; W.T. Pitard, *Ancient Damascus: A Historical Study of the Syrian City-State from Earliest Times until its Fall to the Assyrians in 732–B.C.E.* (Winona Lake, 1987), p. 86.

[128] See with regard to the translation W. Gesenius, R. Meyer et al., *HAHAT* 2.

[129] See especially G. von Rad, *Das formgeschichtliche Problem des Hexateuch* (Stuttgart, 1938) = idem, *Gesammelte Studien zum Alten Testament* 1 (München, 1958), pp. 1–15, 48–65, 90; M.A. Beek, "Das Problem das aramäischen Stammvaters (Deut. XXVI 5)", *OTS* 8 (1950), pp. 193–219, esp. 207; N. Lohfink, *Unsere großen Wörter: Das Alte Testament zu Themen dieser Jahre* (Freiburg, 1977), pp. 76–91, esp. 80–2; A.R. Millard, "A. Wandering Aramean", *JNES* 39 (1980), pp. 153–5; S. Kreuzer, *Die Frühgeschichte Israels in Bekenntnis und Verkündigung des Alten Testaments* (Berlin, 1989), pp. 63–81, 153–80; D.R. Daniels, "The creed of Deuteronomy xxvi revisited", *SVT* 41 (1990), 231–42. Of course, the presumed antiquity of the designation "wandering Aramaean" does not preclude a thorough Deuteronomistic reworking of the Creed, as I have argued in *SVT* 53 (1994), pp. 188–9.

the Chaldaeans in Gen. xi 28, 31, xv 7; Neh. ix 7 is an ana-chronism. However, even at this early date *kśdym* could be under-stood as a designation of Aramaeans.[130]

We now know that toward the end of the Late Bronze Age Amurru was at least in part an Aramaic speaking country.[131] Egyp-tian sources confirm that toward the end of the 13th century B.C. the region of Damascus was populated by Aramaeans.[132] But also *Sūḫu*, located in the upper north of Canaan[133] and homeland of Job's friend Bildad, had become a centre of Aramaic culture by that time.[134] This testifies to the rapid expansion of the Amorite/Aramaic sphere of influence.

Around 1190 B.C. the kingdom of Amurru was destroyed by the Sea Peoples, as is testified by Ramses III and confirmed by an oracle of Balaam (Num. xxiv 23) (*RoY*, pp. 147, 154). Un-doubtedly, large numbers of Amorite refugees fled south then, seeking shelter in the same environment where at that time the early Israelites were living.

2. The many remarkable parallels between Mari and Israel[135] are best explained by assuming a common Amorite background of the two cultures.

Lipiński's statement that the Aramaeans are not attested before 1000 B.C., re-peated in E. Lipiński, "'Mon père était un araméen errant': L'histoire carrefour des sciences bibliques et orientales", *OLP* 20 (1989), pp. 23–47, needs revision in the light of the evidence cited above.

Already the ancient versions took offense at the statement in Deut. xxvi; cf. F. Dreyfus, "'L'Araméen voulait tuer mon père': L'actualisation de Dt 26,5 dans la tradition juive et la tradition chrétienne", in M. Carrez et al. (ed.), *De la Tôrah au Messie, Mélanges H, Cazelles* (Paris, 1981), pp. 147–61.

[130] See for this possibility D.O. Edzard, "Kaldu", *RlA* 5 (Berlin, 1977), pp. 291–2.

[131] De Moor, *ARTU*, p. 118, n. 9. See also I.J. Gelb, "La lingua degli Amoriti", *AANL*, Cl. sc. mor., 13 (1958), p. 152. Amorite *n'm* (note the ending) from the kingdom of Siyannu fought at the side of Ramses II in the battle of Kadesh. Cf. A. Gardiner, *The Kadesh Inscriptions of Ramesses II* (Oxford, 1960), p. 37. The ending *n* in Yaudic, Moabite and the dialect of the Balaam texts should be attributed to the influence of Aramaic-speaking Amorites. According to a text from Emar Aramean Palmyrenians paid each other in the currency of Amurru. Cf. Arnaud (n. 37), No. 21: 16, 18.

[132] M. Görg, *Beitrage zur Zeitgeschichte der Anfänge Israels: Dokumente—Materialien—Notizen* (Wiesbaden, 1989), pp. 157–60; G.G.G. Reinhold, *Die Beziehungen Altisraels zu den aramäischen Staaten in der israelitisch-judäischen Königszeit* (Frankfurt a.M., 1989), pp. 28–9.

[133] J.J. Stamm et al. (ed.) *HALAT* 4, Leiden, 1990, pp. 1335b, with bibliography.

[134] J.A. Brinkman, *A Political History of Post-Kassite Babylonia 1158–722 B.C.* (Roma, 1968), pp. 183–4, n. 1127; Arnaud (n. 37), No. 263: 17–29.

[135] See now A. Malamat, *Mari and the Early Israelite Experience* (Oxford, 1989), with copious bibliography.

3. According to biblical tradition the Amorites dominated the cities and villages in Transjordan (Num. xxxii 4; Deut. iii 5). But also in Cisjordan the ancestors of Israel sojourned among Amorites living in the cities (Gen. xiv 13, xlviii 22; Judg. i 34–5). Now that we know about the expansion and subsequent dispersion of the Amorites towards the end of the Late Bronze Age, these traditions gain credibility.[136] The inhabitants of Amurru were at least in part herdsmen (Weeks [n. 100], pp. 79ff., Pl. 23).

According to Josh. xxiv 2, 15 the early Israelites served the gods of the Amorites and, as we have seen, this is entirely true. In this early period they worshipped not only the Canaanite El, but also other deities, like the Kosharoth, the goddesses overseeing childbirth (Ps. lxviii 7) (cf. *RoY*, p. 119, n. 91; p. 124). Ezekiel's blunt statement "Your father was an Amorite" (Ezek. xvi 3, 45) must have hurt badly exactly because it was at least in part true.[137]

4. As we have seen, it is a simplification to speak of an either-or with regard to the models of peaceful and armed occupation of the land Canaan by the Proto-Israelites. A strong sense of independence (cf. Num. xxiii 9) and a certain aggressiveness (cf. Gen. xlix; Ps. lxviii 2–25) seem to have characterized the early Israelites. Egyptian, Hittite and Canaanite sources testify to the expansionist policies of Amurru and show that its inhabitants were often revolting against their overlords, using the 'Apiru as cheap mercenaries.

The evidence adduced seem to warrant the conclusion that Ugarit and early Israel belonged to the same continuum of Amorite culture.[138]

---

[136] The border description in Josh. xiii 4–5 still presupposes the more restricted meaning of the geographic designation "Amurru". Cf. M. Liverani, "The Amorites", in D.J. Wiseman (ed.), *Peoples of Old Testament Times* (Oxford, 1973), pp. 119–20. Contrary to what some have thought the broader meaning of the gentilic remained in use in the Late Bronze Age. Cf. W.T. Koopmans, *Joshua 24 as Poetic Narrative* (Sheffield, 1990), pp. 444–9; I. Singer, "The 'Land of Amurru' and the 'Lands of Amurru' in the Šaušgamuwa Treaty", *Iraq* 51 (1991), pp. 69–74. Few will share the hypercritical judgement of E.A. Knauf, "Hesbon, Sihons Stadt", *ZDPV* 106 (1990), p. 141: "Am Ende der Bronzezeit kamen keine Israeliten ins Ostjordanland. Kein Mose hat dort die Königreiche Sihons oder Ogs erobert, die keine Amoriten waren."

[137] So with J.T. Luke, "'Your Father Was an Amorite' (Ezek 16: 3, 45): An Essay on the Amorite Problem in OT Traditions", in H.B. Huffmon et al. (ed.), *The Quest for the Kingdom of God: Studies in Honor of G.E. Mendenhall* (Winona Lake, 1983), pp. 221–37.

[138] A similar approach is advocated by Buccellati (n. 122), pp. 246–51.

This is the historical link explaining how Israel could know about the Ugaritic righteous sufferer Daniel just as conversely Ugarit knew the story of the strange god YHWH-El who had appropriated Baal's mountain Zaphon. This finding accords well with the biblical traditions about the origin of the patriarchs in the Aramaic–Amorite milieu of northern Syria, although it now seems likely that they lived rather in the Late Bronze Age than earlier.

However, how can this northern origin be reconciled with the theophany traditions found in Ps. lxviii 8–9 and in some other archaic texts? All of them presuppose that YHWH came from the south instead of the north.[139]

In this case too Ugarit seems to offer a satisfactory explanation. On the basis of their brilliant reconstruction of the history of the cuneiform alphabet Manfried Dietrich and Oswald Loretz have come to the conclusion that the Proto-Ugaritic ruling class must have originated in the south of Canaan, possibly in the Edomite part of Transjordan, from where they moved to the Levant around the middle of the second millennium B.C.[140] This means that the Proto-Israelites and the Proto-Ugaritians moved north from southern Palestine in about the same period and perhaps for the same reasons. The Israelite traditions about the theophany from the south preserve the memory of that migration.

As a matter of fact, we know fairly certainly that a Canaanite variant of this theophany tradition was known in northern Canaan in the small kingdom of Siyannu at the southern border of the kingdom of Ugarit.[141] It is preserved in a number of much later syncretistic hymns in the Papyrus Amherst 63.[142] These hymns describe the theophany in terms that match the imagery of Ps. lxviii remarkably well.[143] The highest god Bethel, with whom YHWH was sometimes

---

[139] Sinai, Kadesh, Seir, Edom, Paran, Teman, Ps. lxviii 8–9, 18; Hab. iii 3; Deut. xxxiii 2; Judg. v 4–5, confirmed by the epigraphical finds at Kuntillet 'Ajrud.

[140] M. Dietrich and O. Loretz, "Das ugaritische Alphabet", *UF* 18 (1986), pp. 3–26; idem and idem, "Die Alphabettafel aus Bet Šemeš und die ursprüngliche Heimat der Ugariter", in *AOAT* 220 (1988) [Festschrift K. Deller], pp. 61–85; idem and idem, *Die Keilalphabete: Die phönizisch-kanaanäischen und altarabischen Alphabete in Ugarit* (Münster, 1988), pp. 297–311.

[141] See for its demarcation M.C. Astour, "The Kingdom of Siyannu–Ušnatu", *UF* 11 (1979), pp. 13–28.

[142] I use the preliminary edition by Vleeming and Wesselius (n. 121); vol. 2 (Amsterdam, 1990).

[143] See especially vol. 2, pp. 29–71.

equated,[144] appears with rainstorms, thunder and fire from Resh,[145] a locality in northern Canaan probably to be identified with Reshbaʻl, east of Hermel,[146] the city of the Ugaritic hero Daniel (*ARTU*, p. 225, n. 6). Apparently, this Resh was situated in *syn'*, Siyannu.[147] We know for certain that, just like Ugarit and early Israel, Siyannu belonged to the Amorite sphere of influence during the Late Bronze Age. It was annexed by Aziru of Amurru, at that time an ally of Egypt, whereas Ugarit had taken sides with the Hittites against Egypt.[148] A few years later, a treaty between Niqmaddu II of Ugarit, Aziru of Amurru and Abdiḫebat of Siyannu speaks explicitly of the differences of opinion in the preceding period.[149]

So we may conclude that not only the legends about king Og[150] travelled north, but also the story of YHWH-El's occupation of Baal's mountain Zaphon and the tradition about his fearful appearance in fire and clouds from a region in southern Canaan. Apparently these earliest settlement traditions of the Israelites were transmitted northward through the channel of Amorite culture.

---

[144] P. Grelot, *Documents araméens d'Égypte* (Paris, 1972), pp. 351–2; Papyrus Amherst 63, XII. 18. See also Gen. xxxi 13, xxxv 7; Jer. xlviii 13.

[145] Cf. Exod. xix 20, xxxiv 2 where *r'š* and *syny* are used in parallelism.

[146] J. Elayi, "Baʼliraʼsi, Rêsha, Reshbaʻl, étude de toponymie historique", *Syria* 58 (1981), pp. 331–41.

[147] Papyrus Amherst 63, X.14, XI.14. There is little reason to assume any direct connection between the names of Siyannu and Sinai, even though a famous Kadesh (on the Orontes) is situated nearby, whereas Kadesh-barnea in the south was totally uninhabited at the time, as reported by R. Cohen, "Les fouilles de Qadesh–Barnéa et les forteresses du Négev", in E.-M. Laperroussaz (ed.), *Archéologie, art et histoire de la Palestine* (Paris, 1986), pp. 87, 95. A remote possibility would be that the frequent combination *hr syny* originally meant "the Siyannite mountain".

[148] Gardiner (n. 131), p. 58; H. Klengel, *Geschichte Syriens im 2. Jahrtausend v.u.Z.* 2 (Berlin, 1969), pp. 318–93.

[149] RS 19.68; Nougayrol (n. 126), pp. 284–6.

[150] W. Röllig, "Eine neue phönizische Inschrift aus Byblos", in R. Degen et al. (ed.), *Neue Ephemeris für Semitische Epigraphik* 2 (Wiesbaden, 1974), pp. 1–15.

RECHTSREFORMEN IN DEUTERONOMIUM XII–XXVI UND IM MITTELASSYRISCHEN KODEX DER TAFEL A (KAV 1)

von

ECKART OTTO

Mainz

I. *Problemstellung*[1]

Es ist ein Charakteristikum des Deuteronomiums, daß gerade in den xii–xxvi programmatisch eröffnenden Kapiteln xii und xiii, dort, wo spezifisch israelitische Motive entfaltet werden, der Einfluß keilschriftlich-assyrischer Sprache und Motivik besonders markant ist. Die Langform der Zentralisationsformel wurde auf dem Hintergrund der akkadischen Phrase *šuma(m) šakānu* (sum. mu.ni.ba.gá.gá.)[2] formuliert.[3] Die vordtr Zentralisationsgesetze in xii 13–28* werden in xiii 2–18* mit drei Rechtssätzen gegen die Propagierung von Fremdreligionen fortgesetzt. In diesem Kapitel ist die Prägung durch Motive neu-assyrischer Vertragstexte und *adê*-Vereidigungen besonders dicht.[4] Vor Verrat an JHWH durch die Verehrung fremder Götter (xiii 3b, 7b, 11b, 14b) wird in Analogie zum politischen Verrat am assyrischen Großkönig gewarnt. Dabei hat die Warnung vor der Verschwörung von *nābî'* und *ḥōlem ḥᵃlôm* in xiii 2–6* eine Parallele in Asarhaddons *adê*-Vereidigung von 672 v.Chr. im Motiv *ina pi-i* LÚ.*ra-gi-me* LÚ.*maḫ-ḫe-e mār* (DUMU) *šá-'i-li a-mat ili* (DINGIR) "aus dem Mund eines

---

[1] Der Beitrag beruht auf einer umfassenden Monographie zur Redaktion von Dtn. xii–xxvi auf ihrem keilschriftrechtlichen Hintergrund, deren Veröffentlichung in SDIO ich vorbereite. Die Stellen im Deuteronomium werden nur mit den Ziffern angegeben.

[2] Cf. *CAD* Š/I, S. 143–4; vgl. F.R. Kraus, "Altmesopotamisches Lebensgefühl", *JNES* 19 (1960), S. (117–32) 128–31.

[3] Cf. N. Lohfink, "Zur deuteronomischen Zentralisationsformel", *Bib* 65 (1984), S. (297–328) 327–8 = ders., *Studien zum Deuteronomium und zur deuteronomistischen Literatur* II (Stuttgart, 1991), S. (147–77) 177. Cf. dort auch zur Setzung von Lang- und Kurzform der Zentralisationsformel als Mittel sekundärer Strukturierung des Textes.

[4] Cf. M. Weinfeld, *Deuteronomy and the Deuteronomic School* (Oxford, 1972), S. 91–100; P.E. Dion, "Deuteronomy 13: The Suppression of Alien Religious Propaganda in Israel During the Late Monarchical Era", in B. Halpern/D. Hobson (Hg.), *Law and Ideology in Monarchic Israel* (Sheffield, 1991), S. (147–216) 199–203.

Propheten, eines Ekstatikers, eines Sohns eines Befragers des Gotteswortes" (SAA II,VI 116,117).[5] Die im engsten Kreis der eigenen
Familie ihren Ausgangspunkt nehmende Rebellion gegen JHWH soll,
wie in der adê-Vereidigung (SAA II, VI 108–22, VII 18–27; cf. Sefire
III 2, 3[6]), durch rücksichtslose Denunzierung engster Familienmit-
glieder im Keime erstickt werden.[7] Die Aufklärung eines Gerüchtes
(xiii 13 *kî-tišmaʿ*) durch gerichtliche Untersuchung in xiii 15 (*šāʾaltā/
nākôn haddābār*) hat Parallelen in den neuassyrischen Landschenkungs-
urkunden K. 211 RS 49; K. 2729 RS 49 (*šaʾal kîn*)[8] und in der Formel
ubtaʾʾerū-š uktaʾʾinū-š[9] des Mittelassyrischen Kodex zur Bezeichnung
öffentlicher Rechtsverfahren[10] sowie das Schlagen einer Stadt mit der
Schärfe des Schwertes in xiii 16a (*hakkeh takkæh ʾæt-yōšᵉbê hāʿîr hahîʾ
lᵉpî ḥæræb*) in Sefire iii 12, 13 *whn qryh hʾnkh tkwh bḥrb*.[11] Wird in xiii
2–18* JHWHs Alleinverehrungsanspruch in Analogie zum politischen
Loyalitätsanspruch des assyrischen Großkönigs, der sich in neuassyrischen Verträgen und Loyalitätseiden niedergeschlagen hat, erhoben, so ist es nur konsequent, wenn die in den neuassyrischen
Vertragstexten auf die beeideten Loyalitätsforderungen folgenden
Flüche auch das Fluchkapitel xxviii tiefgreifend prägten.[12] xxviii 23

---

[5] Cf. S. Parpola/K. Watanabe, *Neo-Assyrian Treaties and Loyalty Oaths* (Helsinki,
1988), S. 33; cf. auch K. Watanabe, *Die adê-Vereidigung anläßlich der Thronfolgeregelung
Asarhaddons* (Berlin, 1987), S. 180. Für einen Überblick über die Staatsverträge
mesopotamischer Tradition cf. B. Kienast, "Der Vertrag Ebla-Assur in rechts-
historischer Sicht", in H. Waetzold/H. Hauptmann (Hg.), *Wirtschaft und Gesellschaft
von Ebla* (Heidelberg, 1988) S. (231–43) 239–43.

[6] Cf. A. Lemaire/J.-M. Durand, *Les inscriptions araméennes de Sfiré et l'Assyrie de Shamshi-
ilu* (Genf, 1984), S. 118.

[7] xiii 9 fin. 10aα (LXX *hagged taggîdænnû*; cf. Weinfeld [Anm. 4], S. 94–5) hat
Parallelen in Sefire III 1, 2 und SAA II, VI 80–2; 119–22 (*pazzuru/qabû*); cf. auch
XIII RS III 15–17 (*pazzuru/šapāru/šamû* [š-St.]). Das Motiv des Bruders derselben
Mutter (XIII 7) hat in diesem Zusammenhang Entsprechung in den neuassyrischen
Texten, während die hethitischen Dienstanweisungenen (cf. E.v. Schuler, *Hethitische
Dienstanweisungen für höhere Hof- und Staatsbeamte—Ein Beitrag zum antiken Recht Kleinasiens*
[Graz, 1957], S. 1, 14, 23) meist auf den gemeinsamen Vater abheben oder auf
unterschiedlich legitme Geburt; cf. Weinfeld (Anm. 4), S. 98–9, Anm. 5.

[8] Cf. J.N. Postgate, *Neo-Assyrian Royal Grants and Decrees* (Rom, 1969), S. 29, 31;
cf. auch Dion (Anm. 4), S. 201–2.

[9] *buʾāru* (G Perf.) vor *kuʾānu* (G Perf.) ist als Hendiadyoin zu verstehen; cf. *AHw*,
S. 109.

[10] Cf. C. Saporetti, *Le leggi medioassire* (Malibu, 1979), S. 14.

[11] Cf. Lemaire/Durand (Anm. 6), S. 119, 145. Dion ([Anm. 4], S. 203) verbindet
tel ʿôlām in xiii 17 mit *til abû-bi*; cf. Kodex Hammurapi (CH) XLIII 79. Zu neuassyrischen Belegen cf. *CAD* A, S. 78.

[12] Cf. D.R. Hillers, *Treaty Curses and the Old Testament Prophets* (Rom, 1964), 30–42;
R. Frankena, "The Vassal Treaties of Esarhaddon and the Dating of Deuteronomy",

hat eine Parallele in SAA II, VI 528–31,[13] xxviii 27–35 in SAA II, VI 419–30, 461–2. Die Abfolge von Flüchen der Geschwüre und Blindheit in xxviii 27–9 erklärt sich aus der Zusammenordnung von *sîn-šamaš*-Flüchen in neuassyrischem Fluchtext (SAA II, VI, 419–24[14]), die, in xxviii 27–9, 34–5 chiastisch angeordnet, xxviii 27–35 zu einem eigenständigen Überlieferungsstück zusammenfassen, das nach einer neuassyrischen *adê*-Vereidigung gestaltet wurde.[15] Es wäre nun aber recht kurzschlüssig, wollte man aus diesen Parallelen in xiii 2–18* und xxviii 23, 27–35* schließen, das vordtr Dtn. sei insgesamt die Urkunde einer nach neuassyrischem Vorbild gestalteten *adê*-Vereidigung Israels auf seinen Gott JHWH als Ablösung seiner Bindung an den assyrischen Großkönig.[16] Nur soviel wird man sagen können, daß das vordtr Dtn auf die assyrische Krise Judas reagiert.[17] Was aber bedeutet das für das Verständnis der Rechtssatzsammlung in xii–xxvi*, die ihre nächste Parallele im vordtn "Bundesbuch", nicht aber in der neuassyrischen *adê*-Vereidigung hat? Wie sind in xii–xxvi* israelitische und keilschriftliche Traditionen in Reaktion auf die neuassyrische Krise miteinander vermittelt? Die Antworten stehen noch aus. Der Vergleich von xii–xxvi* mit der vorgegebenen Tradition

---

OTS 14 (1965), S. (122–54) 129–33, 144–50; Weinfeld (Anm. 4), S. 116–29; D.J. McCarthy, *Treaty and Covenant. A Study in Form in the Ancient Oriental Documents and in the Old Testament* (Rom. ²1981), S. 172–87.

[13] Cf. D.J. Wiseman, "The Vassal-Treaties of Esarhaddon", *Iraq* 20 (1958), S. (1–99) 88; R. Borger, "Zu den Asarhaddon-Verträgen aus Nimrud", *ZA* 54 (1961), S. (173–96) 191–2.

[14] Cf. Weinfeld (Anm. 4), S. 119ff. Zur babylonischen Vorgeschichte des *sîn*-Fluches cf. K. Watanabe, "Die literarische Überlieferung eines babylonisch-assyrischen Fluchthemas mit Anrufung des Mondgottes *Sîn*", *Acta Sumerologica* 6 (1984), S. 99–119.

[15] Cf. G. Braulik, *Deuteronomium* II (Würzburg 1992), S. 206. Frankena ([Anm. 12], S. 130–1, 150) und Weinfeld ([Anm. 4], S. 123) rechnen noch den Deportationsfluch xxviii 36–7 zur Vorlage des Loyalitätseides eines judäischen Königs unter der Voraussetzung, daß, wie im Asarhaddon-Vertrag mit dem König Baal von Tyrus (SAA II, V, IV 14–17), der Deportationsfluch mit der Landesgottheit verbunden wurde.

[16] Cf. Frankena (Anm. 12), S. 150–4; differenzierter Weinfeld (Anm. 4), S. 157. Auf die Parallelität zwischen den futility-curses in xxviii 38–42 (cf. Hillers [Anm. 12], S. 28–9) und den Flüchen in Sefire I A, 27–8 (cf. Weinfeld [Anm. 4], S. 124 mit Anm. 2) und Sefire I A, 30–2; II A, 9 (cf. Hillers [Anm. 12], S. 54–5) sei nur hingewiesen.

[17] Cf. N. Lohfink, "Pluralismus. Theologie als Antwort auf Plausibilitätskrisen in aufkommenden pluralistischen Situationen, erörtert am Beispiel des deuteronomischen Gesetzes", in ders. *Unsere großen Wörter. Das Alte Testament zu Themen dieser Jahre* (Freiburg, 1977), S. 24–43; ders., "Das Deuteronomium", in ders. (Anm. 3), S. (15–24) 22–3.

des Bundesbuches[18] und der Keilschriftrechte[19] ist über die Beschränkung auf den je einzelnen Rechtssatz hinaus auf die Redaktionsstrukturen größerer Rechtssatzeinheiten auszudehnen.

Eine besondere Dichte terminologischer Parallelität kennzeichnet das Familienrecht des Mittelassyrischen Kodex der Tafel A (mass. K.A.) und des Dtn.,[20] so daß es zum Ausgangspunkt des Vergleichs gemacht werden soll. Diese Parallelen gewinnen an Gewicht durch die exklusiven Übereinstimmungen zwischen Dtn. und mass. K.A. im Körperverletzungsrecht (xxv 11–12 par. mass. K.A. § 8)[21] und im Erbrecht (xxi 17 par. mass. K.B. § 1; O. § 3).[22] Die Parallelen zwischen Dtn. und mass. K.A. erhalten weiteres Gewicht durch die Fundumstände des mass. K.A. Aus einer mittelassyrischen Bibliothek, möglicherweise der Schreiberfamilie des Ninurta-Uballitsu stammend,[23] wurde die Tafel A in neuassyrischem Kontext einer Toranlage in Assur zwischen dem Alten Palast und dem Anu-Adad-Tempel gefunden,[24] die keinerlei fortifikatorische Funktion hatte, wohl aber als Gerichtsort gedient haben kann.[25] Der mass. K.A. ist also noch neu-

---

[18] Cf. die tabellarischen Auflistungen der Parallelen durch S.R. Driver, *Deuteronomy* (Edinburg, ³1901), S. IV–VII; H.D. Preuß, *Deuteronomium* (Darmstadt, 1982), S. 104–6; Lohfink (Anm. 3), S. 174.

[19] Cf. die Auflistungen durch G. Seitz, *Redaktionsgeschichtliche Studien zum Deuteronomium* (Stuttgart, 1971), S. 128–30.

[20] xxii 26 ʾên lanna^{ca}râ heṭʾ mawœt = mass. K.A. § 12 II 24 ša sinnilti ḫi-i-ṭu la-áš-šu; § 16 II 60 ḫi-i-ṭu ša aʾīli la-áš-šu; cf. R. Yaron, "The Middle Assyrian Laws and the Bible", *Bib* 51 (1970), S. (549–57) 552; xxii 25 w^{e}hœh^{a}zîq-bāh hāʾîš w^{e}šākab ʿimmāh = mass. K.A. § 12 II 18.19 (LÚ) iṣ-ṣa-ba-as-si it-ti-ak-ši; xxii 26 w^{e}lanna^{ca}râ lōʾ-ta^{ca}śœh dābār = mass. K.A. § 23 III 24, 25 mi-im-ma la-a e-pu-šu; xxii 14 w^{e}śām lāh ^{ea}lîlōt d^{e}bārîm = mass. K.A. § 19 II 84, 85 i-na UGU tap-pa-i-šu a-ba-ta iš-kun.

[21] Cf. C.H. Gordon, "A New Akkadian Parallel to Deuteronomy 25, 11–12", *JPOS* 15 (1935), S. 29–34, mit Hinweis auch auf die Gerichtsurkunde HSS V 43 aus Nuzi; S.M. Paul, "Biblical Analogues to Middle Assyrian Law", in E.B. Firmage u.a. (Hg.), *Religion and Law. Biblical-Judaic and Islamic Perspectives* (Winona Lake, 1992), S. (333–50) 335–9.

[22] Cf. E. Weidner, "Eine Erbteilung in mittelassyrischer Zeit", *AfO* 20 (1963), S. 121–4; E.W. Davies, "The meaning of pî š^{e}nayim in Deuteronomy xxi 17", *VT* 36 (1986), S. 341–7. Die These von R. Westbrook (*Property and the Family in Biblical Law* [Sheffield, 1991], S. 19–20), xxi 15–17 handle nur von der Einstellung des Erblassers zu den Müttern seiner Söhne und den Folgen daraus, harmonisiert das Erbrecht.

[23] Cf. O. Pedersén, *Archives and Libraries in the City of Assur. A Survey of the Material from the German Excavations* I (Uppsala, 1985), S. 31ff.

[24] Cf. J. Jordan, "Aus den Grabungsberichten aus Assur. November bis April 1912", *MDOG* 48 (1912), S. (25–8) 28; W. Bachmann, "Aus den Berichten aus Assur. Berichte über die Grabung am altassyrischen Palast in f 5", *MDOG* 54 (1914), S. (56–9) 58; cf. P.A. Miglus, "Die Stadttore in Assur—das Problem der Identifizierung", *ZA* 72 (1982), S. (266–79) 270, Anm. 31.

[25] Cf. E. Weidner, "Das Alter der mittelassyrischen Gesetzestexte. Studien im Anschluß an Driver and Miles, The Assyrian Laws", *AfO* 12 (1937–9), S. (46–54, Tf. III–VI) 48, sowie bereits W. Andrae, *Der Anü-Adad-Tempel in Assur* (Leipzig, 1909), S. 71.

assyrisch tradiert worden. Ein Fragment der Tafel A aus Ninive[26] belegt die weite Verbreitung.

II. *Rechtsreformen im Mittelassyrischen Kodex der Tafel A*

1. *Redaktionsstrukturen in §§ 12–16*

In den Rechtssätzen des Eherechts in §§ 12–16 werden in einer komplexen Redaktionsstruktur Rechtssätze öffentlichen Strafrechts königlicher Richterjudikatur und gentiles Privatstrafrecht miteinander vermittelt.[27]

Text[28]

KAV 1 II 14–24 (mass. K.A. § 12)

šum-ma aššat (DAM-*at*) *aʾīli* (LÚ) *i-na re-be-e-te te-te-ti-iq aʾīlu* (LÚ) ⌈*iṣ*⌉-

---

[26] Cf. J.N. Postgate, "Assyrian Texts and Fragments", *Iraq* 35 (1973), S. (13–36) 21. Zu mittelassyrischen Texten in neuassyrischen Archiven cf. O. Pedersén, *Archives and Libraries in the City of Assur. A Survey of the Material from the German Excavations* II (Uppsala, 1986), S. 13–19, 44, u.ö. Im Gegensatz zu den altbabylonischen und hethitischen Rechtsüberlieferungen stellt sich in Bezug auf mass. K.A. also nicht das Problem der Traditionskette zwischen keilschriftlichem und israelitischem Recht; cf. dazu M.M. Malul, *The Comparative Method in Ancient Near Eastern and Biblical Legal Studies* (Kevelaer/Neukirchen-Vluyn, 1990), S. 99ff., 113ff.; E. Otto, *Körperverletzungen in den Keilschriftrechten und im Alten Testament. Studien zum Rechtstransfer im Alten Orient* (Kevelaer/Neukirchen-Vluyn, 1991), S. 11ff., 147ff., 165ff.; V.A. Jakobson ("Studies in Neoassyrian Law", *Altorientalische Forschungen* 1 [1974], S. [115–21] 118–19) sieht in dem in der neuassyrischen Eheurkunde ND 2307 Z. 50 (*e-zib-tú idan*ᵃⁿ) verfügten Scheidungsgeld eine neuassyrische Weiterentwicklung des mittelassyrisches Recht repräsentierenden mass. K.A. § 37. Doch ist die Differenz einer Verpflichtung des Ehemanns zur Zahlung im Scheidungsfall in den unterschiedlichen Gattungen von Vertragstext und Rechtssatz begründet, insofern mass. K.A. § 37 V 16 *lib-bu-šu-ma mim-ma id-da-na-áš-še* ("er gibt etwas, wenn er will") die in ND 2307 Z. 50 vertraglich festgelegte Regelung einschließt. Das gilt auch, wenn man mit J.N. Postgate (*Fifty Neo-Assyrian Legal Documents* [London, 1976], Nr. 14, Z. 50 [S. 105]) *e-ṣip-ši* SUM-*an* "er zahlt ihr doppelt zurück (den Brautpreis?)" liest. Entscheidend für die Frage, ob ein Scheidegeld gezahlt wird oder nicht, ist, ob die Eheauflösung durch den Ehemann mit oder ohne Rechtsgrund geschieht (cf. für den altbabylonichen Kontext R. Westbrook, *Old Babylonian Marriage Law* [Horn, 1988], S. 71–9; cf. dazu E. Otto, *ZA* 81 [1991], S. 308–14) und ein beeideter Ehekontrakt besteht oder nicht. Mass K.A. § 37 ist der Redaktionsintention der ursprünglich selbständig tradierten Eherechtssammlung mass. K.A. §§ 25–38 entsprechend (cf. u. II.2) als gelehrter Text nicht an einer umfassenden Regelung der komplexen Möglichkeiten der Ehescheidung orientiert, sondern an der Abgrenzung der Auflösung einer inchoate marriage von der Scheidung einer Vollehe.

[27] Cf. E. Otto, "Das Eherecht im mittelassyrischen Kodex und im Deuteronomium. Tradition und Redaktion in den §§ 12–16 der Tafel A des Mittelassyrischen Kodex und in Dtn 22, 22–29", in M. Dietrich/O. Loretz (Hg.), *Festschrift für K. Bergerhof* (Kevelear/Neukirchen-Vluyn, 1993), S. 259–81.

[28] Transliteration und Übersetzung des Verf.; zur philologischen Kommentierung cf. ders. (Anm. 27).

ṣa-ba-a-sú la-ni-ik-ki-me iq-ṭi-bi-a-áš-še la-a ta-ma-gu-urta-ta-na-ṣa-ar e-mu-
qa-ma iṣ-ṣa-ba-as-si it-ti-ak-ši lu-ú i-na muḫḫi (UGU) *aššat a'ili* (DAM.LÚ)
ik-šu-du-uš ù lu-ú ki-i sinnilta (MÍ) *i-ni-ku-ú-ni še-bu-tu ub-ta-e-ru-uš a'īla*
(LÚ) *i-du-uk-ku ša sinnilti* (MÍ) *ḫi-i-ṭu la-áš-šu*

KAV 1 II 25–9 (mass. K.A. § 13)
šum-ma aššat (DA[M]-*at*) *a'īli* (LÚ) *iš-tu biti* (É-*ti*)-*ša ta-at-ti-ṣi-ma a-na*
muḫḫi (UGU) *a'īli* (LÚ) *a-šar us-bu-ú-ni ta-ta-lak it-ti-ak-ši ki-i aššat* (DAM-
at) *a'īli* (LÚ)-*ni i-de a'īla* (LÚ) *ù aššata* (MÍ-*ma*) *i-duk-ku*

KAV 1 II 30–40 (mass. K.A. § 14)
šum-ma aššat (DAM-*at*) *a'īli* (LÚ) *a'īlu* (LÚ) *lu-ú i-na bīt* (É) *al-tam-me*
lu-ú i-na re-be-te ki-i aššat (DAM-*at*) *a'īli* (LÚ)-*ni i-de it-ti-ak-ši ki-i a'īlu*
(LÚ) *ša aššas* (DAM)-*su a-na e-pa-še i-qa-ab-bi-ú-ni* (LÚ)-*na-i-ka-na e-pu-*
šu šum-ma ki-i aššat (DAM)-*at a'īli* (LÚ)-*ni la-ai-de i-it-ti-a-ak-ši* (LÚ)-*na-*
i-ka-a-nu za-a-ku a'īlu (LÚ) *aššas* (DAM)-*su ú-ba-ar ki-i lib-bi-šu e-pa-a-[s]u*

KAV 1 II 41–57 (mass. K.A. § 15)
šum-ma a'īlu (LÚ) *iš-tu aššat* (DAM)-*ti-šu a'īla* (LÚ) *iṣ-ṣa-bat ub-ta-e-ru-*
ú-uš uk-ta-i-nu-ú-uš ki-la-al-le-šu-nu-ma i-du-uk-ku-šu-nu a-ra-an-šu la-áš-
šu šum-ma iṣ-ṣa-ab-ta lu-ú a-na muḫḫi (UGU) *šarri* (LUGAL) *lu-ú a-na*
muḫḫi (UGU) *dajjānī* (DI.KUD.MEŠ) *it-ab-la ú-ub-ta-e-ru-ú-uš ú-uk-ta-i-*
nu-ú-uš šum-ma mu-ut sinnilti (MÍ) *aššas* (DAM)-*šu i-du-ak ù a-i-la i-duk-*
ak-ma šum-ma ap-pa ša aššatī (DAM)-*šu i-na-ki-is a'īla* (LÚ) *a-na ša re-še-*
en ú-tar ù pa-ni-šu gab-ba i-na-qu-ru ú šum-ma aššas (DAM)-*s[u ú-uš-šar]*
a'īla (LÚ) *ú-[uš-šar]*

KAV 1 II 58–66 (mass. K.A. § 16)
šum-ma a'īlu (LÚ) *ašša[t(*DAM-*at*) *a'īli* (LÚ) *i-na lu-mu-un] pi-i-ša[it-ti-a-*
ak-ši] ḫi-i-ṭu ša a'īli (LÚ) *[la]-⌈áš⌉-šu a'īlu* (LÚ) *sinnilta* (MÍ) *aššas* (DAM)-
su ḫi-i-ṭa ki-i lib-bi-šu e-em-mi-id šum-ma e-mu-qa-a-ma it-ti-ak-ši ub-ta-e-
ru-ú-uš uk-ta-i-nu-ú-uš ḫi-ṭa-šu ki-i ša aššat (DAM-*at*) *a'īli* (LÚ)-*ma*

Übersetzung
mass. K.A. § 12
Wenn die Ehefrau eines a'īlu auf einem Platz vorbeigeht, ein a'īlu
sie ergreift (und) zu ihr sagt: "Ich will mit dir schlafen". (Wenn) sie
nicht einwilligt und sich hütet und er sie aber mit Gewalt ergreift,
mit ihr schläft, sei es, daß man ihn auf der Ehefrau eines a'īlu ergreift, oder Zeugen ihm beweisen, daß er mit der Frau geschlafen
hat, wird der a'īlu getötet. Was die Frau betrifft, gibt es keine Strafe.

mass. K.A. § 13
Wenn die Ehefrau eines a'īlu aus ihrem Haus hinausgeht, zu einem a'īlu in die Wohung geht, er mit ihr schläft, obwohl er weiß, daß sie die Ehefrau eines a'īlu ist, tötet man den a'īlu und die Ehefrau.

mass. K.A. § 14
Wenn ein a'īlu mit der Ehefrau eines a'īlu schläft, sei es in einem Wirtshaus oder auf einem Platz, *obwohl er weiß, daß sie die Ehefrau eines a'īlu ist, wie der a'īlu sagt, daß seine Ehefrau zu behandeln sei, so behandelt man den, der beschlafen hat. Wenn er mit ihr schläft, ohne daß er weiß, daß sie die Ehefrau eines a'īlu ist,* ist der, der beschlafen hat, straffrei. Der a'īlu führt den Beweis gegen seine Ehefrau. Nach seinem Belieben behandelt er sie.

mass K.A. § 15
Wenn ein a'īlu bei seiner Ehefrau einen a'īlu ergreift, *man ihn völlig überführt,* tötet *man* beide. Es gibt für ihn keine Schuld. *Wenn er (ihn) ergreift, sei es, daß er ihn zum König oder zu den Richtern bringt, man ihn völlig überführt, wenn der Ehemann der Frau seine Ehefrau tötet, wird man auch den a'īlu töten. Wenn er die Nase seiner Ehefrau abschneidet, macht man den a'īlu zu einem Verschnittenen und sein ganzes Gesicht zerstören sie. Wenn er aber seine Frau straffrei läßt, läßt er auch den a'īlu straffrei.*

mass. K.A. § 16
Wenn ein a'īlu mit der Ehefrau eines a'īlu *(aufgrund) ihres trügerischen Mundes* schläft, *trifft den a'īlu keine Strafe. Der a'īlu legt seiner Ehefrau eine Strafe nach seinem Belieben auf. Wenn er gewaltsam mit ihr geschlafen hat, man ihn völlig überführt,* ist seine Strafe wie die der Ehefrau des a'īlu.

Die Rechtssätze §§ 12–16 sind konzentrisch redigiert. Die Fälle der Strafschuld von Ehefrau und Konkumbenten in § 14 A und § 16 B bilden einen Rahmen um die Fälle der Strafschuld der Ehefrau bei Straffreiheit des Konkumbenten in § 14 B und § 16 A. In diesen Rahmen stellt der Redaktor § 15 als Sammlung von Verfahrensregelungen, die zweigliedrig strukturiert ist, ein. § 15 A geht von der unmittelbaren Rechtsreaktion in flagranti delicto aus, § 15 B vom öffentlichen Strafverfahren unter Einschaltung von König oder Richtern. Der Redaktor vermittelt die Privatstrafe des Ehemanns an seiner Frau und die damit verbundene Dispositionsverfügung des Ehemanns mit dem öffentlichen Strafrecht, dem der Konkumbent unterliegt, in der Form, daß das Strafmaß, das der Ehemann seiner Frau auferlegt, auch die öffentliche Iudikatur in Bezug auf den Konkumbenten bindet.

Die Intention, privates und öffentliches Strafrecht miteinander zu verbinden, schlüsselt auch die Widersprüche in § 15 auf. In § 15 A erwartet der Interpret aufgrund des Motivs der Selbstjustiz des Ehemanns in flagranti delicto sowie aufgrund der Feststellung der Straffreiheit des Ehemanns eine von ihm vollzogene Privatstrafe.[29] Stattdessen wird er auf eine öffentliche Strafe geführt.[30] In § 15 B erwartet der Ausleger aufgrund der Übergabe des Falles an König oder Richter in Verbindung mit der Formel *ubta"erū-š ukta"inū-š* ein öffentliches Strafverfahren und wird auf eine Privatstrafe geführt. Der Redaktor, dem ein Rechtssatz zur Straffreiheit (*aran-šu laššu*) des Ehefrau und Konkumbenten in flagranti delicto tötenden Ehemannes vorgegeben war,[31] interpretiert in § 15 A die öffentliche Strafe in die private und in § 15 B umgekehrt die private in die öffentliche Strafe hinein und verzahnt so die beiden Rechtsebenen. Dem dient auch die Voranstellung von §§ 12, 13 vor die konzentrisch angeordneten §§ 14–16. Die Rechtssätze §§ 12, 13 sind von §§ 14–16 dadurch abgehoben, daß §§ 12, 13 für die Ehefrau die Todesstrafe in einem öffentlichen Strafverfahren vorsehen und eine privatstrafrechtliche Dispositionverfügung des Ehemannes nicht kennen. Als Grundsatzregelungen in Bezug auf die Rechtsfolgen vor §§ 14–16 gestellt, benennen §§ 12, 13 die Vorausetzungen für die Differenzierungen in §§ 14–16 durch die Vermittlung mit dem Privatstrafrecht des Ehemanns. § 13 widerspricht mit der öffentlichen Bestrafung der Ehefrau der privatstrafrechtlichen Dispositionsverfügung des Ehemannes in § 16 B. Der Redaktor gleicht den Widerspruch durch Einfügung des Suffixes -*ša* in É-*ti-ša* "ihr Haus" aus und deutet den Rechtssatz in Verbindung mit § 46 VI 90 und § 3 A auf die Abwesenheit des Ehemannes, dessen Recht zur Strafsanktion in diesem Falle von der Richterjudikatur übernommen wird. Ohne diesen Ausgleich, der den Kontext von mass. K.A. voraussetzt, gehört der Rechtssatz wie § 12 im Gegensatz zu den dem

---

[29] Cf. nur C. Saporetti, *The Status of Women in the Middle Assyrian Period* (Malibu, 1979), S. 13.

[30] Gegen eine Interpretation von *ubta"erū-š ukta"inū-š* und *i-du-uk-ku-šu-nu* in § 15 II 42, 43, 45 auf Gerüft oder Notgericht (so M. Jastrow, "An Assyrian Law Code", *JAOS* 41 [1921], S. [1–49] 18, Anm. 62, gefolgt von G.R. Driver/J.C. Miles, *The Assyrian Laws* [1935]. *Reprint with Supplementary Additions and Corrections by G.R. Driver* [Aalen, 1975], S. 46, und G. Cardascia, *Les lois assyriennes* [Paris, 1969], S. 121) spricht, daß die Formel *ubta"eru-š ukta"inū-š* im mass. K.A. stets ein öffentliches Gerichtsverfahren bezeichnet. Die von R. Westbrook ("Adultery in Ancient Near Eastern Law", *RB* 97 [1990], S. [542–80] 552–3) vorgeschlagene Deutung auf ein Gerichtsverfahren ex post facto harmonisiert ohne Anhalt am Text.

[31] Die redaktionellen Ergänzungen sind in der Übersetzung kursiv gesetzt; zur Begründung cf. Otto (Anm. 27).

Redaktor in §§ 14–16 vorgegebenen Rechtssätzen des Privatstrafrechts in das öffentliche Strafrecht. Der Redaktor vermittelt gentil-private und öffentliche Gerichtsbarkeit, indem er §§ 12, 13 mit §§ 14–16

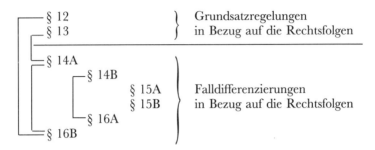

verzahnt. Er verklammert § 13 mit § 14[32] und spannt einen Bogen von § 12 zu § 16,[33] so daß eine kunstvolle Redaktionstruktur entsteht (s.o.). Der Redaktor stellt die Rechtssätze öffentlichen Strafrechts an die Spitze von §§ 12–16, schränkt in §§ 14–16 das Privatstrafrecht auf die Ehefrau als Familienmitglied ein und läßt gegenüber anderen Personen, den Konkumbenten, kein Privatstrafrecht zu, bindet aber das Strafmaß an die privatstrafrechtliche Dispositionsverfügung des Ehemannes. Der Redaktor zielt also auf eine Einschränkung der Privatstrafe gentiler Gerichtsbarkeit zugunsten öffentlicher Strafe der königlichen Richterjudikatur (§ 15 II 47, 48 *lū ana muḫḫi šarri lū ana muḫḫi dajjānē*) und schafft dazu eine komplexe Redaktionsstruktur. Die in §§ 12–16 sichtbar gewordene Intention zur Rechtsreform der Einschränkung gentilen Privatstrafrechts zugunsten der öffentlichen Richterjudikatur des Königs bestätigt sich in der Redaktion des Strafrechts in §§ 1–24, 50–9.

2. *Rechtsreform in der Redaktion von §§ 1–24, 50–9*

Die §§ 1–24, 50–9 bilden einen Rahmen von Rechtssätzen des Strafrechts um §§ 25–49.[34] Die Intention der Redaktion wird paradigmatisch im Abschluß des mass. K.A. in §§ 57–9 deutlich:[35]

---

[32] § 13 II 28* 29* *ki-i* DAM-*at* LÚ-*ni i-de* wird in § 14 II 32 eingefügt und verknüpft mit der Aufsprengung von § 14 in § 14 A-B diesen Paragraphen mit § 16.

[33] § 16 II 60–62 *ḫi-i-ṭu ša* LÚ *la-áš-šu* LÚ.MÍ.DAM-*su ḫi-i-ṭa . . . e-em-mi-id* knüpft an § 12 II 24 *ša* MÍ *ḫi-i-ṭu la-áš-šu*, § 16 II 63 *e-mu-qa-a-ma it-ti-ak-ši* an § 12 II 16 *e-mu-qa-ma iṣ-ṣa-ba-as-si* an.

[34] Cf. Cardascia (Anm. 30), S. 42–3, 46–8, 85 sowie bereits P. Koschaker, *Quellenkritische Untersuchungen zu den "altassyrischen Gesetzen"* (Leipzig, 1921), S. 65.

[35] Cf. zum folgenden E. Otto, "Die Einschränkung des Privatstrafrechts durch öffentliches Strafrecht in der Redaktion der Paragraphen 1–24; 50–9 des Mittel-

Text

KAV 1 VIII 50–3 (mass. K.A. § 57)

lu-ú ma-ḫa-ṣu lu-ú ⌈aꜣ⌉-[. . .] [ša-a ašš] (DAM)-at aꜥ[ꞋIli (LÚ)] ù gal-lu-li di-e-[nu . . .] ša-a [i-na ṭup-pi šaṭ-ru-ú-ni]

KAV 1 VIII 54–7 (mass. KA. § 58)

i-na ḫi-ṭa-a-ni gab-[bi lu-ú na-pa-li lu-ú] na-ka-a-si š[a-a aššat aꜣīli (DAM-at LÚ)] ù gal-lu-li di-e-[nu. . .] ki-i ša-a [i-na ṭup-pi šaṭ-ru-ú-ni]

KAV 1 VIII 58–63 (mass. K.A. § 59)

uš-šar ḫi-ṭa-a-ni ša-[a aššat aꜣīli (DAM-at LÚ)] ša i-na ṭup-pi [šaṭ-ru-ú-ni] aꜣīlu (LÚ) aššas (DAM)-su[i-na-aṭ-ṭu] i-ba-qa-an u[z-né-ša] ú-ḫap-pa ú-la-[ap-pat] a-ra-an-šu la-áš-š[u]

Übersetzung

mass. K.A. § 57

Ob Schlagen oder. . . der Ehefrau eines aꞋilu. . . Blenden, ein Gericht. . . was auf der Tafel geschrieben ist. . .

mass. K.A. § 58

Bei allen Strafen, sei es des Ausreißens oder des Abschneidens, der Ehefrau eines aꞋilu, und des Blendens,[36] ein Gericht. . . gemäß dem, was auf der Tafel steht.

mass. K.A. § 59

Abgesehen von den Strafen für die Ehefrau eines aꞋilu, die auf dieser Tafel niedergeschrieben sind, darf ein aꞋilu seine Ehefrau schlagen, raufen, die Ohren verletzen, durchbohren. Er bleibt straffrei.

Von den konditional eingeleiteten Rechtssätzen des mass. K.A. unterscheiden sich §§ 57–9 formgeschichtlich als erklärende Rechtssätze, die die voranstehenden Paragraphen kommentieren.[37] §§ (57) 58[38] unterstellt die schwere Körperstrafe der Verstümmelung als Privatstrafe in §§ 4, 5, 8, 15, 24 der Aufsicht eines Gerichtes. Nur leichte Körperstrafen ohne bleibenden Körperschaden werden in § 59 von der Aufsicht ausgenommen. §§ 57–9 sind mit der Einschränkung der Privatstrafe des pater familias und ihrer Vermittlung mit der öffent-

---

assyrischen Kodex der Tafel A (KAV 1)", in H. Zwickel (Hg.), *Festschrift für M. Metzger* (Fribourg/Göttingen, 1993), S. 131–66.

[36] Cf. Borger (Anm. 13), S. 195; ders., *TUAT* I/1, S. 91 mit Anm. a.

[37] Cf. Koschaker (Anm. 34), S. 13.

[38] Driver/Miles ([Anm. 30], S. 290–4, 495) ergänzen § 57 nach CH § 127 XXXVIII 31, so daß § 57 dem § 58 entspricht.

lichen Richterjudikatur nicht nur durch ihre Schlußstellung, sondern auch durch ihre den vorangehenden Kontext interpretierende Form erklärender Rechtssätze als Skopus der Redaktion der Tafel A herausgehoben. Ihren Gegenpart haben die Rechtssätze §§ 57–9 in der programmatischen Eröffnung der Tafel A in §§ 1–6:

Text[39]

KAV 1 I 1–13 (mass. K.A. § 1)

[šum-m]a sinniltu (MÍ) *[lu-ú] aššat aʾīli* (DAM.LÚ) *[lu]-ú mārat aʾīli* ([DUMU.M]Í.LÚ) *[a-na] bīt ili* (É. DINGIR) *[ṭ]e-ta-ra-ab [i-na] bit ili* (É. DINGIR) *[mi]-im-ma [ša ili* (DINGIR)] *tal-ti-r[iq ší]-ri-iq* [. . .] *iz-za-qa[p] lu-ú ub-ta-ᴿeᴸ-ru-ú-[ši] lu-ú uk-ta-i-nu-[ú-ši] ba-e-ru-ta* [. . .] *ilu* ([D]INGIR) ᴿiᴸ- *[š]a-ʾ-[ú-lu] [k]-i-i ša-a [ilu* (DINGIR)] *a-na e-pa-še] i-[qa]-ab-[bi-ú-n]-i* ᴿeᴸ-*ep-pu-šu-ú-ši*

KAV 1 I 14–22 (mass. K.A. § 2)

šu[m-ma] sinniltu (MÍ) *[lu-ú] aššat* (DAM-*at*) *aʾili* (LÚ) *lu-ú mārat aʾīli* ([DUMU.MÍ.LÚ) *ši-il-la-ṭu táq-ṭi-bi lu-ú mi-qí-it pe-e ta-ar-ti-i-ši sinniltu* (MÍ) *ši-i-it a-ra-an-ša ta-na-áš-ši a-na mu-ti-ša mārē* (DUMU.MEŠ)-*ša maʾarātē* (DUMU.MÍ.MEŠ)-*ša la-a i-qar-ri-i-bu*

KAV 1 I 23–45 (mass. K.A. § 3)

šumma aʾīlu (LÚ) *lu-ú ma-ri-iṣ lu-ú me-et aššas* (DAM)-*su i-na bītī* (É)-*šu mi-im-ma tal-ti-ri-iq lu-ú a-na aʾīli* (LÚ) *lu-ú a-na sinnilti* (MÍ) *ù lu-ú a-na ma-am-ma ša-ni-em-ma ta-ti-din aššat* (DAM-*at*) *aʾīli* (LÚ) *ù ma-ḫi-ra-nu-te-ma i-du-uk-ku-šu-nu ù šum-ma aššat* (DAM-*at*) *aʾīli* (LÚ) *ša mu-us-sa bal-ṭu-ú-ni i-na bīt* (É) *mu-ti-ša tal-ti-ri-iq lu-ú a-na aʾīli* (LÚ) *lu-ú a-na sinnilti* (MÍ) *ù lu-ú a-na ma-am-ma ša-ni-em-ma ta-at-ti-din aʾīlu* (LÚ) *aššas* (DAM)-*su ú-ba-ar ù ḫi-i-ṭa e-em-mì-id ù ma-ḫi-ra-a-nu ša i-na qa-at aššat* (DAM-*at*) *aʾīli* (LÚ) *im-ḫu-ru-ú-ni šur-qa i-id-da-an ù ḫi-i-ṭa ki-i ša-a aʾīlu* (LÚ) *aššas* (DAM)-*su e-mi-du-ú-ni ma-ḫi-ra-a-na e-em-mi-du*

KAV 1 I 46–56 (mass. K.A. § 4)

šum-ma lu-ú urdu (ÌR) *lu-ú amtu* (GEMÉ) *i-na qa-at aššat* (DAM-*at*) *aʾīli* (LÚ) *mi-im-ma im-ta-aḫ-ru ša urdi* (ÌR) *ù amti* (GEMÉ) *ap-pe-šu-nu uz-né-šu-nu ú-na-ak-ku-su šur-qa ú-mal-lu-ú aʾīlu* (LÚ) *ša aššatī* (DAM)-[*š*]*u uz-né-ša ú-*ᴿ*na-ak-ka*ᴸ-*ás ú šum-ma aššas* (DAM)-*s*[*u*] *ú-uš-šìr*[*uz*]-*né-ša la-a ú-na-ak-ki-is ša urdi* (ÌR) *ù amti* (GEMÉ) *la-a ú-na-ku-su-ma šur-qa la-a ú-ma-lu-ú*

---

[39] Zur philologischen Kommentierung cf. Otto (Anm. 35).

KAV 1 I 57–69 (mass. K.A. § 5)

šum-ma aššat (DAM)-*at aʾīli* (LÚ) *ina bīt aʾīli* (É.LÚ) *ša-ni-e-ma mim-ma tal-ti-ri-iq a-na qa-at 5 ma-an anneke* (AN.NA) *tu-ta-at-tir bēl* (EN) *šur-qí i-tam-ma ma-a šum-ma ú-ša-ḫi-zu-ši-ni ma-a i-na bītī* (É)-*ia ši-ir-qí šum-ma mu-us-sa ma-gi-ir šur-qa id-dan ù i-pa-aṭ-ṭar-ši uz-né-ša ú-na-ak-ka-ás šumma mu-us-sa a-na pa-ṭa-ri-ša la-a i-ma-ag-gu-ur bēl* (EN) *šur-qí i-laq-qé-e-ši ú ap-pa-ša i-nak-ki-is*

KAV 1 I 70–3 (mass. K.A. § 6)

šum-ma aššat (DAM-*at*) *aʾīli* (LÚ) *ma-áš-ka-at-ta i-na ki-i-di tal-ka-ka-an ma-ḫi-ra-a-nu šur-qa i-na-áš-ši*

Übersetzung

mass. K.A. § 1

Wenn eine Frau, *sei es die Ehefrau eines aʾīlu oder die Tochter eines aʾīlu,* zum Tempel geht, und in dem Tempel etwas, was dem Tempel gehört, stiehlt, der Diebstahl (vor Gericht) gebracht wird, wenn *man sie völlig überführt,* die Beweisaufnahme (. . .), befragt man die Gottheit; wie die Gottheit befiehlt, sie zu behandeln, verfährt man mit ihr.

mass. K.A. § 2

Wenn eine Frau, *sei es die Ehefrau eines aʾīlu oder die Tochter eines aʾīlu,* übles Gerede spricht oder sich eine Frechheit anmaßt, trägt diese Frau ihre Schuld. Ihren Ehemann, ihre Söhne und ihre Töchter zieht man nicht zur Rechenschaft.

mass. K.A. § 3

Wenn ein aʾīlu, sei es, daß er krank oder tot ist (und) seine Frau in seinem Hause irgend etwas stiehlt (und) sei es an einen aʾīlu oder eine Frau oder irgendeine andere Person gibt, wird man die Ehefrau des aʾīlu und den Hehler töten. Wenn aber die Ehefrau des aʾīlu, deren Ehemann gesund ist, im Hause ihres Ehemannes stiehlt (und irgend etwas), sei es an einen aʾīlu oder eine Frau, oder irgendeine andere Person gibt, *überführt* der aʾīlu seine Ehefrau und erlegt (ihr) Strafe auf, und der Hehler gibt das, was er aus der Hand der Ehefrau des aʾīlu empfangen hat, zurück, und die Strafe in gleicher Höhe, die der aʾīlu seiner Ehefrau auferlegt, erlegt er dem Hehler auf.

mass. K.A. § 4

Wenn ein Sklave oder eine Sklavin aus der Hand einer Ehefrau irgend etwas empfangen hat, schneidet man die Nase und die Ohren des Sklaven oder der Sklavin ab. Das Gestohlene ersetzen sie. Der a'īlu schneidet seiner Frau die Ohren ab. *Wenn er aber seine Frau straffrei läßt (und) ihre Ohren nicht abschneidet, schneidet man auch nicht die des Sklaven oder der Sklavin ab. Das Gestohlene ersetzen sie nicht.*

mass. K.A. § 5

Wenn die Ehefrau eines Mannes im Haus eines anderen a'īlu irgend etwas stiehlt, was den Wert von 6 Minen Zinn übersteigt, schwört der Besitzer des Gestohlenen: "Ich habe sie nicht angestiftet: 'Begehe Diebstahl in meinem Hause!'" *Wenn ihr Ehemann einverstanden ist, gibt er das Diebesgut zurück und löst sie aus. Ihre Ohren schneidet er ab. Wenn ihr Ehemann nicht zustimmt, sie loszukaufen, nimmt sie der Besitzer des Gestohlenen und schneidet ihre Nase ab.*

mass. K.A. § 6

Wenn die Ehefrau eines a'īlu ein Pfand nach auswärts hingibt, gibt der Empfänger das unrechtmäßig Angeeignete zurück.

Die Rechtssätze §§ 1, 2 formulieren Grundsätze, die das private und öffentliche Strafrecht der königlichen Richterjudikatur einschränken. Wird kultisches Recht des Tempels verletzt, so ist das Gericht des Tempels zuständig. Eine privatstrafrechtliche Verfolgung erübrigt sich. Die Dispositionsverfügung liegt bei der Gottheit. Bei Delikten der Ehefrau gegen Dritte ist eine Noxalhaftung und Haftung weiterer Familienangehöriger ausgeschlossen. Davon abgegrenzt sind die Fälle, in denen der Ehemann durch seine Frau geschädigt wird (§§ 3–6). In allen Fällen von Eigentumsdelikten einer Ehefrau, ausgenommen die gegen den Tempel, hat der Ehemann das Recht zur Privatstrafe an seiner Ehefrau und die Dispositionsverfügung des Strafvollzuges und des Strafmaßes, wenn die Ehefrau den Ehemann bestiehlt und Diebesgut an einen Dritten verhehlt (§§ 3 B, 4) und wenn sie einen Dritten bestiehlt und das Diebesgut in ihr Haus bringt (§ 5) oder nach auswärts verhehlt (§ 6). Auch in diesem Falle gilt aufgrund der engen Beziehung von § 6 als Gegenfall zu § 5 die Privatstrafrechtsregelung aus § 5.[40] Nur im Falle, daß der Ehemann handlungsunfähig ist, tritt die öffentliche Bestrafung ein (§ 3 A). Der Redaktor regelt nicht nur das Privatstrafrecht des Ehemannes gegenüber seiner Frau, sondern stellt einen Zusammenhang zwischen öffentlicher Strafe für

---

[40] Zur Interpretation von § 6 cf. E. Otto, "Die Rechtsintention des Paragraphen 6 der Tafel A des mittelassyrischen Kodex in Tradition und Redaktion", *UF* 23 (1991 [ersch. 1992]), S. 307–14.

tatbeteiligte Dritte und Privatstrafe für die Ehefrau her. Der Ehemann hat kein Zugriffsrecht gegen die tatbeteiligten Dritten. Deren
Bestrafung durch ein öffentliches Gericht ist im Strafmaß an die Dispositionsverfügung des Ehemannes gegenüber seiner Ehefrau gebunden (§§ 3 B, 4). Macht die Frau den Ehemann dadurch zum Hehler,
daß sie das Diebesgut in sein Haus bringt, so hat der Ehemann eine
Dispositionsverfügung hinsichtlich der Noxalhaftung (§ 5), die aber
ausgesetzt ist, wenn die Ehefrau das unrechtmäßig erworbene Gut
nach auswärts gibt. In diesem Falle haftet der Hehler dem Geschädigten gegenüber (§ 6). Die Rechtssätze §§ 1; 2 stehen als Grundsatzregelungen zur öffentlichen Strafverfolgung vor den §§ 3–6, die ein
erstes Themenfeld der Vermittlung von privatem und öffentlichem
Strafrecht anhand der Eigentumsdelikte entfalten. Die Redaktion von
§§ 1–6 entspricht darin der von §§ 12–16. Unterstellen §§ 57–9 die
schweren privatstrafrechtlichen Körperstrafen der Verstümmelung der
Aufsicht öffentlicher Gerichtsbarkeit, so begrenzen §§ 1, 2 die Privatstrafe, indem ihr alle die Tempelgerichtsbarkeit betreffenden Delikte
entzogen werden (§ 1), eine strafrechtliche Noxalhaftung und stell-
vertretende Haftung von Familienmitgliedern prinzipiell ausgeschlossen (§ 2), in §§ 3–6 das Privatstrafrecht auf die Ehefrau eingeschränkt
und für tatbeteiligte Dritte ausgeschlossen wird.

Zwischen §§ 1–6 und §§ 12–16 setzt der Redaktor mit §§ 7–10
(11) Rechtssätze der Angriffe auf eine Person von der ehrverletzen-
den iniuria bis zum Tötungsdelikt. § 7 regelt in einem öffentlichen
Strafverfahren (*ubta″erū-ši*[41]) den Angriff einer Frau auf einen Mann
und § 8 die unvorsätzliche Körperverletzung (*ina ṣālte*[42]) eines Mannes durch eine Frau, die ebenfalls mit öffentlicher Strafe sanktioniert
wird.[43] § 9 ist der Gegenfall, daß ein Mann eine ehrverletzende iniuria
gegenüber einer Frau begeht. Mit §§ 7, 8 wiederholt der Rechtssatz
§ 9 die Sanktion öffentlicher Körperstrafe. Davon hebt sich § 10 (11)
ab. Im Falle des Tötungsdeliktes im eigenen Haus werden dem pater
familias Privatstrafe und Dispositionsverfügung eingeräumt.[44] Die
Privatstrafe als Reaktion auf ein Tötungsdelikt weist darauf hin, daß
die Sanktion der Tötung mittelassyrisch noch in der privatstrafrecht-

---

[41] Ein zu erwartendes *ukta″inū-ši* ist durch Schreiberversehen ausgefallen; cf. Driver/
Miles (Anm. 30), S. 30.
[42] Zur Funktion dieses Motivs cf. Otto (Anm. 26), S. 58–9.
[43] Cf. dazu Gordon (Anm. 21), S. 29–34; Paul (Anm. 21), S. 335–9.
[44] Cf. § 10 I 101 *pa-nu-šu-ma* bezogen auf § 10 I 100 *bēl bīti*.

lichen Institution der Blutrache vollzogen wurde,[45] auf die sich die Dispositionsverfügung bezieht. Der Redaktor schränkt die Blutrache losgelöst von öffentlicher Gerichtsinstanz auf die Bluttat im Hause des Geschädigten ein (cf. § 5) und läßt damit Raum für eine Notwehrreaktion in flagranti delicto. Der Redaktor läßt also eine private Bestrafung nur im Falle der Schädigung durch die Ehefrau oder des Tötungsdeliktes im eigenen Hause zu.

Das gilt auch für §§ 17–21. In diesen Rechtssätzen steht wie in §§ 7–11 nicht die Ehefrau, sondern ein Dritter als Täter im Mittelpunkt. § 17 verknüpft §§ 18–21 mit §§ 12–16. In §§ 18, 19 wird die Verleumdung, in § 20 die homosexuelle Vergewaltigung (RLA IV, 461–3) mit öffentlicher Strafe belegt. Von §§ 17–20 hebt sich § 21 thematisch ab. Wie in §§ 7–9 (10) und §§ 50–2 (53) vor §§ 12–16 und §§ 55–6 geht mit § 21 die Thematik der Körperverletzung dem Familienrecht in §§ 22–4 voraus. Hier wird eine Redaktionsstruktur alternierender Anordnung von familienrechtlichen Rechtssätzen der Delikte geschlechtlicher Beziehungen und des Körperverletzungsrechts erkennbar. In diese Struktur eingebunden unterstreicht § 21 die Rahmungsfunktion von §§ 1–24, 50–9 für §§ 25–49, da §§ 50–2 an § 21 anknüpfen.[46] Der besonderen Thematik der Vermittlung öffentlicher mit privater Strafe entsprechend werden im mass. K.A. die Rechtssätze nicht nur in den Protasen der Fallbeschreibungen, sondern auch in den Apodosen der Rechtsfolgen systematisiert. Den § 21 verbindet mit §§ 18, 19 die öffentliche Strafe der Stockschläge und Fron neben der Geldzahlung. Die infamierende Markierung[47] ist zusätzliche öffentliche Strafe für die Verleumdung. In der Systematik der Rechtsfolgen fügt sich § 21 in eine alternierende Anordnung[48] von Rechtssätzen öffentlicher Strafe in §§ 7–9, 12–13, 18–21 und der Privatstrafe mit Dispositionsverfügung in §§ 10 (11), 14–16. In diese Systematik fügen sich nun auch §§ 22–4, 50–6 ein. Unter Aufnahme eines vorgegebenen

---

[45] Cf. SAA II, VI 256–7 *dāmē kūm dāme lā tatabbakāni*; cf. dazu Watanabe (Anm. 5), S. 156, 185 (Lit.).

[46] Cf. Otto (Anm. 26), S. 81–95. Zur Inklusionstechnik in der Redaktion von Rechtssatzsammlungen cf. ders., *Rechtsgeschichte der Redaktionen im Kodex Ešnunna und im "Bundesbuch". Eine redaktionsgeschichtliche und rechtsvergleichende Studie zu altbabylonischen und altisraelitischen Rechtsüberlieferungen* (Fribourg/Göttingen, 1989), S. 68–78.

[47] Cf. H. Petschow, "Altorientalische Parallelen zur spätrömischen calumnia", *ZSS* (Rom. Abt.) 90 (1973), S. (14–35) 27; C. Locher, *Die Ehre einer Frau in Israel. Exegetische und rechtsvergleichende Studien zu Deuteronomium 22, 13–21* (Fribourg/Göttingen, 1986), S. 361 (Lit.).

[48] Zu dieser Redaktionstechnik cf. Otto (Anm. 46), S. 127–8, 155–6, 175–6.

Rechtssatzes in § 24* formuliert der Redaktor §§ 22–4 als Anwendungs-
fälle von §§ 12–16, wobei die Rechtssätze §§ 22–4 jeweils ihren Ziel-
punkt in Privatstrafe und Dispositionsverfügung haben. In der Systematik der Protasen der Rechtssätze des Rahmens stehen §§ 22–4
zwischen den Rechtssätzen der Körperverletzung in §§ 21, 50–2 und
in der Systematik der Apodosen zwischen den Rechtssätzen öffentlichen Strafrechts in §§ 18–21 und §§ 50–3 (54).

Dieser Systematik fügen sich §§ 50–6 ein, wenn in §§ 55, 56 Rechtssätze familienrechtlicher Delikte geschlechtlicher Beziehungen, verklammert durch §§ 53 (54), auf die der Körperverletzung in §§ 50–2
und Rechtssätze der Privatstrafe auf die der öffentlichen Strafe in §§
50–3 (54) folgen.[49]

Mit der alternierenden Anordnung von Rechtssätzen des Körperverletzungsrechts und des Familienrechts geschlechtlicher Delikte in
den Protasen knüpft der Redaktor eine kleine, §§ 7–24, 50–6 umfas-
sende Struktur:

A:	§§ 7–9 (10)	Körperverletzung
B:	§§ 12–16	geschlechtliche Delikte
	§§ 17–20	Verklammerung
A:	§ 21	Körperverletzung
B:	§§ 22–4	geschlechtliche Delikte
A:	§§ 50–2	Körperverletzung
	§§ 53 (54)	Verklammerung
B:	§§ 55–6	geschlechtliche Delikte

Über diese Struktur schießen §§ 1–6, 57–9 hinaus und erhalten dadurch als äußerer Rahmen der Rechtssätze des mass. K.A. ein be-
sonderes Gewicht. §§ 57–9 schränken durch das Verfahrensrecht die
Privatstrafe zugunsten öffentlicher Rechtsverfahren ein. §§ 1–6 klären
programmatisch den engen Rahmen, innerhalb dessen eine Privatstrafe zulässig ist. Die Verfahrensregelungen in §§ 57–9 heben sich
als erklärende Rechtssätze formgeschichtlich von den voranstehenden
Sätzen ab, die sie verfahrenstechnisch kommentieren, und schließen
§§ 1–24, 50–6 zusammen. Wie §§ 57–9 als Endpunkt der Tafel auf
die Einschränkung der Privatstrafe zielen, so bestimmt die Abgrenzung von privater und öffentlicher Strafe die Redaktionstrukturen von
§§ 1–24, 50–6 in alternierender Anordnung der Apodosen:

---

[49] Cf. E. Otto, "Körperverletzung oder Verletzung von Besitzrechten? Zur Redaktion von Ex 22, 15f. im Bundesbuch und §§ 55; 56 im Mittelassyrischen Kodex
der Tafel A", *ZAW* 105 (1993), S. 153–65.

§§ 1, 2	Grundsätze zur Einschränkung privater und öffentlicher Strafe

A: § 3 A	öffentliche Strafe
B: §§ 3 B–5	Privatstrafe mit Dispositionsverfügung
§ 6	Verklammerung

A: §§ 7–9	öffentliche Strafe
B: § 10 (11)	Privatstrafe mit Dispositionsverfügung
A: §§ 12, 13	öffentliche Strafe
B: §§ 14–16	Privatstrafe mit Dispositionsverfügung
§ 17	Verklammerung
A: §§ 18–21	öffentliche Strafe
B: §§ 22–4	Privatstrafe mit Dispositionsverfügung
A: §§ 50–3 (54)	öffentliche Strafe
B: §§ 55–6	Privatstrafe mit Dispositionsverfügung

§§ 57–9	Verfahrensregelungen zur Einschränkung der Privatstrafe

Die Rechtssätze öffentlicher Strafe schränken die der Privatstrafe ein. §§ 1–3 A begrenzen §§ 3 B–6 und entsprechend §§ 12, 13 die §§ 14–16. § 53 (54) setzt vor §§ 55, 56 einen kräftigen Akzent öffentlicher Strafe. Selbst im Falle einer Schädigung des Ehemanns durch eine Abtreibung als Kapitaldelikt wird ihm kein Recht auf Privatstrafe und Dispositionsverfügung eingeräumt. Die paradigmatisch in §§ 1–6, 12–16, 57–9 erhobene Intention des Redaktors, die Privatstrafe zugunsten öffentlicher Strafverfahren einzuschränken, prägt die Gesamtredaktion von §§ 1–24, 50–9.

Der Redaktor legt mit §§ 1–24, 50–9 einen Rahmen von Rechtssätzen des Strafrechts, die durch die Intention der Rechtsreform strukturiert sind, um eine von ihm übernommene Rechtssatzsammlung des Familienrechts in §§ 25–38.[50] Die Rechtssätze zur inchoativen Ehe und Vollehe sind alternierend im A-B-Schema angeordnet (§§ 25–7/28–9/30–3/34–5/36/37/38) und durch §§ 25–7, 38 gerahmt. Durch §§ 39–48 verknüpft der Redaktor diese rechtliche Sammlung in §§ 25–38 mit dem strafrechtlichen Rahmen in §§ 1–24, 50–9. Die Rechtssätze des Pfandrechts in §§ 39, 44, 48 bilden eine Fachwerkstruktur, deren Zentrum in § 44 die privatstrafrechtliche Dispositionsverfügung auf den Pfandnehmer überträgt. In dieses Fachwerk ist mit §§ 40, 47 ein strafrechtlicher und mit §§ 41–3, 45–6 ein

---

[50] Cf. zur Analyse Otto, Anm. 35.

§§ 1, 2	Grundsätze zur Einschränkung privater und öffentlicher Strafe

A: § 3 A	öffentliche Strafe
B: §§ 3 B–5	Privatstrafe mit Dispositionsverfügung
§ 6	Verklammerung

A: §§ 7–9	öffentliche Strafe
B: § 10 (11)	Privatstrafe mit Dispositionsverfügung
A: §§ 12, 13	öffentliche Strafe
B: §§ 14–16	Privatstrafe mit Dispositionsverfügung
§ 17	Verklammerung
A: §§ 18–21	öffentliche Strafe
B: §§ 22–4	Privatstrafe mit Dispositionsverfügung

A:	§§	25–7	inchoative Ehe
B:	§§	28–9	Vollehe
A:	§§	30–3	inchoative Ehe
B:	§§	34–5	Vollehe
A/B:	§	36	inchoative Ehe/Vollehe
B:	§	37	Vollehe
A:	§	38	inchoative Ehe

§ 39	Pfandrecht
§ 40	Strafrecht
§§ 41–3	Eherecht
§ 44	Pfandrecht
§§ 45–6	Eherecht
§ 47	Strafrecht
§ 48	Pfandrecht

A: §§ 50–3 (54)	öffentliches Strafrecht
B: §§ 55–6	Privatstrafe

§§ 57–9	Verfahrensregeln zur Einschränkung der Privatstrafe durch öffentliche Gerichte

erbrechtlicher Rahmen eingefügt. So ergibt sich obige Redaktions-struktur des mass. K.A.

Mass. K.A. ist das Buch einer Rechtsreform, die das Nebeneinan-der von gentiler Gerichtsbarkeit der Privatstrafe und königlicher Richterjudikatur (cf. 15 II 47, 48)[51] vermittelt. Redaktionelle Ver-

---

[51] Zur Abgrenzung der altbabylonischen Gerichtsinstitutionen cf. A. Walther, *Das altbabylonische Gerichtswesen* (Leipzig, 1917), S. 70ff., 80ff., 105ff.; J.G. Lautner, *Die*

schränkungen wie in § 15 sprechen dagegen, daß die Sammlung als offizielles Gesetzeswerk[52] konzipiert wurde. Die Redaktionsstruktur, die das von Koschaker ([Anm. 34] S. 79ff.) aufgeworfene Problem der leges geminatae löst, widerspricht auch der These, es handle sich um ein aus mehreren Quellen redigiertes privates Rechtsbuch eines "Frauenspiegels". Vielmehr ist der mass. K.A. eine rechtsgelehrte Arbeit im Dienste einer Rechtsreform, die das private Strafrecht zugunsten öffentlichen Strafverfahrens einschränken will und der noch in neuassyrischer Zeit Aufmerksamkeit zuerkannt wurde.[53]

III. *Rechtsreform in Deuteronomium xii–xxvi*

1. *Redaktionsstrukturen in xxii 22–9*

Die Rechtssätze xxii 22–9* sind in einer Redaktionsstruktur zusammengearbeitet, die der von mass. K.A. §§ 12–16 entspricht. Der dtn-vordtr Redaktor des Dtn. nimmt mit xxii 13–21a, 22a, 23, 24a, 25, 27, 28–9, xxiv 1–4a, 5 eine Sammlung von Rechtssätzen des Familienrechts auf,[54] die er durch die *biʾartā*-Formel in xxii 21b, 22b, 24b, durch xxii 26 als redaktionelle Verknüpfung mit xix 2–13*[55] und durch

---

richterliche Entscheidung und die Streitbeendigung im altbabylonischen Prozeßrechte (Leipzig, 1922), S. 68ff.; R. Harris, "On the Process of Secularization under Hammurapi", *JCS* 15 (1961), S. 117–20; dies., *Ancient Sippar. A Demographic Study of an Old Babylonian City (1894–1595 B.C.)* (Leiden, 1975), S. 116–42.

[52] So Driver/Miles (Anm. 30), S. 12–15; Cardascia (Anm. 30), S. 34–6; ders., "La formazione del diritto in Assiria", in A. Theodorides u. a., *La formazione del diritto nel Vicino Oriente Antico* (Neapel/Rom, 1988), S. (51–60) 57–60; cf. dazu E. Otto, "Auf dem Wege zu einer altorientalischen Rechtsgeschichte", *BiOr* 48 (1991), S. (5–14) 8–9.

[53] Zur neuassyrischen Beamtenjudikatur, die den in mass. K.A. § 15 belegten Titel *dajjānu* nicht kennt, cf. K. Deller, "Die Rolle des Richters im neuassyrischen Prozeßrecht", in *Studi in Onore di E. Volterra* VI (Mailand, 1970), S. 639–53; Postgate, *Legal Documents* (Anm. 26), S. 58–62. Zu Rechtsreformen im Kodex Hammurapi cf. zuletzt R. Yaron, "'Enquire now about Hammurabi, Ruler of Babylon'", *Tijds. v. Rechtsgesch.* 49 (1991), S. 223–38; zum Hethitischen Kodex cf. A. Archi, "La formazione del diritto nell' Anatolia ittita", in Theodorides u.a. (Anm. 52), S. 61–75; E. Otto, "Körperverletzung im hethitischen und israelitischen Recht. Rechts- und religionshistorische Aspekte", in B. Janowski/K. Koch/G. Wilhelm (Hg.), *Religionsgeschichtliche Beziehungen zwischen Kleinasien, Nordsyrien und dem Alten Testament im 2. und 1. vorchristlichen Jahrtausend. Akten des internationalen Symposions, Hamburg 17.–21. März 1990* (Fribourg/Göttingen, 1993), S. 391–425.

[54] Cf. E. Otto, "Soziale Verantwortung und Reinheit des Landes. Zur Redaktion der kasuistischen Rechtssätze in Deuteronomium 19–25", in R. Liwak/S. Wagner (Hg.), *Prophetie und geschichtliche Wirklichkeit im alten Israel. FS S. Herrmann* (Stuttgart, 1991), S. (290–306) 291–4, 299–304.

[55] Zusammen mit der *biʾartā*-Formel in xxii 24b ist der dtn Zusatz xxii 26 für die paränetische Formulierung in xxii 24a verantwortlich. Die *biʾartā*-Formel wird dort

die Abschlußformel in xxiv 4b ergänzt. Die Rechtssätze des Eherechts in xxii 22a, 23, 24a, 25, 27–9 formen einen geschlossenen
Block innerhalb des kasuistischen Familienrechts.[56] xxii 23, 24a und
xxii 25, 27 sind durch die Einleitung von xxii 25 mit *w⁽ᵉ⁾im* als Gegenfall
zu xxii 23, 24a und durch den Abschluß der jeweiligen Protasis mit
w⁽ᵉ⁾šākab ʿimmāh eng aufeinander bezogen und in den Protasen konzentrisch strukturiert:

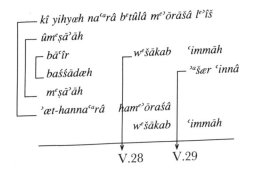

V.28   V.29

Der geschlossenen Rechtssatzeinheit xxii 23–7* werden xxii 22a vor-
an- sowie xxii 28–9 nachgestellt und als Rahmen für xxii 23–7*
miteinander verklammert.[57] xxii 22a hebt sich von den in xxii 23–7*
folgenden Rechtssätzen ab. xxii 23, 24a und xxii 25, 27 differenzieren die Strafschuld nach dem Ort des Geschehens und sind in ihrer
Struktur von dieser Differenzierung bestimmt. Sie traktieren die Fälle am Beispiel der inchoativ verheirateten Frau (*naʿărā bᵉtûlâ mᵉʾōrāśâ
lᵉʾîš*[58]) als Grenzfälle des Eherechts, während xxii 22a von der vollgültig verheirateten Frau (*ʾiššâ bᵉʿūlat baʿal*) handelt und keine Differen-

---

gesetzt, wo der Rechtssatz nicht, wie in xxii 25, 27, 28–9, auf den Aspekt des Schutzes
sozial schwächerer Personen, in diesem Fall der Frau, gedeutet werden kann, da sie
ebenfalls schuldig wurde, so daß der Aspekt der Reinheit des Volkes im Lande
greift (xxii 22, 23–4). Das gilt auch für xxii 21b. Während xxii 13–19 als Schutz-
bestimmung für die junge Frau zu interpretieren ist, ist der Gegenfall xxii 20–21a
durch die *biʿartā*-Formel auf den Reinheitsaspekt gedeutet.

[56] Cf. Otto (Anm. 27).

[57] Cf. die jeweilige Einleitung mit *kî-yimmāṣeʾ*/*yimṣāʾ ʾîš*, die Eröffnung der Protasis
in xxii 22a mit *kî-yimmāṣeʾ ʾîš šōkeb ʾim* und Abschluß in xxii 28 in umgekehrter
Reihenfolge mit *w⁽ᵉ⁾šākab ʿimmah w⁽ᵉ⁾nimṣāʾû*; xxii 28–9 ist von xxii 22a dadurch als
Gegenfall abgegrenzt, daß es in xxii 22a um die todesrechtliche Regelung des Ehe-
bruchs, in xxii 28–9 um die ersatzrechtliche Regelung der Gewalttat gegen ein
unverheiratetes Mädchen geht.

[58] Cf. Westbrook (Anm. 30), S. 574.

zierung der Strafschuld, sondern grundsätzlich die Todesstrafe für Konkumbenten und Ehefrau vorsieht. xxii 22a ist als Grundsatzregelung in Tatbestand und Rechtsfolge (lex generalis) den Rechtssätzen xxii 23–7* vorangestellt, die als leges speciales die lex generalis in xxii 22a differenzieren. xxii 22a konstatiert die prinzipielle Todeswürdigkeit von Ehefrau und Konkumbenten. In der Rahmenstruktur von xxii 22a, 28–9 wird von xxii 22a als Grundsatzregelung des Todesrechts der ersatzrechtliche Fall xxii 28–9 abgegrenzt, während xxii 23–7* in konzentrischer Struktur angeordnet die Grundsatz-

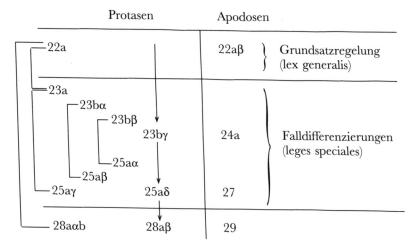

regelung zum Todesrecht in xxii 22a differenzieren. Wie der Redaktor xxii 22a mit xxii 28–9 zu einen Rahmen für xxii 23–7* verklammert, so verzahnt er auch xxii 22a, 28–9 mit xxii 23–7*,[59] so daß sich obige Struktur für xxii 22–9* ergibt.

In xxii 22–9* sind durch die redaktionelle Struktur Rechtssätze unterschiedlicher Herkunft miteinander vermittelt.[60] xxii 22a geht auf einen partizipial formulierten Rechtssatz[61] des im Ursprung familiengebundenen *môt-yûmāt*-Rechts (cf. Lev. xx 10, xviii 20; Ex. xx 14

---

[59] Cf. die Wiederaufnahme der Eröffnung von xxii 22a mit *ʾîš haššokeb ʿim hāʾiššâ* am Ende von xxii 22a, die der Verknüpfung mit den Versen xxii 23, 25, 28 dient, die mit *wᵉšākab ʿimmāh* daran anknüpfen. Die Rechtsfolgebestimmung *ûmet hāʾîš ... lᵉbaddô* in xxii 25a knüpft an xxii 22a *ûmetû gam-šᵉnêhæm*, die Definition der jungen Frau als *naʿrā bᵉtûlâ ʾašær lōʾ-ʾōrāśâ* in xxii 28–9 an xxii 23–7* *naʿrā bᵉtûlâ mᵉʾōrāśâ lᵉʾîš* an.

[60] Cf. Otto (Anm. 54), S. 292–3, 302.

[61] Cf. Seitz (Anm. 19), S. 120; Preuß (Anm. 18), S. 125–6.

par. Dtn. v 18[62]) zurück und ist nur oberflächlich der kasuistischen Form angeglichen worden. xxii 28–9 gehört wie Ex. xxii 15–16[63] in das kasuistische Konfliktregelungsrecht der Torgerichtsbarkeit. Durch die Redaktion werden das Recht gentiler Gerichtsbarkeit des pater familias und der lokalen Gerichtsinstitution miteinander verzahnt. In den so geschaffenen Rahmen fügt der Redaktor die Falldifferenzierungen in xxii 23–7* ein, die, wie die Eröffnung mit *kî yihyæh* zeigt, xii 22a voraussetzen.

Die Struktur von xxii 22–9* gleicht auffällig der von §§ 12–16 des mass. K.A. Jeweils werden Rechtssätze als Grundsatzregelungen vorangestellt, die, in einen die Einheit umgreifenden Rahmen eingefügt, durch konzentrisch angeordnete Rechtssätze differenziert und mit der konzentrischen Rechtssatzeinheit intensiv verklammert werden. In beiden Fällen werden durch diese Struktur Rechtssätze unterschiedlicher Herkunft miteinander vermittelt und ausgeglichen. Die in den Rahmen xxii 22a, 28–9 eingefügten Falldifferenzierungen in xxii 23–7* setzen, wie die Eröffnung mit *kî yihyæh* zeigt, xxii 22a voraus. Die Ausdifferenzierungen werden anhand der inchoativ verheirateten Frau als Grenzfall zwischen der vollgültig verheirateten (xxii 22a) und der unverheirateten Frau (xxii 28–9) abgehandelt, die von der unverheirateten Frau abgegrenzt und wie eine vollgültig verheiratete Ehefrau behandelt wird,[64] so daß auch die Vergehen einer vollgültig verheirateten Frau in die Differenzierungen in xxii 23–7* eingeschlossen sind.[65]

---

[62] Zum Zusammenhang dieser Prohibitive mit dem *môt-yûmāt*-Recht cf. E. Otto, "Der Dekalog als Brennspiegel israelitischer Rechtsgeschichte", in J. Hausmann/ H.J. Zobel (Hg.), *Alttestamentlicher Glaube und biblische Theologie. FS H.D. Preuß* (Stuttgart, 1992), S. 59–68. Zur Bindung dieses Rechts an die Familie cf. Otto (Anm. 26), S. 138–46; G. Liedke, *Gestalt und Bezeichnung alttestamentlicher Rechtssätze. Eine formgeschichtlich-terminologische Studie* (Neukirchen-Vluyn, 1971), 120–35; E. Lipiński, "Prohibitive and Related Law Formulations in Biblical Hebrew and in Aramaic", *PWCJS* 9 (1988), S. 25–39.

[63] Cf. E. Otto, "Zur Stellung der Frau in den ältesten Rechtstexten des Alten Testamentes (Exodus 20,14; 22,15f.) - Wider die hermeneutische Naivität im Umgang mit dem Alten Testament", *ZEE* 26 (1982), S. (279–305) 284–9; ders. (Anm. 49).

[64] Cf. CE § 26; cf. dazu Otto (Anm. 46), S. 29ff.; ders., Rezension von R. Yaron, *The Laws of Eshnunna* (²1988), *VT* 40 (1990), S. (361–9) 362–3; Westbrook (Anm. 26), S. 34–8; cf. dazu Otto (Anm. 26).

[65] Cf. A. Tosato, *Il matrimonio israelitico. Una teoria generale* (Rom, 1982), S. 94, 110, Anm. 117. Wenn L. Stulman ("Sex and Familial Crimes in the D Code: A Witness to Mores in Transition", *JSOT* 53 [1992], S. [47–63] 58–60) ein Abwandern des ursprünglich in der Familie beheimateten Familienrechts an das Torgericht annimmt, so ist ihm zuzustimmen. Nicht begründet dagegen und durch die konzentrische Struktur eher ausgeschlossen ist die damit verbundene These, in xxii 23–4 liege ein gegenüber xxii 25–7 älteres Überlieferungsstadium vor.

Dieses Auslegungsverhältnis von Rechtssätzen der vollgültig und der inchoativ verheirateten Frau in xxii 22a/23, 24a, 25, 27[66] hat eine Parallele in CH §§ 129, 130.[67] Wie in den Keilschriftrechten schlägt sich in dieser Art der Aufweitung von Rechtssätzen durch Grenzfallbestimmungen eine rechtsgelehrte Beschäftigung nieder,[68] die in der Schreibergelehrsamkeit ihren Ort hat.[69] In der Differenzierung zwischen Ehebruch und Vergewaltigung folgt der Redaktor einem auch keilschriftlich u.a. in mass. K.A. §§ 12; 13; CE §§ 26–8; CH §§ 129, 130 und heth. K. §§ II 83, 84[70] breit belegten Schema. Das wirft nun auch ein Licht darauf, daß Rechtssätze unterschiedlicher Herkunft in mass. K.A. §§ 12–16 und xxii 22a, 23–9* in ähnlicher Strukturierung redigiert wurden. Wie in §§ 12–16 des mass. K.A. werden in xxii 22–9* Rechtssätze privaten und öffentlichen Rechts miteinander verzahnt. Vermittelt mass. K.A. §§ 12–16 Rechtssätze des Strafrechts der Familie und königlichen Richterjudikatur, so wird in xxii 22–9* ein Rechtssatz des Todesrechts in xxii 22a, das ursprünglich Grenzrecht der Familie war, mit dem kasuistischen Konfliktregelungsrecht in xxii 28–9, das in lokaler Gerichtsinstitution des "Torgerichts" beheimatet war, in chiastischer Rahmung verbunden und in rechtsgelehrter Ausgestaltung in xxii 23, 24a, 25, 27 differenziert. Der Redaktor bedient sich dabei eines Redaktionsmusters, das im assyrischen Recht eine Parallele hat. Von dieser Einsicht ausgehend eröffnet sich der Blick auf die dtn Redaktion in xii–xxvi.

2. Die Auslegung des "Bundesbuches" in xii–xxvi

Der deuteronomischen Redaktion in xii–xxvi liegt eine stellenweise mehrschichtige deuteronomistische Bearbeitung auf, die die Endgestalt von xii–xxv u.a. am Dekalog orientiert.[71] Die dtr Bearbeiter bedienen

---

[66] Cf. Otto (Anm. 27).

[67] Cf. Westbrook (Anm. 64), S. 35; Otto (Anm. 46), S. 32–3.

[68] Cf. B.L. Eichler, "Literary Structure in the Laws of Eshnunna", in: F. Rochberg-Halton (Hg.), *Language, Literature and History. Philological and Historical Studies Presented to E. Reiner* (New Haven, Conn., 1987), S. 71–84.

[69] Cf. Otto (Anm. 26), S. 164–87; ders., "Town and Rural Countryside in Ancient Israelite Law. Reception and Redaction in Cuneiform and Israelite Law", *JSOT* 57 (1993), S. 3–22; cf. auch zur Schreiberausbildung D.W. Jamieson-Drake, *Scribes and Schools in Monarchic Judah. A Socio-Archeological Approach* (Sheffield, 1991), S. 147–59; B.S. Jackson, "Practical Wisdom and Literary Artifice in the Covenant Code", *Jewish Law Association Studies* 6 (1992), S. 65–94.

[70] Cf. J. Friedrich, *Die hethitischen Gesetze* (Leiden, ²1971), S. 86; J. Grothus, *Die Rechtsordnung der Hethiter* (Wiesbaden, 1973), S. 35.

[71] Cf. G. Braulik, *Die deuteronomischen Gesetze und der Dekalog. Studien zum Aufbau von Deuteronomium 12–26* (Stuttgart, 1991), S. 23–114.

sich der ihnen vorgegebenen dtn Rechtssatzsammlung.[72] Auf die als Hauptgesetze voranstehenden Gebote der Kulteinheit in xii 13–22, 26–8* und Kultreinheit in xiii 2–18* folgen in xiv 22–xv 23* privileg-rechtliche Aussonderungsbestimmungen. Die Privilegrechtsbestimmung des Jahreszehnts in xiv 22–7 bildet als Bestimmung *šānâ* (*b*ᵉ)*šānâ* (xiv 22, xv 20) mit der entsprechenden Erstgeburtsbestimmung in xv 19–23 einen Rahmen[73] für die Bestimmungen des Drittjahreszehnts (xiv 28–9), der *š*ᵉ*miṭṭâ* (xv 1–2, 7–10, 11b) und der ebenfalls am 6/7-Schema des Privilegrechts[74] orientierten Sklavenfreilassung im 7. Jahr (xv 12–18). Diese Privilegrechtsbestimmungen in xiv 22–xv 23* for-men mit denen von Erstlingen und Drittjahreszehnt in xxvi 2*, 5a*, 10–13*[75] einen Rahmen. Die Aussonderungsbestimmungen in xxvi 2–13* knüpfen an die Bestimmungen in xiv 22–9 an und führen sie weiter.[76] Die theologische Mitte von xvi 2*, 5a*, 10–13* in den Be-

---

[72] Cf. A.D.H. Mayes, *Deuteronomy* (London, 1979), S. 42–3. Zur Begründung der literarischen Abhebung des vordtr Grundbestandes der dtn Redaktion in xii 13, 14a, 15–22, 26–8, xiii 2a, 3b, 4a, 6a*, b, 7*, 9–18, xiv 22–9, xv 1–2, 7–10, 11b, 12–23, xvi 1–17, 18*, 19, xvii 2, 3*, 4, 5*, 6–10, 12–13, xviii 1*, 3–4, 5*, 6–8, xix 2a, 3b, 4–6, 10–13, 15–21, xxi 1*, 2–5*, 6–9, 15–xxii 7a, 8–29, xxiii 16–26*, xxiv 1*–7, 10–xxv 12, xxvi 2*, 5a*, 10–13* von dtr Überarbeitung cf. E. Otto, "Vom Bundesbuch zum Deuteronomium. Die deuteronomische Redaktion in Dtn 12–26", in G. Braulik/W. Groß/S.E. McEvenue (Hg.), *Biblische Theologie und gesellschaftliche Wandel. FS N. Lohfink* (Freiburg, 1993), S. 260–78.

[73] Cf. die lexematischen Bezüge *ʾkl lipnê yhwh* ʾ*ᵃlôhêkā* + *māqôm*-Formel sowie die Zweigliedrigkeit von Grundsatz- und Einschränkungsregel in xiv 22–3/24–6 par. xv 19–20/21–3.

[74] Cf. E. Otto, "Art *šæbaʿ, šābûʿôṭ*", *THWAT* VII (1992), S. 1017–18. Das Privileg-recht Jahwes ist weder mit vorjehowistischer Überlieferung in Ex. xxxiv (zur Analy-se cf. Otto [Lit.]) noch mit einer Sammlung in xii–xviii* zu verbinden, sondern ist durch die Aussonderungen für Jahwe als Privileg, in der Regel im 6/7-Schema, in BB und Dtn. gekennzeichnet.

[75] Zur Analyse cf. Seitz (Anm. 19), S. 243–8; S. Kreuzer, *Die Frühgeschichte Israels in Bekenntnis und Verkündigung des Alten Testaments* (Berlin, 1989), S. 149–82. Zu xxvi 6–9 cf. auch N. Lohfink, "Dtn 26, 6–9: Ein Beispiel altisraelitischer Geschichts-theologie", in ders., *Studien zum Deuteronomium und zur deuteronomistischen Literatur* I (Stutt-gart, 1990), S. 291–303.

[76] xxvi 12a *kol-maʿśar t*ᵉ*bûʾāt*ᵉ*kā* nimmt wörtlich anknüpfend xiv 28 auf, setzt mit *kî t*ᵉ*kalleh la'ser* xiv 28 *tôṣîʾ* ... *w*ᵉ*hinnaḥtā* als abgeschlossen voraus und schlägt einen Bogen zu xiv 22 ʿ*aśśer t*ᵉ*ʿaśśer ʾet kol-t*ᵉ*bûʾâ*. xxvi 2a *kol-p*ᵉ*rî haʾᵃdāmâ* faßt die Aufzäh-lung der Früchte in xiv 23 zusammen. Mit dem Lexem *reʾšît* wird das aus der Ver-klammerung von xiv 22–7 mit xv 19–23 stammende Motiv der *b*ᵉ*kôrōt* (xiv 23) as-soziiert. xxvi 2b* *hlk* + *māqôm*-Formel (ohne *l*ᵉ*šakken š*ᵉ*mô šām* [dtr]) nimmt xiv 25bβ auf. xxvi 11 faßt zitierend das Motiv der Freude und Fürsorge für den Leviten in xiv 26bβ, 27a zusammen. *š*ᵉ*nat hamma* ᵃ*śer* in xxiv 12a verweist auf *š*ᵉ*nat haš*š*miṭṭâ* in xv 9 (cf. N. Airoldi, "La cosidetta 'decima' israelitica antica". *Bib* 55 [1974], S. [179–210] 206–7, Anm. 1). xxvi 12b faßt die Gebote der Speisung der personae miserae in xiv 29 zusammen. *haqqōdæš* in xxvi 13 weist zurück auf *taqdîš* in xv 19.

kenntnissen xxvi 5aβ, 10a, 13aβb hat ihren Ausgangspunkt in xiv
23b. Erst in xxvi 2*, 5a*, 10–13* wird deutlich, inwiefern die Darbringung von Zehntem und Drittjahreszehntem JWWH-Furcht ler-
nen läßt.

Die privilegrechtlichen Aussonderungsbestimmungen in xiv 22–xv
23* und xxvi 2–13* bilden einen Rahmen um die Festordnung in
xvi 1–17, die Gerichtsordnung in xvi 18–xviii 8* und die materiale
Rechtsordnung in xix 2–xxv 12*.

Die drei jeweils konzentrisch strukturierten Festordnungen in xvi
1–15[77] werden durch die Wallfahrtsbestimmungen in xv 19–23 und
xvi 16–17[78] mit den privilegrechtlichen Rahmen der Aussonderungsbestimmungen in xiv 22–xv 23* verzahnt. Legt xv 19–23 den Ort
der Opfergabe fest, so regelt xvi 16–17 den zeitlichen Aspekt. Wie
der privilegrechtliche Rahmen in xiv 22–xv 23* folgert die Festordnung
in xvi 1–17 Verfahrensregelungen aus dem Hauptgebot der Kultzentralisation in xii 13–22*.[79] Die vordtr Gerichtsordnung in xvi
18*, 19, xvii 2-7*, 8-13*, xviii 1-8*[80] zieht die Konsequenzen aus der
Kultzentralisation für das Gerichtswesen. Schlüssel zur Interpretation
ist die Abfolge von xvii 2–7* und xvii 8–13*. An xiii 2–18* anknüpfend regelt xvii 2–7* als "Modellprozeß mit eingebauter Zweizeugen-

[77] Zur Strukturierung der Festordnungen in Siebenergruppierungen cf. G. Braulik,
"Die Funktion von Siebenergruppierungen im Endtext des Deuteronomiums", in
F.V. Reiterer (Hg.), *Ein Gott—eine Offenbarung. FS N. Füglister* (Würzburg, 1991),
S. (37–50) 41.

[78] Cf. die gemeinsamen Lexeme *šānâ bᵉšānâ*, *zᵉkûrᵉkā/hazzākār* sowie die gemeinsame *māqôm*-Formel. Zur Übergangs- und Verklammerungsfunktion von xv 19–23 cf.
auch Mayes (Anm. 72), S. 253.

[79] Cf. zur Verklammerung von Fest- und Gerichtsordnung mit xii 13–19 W.S.
Morrow, *The Composition of Deuteronomy 14, 1–17, 1* (Ph.D. Diss., University of Toronto, 1988), S. 493–500.

[80] Zu dtr Ergänzungen cf. U. Rüterswörden, *Von der politischen Gemeinschaft zur
Gemeinde. Studien zu Dt 16, 18–18, 22* (Frankfurt M., 1987), S. 11ff., 31ff., 39ff., 67ff.,
xvii 14–20, xviii 9–22 ist gegen U. Rüterswörden, gefolgt von K. Zobel (*Prophetie und
Deuteronomium. Die Rezeption prophetischer Theologie durch das Deuteronomium* [Berlin, 1992],
S. 110ff.), nicht Teil eines dtn-vordtr "Ämtergesetzes". xvii 14 ist mit xix 1 dtr
aufgrund der Parallelen in vii 1, viii 7 und der Nähe zu xii 29 (dtr; cf. N. Lohfink,
"Kerygmata des Deuteronomistischen Geschichtswerkes", in J. Jeremias/L. Perlitt
[Hg.], *Die Botschaft und die Boten. FS H.W. Wolff* [Neukirchen-Vluyn, 1981], S. 87–
100) und nicht von xvii 15 abzulösen; cf. N. Lohfinks Rezension der Arbeit von
U. Rüterswörden in *ThLZ* 113 (1988), S. 425–30, der zurecht feststellt, daß ohne
xvii 15 kein Königsgesetz zustande komme. Dasselbe gilt für das Prophetengesetz,
das ohne xviii 16, 20 (dtr) wenig plausibel ist. Erst die dtr Erweiterung redigiert
xvi 18–xviii 22 zu einem "Ämtergesetz", das im Rahmen eines dtr Verfassungs-
entwurfs gerade das zum Programm erhebt, was Rüterswörden der deuteronomischen
Schicht zuweist.

regelung"[81] den eindeutig aufgeklärten Fall, der vor der lokalen Gerichtsbarkeit verhandelt wird, xvii 8–13* dagegen den nicht durch Zeugen aufgeklärten Fall, der vor der Kultzentralisation am Lokalheiligtum durch kultischen Rechtsentscheid entschieden wurde (Ex. xxii 7–8[82]), nun aber der Gerichtsbarkeit am Zentralheiligtum unter Beteiligung levitischer Priester zukommt.[83] Das am Zentralheiligtum angesiedelte Gericht ist also nicht Berufungsinstanz für die Ortsgerichte, sondern Nachfolgeinstitution der Lokalheiligtümer für deren kultischen Rechtsentscheid. Der Ordnung der profanen Lokalgerichtsbarkeit in xvii 2–7* ist das Ämtergesetz in xvi 18–19*, der Ordnung der kultischen Zentralgerichtsbarkeit in xvii 8–13* das Ämtergesetz in xviii 1–8* zugeordnet. Die Ämtergesetze xvi 18–19*, xviii 1–8* rahmen also die lokalen und zentralen Gerichtsordnungen in xvii 2–13*.

In der materialen Rechtsordnung in xix 2–xxv 12* formt der deuteronomische Redaktor ein Fachwerk aus den im A-B-Schema alternierender Anordnung redigierten Reihen sozialer Bestimmungen in xxii 1–7a, 8–12; xxiii 16–26*, xxiv 6–7, 10–22, xxv 1–4,[84] in das die kasuistischen Rechtssätze des mit dem Prozeßrecht in xix 15–21, xxi

---

[81] Cf. N. Lohfink, "Die Sicherung der Wirksamkeit des Gotteswortes durch das Prinzip der Schriftlichkeit der Tora und durch das Prinzip der Gewaltenteilung nach den Ämtergesetzen des Buches Deuteronomium (Dtn 16, 18–18, 22)", in ders. (Anm. 75), S. (305–23) 306.

[82] Cf. H. Niehr, *Rechtsprechung in Israel. Untersuchungen zur Geschichte der Gerichtsorganisation im Alten Testament* (Stuttgart, 1987), S. 54–5, 87–91. Zum kultischen Rechtsentscheid in Israel cf. auch T.S. Frymer-Kensky, *The Judicial Ordeal in the Ancient Near East* (Ph.D. Diss., Yale University, New Haven, Conn., 1977), S. 474–80.

[83] Cf. Lohfink (Anm. 81), S. 307–8; B.M. Levinson, *The Hermeneutics of Innovation: The Impact of Centralization upon the Structure, Sequence, and Reformulation of Legal Material in Deuteronomy* (Ph.D. Diss., Brandeis University, Waltham, Mass., 1991), S. 325–404. Eine Herauslösung von xvii 2–7* aus dem Kontext und Anbindung an xiii* oder eine Eintragung von xiii* in xvii* (cf. H. Seebaß, "Vorschlag zur Vereinfachung literarischer Analysen im dtn Gesetz", *BN* 58 [1991], S. [83–98] 92) verkennt diesen Zusammenhang.

[84] Cf. Otto (Anm. 54), S. 295–8, 304–6. In xxii 1–12* werden Aufforderungen zur sozialen Verantwortung (xxii 1–4, 6–7a) mit Verboten unerlaubter Mischungen (xxii 5, 9–11), in xxiii 16–26* soziale Gebote (xxiii 16–17, 20 [21; cf. dazu L. Perlitt, "'Ein einzig Volk von Brüdern': Zur deuteronomischen Herkunft der biblischen Bezeichnung 'Bruder'", in D. Lührmann/G. Strecker (Hg.), *Kirche. FS G. Bornkamm* (Tübingen, 1980), S. (27–52) 34–5], 25–6) mit kultisch thematisierten Rechtssätzen (xxiii 18–19, 22–4) und in xxiv 6–7, 10–22, xxv 1–4 Sozialgesetze (xxiv 6, 10–15, 17–22; xxv 4) mit Strafrechtssätzen (xxiv 7, 16, xxv 1–3) verbunden. Die Reformidee des Ausschlusses der Noxalhaftung und Haftung weiterer Familienangehöriger bei Delikten einer Ehefrau in mass. K.A. § 2 (cf. o. II.2) berührt sich mit der Individualisierung der Strafverfolgung in xxiv 16, die eine generationsübergreifende Haftung der Söhne für die Väter ausschließt; cf. bereits A.F. Puukkoo, "Die alt-

22–3 verzahnten Blut- sowie Körperverletzungsrechts in xix 2a, 3b, 4–6, 10–13, xxi 1*, 2*–9, xxv 11–12 und Familienrechts in xxi 15–21, xxii 13–29, xxiv 1–4*, xxv 5–10 eingefügt und durch xxiv 5 mit der Reihe in xxiv 6–xxv 4* verzahnt wurden.[85] Innerhalb des Familienrechts rahmen die mit *kî-yiqqaḥ ʾîš ʾiššâ* eingeleiteten, die Abneigung des Ehemanns voraussetzenden Rechtssätze in xxii 13–19,[86] xxiv 1*–4, (5) den geschlossenen, jeweils mit *kî-yimmāṣeʾ/yimṣaʾ ʾîš* eingeleiteten Block in xxii 22–9. Um diese das Verhältnis von Mann und Frau regelnden Rechtssätze sind mit xxi 15–21, xxv 5–10 die den Erbfall betreffenden Rechtssätze gelegt. Der Redaktor redigiert die materiale Rechtsordnung in xix 2–xxv 12* unter den Gesichtspunkten sozialer Verantwortung und Reinheit des Volkes im Lande. Das Motiv der sozialen Verantwortung hat seinen theologischen Begründungszusammenhang in den auf diesen Aspekt interpretierten Aussonderungsbestimmungen in xiv 22–xv 23* und xxvi 2–13*. Durch die Inklusionsstruktur des privilegrechtlichen Rahmens werden in der dtn Redaktion auch Fest- und Gerichtsordnung der JHWH-Herrschaft unterstellt. Doch leitet sich aus dem sozial interpretierten Privilegrecht der Aussonderungsbestimmungen noch nicht deren zentraler Aspekt der Kultzentralisation ab, der im Motiv der Reinheit des auf das eine erwählte Heiligtum bezogenen Volkes im Lande im materialen Recht in xix 2–xxv 12* eine Entsprechung hat. So weist die Redaktionsstruktur in xiv–xxvi* auf die Hauptgesetze in xii, xiii*, die mit dem privilegrechtlichen Rahmen der Aussonderungsbestimmungen sowie der Fest- und Gerichtsordnung intensiv verzahnt sind. Die Entfaltung von xii 13, 14a, 17–18 in xii 20–2, 26–8 wird im privilegrechtlichen Rahmen in xiv 22–9, xv 19–23, xxvi 2–13* fortgesetzt. Die Festordnung knüpft in xvi 2, 5–7, 10–11, 15–17 an

---

assyrischen und hethitischen Gesetze und das Alte Testament", *StOr* 1 (1925), S. (125–66) 128–9. Hier wie dort schlägt sich in dieser Begrenzung der Einfluß staatlicher Rechtspflege nieder; cf. B. Halpern, "Jerusalem and the Lineages in the Seventh Century BCE: Kinship and the Rise of Individual Moral Liability", in ders./ Hobson (Hg.) (Anm. 4), S. (11–107) 17.

[85] Die "Kriegsgesetze" in xx 1–20, xxi 10–14, xxiii 10–15, xxv 17–19 sind dtr bearbeitete und eingefügte Programmtexte (cf. Preuß [Anm. 18], S. 120–1, 139–40), die unter Verwendung älteren Materials (cf. A. Rofé, "The Laws of the Warfare in the Book of Deuteronomy: Their Origins, Intent and Positivity", *JSOT* 32 [1985], S. 23–44), das aber von der dtn Redaktion in xii–xxvi* unabhängig ist, gestaltet wurden. xxiv 5 konnte wie die dtn Fluchttradition (xxviii 30, cf. xx 5–7) Anknüpfungspunkt für die dtr Redaktion sein.

[86] xxii 20–21a (vordtn Ergänzung; cf. Mayes [Anm. 72], S. 309) dient bereits in der vordtn Familienrechtssammlung der redaktionellen Verknüpfung von xxii 13–19 mit xxii 22–9*; cf. Otto (Anm. 54), S. 291–5, 299–304.

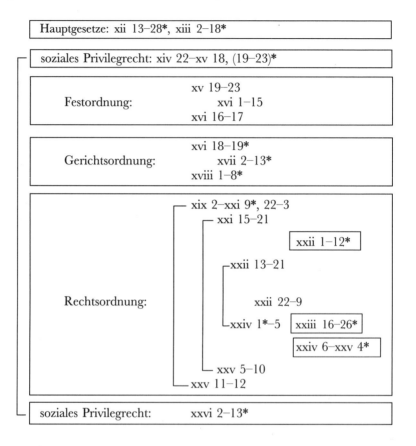

Hauptgesetze: xii 13–28*, xiii 2–18*

soziales Privilegrecht: xiv 22–xv 18, (19–23)*

Festordnung: xv 19–23, xvi 1–15, xvi 16–17

Gerichtsordnung: xvi 18–19*, xvii 2–13*, xviii 1–8*

Rechtsordnung:
xix 2–xxi 9*, 22–3
xxi 15–21
xxii 1–12*
xxii 13–21
xxii 22–9
xxiv 1*–5   xxiii 16–26*
xxiv 6–xxv 4*
xxv 5–10
xxv 11–12

soziales Privilegrecht: xxvi 2–13*

xii 13, 14a, 26–8 und die Gerichtsordnung in xvii 2–7* an xiii 2–18* an. xii 13–22*, 26–8, xiii 2–18* eröffnen als Hauptgesetze das Korpus der privilegrechtlich gerahmten Rechtssätze in xiv–xxvi*, so daß sich obige Redaktionsstruktur ergibt.

xii 20–2, 26–8 wird unter die Hauptgesetze eingeordnet, während die übrigen Ausführungsbestimmungen zu xii 14a, 17 in xiv 22–9; xv 19–23* und xxvi 2–13* in die leges speciales verwiesen werden, weil xii 20–2, 26–8 wie xii 13, 14a, 15–19[87] Auslegung des Altargesetzes des Bundesbuches (BB) in Ex. xx 24 ist.[88] xii 13–28* ist also als Auslegung des Altargesetzes dem durch das Privilegrecht gerahmten

---

[87] Cf. Lohfink (Anm. 3), S. 168–77.
[88] Cf. Levinson (Anm. 83), S. 193–207. Zur Aufnahme von Ex. xxii 19a in xiii* cf. Dion (Anm. 4), S. 197, Anm. 1 (mit Hinweis auf Lohfink), sowie Seebaß (Anm. 83), S. 87.

Korpus der Rechtssätze in xix–xxvi* vorangestellt worden, so wie das Altargesetz dem BB voransteht. Vom BB her schlüsselt sich auch der Rahmen der privilegrechtlichen Aussonderungsbestimmungen im 6/7-Schema in xiv 22–xv 23*, xxvi 2–13* auf. In der Endgestalt des vordtr BB wird das Korpus der Rechtssätze in Ex. xxi 2–xxiii 12 durch die Bestimmungen von Sklavenbefreiung (Ex. xxi 2–11) sowie *š^emiṭṭâ* und Ruhetag (Ex. xxiii 10–12), die ebenfalls im 6/7-Schema der Privilegrechtstheologie strukturiert sind, gerahmt.[89] Das Privilegrecht in Ex. xxi 2–11, xxiii 10–12 rahmt die aus ursprünglich selbständigen Rechtssatzsammlungen des Todesrechts (Ex. xxi 12–17), Körperverletzungsrechts (Ex. xxi 18–32) und Sachenrechts (Ex. xxi 33–xxii 14) zusammengefügte Ordnung des materialen Rechts in Ex. xxi 12–xxii 19a. Zentrum des vordtr BB bildet die Zusammenordnung von Sozialrecht und Privilegrecht als Abschluß der Ordnung des materialen Rechts in Ex. xxii 20–6*, 28–9, auf die die Gerichtsordnung in Ex. xxiii 1–8 folgt, so daß sich folgender Aufbau des BB ergibt:[90]

---

[89] Zu Abgrenzung und Redaktionsgeschichte cf. E. Otto, *Wandel der Rechtsbegründungen in der Gesellschaftsgeschichte des antiken Israel. Eine Rechtsgeschichte des "Bundesbuches" Ex XX 22–XXIII 13* (Leiden, 1988), S. 9–56. Zu den jüngsten Analysen des BB durch L. Schwienhorst-Schönberger, *Das Bundesbuch (Ex 20, 22–23, 33). Studien zu seiner Entstehung und Theologie* (Berlin, 1990), und Y. Osumi, *Die Kompositionsgeschichte des Bundesbuches Exodus 20, 22b–23, 33* (Fribourg/Göttingen, 1991); cf. E. Otto, "Vom Profanrecht zum Gottesrecht: Das Bundesbuch", *ThR* 56 (1991), S. 421–7; ders., "Die Kompositionsgeschichte des alttestamentlichen 'Bundesbuches' Ex 20, 22b–23, 33", *WZKM* 83 (1993), S. 153–65. Zur Problematik der Aussonderung einer profanen Rechtssatzsammlung der *mišpaṭim* in Ex. xxi 2–xxii 17 cf. auch J.M. Sprinkle, *A Literary Approach to Biblical Law: Exodus 20:22–23:19* (Ph.D. Diss. Hebrew Union College, Cincinnati, 1991), S. 477–53, et passim. Bedauerlicherweise begründet Sprinkle seine konsequent synchrone Interpretation des BB nicht mit einer Analyse der Textstrukturierung des vorliegenden Textes; cf. dazu den weiterführenden Vorschlag von N. Lohfink, "Poverty in the Laws of the Ancient Near East and of the Bible", *ThSt* 52 (1991), S. (34–50) 40–1.

[90] Cf. Otto, *Rechtsbegründungen* (Anm. 89), S. 9–11, 54–6. Diese Redaktionsstruktur ist aus der Verbindung der zwei Rechtssatzsammlungen Ex. xx 24–6, xxi 2–xxii 26* und xxii 28–xxiii 12* entstanden und setzt die Redaktionsstrukur der Rechtssatzsammlung Ex. xxii 28–xxiii 12* fort, in der die Gerichtsordnung in Ex. xxiii 1–3 (4–5) 6–8 durch das Privilegrecht im 6/7-Schema in Ex. xxii 28–9, xxiii 10–12 gerahmt wird; cf. Otto, *Rechtsbegründungen*, S. 45–51. Für die Traditionsgeschichte dieser sich des Privilegrechts bedienenden Redaktionsstruktur ist es bedeutsam, daß die Redaktion dieser Rechtssatzsammlung in priesterlichen Kreisen des spätvorexilischen Juda zu vermuten ist; cf. Otto, S. 50–1. Zur dtr Überarbeitung in Ex. xx 22, 23, xxi 1, xxii 19b, 20aβb, 21, 23, 24b, 30, xxiii 9, 13, (14–33) cf. Otto, *Rechtsbegründungen* (Anm. 89), 4–8; ders. (Anm. 74), S. 1022–3 (zu xxiii 14–19). N. Lohfink ("Gibt es eine deuteronomistische Bearbeitung im Bundesbuch?", in C. Brekelmans/J. Lust [Hg.], *Pentateuchal and Deuteronomistic Studies* [Leuven, 1990], S. 91–113) rechnet mit einer entsprechenden vordtn Überarbeitung; cf. dazu Schwienhorst-Schönberger (Anm. 89), S. 346–8.

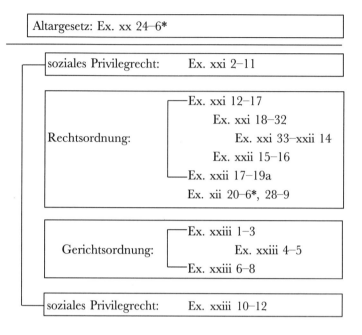

xii–xxvi* legt, beginnend mit dem Altargesetz,[91] das BB aus.[92] Im privilegrechtlichen Rahmen in xiv 22–xv 23* werden mit xv 1–18* die den Rahmen des BB bildenden Rechtssätze im 6/7-Schema zu Sklavenrecht[93] und *šᵉmiṭṭâ* in Ex. xxi 2–11, xxiii 10–11 in das Zentrum des Rahmens gerückt und durch die unter das Zentralisationsgebot fallenden Zehnt- und Erstgeburtsgebote in xiv 22–9, xv 19–23 unter Aufnahme von Ex. xxii 28–9 gerahmt und mit den Hauptgeboten in xii 13–28*, xiii 2–18* und der Festordnung in xiv 1–17 verzahnt. Da es dem dtn Redaktor um eine Reform unter dem Gesichtspunkt des Hauptgebotes der Kultzentralisation geht, hat er das Ruhetagsgebot Ex. xxiii 12 nicht aufgenommen. Unter dem Gesichtspunkt der Kultzentralisation stellt der Redaktor an den Rahmen xiv 22–xv 23* anknüpfend die Institutionsordnung von Kult und Gericht vor die materiale Rechtsordnung. Mit xvi 1–17 reformiert er eine Ex. (xxiii 14–19*); xxxiv 18–23, 25*, 26[94] entsprechende Fest-

---

[91] Cf. Levinson (Anm. 83), S. 325–404.
[92] Cf. Otto (Anm. 72).
[93] Zur Anknüpfung an Ex. xxi 2–6 in xv 12–18 cf. F. Horst, "Das Privilegrecht Jahwes", in ders., *Gottes Recht* (München, 1961), S. (17–154) 98–9; Mayes (Anm. 72), S. 249–53.
[94] Zum überlieferungsgeschichtlichen Verhältnis zwischen Ex. xxxiv 18–26* und

ordnung.[95] Die Gerichtsordnung in xvi 18–xviii 8* knüpft in der Eröffnung in xvi 18*, 19 an die Gerichtsordnung des BB in Ex. xxiii 6, 8, an.[96] In xix 15–21 wird die Gerichtsordnung (xvii 6) mit dem Blutrecht der materialen Rechtsordnung in xix 2–xxv 12* verzahnt. Milt ῾ed ḥāmās wird an Ex. xxiii 1 angeknüpft und durch die Zweizeugenregelung der Appell wahren Zeugnisses in Verfahrensrationalität überführt. Die aus dem BB übernommene Talion in xix 21 verklammert das Prozeßrecht mit dem Blutrecht in xix 2–13*[97] wie xxi 22–3 mit dem Familienrecht in xxi 15–21, xxiii 13–29, xxiv 1*–5. Die so mit der Gerichtsordnung in xvi 18–xviii 8* verzahnte materiale Rechtsordnung in xix 2–xxv 12* ist durch die Auslegung von Rechtssätzen des BB strukturiert. Aus der materialen Rechtsordnung des BB werden vom dtn Redaktor neben Ex. xxi 23–4 und Ex. xxii 19a Sätze des Todesrechts in Ex. xxi 12–17 und des sozialen Ethos in Ex. xxii 20–6*, xxiii 4–5 rezipiert. Die Sätze des sozialen Ethos werden in xxii 1–4 (Ex. xxiii 4–5),[98] xxiii 20 (Ex. xxii 24*) und xxiv 10–

---

xxiii 14–19 cf. Otto (Anm. 74), S. 1022–3 ders., *ThR* 56 (Anm. 89), S. 426–7.

[95] Cf. G. Braulik, "Leidensgedächtnisfeier und Freudenfest. 'Volksliturgie' nach dem deuteronomischen Festkalender (Dtn 16, 1–17)", *ThPh* 56 (1981), S. 335–57 = ders., *Studien zur Theologie des Deuteronomiums* (Stuttgart, 1988), S. 95–121; ders., "Die Freude des Festes. Das Kultverständnis des Deuteronomiums-die älteste Festtheorie", in W. Ernst u.a. (Hg.), *Theologisches Jahrbuch 1983* (Leipzig, 1983), S. 19–54 = ders., a.a.O., S. 161–218.

[96] Während Ex. xxiii 1–3, 6–8 weder dem Reichen noch dem Armen aufgrund seiner sozialen Stellung einen Vorteil gewährt (cf. dazu S. Herrmann, "Weisheit im Bundesbuch. Eine Miszelle zu Ex 23, 1–9", in Hausmann/Zobel [Hg.] [Anm. 62], S. 56–8), nimmt der dtn Redaktor nur die gegen den sozial Starken gerichteten Sätze auf und spitzt die Gerichtordnung der Rahmung im Privilegrecht entsprechend sozial zu. Die Auslassung von Ex. xxiii 7 ist in der sozialen Zuspitzung, die sich auch in der Aufnahme von Ex. xxiii 6 in xxiv 17a niederschlägt, konsequent und kein Argument, um einen literarischen Zusammenhang zwischen der dtn Gerichtsordnung und der des Bundesbuches in Abrede zu stellen; gegen Rüterswörden (Anm. 80), S. 21–2.

[97] Die in xix 21 angefügte Talion legt das in xix 19a formulierte talionische Prinzip der Todessanktion für falsche Anklage eines Kapitaldeliktes (cf. dazu H. Petschow, "Ein Fall von 'Talion' bei falscher Anschuldigung in Ur III", *AfO* 35 [1988], S. 105–8) aus und schlägt mit der talionischen Formulierung *næpæš bᵉnæpæš* einen Bogen zurück in das Blutrecht in xix 6, 11. Die Aufzählung der talionischen Körperstrafen hat in diesem am Blutrecht orientierten Zusammenhang nur die Funktion, das erste Glied zu unterstreichen und setzt damit die Interpretation der Talion im BB voraus; cf. E. Otto, "Die Geschichte der Talion im Alten Orient und Israel", in D.R. Daniels u.a. (Hg.), *Ernten, was man sät. FS K. Koch* (Neukirchen-Vluyn, 1991), S. (101–30) 117–24.

[98] Cf. dazu G. Barbiero, *L'asino del nemico. Rinuncia alla vendetta e amore del nemico nella legislazione dell' Antico Testamento (Es. 23, 4–5; Dt. 22, 1–4; Lv. 19, 17–18)* (Rom, 1991), S. 72–202. Zu den ethischen Bestimmungen des BB cf. auch E. Otto, "Sozial- und rechtshistorische Aspekte in der Ausdifferenzierung eines altisraelitischen Ethos

13, 17 (Ex. xxii 25–6)[99] in die alternierend angeordneten Reihen des
sozialen Ethos in xxii 1–12*, xxiii 16–26*, xxiv 6–xxv 4* aufgenommen, die die materiale Rechtsordnung in xix 2–xxv 12* strukturie-
ren. Die materiale Rechtsordnung in xix 2–xxv 12* wird wie die des
BB durch Rechtssätze zu Tötungsdelikt und Asyl (Ex. xxi 12–14)
eingeleitet, die in xix 2–13* direkt an Ex. xxi 12–14 anknüpfen.[100]
Stellt Ex. xxi 12 den Tötungsfall mit undifferenzierter todesrechtlicher
Sanktion als lex generalis vor die Falldifferenzierung zwischen Körperverletzung mit Todesfolge und Mord in Ex. xxi 13–14, so kehrt
xix 2–13* diese Reihenfolge um. Der dtn Redaktor ist primär an der
Falldifferenzierung in Ex. xxi 13–14 interessiert, weil sie mit der Asyl-
funktion der lokalen Heiligtümer (*māqôm/mizbeaḥ*) verbunden ist.
Wiederum ist das Hauptgebot der Kultzentralisation in xii 13–28*
der hermeneutische Schlüssel des dtn Redaktors in der Rezeption
des BB.

In der alternierend Sätze des sozialen Ethos und des Strafrechts
anordnenden Reihe xxiv 6–xxv 4* legt xxiv 7 den Rechtssatz des
môt-yûmāt-Rechts in Ex. xxi 16 aus. Der dtn Redaktor hat also die
Rezeption der materialen Rechtsordnung des BB konsequent auf das
Todesrecht (Ex. xxi 12–16) sowie das soziale Ethos (Ex. xxii 20–6*,
xxiii 4–5) beschränkt und das Körperverletzungsrecht (Ex. xxi 18–
22, 25–32) sowie das Sachenrecht der *yᵉšallem*-Gesetze (Ex. xxi 33–
xxii 14) übergangen, während er das restliche BB mit Ex. xx 24–6,
xxii 19a in den Hauptgeboten xii 13–28*, xiii 2–18*, mit Ex. xxi 2–
11, xxii 28–9, xxiii 10–11 in der privilegrechtlichen Rahmung xiv
22–xv 23*, mit Ex. xxiii 1, 6, 8 in der Gerichtsordnung xvi 18–xviii
8* rezipiert hat. Das konsequente Auslassen des Körperverletzungs-

---

aus dem Recht", *Osnabrücker Hochschulschriften. Schriftenreihe des FB 3*, 9 (1987), S. 135–61.

[99] Ob xxiv 17–18 auch an Ex. xxii 20–1 (xxiii 9) anknüpft, oder umgekehrt Ex.
xxii 20aα durch Ex. xxii 20aβb, 21 im Sinne von xxiv 17–18 dtr erweitert wurde,
entscheidet sich daran, ob die überarbeitende Pluralschicht im BB als vor- oder
nachdtn interpretiert wird; Lit. cf. o. Anm. 90. Zur These von G.A. Chamberlain
(*Exodus 21–23 and Deuteronomy 12–26. A Form-Critical Study* [Th.D. Diss., Boston
University, 1977], S. 108–70), Ex. xxi 2–xxii 15, (16) zeige ein Geffälle vom BB
zum Dtn, während in Ex. xx 22–xxi 1, xxii 17–xxiii 19, 20–23 das Verhältnis
umgekehrt sei, cf. Otto, *Rechtsbegründungen* (Anm. 89), S. 8.

[100] Die sich aus dem literarischen Wachstumsprozeß von Ex. xxi 12, 13–14 erklärende Abfolge der Konjunktionen ᵓašær mit nachgeordnetem wᵉkî wird in xix 4b, 5,
11 wiederholt, was auf eine direkte Abhängigkeit hinweist. Dagegen ist eine direkte
literarische Abhängigkeit zwischen xxi 18–21* und Ex. xxi 15, 17 nicht wahrscheinlich zu machen; cf. E. Bellefontaine, "Deuteronomy 21, 18–21: Reviewing the Case
of the Rebellious Son", *JSOT* 13 (1979), S. (13–31) 15–16. xxi 18–21* war schon
vordtn mit xxi 15–17 als Gegenfall verbunden.

und Sachenrechts des BB ist darin begründet, daß der dtn Redaktor in diesen Rechtssätzen, die keinen unmittelbaren Bezug zu der in den Hauptgeboten zur Sprache gebrachten Reformintention haben, das BB nicht auslegt, sondern ergänzt. Im BB beschränkt sich das Familienrecht auf Ex. xxii 15–16.[101] Entsprechend entfaltet der dtn Redaktor breit das Familienrecht in xxi 15–xxii 29*, xxiv 1–5, xxv 5–10. Umgekehrt wird das im BB breit entfaltete Körperverletzungs-recht auf xxv 11–12, einen Rechtssatz, der große Nähe zu mass. K.A. § 8 hat,[102] eingeschränkt. Im kasuistischen Recht legt der dtn Redaktor also das BB nicht aus, sondern ergänzt es.

IV. *Zusammenfassung: Schriftauslegung im Dienste der Reform als Antwort auf die neuassyrische Krise*

Dtn. xii–xxvi* ordnet als Auslegung des BB unter dem Gesichtspunkt der Kultzentralisation Fest-, Gerichts- und Rechtsordnung neu. Das dem BB vorangestellte Altargesetz in Ex. xx 24–6 wird zum Haupt-gebot der Kultzentralisation in xii 13–28* ausgebaut. Aus dem BB wird die folgende Rahmung durch privilegrechtliche Aussonderungs-bestimmungen in xiv 22–xv 23*, xxvi 2–13* übernommen. Die Kult-zentralisation bestimmt die Anordnung der privilegrechtlichen Bestim-mungen, wenn xv 1–18* durch xiv 22–9, xv 19–23* gerahmt wird. Der Reformintention folgend stellt der dtn Redaktor vor die mate-riale Rechtsordnung die Institutionsordnungen in xvi 1–xviii 8*, die im BB in Ex. xxiii 1–8, (14–19) der materialen Rechtsordnung fol-gen. Über das BB hinausgehend stellt der Redaktor die Festordnung in xvi 1–17 vor die Gerichtsordnung in xvi 18–xviii 8*. In der ma-terialen Rechtsordnung, die er unter den Gesichtspunkten sozialer Verantwortung und Reinheit des Volkes im Lande redigiert,[103] er-gänzt der Redaktor das BB und regelt mit dem Familienrecht den Rechtsbereich, der im BB ungeregelt bleibt. Kult- und Prozeßrecht sollen also unter dem Aspekt der Kultzentralisation reformiert wer-den. Der dtn Redaktor leistet diese Aufgabe durch Auslegung des BB. Wie die Ergänzung der materialen Rechtsordnung durch das

---

[101] Die einzige Überschneidung in den kasuistischen Rechtssätzen von Ex. xxii 15–16 mit xxii 28–9 geht nicht auf direkte Übernahme zurück, da xxii 28–9 schon vordtn fest in den Kontext von xxii 22–9* integriert war; cf. Otto (Anm. 27). Zum rechtshistorischen Gefälle cf. Otto (Anm. 63), S. 286–7.

[102] Cf. Paul (Anm. 21), S. 335–9. Braulik ([Anm. 15], S. 189) interpretiert xxv 11–12 als Abgrenzung von Ex. xxii 22.

[103] Cf. Otto (Anm. 54), 291–306.

Familienrecht des Dtn. zeigt, sollte durch die Auslegung das BB nicht
außer Kraft gesetzt werden, sondern weiterhin gültig bleiben.[104]

Die Intention der Reform verbindet das Dtn. mit dem Mittelassyrischen Kodex der Tafel A. Geht es in diesem Kodex um die Einschränkung der gentilen Privatstrafe zugunsten der Strafe öffentlicher
Gerichtsinstitutionen königlicher Richterjudikatur, so zieht das Dtn.
in xii–xxvi* die Konsequenzen für Kult und Gericht aus der Kultzentralisation. Die grundlegende Strukturierung von xii–xxvi* stammt
nicht aus der Tradition der Keilschriftrechte, sondern aus der Exegese
des BB. Dennoch zeigt die Redaktion in xii–xxvi* einige nicht aus
dem BB ableitbare Züge. In der Redaktion der materialen Rechtsordnung des BB wurde die Sammlung der $y^e\check{s}allem$-Sätze in Ex. xxi
33–xxii 14, die ihrerseits aus ursprünglich selbständigen Sammlun-
gen redigiert wurde,[105] mit der Sammlung des Körperverletzungsrechts
in Ex. xxi 18–32[106] zusammengefügt und durch das Todesrecht in
Ex. xxi 12–17, xxii 17–19a gerahmt.[107] Im Dtn. wird dagegen die
materiale Rechtsordnung in xix 2–xxv 12* durch ein Fachwerk von
Rechtssätzen im A-B-Schema alternierender Anordnung strukturiert,
das die kasuistischen Rechtssätze der Rechtsordnung mit der Redaktionsintention des Rahmens und der Hauptgebote vermittelt. Dieses
Redaktionsverfahren, das am BB keinen Anhalt hat, wird auch im
Mittelassyrischen Kodex angewandt. Wie im Dtn. wird eine Rechtssatzsammlung des Familienrechts (mass. K.A. §§ 25–38) durch eine
Fachwerkstruktur (mass. K.A. §§ 39–49) auf den Rahmen und seine
Redaktionsintention bezogen. Anders als im mass. K.A., in dem die
Fachwerkstruktur an die Sammlung des Familienrechts angefügt wird,
ist sie mit xxii 1–12*, xxiii 16–26*, xxiv 6–xxv 4 in das Familienrecht einbezogen worden. Die Voranstellung von Hauptgesetzen vor
das folgende Korpus von Rechtssätzen als differenzierende leges
speciales hat, wie der Vergleich von xxii 22–9 mit mass. K.A. §§ 12–
16 gezeigt hat (cf. dazu o. II. 1), eine auf keilschriftliche Redaktions-

---

[104] Auf diesem Hintergrund wird auch die Einfügung des BB in die nachdtr Sinai-
perikope verständlich.

[105] Cf. Otto, *Rechtsbegründungen* (Anm. 89), S. 12–24; ders., "Die rechtshistorische
Entwicklung des Depositenrechts in altorientalischen und altisraelitischen Rechts-
korpora", *ZSS (Rom. Abt.)* 105 (1988), S. (1–31) 16–27.

[106] Cf. Otto, *Rechtsbegründungen* (Anm. 89), S. 24–31; ders., "Die Rechtssystematik
im altbabylonischen 'Codex Ešnunna' und im altisraelitischen 'Bundesbuch'. Eine
redaktionsgeschichtliche und rechtsvergleichende Analyse von CE §§ 17; 18; 22–28
und Ex 21, 18–32; 22, 6–14; 23, 1–3, 6–8", *UF* 19 (1987), S. (175–197) 187–94.

[107] Cf. dazu Otto, *Rechtsbegründungen* (Anm. 89), S. 9–10, 40–4.

technik zurückgehende Tradition. Während im BB das Altargesetz
in Ex. xx 24–6 keine das folgende Korpus der Rechtssätze struktu-
rierende Funktion hat, sind in xii–xxvi* die Rechtssätze auf das Gebot
der Kultzentralisation in xii 13–28* bezogen.

Keinen Anhalt am Bundesbuch oder am Mittelassyrischen Kodex
hat schließlich das Hauptgesetz der Kultreinheit in xiii 2–18*. Die
drei Rechtssätze sind unter intensiver Nutzung von Motiven der neuassyrischen adê-Vereidigungen und -Verträge formuliert worden (cf.
o. I). In Anknüpfung an Ex. xxii 19a (cf. o. Anm. 88) wurde das
Hauptgesetz der Kultreinheit als Entfaltung des Alleinverehrungsanspruches JHWHs[108] in Analogie zum neuassyrischen Loyalitätseid
gegenüber dem Großkönig gestaltet. Die Ausgestaltung des Haupt-
gesetzes der Kultreinheit in xiii 2–18* unter neuassyrischem Einfluß
hat in der dtn-vordtr Redaktion ein Widerlager in dem ebenfalls unter
Einfluß der neuassyrischen adê-Vereidigungen dtn gestalteten Fluchtext in xxviii 23–42*.[109] Das Hauptgesetz xiii 2–18* und der Fluchtext xxviii 23–42* entsprechen den Gattungselementen von Vertrags-
oder Eidesbestimmungen und Flüchen, die die Gattung des neuassyrischen Loyalitätseides und -vertrages konstituieren. Der dtn Redaktor
interpretiert das Reformwerk der Auslegung des BB in xii–xxvi* als
Loyalitätseid gegenüber JHWH. Israelitisches Proprium der Exegese
des BB unter den Aspekten der Hauptgebote von Kulteinheit und
Kultreinheit des göttlichen Alleinverehrungsanspruches, gelehrte Redaktionsverfahren, die auch der in neuassyrischem Kontext gefundene
Mittelassyrische Kodex kennt, und die neuassyrischen Motive der adê-
Vereidigungen und -Verträge greifen in der dtn Redaktion von xii–
xxvi* ineinander[110] und begründen so das deuteronomische Reformwerk theologisch als Loyalitätsverpflichtung vor dem Gott Israels.[111]

---

[108] Die Forderung der Kultreinheit in xiii 2–18* hat ihre Voraussetzung in JHWHs
Alleinverehrungsanspruch.

[109] Zur dtr Überarbeitung cf. Preuß (Anm. 18), S. 156–7. Eine pauschale dtr
Ableitung der Flüche ist angesichts der neuassyrischen und aramäischen Parallelen
unzulässig; cf. Braulik (Anm. 15), S. 206.

[110] Damit löst sich die von N. Lohfink ("'d[w]t im Deuteronomium und in den
Königsbüchern", *BZ* NF 35 [1991] S. [86–93] 91–3) im Anschluß an den Gebrauch
von 'edô(ô) t im Dtn erörterte Alternative, das vordtr Dtn als privilegrechtlichen Text
in Analogie zum keilschriftlichen Loyalitätseid oder als eine gelehrte Schreiberarbeit
im Anschluß an B. Couroyer ("'édût: Stipulation de traité ou enseignement?", *RB*
[1988], S. 312–31) zu verstehen.

[111] Cf. E. Otto, "Aspects of Legal Reforms and Reformulations in Ancient
Cuneiform and Israelite Law", in B.M. Levinsin (Hg.), *Theory and Method in Biblical
and Cuneiform Law* (Sheffield, 1984), S. 158–94.

LE PENTATEUQUE, LE DEUTÉRONOMISTE ET SPINOZA[1]

par

PAOLO SACCHI
Torino

Je crois qu'il est évident pour tout le monde que la recherche sur le Pentateuque procède aujourd'hui en tâtonnant. Le professeur de Pury a introduit son beau livre *Le Pentateuque en question*, en citant une phrase de Otto Eckart: "Nous trouvons-nous aujourd'hui devant un bouleversement dans les recherches sur le Pentateuque?" La réponse était affirmative (p. 9). Je voudrais aujourd'hui proposer un diagnostic de la situation semblable à celui fait par de Pury, mais avec quelques différences. Dans le terme "bouleversement" il y a bien le sens d'une révolution; mais on y perçoit aussi l'espoir que cette révolution puisse donner de bons fruits. Moi, je ne suis pas aussi optimiste que de Pury: c'est la façon même de se poser devant le texte, qui, à mon avis, est aujourd'hui fautive. C'est ce qui a produit dans le domaine de la recherche sur le Pentateuque un éventail d'opinions beaucoup plus large que dans d'autres domaines de la recherche.

Les difficultés d'aujourd'hui plongent, comme il est naturel, leurs racines dans le passé. C'est pourquoi je voudrais attirer l'attention sur quelques problèmes du passé, qui ont conditionné et conditionnent encore notre façon de nous poser devant le texte du Pentateuque.

En principe, je crois que l'on peut retenir la validité de l'affirmation suivante: pour pouvoir appliquer la méthode philologico-critique de la tradition et exégèse d'un texte, il faut, en premier lieu, avoir devant nous un texte. Mais pour avoir la possibilité de définir "texte" un ensemble de mots, il n'est pas suffisant que nous lisions des mots l'un après l'autre. Il faut bien aussi qu'ils soient disposés d'une telle façon qu'ils forment une œuvre, c'est à dire un écrit qui fut composé ayant un commencement, un développement et une conclusion du récit. C'est ce que nous appelons la structure de l'œuvre. Or, tous ces éléments peuvent se disposer dans une structure seulement

---

[1] Les références abrégées dans les notes renvoient aux ouvrages cités dans la bibliographie, pp. 287–8.

s'il y a une intelligence qui organise tout l'ensemble. Cette intelligence qui se reflète et se révèle dans l'œuvre est ce que nous appelons "auteur". Ce terme est approprié aussi bien si l'auteur a écrit son ouvrage en tirant le sujet seulement de son monde imaginaire, que s'il a employé des sources, comme il arrive toujours pour les historiens. Nos ancêtres, les philologues du XVIᵉ siècle et du XVIIᵉ siècle ont appliqué ce principe d'instinct, sans le formaliser. Mais il est évident qu'entre le commencement de l'ère moderne et notre situation contemporaine doit bien s'être produit un phénomène qui a provoqué un changement profond et radical dans la perspective de la recherche.

Si nous laissons de côté la philologie des biblistes et si nous prenons en considération une science moderne telle que la sémiologie, en tant que science qui peut être appliquée à un texte littéraire, on trouve la formulation suivante du problème de l'"auteur en relation avec le texte": "l'auteur est un élément nécessaire de la communication littéraire."[2] J'ai tiré ces mots d'un livre de C. Segre, un sémiologue qui s'occupe de l'interprétation des textes littéraires. Devons-nous penser que la Bible, en tant que texte sacré, n'est pas un texte littéraire? Dans ce cas il faudrait abandonner notre métier. De Pury n'a pas de doute sur ce point: le Pentateuque est défini explicitement "ouvrage littéraire" (p. 17).

Or, nous voyons que la philologie biblique, surtout celle du Pentateuque, ignore presque totalement le terme d'auteur. On parle toujours de rédacteur. Et pour cause, si l'on accepte la perspective, avec laquelle la plupart des chercheurs vise le texte: le rédacteur est une figure plus nuancée que celle de l'Auteur. Elle correspond à une image du texte ayant des contours imprécis, selon laquelle on peut regarder les éléments fondamentaux de l'œuvre d'une façon très souple; on peut même les ignorer. Il n'est plus nécessaire que l'œuvre ait

---

[2] Cf. C. Segre, *Avviamento*, p. 8: "L'autore è elemento imprescindibile della comunicazione letteraria, in quanto mittente del messaggio." Ces mêmes principes sont présentés par de Pury, p. 53.

En ce qui concerne le rapport entre le texte et son auteur et surtout sur la manière dont nous pouvons nous représenter l'auteur, cf. encore Segre, p. 13, qui se réfère à beaucoup d'autres études et en particulier à W.C. Booth, *The Rhetoric of Fiction* (Chicago–London, 1961). On ne peut pas atteindre la figure historique de l'auteur, mais on doit se contenter "dell'autore quale si rivela nell'opera; un autore depurato dei suoi tratti reali, e caratterizzato da quelli che l'opera postula ... Viene chiamato autore implicito".

son commencement, son développement, sa conclusion, sa perspective de quelque façon unitaire.

Le rédacteur, si on veut le définir selon la formulation la plus radicale, est une figure d'écrivain qui se borne à recueillir des ouvrages, ou plus souvent des passages appartenant à des ouvrages qui avaient été déjà écrits auparavant. Sa fonction est seulement de faire des sélections; en outre, cette opération de sélection est très souvent considérée comme la dernière d'une série d'opérations semblables, qui avaient été déjà faites dans le passé. Or, il va de soi que, si les choses se passèrent réellement de cette façon, l'ouvrage final ne pouvait avoir qu'une structure très faible, même variable d'une de ses parties à l'autre. Celui qui avait écrit une œuvre ainsi conçue par les savants ne pouvait plus être appelé auteur, mais il fallait lui donner un nom ayant une signification plus nuancée. Si nous tenons comme valable cette image de la formation du texte, il s'ensuit que l'interprétation générale de l'ouvrage devient très incertaine comme aussi bien celle de chaque partie, car nous la lisons en la pensant située hors de son contexte d'origine.

Or, le problème est de savoir si cette façon de se poser devant le texte du Pentateuque vient des choses elles-mêmes, ou bien si elle s'est produite à cause de quelques phénomènes étrangers à la philologie, ayant pénétré dans la recherche de l'extérieur. Si c'est ce deuxième cas qui s'est avéré, il faudra prendre en considération la nécessité de considérer tout le problème du Pentateuque dans une lumière nouvelle.

Au commencement de l'ère moderne les philologues qui s'occupaient du Pentateuque lisaient un ouvrage aux contours bien précis, ayant son texte et son auteur, le texte allant du premier verset de la Genèse jusqu'à la fin du Deutéronome. L'auteur était Moïse, un homme qui vécut dans un temps déterminé. En d'autres termes, le Pentateuque avait alors des coordonnées historiques et littéraires qui en permettaient l'exégèse d'une façon correcte au point de vue scientifique. La compréhension du Pentateuque commença à faire problème à partir du moment où l'on trouva des difficultés pour le lier à celui que la tradition considérait comme son auteur depuis plus de quinze siècles. Moïse décrivant sa mort faisait problème, mais c'était une difficulté qui naissait justement du fait que l'on considérait le Pentateuque comme l'œuvre de Moïse.

Le problème devenait plus difficile si l'on prenait en considération des propos tels que "alors les Cananéens étaient dans le pays." On aurait pu recourir à la conception d'interpolation, mais on préféra une solution plus simple, qui s'imposa: on admit l'existence d'un auteur beaucoup plus tardif que Moïse. On proposa le nom d'Esdras.[3]

Toutefois, même si l'on déplace le Pentateuque de plus de mille ans, on peut encore employer correctement la méthode philologique, car c'est bien encore un texte avec son auteur que nous avons devant nous. Il est évident que le cadre historique, dans lequel l'ouvrage avait été composé, avait changé: Moïse, n'étant plus l'auteur de l'ouvrage, mais tout simplement son personnage principal, devait être récupéré à travers le monde imaginaire du nouvel auteur. Il y avait aussi le problème du rapport entre cet Auteur et ses sources. Tout cela créa, et c'est bien naturel, des problèmes aux théologiens et aux hommes de foi en général. Mais on ne peut pas résoudre un problème théologique ou de foi, entremêlant philologie, histoire et théologie.

Au cours du XVIIe siècle naquit un nouveau problème concernant le Pentateuque. Moïse, donc, n'était plus l'Auteur du Pentateuque: or, une fois perdu le rapport entre l'ouvrage et son auteur, c'était l'ouvrage lui-même qui était discuté, car la seule raison qui permettait de considérer le Pentateuque comme une unité, était l'unité de l'Auteur. C'est Spinoza qui le premier vit et comprit la portée de la nouvelle perspective et qui l'exploita avec cohérence. C'est Spinoza qui comprit parfaitement que, si le Pentateuque avait perdu son auteur, il avait aussi perdu, en même temps, son texte.[4]

Dans des pages peu nombreuses, mais d'une clarté exemplaire, il affirma que le Pentateuque ne pouvait pas être considéré comme un ouvrage, car il fallait tenir compte des liens bien clairs existant entre le Pentateuque et les livres qui le suivaient. Ces liens imposaient la nécessité de chercher non plus l'auteur du Pentateuque, mais celui de l'ouvrage qui, ayant commencé son récit avec la création du monde, le terminait en l'an 561 av. J.-C., date du dernier événement connu—connu par l'ouvrage, connu par l'auteur. Il fallait donc situer l'auteur de l'ouvrage "Pentateuque-Livres des Rois" au temps de la fin de l'exil. Le nom proposé avec quelque doute fut encore une fois celui d'Esdras, mais ce n'était plus l'auteur du Pentateuque, dont il était question.[5] C'était un aperçu qui aurait pu conduire la recherche biblique sur une ligne entièrement différente de celle qui a été suivie.

---

[3] Cf. de Pury, p. 13. et H.J. Kraus, *L'Antico Testamento nella ricerca storico-critica dalla riforma ad oggi* (Bologna, 1975) (deuxième édition allemande du 1969), p. 65, qui renvoient à Masius; mais le nom d'Esdras devait déjà circuler depuis longtemps si Carlestade (mort en 1541) avait déjà repoussé cette hypothèse.

[4] Cf. surtout le ch. VII du *Tractatus*.

[5] Dans le ch. VIII du *Tractatus* Spinoza aborde beaucoup de problèmes concer-

Spinoza eut un autre mérite aussi. Il comprit parfaitement que la difficulté la plus grave concernant sa thèse était constituée par le Deutéronome. Il résolut le problème, en admettant que le Deutéronome avait été écrit indépendamment du reste du Pentateuque et qu'il fut inséré à la place où nous le trouvons actuellement, en un deuxième temps. Certes, sa solution n'est pas valable, si on la considère dans ses détails, car elle est centrée entièrement sur la figure d'Esdras, bien qu'il s'agisse d'un Esdras beaucoup plus ancien que ce que nous pensons aujourd'hui. En outre, il eut le mérite de comprendre que certains décalages existant entre différentes parties du texte devaient dériver de la juxtaposition de sources différentes. Mais il ne songea pas du tout à identifier et à classer ces sources, si elles n'étaient indiquées dans les livres bibliques eux-mêmes. Rendtorff a parfaitement raison, en affirmant qu'il ne croit pas à l'existence de ces sources clairement établies, car la recherche n'a jamais été capable d'en identifier ne serait-ce qu'une seule.[6]

De Pury synthétise ainsi la manière avec laquelle on posa le problème du Pentateuque dans la deuxième moitié du XVIIe siècle: "dès le moment où l'on plaçait avec Spinoza et Richard Simon, l'édition ou la rédaction du Pentateuque à l'époque d'Esdras, il devenait indispensable d'expliquer la 'préhistoire' de cet ouvrage littéraire, c'està-dire de trouver un 'pont' entre le *terminus a quo*, que représentait la période des événements fondateurs et le *terminus ad quem* constitué par la rédaction finale à l'époque d'Esdras. La question des sources devenait ainsi la question du devenir du Pentateuque. Simon postula une chaîne de tradition allant de Moïse à Esdras" (p. 17). Je relève le mot "postuler" employé par de Pury: il s'agit bien d'un postulat,

---

nant le Pentateuque et les livres historiques, en distinguant avec clarté les questions historico-philologiques de celles théologiques.

[6] Rendtorff (dans de Pury, p. 84) écrit: "Mais je conteste qu'il soit plausible d'admettre l'existence des 'sources' indépendantes *écrites*, qui auraient d'abord existé chacune pour elle-même et qui n'auraient été agencées ensemble qu'au cours d'un stade rédactionnel secondaire. La principale raison de mon doute tient au fait qu'il n'est pas possible—et qu'il n'a jamais été possible au cours de l'histoire de la recherche—de reconstruire à peu près complètement ne serait-ce que l'une de ces supposées 'sources'." Je suis d'accord qu'il n'est pas possible de reconstruire de sources antérieures, mais cela ne peut signifier que nous ne sommes pas à même d'identifier, ne serait-ce que quelques fois, l'existence de sources dans le texte constitué que nous possédons. Je pense qu'il faut savoir se contenter de ce qui est possible. Les deux récits de la Genèse, qui racontent les aventures d'Abraham et de Sarah auprès du pharaon ou du roi de Gérar, dérivent sans aucun doute de deux milieux différents, bien qu'il ne soit possible d'établir ni à quels ouvrages pouvait appartenir chaque récit, ni de quel milieu il provenait. La tradition orale est un escamotage pour nuancer les termes du problème et ainsi l'éviter.

car il est tout à fait impossible d'écrire l'histoire de la préhistoire.

Dans les propos du prof. de Pury on perçoit parfaitement les exigences de la recherche moderne et je pense aussi qu'il a bien compris la pensée de Simon; mais celle de Spinoza était différente. On ne peut pas placer les deux savants, bien que contemporains, sur le même niveau. Richard Simon critiqua fortement Spinoza, mais son point de vue était surtout théologique; il lui reprocha "toutes les conséquences fausses et pernicieuses (naturellement pour la religion), que Spinoza a prétendu tirer de ces changements ou additions",[7] que la critique était en train de découvrir dans le texte du Pentateuque. Mais le problème véritable n'était pas là: c'est que Spinoza, en suivant peut-être Masius et d'autres encore, regardait le texte du point de vue de l'Auteur. Il avait déjà formulé son principe général pour l'interprétation d'un texte quelconque: il faut chercher en premier lieu son Auteur "qui il était, en quelle occasion, en quel temps, pour qui et enfin en quelle langue il écrivit."[8] Ce principe est d'une modernité frappante.

En rapportant ce principe philologique au Pentateuque, Spinoza put affirmer: "Ayant pris en considération les trois éléments suivants, c'est-à-dire l'unité du sujet de tous ces livres, leur enchaînement et le fait qu'ils sont *apographa* écrits beaucoup de siècles après les événements racontés, nous concluons ... que tous ces livres furent écrits par un seul historien."[9] Il fallait donc faire partir toute recherche de l'Auteur; le problème des sources prenait un sens seulement à la lumière de celui qui les employa, c'est-à-dire l'Auteur.

Or, le problème des sources, que la philologie est bien à même d'aborder, bien que dans les limites que nous avons mentionnées ci-

---

[7] Les mots cités sont tirés de la préface de l'*Histoire Critique*, dont les pages ne sont pas numérotées.

[8] Spinoza, *Tractatus*, § 3: "Quisnam fuerit, qua occasione, quo tempore, cui et denique qua lingua scripserit." Comme on le voit bien, Spinoza avait une conception de l'auteur purement historique. A cet égard la science a fait un grand progrès, en reconnaissant la différence entre l'auteur historique et l'auteur implicite. Voir n. 2. La conception rigide de l'auteur, qu'avait Spinoza, fut sans aucun doute la cause qui favorisa les idées de Simon, qui se sont imposées.

[9] Cf. le ch. VIII du *Tractatus*: "Ex his igitur tribus consideratis—nempe simplicitate argumenti horum omnium librorum, connexione, et quod sint apographa multis post saeculis a rebus gestis scripta, concludimus ... eos omnes *ab uno solo historico* scriptos fuisse." Cet auteur doit avoir vécu après le dernier événement qu'il a raconté. Spinoza avança le nom d'Esdras avec quelque doute, mais tout en ayant conscience qu'il ne s'agit que d'une hypothèse, cependant il la considéra presque sûre. Il va de soi que Spinoza envisageait Esdras plus ancien que nous ne le pensons. En ce qui concerne la signification du mot "apographa" chez Spinoza, cf. le

dessus, devint pour Simon[10] surtout le problème de la *tradition* qui aurait transmis le texte à partir de Moïse jusqu'à la rédaction finale. Cette façon de poser le problème a inauguré la critique moderne, en l'introduisant dans une voie sans issue, car il s'agit d'un problème, qui, tout en étant très important, ne peut pas être posé. Pour le dire avec les paroles de Momigliano, il n'est pas suffisant que les questions que l'on pose à un texte soient intelligentes, il faut aussi qu'il soit à même de répondre.

Si, après avoir affirmé que Moïse ne pouvait pas être l'auteur du Pentateuque, on cherche à sauver son rapport avec le texte par la formule que Moïse était celui qui avait donné naissance à la chaîne d'une tradition se continuant jusqu'à la constitution du texte, cela n'est plus un sujet que la philologie peut aborder. Il s'agit d'hypothèses destinées à rester telles. C'est le cas des scribes-prophètes qui, selon Simon, auraient transmis les mémoires de la civilisation et de la religion hébraïques de son fondateur, Moïse, à Esdras. On peut supposer qu'auprès du palais et auprès du temple de Jérusalem il y avait des scribes qui devaient bien écrire quelque chose, mais je ne sais ni auprès combien d'autres temples on avait l'habitude de recueillir les mémoires du passé, ni comment on groupait les matériaux. Nous pouvons considérer comme certain, au niveau historique, que Moïse fut le premier législateur juif, mais nous ne pouvons pas reconstruire les maillons, les démarches de la tradition antérieure aux textes écrits.

La philologie peut indiquer qu'un auteur a employé une source, mais elle n'est à même d'indiquer aucune des infinies possibilités de combinaisons des sources avant la constitution du texte. En d'autres termes, on ne peut pas faire l'histoire de la préhistoire, car l'histoire se fait seulement par les documents: ce sont les termes eux-mêmes du problème qui sont en contradiction entre eux. L'existence de cette chaîne de la tradition ne pourra jamais être démontrée.

Il est clair que le problème de la tradition antérieure à l'écriture ne provient ni de la philologie, ni de l'historiographie. C'est un problème de foi, ou mieux, c'est un problème qui découle du désir de ne pas perdre entièrement le lien entre l'Auteur-Moïse et le Pentateuque, car sa valeur religieuse paraissait être liée à sa personne.

---

commentaire du *Tractatus* de A. Droetto et E. Giancotti Boscherini (Torino, 1972), p. 254: "'Apographi' vuol dire per Spinoza che i libri esaminati non appartengono né agli autori, né all'epoca a cui sono attribuiti."

[10] Cf. pp. 3–4, mais c'est un *leitmotiv* de l'ouvrage entier.

Aujourd'hui la philologie concentre de nouveau son attention sur le texte que nous possédons, car on commence à prendre conscience que l'effort de connaître ce qui n'est pas connaissable est vain et inutile. Mais on a encore de la peine à accomplir la démarche définitive, c'est-à-dire à se poser le problème de l'Auteur, ce même problème à partir duquel la recherche moderne a pris naissance. Je tire encore quelques propos de la belle œuvre de de Pury: "L'intérêt des chercheurs... se porte actuellement sur la 'forme finale' ('Endgestalt') ou la forme 'canonique' du Pentateuque. Mais les questions à ce propos sont nombreuses; comment reconnaître la rédaction finale? Et, surtout, comment faut-il se représenter cette rédaction finale? S'agit-il d'un acte de compilation... Ou la rédaction finale est-elle simplement une ultime couche de rédaction venue réinterpréter ou réadapter un Pentateuque déjà constitué...?" (pp. 69–70). Comme on le voit bien, il s'agit toujours d'identifier une rédaction; le problème de l'Auteur a bien disparu de la recherche d'aujourd'hui.

A mon avis, de Pury a parfaitement cerné le problème de la recherche actuelle, mais il a encore formulé les questions à l'aide de l'ancienne terminologie. La question fondamentale est la première posée par de Pury: "Comment reconnaître la rédaction finale?" Il va de soi que de Pury, en parlant de la rédaction finale, ne veut pas indiquer le texte que nous possédons. Dans ce cas il n'y aurait pas de problèmes. Par "rédaction finale" il doit bien entendre quelque chose de différent. Je crois qu'il envisage l'état du texte, une fois que l'on a identifié toutes les interpolations et adjonctions successives. Mais successives à quoi? Evidemment à ce qu'il appelle la rédaction finale, qui ne coïncide pas avec l'état final du texte.

Cette rédaction ou compilation finale, qui ne coïncide pas avec le texte tel que nous le lisons, ne peut être interprétée comme une couche quelconque, qui se caractérise seulement par le fait qu'elle est la dernière, car c'est à cette couche qu'il faut attribuer la structure générale de l'œuvre. Or, si nous ne sommes pas disposés à admettre qu'il y avait une intelligence de cette sorte aux abords de l'histoire, capable d'envisager et de créer la structure future, il faut bien reconnaître que l'ouvrage que nous possédons est le résultat du travail d'un Auteur, qui employait les matériaux dont il disposait selon son idéologie et selon les conditionnements historiques que lui imposait la situation où il vivait. C'était vraisemblablement l'époque des accords et des compromis entre la maison royale (Zerubbabel) et le sacerdoce en exil.

C'est seulement si l'on accepte cette façon de se poser devant le texte, qu'on pourra aller de l'avant. Seulement alors on pourra parler clairement d'interpolations et de sources. Si l'on continue de considérer la formation du texte comme un processus presque naturel de tradition, les mots "source" et "interpolation" n'ont pas de sens, car les sources et les interpolations deviennent, elles aussi, des couches de la tradition.

Or, je suis sûr que dans l'ensemble "Genèse-Rois" il y a une structure générale, que nous pouvons percevoir, comme l'avait bien vu Spinoza, dans la continuité du récit. Une étude récente telle que celle de Hughes a montré que le récit se développe soutenu par une chronologie artificielle, au moins avant l'époque des royaumes divisés. Si la chronologie historique, qui arrive à peu près à la fin du Xe siècle av. J.-C., est la preuve du sérieux avec lequel notre Auteur travailla, malgré quelques fautes évidentes et des conjectures discutables,[11] la chronologie artificielle, concernant les époques antérieures, est la preuve la meilleure de l'existence d'une idéologie organisant l'ensemble. Cela reste valable, même si l'on considère les variantes de la Septante concernant la chronologie antérieure à la monarchie. Les variantes concernent toujours les centaines, non pas les dizaines, ni les unités. Il s'agit donc d'une nouvelle interprétation globale et idéologique des grandes périodes de l'histoire d'Israël, ne touchant pas à l'unité de la conception originaire de l'œuvre.

Une réflexion toute particulière est due à l'œuvre de Wellhausen. J'ai cité son œuvre, tout en sachant que beaucoup de choses qu'il a dites avaient été déjà proposées, mais il faut bien avoir un point de repère précis pour conduire un raisonnement, et, en tout cas, le point de repère de Wellhausen est très intelligent. Pour lui, il était clair que le Pentateuque ne pouvait pas être cerné, du point de vue philologique, comme un ouvrage, car le récit comprenait au moins un livre en plus, celui de Josué. C'était l'Hexateuque. Il comprit encore que le problème philologique concernait les sources, conçues par lui comme textes écrits en nombre limité et bien discernables. En envisageant ainsi la composition de l'ouvrage, il cherchait à répondre aussi bien à la question des sources qu'à celle de la chaîne de la

---

[11] Je pense, par exemple, à l'arrangement des événements et de la succession des rois des dernières années du royaume d'Israël. Dans la documentation, que l'Auteur avait à sa disposition, il devait bien y avoir des trous, dont il se rendait compte et qu'il chercha à compléter à l'aide de véritables conjectures. Cf. G. Garbini, "I sigilli del regno d'Israele", *OrAnt* 21 (1982), pp. 163–76, p. 173.

tradition, car les sources ainsi identifiées, constituaient en même temps
les maillons de la tradition dont on était à la recherche et en prou-
vaient l'existence, même si leur datation était trop basse pour atteindre le temps de Moïse.

En suivant cette méthode, il arriva, en procédant à rebours dans
le temps, jusqu'à RJE, dans lequel les éléments J et E étaient encore
discernables avec une clarté suffisante, mais après il aborda le problème
impossible, c'est-à-dire identifier les couches de J et de E. Comme il
est bien connu, il en proposa trois pour chacune des deux sources,
tout en n'approfondissant pas la question.[12]

Ce furent ses successeurs qui concentrèrent leur attention sur cet
aspect du problème. A ce propos, le nom de Gunkel émerge. Les
sources de Wellhausen se sont changées de sources écrites en traditions orales. Il est clair que ces traditions sont conçues comme orales
dans le but de rendre le schéma de Wellhausen moins rigide. En
faisant ainsi, on a la possibilité de passer des récits les plus anciens
au texte écrit, que nous possédons, d'une façon progressive et gra-
duelle, qui s'adapte bien à l'hypothèse. Cette conception de la formation du texte est l'image visible, projetée dans l'histoire, de l'hypothèse elle-même; ce n'en est pas la preuve.

Comme il est bien connu, Noth a donné naissance à la théorie du
Tétrateuque. Une fois encore la coupure que la philologie moderne
cherche entre le Pentateuque et les livres qui suivent, ne coïncide
pas avec la fin du Pentateuque. C'est qu'il n'est pas possible de la
poser là.

Nous ne pouvons que nous fonder sur le texte que nous avons et
qui montre, dans les grandes lignes, une unité qui va du premier
chapitre de la Genèse à la fin des livres des Rois, à l'exception du
Deutéronome, qui apparaît comme une grande interpolation au sein
de l'œuvre originaire. Pour reconstruire cette œuvre, il faut partir de
l'ensemble entier de la tradition écrite pour éliminer toutes les adjonctions successives à l'œuvre originaire, c'est-à-dire à l'œuvre de
l'Auteur. Seulement à ce moment je pourrai poser à l'ensemble
ouvrage-Auteur les grandes questions de la philologie: quels étaient
ses buts, quelles sources il employa, même s'il n'est pas possible d'établir si elles étaient seulement écrites ou bien aussi orales.

---

[12] Cf. Wellhausen, pp. 207–8. En ce qui concerne l'incertitude des relation entre
J et E il écrit: "Freilich ist es mir nicht gelungen, den Faden von J und E durch das
Ganze zu verfolgen." La distinction des couches à l'intérieur de J et E est encore
moins plausible.

Quelqu'un a pensé que les récits du Jahviste avaient été ajoutés à l'œuvre du Deutéronomiste en un deuxième temps.[13] Mais à ce propos, une observation s'impose: la grille chronologique, dans laquelle les événements antérieurs à la monarchie divisée sont insérés, est totalement dérivée d'une conception globale de l'histoire, qui n'a rien à faire avec les documents historiques. Or, puisque le livre des Juges est déjà bien inséré dans cette grille et que son Auteur/Rédacteur est reconnu être le même que celui des livres historiques, il s'ensuit que la chronologie que j'ai appelée artificielle, n'est pas caractéristique du seul Pentateuque. Nous avons, donc, une preuve ultérieure de l'unité de méthode liant le Pentateuque (ou mieux, le Tétrateuque) aux livres successifs. Il est vrai que des études récentes ont démontré que des fragments d'une chronologie quelque peu différente sont restés dans le texte que nous avons:[14] il s'agit vraisemblablement de restes appartenant à des sources, qui ont été mal assemblées par l'Auteur. Ces sources sont bien discernables à la lumière de ce décalage.

En ce qui concerne la thèse contemporaine des "Grandes Unités", il me semble qu'il s'agit d'une façon plus rationnelle, au sens de plus simple, de toucher à une tradition antérieure au texte. Toutefois il est suffisant d'observer qu'une "Grande Unité" n'est qu'une subdivision du texte que nous avons, une sorte de division en chapitres, pour comprendre que ces unités n'existèrent pas du tout avant le texte que nous avons. La "Grande Unité" constituée par des ouvrages ayant déjà quelque structure littéraire, et dont l'existence était plus probable en soi-même, se substitue à l'unité de la *Formgeschichte* classique, qui s'appuyait surtout sur le sujet de chaque passage. Je voudrais citer ici la belle étude de Ha, portant sur le chapitre xv de la Genèse. Ha a bien démontré que la multiplicité des thèmes ne s'oppose point à l'unité de l'Auteur. Je souligne que l'unité d'Auteur est autre chose que la rédaction finale.

Je répète: je n'exclus pas que l'Auteur de l'ensemble "Genèse-Rois" ait employé des sources, même beaucoup de sources. C'est leurs contours seulement que nous pouvons entrevoir quand leur idéologie s'oppose, çà et là, à celle de l'Auteur, qui semble avoir écrit son œuvre en s'intéressant plus à la continuité chronologique du récit qu'à l'idéologie de ses sources. On peut citer, par exemple, les textes

---

[13] Cf. Van Seters *Der Jahwist*; voir aussi Schmid.
[14] Cf. Hughes, *Secrets of the Times*.

concernant la monarchie unifiée et leur attitude quelques fois favorable et d'autres fois contraire à la monarchie. Ce phénomène est
évident surtout à propos du règne de Saül, dont le récit même des
événement nous fait problème. Puisque, selon notre Auteur, il fut élu
roi trois fois, il est naturel de songer à des sources différentes. Toutefois le récit paraît bien structuré au moins d'un point de vue formel. L'Auteur avait bien à sa disposition plusieurs textes, mais je ne
crois pas que l'on puisse en établir le nombre et surtout que l'on
puisse attribuer chaque verset à l'une ou à l'autre source.

Conclusions

(1) Il me semble que la question du Pentateuque est dépassée. Il est
    simplement la première partie de l'ouvrage "Genèse-Rois".
(2) On devrait abandonner le terme de Rédacteur et adopter celui
    d'Auteur.[15]
(3) La théorie classique des quatre sources du Pentateuque doit être
    abandonnée, même si l'on doit continuer à mettre à profit tant
    de notions particulières que la recherche moderne a établies.
(4) Le Deutéronome doit être considéré comme un ouvrage à part,
    qui n'a rien à faire avec l'Auteur de l'ensemble "Genèse-Rois".[16]
(5) Un problème particulier est soulevé par les textes "sacerdotaux"
    (P), car ils représentent une source aux contours suffisamment
    précis. Comme l'Auteur de l'ensemble "Genèse-Rois" montre par
    son idéologie qu'il appartient au milieu du palais (même du pa-
    lais en exil), les textes de la source P montrent, toujours, par leur
    idéologie, qu'ils dérivent du milieu du temple, qui était en exil
    lui-aussi. Le problème est de savoir combien d'entre eux ont été
    insérés dans l'ouvrage général par notre Auteur et combien ont
    été insérés après. Si nous datons l'œuvre de notre Auteur de la
    deuxième moitié du VIe siècle av. J.C., au temps des négociations

---

[15] Il est curieux de remarquer ce qu'on pourrait appeler la viscosité de la recherche: dans mon premier article sur l'Auteur j'ai proposé l'abbréviation R1!
[16] J'avais essayé d'abord d'insérer le Deutéronome aussi dans l'ouvrage de notre
Auteur, en considérant comme interpolations tous les passages, qui n'étaient pas
d'accord avec son idéologie (cf. Sacchi [1987], p. 76). Mais c'est une hypothèse plus
simple, et donc plus probable, que de considérer le Deutéronome comme ouvrage
autonome, qui fut inséré à la place où nous le trouvons dans un deuxième temps.
Cf. Sacchi, *Henoch* 10 (1988), p. 250, et "Giosuè", p. 348. Voir aussi Ha. Ha montre qu'il y a bien des différences entre l'idéologie du pacte en Gen. xv et dans le
Deutéronome.

entre la maison royale et le sacerdoce en exil, qui se conclurent avec l'accord entre Zorobabel et Josué, il est possible que l'insertion des textes dits sacerdotaux ait été faite par notre Auteur lui-même.

(6) Cependant, il est évident que des interpolations furent apportées au texte de l'Auteur dans les époques successives. Puisqu'il s'agit d'interpolations au véritable sens du mot, elles doivent être identifiées, en se fondant sur des principes stylistiques et formels, auxquels doit correspondre une idéologie caractéristique, différente de l'idéologie de l'Auteur. Les passages universalistes[17] et ceux nomistes[18] font bien partie de ces interpolations.

Petite bibliographie méthodologique

J.N. Aletti, "L'approccio narrativo applicato alla Bibbia: stato della questione e proposte", *RivBibl* 39 (1991), pp. 257–76.

D'A.S. Avalle, *Principi di critica testuale* (Padova, 1978²). Important surtout pour ce qui concerne la conception de l'originel.

E. Blum, *Die Komposition der Vätergeschichte* (Neukirchen-Vluyn, 1984).

P.G. Borbone, *Il libro del profeta Osea; edizione critica del testo ebraico* (Torino, 1990).

C.H.W. Brekelmans, "Eléments deutéronomiques dans le Pentateuque", *RechBibl* 8 (1966), pp. 77–91.

G. Contini, *Breviario d'ecdotica* (Milano-Napoli, 1986).

E. Cortese, "Gios., 21 e Giud 1 (TM o LXX?) e l'abbottonatura del 'Tetrateuco' con l'opera deuteronomistica", *RivBibl* 33 (1985), pp. 375–94.

E. Cortese, "Il Pentateuco oggi: la teoria documentaria in crisi?", *Scuola Catt* iii (1983), pp. 79–88.

A. de Pury (Editeur), *Le Pentateuque en question* (Genève, 1989).

J. Ha, *Genesis 15: A Theological Compendium of Pentateuchal History* (Berlin, 1989).

J. Hughes, *Secrets of the Times: Myth and History in Biblical Chronology* (Sheffield, 1990).

N. Marconi, "Contributi per una lettura unitaria di Gen 37" *RivBibl* 39 (1991), pp. 277–303.

A. Masius, *Josuae imperatoris historia illustrata atque explicata* (Anvers, 1574).

A.H.D. Mayes, *The Story of Israel between Settlement and Exile; A Redactional Study of the Deuteronomistic History* (London, 1983).

C. Milikowsky, "The Status Quaestionis of Research in Rabbinic Literature", *JJS* 39 (1988), pp. 201–11.

H. Mölle, *Genesis 15. Eine Erzählung von den Anfängen Israels* (Würzburg, 1988).

S Mowinckel, *Tetrateuch-Pentateuch-Hexateuch* (Berlin, 1964).

M. Nobile, "Un contributo alla lettura sincronica della redazione Genesi-2Re, sulla base del filo narrativo offerto da 2Re 25, 27–30", *Antonianum* 61 (1986), pp. 207–24.

M.A. O'Brien, *The Deuteronomistic History Hypothesis: A Reassessment* (Freiburg [(Schweiz)]-Göttingen, 1989).

---

[17] Cf. J. Hoftijzer, *Die Verheissungen an die drei Erzväter* (Leiden, 1956).

[18] Voir, par exemple, les mots *kl htwrh* en Jos. i 7, qui sont sans aucun doute une adjonction postérieure, ou bien le chapitre 24 de la Genèse. Cf. A. Rofé, "An Inquiry into the Betrothal of Rebekah", en *Festschrift Rendtorff* (Neukirchen, 1990), pp. 27–39.

R. Rendtorff, "Zur Komposition des Buches Jesaja", *VT* 34 (1984), pp. 295–320.

A. Rofé, *Storie di profeti* (Brescia, 1991).

M. Rose, *Deuteronomist und Jahwist. Untersuchungen zu den Berührungspunkten beider Literaturwerke* (Zürich, 1981).

P. Sacchi, "Il più antico storico di Israele: un'ipotesi di lavoro", Atti del Convegno *Le Origini d'Israele* (Roma, 1987), pp. 65–86.

P. Sacchi, Compte rendu de J. Van Seters, *Der Jahwist als Historiker*, *Henoch* 10 (1989), pp. 247–50.

P. Sacchi, Compte rendu de J. Hughes, *Secrets of the Times. Myth and History in Biblical Chronology*, *Henoch* 13 (1991), pp. 239–42.

P. Sacchi, Compte rendu de A. de Pury, *Le Pentateuque en question*, *Henoch* 13 (1991), pp. 101–8.

P. Sacchi, Compte rendu de H. Ha *Genesis 15*, *Henoch* 13 (1991), pp. 108–9.

P. Sacchi, "Giosuè 1, 1–9: dalla critica storica a quella letteraria", en *Storia e tradizioni di Israele; scritti in onore di J.A. Soggin* (Brescia, 1991), pp. 237–54.

P. Schäfer, "Research into Rabbinic Literature: An Attempt to define the Status Quaestionis", *JJS* 37 (1986), pp. 139–52.

P. Schäfer, "Once again the Status Quaestionis in Research in Rabbinic Literature; an Answer to Ch. Milikowsky", *JJS* 40 (1989), pp. 89–94.

H.H. Schmid, *Der sogenannte Jahwist* (Zürich, 1976).

C. Segre, *Semiotica filologica; Testo e modelli culturali* (Torino, 1979).

C. Segre, *Avviamento all'analisi del testo letterario* (Torino, 1985).

R. Simon, *Histoire critique du Vieux Testament* (Rotterdam, 1685²).

B. Spinoza, *Tractatus theologico-politicus*, en *Opera*, herausg. von C. Gebhardt (Heidelberg, 1924–5) III.

J. Van Seters, *In Search of History. Historiography in the Ancient World and the Origins of Biblical History* (New Haven, Connecticut, et London, 1983).

J. Van Seters, "The Primeval Histories of Greece and Israel Compared", *ZAW* 100 (1988), pp. 1–22.

J. Van Seters, *Der Jahwist als Historiker*, traduit de l'anglais (Zurich, 1987).

J. Van Seters, "Recent Studies on the Pentateuch. A Crisis in Method", *JAOS* 99 (1979), pp. 663–73.

P. Weimar, *Genesis 15. Ein redaktionskritischer Versuch*, en *Die Väter Israels*, en *Fests. J. Scharbert* (Stuttgart, 1989), pp. 361–411.

Helga Weippert, "Das deuteronomistische Geschichtswerk; sein Ziel und Ende in der neueren Forschung", *ThRund* NF 50 (1985), pp. 213–48.

J. Wellhausen, *Die Composition des Hexateuchs und der historischen Bücher des Alten Testaments* (Berlin, 1899³).

ERWÄGUNGEN ZUR GESCHICHTE DER AUSSCHLIESSLICHKEIT DES ALTTESTAMENTLICHEN GLAUBENS

von

WERNER H. SCHMIDT

Bonn

Theologie kann als eine auf Grund eines persönlichen "Standpunkts", einer vorausgesetzten Entscheidung entworfene, so auf zustimmender, innerer Anerkennung aufruhende Wissenschaft erscheinen; Religionswissenschaft gilt demgegenüber als von außen beobachtende, auf Wertungen verzichtende Wissenschaft. Sind die damit angedeuteten Gegenüberstellungen wie "von innen—von außen betrachtend", "persönlich beteiligt—neutral beschreibend" aber sachgemäß, dem theologischen wie religionswissenschaftlichen Versuch der Einfühlung und Auslegung angemessen? Von der Exegese her läßt sich ein Stück weit zwischen Theologie und Religionswissenschaft vermitteln; denn beiden kommt die Aufgabe der Interpretation zu.

Auch religionsgeschichtliche Fragestellung richtet sich auf die Eigenart eines Phänomens, hat zum einen in vielfältigen Einzelheiten Zusammenhänge aufzuspüren, zum andern im Rahmen des Vergleichbaren Gemeinsamkeiten und Unterschiede aufzudecken, um so zugleich das Typische wie das Individuelle, das Charakteristische oder gar Einmalige zu erkennen.[1]

I

Der Glaube richtet sich auf Unbedingtes, ist selbst aber bedingt, durch die Geschichte, namlich die vorgegebene Überlieferung wie die

---

[1] Diese Absicht verfolgte schon die sog. Religionsgeschichtliche Schule: Stellt man Israel "in die Entwicklungsgeschichte des Orients" und macht mit dem "Vergleichen" Ernst, so können "das AT und seine Religion dadurch nicht verlieren, sondern nur gewinnen". Es sind nicht nur "Verbindungsfäden" zur Umwelt zu ziehen. "Das letzte Ziel der Forschung" ist, "die Abweichungen, die andersartigen Färbungen, die Akzentverschiebungen festzustellen", "die Originalität Israels, seiner Literatur und seiner Religion" zu erfassen; das Besondere tritt "durch den Gegensatz nur um so schärfer heraus". So H. Greßmann, "Die Aufgaben der alttestamentlichen Forschung", *ZAW* 42 (1924), S. 1–33, bes. 10.

jeweilige Situation, geprägt. Er bekennt in der Anrede: "Du, Gott, von Ewigkeit zu Ewigkeit"[2] und kann um eine Zeit wissen, in der er noch nicht war: Die Väter "verehrten andere Götter" (Jos. xxiv 2).

So vermag der Glaube zwischen der von ihm formulierten Wahrheit und sich selbst zu unterscheiden; er weiß um eine Zeit, in der es ihn noch nicht gab. Damit legt die für neuzeitliches historisches Denken selbstverständliche und unabdingbare Betrachtung des Glaubens aus dem Blickwinkel der Geschichte an das Alte Testament[3] keinen seinem Selbstzeugnis widersprechenden, ihm völlig fremden und von außen aufgenötigten Maßstab an.

Das zeitlich und räumlich unendlich weit ausgreifende Bekenntnis "Im Anfang schuf Gott Himmel und Erde" (Gen. i 1), das die Ausschließlichkeit mit der Unterscheidung von Gott und Welt aussagt, mag aus einer bestimmten Situation mit den sich in ihr ergebenden Anforderungen erwachsen sein, bildet an seinem Ort aber zugleich das Tor, das der Leser oder Hörer durchschreiten muß, um in das Alte Testament hineinzukommen. Ursprünglich als Einleitung für die Priesterschrift um die Exilszeit verfaßt, stellt dieser Satz eine zusammenfassende, überschriftartige Themaangabe dar, welche die in Gen. i aufgenommenen Traditionen deutet und den folgenden Geschehensverlauf—untergründig prägend—begleitet.[4] Im gegebenen Kontext gilt jenes Bekenntnis darüber hinaus dem Pentateuch oder gar dem Alten Testament insgesamt. Der Satz umreißt den Horizont, vor dem die folgenden Texte einschließlich der in ihnen erhaltenen älteren Überlieferungen gelesen und verstanden werden sollen.

Religionsgeschichtliche Rückfrage, welche die Traditionen aus diesem gegebenen Kontext löst, liest sie in einer anderen Richtung, d.h. gegen die Intention des vorliegenden Zusammenhangs, der die in dem Bekenntnis von Gen. i 1 ausgesprochene Ausschließlichkeit voraussetzt.

---

[2] Ps. xc 2. "Sie vergehen—du aber bleibst" Ps. cii 27; vgl. xciii 2; Jes. xi 28, xliii 10; Hab. i 12; Gen.i 1.

[3] Israel weiß, daß es entstand, als andere Völker längst existierten (vgl. die Völkertafel Gen. x; auch Gen. v). Das Alte Testament bewahrt die Erinnerung daran, daß das Land nicht Israels Eigentum von uran war oder das Königtum in einem bestimmten Zeitpunkt der Geschichte aus Vorbildern der Umwelt entlehnt wurde. Auch kann das Alte Testament Epochen seines Gottesverständnisses unterscheiden—vor allem die Erzväterzeit vom Jahweglauben (Ex. vi 3 u.a.).

[4] Ist dieser "Anfang" (vgl. zuletzt E. Jenni, "Erwägungen zu Gen 1,1 'am Anfang'", *Zeitschrift für Althebraistik* 2 [1989], S. 121–7) nicht zugleich der Einsatz der—von der Priesterschrift dargestellten—Geschichte?

Eine entsprechende Spannung wird gelegentlich ausdrücklich.

So wird die Begegnung der "drei Männer" mit Abraham (Gen. xviii 2) vorweg gedeutet (xviii 1): "Jahwe erschien ihm."
In der Szene der Begegnung Abrahams mit Melchisedek wird "El Eljon", wohl Name eines oder des Stadtgottes von (Jeru-)Salem, ausdrücklich gedeutet als "Jahwe, der höchste Gott".[5]
Überhaupt konnte das Alte Testament die vielfältigen, zumal in der Genesis vorkommenden Gottesnamen wie "El Olam" bewahren, weil "El" nicht nur als Name eines bestimmten Gottes, sondern auch als Appellativ "Gott" deutbar ist. Im Nachhinein lassen sich die ehemaligen Eigennamen als Beinamen oder Attribute des einen Gottes verstehen: "Ewiger Gott" (Gen. xxi 33; vgl. xvi 13 u.a.).

Darum können dieselben Prädikationen höchst unterschiedlich—gleichsam religionsgeschichtlich und theologisch—akzentuiert werden. Religionsgeschichtliche Sichtweise, die dem Ablauf der Geschichte folgt und dabei fremde Einflüsse hervorhebt, und theologisches Verständnis, welches das Bekenntnis des Glaubens zur Identität des einen Gottes wahrt, stellen sich hier als zwei Aspekte einer "Sache" bzw. derselben Aussage heraus, die sich keineswegs gegenseitig ausschließen, sondern ineinander liegen oder gar sich wechselseitig aufeinander beziehen können.[6]
Der vorliegende alttestamentliche Text sagt die Ausschließlichkeit aus oder will sie aussagen; erheblich schwerer fällt es, ihre Bedeutung in der Geschichte bis zur Frühzeit zurückzuverfolgen.

II

Um die Zeit des babylonischen *Exils* (6.Jh.) finden sich in unterschiedlichen Literaturbereichen, so in der Priesterschrift, zumal bei dem Propheten Deuterojesaja und im deuteronomisch-deuteronomistischen Schrifttum monotheistische oder monotheistisch klingende Aussagen. Fragt man von diesen jüngeren Zeugnissen vorsichtig-tastend in die ältere Zeit zurück, gewinnt man zugleich einen Einblick in die überraschende *Vielfalt* der Ausdrucksmöglichkeiten für die Ausschließlichkeit des Glaubens.[7]

---

[5] Gen. xiv 18ff., bes. v 22; vgl. Ps. xlvii 3, u.a. Auch Dtn. xxxii 8-9 läßt sich nur isoliert vom Kontext polytheistisch deuten.
[6] In Fällen wie Gen. xiv 22 können sich religionswissenschaftliche und theologische Fragestellung treffen, weil der Religionswissenschaftler beobachten kann, wie das ursprünglich Fremde zum Ausdruck eigener Identität wird, was der Theologe als Bekenntnis versteht, nachsprechen und weitergeben kann.
[7] Der folgende kurze Abriß nimmt Formulierungen auf aus: "Die Frage nach der

Jener die *Priesterschrift* eröffnende Satz (Gen. i 1) klingt eindeutig monotheistisch; er ist nicht eigentlich ein Urteil, daß Gott, nur ein Gott, existiert, sondern ein Bekenntnis zum Wirken des Schöpfers und damit zum Dasein Gottes. Weder das Chaos noch die Gestirne bilden mythisch-persönliche, aus sich tätige Mächte, und der Erde wird durch Gottes Wort die Fähigkeit zur Fruchtbarkeit erst zugesprochen. Zwar fehlt eine Feststellung wie "außer ihm ist keiner", jedoch bleibt für andere göttliche Kräfte in der Schöpfungsgeschichte kein Betätigungsfeld.[8]

Innerhalb derselben Quellenschrift wird gegenüber Abraham und seinen Nachkommen die Forderung ausschließlichen, "untadelig-vollkommenen" Verhaltens (Gen. xvii 1) erhoben, die mit der sog. Selbstvorstellung "Ich bin . . ." an das erste Gebot erinnert:

"Ich bin El Schaddai. Wandle vor mir,
und sei vollkommen / ganz!"[9]

Der Zuwendung Gottes soll die ungeteilte Ganzheit der Zuwendung Abrahams zu Gott entsprechen. Darüber hinaus betont die Priesterschrift die Identität des einen Gottes im Wandel der Zeiten und Namen (Ex. vi 2–3). Im Fortgang dieser Erzählung kann Gott selbst ankündigen (Ex. xii 12): "An allen Göttern Ägyptens werde ich Strafgerichte vollstrecken."

Diese Zukunftsansage bezeugt zwar die Überlegenheit des einen Gottes auch im Ausland, damit die Ohnmacht der anderen Götter. Wird aber deren Existenz bestritten?

Einheit des Alten Testaments—im Spannungsfeld von Religionsgeschichte und Theologie", *JBTh* 2 (Neukirchen-Vluyn, 1987), S. 33–57, bes. 42ff.; "'Jahwe und . . .' Anmerkungen zur sog. Monotheismus-Debatte", in *Die Hebräische Bibel und ihre zweifache Nachgeschichte*, FS R. Rendtorff (Neukirchen-Vluyn, 1990), S. 435–47; "Monotheismus", *TRE* 23 (1994), S. 237–48; vgl. zur näheren Begründung auch: *Alttestamentlicher Glaube in seiner Geschichte* (Neukirchen-Vluyn, [7]1990), bes. § 6b und § 11.

[8] Es treten nicht einmal (wie etwa Ps. ciii 20ff.) Schöpfungsmittler auf. Höchstens klingt in der Ankündigung "Wir wollen Menschen machen" (Gen. i 26) die Anrede an einen Kreis Gott zugehöriger, ihm untergeordneter Wesen, etwa himmlischer Heerscharen, nach (vgl. Gen. iii 22; xi 7J; Jes. vi 8, u.a.). Da die Priesterschrift diese Vorstellung sonst nicht bezeugt, liegt es näher, an einen sog. Plural deliberationis, genauer an ein Selbstgespräch zur Kundgabe des bevorstehenden Tuns, zu denken. Besteht, wenn die Existenz anderer Götter nicht—ausdrücklich—geleugnet wird, in Gen. i gleichsam ein "impliziter" Monotheismus?

[9] "Das Wort ist gewiß eine Vorwegnahme des Dekalogs" (K. Elliger, "Sinn und Ursprung der priesterlichen Geschichtserzählung", in *Kleine Schriften zum Alten Testament* [München, 1966], S. 144–98, bes. 197). Zu "untadelig, vollkommen" vgl. Gen. vi 9; Dtn. xviii 13; auch Jos. xxiv–14; 2 Sam. xxii 24; Ps. xv 2; sachlich 1 Kön. viii 61, ix 4, xi 4 u.a.

Der Prophet *Deuterojesaja* betont mit ungewöhnlich scharfen, kaum überbietbaren Worten, die Jahwe aus jeder möglichen Göttergenealogie ausnehmen und die Existenz anderer Götter ausschließen, im Rahmen seines tröstend-heilvollen Zuspruchs an die Exilierten:

> Vor mir wurde kein Gott gebildet,
> und nach mir wird keiner sein. (Jes. xliii 10)
>> Ich bin der Erste und ich der Letzte,
>> außer mir ist kein Gott.[10]

Falls solche monotheistisch klingenden Aussagen im strengen, eindeutigen Sinne monotheistisch gemeint sind: "außer mir ist kein", d.h.: "gibt es keinen Gott", dann hält der Exilsprophet diese (theoretische) Einsicht kaum durch; denn er setzt sich, sei es auch ironisch-spielerisch, mit den Völkern bzw. ihren Göttern auseinander:

> Tut kund, was hernach kommen wird,
> damit wir erkennen, daß ihr Götter seid![11]

Ausdrücklich zieht Deuterojesaja die Folgerung (xli 24, 29): "Euer Tun ist nichts", bestreitet also zumindest mit dem Sein, der Existenz, *zugleich* die *Wirksamkeit* und das Zukunftswissen der Götter. Sie "nützen nichts". Es ist möglich, sie zu "wählen", aber: "ein Greuel, wer euch erwählt".[12]

Wäre diese Argumentation nötig, wenn der Exilsprophet als selbstverständlich voraussetzt, daß Götter überhaupt nicht existieren? Gewiß

---

[10] Jes. xliv 6; vgl. xli 4, xlv 5–6, 18, xlvi 9 u.a. Beide Zitate entstammen der Redeform der Gerichtsreden, in denen sich der Exilsprophet im Namen Jahwes mit den Völkern bzw. deren Göttern auseinandersetzen muß. Im Anschluß an die Botschaft der vorexilischen Propheten, deren Unheilsankündigung sich durch den Verlauf der Geschichte bestätigt hatte, gilt die Zukunftsansage als Wahrheitsbeweis—gleichsam für die Gottheit Gottes.

[11] In der Gerichtsrede Jes. xli 22–3; vgl. xli 26, xliv 6–8. Anscheinend können die Götter der Völker selbst aufgerufen werden, obwohl sie dann nicht zu Wort kommen. In prophetischer Vorwegnahme der Zukunft sagt Jes. xlvi 1–2 den Sturz von Bel und Nebo an. Wird hier zwischen den Göttern bzw. ihren Namen und "ihren Bildern" unterschieden? Die Argumentation zielt wiederum auf die Kraftlosigkeit und den Niedergang der Götter. Sie werden "getragen" oder müssen getragen werden, Jahwe trägt selbst, gibt unermüdlich Kraft (xl 28–9). Wird mit der Anrede oder dem Namen der Götter nicht irgendein mögliches Sein vorausgesetzt? Gewiß tritt der Prophet in einem Lebensraum auf, in dem Götter vorgestellt werden und ihre Existenz als selbstverständlich hingenommen wird. Paßt er sich dieser Welt in seiner Redeweise an, formuliert und argumentiert in einem Übergangsfeld des Glaubens und Denkens mit einer seiner Absicht eigentlich unangemessenen, nur spielerisch gebrauchten Sprache? Wie wird diese Einschränkung aber am Text erkennbar? Oder denkt der Prophet einheitlich?

[12] Jes. vii 24; vgl. Jos. xxiv 15.

bedeuten sie nichts; "sind" sie auch nicht? Seine Verkündigung ent-
spricht—gleichsam spiegelbildlich—der Folgerung: "Außer mir ist kein
Helfer".[13] Demnach ist das eigentliche Ziel von Deuterojesajas Bot-
schaft und Argumentation zumindest nicht nur ein "theoretischer"
Monotheismus, vielmehr soteriologisch die Heilszusage: der eine, wahre
Gott ist "allein" Schöpfer (Jes. xliv 24) und Erlöser.[14]

Im *Deuteronomium* und deuteronomistischen Geschichtswerk steht der
Ausschließlichkeitsanspruch des Glaubens, mannigfach variiert und
nuanciert, im Mittelpunkt der Darstellung und wird zum Maßstab
der Geschichte.[15] Dabei findet sich im Deuteronomium neben der
vielfach erhobenen Warnung, "anderen Göttern" zu dienen,[16] das
monotheistisch klingende Bekenntnis, daß "Jahwe (allein) Gott ist im
Himmel oben wie auf der Erde unten und keiner sonst".[17] Beide
Äußerungen gehören vermutlich verschiedenen literarischen Schichten an. Jedoch stehen die den Polytheismus voraussetzende und die
(jüngere) monotheistisch wirkende Aussage in einem Buch vereint
nebeneinander. Demnach läßt sich seine Intention kaum mit dem
Begriff "Monotheismus", sondern eher mit dem Bekenntnis (Schᵉma)
wiedergeben, das die Existenz anderer Götter zumindest nicht
ausdrück-lich leugnet:

> "Höre, Israel, Jahwe, unser Gott,
> Jahwe ist *einer*."[18]

Spricht das Bekenntnis, das in seiner Situation (im 7.Jh.?) nach verschiedenen Richtungen auslegbar ist, die Eigenart oder Einzigkeit dieses
Gottes gegenüber der kanaanäischen Religion mit dem Baalkult aus

---

[13] Jes. xliii 11 im Anschluß an Hos. xiii 4; vgl. Jes. xliii 3, xlv 21. So kann
Deuterojesaja zugleich erwarten, daß alle Welt den einen Gott anerkennt (xlv 14,
23ff. u.a.).

[14] Schon G. v. Rad, *Theologie des Alten Testaments* I (München, ⁴1962), S. 225,
betont: Der Exilsprophet spricht den "auch der theologischen Reflexion bewußt ge-
wordenen Monotheismus ... nicht als eine religionsphilosophische Wahrheit aus".
H. Wildberger ("Der Monotheismus Deuterojesajas", in *Jahwe und sein Volk* [Mün-
chen, 1979], S. 249–73, bes. 254) gesteht zu: Die monotheistischen Aussagen sind
"dem soteriologisch-seelsorgerlichen Interesse untergeordnet", sind aber "ernst zu
nehmen"; denn sie eröffnen "einen neuen Horizont". Vgl. auch H. Klein, "Der
Beweis der Einzigkeit Jahwes bei Deuterojesaja", *VT* 35 (1985), S. 267–73; R.G.
Kratz, *Kyros im Deuterojesaja-Buch* (Tübingen, 1991), bes. S. 193.

[15] Vgl. Dtn. xiii; Jos. xxiii 6ff.; 1 Kön. xi 2, 4; 2 Kön. xvii 35–6 u.v.a. Auf einen
Monotheismus zielen Aussagen wie 2 Sam. vii 22; 1 Kön. viii 60; 2 Kön. v 15, xix
19 u.a.

[16] Dtn. v 7, vi 14, vii 4, 16, xii 2–3, xiii 1ff. u.a.

[17] Dtn. iv 39; vgl. iv 35, xxxii 39.

[18] Dtn. vi 4; vgl. "einer, einzig" Sach. xiv 9; Mal. ii 10; Hi. xxxi 15.

oder eher die Einheit Jahwes gegenüber der Vielheit der Jahwekult-
stätten? Beide Absichten können sich auch verbinden, wenn das Bekenntnis zur Einheit Jahwes zugleich die Vielfalt der Baalverehrung
abwehrt.[19] Erst in seiner gewichtigen Wirkungsgeschichte scheint es
(im Anschluß an Dtn. iv 35ff.) "monotheistisch" verstanden worden
zu sein.[20]

Bestimmt die Ausschließlichkeitsforderung zunächst das Verhältnis
des Menschen zu Gott, so wird hier (Dtn. vi 4) ein Satz "über" Gott
selbst formuliert. Allerdings wird aus einer solchen Grenzaussage
sogleich wieder die Folgerung für menschliches Verhalten gezogen
(vi 5): Gott "mit ganzem Herzen (etwa: Denken, Sich-Entscheiden),
mit ganzer Seele (wohl: Ausrichtung, Verlangen) und mit ganzer Kraft
zu lieben"; in dieser ungeteilten Zuwendung[21] spiegelt sich die Ausschließlichkeit des Glaubens wider.

---

[19] Nach der frühen Untersuchung von W.F. Bade ("Der Monojahwismus des
Deuteronomiums", *ZAW* 30 [1910], S. 81–90, bes. 89) will Dtn. vi 4 "betonen, daß
Jahwe eine *Einheit*, nicht eine *Mehrheit*, ist. Der ... Monotheismus einer späteren
Zeit erst hat den Satz zu einem Losungswort gegen den Polytheismus gemacht." In
den Inschriften von Kuntillet ʿAǧrud scheint der Gottesname "Jahwe von Samaria"
bezeugt zu sein; vgl. u. Anm. 65. Nicht ausdrücklich erwähnt, aber naheliegend ist
der Bezug zur Forderung der Kultzentralisation, zumal wenn Dtn. vi 4ff. den entsprechenden Gesetzen Dtn. xxiiff. nachträglich als Deutung vorangestellt wurde: Ist
die "Einheit" Gottes auch ein Grund für die Einheit der "erwählten" Kultstätte?
Noch andere Auslegungen werden erwogen, wie: "Nur als der Gott Israels ist Jahwe
'einzig', als der von Israel allein geliebte Gott ist er einzigartig" (G. Braulik, *Deuteronomium 1–16,7* [1986], S. 56 z.St.). Vgl. zur Auslegung etwa N. Lohfink, "Gott im
Buch Deuteronomium" (1976), in *Studien zum Deuteronomium und zur deuteronomistischen
Literatur* II (Stuttgart, 1991), S. 25–53; E. Nielsen, "'Weil Jahwe unser Gott ein Jah-
we ist' (Dtn 6,4f)", in *Beiträge zur alttestamentlichen Theologie*, FS W. Zimmerli (Göttin-
gen, 1977), S. 288–301; M. Rose, *Der Ausschließlichkeitsanspruch Jahwes* (Stuttgart, 1975),
S. 134ff.; M. Peter, "Dtn 6,4—ein monotheistischer Text?", *BZ* NF 24 (1980),
S. 252–62; H.D. Preuß, *Deuteronomium* (Darmstadt, 1982), S. 178 (Lit.); R.W.L.
Moberly, "Yahweh is one': the translation of the Shema", in J.A. Emerton (Hg.),
Studies in the Pentateuch, *SVT* 41 (1990), S. 209–15.

[20] Im vorliegenden Kontext wird das Bekenntnis Dtn. vi 4 durch die vorangestell-
ten "monotheistischen" Aussagen (iv 35, 39) ausgelegt und später auch in diesem
Sinne verstanden; so zitiert es Mk. xii 28ff. in Verbindung mit und im Sinne von
Dtn. iv 35: "Er ist einer, und kein anderer ist außer ihm."
Daß "der Monotheismus bereits im Deuteronomium geboren" wird (G. Braulik,
"Das Deuteronomium und die Geburt des Monotheismus", in *Studien zur Theologie
des Deuteronomiums* [Stuttgart, 1988], S. 257–300, bes. 288; vgl. 290–1), bleibt angesichts
ähnlicher Aussagen um die Exilszeit unsicher. Sie sind bei Deuterojesaja breiter
bezeugt, in seiner Gesamtbotschaft stärker verankert und auch sicherer in die Exils-
zeit datierbar. Gehört der Abschnitt Dtn. iv 27ff., da die Zerstreuung "unter die
Völker" (Plural) vorausgesetzt ist, nicht eher in nachexilische Zeit? So liegt hier eher
Einfluß Deuterojesajas vor. Vgl. auch D. Knapp, *Deuteronomium 4* (Göttingen, 1987),
S. 104–5.

[21] Die Priesterschrift nimmt in anderer Sprache diese Tendenz durch die Forderung der Ganzheit auf; vgl. o. Anm. 9.

Der Prophet *Jeremia* vergleicht (gegen Ende des 7.Jh.) in einem eindrucksvollen Bild die lebenspendende Kraft des einen Gottes mit den Fähigkeiten der Götter, um nicht ihre Existenz, aber ihre Verläßlichkeit zu leugnen und auf den beständigen Grund des Vertrauens zu verweisen:

> Zweifaches Unrecht beging mein Volk:
> Mich verließen sie,
> den Quell lebendigen Wassers,
> um sich Zisternen zu hauen,
> rissige Zisternen, die das Wasser nicht halten.[22]

"Sie sind keine Götter", d.h.: nicht eigentlich, nicht in Wahrheit Götter; denn sie "nützen nichts":[23]

Wie Jeremia hier die Ausschließlichkeit des Glaubens nicht gesetzlich-fordernd, sondern feststellend, ja anschaulich und insofern trotz der Anklage lockend-werbend ausspricht, so kann sie schon der Prophet *Hosea* (im 8.Jh.) als Aussage und Zuspruch formulieren:

> Ich bin Jahwe, dein Gott,
> vom Land Ägypten her.
> Einen Gott neben mir kennst du nicht,
> und einen Helfer außer mit gibt es nicht.
> (Hos. xiii 4; vgl. xii 10; aufgenommen Jes. xliii 11)

Schon hier sind wesentliche Elemente der Einleitung des Dekalogs miteinander verbunden: die sog. Selbstvorstellungsformel "Ich bin Jahwe", erweitert um die Huldbezeugung "dein Gott", der geschichtliche Rückbezug als Orts- oder auch Zeitangabe "vom Land Ägypten her" und die Aussage der Ausschließlichkeit.[24]

Da die sog. Selbstvorstellungsformel nicht typisch prophetisch ist,

---

[22] Jer. ii 13. Muß Jeremia bei seinem Auftrag erfahren, daß Gott ihm vom "Quell lebendigen Wassers" zum "Trugbach" (xv 18) wird, so kann der Hiob-Dialog diese Einsicht in seinen Klagen und Anklagen (vii 12ff., ix 12ff., xvi 19ff., xix 6ff.; vgl. Hi. xii 1ff. mit Jer. xx 14ff.) angesichts menschlichen Leids verallgemeinern. Beide halten an Gott in der Anrede fest.

[23] Vgl. "nichts-nutzig" Jer. ii 8, 11; auch xi 12; Jon. ii 9; Jes. xliv 9–10, 17 u.a.

[24] "Hos 13, 4 ist (zusammen mit 12, 10) das älteste datierbare Zeugnis im Alten Testament für die Verbindung von Selbstvorstellung Jahwes (Dekaloganfang) und erstem Gebot; ob diese Verbindung Hosea schon vorgegeben war, wie man meist annimmt [W. Zimmerli u.a.] oder aber von ihm geschaffen wurde [F.-L. Hoßfeld, *Der Dekalog* (Freiburg/Göttingen, 1982), S. 264], ist nicht mehr nachweisbar" (J. Jeremias, *ATD* 24/1 [Göttingen, 1983], S. 163). Dabei erinnert der Rückverweis auf die Geschichte "von Ägypten her" (auch Hos. xii 10) mit dem zeitlichen Beginn dieser Beziehung zugleich an die Erfahrung der Rettung oder "Hilfe".

scheint der Prophet eher eine vorgegebene Redeform abgewandelt aufzunehmen. Jedenfalls legt er die Alleinverehrung von der Einsicht aus, daß dieser Gott der alleinige "Helfer" ist; so ergibt sich die Forderung aus der Zusage.

Der Prophet *Jesaja*, der Gott "auf einem hohen und erhabenen Thron" sieht und die weltweit ausgreifende Proklamation "Die Fülle der ganzen Erde ist seine Herrlichkeit" vernimmt,[25] bringt die Exklusivität nicht als Forderung oder Anklage, sondern im Rahmen seiner Gerichtsansage (ii 17) bereits als Zukunftserwartung zur Geltung:

> Erhaben ist Jahwe *allein* an jenem Tag.[26]

Nach *Amos'* Botschaft[27] ahndet Jahwe auch Vergehen, von denen Israel nicht betroffen ist (ii 1), und hat Macht über die Nachbarstaaten hinaus[28] bis an die Grenzen des Kosmos: Weder im Himmel oder in der Unterwelt noch in der Tiefe des Meeres gibt es vor Gott eine Fluchtstätte.[29] In solcher Einsicht sprengt Jahwe die Schranken eines "Nationalgottes", zumal sich dieser "Volksgott" gegen sein eigenes Volk wendet.

Demnach gehen die ältesten sog. Schriftpropheten des 8.Jahrhunderts wie selbstverständlich von der Ausschließlichkeit des Glaubens aus, bezeugen sie in unterschiedlicher Sprache und beziehen sie in je eigener Weise auf ihre Wirklichkeit. Von den sog. Vorschriftpropheten, deren—schwer eindeutig abzugrenzende und zu datierende—Überlieferung nur in Erzählzusammenhängen erhalten ist, trat insbesondere

---

[25] Jes. vi 1, 3. Ähnlich bezeugen Psalmen, die in der Regel als älter angesehen werden, eine doppelte Einsicht: zum einen die Überlegenheit oder Vorherrschaft Jahwes über andere Götter oder Gottwesen (Ps. xxix 1; vgl. Ps. lxxxii; auch lxxxix 6ff., xciii 4 u.a.), zum andern die Prädikation Jahwes als "König über die ganze Erde" (Ps. xlvii 3, 8) oder das Bekenntnis: "Jahwe gehört die *Erde* und was sie erfüllt" (Ps. xxiv 1–2; vgl. lxxiv 16, lxxxix 12, xcv 5). Vgl. M. Metzger, "Eigentumsdeklaration und Schöpfungsaussage", in FS H.J. Kraus (Neukirchen-Vluyn, 1983), S. 37–51; H. Spieckermann, "Die ganze Erde ist seiner Herrlichkeit voll", *ZThK* 87 (1990), S. 415–36.

[26] Die Aussage bringt schon früh (im 8.Jh.) alttestamentliche Zukunftserwartung auf einen Nenner. Sie setzt wohl Amos' (wie viii 2, vi 8) oder Hoseas (i 6, 9 u.a.) Einsichten von einem tiefen Einschnitt voraus, formuliert die Gerichtsansage aber nicht als Kritik oder gar "Ende", vielmehr "positiv" und—in weisheitlicher Tradition—allgemein wie Jes. xxxi 3 u.a.).

[27] In den Worten dieses ältesten Schriftpropheten macht kein Baal Jahwe "den Rang streitig . . . Die Einzigkeit der Gottheit Jahwes in Israel und der Völkerwelt ist kein Gegenstand seiner Botschaft, sondern deren selbstverständliche Voraussetzung" (H.W. Wolff, *BK* XIV/2 [Neukirchen-Vluyn, ²1975], S. 122).

[28] Am. v. 27, vi 14, ix 7; vgl. Jes. v 26ff., x 5–6; Jer. iv 5ff., u.a.

[29] Am. ix 2–3; vgl. Ps. cxxxix 7ff.

Elija (im 9.Jh.) für die Ausschließlichkeit des Glaubens ein. Fordert
Elija ("Mein Gott ist Jahwe") in einer dramatischen, wunderhaften
Szene zur Alternative zwischen Baal und Jahwe auf,[30] so klagt er
nach einer anderen—gegenwärtigem Wirklichkeitsverständnis leichter zugänglichen—Erzählung bereits an, geht damit aber davon aus,
daß diese Eigenart des Glaubens dem Angeredeten bekannt ist, damit er den Schuldaufweis einsehen kann:

> Ist denn kein Gott in Israel,
>   daß du sendest Baal Sebub (Sebul), den Gott von Ekron,
> zu befragen?[31]

Ein solches Wort bestreitet nicht die Existenz des fremden Gottes,
nicht einmal dessen Bedeutung an seinem Ort oder für ein anderes
Volk, schließt aber in Israel die Wendung zu einem anderen Gott
aus: Jahwe ist der allein zuständige Nothelfer.

Gewiß sind die Propheten nicht repräsentativ für die Mehrheit
ihres Volkes, setzen aber als selbstverständlich voraus, daß es—im
Fall Elijas zumindest der König—um die Ausschließlichkeit wissen kann
und sollte.

Ist das Bekenntnis "Jahwe allein" erst einer Bewegung der Zeit
Elijas zu verdanken?[32] Sie hat die Ausschließlichkeit kaum hervorge-
bracht; eher wurde sie dieser Eigenart des Glaubens stärker gewahr
und bewußt, hat sie in der—zunehmenden—Auseinandersetzung mit
dem Baalkult[33] entfaltet und zugespitzt.

So führt das Urteil sachlich weiter: In dieser Epoche vollzog sich
der Übergang von einer "integrierenden" zur "intoleranten"—bzw.
von einer "unpolemischen" zu einer "polemischen"—Monolatrie.[34]

---

[30] 1 Kön. xviii 21 mit dem Ziel: Jahwe "Gott in Israel" (v 6) bzw. "der Gott"
(v 37, 39). Vgl. 1 Kön. xix; auch 2 Kön. ix.

[31] 2 Kön. i 6 (auch vi 3); vgl. G. Hentschel, "Elija und der Kult des Baal", in
E. Haag (Hg.), *Gott, der einzige* (Freiburg, 1985), S. 54–90; auch St. L. McKenzie,
The Trouble with Kings, SVT 42 (Leiden, 1991), S. 93–4; A. Lemaire, "Joas, roi d'Israël
et la premiere rédaction du cycle d'Elisée", in C. Brekelmans–J. Lust (Hg.), *Pentateuchal
and Deuteronomistic Studies* (Leuven, 1990), S. 245–54. 2 Kön. i 6 enthält die Charak-
teristika der Schriftprophetie noch nicht; umgekehrt setzt Amos die Ausschließlichkeit voraus.

[32] So B. Lang, in B. Lang (Hg.), *Der einzige Gott* (München, 1981), S. 58ff.; noch
weiter geht H. Vorländer (ebd. S. 93ff.); vgl. auch F. Stolz, in O. Keel (Hg.), *Monotheismus im Alten Israel und seiner Umwelt* (Fribourg, 1980), S. 154ff., 174ff.

[33] Vgl. noch Hos. ii, iii 1, iv 12ff.; auch Num. xxv; Ri. vi u.a.

[34] So F.-L. Hossfeld, "Einheit und Einzigkeit Gottes im frühen Jahwismus", in
M. Böhnke–H. Heinz (Hg.), *Im Gespräch mit dem dreieinen Gott*, FS Breuning [Freiburg,
1985], S. 57–74, bzw. E. Zenger, in *Gott, der einzige* (o. Anm. 31), S. 50ff., bes. 53.

Gibt es "Integration" jedoch ohne "Intoleranz", Übernahme ohne Auswahl oder gar Abstoßung?[35]

Gehen auch erzählende Traditionen oder Texte in eine ähnlich frühe Zeit zurück?

Nach *elohistischer* Darstellung offenbart sich Gott auch einem ausländischen König (Gen. xx 3, 6–7), wie auch die Josephserzählung (xli 25, 28) sagen kann: "Gott hat dem Pharao (im Traum) angekündigt, was er tun will."

Vor allem zeigt bereits der *jahwistische* Erzählstrang, der im Grundbestand in die frühe Königszeit zurückreichen kann,[36] eine erstaunliche Konzentration theologischer Aussagen, bezeugt Jahwe als Schöpfer und Erhalter (Gen. ii 4bff, viii 22), welcher Unheil sendet, Heil gewährt und aus der Not befreit.[37]

Nach solchen erzählenden Überlieferungen schließt Jahwes geschichtliches Wirken schon früh Bereiche der *Natur*[38] ein aber auch das Leben des *einzelnen*, die "persönliche Frömmigkeit"?[39] Vermutlich hat sich, zunächst allgemein geurteilt, eine Religion überhaupt dem Problem zu stellen: Wie lassen sich ihre—auf eine Gruppe bezogenen, mehr oder weniger grundsätzlichen—Einsichten mit dem Alltagsleben des Menschen, seinen Nöten und Wünschen, verbinden, oder wieweit bedarf es hier einer Ergänzung durch eine andere Ausrichtung und Praxis? D.h. im Fall Israels: Wie lassen sich die zunächst

---

[35] Fremde Vorstellungen, selbst kanaanäische Überlieferungen vom Gott El (Gen. xiv 18ff., Num. xxiii 22; Ps. xlvii, lxxxii, u.a.), konnten letztlich nur umgeformt und unter Abweisung des Unannehmbaren (vgl. beispielsweise die Züge, die der Gott El im ugaritischen Epos Schachar und Schalim trägt) angeeignet werden. Vgl. u. Anm. 83.

[36] Die—stark umtrittene—Datierung des jahwistischen Werks (ohne redaktionelle Zusätze, die ebenfalls den Jahwenamen gebrauchen) in die frühe Königszeit, wohl vor der sog. Reichsteilung 926 v. Chr., bleibt doch wohl die wahrscheinlichere Lösung; vgl. W.H. Schmidt, "Ein Theologe in salomonischer Zeit? Plädoyer für den Jahwisten", *BZ* NF 25 (1981), S. 82–102; H. Seebaß, "Jahwist", *TRE* 16 (1987), S. 441–5; K. Berge, *Die Zeit des Jahwisten*, BZAW 186 (Berlin, 1990); auch A. Schart, *Mose und Israel im Konflikt* (Freiburg/Göttingen, 1990), S. 240–1.

[37] Jahwe, Schöpfer der Lebewesen (Gen. ii 7ff.), gibt den Rhythmus von Saat und Ernte (viii 22; vgl. ii 5), das Brot (Ex. xvi 4), sorgt für den Menschen, selbst noch den Ungehorsamen (Gen. iii 21, iv 15; vgl. vii 16b), befreit aus der Not (Gen. xvi 7a, 11ff., xxiv 32–3; Ex. iii 8, u.a.), sendet Heil wie Unheil (Gen. vi 7, xii 17, xviii–xix, xxix 31 u.a.); zwar trifft Noachs Fluch Kanaan zum Vorteil Sems, doch der segen gilt nicht Sem, sondern dem Gott Sems, Jahwe (ix 25–6).

[38] Vgl. Ex. xv 22ff.–xviii; Num. xi, xx u.a.

[39] Vgl. R. Albertz, *Persönliche Frömmigkeit und offizielle Religion* (Stuttgart, 1978); jetzt ders., *Religionsgeschichte Israels in alttestamentlicher Zeit* 1 (Göttingen, 1992).

die Gemeinschaft betreffenden Aussagen auf das Schicksal des einzelnen anwenden?

Nach der alttestamentlichen Überlieferung galt Jahwe nicht nur als Staats-, Landes- oder Volksgott, sondern war, wie die Erzählung von Hanna beispielhaft zeigt, zugleich für die Not des einzelnen zuständig.[40] Auch die ältere Spruchweisheit oder individuelle Klagepsalmen,[41] zugespitzt in Jeremias Konfessionen oder gar in Hiobs Anklagen, beziehen menschliches Schicksal auf Jahwe.

III

Das *Bundesbuch*, das sicher vordeuteronomisch ist und in seinem Kern in frühkönigliche oder gar vorstaatliche Zeit[42] zurückgehen wird, enthält als Rechtssammlung wiederum ältere Rechtssätze. Unter ihnen hat sich eine anscheinend recht frühe, Tat und Folge verknüpfende Formulierung erhalten, die, um eindeutig zu bleiben, späterer (eingeklammerter) Ergänzungen bedurfte:

> Wer (anderen) Göttern opfert (es sei denn Jahwe allein),
> wird gebannt. (Ex. xxii 19)

Hier liegt vermutlich die älteste Fassung der Exklusivität des Glaubens mit Forderungscharakter vor. Jener Rechtssatz: "Wer Göttern opfert, wird gebannt", der späterer Zeit nur mit den angedeuteten Erweiterungen verständlich oder eindeutig erscheint, macht auch deshalb einen alten Eindruck, weil mit dem Verb *zbḥ* "opfern" nicht nur wie später das Schlachtopfer, sondern allgemein jedes Opfer, "zusammenfassend der Opferkult",[43] bezeichnet wird. Mit seiner knap-

---

[40] 1 Sam. i; vgl. Gen. xvi, xxi, xxix 32–3; auch Rut. Ein ähnliches Zeugnis können die Eigennamen enthalten; J.H. Tigay, *You shall have no other Gods. Israelite Religion in the Light of Hebrew Inscriptions* (Atlanta, 1986); ders., "Israelite Religion. The Onomastic and Epigraphic Evidence", in *Ancient Israelite Religion*, FS F.M. Cross (Philadelphia, 1987), S. 157–94; J.D. Fowler, *Theophoric Personal Names in Ancient Hebrew* (Sheffield, 1988); J.C. de Moor, *The Rise of Yahwism* (Leuven, 1990), S. 10ff.

[41] Amos' Fürbitte (vii 2, 5) setzt mit Anrede, Bitte und Begründung die Struktur des individuellen Klagelieds voraus; vgl. auch Jes. viii 17 "ich hoffe"; Mi. i 8 u.a.

[42] Vgl. etwa G. Wanke: *TRE* 7 (1981), S. 412–15; F. Crüsemann, "Das Bundesbuch. Historischer Ort und institutioneller Hintergrund", in *SVT* 40 (1988), S. 27–41; ders., *Die Tora* (München, 1992),; E. Otto, *Wandel der Rechtsbegründungen in der Gesellschaftsgeschichte des antiken Israel* (Leiden, 1988); L. Schwienhorst-Schönberger, *Das Bundesbuch (Ex. 20, 22–23, 33)*, *BZAW* 188 (Berlin, 1990); Y. Osumi, *Die Kompositionsgeschichte des Bundesbuches Exodus 20,22b–23,33* (Freiburg/Göttingen, 1991).

[43] R. Rendtorff, *Studien zur Geschichte des Opfers im alten Israel* (Neukirchen-Vluyn, 1967), S. 38. Dieselbe "Opfer"-Handlung ist auch sonst in alten Überlieferungen

pen Form, die eine klar umrissene Handlung mit einer harten Fol-ge[44] verbindet, ähnelt der Satz den frühen Todesrechtssätzen.[45]

Untersagt eine solche Formulierung nur eine bestimmte—wohl öffentlich vollzogene, insofern leicht erkennbare—Handlung, sei es das Opfern am Altar oder auch die Proskynese,[46] so scheint eine wohl jüngere pluralische Wendung (Ex. xxiii 13) bereits eine weitere, allgemeinere Bedeutung zu haben:

Den Namen anderer Götter sollt ihr nicht anrufen,
und er soll aus deinem Munde nicht gehört werden.

Sie verbietet den (kultischen) Anruf[47] der Namen anderer Götter und—in einer singularischen, vermutlich sachlich verschärfenden Erweite-rung—das Aussprechen; die Namen fremder Götter sollen überhaupt nicht in den Mund genommen werden.

Demgegenüber ist das erste Dekaloggebot, das durch das göttliche Ich geprägt ist, eindeutig "von allen Fassungen die allgemeinste und die am wenigsten spezifizierte";[48] denn es verbietet jegliches Verhal-ten zu fremden Göttern, schließt also Opfern, Verehren oder Anru-fen ihrer Namen, nicht nur öffentliche, sondern auch private, ande-ren nicht ohne weiteres einsichtige Handlungen, ein:

(Gen. xxxi 54, xlvi 1; Ex. xviii 12; auch v 3 u.a.) bezeugt.

[44] Die Gemeinschaft ahndet die Übertretung. Zum Weihe-Akt des "Bannens", sei es durch Tötung oder Ausschluß aus der Gemeinschaft, vgl. C. Brekelmans, *THAT* I (1971), Sp. 635–9; N. Lohfink, *ThWAT* III (1982), Sp. 192–213.

[45] Vgl. Ex xxi 12, 15–17.

[46] Der dem Dekaloggebot formal vergleichbare Prohibitiv: "Du sollst nicht nie-derfallen vor einem anderen Gott" (Ex. xxxiv 14; abgewandelt aufgenommen Ps. lxxxi 10) wird—vor allem wegen der ungewöhnlichen, ja einmaligen singularischen Formulierung 'el 'aher "anderer Gott"—ebenfalls für die "älteste Formulierung des Fremdgötterverbots" gehalten; so F.-E. Wilms, *Das jahwistische Bundesbuch in Exodus 3* (München, 1973), S. 157; vgl. G. Schmitt, *Du sollst keinen Frieden schließen mit den Bewohnern des Landes* (Stuttgart, 1970), S. 26; E. Otto, *Das Mazzotfest in Gilgal* (Stutt-gart, 1975), S. 210; bes. J. Halbe, *Das Privilegrecht Jahwes Ex 34,10–26* (Göttingen, 1975), S. 119ff., L. Schwienhorst-Schönberger (o. Anm. 4?), S. 316ff. Allerdings begegnet dieses Gebot durch das einleitende "denn" nur in abhängiger Stellung, ist also stärker in den Kontext eingebunden; außerdem erfährt es selbst nochmals eine Begründung durch den Verweis auf Jahwes über die Ausschließlichkeit wa-chenden "Eifer".

[47] Vgl. Jos. xxiii 7; auch Jes. xxvi 13; dazu W. Schottroff, *'Gedenken' im Alten Orient und im Alten Testament* (Neukirchen-Vluyn, ²1967), S. 248–9; *THAT* I (1971), Sp. 507–18, bes. 513; etwas anders H. Eising, *ThWAT* II (1977), Sp. 571–93: Es ist verbo-ten, "den Namen anderer Götter zu preisen, d.h. sich zu ihnen zu bekennen" (S. 584).—Vgl. noch Wendungen wie Ex. xxiii 24; Lev. xix 4, xxvi 1 u.a.

[48] G.v. Rad (o. Anm. 14), S. 217. Man "versucht, den Fall der Fremdgottverehrung allgemein und umfassend zu formulieren" (H. Gese, *Vom Sinai zum Zion* [München,

"Es soll(en) für dich nicht andere Götter sein
vor mir" bzw. "mir gegenüber".[49]

Auch die Formulierung "andere Götter" ist "sicher im weitesten Sinne des Wortes zu verstehen".[50] Ihre Existenz wird als selbstverständlich hingenommen, so vorausgesetzt. Nicht das Sein der Götter, vielmehr ihre Zuständigkeit für diejenigen, denen die Zuwendung "dein
Gott" (Ex. xx 2) gilt, sowie ihre Wirksamkeit wird bestritten.

IV

Sucht man sich noch weiter zurückzutasten, so wird es bei vorsich-
tigem Urteil immer schwerer, eine eindeutige Entscheidung zu fällen. Immerhin besingt das *Deboralied*, das im Kern vermutlich auf
vor-jerusalemischer, ja vorstaatlicher Überlieferung (etwa des 11.Jh.)
beruht, die Bindung an Jahwe oder gar "die Heilstaten Jahwes" (Ri.
v 11).[51] In der Frühzeit scheint Israel eben im Krieg die Hilfe Jahwes

---

1974], S. 67 Anm. 14). Vgl. W.H. Schmidt, "Überlieferungsgeschichtliche Erwägungen zur Komposition des Dekalogs", in *Congress Volume: Uppsala 1971*, SVT 22 (1972),
S. 201–20, bes. 204–5. Auch nach Hossfeld (o. Anm. 24, S. 267) verzichtet Ex. xx
3 "auf jede kultische Konkretion der Verehrung". Ist mit der Charakterisierung
"Abstraktion zum inhaltsleersten ... Ausdruck des Gottesverhältnisses, zur Haben-
Relation" (ebenda) die Tendenz aber angemessen beschrieben? Eher handelt es sich
um einen möglichst inhaltsweiten Ausdruck.

    N. Lohfink betont, daß der Dekalog—im Vergleich mit einer Wendung wie "an-
deren Göttern nachgehen"—im ersten Gebot "gerade nicht typisch dt/dtr spricht
und daß es möglich ist, daß er der dt/dtr Sprache und Theologie vorausliegt"
(N. Lohfink, "Die These vom 'deuteronomistischen' Dekaloganfang", in *Studien zum
Pentateuch*, FS W. Kornfeld [Wien, 1977], S. 101–25, bes. 108).

[49] Die Verbindung *'al-pᵉnê* enthält verschiedene Bedeutungsnuancen, wie "vor dem
Angesicht, in der Gegenwart von" (Ex. xxxiii 19, xxxiv 6 u.a.), "zum Nachteil von"
(Dtn. xxi 16), "vor das Gesicht, gegen" (Gen. xvi 12; vgl. Neh. ii 2), "ins Antlitz,
offen" (Hi. i 11; Jes. lxv 3), umfaßt also "Gegenwart und Konfrontation zugleich".
So H. Simian-Yofre, *ThWAT* VI (1988), Sp. 629–59, bes. 656; vgl. J. Reindl, *Das
Angesicht Gottes im Sprachgebrauch des Alten Testaments* (Leipzig, 1970), bes. S. 45–6; A.S.
v.d. Woude, *THAT* II (1976), Sp. 432–60, bes. 459. Die Wiedergabe "über mich
hinaus" (M. Weippert [u. Anm. 75], S. 147) schwächt eher ab. E. König, *Hebräisches
und aramäisches Wörterbuch zum Alten Testament* (Leipzig, 6.7 1936), S. 367, und L. Köhler,
ThR (1929), S. 174; KBL, S. 767, übersetzen zuspitzend: "(mir) zum Trotz".
    "Vielleicht ist die zwischen *örtlichem* 'vor meinem Antlitz" und 'in mein Angesicht'
als *feindselige* Herausforderung *schillernde* Bedeutung gewollt." (So A. Schenker, "Der
Monotheismus im ersten Gebot, die Stellung der Frau im Sabbatgebot und zwei
Sachfragen zum Dekalog" [1985], *Text und Sinn im Alten Testament* [Freiburg/Göttin-
gen, 1991], S. 187–205, bes. 190.)

[50] G.v. Rad (o. Anm. 14), S. 221. Der Ausdruck "andere Götter" kann schon
früh in Hos. iii 1 bezeugt sein, falls er dort nicht einen Zusatz darstellt, was aber
schwer eindeutig zu entscheiden bleibt.

[51] Vgl. J. Jeremias, *Theophanie* (Neukirchen-Vluyn, ²1977), bes. S. 183ff.; H.-J. Zobel,

erfahren zu haben. Wirkt er—ohne Begleiter oder Begleiterin—nicht wie ein "Nationalgott", wenn er wie Kamosch für "das Volk des Kamosch" (Num. xxi 29), die benachbarten Moabiter sorgt?[52]

Geben schließlich die im *Exodusbuch* bewahrten, so verschiedenartigen *Überlieferungen* von Moses Berufung (Ex. iii), vor allem von der Rettung am Meer (Ex. xiv–xv) oder der Theophanie am Sinai (xix 16ff., xxiv 10–11)—anders als etwa die Tradition von Abrahams Begegnung mit dem Heiligen: "*Drei* Männer standen vor ihm"[53]—in ihrem überlieferungsgeschichtlichen Grundbestand nicht bereits auf je ihre Weise die alleinige Zuwendung des Gottes Jahwe zu den Betroffenen[54] wieder?

Auch nach anderen, höchst verschiedenartigen und alt wirkenden Traditionen bekannte sich Israel oder die später "Israel" genannte Verehrergruppe in—mehr oder weniger offiziellen—gottesdienstlichen Handlungen (nur) zu Jahwe. So wirkt die Überlieferung von einem gemeinsamen Kult mit den Midianitern überraschend, wenn nicht anstößig, weil sie späteren Vorstellungen und Gepflogenheiten widerspricht und sich schon aus den Gegebenheiten der Richterzeit[55] kaum mehr erklären läßt: "Moses Schwiegervater, Priester von Midian" "nahm" Opfer "für Gott, und alle Ältesten Israels kamen herbei um

---

"Der frühe Jahwe-Glaube in der Spannung von Wüste und Kulturland", *ZAW* 101 (1989), S. 342–65; H. Schulte, "Richter 5. Das Debora-Lied", in *Die hebräische Bibel und ihre zweifache Nachgeschichte. FS R.* Rendtorff (Neukirchen-Vluyn, 1990), S. 177–91; anders U. Bachmann, *Das Deboralied zwischen Geschichte und Fiktion* (St Ottilien, 1989).

[52] Vgl. Ri. xi 23–4 mit der Mescha-Stele (H. Donner–W. Röllig, *Kanaanäische und aramäische Inschriften* [Wiesbaden, 1962], Nr. 181; W. Beyerlin [Hg.], *Religionsgeschichtliches Textbuch zum Alten Testament* [Göttingen, ²1985], S. 253ff.); auch 1 Sam. xxvi 19; 1 Kön. xx 23; 2 Kön. v 17.

[53] Gen. xviii 2; vgl. xix 1, xxviii 12, xxxii 2–3 u.a. So scheinen sich in der Genesis einerseits Vorformen der Zuwendung eines Gottes zu einer Gruppe (Gen. xxxi 53; vgl. iv 15 u.a.), andererseits noch polytheistische Vorstellungselemente zu bewahren; sie werden nachträglich—grob geurteilt: auf Grund der im Exodusbuch enthaltenen Anstöße des Jahweglaubens—im Sinne der Ausschließlichkeit (wie Gen. xviii 1) gedeutet. Gen. xxxv 2–4 berichtet von Abgrenzung durch Vergraben von "fremden Göttern" und Schmuck.

[54] Innerhalb der Darstellung des Exodusbuches, das die Macht Jahwes im Ausland bezeugt (Ex. vii–xiv; vgl. Gen. xii 17), kommt noch vor den Rechtssammlungen (Ex. xxff.) die Andersartigkeit des Jahweglaubens gegenüber der (ägyptischen) Umwelt in der Szene von der ersten Begegnung zwischen Mose und dem Pharao mit der Frage und Aussage des Pharaos Ex. v 2 audeutend zum Ausdruck: "Wer ist Jahwe? . . . Ich kenne Jahwe nicht." Dieses Erzählmotiv (vom Opferfest in der Wüste Ex. v 1–3 u.ö.) scheint die Einsicht weiterzugeben, daß Jahwe kein ägyptischer Gott ist, sich so von den Landesgöttern unterscheidet.

[55] Vgl. Ri. vi–vii; auch Num. xxv 6ff. u.a.

zusammen mit Moses Schwiegervater vor Gott ein Mahl zu halten."[56] Zwar wird der Name Gottes hier, im Höhepunkt und Kern der Szene (Ex. xviii 12), nicht genannt, nach dem Kontext ist es aber nur *eine* Gottheit, und zwar Jahwe.[57]

Im allgemeinen werden nach der üblichen Anschauung priesterliche Aufgaben auf Aaron zurückgeführt; demgegenüber verbinden verstreute Nachrichten Mose mit Kulttraditionen.[58] So findet sich im Rahmen von Moses Verhandlungen mit dem Pharao in der älteren Erzählschicht die Überlieferung von einem Opferfest in der Wüste "für Jahwe".[59]

In so unterschiedlichen Geschichten mit wechselnden Haftpunkten wird nirgends eine Jahwe beigesellte Gottheit erwähnt. Die Eigenart solcher Überlieferungen, nur von Jahwe zu reden, wird durch den in anderem Zusammenhang erhaltenen Namen "Der (vom) Sinai"[60] in gewisser Weise bestätigt.

Gibt es wirklich genügend Anhaltspunkte für die Annahme einer durchgängigen Übermalung jener im Exodusbuch bewahrten, teils für Israels Glauben grundlegenden Traditionen? Es ist kaum vorstellbar, daß sie ursprünglich von "Jahwe und ...", sei es einer weiblichen oder männlichen Gottheit, berichtet hätten und in dieser ent-

---

[56] Ex. xviii 1, 12; vgl. ii 16, iii 1, auch xxiv 11. So kann das Alte Testament auf menschlicher Ebene von "Israel und" erzählen. Nach Ex. xii 38 (vgl. Num. xi 4) schloß sich Israel allerlei "Mischvolk" an.

[57] Vgl. explizit das vorhergehende—wohl jüngere—Bekenntnis Ex. xviii 11; zur Verbindung Jahwes mit Midian auch die alte Überlieferung Ex. iv 24–5.

[58] Vgl. auch Ri. xviii 30; 2 Kön. xviii 4 u.a.

[59] Ex. v 1, 3 u.a.; dazu W.H. Schmidt, *Exodus 1–6*, *BK* II/1 (Neukirchen-Vluyn, 1988), S. 251ff. Vgl. auch Ex. xvii 15–16; ähnlich Ri. vi 24. Selbst die Erzählung vom sog. Goldenen Kalb, die mit der doppeldeutigen Formulierung "Dies sind deine Götter" bzw. "Dies ist dein Gott" (Ex. xxxii 8; vgl. 1 Kön. xii 28) Ausschließlichkeitsgebot und Bilderverbot zu einer Frontstellung vereint, bezieht das Kultobjekt ausdrücklich allein auf den Gott (Jahwe), der Israel "aus Ägypten geführt hat".

[60] Ri. v 4–5; vgl. Dt. xxxii 2; Ps. lxviii 8–9. Diese Aussage findet ihrerseits eine Stütze in dem auf einer Inschrift von Kuntillet ʿAğrud anscheinend bezeugten Namen "Jahwe von Teman" (vgl. Hab. iii 3) sowie in den ägyptischen Zeugnissen von den Schasu Jhw ("Nomaden des [Berges] Jhw"?). Vgl. etwa Jeremias (o. Anm. 51), S. 8–9; P. Maiberger–C. Dohmen, *ThWAT* V (1986), Sp. 823–4; E.A. Knauf, *Midian* (Wiesbaden, 1988), S. 46ff. Daß der "Gott Israels" (Gen. xxxiii 20; Ri. v 5 u.a.) nicht in dem von dieser Verehrergruppe (später) bewohnten Land, in Palästina, beheimatet ist, ist nachträglich schwerlich erfindbar und aus den Gegebenheiten nach Errichtung des Jerusalemer Tempels oder gar aus noch jüngerer Zeit kaum mehr erklärbar. Wenn sich für den Gottesnamen Jahwe in Syrien-Palästina kaum vergleichbare, echte Parallelen finden, entspricht dies jenem nach Süden weisenden Zeugnis von Ri. v 4–5 u.a. Vgl. W.H. Schmidt (o. Anm. 59), S. 169ff.

scheidenden Hinsicht nachträglich korrigiert worden wären. Trotz mancher späterer Ausgestaltungen und Ergänzungen geben jene Überlieferungen von sich aus keinen Anlaß, eine tiefgreifende "Zensur" zu vermuten, welche "die Erinnerungen an die polytheistische Vergangenheit getilgt hat".[61]

Diese Exodustradition—bzw. die Gruppe, die sie pflegte—drang erst in Palästina ein, war dort nicht seit je beheimatet, brachte also andere, neue Impulse in das Land. Wie kam es, daß sich der Glaube an Jahwe vom Sinai bei den mancherlei in "Israel" aufgegangenen Gruppen oder gar Stämmen durchsetzte?[62] Was gab den Anstoß, den Anlaß zum Übertritt, bei den im Land ansässigen Kanaanäern, soweit sie sich an Israel anschlossen? Jedenfalls wird man urteilen dürfen: Je kleiner die einwandernde Gruppe und je höher der einheimische Bevölkerungsanteil in Israel war, desto auffälliger wird die Übernahme des Jahweglaubens.[63]

Wie immer sich das "Israel" in Palästina bildete, jene Impulse waren so stark und prägend, daß es die Ursprünge der Gemeinschaft zwischen Gott und Volk—über die Verheißungen an die Väter hinaus—in der Mosezeit suchte und sich in das Land "geführt" verstand.

Vermutlich war die Situation im späteren Süd- und Nordreich recht unterschiedlich, überhaupt regional und zeitlich verschieden. Immerhin zeigt sich die grundlegende Bedeutung der Exodustradition, die zunächst eher im Norden, eben in "Israel", gepflegt wurde, im 8.Jahrhundert in der Einwirkung auf die Botschaft des Propheten Hosea, der die Zusage "Jahwe, dein Gott vom Land Ägypten her"—gemeinsam mit der Ausschließlichkeit—bezeugt und wohl voraussetzt.[64]

Nun lassen archäologische Funde, seien es Inschriften, nach denen Jahwe mit einer Göttin—bzw. einem weiblichen Kultsymbol—

---

[61] Vgl. F. Stolz, in *Monotheismus* (o. Anm. 32), S. 167; zum Exodusbuch vgl. den Forschungsüberblick: W.H. Schmidt, *Exodus, Sinai und Mose* (Darmstadt, 1983; ³1995).

[62] "Empfahl sich" der Gott, der die von einem Streitwagenkorps Verfolgten retten konnte (Ex. xv 21 u.a.), in einer Situation, in der man sich gegenüber der Übermacht der Kanaanäer mit ihren "eisernen Wagen" (Jos. xvii 16; Ri. i 19; vgl. i 27ff.; 1 Kön. xx 23 u.a.) zu behaupten hatte?

[63] Nach K. Koch (*Spuren des hebräischen Denkens* [Neukirchen-Vluyn, 1991], S. 63 "besteht *das* Problem der israelitischen Frügeschichte darin, wieso und auf welche Weise sich die Verehrung eines Gottes aus der südlichen Wüste . . . bei den Menschen durchgesetzt hat, die vordem der Vielzahl kanaanischer Götter gehuldigt haben. Je weniger Israeliten tatsächlich eingewandert sind, desto größer das Rätsel . . . "

[64] Vgl. Hos. xii 10, xiii 4, auch ii 17; Am. ix 7. Der Gottesname oder die Gottesbezeichnung El wird, wie schon die Bileamsprüche (Num. xxiii 22, xxiv 8) zeigen, durch die Herausführung näher bestimmt.

verbunden ist,[65] oder auch verschiedenartige bildliche Darstellungen[66] noch in der Königszeit auf polytheistische Züge—zumindest im Volksglauben—schließen. Die Wirklichkeit war anscheinend komplexer, als die biblischen Texte von sich aus zu erkennen geben. Ist es aber schon möglich, das Gewicht der Inschriften, das schwer abzuwägen bleibt, so angemessen einzuschätzen, daß sich ein Panorama, ein Bild der Gesamtsituation Israels, zeichnen läßt? Erst recht bleibt angesichts möglicher neuer Funde Unvorhersehbares und Unwägbares.

Möchte man die Bedeutung der verschiedenartigen im Exodusbuch bewahrten Überlieferungen, zumal auf Grund der gefundenen Inschriften, einschränken, wird man eher der Auffassung zuneigen: Mit und neben dem gleichsam "offiziellen" Strang trug in älterer— vorstaatlicher, frühköniglicher—Zeit vielleicht nur ein (kleinerer) Kreis das Bekenntnis zu dem einen Gott, während ein (größerer) Teil der Bevölkerung es zumindest im praktischen Lebensvollzug weniger ernst nahm.[67] So braucht man keine tiefgreifende "Zensur", für welche die

---

[65] In den Inschriften selbst kommt der Vorrang oder die Überordnung Jahwes zur Geltung: Jahwe hat "durch seine Aschera"(?) gerettet (Chirbet el-Qom). Ein Segensspruch (Kuntillet ʿAğrud) wird nach der Erwähnung von Jahwe und "seiner Aschera" nicht im Plural, sondern im Singular fortgesetzt: "*Er* möge segnen . . . "

Ist Aschera, ob nun Eigenname, Erscheinungsform oder Kultsymbol, nur eine Art Mittlerin Jahwes? Ist die Rolle vergleichbar, die in weit späterer Zeit die Weisheit spielt (z.B. Prov. iii 19 "durch Weisheit")?

Wesentliche Texte sind zusammengestellt bei K.A.D. Smelik, *Historische Dokumente aus dem alten Israel* (Göttingen, 1987), S. 137ff., 144, 161 (Lit.); *TUAT* II/4 (1988), S. 556ff., 561ff.; G.I. Davies, *Ancient Hebrew Inscriptions* (Cambridge, 1991), S. 78ff., 105–6; zur vielfältigen Diskussion u.a.: J.A. Emerton, "New Light on Israelite Religion", *ZAW* 94 (1982), S. 2–20; P. Höffken, "Eine Bemerkung zum religionsgeschichtlichen Hintergrund von Dtn 6,4", *BZ* NF 28 (1984), S. 88–93; J. Day, "Asherah in the Hebrew Bible and Northwest Semitic Literature", *JBL* 105 (1986), S. 385–408; D.N. Freedman, "Yahweh of Samaria and his Asherah", *BA* 50 (1987), S. 241–9; verschiedene Beiträge in FS F.M. Cross (o. Anm. 40); J.M. Hadley, "The Khirbet el-Qom Inscription": *VT* 37 (1987), S. 50–62, "Some drawings and inscriptions on two pithoi from Kuntillet ʿAjrud", S. 180–213; S. Schroer, *In Israel gab es Bilder* (Freiburg/Göttingen, 1987), S. 21ff.; S.M. Olyan, *Asherah and the Cult of Yahweh in Israel* (Atlanta, 1988); K. Koch, "Aschera als Himmelskönigin", *UF* 20 (1989), S. 97–110; O. Loretz, *Ugarit und die Bibel. Kanaanäische Götter und Religion im Alten Testament* (Darmstadt, 1990), S. 83ff.; O. Keel–C. Uehlinger, *Göttinnen, Götter und Gottessymbole* (Freiburg, 1992), S. 237ff.; M. Dietrich–O. Loretz, *Jahwe und seine Aschera* (Münster, 1992).

[66] Vgl. P. Welten, "Bilder" (II), *TRE* 6 (1980), S. 517–21; Schroer (Anm. 65); H. Weippert, *Palästina in vorhellenistischer Zeit* (München, 1988); C. Uehlinger, "Götterbild", *Neues Bibel-Lexikon* I (Zürich, 1991) Sp. 871–92; Keel-Uehlinger (o. Anm. 65).

[67] Erinnert sei an das gewiß zugespitzte, Elija zugeschriebene Urteil "Ich allein bin übriggeblieben" (1 Reg. xiv 14; vgl. xviii 22), obwohl es voraussetzt, daß die Situation der Jahwegläubigen früher anders war.

alttestamentlichen Texte selbst keinen Anhalt liefern, zu vermuten, kann aber zugestehen: Die uns erhaltene Überlieferung bewahrt, möglicherweise auswählend, die Hauptlinie; anderes, wohl mehr volkstümliche Vorstellungen, mag ausgeschlossen worden sein.

Überhaupt bezeugt das Alte Testament selbst in erzählenden wie prophetischen Texten mit offenem Eingeständnis, daß der Glaube von der Früh- bis zur Spätzeit Anfechtungen ausgesetzt war und die Ausschließlichkeit nicht durchhielt.[68] Allerdings berichtet das Alte Testament von dieser Situation nicht ohne Wertung, nämlich nicht ohne Vorwurf. Beschreibt es eine Szene, in der die Verehrung von "Jahwe und..." eine gültige Möglichkeit oder Wirklichkeit war? Mag heutiger religionsgeschichtlicher Fragestellung eine Form des "Polytheismus", die Jahwe neben andere mehr oder weniger gleichberechtigte Gottheiten stellt, als für die damalige Zeit selbstverständliche Gegebenheit erscheinen,[69] so setzt das Alte Testament mit seiner kritischen Haltung—zumindest implizit—eine Art "Maßstab" voraus, von dem her es klagend-anklagend urteilt.[70]

"Ein Jahwekultus ohne das Erste Gebot ist nicht vorstellbar"; dieses Urteil G.v. Rads[71] hebt ein Wahrheits- oder Wesensmoment hervor,

---

[68] Vgl. etwa Num. xxv; Ri. vi; 2 Kön. i; Hos. i ff.; Jer. ii, xliv; Ez. viii; Jes. lxv u.v.a.

[69] Nach Lang ([o. Anm. 32] S. 53–4, 56, 62) herrscht im Israel der Königszeit "eine polytheistische Religion vor, die sich von den Religionen ihrer Umwelt nicht unterscheidet". Die Israeliten sollen "je ihren persönlichen Schutzgott", "auch Jahwe" und "Ressortgötter verehrt" haben, schließlich eine "Liebesgöttin, die ihre Statue im Heiligtum besitzt". Gibt es dafür tragfähige Belege? Selbst der "Kampf zwischen Jahwe und Baal hält sich noch ganz im Rahmen des Polytheismus". Allerdings räumt Lang (S. 60) eine gewichtige Besonderheit ein: "Daß Jahwe zum Gegner Baals werden kann, muß auch in seinem *Wesen* begründet liegen". Jahwe fehlt "jede Einbindung in eine Götterfamilie... Jahwe erscheint als Einzelgänger, der außerhalb der gewöhnlichen Bindungen steht."

[70] Das durch die wachsende Vielzahl von Inschriften verschärft aufgeworfene Problem darf man andeutend mit einer dem Alten Testament eigentlich unangemessenen, einer anderen Welt entstammenden Begrifflichkeit so umschreiben: Deuten sich schon früh "Heterodoxie" und "Orthodoxie" an, oder geht diese Unterscheidung erst allmählich aus einer Vielfalt von ursprünglich gleichwertigen Möglichkeiten hervor? Besteht bereits die Möglichkeit des "Abfalls", oder sind anfangs alle Wege offen und beliebig? Gibt es ansatzweise eine Art—zunächst vielleicht unausgesprochener, nicht schriftlich fixierter—"Norm", an der gemessen werden kann? Ist die Abweichung vom Jahweglauben also schon bald erkennbar und, wenn ja, an welchem Maßstab?—Läßt sich damit zugleich eine Eigenart oder ein eigenständiges Strukturelement ermitteln, das sich mit anderem verbinden, fremdem Einfluß unterliegen und so sich "mischen" kann?

[71] (o. Anm. 14), S. 39; ähnlich S. 223: "Die gesamte Kultgeschichte Israels ist ja ein einziger Kampf um die Gültigkeit des Ersten Gebotes." Vgl. demgegenüber die Einwände von B.J. Diebner, "Gottesdienst II. Altes Testament", TRE 14 (1985), S. 5–28.

überbetont jedoch den Forderungscharakter. Die Unvereinbarkeit mit anderen Kulten mag erst später empfunden sein; so wird die Ausschließlichkeits*forderung* jünger sein und die Notwendigkeit der Abgrenzung widerspiegeln, der es in der Frühzeit (so) noch nicht bedurfte.[72] War die Beziehung Jahwes zum "Volk (bzw. zur Mannschaft) Jahwes" (Ri. v 11, 13) aber nicht seit je einzig?

Nach diesem (kurzen) Gang durch die Glaubensgeschichte darf man wohl *vier* Phänomene, Aspekte oder gar Stadien unterscheiden:

(a) Das Zeugnis von der alleinigen Zuwendung des Gottes Jahwe zu einer Gruppe bzw. von der Gebundenheit dieser Gruppe, des Volkes oder auch Staates,[73] an Jahwe.

> Möchte man dieses Verhältnis so charakterisieren: Jahwe war "Nationalgott", dann hat man hinzuzufügen, daß schon nach frühen Zeugnissen sein Wirkungsbereich über Volk und Land hinausragen, auch individuelles Geschick einbegreifen oder bestimmen konnte; erst recht sind zumindest seit Amos prophetische Einsichten mit jener Bezeichnung nicht mehr angemessen erfaßbar.

(b) Die Formulierung dieses Verhältnisses mit Gebotscharakter, sei es in einem Rechtssatz oder einer Forderung, schließlich zugespitzt in der allgemeinen Gestalt des Ersten Gebots.

(c) Das Bekenntnis zur Einheit Gottes: "Jahwe ist einer" (Dtn. vi 4).

(d) Die monotheistische—oder monotheistisch klingende—Aussage oder Zuspitzung des Bekenntnisses.

Diese Phänomene folgen allem Anschein nach aufeinander, bilden aber keine sich ablösenden "Entwicklungsstufen". Die letzte führt die vorhergehenden weiter, ruht aber auf ihnen auf, löst sie nicht (zu-

---

[72] "Vielleicht setzt . . . das erste Gebot die geschichtliche Erfahrung voraus, daß der Jahweglaube fremdem Kult ausgesetzt ist . . . Sollte sich der Jahweglaube tatsächlich erst in der Begegnung mit dem kanaanäischen Pantheon vom Polytheismus abgegrenzt haben und damit der Differenz Einheit Vielheit bewußt geworden sein, so ist jedenfalls die Zuwendung Gottes zum Menschen bzw. zu einer bestimmten Gruppe seit je einzig" (W.H. Schmidt, *Das erste Gebot* [München, 1969], S. 13). Nach G. van der Leeuw (*Phänomenologie der Religion* [Tübingen, ²1956], S. 199) bezieht sich das Bekenntnis zunächst auf die Macht die erfahrenen Gottes: "Die Einzigkeit Gottes ist nicht eine Negation seiner Vielheit, sondern eine leidenschaftliche Affirmation seiner Gewaltigkeit."

[73] Trotz vorgegebener Bauform, Keruben, ehernem Meer, eherner Schlange und anderen, nach altorientalischen Vorbildern angefertigten Darstellungen, Symbolen oder Kultgeräten wurde nach 1 Kön. vi–viii der von Salomo errichtete Tempel Jahwe (vgl. viii 12–13) geweiht; auch dort ist von einer gleichrangig neben ihm

mindest nicht ohne weiteres) ab; so sind sie in ihr nicht aufgehoben, sondern behalten ihren Sinn und ihr Recht. Wäre ein "Monotheismus" ohne sie nicht auch zu mißverständlich?

Die längst vertraute Frage nach "Alter und Aufkommen des Monotheismus"[74] mit der neuerdings geführten sog. Monotheismus-Debatte weist mit Recht auf die Geschichte des Glaubens hin—auf einen Werdegang, der sich mit dem Gedanken der "Entwicklung" oder "Ent-faltung" nicht ausreichend erfassen läßt. Zugleich wird die Problemstellung jedoch nicht unerheblich verschoben, indem nach einem "Theismus" gesucht und dieser als Maßstab genommen wird.

Ist der Vergleich "Polytheismus—Monotheismus" nicht zu grob, um den Sachverhalt gerecht zu erfassen? Auch die einschränkende Gegenüberstellung von "theoretischem" und "praktischem Monotheismus"[76] deutet zwar bestehende Unterschiede in der Geschichte des Glaubens an dem einen Gott an, bleibt aber unbefriedigend. Wo fällt es schwerer, eine Grenze zwischen Theorie und Praxis zu ziehen als bei der Gottesverehrung? Wie kann sie sich mit "Theorie" begnügen, und wo fängt "Praxis" an? Wäre es dem Phänomen nicht angemessener, zu fragen, ob und wie die Ausschließlichkeit des Glaubens zum Ausdruck kommt?

---

stehenden Gottheit keine Rede. Sind das "Eifersuchtsbild" und andere Darstellungen, die der Prophet Ezechiel (viii 5ff.) kurz vor dem Exil—als Anlaß für die Gerichtsdrohung—schaut, nicht eher Einführungen späterer, etwa assyrischer Zeit (vgl. 2 Kön. xxi 5ff., bes. v 7; auch xxiii 4ff.)?

[74] B. Balscheit, *Alter und Aufkommen des Monotheismus in der israelitischen Religion*, BZAW 69 (Berlin, 1938). Schon J. Wellhausen (*Israelitische und jüdische Geschichte* [Berlin, ⁹1958], S. 29, 32] urteilte: "Der Monotheismus war dem alten Israel unbekannt"; Jahwe war "von Haus aus der Gott Israels und wurde dann viel später der universale Gott".

[75] Vgl. zur Diskussion außer einer Reihe von Aufsätzen vor allem die drei Sammelbände: Keel (o. Anm. 32); Lang (o. Anm. 32); Haag (o. Anm. 31) mit einem Forschungsüberblick von Norbert Lohfink (S. 9ff.); auch de Moor (o. Anm. 40); H. Niehr, *Der höchste Gott*, BZAW 190 (Berlin, 1990); M. Weippert, "Synkretismus und Monotheismus", in J. Assmann–D. Harth (Hg.), *Kultur und Konflikt* (Frankfurt/M., 1990), S. 143–79. M.Th. Wacker–E. Zenger, *Der eine Gott und die Göttin* (Freiburg, 1992); Keel-Uehlinger (o. Anm. 65), S. 2ff.

[76] "Einen theoretischen Monotheismus kennt Israel nicht"; alttestamentlicher Glaube "kämpft nicht um ein gereinigtes Welt- und Götterbild, sondern läßt das Phänomen fremder Götter" zu, "nimmt diesen aber alle Macht" (W. Zimmerli, *Grundriß der alttestamentlichen Theologie* [Stuttgart, 1985], S. 34). Es "hat sich sehr bald ein praktischer Monotheismus in Israel herausgebildet, für den die Verehrung anderer Götter als illegitim gelten mußte" (R. Rendtorff, "Die Entstehung der israelitischen Religion als religionsgeschichtliches und theologisches Problem", in *Gesammelte Studien zum Alten Testament* [München, 1975], S. 119–36, bes. 133).

V

Mit der Ausschließlichkeit des Glaubens ist wohl ein Impuls gesetzt, ihre Bedeutung aber nicht von vornherein gegeben. Ihre Implikationen und *Konsequenzen* ergeben sich erst im Laufe der Geschichte[77] so daß sich angesichts wechselnder Situationen neue Aspekte und Sinndeutungen erschließen.

Ein Großteil altorientalischer Mythen, etwa von Göttergeburt oder Göttertod, entfällt zumindest in der Auswirkung; entsprechend kann die Kosmogonie nicht als Theogonie dargestellt werden. Die Vorstellung einer göttlichen Ehe wird von den Propheten[78] auf die Beziehung Gott-Volk übertragen und für den Schuldaufweis benutzt, ist darum letztlich nur als Metapher verwendbar. Die Gestirne gelten der Schöpfungsgeschichte[79] nicht als mythisch-göttliche, menschliches Schicksal bestimmende Größen, sondern sind weltliche Phänomene, gleichsam "Lampen", die ihre Aufgabe erfüllen: die Erde zu beleuchten und die Zeiten zu unterscheiden.

Bei der Übernahme fremder, altorientalisch vorgegebener Vorstellungen, Motive oder Attribute können sich charakteristische, durch die Ausschließlichkeit angestoßene Umwandlungen vollziehen. So spitzt sich die Frage, die vergleichend nach dem Unvergleichlichen sucht: "Wer gleicht Jahwe unter den Göttersöhnen?" (Ps. lxxxix 7) zu: "Wer ist Gott als *nur* Jahwe?"[80] Von dem "Höchsten", der "erhaben über alle Götter" (Ps. xcvii 9) ist, wird bekannt (lxxxiii 19): "Du *allein* bist der Höchste über die ganze Erde."[81] Die altorientalisch vorgegebene Vorstellung vom "großen König über alle Götter" (Ps. xcv 3) gestaltet sich durch die Ausschließlichkeit des Bekenntnisses zu dem "einen, einzigen" Gott (Dtn. vi 4) umgeprägt, zu der die Welt umgreifenden Erwartung:

---

[77] Deutlich ist der Vorgang ja bei dem Bereich der Fruchtbarkeit in der Natur. Nach der jahwistischen Darstellung hatte Jahwe "noch nicht regnen lassen" (Gen. ii 5; vgl. viii 22); dennoch bleibt umstritten, ob er die Vegetation schenkt (1 Kön. xviii ff.; Hos. iiff.; Jer. ii u.a.).

[78] Hos. i, ii; Jer. iii; Ez. xvi, xxiii u.a.

[79] Gen. i 14ff.; vgl. Jes. xl 26; Ps. xix 5, xxiv 16, cxxxvi 7ff. u.a.

[80] Ps. xviii 32; vgl. 2 Sam. vii 22; 1 Kön. viii 23.

[81] Entsprechend wird von dem Gott "im Kreis der Heiligen" (lxxxix 6–8) ausgesagt (1 Sam. ii 2): "Niemand ist heilig wie Jahwe." Überhaupt dringt die im Rechtssatz (Ex. xxii 19) begegnende Praktikel "allein" in Aussagen von und vor Gott ein: "du allein bist Gott", Ps. lxxxvi 10, vgl. lxxii 18, lxxxiii 19, cxxxvi 4, cxlviii 13; 2 Kön. xix 15; Dtn. xxxii 12; Jes. ii 17, xliv 24; Hi. x 8; Neh. ix 6 u.a. "Ich will kundtun deine Gerechtigkeit allein" (Ps. lxxi 16) bis hin zum Schuldbekenntnis (Ps. li 6 gegenüber 2 Sam. xii 13): "An dir allein habe ich gesündigt."

Jahwe wird König werden über die ganze Erde;
an jenem Tag wird Jahwe *einzig* sein
und sein Name *einzig*.[82]

So ist die Übernahme fremden Guts ein höchst kritischer Prozeß, der eine Auseinandersetzung verrät: Unverträgliches wird abgelehnt, aus den vielfältigen Möglichkeiten, welche die Umwelt anbietet, wird gleichsam eine Auswahl getroffen, das Aufgenommene wird durch Umgestaltung dem Eigenen angeglichen. Durch diese Eingliederung verwandelt sich ursprünglich Fremdes in Eigenes.[83] Zeigt sich in diesem Vorgang, der bereichert, ohne Entscheidendes aufzugeben, nicht auch eine Kraft des Glaubens?

Dämonische Mächte können Gott als seinen Willen ausführend Boten unterstellt werden.[84] So kann der Mensch ein Unglück oder unheilvolles Geschehen nicht dem unberechenbaren Willen eines Dämons oder dem bösen Wirken einer Gottheit zuschreiben und von der Macht, die ihn verfolgt, zu einem ihm wohlgesonnenen Nothelfer fliehen. Was heißt—nach langem theologischem Nachdenken—also Ausschließlichkeit des Glaubens?

---

[82] Sach. xiv 9; vgl. Jes. ii 17, xxiv 23, lx 19–20; Zeph. ii 11 u.a. Nach der Hoffnung später Zeit können die Völker (Jes. xlv 6, 14, 23–4; vgl. ii 2–4, xix 21ff.; auch 1 Kön. viii 43; Ps. c u.a.) oder gar die Toten in den Kreis derer einbezogen werden, die Gottes Macht anerkennen (Ps. xxiii 28ff.; vgl. lxxiii 23ff.; Jes. xxv 8, xxvi 19; Hi. xxvi 5–6; Dan. xii 2 u.a.). Dabei braucht die Ausschließlichkeit des Glaubens nicht einen Ausschließlichkeitsanspruch der eigenen Gruppe zu bedeuten (Mi. iv 5; vgl. 2 Kön. v 17–18 u.a.).

[83] "Es gehört zum Wesen des alttestamentlichen Glaubens, daß er 'polemischen und usurpierenden Charakter trägt, daß er nicht in sich selbst ruht, sondern in steter Auseinandersetzung lebt, aus den anderen Religionen assimilierbare Gedanken, Vorstellungen und Begriffe an sich reißt und sie umformend sich eingliedert', aber auch scharf von sich weist, was ihn gefährdet" (E. Würthwein, *Wort und Existenz* [Göttingen, 1970], S. 198, mit einem Zitat von J. Hempel, *ZAW* 54 [1936], S. 293–4; vgl. ThR 36 [1971], S. 201). Von der "Forderung der Alleinverehrung Jahwes aus konnte die Übernahme neuer Elemente aus den Traditionen anderer Religionen niemals einfach in der Form der Addition des Neuen zum schon Vorhandenen hinzu geschehen, sondern es mußte sich jeweils ein Prozeß der Assimilation und Resorption vollziehen, bei dem das Aufgenommene so weit umgeformt wurde, daß es sich dem schon Vorhandenen einfügen ließ, anderes aber als nicht assimilierbar abgestoßen wurde" (Rendtorff [o. Anm. 76], bes. S. 133–4; vgl. 150).

[84] Die Dämonen sind Jahwe als seinen Willen ausführende Engel unterstellt—so der "Verderber" bzw. "Würgeengel" der Passanacht Ex. xii 23 oder der Pestengel 2 Sam. xxiv 17 (vgl. Num. xii 21ff. u.a.). Dämonische Züge sind gleichsam in Gott integriert—so der Flußdämon, mit dem Jakob ringt (Gen. xxxii 23ff.; Hos. xii 4). Vgl. noch Ri. ix 23; 1 Sam. xvi 14; 1 Kön. xxii 19ff.; auch Am. ix 3 u.a. Selbst der Satan ist, obwohl Versucher oder "Widersacher", kein widergöttliches Prinzip,

(a) Außer dem einen Gott sind andere Nothelfer nicht möglich; sie werden ausgeschlossen.

(b) Andere Nothelfer sind nicht nötig, da der eine Gott in allen Lebensbereichen wie in der ganzen Welt wirkt.

Wie schon frühe Erzählungen berichten, kann Jahwe unfruchtbar oder fruchtbar machen;[85] so empfängt, wie Hiob zugespitzt bezeugt, der Mensch *Gut und Böse* aus derselben Hand, begegnet in Zorn und Gnade demselben Gott:

> "Das Gute nehmen wir von Gott,
> und das Böse sollten wir nicht annehmen?"
> "Jahwe hat es gegeben, Jahwe hat es genommen;
> der Name Jahwes sei gelobt".[86]

Ein solcher Lobpreis, der den Gott anerkennt, der die Gaben des Lebens schenkt und zurückfordert, ist gleichsam die Anwendung der Ausschließlichkeit des Glaubens auf das eigene Schicksal, auf die Polarität menschlicher Erfahrungen, wie vielfältig die Klagelieder des Psalters und selbst noch der skeptische "Prediger" bezeugen:

> "Am Tage des Glücks sei guter Dinge,
> und am Tage des Unglücks merke dir:
> Auch diesen hat Gott gemacht—wie jenen."[87]

---

sondern wirkt nur in dem Rahmen oder Handlungsspielraum, den Gott ihm zuvor freigegeben hat (Hi. i–ii).

Mag die Volksreligion andere als die im Alten Testament dargestellten Züge tragen, so schränkt jedenfalls in der Konsequenz die Forderung gänzlicher Hinwendung zu dem einen Gott die Dämonenvorstellungen stark ein. "Geschah in Israel aber ein Unheil, dann hatte man nicht den Weg zu einer anderen Gottheit frei. Auch konnte man es nicht auf irgendwelche mißgünstigen Dämonen zurückführen; denn Jahwe hat alles Dämonische in sich aufgesaugt, es gab keine Kausalität neben ihm ... So mußte man sich an den wenden, der schlug." Der Glaube an Jahwe hat "mit seinem Ausschließlichkeitsanspruch die Dämonen weitgehend verdrängt" (L. Wächter, *Der Tod im Alten Testament* [Berlin, 1967], S. 29, 41, im Anschluß an P. Volz, *Das Dämonische in Jahwe* [Tübingen, 1924], S. 9, 31). Etwas anders G. Wanke ("Dämonen II, *TRE* 8 [1981], S. 275–7), der aber auch betont: Der "Alleinigkeitsanspruch Jahwes hat die Ausbildung einer ausgeprägten Dämonologie verhindert"; die "Aspekte des Bedrohlichen und Unheimlichen wurden ... integriert", so daß "entsprechende Vorstellungen in alttestamentlichen Texten selten explizit bezeugt sind" (S. 275). Vgl. K. Seybold, *Das Gebet des Kranken im Alten Testament* (Stuttgart, 1973), S. 40.

[85] Vgl. Gen. xxix 31ff.; 1 Sam. i; auch Rut.

[86] Hi. ii 10, i 21.

[87] Koh. vii 14; vgl. Spr. xvi 4.

Da die Ausschließlichkeit des Glaubens letztlich nicht erlaubt, Widriges auf andere Mächte zurückzuführen, sucht das Alte Testament das Dasein mit seinen Höhen und Tiefen, in seiner Gesamtheit einschließlich seiner Widersprüchlichkeit, auf Gott zu beziehen, so die Einheit des Glaubens zu wahren, ohne das Mangelhafte und Negative der Wirklichkeit zu übersehen, zu verschweigen oder zu beschönigen.

Weil der Mensch das Schicksal einschließlich des ihm schwer Erträglichen als Geschick versteht, ist eine—ähnlich gelegentlich schon im alten Orient[88] begegnende—Formulierung, welche die Vielfalt und Gegenseitigkeit menschlicher Erfahrung zu umfassen sucht, für das Alte Testament in hohem Maße charakteristisch; es erscheint als grundlegendes Bekenntnis, daß Gott—mit einer kaum zufälligen Reihenfolge der Verben, in der sich eine Perspektive oder Intention andeutet—"tötet und lebendig macht",[89] einreißt und aufbaut, ausreißt und pflanzt,[90] "erniedrigt" und "erhöht",[91] Licht wie Finsternis, Heil wie Unheil schafft.[92] Dabei können sich die Ausschließlichkeit und dieses doppelseitige Handeln Gottes ausdrücklich verbinden:

Ich bin es, und außer mir ist kein Gott.
Ich töte und mache lebendig,
ich zerschlug und werde heilen. (Dtn. xxxii 39)

---

[88] "Die Schwache lasse ich ins Haus eintreten, die Starke vertreibe ich daraus" heißt es im Inanna-Hymnus (A. Falkenstein—W.v. Soden, *Sumerische und akkadische Hymnen und Gebete* [Zürich/Stuttgart, 1953], S. 231). W. Zimmerli (*Ezechiel*, BK XIII/1 [Neukirchen-Vluyn, 1969, ²1979], S. 389) findet hier einen "Hinweis auf die rätselhaft launische ... Freiheit" der Gottheit. Vgl. auch H. Ringgren, *ThWAT* IV (1984), Sp. 764–7.

[89] 1 Sam. ii 6–7; Dtn. xxxii 39; 2 Kön. v 7; vgl. Hi. v 18; Ez. xvii 24; Jes. xix 22; auch Zeph. i 12; Jer. x 5; dann Ps. xc, civ 29–30; Gen. iii 19 u.a.

[90] Jer. i 10 u.a. Es handelt sich um eine wohl im Anschluß an xlv 7 von der Redaktion formulierte Zusammenfassung der Botschaft Jeremias; dazu S. Herrmann, *Jeremia* (Darmstadt, 1990), S. 75–6; A. Graupner, *Auftrag und Geschick des Propheten Jeremia* (Neukirchen-Vluyn, 1991), S. 162–3. Zur Sache vgl. auch Jer. xxiv 5, 8, xxxii 15. Wird Jer. xviii 7ff. weit über die exilisch-nachexilische Situation hinaus Gottes Handeln an Völkern und Staaten grundsätzlich-lehrsatzmäßig bedacht, so umfaßt es wiederum Gutes und Böses, Gericht und Heil; vgl. J. Jeremias, *Die Reue Gottes* (Neukirchen-Vluyn, 1975), bes. S. 83ff.

[91] Ez. xvii 24; vgl. auch Ex. xv 26; Hos. vi 1; Hi. 18; Jes. xxx 26; Jer. xxxi 10; 2 Kön. xx u.a.; dazu N. Lohfink, "Ich bin Jahwe, dein Arzt" (Ex. xv 26), in *"Ich will euer Gott werden"* (Stuttgart, 1981), S. 11–73; J. Scharbert, "Krankheit" (II), *TRE* 19 (1990), S. 680–3; ders., "Leiden" (I), *TRE* 20 (1990), S. 670–2 (Lit.) H. Niehr, "JHWH als Arzt", *BZ* NF 35 (1991), S. 3–17.

[92] Jes. xlv 7; vgl. H. Haag, "Ich mache Heil und erschaffe Unheil" (Jes. xlv 7),

Alttestamentlicher Glaube umgreift so mehr und mehr Geschichte und Natur, Vergangenheit wie Zukunft, Fernes und Nahes, Strukturelles und Kontingentes, Universales und Individuelles.[93] Selbst die Spruchweisheit urteilt: "Unterwelt und Abgrund liegen offen vor Jahwe, wieviel mehr die Herzen der Menschen!"[94]

---

in ders., *Das Buch des Bundes* (Düsseldorf, 1980), S. 210–15; W.H. Schmidt, "Gott und Böses", *EvTh* 52 (1992), S. 7–22.

[93] Vgl. etwa Ps. ciii 1–2, 19ff.

[94] Spr. xv 11; vgl. xvi 1ff.; auch Am. ix 2; Jes. vii 11; Ps. cxxxix 8; Hi. xiv 13, xxvi 5–6 u.a.

QUELQUES EXEMPLES DE SOMMAIRES PROLEPTIQUES DANS LES RÉCITS BIBLIQUES

par

JEAN LOUIS SKA
Rome

"Après ces événements, Dieu mit Abraham à l'épreuve." H. Gunkel avait déjà remarqué que ce demi-verset bien connnu de la Genèse (xxii 1a) est une sorte de titre (*Überschrift*); il donne deux autres exemples du même phénomène (Gn. xviii 1a, l'apparition de YHWH à Abraham aux chênes de Mamré, et 2 R. ii 1a, l'ascension d'Élie).[1] Dans ces troix cas, le narrateur fournit en quelques mots à ses lecteurs une information essentielle sur le récit qui va suivre.

Ce procédé, que nous appelons "sommaire proleptique", se définit comme une formule concise qui anticipe et introduit le récit consécutif. Il se distingue du sommaire normal qui résume une série d'actions ou d'événements avant de passer à la scène ou l'épisode suivant, tout comme des "sommaires" qui peuvent conclure une narration. Il ne faut pas non plus le confondre avec la "reprise" qui signale la fin d'une digression ou d'une interpolation[2] Notre "sommaire proleptique" correspond, en gros, aux titres et sous-titres de nos œuvres modernes.

Retrouve-t-on ce précédé ailleurs? Dans quels genres de récits? Pour quelles raisons certains récits adoptent-ils cette stratégie? Cette étude tentera de répondre à ces questions.

1. *Formules contenant le verbe ʿśh*

Les formules *wayyaʿaś(ü) kēn* ou *wayyaʿaś(ü) ka'ašer* . . . remplacent souvent le récit de l'exécution d'un ordre qui vient d'être donné (Gn. vi 22, vii 5, xlii 25, xliv 2; Ex. xvii 6b, 10, xl 16; Lv. viii 36, xvi 34 . . .).[3]

---

[1] *Genesis* (Göttingen, ³1910), p. 193; cf. p. 236.
[2] C. Kuhl, "Die "Wiederaufnahme"—ein literarkritisches Prinzip?", *ZAW* 64 (1962), pp. 1–11; et, plus récemment, M. Anbar, "La reprise", *VT* 38 (1988), pp. 385–98.
[3] Sur la formule d'exécution (*Ausführungsformel*), voir H. Ringgren, *TWAT* VI, col. 421–2.

Dans tous ces cas, la formule d'exécution équivaut au "sommaire" bien connu des critiques littéraires.[4]

Dans d'autres cas, cependant, la formule est suivie d'un récit qui décrit avec plus ou moins d'ampleur ce que celle-ci vient de résumer en quelques mots. Dans tous ces textes, la formule fait charnière entre le discours qui contient un ordre, une promesse ou une annonce, et le récit qui en décrit l'exécution ou l'accomplissement.[5] Bien que le premier verbe de la section narrative qui suit le verbe *wayya'aś(û)* soit un verbe narratif (*wayyiqṭōl*), il n'y a donc pas succession au sens strict.[6] Pour ne citer qu'un exemple, en Ez. xii 1–6, Dieu donne au prophète Ézéchiel l'ordre de mimer la déportation des exilés. Au *v.* 7a apparaît la formule *wā'a'aś kēn ka'ăšer ṣuwwêtî* ("et j'agis comme j'en avais reçu l'ordre"); suit un court récit de l'exécution de cet ordre (*v.* 7b).

Pourquoi ajouter un récit alors que la formule d'exécution suffit dans bien des circonstances? En général, la présence d'un récit souligne une relation particulière entre le dire et le faire, entre le discours et les événements ou les actions. Ainsi, le récit des plaies d'Égypte signale à deux reprises la conformité entre les paroles de Moïse et l'action divine par la tournure: *wayya'aś yhwh kid^ebar mōšeh* (Ex. viii 9, 27). YHWH agit selon la parole de son envoyé alors qu'on attendrait l'inverse. La même observation étonnante réapparaît à deux autres endroits avec des formules similaires. YHWH annonce à Moïse la plaie de la vermine (Ex. viii 16–19), puis il agit comme il l'avait dit (*wayya'aś yhwh kēn*, *v.* 20a). Un bref récit développe ce sommaire (*v.* 20b). Le même schéma se retrouve en Ex. ix 1–6 (la peste du bétail), avec le syntagme *wayya'aś yhwh 'et-haddābār hazzeh* (*v.* 6aα) entre l'annonce (*vv.* 1–6) et la narration (*v.* 6aββ). Le caractère juridique et

---

[4] Pour la terminologie, voir entre autres G. Genette, *Figures III* (Paris, 1972), p. 129. Le "sommaire" se distingue de la "scène" par son rapport au temps. Dans un "sommaire", le "temps racontant" (temps nécesaire pour raconter les événements) est beaucoup plus court que le "temps raconté" (la durée supposée des événements racontés). Dans une "scène", au contraire, temps racontant et temps raconté sont presque égaux, surtout dans les dialogues.

[5] Principaux exemples: Gn. xxi 1, xxix 28, xlii 20, xlv 21, l 12; Ex. vii 6, 10, viii 9, 13, 20, 27, ix 6, xvi 17, xviii 24, xxxii 28, Lv. viii 4; Nb. ii 34, viii 3, xxiii 2; Jos. iv 8; ix 26, x 23, xi 9; Jg. xxi 23; 1 Sam. vi 10, xvi 4; 2 Sam. v 25; 1 R. xvii 5, xxi 11; 2 R. viii 2, xi 9; Isa. xx 2; Jr. xxxvi 8, 9–13; Ez. xii 7; Esd. x 16.

[6] S.R. Driver, *A Treatise on the Use of the Tenses in Hebrew* (Oxford, ³1892), pp. 81–2 (§ 75); voir aussi P. Joüon-T. Muraoka, § 118 ij.

prophétique de ces récits explique cette insistance sur le rapport étroit qui unit parole et événement.[7]

Dans d'autres cas, le texte met en évidence l'exécution fidèle d'un ordre, comme pour Élie (1 R. xvii 5; cf. *v.* 24) ou Ézéchiel (Ez. xii 7, voir *supra*). En général, le récit mentionne l'exécution parce que cette dernière comporte quelque difficulté, par exemple lorsque Samuel doit chercher un successeur à Saül (1 Sam. xvi 4–13), que la Shunammite doit s'exiler au pays des Philistins (2 R. viii 2) ou que les juges doivent régler la question délicate des mariages mixtes selon les normes édictées par Esdras (Esd. x 16–17).

Pour certains récits, c'est le caractère exceptionnel de l'événement qui explique la présence d'un sommaire suivi d'une narration. La naissance d'Isaac en est un bon exemple (Gn. xxi 1–2); l'invraisemblance de la promesse divine justifie la narration de son accomplissement. Dans le récit de la vigne de Nabot, le récit décrit l'exécution du plan de Jézabel pour souligner que l'implacable reine est arrivée à ses fins (1 R. xxi 11–13). Dans le cas de Jacob, en Gn. xxix 28–30, le narrateur montre que le héros s'exécute à son plus grand dam après avoir été trompé. Dans celui de Jos. ix 26–7, l'honnêteté de Josué contraste avec la ruse des Gabaonites. Nous rangeons aussi dans cette catégorie le récit de l'enlèvement des filles de Silo par les Benjaminites (Jg. xxi 23) ou celui du transport de l'arche depuis la Philistie jusqu'à Beth Shemesh (1 Sam. vi 10).[8]

Dans le même ordre d'idée, l'exécution de certains ordres mérite une attention particulière parce qu'elle a valeur fondatrice. Elle coïncide avec le début d'une institution juridique (Ex. xviii 24–5) ou cultuelle (Lv. viii 4; Nb. viii 3), ou l'institution d'un ordre social (Jos. ix 26–7). Nb. ii 34 signale la première fois que les tribus ont adopté l'ordre de marche dans le désert tel qu'il a été expliqué par YHWH à Moïse. Ex. xxxii 27, 28–9 appartient au même type de textes. En fait, les *vv.* 28–9 ne décrivent pas l'exécution de l'ordre du *v.* 27, mais le résultat de cette exécution (*v.* 28b) et ses conséquences pour les lévites (*v.* 29). C'est ce dernier point que le récit veut mettre en évidence.[9]

---

[7] D.J. McCarthy, "Moses' Dealings with Pharaoh: Ex 7, 8–10, 27", *CBQ* (1965), pp. 336–47 = *Institution and Narrative* (Rome, 1985), pp. 115–26.

[8] Autres exemples du même type: 2 R. viii 2a (sommaire) et viii 2b (exécution); xviii 3 (sommaire) et 4–8 (détails); Jr. xxxvi 8 (cf. *v.* 10).

[9] Voir E. Blum, *Studien zur Komposition des Pentateuch* (BZAW 189; Berlin–New York, 1990), p. 56.

Ces observations confirment l'opinion selon laquelle l'expression *way^ehî kēn* de Gn. i 7, 9, 11, 15, 24, 30 n'est pas nécessairement le signe de la présence de deux sources (un *Wortbericht* et un *Tatbericht*).[10] Elle est dans quelques cas accompagnée d'une expression proche de la formule d'exécution (*vv.* 7a, 16a, 25a avec le verbe *ʿśh*) ou suivie d'un récit d'exécution (*v.* 12, 16–18, 25). Dans ces trois derniers cas, elle joue le rôle de résumé proleptique. Il en va de même dans le récit de Jg. vi 37–8 et 39–40. La première fois, le récit utilise l'expression *way^ehî kēn* comme charnière et résumé proleptique (*v.* 38a); la seconde fois, on trouve la formule d'exécution (*v.* 40a). Les deux formules ont la même fonction. 2 R. vii 17–20 présente un cas similaire (voir v. 20a).[11]

Ces exemples ne comportent guère de difficultés. Leur analyse a cependant permis de se familiariser avec le procédé avant d'affronter des textes plus élaborés.

2. *L'usage d'un terme clé*[12]

Souvent le sommaire contient un mot clé qui sera répété par la suite. Ex. ii 15 fournit un premier exemple de cette technique. La fin du verset décrit l'arrivée de Moïse au pays de Madian de la façon suivante: *wayyibraḥ mōšeh mipp^enê par^ʿōh wayyēšeb b^{eʾ}ereṣ-midyān wayyēšeb ʿal-habb^{eʾ}ēr*-"Moïse s'enfuit de chez Pharaon et il s'établit dans la terre de Madian et il s'assit auprès du puits". Le verbe *wayyēšeb* n'a pas la même signification dans les deux dernières propositions de ce verset et cette construction a depuis longtemps fait problème. Wellhausen pensait que les deux *wayyēšeb* appartenaient à deux récits différents qu'il attribuait cependant à J.[13] A première vue, le récit des déboires de Moïse en Égypte (ii 11–15) pourrait se conclure par la phrase *wayyēšeb b^{eʾ}ereṣ midyān* et le récit de la rencontre auprès du puits (ii 15–23) commencer par *wayyēšeb ʿal-habb^{eʾ}ēr*. Cependant, cette première impression se heurte vite à de fortes objections.

---

[10] Opinion de W.H. Schmidt, *Die Schöpfungsgeschichte der Priesterschrift. Zur Überlieferungsgeschichte von Genesis 1, 1–2,4a und 2,4b–3,24* (Neukirchen-Vluyn, ²1967).

[11] Ceci va dans le sens de la thèse de O.H. Steck, *Der Schöpfungsbericht der Priesterschrift* (Göttingen, ²1981).

[12] E. Zenger, *Die Sinaitheophanie. Untersuchungen zum jahwistischen und elohistischen Geschichtswerk* (Würzburg, 1971), pp. 55–6, signale quelques autres exemples: Gn. ii 8, vii 11, xxxvii 5; Ex. xix 1; Lv. xvii 5.

[13] J. Wellhausen, *Die Composition des Hexauteuchs und der historischen Bücher des Alten Testaments* (Berlin, ³1899), p. 69. Le syriaque et la LXX ont un texte plus coulant.

En premier lieu, le procédé de la répétition de deux verbes identiques ou de même racine à très courte distance est un trait caractéristique de cette page de l'exode.[14] Ensuite, la scène de la rencontre auprès du puits requiert une indication de lieu dans son introduction et celle-ci accompagne le premier *wayyēšeb*.[15] Enfin, cette scène de la rencontre auprès du puits suit un schéma bien connu dont le premier membre décrit le voyage d'un homme à l'étranger, ce qui est le contenu de la première partie du *v.* 15.[16] Pour ces raisons, il convient d'interpréter le *v.* 15 et spécialement le syntagme *wayyēšeb bᵉʾereṣ midyān* comme une phrase à double fonction. Elle termine le récit des premières initiatives de Moïse adulte et elle introduit le récit de la rencontre auprès du puits dont elle est le "sommaire proleptique".[17] Ce fait est confirmé par la répétition du verbe clé *yšb* au *v.* 21 (Schmidt [n. 14], p. 83).

Ainsi, dans la composition actuelle de Ex. ii, le récit de la rencontre auprès du puits ne peut être séparé de l'épisode qui précède, même s'il suit un schéma propre et s'il a pu exister sous forme indépendante.

Dans certains cas, le procédé est rédactionnel. Ex. xl 17, par exemple, résume en une phrase la construction de la demeure et se conclut par ces mots: *hûqam hammiškān* ("la demeure fut dressée"). Suit une description détaillée de toute l'opération (*vv.* 18–33).[18] Celle-ci est en général considérée comme rédactionnelle parce qu'elle reprend des éléments épars de Ex. xxv–xxx.[19] Elle se raccroche au *v.* 17 par le biais du verbe *qûm* utilisé aux *v.* 18 (2x) et 38 sous la forme *wayyāqem*

---

[14] B.S. Childs, *Exodus. A Commentary* (London–Philadelphia, 1974), p. 29; W.H. Schmidt, *Exodus* (Neukirchen-Vluyn, 1988), p. 83. Par exemple, *wayyigdal*, *vv.* 10 et 11; *wayyarʾ*, *vv.* 11 (2x) et 12; *makkeh, wayyak, takkeh*, *vv.* 11, 12 et 13: *wayyēṣēʾ*, *vv.* 11 et 13; *halᵉhorgēnî, hāragtā, lahărōg*, *vv.* 14 et 15. Voir surtout la transition entre Ex. ii 10–15 (*wayyigdal*).

[15] Schmidt (n. 14), p. 83; cf. *v.* 16: *kōhēn midyān*. Cet auteur se refuse à voir différentes sources dans cette fin du *v.* 15.

[16] Autres textes: Gn. xxiv; xxix 1–14; cf. 1 R. xvii 10. Voir R. Alter, *The Art of Biblical Narrative* (New York, 1981), p. 52; R.C. Culley, *Studies in the Structure of Hebrew Narrative* (Philadelphia—Missoula, 1976), p. 42.

[17] Cette fonction du premier *wayyēšeb* a été reconnue par M. Greenberg, *Understanding Exodus* (New York, 1969), p. 46 (autres exemples: Gn. xxxvii 21, xlii 20); Schmidt (n. 14), p. 83, pour qui la fin du *v.* 15 sert de transition (*Überleitung*) ou de sous-titre (*Überschrift*).

[18] Exemple cité par Driver; voir n. 6.

[19] B. Baentsch, *Exodus-Leviticus-Numeri* (Göttingen, 1903), p. 304, attribuait les *vv.* 16 et 18–33 à Ps et le *v.* 17 à P. M. Noth est du même avis; voir *Das zweite Buch des Mose. Exodus* (Göttingen, ²1961), p. 227. La plupart des exégètes sont de la même opinion.

dans les trois cas. Dans le texte actuel, le *v.* 17 introduit par conséquent de façon proleptique la section qui suit immédiatement.

1 Sam. x 9b affirme que tous les signes annoncés par Samuel à
Saül se sont accomplis. Le récit suivant, toutefois, décrit la rencontre
de Saül avec les prophètes de Guivéa (*vv.* 10–12), le troisième des
signes annoncés (*vv.* 5–6).[20] Certains auteurs estiment que le texte a
été retravaillé et que l'anecdote des *vv.* 10–12 a été insérée après
coup.[21] En effet, elle ne décrit que l'un des trois signes annoncés par
Samuel et ce signe est plutôt négatif, contrairement à ce que pré-
voyaient les *vv.* 5–6. Le sommaire final (*v.* 9b) est devenu par cette
opération un sommaire proleptique, au moins en partie.

3. *Les récits de théophanie*

Dans son commentaire sur la Genèse ([n. 1] p. 193), Gunkel observe
que Gn. xviii 1a est un titre, comme nous l'avons dit plus haut. Il
ajoute cependant de suite que ce demi-verset ne faisait pas partie du
récit (*Sage*) primitif qui commence avec le *v.* 1b. Quelques exégètes
l'ont suivi.[22] Faut-il leur emboîter le pas?

En réalité, ils tirent argument de la nature de Gn. xviii 1a. Ce
verset contient une réflexion d'ordre théologique, ce qui serait le propre
d'une époque tardive. Les récits anciens, au contraire, sont plus spon-
tanés et ne se préoccupent pas de l'effet qu'ils peuvent produire. Le
verset doit donc être plus récent que le reste du chapitre.

Cependant, il est curieux de constater que quatre récits bibliques
de théophanie commencent de manière très semblable (Gn. xviii 1a;
Ex. iii 2a; Jg. vi 12, xiii 3).[23] Chaque texte débute par la même

---

[20] Exemple cité par Driver; voir n. 6.

[21] W. Richter, *Die sogenannten Berufungsberichte. Eine literaturwissenschaftliche Studie zu 1 Sam 9, 1–10, 16, Ex 3f. und Ri 6, 11b–17* (Göttingen, 1970), pp. 21–2; L. Schmidt, *Menschlicher Erfolg und Jahwes Initiative. Studien zur Tradition, Interpretation und Historie von Gideon, Saul und David* (Neukirchen-Vluyn, 1970), pp. 66–7; P.K. McCarter, *1 Samuel* (Garden City, 1980), p. 183.

[22] R. Kilian, *Die vorpriesterlichen Abrahamsüberlieferungen literarkritisch und traditionsgeschichtlich untersucht* (BBB 24; Bonn, 1966), pp. 25–6 et 96–7; C. Westermann, *Genesis 12–36* (Neukirchen-Vluyn, 1981), pp. 335–6. J. Van Seters, *Abraham in History and Tradition* (London-New Haven, Conn., 1975), pp. 202–8, considère que le chapitre a amal-gamé deux récits, celui de l'annonce de la naissance d'Isaac (*vv.* 1a, 10–14) et celui de l'hospitalité donnée à des dieux (*vv.* 1b–9). Voir aussi la contribution de J. Loza dans ce même volume.

[23] Pour Ex. iii 2a, voir Childs (n. 14), p. 49, qui considère ce demi-verset comme une "superscription" analogue à Gn. xviii 1. Le *v.* 2b décrit la "chronological sequence".

forme du verbe *r'h* au *nif'al (wayyērā')*. Le sujet est *yhwh* en Gn. xviii 1 et *mal'ak yhwh* dans les trois autres. Le destinataire de l'apparition est introduit par la préposition *'el*. La construction de Gn. xviii la se retrouve exactement en Jg. vi 12a: *wayyērā' 'ēlāyw (mal'ak) yhwh*. L'ordre des mots diffère légèrement en Ex. iii 2a: *wayyērā' mal'ak yhwh 'ēlāyw*. Jg. xiii 3 mentionne explicitement que l'ange apparaît à la femme de Manoah et non à son mari, comme on pourrait s'y attendre *(wayyērā' mal'ak yhwh 'el-hā'iššâ)*.[24] En outre les quatre récits mentionnent le lieu de l'apparition. Gn. xviii la et Ex. iii 2a le précisent au moyen de la préposition *b*ᵉ: *b*ᵉ*ēlōnê mamrē'* (Gn. xviii 1a); *b*ᵉ*labbat-'ēš mittôk hass*ᵉ*nēh* (Ex. iii 2a). En Jg. vi 12 et xiii 3, cette précision est superflue puisque le verset précédent contient une indication de lieu, le chêne d'Ophra (vi 11) ou Çoréa (xiii 2).

Chacun de ces récits reprend ensuite le verbe *r'h* sous différentes formes. Gn. xviii 2a et Ex. iii 2b utilisent une construction presque identique qui introduit un changement de "perspective".[25] Dans le sommaire proleptique de Gn. xviii 1a et Ex. iii 2a, le narrateur s'était adressé à son lecteur en usant de sa perspective de narrateur omniscient. Ensuite, ce narrateur adopte le "point de vue" du personnage, Abraham ou Moïse, qui ne sait pas (encore) qui lui apparaît. La particule *w*ᵉ*hinnēh* signale ce changement (Gn. xviii 1a: *wayyiśśā' 'ênāyw wayyar' w*ᵉ*hinnēh* . . .; Ex. iii 2a: *wayyar' w*ᵉ*hinnēh* . . .).[26] Le verbe *r'h* revient deux fois en Gn. xviii 2. Ex. iii 2–4 contient six emplois de la racine *r'h* en trois versets.[27]

Les deux récits des Juges se terminent par une scène de reconnaissance qui utilise le verbe *r'h* (Jg. vi 22[2x], xiii 20–3[4x]). Jg. vi 11–24 est, de l'avis de la majorité des exégètes, une composition rédactionnelle.[28] Il est raisonnable de penser que le rédacteur a donc

---

[24] Pour la répétition du nom d'un acteur au début d'une scène, voir R.E. Longacre, *Joseph. A Story of Divine Providence* (Winona Lake, 1989), pp. 141–7 ("Participant Reference").

[25] Terminologie de Genette, *Figures III*, pp. 184 et 203. Pour plus de détails à ce propos voir J.L. Ska, *"Our Fathers Have Told us". Introduction to the Analysis of Hebrew Narratives* (Rome, 1990), pp. 65–82.

[26] Fait constaté pour la première fois par J.P. Fokkelman, *Narrative Art in Genesis. Specimens of Stylistic and Structural Analysis* (Assen–Amsterdam, 1975), p. 54. Voir Ska (n. 25), p. 68. La particule *w*ᵉ*hinnēh* introduit un "discours indirect libre" (*erlebte Rede*); sur ce point, voir M. Weiss, "Einiges über die Bauformen des Erzählens in der Bibel", *VT* 13 (1963), pp. 456–75.

[27] Childs (n. 14), p. 70; G. Fischer, *Jahwe, unser Gott. Sprache, Aufbau und Erzähltechnik in der Berufung des Mose (Ex 3–4)* (Göttingen–Freiburg Schweiz, 1989), pp. 69–72.

[28] Voir U. Becker, *Richterzeit und Königtum. Redaktionsgeschichtliche Studien zum Richterbuch*

consciemment créé un "récit de reconnaissance" en insérant le "sommaire proleptique" du v. 12a en fonction des *vv.* 21–4 présents dans sa *Vorlage*. Sinon, pourquoi avoir ajouté une seconde introduction après le *v.* 11a? L'explication la plus simple est qu'il a voulu se conformer à un modèle connu en retravaillant le récit que lui avait légué la tradition.

Le récit de Jg. xiii est plus unifié. Il a amalgamé plusieurs motifs, entre autres le schéma d'un récit d'annonce de naissance avec celui d'une théophanie qui culmine dans un acte de reconnaissance.[29] Même les essais les plus récents considèrent que les *vv.* 3 et 20–4 font partie d'une même source.[30] Or, la racine *r'h* y réapparaît cinq fois (sept en comptant le *v.* 6). Une fois encore, le "résumé proleptique" introduit un des thèmes centraux du récit et l'un des mots clés de son tissu linguistique.

Ce premier parcours a permis de mieux cerner une des techniques du résumé proleptique. Le récit commence par un verbe au *wayyiqṭōl* dont la racine est reprise plus d'une fois au cours du récit soit au début (Gn. xviii et Ex. iii), soit à la fin (Jg. vi et xiii). Dans ces récits de théophanies, la racine *r'h* introduit le thème de la "reconnaissance" qui est traité ensuite de façon particulière dans chaque récit.

Il est à présent possible de revenir au problème de Gn. xviii 1a. Au vu des analyses précédentes, il ne semble pas opportun d'attribuer ce "titre" à un interpolateur. Les similitudes entre Gn. xviii 1–2 et Ex. iii 2–4 sont trop nombreuses pour qu'on traite les deux textes de façon différente. A cela s'ajoute que la formule *wayyērā' yhwh/'ĕlōhîm/mal'ak yhwh/'elōhîm/kᵉbôd yhwh* est la façon habituelle d'introduire un récit d'apparition.[31] En particulier, l'introduction de Gn. xviii 1a est semblable à celle d'un autre récit d'annonce de naissance, Jg. xiii 3. Enfin, à notre connaissance, aucun récit ne commence par un participe suivi de la formule *wayyiśśā' 'et-ʿênāyw wayyar' wᵉhinnēh*,[32]

(Berlin–New York, 1990), pp. 145–51. Le récit de vocation (*vv.* 11b–17) a été inséré dans un récit plus ancien (*vv.* 11a, 18–19, 21–4) qui décrivait la fondation d'un sanctuaire (récit étiologique).

[29] W. Richter, *Traditionsgeschichtliche Untersuchungen zum Richterbuch* (Bonn, 1963), pp. 140–4.

[30] Par exemple, K.F.D. Römheld, "Von den Quellen der Kraft (Jdc 13)", *ZAW* 104 (1992), pp. 28–52; pour ce dernier, le texte primitif comportait les *vv.* 2–4, 5aγ, 6–8*, 10–11a, 13–14a, 15–19a, 20–4.

[31] Gn. xii 7, xvii 1, xxvi 2, 24, xxxv 9; Ex. iii 2; Nb. xvi 19, xvii 7, xx 6; Jg. vi 12, xiii 2 . . . Pour plus de détails, voir H.F. Fuhs, "*rā'āh*", *TWAT* VIII, col. 258–60.

[32] Pour une liste de textes où figurent cette expression, voir C. Conroy, *Absalom,*

ce qui serait le cas si Gn. xviii 1a était une interpolation. Quant à dire que les récits anciens évitent les réflexions d'ordre théologique, c'est un présupposé difficile à démontrer.

4. Les livres de Jonas et de Ruth

Jonas iii 5

Ce verset peut aussi s'interpréter comme un sommaire proleptique.[33] Certains rejettent cette idée et pensent au contraire que le *v.* 5 dépeint la première réponse des Ninivites, réponse individuelle et spontanée. Ensuite, lorsque la nouvelle a atteint le palais royal, arrive la réponse officielle des autorités qui étendent le jeûne également aux animaux.[34]

Est-il possible choisir? La seconde hypothèse nous paraît forcer quelque peu le sens du texte. Elle ne va pas non plus sans quelques difficultés. Pour quelle raison le roi fait-il proclamer par décret un jeûne alors que toute la population "des plus grands jusqu'aux plus petits" (*v.* 5b) l'avait déjà spontanément commencé? Si le décret royal a pour premier but d'inclure les animaux dans les rites pénitentiels, cela ne ressort en aucune façon du texte de Jon. iii 7. Ou bien le jeûne du *v.* 5 fait double emploi avec celui du *v.* 7, ou bien il faut comprendre le v. 5 comme une prolepse. Or, le *v.* 5, en parlant des "grands" et des "petits", laisse entendre que la maison royale fait partie de ces Ninivites qui ont immédiatement cru à la parole du prophète. L'expression "du plus grand au plus petit" est en effet un mérisme qui désigne la totalité des habitants et qui inclut donc le roi et sa cour.[35] De ce fait, il faut admettre que le récit raconte deux fois la conversion des Ninivites, une fois de façon synthétique (*v.* 5), et une seconde, en donnant le détail de tout le processus (*vv.* 6–10).

Absalom! Narrative and Language in 2 Sam 13-20 (Rome, 1978), p. 71, n. 110; H.-W. Jüngling, *Richter 19–Ein Plädoyer für das Königtum. Stilistische Analyse der Tendenzerzäh-lung Ri 19, 1–30a; 21, 25* (Rome, 1981), pp. 177-8, n. 574; voir aussi pp. 183–4 et n. 583.

[33] H.W. Wolff, *Dodekapropheton 3. Obadja und Jona* (Neukirchen-Vluyn, 1977), pp. 120, 124, 136; N. Lohfink, "Jona ging zur Stadt hinaus (Jon 4, 5)", *BZ NF* 5 (1961), pp. 185–203, p. 197, n. 39, reste indécis.

[34] Voir T.T. Perowne, *Obadiah and Jonah* (Cambridge, 1883, 1905), pp. 77–78, et surtout J.M. Sasson, *Jonah. A New Translation with Introduction, Commentary, and Interpretation* (New York, 1990), p. 247.

[35] Sur cette expression, voir J. Krašovec, *Der Merismus im Biblisch-Hebräischen und Nordwestsemitischen* (Rome, 1977), p. 57. Principaux parallèles: Jr. xvi 6; Est. i 5, 20; 2 Ch. xxxi 15, xxxiv 30. On pourrait objecter que Est. i 5, 20 n'inclut pas le roi dans

Ce procédé n'est pas rare dans le livre de Jonas. À plusieurs reprises, le narrateur décrit la réaction immédiate des acteurs avant d'expliciter leur démarche. C'est le cas des marins en Jon. i 5, 10, 16,
des Ninivites dans le texte qui vient d'être étudié, de Jonas lui-même
en Jon. iv 1, et de Dieu en iv 4.[36] Jon. iii 5 n'est donc pas isolé et
le but de ce sommaire saute aux yeux: le narrateur insiste sur la
rapidité de la conversion dans le cas des marins comme dans celui
des Ninivites pour faire ressortir, par contraste, la lenteur de Jonas.

Ruth i 6, ii 3, iii 6

Le livre de Ruth utilise trois fois le procédé du "sommaire proleptique".
Dans les deux premiers cas, le sommaire emploie le terme clé de la
scène qu'il introduit, le verbe *šûb* ("retourner") en i 6 et le verbe *lqt*
("glaner") en ii 3.[37] Dans les deux cas, ce verbe est répété douze fois
dans le chapitre en question.[38]

En i 6 comme en ii 3, le verbe du sommaire ne peut exprimer la
succession. Le retour n'est pas raconté en i 6, mais il est l'objet de
tout le chapitre. Au ch. ii, il paraît moins facile d'identifier le résumé
proleptique du *v.* 3. Quelques bonnes raisons militent cependant en
faveur de cette opinion. La glane occupe tout le chapitre et ne se
limite certainement pas à ce verset. D'autre part, Ruth n'a glané
que dans le champ de Booz, comme il ressort de sa conversation
avec Noémi au *v.* 19. Or, Ruth n'est arrivée dans ce champ qu'au
v. 3b. Pour certains commentateurs, il faut même aller jusqu'au *v.* 15
pour que Ruth puisse commencer à glaner, après en avoir reçu
l'autorisation de Booz.[39] En effet, d'après le *v.* 7, Ruth a demandé

---

la totalité des citoyens décrite par le mérisme "du plus petit au plus grand". Mais
la difficulté n'est qu'apparente. Le texte parle d'un décret du roi pour tous les habitants
de l'empire. Le roi occupe dans ce récit la place de Jonas en Jon. iii 5; le mérisme
désigne dans le cas de Est. i 5.20 tous les citoyens de l'empire perse et dans celui
de Jon. iii 5 tous les Ninivites sans exception, donc aussi le roi.

[36] Wolff (n. 33), p. 124, et Lohfink, "Jona", article cité n. 33.

[37] Fait constaté par R.L. Hubbard, *The Book of Ruth* (Grand Rapids, 1988), pp. 99
et 140 ("summary-introduction"); E.F. Campbell, *Ruth* (Garden City, 1975), p. 92:
"a sort of summation of the action", as in i 6: "Here is what this episode is about
and here is how it happened". P. Joüon, *Ruth. Commentaire philologique et exégétique*
(Rome, ²1986), pp. 35–6, considère que le *v.* 7 est redondant.

[38] H.W. Hertzberg, *Die Bücher Josua, Richter, Ruth* (Göttingen, ²1959), p. 265;
W. Dommershausen, "Leitwortstil in der Ruthrolle", *Theologie im Wandel* (München-
Freiburg i.Br., 1967), pp. 394–408, sp. pp. 395–6 et 398–9; E. Zenger, *Das Buch
Ruth* (Zürich, 1986), p. 18.

[39] J.M. Sasson, *Ruth. A New Translation with a Philological Commentary and a Formalist-*

au chef des moissonneurs la permission de glaner. Mais le texte ne dit rien de la réponse de celui-ci. Le reste du verset est difficile à traduire et il est malaisé d'en tirer un argument solide.[40] Mais le *v.* 15 débute par une expression qui ne suggère pas que Ruth ait continué à glaner; elle décrit plutôt le début d'une action: *wattāqom l^elaqqēṭ*.[41] Quoi qu'il en soit, il n'y a pas succession entre les verbes *watt^elaqqēṭ* et *wayyiqer* du *v.* 3, et cela suffit pour que le premier soit proleptique.

Le sommaire du ch. iii est différent sous deux aspects. En premier lieu, il s'agit d'une simple formule d'exécution identique à celles analysées au début cette étude. En second lieu, Ruth ne suit pas les conseils de Noémi, contrairement à ce qu'elle promet au *v.* 5 et à ce que la narrateur affirme au *v.* 6.[42] En l'occurrence, elle n'attend pas que Booz lui dicte sa conduite, elle prend elle-même l'initiative (*v.* 9). Dans sa première réponse à Booz, Ruth prononce un mot lourd de sens dans tout le récit, *gō'ēl* ("rédempteur"). C'est d'ailleurs ce mot qui fournit la clé du dénouement final. Ce mot, contrairement aux autres, n'est pas employé douze fois dans le chapitre, mais sept.[43] Dans tout le livre, il apparaît vingt-quatre fois.

Le résumé réserve donc une surprise au lecteur qui se voit confronté à un élément imprévu. Pourquoi le récit procède-t-il de la sorte? La réponse se trouve en partie dans le *v.* 9b.

En réalité, Ruth propose à Booz de l'épouser et elle en donne la raison: "car tu es un *gō'ēl*", *kî gō'ēl 'āttâ*.[44] Le résumé proleptique de Rt. iii 6 a donc mis le lecteur sur une fausse piste. Il s'attendait à

Folklorist Interpretation (Baltimore–London, 1979; Sheffield, ²1989), p. 44: "Ruth did not begin gleaning until the end of her interview with Boaz". Voir aussi pp. 44, 48, 50, 56. Même explication chez Campbell (n. 37), p. 96, et Hubbard (n. 37), pp. 148–50.

[40] Voir D. Barthélemy, *Critique textuelle de l'Ancien Testament* 1: *Josué, Juges, Juges, Ruth* . . . (Fribourg/Suisse Göttingen, 1982), pp. 132–3, et les commentaires.

[41] J. Gamberoni, "*qûm*", *TWAT* VI, col. 1257–8.

[42] Campbell (n. 37), p. 121; Hubbard (n. 37), pp. 206 et 212.

[43] Dommershausen (n. 38), p. 405.

[44] Sasson (n. 39), pp. 80–2, propose de lire le *kî* comme un *kî* affirmatif ("indeed"; Joüon-Muraoka § 164 f.). Ceci dépend en grande partie de son exégèse de Ruth qui sépare totalement le mariage de la "rédemption". Cette dernière ne joue que dans le cas du rachat du champ de Noémi (Rt. iv 3). Pour une critique, voir Hubbard (n. 37), pp. 212–13, n. 36. A notre avis, les *vv.* 10–13 ne vont pas dans le sens de l'interprétation de Sasson. Nulle part il n'y est question de champ ou de propriété à racheter; c'est bien Ruth qui doit être "rachetée", selon les suffixes du *v.* 13 (*yig'ālēk, l^ego'ŏlēk ûg^e'altîk*).

voir une Ruth soumise à sa belle-mère et il admirera d'autant plus l'audace d'une initiative qui se révélera décisive.[45]

Conclusion. Ces quelques exemples ont montré à suffisance que le phénomène du sommaire proleptique est assez répandu dans les récits bibliques. Certains particularités stylistiques, l'emploi de mots clés et les anomalies dans l'emploi du *wayyiqtol* sont les principaux signes qui permettent de déceler sa présence.[46]

---

[45] A propos du mariage de Ruth, les commentaires répètent à l'envi qu'il n'existe aucun parallèle biblique où le rédempteur doive également assumer les responsabilités du *levir*. Les lois sont distinctes; celle du lévirat se trouve en Dt. xxv 5–10 et celles sur la rédemption principalement en Lv. xxv, et il n'y a aucun contact entre elles. Cependant, un texte poétique peut éclairer Rt. iii 9. Il s'agit d'Isa, xliv 1–8. Dans les deux textes, il est question d'une veuve sans enfants qui est épousée par un *gōʾēl*, Dieu en Is. xliv 5, 8, Booz dans le livre de Ruth. On peut en conclure qu'à l'époque du second Isaïe, il était possible de lier les devoirs du *gōʾēl* avec celui de *levir*. Le livre de Ruth pourrait présenter une sorte de parabole offrant à la communauté postexilique les moyens juridiques et religieux de résoudre certains problèmes posés par la présence en son sein d'étrangers et surtout de femmes étrangères (Esdras et Néhémie, Dt. xxiii 4). Voir aussi A. Lemaire, "Une inscription phénicienne découverte récemment en Cilicie et le mariage de Ruth la Moabite", *EI* 20 (1989), pp. 124*–9*.

[46] Le procédé n'est nullement limité aux narrations bibliques. Il se retrouve dans les listes (*ʾēlleh tōlᵉdōt*, *ʾēlleh šᵉmôt*...), dans le textes juridiques (Ex. xxi 1, xxv 1, 4; Lv. xxiii 1; Dt. iv 44–5, xii 1, xxviii 69...) et prophétiques (Isa. i 1, ii 1, vi 1; Jr. i 1; Os. i 2a; Abd. i 1a; Mi. i 1...); il est proche de la cinquième règle de Hillel, *kᵉlāl ûpᵉrāt* ("le général et le singulier").

HISTOIRE DU TEXTE DES LIVRES HISTORIQUES ET HISTOIRE DE LA COMPOSITION ET DE LA RÉDACTION DEUTÉRONOMISTES AVEC UNE PUBLICATION PRÉLIMINAIRE DE 4Q481A, "APOCRYPHE D'ÉLISÉE"

par

JULIO TREBOLLE
Madrid

Cette conférence cherche à développer une ligne de travail suivie dans des publications précédentes et en particulier dans un article de 1986, qui commençait avec les affirmations suivantes:

> L'étude des manuscrits bibliques de la mer Morte, en particulier de 4QSam[b], a révélé la *pluralité des formes textuelles* dans lesquelles se transmettait le texte des Livres historiques à l'époque perse et hellénistique. La critique littéraire historique (Literarkritik) détecte aussi une *pluralité de rédactions* deutéronomistes dans ces mêmes livres.
>
> Cet article veut montrer que la pluralité des formes textuelles et la pluralité des rédactions sont des phénomènes à mettre en relation. La recherche doit partir de l'analyse de *l'histoire de la transmission du texte*, des attestations les plus récentes aux plus anciennes, pour examiner ensuite *l'histoire de la rédaction* des livres qui forment l'histoire deutéronomiste... Il est très significatif que les livres qu'a affectés la rédaction deutéronomiste (livres historiques et Jérémie), se présentent à Qoumrân et dans la Septante sous une forme textuelle "plus brève" que celle du TM. Les additions du TM correspondent parfois justement à des passages d'origine deutéronomiste. Ainsi Jug. vi 7–10 est absent du ms. 4QJug[a] et 1 Rois vii 11–14 ne se trouve pas dans l'ancienne Septante.[1]

L'omission à Qoumrân et dans la Septante de textes considérés comme deutéronomistes invitait à étudier quelle pourrait être la contribution de l'histoire du texte à l'étude de l'histoire de la rédaction deutéronomiste. Le ms. 4QJug[a], que j'ai publié entre-temps, offre en plus

---

[1] J. Trebolle Barrera, "Historia del texto de los libros históricos e historia de la redacción deuteronòmista (Jueces 2,10–3,6)", *Salvación en la Palabra, Homenaje A. Díez Macho* (Madrid, 1986), pp. 245–55. Édition préliminaire de 4QJug[a] par l'auteur dans "Textual Variants in *4QJudg[a]* and the Textual and Editorial History of the Book of Judges", *RQ* 14 (1989), pp. 229–45.

des coïncidences frappantes avec le texte antiochien et avec celui de la Vieille Latine, qui représentent en Juges, comme d'ailleurs en Samuel-Rois, le texte, ou un texte, très proche de l'ancienne Septante, laquelle à son tour traduit un texte hébraïque ancien d'un courant textuel différent de celui transmis par le TM.

La contribution de l'histoire du texte à celle de la rédaction deutéronomiste se situe au carrefour où la critique textuelle et la critique littéraire ne peuvent que se rencontrer, c'est-à-dire, aux points de suture, de reprise ou de transposition qui unissent les différentes unités de la composition des livres historiques. C'est à ces points-là que les rédacteurs, éditeurs et glossateurs ont laissé, dans la tradition manuscrite, le plus de traces de leur travail. Ces points précis offrent les meilleurs indices pour l'étude des différentes traditions textuelles connues par le TM et les LXX.

L'article de 1986 proposait l'exemple d'une reprise (*Wiederaufnahme*) ou transposition présente dans l'ancienne Septante (préservée par le texte antiochien des mss gln-dpt et de Théodoret) de Jug. ii 10 // iii 5: "Et les Israélites habitèrent au milieu des Cananéens, des Hittites, des Hivvites, des Perizzites, des Amorites, des Jébuséens et des Girgashites, ils épousèrent leurs filles et ils donnèrent leurs propres filles à leurs fils (TM + *et ils servirent leurs dieux*)." Cette reprise atteste un niveau de composition antérieur à l'insertion de tous les matériaux deutéronomistes de Jug. ii 11–iii 4. A ce premier stade de l'histoire deutéronomiste, les livres de Josué et Juges étaient à la fois délimités et liés par une reprise, un *custos*, formé par les versets de Jos. xxiv 27–31 sur la mort de Josué, répétés en Jug. ii 6–10. Après cela, le texte continuait en se référant aux peuples cananéens et passait directement à l'introduction deutéronomiste, très brève, au récit d'Éhud (Jug. iii 12–30*), comme l'indique le *custos* à la fin du Livre de Josué, LXX xxiv 33b: "les Israélites servirent (Astarté et) les dieux des peuples d'alentour et Yahvé les livra entre les mains de Églon, roi de Moab, pendant dix-huit ans."

La contribution de l'histoire du texte biblique à l'étude de la rédaction deutéronomiste est plus perceptible et aussi plus prometteuse dans l'étude de la composition—ordre et rapport entre les différentes unités littéraires—qu'en ce qui concerne la rédaction proprement dite—forme et contenu des unités deutéronomistes elles mêmes. Un demi-siècle d'études de l'histoire deutéronomiste en suivant les traces de M. Noth et la méthode et les buts de la critique de la rédaction, a laissé de côté les études d'histoire du texte et de critique de la composition qui prévalurent dans les grands commentaires des livres de Samuel par J. Wellhausen et S.R. Driver et encore des livres des Rois par J.A. Montgomery. Depuis l'époque de Noth on a cru pouvoir travailler sur un terrain textuel sûr, celui du TM, corrigé assez rarement à l'aide des versions, considérées plutôt comme des traductions targoumiques et paraphrastiques et, en conséquence, souvent délaissées.

L'examen des manuscrits bibliques de la grotte IV a donné un nouvel essor aux études de critique textuelle des livres historiques, mais leur influence sur l'exégèse actuelle est presque nulle. La critique textuelle après Qoumrân ouvre de nouvelles possibilités pour l'étude de la composition des livres, c'est-à-dire, de l'ordre, susceptible de plusieurs changements, et du rapport entre les différentes unités de composition, avec indépendance des cadres d'interprétation qui leur furent imposées, souvent postérieurement, par les rédacteurs deutéronomistes.

1. Les nouveaux manuscrits de Qoumrân "à la frontière du texte biblique": Apocryphe d'Élisée (4Q481a)

Les manuscrits bibliques de Qoumrân publiés dernièrement rapprochent l'histoire du texte et l'histoire de la formation littéraire des livres bibliques, même ceux de la Torah, beaucoup plus que ce qu'on pouvait imaginer jusqu'à ces dernières années.

L'étude des premiers manuscrits bibliques trouvés dans la grotte I confirma la fidélité de la transmission du TM, bien qu'il soit nécessaire de corriger aujourd'hui certaines lectures et interprétations des premières années des études qoumrâniennes, trop influencées par le TM. L'exégèse de l'Ancien Testament en est restée pratiquement à la première impression donnée par l'étude de ces premiers textes de Qoumrân. L'étude postérieure des manuscrits de la grotte IV, en particulier de Samuel et de Jérémie, ainsi que l'identification de la recension proto-théodotionique ou *kaige* dans ces mêmes livres et dans ceux des Juges et des Rois, livres affectés précisément par la rédaction deutéronomiste, confirmèrent la fidélité de la version grecque de la Septante à son original hébreu. Celui-ci était un texte en général plus bref que le TM, avec des variantes fréquentes et un ordre parfois différent des unités de composition. Mais les nouveaux manuscrits publiés récemment débordent absolument le cadre dans lequel se sont développés depuis toujours l'étude du texte et l'exégèse biblique, cadre délimité par le TM d'un côté et la version de la Septante de l'autre.

Ces nouveaux manuscrits se réfèrent pour la plupart aux livres de
la Torah, ce qui est d'autant plus significatif que leur texte conso-
nantique était en principe plus fermement établi que celui des autres
livres bibliques. Le ms. 4QpaleoExod^m représente une forme textuelle
"proto-samaritaine" caractérisée par l'addition çà et là d'autres passages d'Exode ou de Deutéronome. Plus surprenant est le fait que
d'autres manuscrits bibliques, comme 4QDeut^n et 4QDeut^j, présentent des ajouts empruntés à des traditions qui ne sont pas connues
par les textes canoniques, ou bien, comme 4QNum^b, remanient des
textes d'autres livres canoniques. En outre, des textes non-bibliques
déjà connus comme Le Rouleau du Temple, 4QFlor, 4QTest et
4QCatena^a, ainsi qu'une autre série de textes nouveaux, Psaumes de
Josué, Pseudo-Ezéchiel, Pseudo-Moïse et surtout 4QPP ("Paraphrase
du Pentateuque"), présentent des phénomènes semblables.[2] Il est
possible de considérer ces textes "à la frontière du texte biblique"
comme des "réécritures" de ce dernier, mais on insistera plutôt sur
le caractère biblique des ajouts qu'ils offrent.

L'ouvrage que l'on peut nommer Apocryphe d'Élisée (4Q481a),
dont je fais ici une présentation préliminaire,[3] renferme une problématique identique: les trois petits fragments conservés reproduisent
le texte de 2 Rois ii (?-) 14–16 avec d'autres passages qui ne correspondent pas à un texte biblique connu.

FRAGMENT 1

](sau)vèrent/-ont? lui là-bas?[.	שעו לו להנא[.[1
] ... [] .... [	] .... [] .. [2

FRAGMENT 2

m	א° כי [	1
a	אלי[שׁע	2
r	ו] ׳על אלישע ויראו	3
g	ע[ויבאו לקרת	4
	חמשים אנשׁים[	5
	ה[הר]ים	6

[2] Cf. les textes publiés par N. Jastram, J.A. Duncan, E. Tov et S.A. White en
J. Trebolle Barrera et L. Vegas Montaner (ed.), *The Madrid Congress. Proceedings of the
International Congress on the Dead Sea Scrolls, Madrid 18–21 March, 1991* (Leiden et Ma-
drid, 1992).

[3] Je remercie le Prof. John Strugnell qui m'a confié l'édition de ce manuscrit et
le Prof. Émile Puech pour son aide dans l'étude paléographique.

Reconstruction

כי יא[1

אלי[שע   2

ו[יעל אלישע ויראו   3

בני הנביים אשר ביריחו (אתו) מנגד ויאמרו נחה רוח אליהו על אליש[ע ויבאו לקרת   4

(אלישע) וישתחוו לו ארצה ויאמרו אליו הנה נא יש את עבדיך [המשים אנשים   5

בני חיל ילכו נא ויבקשו את אדניך פן נשאו רוח יהוה וישלכהו באחר ה[הר]ים   6

Traduction

1   ] . . car

2   Éli]sée

3   et]monta Élisée. Et virent

4 les frères prophètes qui étaient à Jéricho (*lui*) de loin et dirent: "L'esprit d'Élie s'est reposé sur Élisée!";] ils vinrent à la rencontre

5 (*d'Élisée*) et se prosternèrent à terre devant lui. 16 Ils lui dirent: "Il y a ici avec tes serviteurs] cinquante hommes

6 braves, Permets qu'ils aillent à la recherche de ton maître; peut-être l'esprit de Yahvé l'a-t-il enlevé et jeté sur quelque m]ontag[ne.."

Variantes

1.3 ויעבר TM { ו[יעל.

1.3 ויראו } TM ויראהו, MSS LXX^L Syr Amr. וא-. Le grec antiochien a plus tard la nécessaire référence pronominale: ἐξ ἐναντίας] + ἀναστρέφοντα αὐτόν.

1.4 La lecture לקרת (TM לקראתו) sans pronom suppose le nom Élisée au commencement de la ligne suivante.

FRAGMENT 3

1	]? et lui	m	ף והוא[	1
2	] en face de lui	a	לנגדו[	2
3	]? en lamentation et il dit	r	בקינה וייאמר . [	3
4	]? et seigneur et non	g	ב. ואדון ולוא.[	4
5	pré]leva en Juda		נ[שא ביהודה	5
6	] vac?		vac?[	6

Le manuscrit est écrit dans une écriture de chancellerie ou formelle asmonéenne tardive ou hérodienne ancienne des environs de 50–25

J. Trebolle, 4Q481a, ''Apocryphe d'Élisée'', Photo PAM 43.550

av.C.[4] Le texte du frg. 2, ll. 3–6 correspond à 2 Rois ii (?-)14–16. La variante de la l. 3, *w]y'l*, ainsi les mots de la l. 1, *]y' ky*, impossibles à identifier dans le contexte précédent, rendent inutile tout effort de reconstitution du texte des lignes 1–3. Ce texte ne correspondait pas, au moins partiellement, au TM connu. Le mot *qynh* du frg. 3, l. 3, fait penser à un texte de "lamentation", qui commencerait à partir du mot suivant, "et il dit" (cf. 2 Chron, xxxv 25). Étant donnée la similitude des lettres *y/w*, on peut penser aussi au mot *qwnh* et à une référence dans le domaine de la propriété, cultuelle ou autre. On ne peut deviner dans quel but le texte se réfère à "Juda" (*byhwdh*, l. 5).[5]

On doit souligner ici l'importance de la variante de la l. 3, *wyr'w* (TM *wyr'hw*), coïncidant avec celle des manuscrits hébraïques médiévaux (MSS) Kennicott 155, 225 et 240, du grec antiochien et des versions syriaque et arménienne. La coïncidence, dans les livres des Rois, de la série de témoins formée par MSS, Chron, LXX[L] (mss boc₂e₂), VL, Syr, Arm et Josèphe, tous opposés au TM, relève d'un courant textuel hébreu pré-massorétique ou non-massorétique.[6] Faute du pronom suffixe, on doit attendre l'accusatif *'tw*, selon l'expression de 2 Rois iv 25, *wyhy kr'wt 'yš h'lhym 'th mngd*.[7]

Le peu de texte conservé ne permet pas de tirer de grandes conclusions, mais il nous oblige à nous demander si nous avons affaire ici à un manuscrit biblique ou non-biblique et quels sont les critères pour établir si un texte est biblique ou s'il ne l'est pas. L'étude des nouveaux textes "frontières", "anthologiques" ou "paraphrastiques", ne sera pas sans conséquences pour l'étude textuelle et littéraire des livres

---

[4] Il n'est plus possible de connaître avec certitude quel était l'ordre des fragments dans le rouleau. D'après la forme des cassures, on peut supposer que les frgs 2 et 3 étaient superposés. Ils appartenaient sûrement à deux colonnes différentes. Le décompte des lettres en suivant le TM donne à supposer que le nom *'ly[š'* (frg. 3, l. 2) suivait le verbe *wy'mr* (v. 14).

[5] Une tache d'encre au commencement de la ligne entre les lignes 3 et 4 peut correspondre à la partie inférieure d'une *nun* ou d'un *kaf* finals (l. 3) ou à la partie supérieure d'un *lamed* (l. 4).

[6] Pour ce qui concerne le texte des Rois même M.H. Goshen-Gottstein est prêt à reconnaître: ". . . we may have to reckon, with different 'breadths' of the 'central current' and different strenghts of the 'trickle' from the side", "Hebrew Biblical Manuscripts: Their History and Their Place in the HUBP Edition", *Bib.* 48 (1967), pp. 243–90, cf. p. 275.

[7] Dans sa discussion de la leçon du texte antiochien καὶ εἶδον (. . .) ἐξ ἐναντίας ἀναστρέφοντα αὐτόν (LXX[L]), D. Barthélemy considère seulement la correspondance ἀναστρέφοντα = *mngd*, mais non celle de αὐτόν = *'tw* (au lieu de TM *wyr'hw*), qui semble être exigé aussi par 4Q481a, cf. *Critique textuelle de l'Ancien Testament 3: Ézéchiel, Daniel et les 12 Prophètes* (Fribourg-Göttingen, 1992), p. xlvi.

historiques, et surtout pour l'analyse des nombreuses transpositions attestées dans les livres des Rois et de certains passages auxquels on pourra difficilement dénier le titre de bibliques, mais qui sont souvent qualifiés de "paraphrases targoumiques", "miscellanées" ou "suppléments", 1 Rois LXX ii 35a–o, 46a–l, xii 24a–z, etc.

2. *Considérations méthodologiques*

L'étude de l'histoire du texte doit précéder, en principe, celle de l'histoire de la rédaction, bien qu'il faille souligner que les deux deviennent de plus en plus inséparables. Autrement l'exégète qui cherche à reconstruire l'histoire de la rédaction littéraire risquerait de travailler sur la base d'un texte tardif et, par conséquent, d'attribuer aux rédacteurs deutéronomistes le travail d'éditeurs postérieurs. Un des piliers de la théorie de M. Noth sur la rédaction deutéronomiste— 1 Rois vi 1, où on établit la date de la construction du Temple "En la quatre cent quatre-vingtième année après la sortie des Israélites d'Égypte",—se trouve différemment placé dans le TM et dans les LXX; le reste du verset ne fait que répéter les données des vv. vi 37–38a, qui, selon l'ordre attesté par la Septante, suivaient presque immédiatement: v 15–30, 32b, vi 1a, v 31–32a, vi 37–38a, 2–10. Cet ordre est antérieur à celui du TM comme le prouvent les maladresses textuelles que la transposition de vi 37–38a a provoquées aux points d'insertion du TM (vi 36 et vii 12b), les unités vi 2–36 et vii 13–51, qui devaient se suivre sans interruption comme l'atteste l'hébreu de la LXX, ayant été ainsi disloquées. La référence chronologique à la sortie d'Égypte est l'œuvre d'exégètes qui aimaient établir des rapports entre les différents livres et entre les grands événements bibliques.

La recherche sur les livres historiques souffre encore du manque d'une édition critique du texte grec dans la collection de Göttingen.[8] On ne pourra faire cette édition sans regarder de près l'histoire du texte hébreu et même sans connaître sa formation littéraire. Il est tout aussi vrai qu'on ne pourra pas connaître l'histoire textuelle et littéraire du texte hébreu sans tenir compte de l'histoire parallèle du texte grec. Les variantes textuelles les plus importantes ne sont pas celles produites par "erreur" des copistes au cours de la transmission

---

[8] L'édition d'A. Rahlfs pèche par un préjugé défavorable au texte antiochien, *Lucians Rezension der Königsbücher* (Göttingen, 1911).

du texte, mais plutôt les vastes transpositions et additions dont l'origine remonte à une époque où le processus d'édition n'était pas encore stabilisé, comme c'est le cas au second siècle ap. J.-C. pour les écrits du Nouveau Testament. Ces variantes se produisaient en groupe, les unes provoquant les autres. La transposition ou interpolation d'une pièce littéraire engendrait des tensions et des corruptions dans le texte, particulièrement aux points de suture où l'on avait fait l'insertion. L'étude textuelle permet de déceler plusieurs cas de reprise. Ainsi, par exemple, une répétition dans le texte antiochien de Jug. ix 16 et 19 (*'m b'mt wbtmym 'śytm 'm 'by/yrb'l w'm bytw*) délimite avec précision l'insertion deutéronomiste des *vv.* 16b–18.

Le texte de la reprise a été conservé parfois par le TM et parfois par les LXX et il peut se trouver avant ou après le passage interpolé. Ainsi l'insertion de viii 30–5 est signalée par le double emplacement possible des phrases de Jos. ix 1–2, avant (LXX) ou après (TM) l'unité insérée. Une reprise dans la Septante (gn-dhptw ἀλλὰ διάδος αὐτὴν ταῖς φυλαῖς Ἰσραὴλ εἰς κληρονομίαν ὃν τρόπον ἐνετειλάμην σοι) indique les points d'insertion de Jos. xiii 2–6a avec plus de précision que ne l'ont fait les critiques modernes. L'interpolation de Jug. ii 22 est marquée par une reprise dont le texte est plus complet dans les LXX (καὶ ἀφῆκεν) que dans le TM. La glose de Jug. ix 24 est délimitée par une transposition présente dans le grec antiochien aux *vv.* 23 et 25 (καὶ ἠθέτησαν οἱ ἄνδρες Σικίμων ἐν τῷ οἴκῳ Ἀβιμέλεχ (*et constituerunt principes Sicimorum super Abimelec* VL) ... καὶ ἐπισυνέστησαν τῷ Ἀβιμέλεχ οἱ ἄρχοντες Σικίμων καὶ οἱ ἄνδρες αὐτῆς.[9]

Chacun des livres historiques a eu sa propre histoire de rédaction deutéronomiste. C'est surtout le cas du livre des Juges. Il faut souligner ici que chaque livre a eu de même une histoire éditoriale propre, si bien que les caractéristiques acquises pendant le processus d'édition ne doivent pas être prêtées aux étapes de la rédaction deutéronomiste. Des éléments qu'on considère comme typiques d'une rédaction nomiste peuvent être plutôt caractéristiques d'une révision du texte, qui n'a affecté qu'un livre ou l'autre selon une division des livres différente de celle du TM. Dans la *Vorlage* de la Septante la division entre 2 Samuel et 1 Rois était située entre 1 Rois ii 11 et 12 (cf. LXX^L). Le mot *twrh*, qui n'apparaît pas dans 1 Rois ii 12–xx

---

[9] Plusieurs cas semblables ont été signalés par l'auteur, *Centena in libros Samuelis et Regum. Variantes textuales y composición literaria en los libros de Samuel y de Reyes* (Madrid, 1989).

(section non recensée du grec), se trouve, au contraire, 11 fois dans les sections 1 Rois i 2–11 et 1 Rois xx–2 Rois, celles dont le texte de la Septante fut recensé par les "devanciers d'Aquila". Cela est plus significatif du fait que les mots voisins, assez fréquents en 1 Rois ii 12–xx, *ḥwqym/ḥqwt* (11x), *mšpṭym* (8x) et *mṣwt* (10x), deviennent plus rares dans les autres sections, 6, 1 et 7 fois respectivement.[10]

L'ancienne Septante traduisait le mot *ḥq/ḥqh* par πρόσταγμα (1 Rois iii 14, viii 58, 61, ix 4, 6, 11, xi 38), mais la recension rabbinique remplaça πρόσταγμα par δικαίωμα. Voilà une nouvelle caractéristique *kaige* à ajouter à la liste de celles qui ont été repérées jusqu'à présent (1 Rois ii 3; 2 Rois xvii 13, 19, 34, 37, xxiii 3; cf. aussi 1 Rois xi 34 dans un ajout hexaplaire; il est significatif que le texte antiochien préserve la version ancienne πρόσταγμα dans les sections *kaige*, 1 Rois ii 3 et xxiii 3). Le mot *mṣwh* est traduit habituellement par ἐντολή et *mšpṭ* par κρίματα, mais en 1 Rois ἐντολή semble traduire également *mṣwh* et *mšpṭ*. Il faut signaler que le texte grec est parfois plus bref (ignore 1 Rois vi 12, xi 33, 34 et 2 Rois xvii 5) et plus régulier dans l'emploi de la paire fondamentale des mots *ḥqym wmṣwt/mšpṭym* (1 Rois iii 14, viii 58, 61, ix 4, 6, xi 11, 38).[11]

De même le verbe *š'l* (*mn*), utilisé 11 fois en 1 Rois ii 11–xxi 29, est remplacé par *drš*, 12 fois, en 1 Rois xxii–2 Rois.[12] Le verb *ḥrš*, "se taire", utilisé en 1 Sam. vii 8, x 27; 2 Sam. xiii 20, xix 22; 2 Rois xviii 36 (pris de Isa. xxxvi 21) cède la place au verbe *ḥšh* précisément à partir de 1 Rois xxii (xxii 3; 2 Rois ii 3, 5, vii 9).

---

[10] *twrh*: 1 Rois ii 3; 2 Rois x 31, xiv 6, xvii 13, 34, 37, xxi 8, (xxii 8), xxii 11, xxiii 24, 25. Le seul cas en 1–2 Samuel, 2 Sam vii 19, n'est pas à considérer.
Section 1 Rois ii 12–1 Rois xx: ḥwqym/ḥqwt, iii 3, 14, vi 12, viii 5–8, 61, ix 4, 6, xi 11, 33, 34, 38; *mšpṭym*, iii 11, 28, vi 12, viii 45, 49, 58, ix 4, xi 33; *mṣwt*, ii 43, iii 14, vi 12, viii 58, 61, ix 6, xi 34, 38, xiv 8, xviii 18 (>LXX).
Sections 1 Rois i 1–ii 11 et 1 Rois xx–2 Rois: ḥwq/ḥqh, 1 Rois ii 3; 2 Rois xvii 13, 15 (>LXX), 34 (glose?), 37, xxiii 3; *mšpṭ*, 2 Rois xvii 37; *mṣwh*, 2 Rois xvii 13, 16, 19, 34, 37, xviii 6, xxiii 3.
[11] Cf. N. Lohfink, "Die *huqqîm ûmišpāṭîm* im Buch Deuteronomium und ihre Neubegrenzung durch Dtn 12,1", *Studien zum Deuteronomium und zur deuteronomistischen Literatur II* (Stuttgart, 1991), pp. 229–56, cf. p. 241.
[12] *drš* (*'t yhwh* ou *bb'l*), 1 Rois xxii 5, 7, 8; 2 Rois i 2, 3, 6, 16, 16, iii 11, viii 8, xxii 13, 18. En 1–2 Samuel on utilise toujours *š'l*, sauf dans un cas de glose en 1 Sam ix 9 (*drš*). L'usage de *drš* en 1 Rois xiv 5 est aussi l'exception qui confirme la règle: tout le passage de 1 Rois xiv 1–20 était absent de l'hébreu traduit par la Septante; il reproduit une version hébraïque récente de l'histoire de Jéroboam. L'ancienne Septante utilisait ἐπερωτᾶν pour traduire aussi bien *š'l* que *drš*. En 2 Rois le verbe *drš* est traduit par ἐπιζητεῖν; la seule exception est aussi significative, puisqu'elle préserve une lecture de l'ancienne Septante qui n'a pas de correspondance dans le TM, 2 Rois i 2 καὶ ἐπορεύθησαν ἐπερωτῆσαι (δι' αὐτοῦ).

On peut formuler l'hypothèse selon laquelle les éléments recensionnels du grec, en particulier les additions hexaplaires, correspondent à des formes récentes de l'hébreu. Ainsi, par exemple, l'édition hébraïque de Rois représentée par l'ancienne Septante (LXX^L)' ne connaissait pas le nom d'un dieu *molek* (μολόχ), mais celui de *milkōm* (μελχύλ ou βασιλέα αὐτῶν). La forme dépréciative *molek* fut introduite dans le texte protomassorétique et elle passa plus tard à la tradition textuelle grecque. Cette interpolation provoqua un doublet dans le TM, 1 Rois xi 5 et 7, avec des répétitions (*mlkm/mlk, 'mnym/ bny 'mwn* et *šqs/'lhy*) que l'original de la Septante ne connaissait pas (cf. 1 Rois xi 33 et 2 Rois xxiii 13).

3. *Histoire du texte et structure de la rédaction deutéronomiste (2 Rois xvii 2 et 1 Rois xiv 22)*

En 2 Rois xvii 2, le TM lit "(Osée) fit ce qui déplaît à Yahvé, *non pas pourtant comme* (*rq l' k-*) les rois d'Israël ses prédécesseurs", tandis que la Septante (LXX^L et VL) a "plus que tous" (παρὰ πάντας τοὺς γενομένους = *mkl 'šr hyw*). Selon B. Stade, C.F. Burney, J.A. Montgomery, M. Cogan−H. Tadmor, etc., le grec est secondaire: le traducteur ne pouvait que considérer comme le pire des rois d'Israël celui qui fut responsable de la disparition du royaume. Il est préférable de s'abstenir de juger des possibles tendances des traducteurs et de s'en tenir aux éléments formels du texte. La lecture du TM, *rq l' k-*, se trouve aussi en 2 Rois iii 2 et xiv 3, accompagnée dans les deux cas d'une raison qui justifie la disculpation du roi: Joram "supprima la stèle de Baal que son père avait faite" et Amasias "ne mit pas à mort les fils des meurtriers", accomplissant ainsi la loi de Moïse (Dt. xxiv 6). Ces deux textes sont des ajouts "nomistes" (DtrN) ou même plutôt des gloses plus récentes.[13]

La lecture attestée par la Septante (*'šh hyšr/hr'*) *mkl* se trouve encore cinq fois, 2 Rois xiv 9, 22, xvi 25, 30, 33 (cf. aussi 2 Rois xxi 9, 11), toujours dans des passages qui appartiennent à une couche ancienne de la rédaction deutéronomiste, antérieure en tout cas aux éléments de rédaction "nomiste". Cela invite à supposer qu'en 2 Rois

---

[13] E. Würthwein, *Die Bücher der Könige* (Göttingen, 1984), pp. 279 et 371. En 2 Rois iii 2−3 la reprise *rq . . . rq* indique les limites de l'ajout; la seconde adversative ne fait pas référence à la première (ainsi Würthwein), mais elle suivait la formule précédente.

xvii 2 la lecture *mkl* (LXX) est également plus ancienne que celle du TM *rq l' k-*.

Cette hypothèse permet de récupérer un élément significatif de la structure deutéronomiste du livre des Rois. L'expression de refus absolu, *mkl*, s'applique seulement au premier et au dernier roi d'Israël, Jéroboam et Osée, ainsi qu'à Omri et Achab, spécialement visés par les historiens deutéronomistes. Pour le royaume de Juda, ce refus absolu ne vise que Roboam (1 Rois xiv 22, 24), premier roi de la monarchie divisée, et Manassé (2 Rois xxi 11), successeur d'Ézéchias et prédécesseur de Josias. Seuls le fondateur de la dynastie, David, et Ezéchias et Josias sont loués sans réserves.

La distribution des jugements pleinement élogieux ou absolument condamnatoires constitue sans doute un principe de structuration de la rédaction deutéronomiste, plus précisément de la rédaction josianique des livres de Rois.[14] La lecture *mkl*, attestée par l'ancienne Septante en 2 Rois xvii 2, est le chaînon qui permet de reconnaître la structure concentrique de la composition de ce livre. Josias, le dernier roi, fait pendant au premier, David, Manassé à Roboam, et Osée à Jéroboam. La variante du TM répond à des soucis exégétiques analogues à ceux qui se manifestent en 2 Rois iii 2 et xiv 3.

De même, les formules qui introduisent les règnes de Roboam et Josias se correspondent. La formule de Roboam en LXX xii 24a, "Roboam fit le mal aux yeux de Yahvé et il ne marchait pas sur le chemin de son père, David", ignore les interpolations deutéronomistes introduites en TM xiv 22 et son texte coïncide avec celui de la formule de Josias, sauf pour l'opposition "fit le mal"—"fit le bien" (2 Rois xxii 2). Il n'est pas facile d'imaginer comment un rédacteur ou midrashiste tardif aurait pu prendre pour modèle la formule de Josias et, en même temps, expurger les additions deutéronomistes de la formule de TM xiv 22.

En plus, l'emplacement de la formule initiale de Roboam immédiatement après la formule finale de Salomon suit de près la loi de composition des livres des Rois, selon laquelle toute unité littéraire doit être encadrée par les formules initiale et finale du règne correspondant. Le TM s'écarte de cette loi, puisque, le cadre du règne de

---

[14] Cela vient à l'appui du courant d'opinion, auquel j'adhère, favorable à l'existence d'une première rédaction deutéronomiste à l'époque de Josias, avant l'Exil en tout cas; cf. F.M. Cross, *Canaanite Myth and Hebrew Epic. Essays in the History of the Religion of Israel* (Cambridge, Mass., 1982), pp. 274–89.

Roboam devant suivre celui de Salomon, tout le matériel de 1 Rois xii 1–24 se trouve hors de tout cadre de composition. La disposition du texte grec correspond ici à la structure de la première histoire deutéronomiste, tandis que le TM répond à un souci de mettre en rapport la division du royaume (ch. xii) avec les méfaits de Salomon (ch. xi) et de présenter Jéroboam comme un "satan" de Salomon, plutôt que comme l'antagoniste de Roboam à l'assemblée de Sichem.

Toute discussion sur une addition quelconque de la LXX est liée à une problématique qui ne laisse pas de susciter des réactions très opposées: la question du statut des "suppléments" de la Septante, en particulier en 1 Rois ii et xii. Je continue à penser que le texte le plus court de 1 Rois iii–xi, attesté par la LXX, correspond à celui d'une édition de 1 Rois antérieure à celle connue par le TM. Les "suppléments" correspondent à des matériaux hébreux qui n'avaient pas trouvé place dans le "corps principal" de la composition connue par la Septante. Ils étaient restés dans des collections plus ou moins souples autour du motif de la sagesse de Salomon. L'édition transmise par le TM distribua les matériaux de ces suppléments à l'intérieur du corps principal, et les plaça aux endroits qui semblaient les plus adéquats. Certaines pièces de la composition qui formaient une unité autour d'un même sujet furent ainsi disloquées. Entre les *vv.* iv 7–19, <...> v 7–8, 2–4, fut inséré le matériel de TM iv 20, v 16 (LXX ii 46a–i). Le mot "Juda" servit de mot-crochet pour l'insertion.

4. *Histoire du texte et composition deutéronomiste: transpositions en 2 Rois x et xiii*

Le texte que je propose maintenant à discussion semble à première vue outrancier. La VL présente le récit de la mort d'Élisée, 2 Rois xiii 14–21, à la fin du règne de Jéhu, après x 31.[15] J'avance déjà mon opinion: la transposition s'est effectuée à l'intérieur du courant textuel du TM et non pas au niveau de la traduction grecque ou de la transmission textuelle de la VL. La transposition effectuée dans le TM a laissé plusieurs traces et bouleversé complètement le texte, surtout aux points de suture du nouveau et de l'ancien emplacement.

Selon Barthélemy, en 2 Rois xiii 23 la Septante omet TM *'d 'th*, "jusqu'à présent", un cas de modernisation exégétique de la part du

---

[15] Cf. B. Fischer, "Palimpsestus Vindobonensis", *Beiträge zur Geschichte der lateinischen Bibeltexte* (Freiburg, 1986), pp. 308–438, cf. p. 379.

traducteur grec.[16] En fait l'ancienne Septante n'omet pas cette expression. Son texte n'est pas ici celui de LXX^B (*kaige*), mais bien celui des manuscrits lucianiques boc$_2$e$_2$, qui attestent que l'hébreu traduit par l'ancienne Septante ignorait complètement le texte du *v.* 23 à l'emplacement du TM, parce qu'il s'y trouvait bien avant, après xiii 7, l'expression *'d 'th* (ἕως τοῦ νῦν) comprise.

Le TM présente ici une série d'anomalies. Les formules initiale et finale du règne de Joas se trouvent l'une après l'autre (xiii 10–11, 12–13), si bien qu'elles laissent hors de tout cadre les matériaux des *vv.* 22, 24–5, allant ainsi une fois de plus à l'encontre d'une des lois de la composition du livre (*supra*). La formule de conclusion (xiii 12–13) est encore répétée en xiv 15–16. Primitivement après le *v.* 7 (LXX^L), le *v.* 23 a été déplacé, le *v.* 22 n'étant qu'une reprise du *v.* 4b.

Par contre, dans le texte hébreu traduit par la Septante, les formules initiale (*vv.* 10–11) et finale (après le *v.* 25, cf. mss boc$_2$e$_2$) encadraient la notice de *vv.* (22), 24–5 sur la victoire de Joas contre les Araméens. L'original de la Septante (LXX^L omet xiv 15) ne connaissait pas non plus la répétition qu'on a signalée dans le TM.

Les petits détails sont souvent encore plus parlants. Le texte de xiii 7 attesté par LXX^L est plus bref que celui du TM (*v.* 23): καὶ μετεμελήθη (*nḥm*) κύριος καὶ ᾤκτειρεν αὐτούς—TM *wyḥn yhwh 'tm wyrḥmn wypn 'lyhm*, reproduit par le texte *kaige* de LXX^B καὶ ἠλέησεν κύριος αὐτοὺς καὶ οἰκτίρησεν αὐτοὺς καὶ ἐπέβλεψεν πρὸς αὐτούς. L'innovation littéraire du TM manifeste une tendance antianthropomorphique ("Yahvé fit grâce" au lieu de "se repentit") et s'est produite probablement à partir de la paire de mots *ḥnn/pnh 'l*, qui se trouve aussi en Ps. xxv 16, lxxxvi 16 et cxix 132.

Le *sadran* qui a inséré en TM xiii 14–20 le récit sur la mort d'Élisée a dû réordonner les unités dans le TM comme on vient de le signaler. Son propos était d'identifier le "libérateur" d'Israël (*v.* 5) comme étant Élisée. Il a dû remplacer pour cela le mot "libération" (σωτηρία = *tšw'h* ou *yšw'h*)[17] par "libérateur" (*mwšy'*), qui ne se trouve plus en 1–2 Rois.[18] L'hébreu de la Septante avait le même mot *tšw'h*

---

[16] D. Barthélemy et al., *Critique textuelle de l'Ancien Testament* 1 (Fribourg-Göttingen, 1982), p. 402.

[17] *tšw'h*: Jug. xv 18; 1 Sam. xi 9, 13, xix 5; 2 Sam. xix 3, xxiii 10, 12; 2 Rois v 1, xiii 17, 17; 1 Chron. xi 14, xix 22; 2 Chron. vi 41; *yšw'h*: 1 Sam. ii 1, xiv 45; 2 Sam. x 11, xxii 51.

[18] Cf. Dt. xxii 27, xxviii 29, 31; Jug. iii 9, 15, xii 3; 1 Sam. x 19; 2 Sam. xxii 3, 42.

aux *vv.* 5 et 17, et celui qui donnait la "libération" était Yahvé dans les deux cas, comme aussi en 2 Rois v 1 (*ky bw ntn yhwh tšwʻh lʾrm*).

Après le récit sur la mort d'Élisée la VL présente le texte *et Ieu non observauit ire in uiam Domini Dei Israel ex toto corde suo* qui correspond à celui du TM x 3la, sauf pour la variante très significative *uiam domini* au lieu de TM "la Torah de Yahvé", *twrt yhwh* (cf. *supra*). Au ch. x le récit était encadré par la reprise du *v.* x 29a répété au *v.* 31, semblable à celle de xiii 2b/6a qui délimite l'insertion deutéronomiste de *vv.* 3–5.

Le moins qu'on puisse dire en conclusion c'est que le récit de la mort d'Élisée faisait partie du cycle d'Élisée, 2 Rois iv–ix, et qu'il n'avait pas trouvé d'emplacement défini dans la composition du livre. Selon le récit attesté par la VL, Élisée se trouve avec Jéhu (841–814/3) à l'occasion d'une bataille à *Aseroth, in Aseroth quae est contra faciem Samariae*, nom de lieu inconnu de la Bible mais mentionné dans les ostraca de Samarie à l'époque de la dynastie de Jéhu (*Haṣeroth*).[19] La transposition du récit au ch. xiii a fait d'Élisée un octogénaire, qui participe avec Joas (798–782/1) contre Ben-Hadad III à la bataille d'Apheq (xiii 17).

L'étude de l'histoire du texte, des livres de Rois en particulier, permet de reconnaître un stade éditorial des livres dans lequel plusieurs unités littéraires gardaient encore leur intégrité et leur indépendance à l'égard des autres. L'édition connue par le TM éparpilla souvent les matériaux des unités mineures entre ceux des unités plus grandes et opéra d'autres déplacements et changements mineurs ainsi que des ajouts exégétiques. L'exégèse pratiquée sur la seule base du TM arrive souvent à fragmenter le texte plus qu'il ne l'était à un stade d'édition plus ancien. En 1 Rois x 36 l'ancienne Septante (LXX[L] VL) transmet le texte complet et bien structuré de la notice sur le coup d'état contre Ochozias, en toute indépendance du récit prophétique sur la révolte de Jéhu. Le TM éparpilla les matériaux de la notice au long de ce récit, interrompant celui-ci à plusieurs reprises (viii 28, ix 14, 27, 28). De même la Septante préserve dans son intégrité le récit de Shiméï (1 Rois ii 35l–o, 36–46a), dont le TM offre la première partie (sans l'introduction originale) entre les matériaux recueillis dans le testament de David (ii 8–9), et la seconde partie

---

[19] Probablement ʻAṣire eš-Šemāliye, au nord de Sichem, cf. Y. Aharoni, *The Land of the Bible. A Historical Geography* (London, 1979²), p. 436.

après les récits de la succession (ii 36–46). Une reprise (LXX^L VL *wymt dwd wyškb ʿm ʾbtyw*, ii 1a, 10a) signale l'insertion du testament de David (ii 1b–9).

Après avoir plaidé pour une étroite relation entre l'histoire du texte et l'histoire de la composition-rédaction deutéronomiste, je voudrais rappeler que, devant les tendances actuelles à une chronologie basse pour la rédaction des livres historiques et à une chronologie haute pour la "canonisation" des livres et la fixation de leur texte et aussi pour la formation d'une bonne part de la littérature pseudépigraphique trouvée à Qoumrân, il faut laisser du temps au temps pour que les deux histoires, littéraire et textuelle, aient pu naître, suivre leur cours et finalement laisser la place à l'histoire d'autres corps de littérature. Quatre points de repère doivent orienter, je crois, toute recherche: (1) l'époque de Josias avant l'Exil, avec une première rédaction deutéronomiste étroitement liée à la rédaction et à l'idéologie du premier Isaïe (la reprise d'Isa. xxxvi–xxxix et 2 Rois xviii 13–xx 19 unissant les deux rouleaux); (2) l'époque de l'Exil, avec une deuxième rédaction deutéronomiste liée à celle du livre de Jérémie (la reprise de Jer. lii et 2 Rois xxiv 18–xxv 30 unissant aussi les "explicit" des deux rouleaux); (3) l'époque postexilique, dans laquelle le Sacerdotal et le Chroniste réélaborent les livres historiques, et finalement (4) l'époque de la version grecque, où la *Vorlage* choisie jouissait de la plus grande autorité. L'école deutéronomiste créa tout un langage et tout un monde d'idées qui perdurèrent jusqu'à l'époque de Qoumrân et qui pouvaient toujours se manifester en des ajouts exégétiques ou en des retouches éditoriales.

ISAIAH XI 11–16 AND THE REDACTION OF ISAIAH I–XII

by

H.G.M. WILLIAMSON
Oxford

The Masoretic Text of the first half of Isa. xi 11 reads

> *wᵉhāyâ bayyôm hahû᾽ yôsîp ᾽ᵃdōnāy šēnît yādô*
> *liqnôt ᾽et-šᵉ᾽ār ᶜammô.*

Although this can certainly be construed as it stands without emendation,[1] most commentators favour reading *šᵉ᾽ēt* in place of *šēnît*, so giving rise to the translation: "In that day the Lord will again extend his hand to recover the remnant which is left of his people". The use of the common idiom *nś᾽ yd* and comparison with Isa. xlix 22 in particular make this proposal attractive, and it will tentatively be adopted here.

Two main ways of understanding the verse have generally been advanced. One group of commentators thinks that there is a reference to the first exodus; God is about to move again as he did on that previous occasion.[2] Others, however, suggest that the reference is to the first return from exile in the time of Cyrus, with which also the returns at the time of Ezra and Nehemiah may have been associated.[3] It is common to both these approaches, however, that they consider that what God is about to do again is to "recover the remnant of his people".

---

[1] See the Additional Note at the end of this article for a discussion of the text and of the major emendations which have been proposed.

[2] So, for instance, Franz Delitzsch, *Commentar über das Buch Jesaia* (Leipzig, 1889⁴), p. 197; G.B. Gray, *A Critical and Exegetical Commentary on the Book of Isaiah I–XXVII* (Edinburgh, 1912), p. 225; P. Auvray, *Isaïe 1–39* (Paris, 1972), p. 147. We may also note here the suggestion of O. Procksch, *Jesaia 1* (Leipzig, 1930), p. 157, that it refers back to v. 10 immediately preceding. In my opinion, however, v. 10 was added later, as a link between vv. 1–9 and 11–16.

[3] So, for instance, B. Duhm, *Das Buch Jesaia* (Göttingen, 1922⁴), p. 109; K. Marti, *Das Buch Jesaja* (Tübingen, 1900), p. 114; G. Fohrer, *Das Buch Jesaja 1: Kapitel 1–23* (Zürich, 1966²), p. 171; H. Wildberger, *Jesaja 1: Jesaja 1–12* (Neukirchen-Vluyn, 1980²), pp. 467–8; O. Kaiser, *Das Buch des Propheten Jesaja, Kapitel 1–12* (Göttingen, 1981⁵), p. 250.

A quite different interpretation, however, would seem to be justified when it is recognized that from a grammatical point of view what the Lord is about to do again is not so much to recover his people as to raise or extend his hand. If we then ask when he did *this* for the first time, we are led to consider the fact that in the previous chapters there is a repeated refrain to the effect that "for all this his anger is not turned away, and his hand is stretched out still" (v 25, ix 11, 16, 20, x 4). Since, as J. Vermeylen has pointed out,[4] xi 11–16 makes reference to at least one other theme from these chapters, namely the dispute between Ephraim and Judah (xi 13; cf. ix 20), the possibility that this is another example of the same process is attractive.

The case becomes more than merely an attractive possibility, however, when we look further at the passage introduced by v 25 in particular. There, the reference to God's hand in *v.* 25 is followed in *v.* 26 by the statement that God will "raise an ensign to the nations", and this is precisely the same in xi 12, following *v.* 11; indeed, the phraseology in both cases is identical: *w⁽ᵉ⁾nāśā' nēs laggôyīm*. Furthermore, we are told that the nations will come "from afar . . . from the ends of the earth" in v 26, and in xi 12 that the outcasts of Israel and the dispersed of Judah will be gathered "from the four corners of the earth". With three elements occurring in the same order in the two passages (God's hand; the ensign; from afar), it is hard to escape the conclusion that the one has been framed with an eye on the other.

Of course, the differences between the two passages should not be overlooked. In ch. v, God's hand is stretched out in judgement against his people, while in ch. xi it is raised again, but this time to restore them; in ch. v the nations are summoned by God's ensign to execute

---

[4] *Du prophète Isaïe à l'apocalyptique. Isaïe, I–XXXV, miroir d'un demi-millénaire d'expérience religieuse en Israël* 1 (Paris, 1977), p. 278, n. 4. Vermeylen considers the interpretation of xi 11 advanced above, but rejects it. Instead, he prefers to associate our verse with x 32, which he thinks the redactor would have understood as a reference to God waving his hand in protection of Zion, rather than as an attacker "shaking his fist" in enmity at the city. Consequently, Vermeylen proposes to read *hēnîp* or *y⁽ᵉ⁾nôpēp* instead of *yôśîp* in xi 11, comparing xi 15 and x 32 respectively for these alternative forms, and so to leave *šᵉnît* unchanged. Both steps in this argument are problematic. No good reason is given why the redactor should have misinterpreted x 32 in a manner which runs so contrary to the clear sense of the context (the change in subject to the Lord acting in judgement on the enemy is emphatically marked at the start of x 33), while the proposed emendation of xi 11 is entirely conjectural.

his judgement on his people, but in ch. xi to assist, we are bound to assume, in their recovery (this theme becomes explicit in xlix 22); and whereas in ch. v it is the hostile nations which come from afar, in ch. xi it is the dispersed people of Israel and Judah. In other words, ch. xi explicitly reverses the threatening tone of ch. v, a difference in tone maintained throughout the two paragraphs which have thus been introduced.

Pursuing these observations further, we should remember next that v 25–9 (30) is generally thought to have been relocated from an original literary setting somewhere between ix 7 and x 4 where it seems to belong because of the refrain already cited. Exactly where it might have come in that passage is a matter of continuing debate amongst the commentators, and one which need not detain us here.[5] It is sufficient to observe that the case for some such transposition is strong.[6]

How and why the passage was transposed, however, has been less satisfactorily answered. Usually it is thought to have been the result of some error in transmission, so that a number of commentaries, and even at least one translation of the Bible,[7] rearrange the material into what they consider to have been the original, correct order. Our observations point to a different solution, for it should not escape notice that v 25–30 comes at the end of a major section of the book, just as xi 11–xii 6 does. It is thus highly satisfying from the point of view of redaction criticism to find that two concluding sections

---

[5] In addition to the commentaries, cf. R. Fey, *Amos und Jesaja, Abhängigkeit und Eigenständigkeit des Jesaja* (Neukirchen-Vluyn, 1963), pp. 83–88; H. Donner, *Israel unter den Völkern. Die Stellung der klassischen Propheten des 8. Jahrhunderts v. Chr. zur Aussenpolitik der Könige von Israel und Juda* (*SVT* 11; Leiden, 1964), pp. 66–75; J. Vollmer, *Geschichtliche Rückblicke und Motive in der Prophetie des Amos, Hosea und Jesaja* (*BZAW* 119, Berlin, 1971), pp. 130–44; H. Barth, *Die Jesaja-Worte in der Josiazeit. Israel und Assur als Thema einer produktiven Neuinterpretation der Jesajaüberlieferung* (Neukirchen-Vluyn, 1977), pp. 109–12; Vermeylen, pp. 177–86; C.E. L'Heureux, "The Redactional History of Isaiah 5.1–10.4", in W.B. Barrick and J.R. Spencer (ed.), *In the Shelter of Elyon. Essays on Ancient Palestinian Life and Literature in Honor of G.W. Ahlström* (Sheffield, 1984), pp. 99–119.

[6] *Pace* W. Dietrich, *Jesaja und die Politik* (Munich, 1976), pp. 186–87; R.B. Chisholm, "Structure, Style, and the Prophetic Message: An Analysis of Isaiah 5:8–30", *BibSac* 143 (1986), pp. 46–60, and W.P. Brown, "The So-Called Refrain in Isaiah 5:25–30 and 9:7–10:4", *CBQ* 52 (1990), pp. 432–43. The present sequence is also apparently assumed to be original by J.H. Hayes and S.A. Irvine, *Isaiah. The Eighth-century Prophet* (Nashville, 1987), pp. 99 and 106–7, and by Y. Gitay, *Isaiah and his Audience. The Structure and Meaning of Isaiah 1–12* (Assen, 1991), pp. 87–116.

[7] Cf. the *New English Bible*. The canonical order has correctly been restored, however, by the *Revised English Bible*.

are introduced by closely parallel material, the one referring to God's judgement, following the lengthy and varied invective of ii 6–v 24,[8] and the other, referring to God's salvation, following the material in vi 1–xi 9 which in the present form of the book, at least, includes a good deal of more hopeful material. It is true that these chapters are not so consistently hopeful as ii–v are threatening, but the change in tone between the two sections is still marked, and it is worth bearing in mind that some passages which may have been threatening in tone when originally written were certainly re-read as conveying promise (and further positive material added to them subsequently) in later times. (I shall seek to refine this initial impression later on.)

There is good reason to believe, therefore, that the transposition of v 25–9 (30) to its present position was consciously undertaken by the same redactor who composed xi 11–16 (and ch. xii, in my opinion). What is more, his procedure, which on the face of things appears in two respects to be rather clumsy, now receives adequate explanation.

First, there is the oddity that the passage which seems to have been removed from its original setting begins with an unattached "therefore". Although in a general way this can, of course, be read in the present form of the text as referring to the material which precedes it, it is nevertheless awkward in that *v.* 24 itself rounds off the section with its own introductory "therefore". If, however, the redactor was attempting to locate material here which could serve as a balance to his conclusion of the following main section in xi 11–16, then his choice becomes intelligible. Not only did he need, of course, to begin this passage with a reference to God's outstretched hand which the refrain provided, but he drew particular attention to this element by choosing the one and only example of the refrain which is itself immediately preceded by another reference to this same point: "Therefore the anger of the Lord was kindled against his people, and he stretched out his hand against them and smote them" (v 25*a*). This element is not found in any of the other examples of the refrain in chs ix–x. It is thus clear that the redactor chose to move precisely this material from its original setting because it was particularly suited by repetition of the crucial element for the wider

---

[8] In common with most commentators, I accept the view that iv 2–6 is distinctly later in date; see recently Vermeylen, pp. 152–7, and M.A. Sweeney, *Isaiah 1–4 and the Post-Exilic Understanding of the Isaianic Tradition* (*BZAW* 171; Berlin and New York, 1988), pp. 179–81. Without it, ii 6–v 24 is entirely invective of one sort or another.

purposes on which he was engaged. Furthermore, the double reference to the anger of the Lord in the first and last lines of the verse
also suited his intention in the final rounding-off passage at xii 1.

Second, commentators have often drawn attention to the fact that
in v 26 there is a curious reference to the plural "nations" in a
context which obviously referred originally to only a single nation
(cf. the singular *lô* in the next clause and the singular verb *yābô'*
immediately after that); they therefore propose emending the plural
laggôyīm to the singular *l^egôy*, explaining the error as due to a mistaken division of the words: the final *mem* should be attached to the
following word, which is then to be read as *mimmerḥāq* (cf. Jer. v 15).
There is no reason to doubt that this, or something very like it, was
what Isaiah himself would have written when this verse stood in its
original position, but comparison with xi 12 (as well as with xlix 22)
indicates that the alteration was not caused by scribal error, nor even,
as Gray suggests, by "a scribe who wished to assimilate to 11¹²", but
rather by the deliberate activity of the redactor who was forging a
link between this passage and his composition in xi 11–16. He thereby
involves the nations at large in the judgement of his people just as
he envisages the time when they will assist in their restoration.

So far, our discussion of v 25–30 has gone only so far as to suggest that the redactor was responsible for giving it its new and present
setting in the book. With one slight alteration (the substitution of the
plural for the originally singular "nation"), it seems that his purpose
was adequately achieved by using inherited material in a new setting. It could now serve to round off the condemnations of the first
section in the book, and he used it as a basis for constructing a new
parallel conclusion to what he took to be the second, more hopeful,
section at xi 11–16. The question naturally arises next whether in
the process he has added anything on his own account to this inherited material.

In answering this question, attention quickly falls on the concluding verse of the passage, v 30:

> They will growl over it on that day,
>   like the roaring of the sea.
> And if we look to the land,
>   behold, darkness closing in;
> and the light is darkened by its clouds.[9]

---

[9] Though the general sense of the second line is clear, several of its details remain

This verse is widely regarded as an addition to the previous paragraph.[10] Attention is drawn to the tell-tale phrase "on that day", to
the development in a new direction of the catchword "growl (*w^eyin-*
hōm)" (vv. 29 and 30), and to the widening of the scope of the prophecy
from a military defeat in *vv.* 26–9 to a more mythologically expressed
universal catastrophe in *v.* 30. In addition, *v.* 29 gives the strong
impression of being itself a conclusion that expects no continuation.

Differences of opinion arise, however, when we turn to the interpretation of the first line: who is growling over whom? A considerable number of commentators think that the glossator has sought to
reverse the gloom of the previous paragraph—either God or some
unnamed subject is now going to growl over Assyria (*'ālāw*), so that
eventually there will be unrelieved darkness for the country which
once oppressed Israel.[11] Against this, however, it must be observed
that the first word of the verse—*w^eyinhōm*, "and he will growl"—
exactly repeats the same word from *v.* 29, and since there is no
indication of a change of subject, it is more natural to suppose that
the one responsible for the addition picked it up with the intention
of developing the meaning which it has there rather than of using it
in some completely different way. On this view, the lion of *v.* 29,
representing Assyria, remains the subject, and the object over which
he growls remains the prey, representing Israel.[12] However, as we have

---

obscure. Because the root *nbṭ* is elsewhere attested only in the *hiph'il*, I cautiously
propose revocalizing the first word *w^enabbīṭ* with the Vulgate. The Masoretic division
of the line, which implies alternating light and darkness, is probably a consequence
of the "optimistic" reading of the first line, rejected above; with most commentators,
the *zāqēph qāṭôn* should be moved to *ṣar*, and the following word vocalized *w^e'ôr* in
consequence. Even with these slight alterations, the text does not read entirely
smoothly, and the possibility of more deep-seated corruption cannot be dismissed.

[10] It is not clear why R.E. Clements, *Isaiah 1–39* (Grand Rapids and London,
1980), p. 70, limits the addition to the second half of the verse only, especially in
view of the fact that two of the main reasons for detecting an addition here in the
first place come in the first half of the verse. He gives no reason for his position,
and indeed offers no comment on the first half of the verse. Nor is the suggestion
of Procksch (pp. 97–100) convincing; he thinks that the verse originally belonged
with 25*a*. He bases this on metrical considerations in large part, but is able to do
so only following radical surgery on *v.* 30. Among the casualties of this operation is
the phrase "on that day", but there is no evidence whatsoever for deleting it, and
it is itself one of the markers of the secondary nature of the verse.

[11] So, for instance, Duhm, p. 63; Marti, p. 62; J. Becker, *Isaias—der Prophet und
sein Buch* (Stuttgart, 1968), pp. 50–1; Kaiser, p. 116; Barth, p. 193; Vollmer, p. 135;
Vermeylen, p. 185. Gray, pp. 98–9, seems to be unable to decide.

[12] So, for instance, Delitzsch, p. 120; W. Eichrodt, *Der Heilige in Israel Jesaja 1–12*
(Stuttgart, 1960), p. 118; and in part Wildberger, pp. 226–7. Barth's objection to

already noted, the effects are now drawn in an even more terrifying manner by the suggestion that this will mark a return to the conditions of the primeval chaos. There is thus every reason to regard v 30 as a redactional addition, and no objection to ascribing it to the same redactor as the one responsible for moving v 25–9 to its present position. It serves to strengthen the note of judgement with which he rounded off the passage on the prophetic indictment of Israel.

The similarity of this verse with viii 22 has often been noted:[13]

> And they will look to the earth,
> > but behold, distress and darkness,
> > > the gloom of anguish;
> > and they will be thrust into thick darkness.[14]

The first phrase, w^e-el-$\dot{}eres$ $yabb\hat{\imath}t$ $w^ehinn\bar{e}h$, is just like the start of v 30b, $w^enibbat$ $l\bar{a}\dot{}\bar{a}res$ $w^ehinn\bar{e}h$. The expression $\sqrt{nbt}$ $l/\dot{}l$ $(h)\dot{}rs$ occurs only six times in the Hebrew Bible, three times with God as subject (Ps. cii 20, civ 32; Job xxviii 24), and three times with a human subject—in the two passages under consideration and at Isa. li 6. Our two passages are alone, however, in being followed in each case by $w^ehinn\bar{e}h$. In addition, both passages go on to speak of a time of oppression under the image of deep darkness, $\dot{h}\bar{o}\check{s}ek$ sar in v 30 and $sar\hat{a}$ $wa\dot{h}^a\check{s}\bar{e}k\hat{a}$ in viii 22. There can thus be no doubt that there is a close association between them.

It seems, furthermore, that viii 21–2 has also been added into its present context by a redactor. Although a few scholars have sought to defend the unity of vv. 19–22,[15] the majority hold firmly to the

---

this interpretation, that "eine Fortsetzung der Unheilsaussage im Blick auf den 5,26–29 Angegriffenen über V29 hinaus nur einen Rückschritt und eine Abschwächung bedeuten könnte", would be applicable only if this were all part of a single composition. In the case of an appendage, such a "Rückschritt" poses no problem, while the development of the image through the rest of v. 30 can hardly be called an "Abschwächung".

[13] First, apparently, by the LXX (cf. J. Ziegler, *Untersuchungen zur Septuaginta des Buches Isaias* [Münster, 1934], pp. 138–9), and most recently by B.W. Anderson, "'God with Us'—In Judgment and in Mercy: The Editorial Structure of Isaiah 5–10 (11)", in G.M. Tucker, D.L. Petersen, and R.R. Wilson (ed.), *Canon, Theology, and Old Testament Interpretation. Essays in Honor of Brevard S. Childs* (Philadelphia, 1988), pp. 230-45.

[14] Or "gloom with no brightness", if the proposal to emend $m^enudd\bar{a}\dot{h}$ to $minn\bar{o}gah$ is adopted; cf. Amos v 20.

[15] E.g. G.R. Driver, "Isaianic Problems", in G. Wiessner (ed.), *Festschrift für Wilhelm Eilers* (Wiesbaden, 1967), pp. 43–57 (43–9); C.F. Whitley, "The Language and Exegesis of Isaiah 8₁₆₋₂₃", *ZAW* 90 (1978), pp. 28–43; Vermeylen, pp. 229–30.

view that 21–2 should be taken independently.[16] That observation does not, however, settle the question of authorship, on which opinions are divided. While the majority find here an Isaianic fragment,[17] not a few others think of a later exilic[18] or post-exilic[19] composition.

Naturally, in the case of so short a fragment it is difficult to reach an absolutely firm decision on the matter, but such evidence as there is favours the case for authenticity, while the arguments to the contrary are weak. Wildberger adduces three positive arguments: metre and style, the reference to "his king" in v. 21, which should apply to the pre-exilic period, and vocabulary; although most of the vocabulary of the passage is general (having parallels both in Isaiah and elsewhere), he is particularly struck by the similarity with out passage of *b^e'ereṣ ṣārâ w^eṣûqâ* "through a land of trouble and anguish", in xxx 6, the more so in view of the fact that *ṣûqâ* occurs elsewhere only at Prov. i 27. Negatively, Wildberger also makes the point (along with many others) that there is nothing to prevent Isaianic authorship.

Of these arguments, the second is undoubtedly the strongest; it is difficult to see what sense could be made of the verse once the monarchy had ceased to exist.[20] The argument from vocabulary adds some weight to the case, but of course the possibility of later imitation means that it cannot be decisive. As to the negative argument, this is certainly true as far as it goes. Clements, for instance, dates the fragment late simply on the ground that *vv.* 19–20 are an addition; therefore, he assumes, 21–2 must have been added after that.[21] But the conclusion does not follow from the observation. If 19–20

---

[16] The brief remarks of Gray, p. 157, are usually considered decisive.

[17] E.g. Duhm, p. 87; Marti, p. 90; Procksch, p. 142; A. Alt, "Jesaja 8,23–9,6. Befreiungsnacht und Krönungstag", in *Festschrift Alfred Bertholet zum 80. Geburtstag gewidmet* (Tübingen, 1950), pp. 29–49 = *Kleine Schriften zur Geschichte des Volkes Israel* 2 (Munich, 1953), pp. 206–25; Fohrer, pp. 134–5; Wildberger, p. 357; K. Jeppesen, "Call and frustration. A new understanding of Isaiah viii 21–22", *VT* 32 (1982), pp. 145–57; J. Høgenhaven, *Gott und Volk bei Jesaja. Eine Untersuchung zur biblischen Theologie* (Leiden, 1988), pp. 103–5; A. Laato, *Who is Immanuel? The Rise and the Foundering of Isaiah's Messianic Expectations* (Åbo, 1988), pp. 188–9; Gray, p. 157, is again undecided.

[18] E.g. Barth, pp. 153–4; Vermeylen, pp. 228–30; Clements, pp. 102–3.

[19] E.g. Kaiser, p. 193, n. 16.

[20] G.C. Heider's proposal to emend *b^emalkô* to *b^emōlek* is unconvincing; cf. *The Cult of Molek. A Reassessment* (Sheffield, 1985), pp. 328–32. In joining *vv.* 19–20 and 21–2, he fails to explain the switch to singular verbs in the latter, has to assume the unexpressed "Sheol" as the antecedent for *bāh*, and conjecturally deletes the suffix on *b^emalkô*.

[21] See both his commentary and "The prophecies of Isaiah and the fall of Jerusalem in 587 B.C.", *VT* 30 (1980), pp. 421–36 (427).

are indeed an addition (a matter which we need not decide here), it does not follow that 21–2 could not already have been in place before they were added. The position of 19–20 was no doubt governed by the link between "the teaching and the testimony" in *vv.* 20 and 16. Similarly, Barth's reasons for dating 21–2 to the exilic period rest merely on the similarity between the description of the time of distress, such as hunger, with the conditions attested by Jeremiah and Lamentations for the time of the fall of Jerusalem. This argument, too, is insignificant; such conditions were common at any time of military catastrophe, and they would have been known—even from first-hand experience—long before the final downfall of Jerusalem.[22] On balance, then, the case in favour of the authenticity of this passage, or at the very least for a pre-exilic origin, seems to be the stronger.

At this point, a further argument needs to be brought into the discussion. As already noted, most commentators believe that these two verses are fragmentary. This is because the first word of the passage, the verb *'ābar*, "to pass over/through", lacks a subject, and the suffix on the second word, *bāh*, "(through) it" (feminine singular) lacks an antecedent.[23] That being the case, it is difficult to believe that these verses were written specifically for their present context. Even someone writing an addition could be expected to make his composition fit the context and not to introduce unattached verbs and suffixes. Nor is there any evidence that something has dropped out from the start of the passage, as implied by Wildberger's row of dots at the start of his translation. The obvious conclusion is that these words have been secondarily transferred to their present position from their original context, which was presumably at some other point in the early form of the collection of Isaianic material.[24]

Barth seeks to evade this conclusion with three arguments, but they are not all convincing. First, he maintains that appeals to fragment hypotheses should be a last resort. In these early chapters of Isaiah, however, there are so many well attested examples of material being rearranged for later redactional purposes that even as a last resort

---

[22] This is not to deny, of course, that later readers may have understood these verses in the way that Barth and Clements suggest.

[23] Against Vermeylen's attempt to overcome this, cf. Høgenhaven, p. 104.

[24] It is not necessary in the context of the present discussion to decide where these verses may once have stood or what exactly their point of reference may originally have been; for a speculation about the former, cf. P.W. Skehan, "Some Textual Problems in Isaia", *CBQ* 22 (1960), pp. 47–55 (48–51), and for discussion of the latter, cf. Høgenhaven, p. 105.

such a hypothesis is by no means unlikely. Second, with an appeal to GK § 144*d*, he proposes that the verb may be construed as having an indefinite personal subject, "one" or "they"; that is certainly a reasonable possibility. Third, to explain the unattached feminine singular suffix on *bāh*, he draws attention to an apparently similar phenomenon at iii 25–6 and v 14; since in these two cases Jerusalem is the implied point of reference, he suggests that the same may be true here. Unfortunately, however, he does not observe that the two passages to which he refers are not so straightforward as he implies. iii 25–6 must certainly once have been the direct continuation of iii 16–17 before the addition of the prose material in *vv.* 18ff. The feminine singular suffixes in 25–6 (both second and third person) then relate easily enough to the mention of Zion in 16–17. At v 14, there is also evidence that the feminine singular suffixes may once have had an explicit antecedent. The verse's introductory "therefore" sits uneasily after the "therefore" of *v.* 13 and suggests, as many have recognized, that this verse has been given its present position as part of the redactional compilation of the "Woe!" cycle in v 8–24.[25] It is therefore probable that this verse too once stood in a context where the suffix's antecedent was made clear. Barth's case against the fragmentary nature of viii 21–2 thus fails, and accordingly I conclude that at this point some words of Isaiah have been relocated from elsewhere by a later redactor.

Following viii 21–2 there is a short addition (viii 23*a*) which has clearly been introduced to link what precedes with what follows. Although there are a number of uncertainties about the text of this line, the use of the words *mû'āp* and *mûṣāq* are obviously intended to pick up on viii 22. Similarly, on the assumption that the negative *lō'* of the MT is sound (which then implies that the introductory *kî* should be understood as an adversative), there is also a connection with the following passage: those who have walked in darkness (as in viii 22)

---

[25] Cf. J.A. Emerton, "The textual problems of Isaiah v 14", *VT* 17 (1967), pp. 135–42, and Vermeylen, p. 172, for references. B.W. Anderson (n. 13) acutely observes that there are several "double therefores" in Isaiah, and suggests that this may be a mark of the work's redaction. He is careful to draw a distinction between this and original composition, however. ("These rhetorical uses of the 'double therefore' do not necessarily indicate that the present text of Isa. 5:13, 14 is original.") Since we have already noted that a further instance was created by the addition of v 25ff., I am tempted to suggest that this may be an indicator of our redactor's hand. It may not be coincidental that v 14 "mythologizes" the judgement of the people, just as v 30 does.

will not do so for ever, for light and joy will follow (ix 1–2). The addition may also, therefore, testify to an understanding of the first part of the passage (viii 23*b*) as contrasting a "former time" of oppression followed by a "latter time" of glory.[26]

It appears, therefore, in the light of this discussion, that viii 21–23*a* has been compiled along exactly the same lines as those I suggested for v 25–30. A fragment of Isaianic material has been put in a new setting, and it has been followed by a brief addition which links up with the fragment by means of verbal association. Moreover, since viii 22 is part of the material which was relocated from elsewhere in Isaiah's work, it must be concluded that the similarities between it and v 30, as described above, are to be explained by the redactor imitating at v 30 the kind of sentiments and expressions which he learnt from viii 22.

Brief mention may be made here of the probability that the same style of redactional composition also characterizes the introduction to ch. ii, though space precludes full justification in the case of a passage which has been discussed so frequently. Suffice it to observe for now that ii 2–4 are likely to have been an independent composition (incorporated also at Mic. iv 1–4) which has been worked into its present context by the addition of *v.* 5. There are in this verse clear echoes both of *vv.* 3 and 4 preceding (*bêt ya⁽ᶜᵃ⁾aqōb* and *lᵉkû wᵉnēlᵉkâ*) and of *v.* 6 following (*bêt ya⁽ᶜᵃ⁾qōb*). Furthermore, it is suggestive, in view of the imagery found in v 30 and viii 21–23*a*, that ii 5 also introduces the metaphor of light to express God's instruction. Should the hand of our redactor be thus attested at the start of ch. ii, it would be attractive to think that the form of the work for which he was responsible may in fact have started here, with the heading in ii 1.

Following my comparison of v 25–30 and xi 11–16, I suggested that they served as redactional summaries of the general tone and tenor of the two large preceding blocks of material for which they served as conclusions and that this was more obvious and clear-cut in the case of the former than of the latter. The discussion of viii

---

[26] This may itself be a redactional re-reading of the passage, if J.A. Emerton is correct in his understanding of the original sense of the verse; cf. "Some Linguistic and Historical Problems in Isaiah viii. 23", *JSS* 14 (1969), pp. 151–75. By the same token, the present discussion is not affected by the uncertainty whether viii 23*b* was always joined to the following passage or whether this connection too was made only later.

21–23*a*, which I have ascribed to the same redactional level, may help to refine and clarify this state of affairs. The pre-exilic material in chs vi–xi appears to combine passages of judgement and of promise, but to judge from the conclusion of ch. xi (together with ch. xii) the redactor understood its predominant characteristic as that of promise. viii 22–23*a*, as assembled by him, helps to explain how and why this was so, for it indicates a clear "before" and "after" schematization in his interpretation of the history of Judah. If, as I have suggested, he originally added it immediately following viii 18, which concludes the first-person account in chs vi and viii, often described as the prophet's "memoir", it would have served admirably to effect a transition from the pessimism of viii 16–18 to the hopeful oracle in viii 23*b*–ix 6. In addition, it would serve to establish an interpretative framework within which to read the threatening passage ix 7–x 4, followed by the announcement in x 5ff. that Assyria would herself be judged after executing God's judgement on his people. It thus explains why, from his point of view, threatening material could be included within a section whose overall impact he took to be positive. Moreover, its location at the end of the first-person material, which clearly constitutes some sort of a literary section within the book, accords well with his procedure in the other two passages. Finally, since on other grounds, which go far beyond the strict limits of Isa. i–xii, I believe that viii 16–18 and viii 23*b*–ix 6 were of particular significance to him, it is not surprising to find evidence for his intervention at this point. Whether we may conclude from this that he was also responsible for the present setting of viii 23*b*–ix 6 or whether it was already located here in the material which he inherited cannot be determined on the basis of the evidence presented in this limited study alone.

Before drawing a few conclusions, it is important to stress that the discussion has been consciously restricted to a line of evidence which arises directly out of our starting point in xi 11–16. A much fuller study would be required to determine whether, for instance, there is evidence for the work of this same redactor elsewhere in Isaiah, and how extensive may have been the version of the book which he produced.

That having been said, however, two points give us some indication of his setting. First, it seems most likely that he wrote from the point of view of one for whom the judgement was already past. While inevitably such matters cannot be proved, this is the most natural conclusion to draw from the arrangement of his material and from the transitional function of viii 20–23a, already described, in particular.

Second, however, it appears from xi 11–xii 6 that the salvation still lies in the future, from his point of view. This conclusion rests not only on the repeated "in that day" (xi 11, xii 1, 4), but also on the fact that he combines the hope of return with the reunification of the divided house of Israel in xi 12–13. Since the latter hope cannot be a *vaticinium ex eventu* but must be looking towards the future, the probability is that the reference to the return is as well.[27] This is one reason, among others, why I am not able to follow O.H. Steck in taking xi 11–16 along with xxvii 12–13, xxxv and lxii 10–12 as part of a single redactional level.[28]

The consequence of these two conclusions seems clear, though a host of objections and related issues would require to be examined before it could be advanced in any other than the most tentative manner. Our redactor must be set in the exilic period, must have come to terms with the theological impact of God's judgement on his people and be anticipating a time of restoration and return. And if anyone should make so bold as to respond that that puts him indistinguishably close to the time and outlook of Deutero-Isaiah, I should not be inclined to disagree.

Additional Note

There are two ways in which sense can be made of the MT of Isa. xi 11 as it stands. One is to suppose that *yôsîp* governs the infinitive *liqnôt* and that *yādô* is an adverbial accusative, as in the marginal reading of the *Revised Version*: "And it shall come to pass in that day, that the Lord shall again the second time recover with his hand the remnant of his people". Such a rendering (which is not supported by the LXX; see below) appears to be forced, however, for it gives peculiar sense ("to recover with his hand") and results in a strange word order, the effect of which is to emphasize *yādô* in a manner which is not developed in the context. An additional difficulty is that *šēnît* is redundant after *yôsîp*. (J.G. Janzen, kindly commenting on

---

[27] Ezek. xxxvii is sufficient to show that such a hope for reunification need not necessarily be post-exilic.

[28] Cf. *Bereitete Heimkehr. Jesaja 35 als redaktionelle Brücke zwischen dem Ersten und dem Zweiten Jesaja* (Stuttgart, 1985), and *Studien zu Tritojesaja* (BZAW 203; Berlin and New York, 1991).

an earlier draft of this article, has reminded me that *yôsîp ʿôd* is common in Biblical Hebrew, and that this aspect of the present text need not be considered strange by analogy. But the absence of parallels to the usage of our verse suggests that *yôsîp šēnît* may have been as unlikely in Hebrew as would be the English "again a second time" by comparison with the expected "yet again".)

The alternative way to explain the MT is to assume that *yādô* is the direct object of *yôsîp* and that it has the meaning "his strength". This is the approach adopted by the Targum ("The Lord will add [*ywsyp*] his strength [*gbwrtyh*] a second time . . ."). In support of this approach, appeal might be made to *yōsîp ʾōmeṣ* in Job xvii 9, though the sense required there, "will grow stronger", is hardly suitable with the Lord as its subject.

It is thus difficult to escape the conclusion that the LXX was probably right to find in *šēnît* an infinitive that could both be dependent upon *yôsîp*, used as an auxiliary verb in its commonest sense, and govern *yādô* as its accusative object. LXX has τοῦ δεῖξαι, "to show" (LXX's continuation τὴν χεῖρα αὐτοῦ τοῦ ζηλῶσαι clearly arises from reading *lqnwt* in the light of *qnʾ* rather than *qnh*), and although it is not attested elsewhere as a translation of *nśʾ* (cf. E. Hatch and H.A. Redpath, *A Concordance to the Septuagint* [Oxford, 1897], p. 286), commentators have generally used this evidence to support an emendation of *šēnît* to *śᵉʾēt*. *nāśāʾ yād* occurs in a closely comparable context at xlix 22, and the proposed emendation removes the grammatical difficulties already noted, overcomes, of course, the oddity of *šēnît* following *yôsîp*, and is sufficiently close to the consonantal text of the MT to be explained as a scribal slip in the course of the transmission of the text.

This seems the most likely solution to me, though not surprisingly other suggestions have been advanced. (For Vermeylen, cf. n. 4 above; for some others that do not require discussion, cf. Wildberger, p. 463.) The most influential alternative has been that of D. Winton Thomas ("The Root *šnh = sny* in Hebrew II", *ZAW* 55 [1937], pp. 174–6), who attempted to relate *šēnît* to a root *šnh* in Hebrew which he and a number of other scholars have argued has cognates in Arabic, Syriac and, probably, Ugaritic, and which means "to be, or become, high, exalted in rank; to shine"; if *šēnît* be read as the *piʿel* infinitive construct *šannôt*, it gives us a meaning apparently similar to *śᵉʾēt* but has the advantage of keeping closer to the MT.

While many now accept the existence of this root in Classical

Hebrew (cf. J.J. Stamm et al., *Hebräisches und Aramäisches Lexikon zum Alten Testament* iv [Leiden, 1990], pp. 1477–8, though it is rejected by Wildberger), Winton Thomas's proposal for our particular verse has not found such favour; see, for instance, J.A. Emerton's review of the evidence which supports the probability of a root *šnh* II in Hebrew while nevertheless retaining the MT of Isa. xi 11; "The Meaning of *šēnā'* in Psalm cxxvii 2", *VT* 24 (1974), pp. 15–31. (Emerton defends the MT on the ground that "it would not be surprising if there were an otiose expression in a late prophetic verse like Isa. xi 11", p. 28. He does not explain, however, why late prophetic verses should be more susceptible to otiose expressions than others.) Indeed, it is not certain that the postulated root, which seems usually to relate to being high in the sense of exalted of rank, also had the meaning of being physically high. Of course, the two ideas are closely related, as *nś'* itself shows, but the development required to make sense of Isa. xi 11 adds a further hypothetical element which contrasts with the solid attestation of the expression *nāśā' yād* and the support of the close parallel with xlix 22.

SUPPLEMENTS TO VETUS TESTAMENTUM

2. POPE, M.H. *El in the Ugaritic texts*. 1955. ISBN 90 04 04000 5
3. *Wisdom in Israel and in the Ancient Near East*. Presented to Harold Henry Rowley by the Editorial Board of Vetus Testamentum in celebration of his 65th birthday, 24 March 1955. Edited by M. NOTH and D. WINTON THOMAS. 2nd reprint of the first (1955) ed. 1969. ISBN 90 04 02326 7
4. *Volume du Congrès* [International pour l'étude de l'Ancien Testament]. Strasbourg 1956. 1957. ISBN 90 04 02327 5
8. BERNHARDT, K.-H. *Das Problem der alt-orientalischen Königsideologie im Alten Testament*. Unter besonderer Berücksichtigung der Geschichte der Psalmenexegese darge-stellt und kritisch gewürdigt. 1961. ISBN 90 04 02331 3
9. *Congress Volume*, Bonn 1962. 1963. ISBN 90 04 02332 1
11. DONNER, H. *Israel unter den Völkern*. Die Stellung der klassischen Propheten des 8. Jahrhunderts v. Chr. zur Aussenpolitik der Könige von Israel und Juda. 1964. ISBN 90 04 02334 8
12. REIDER, J. *An Index to Aquila*. Completed and revised by N. Turner. 1966. ISBN 90 04 02335 6
13. ROTH, W.M.W. *Numerical sayings in the Old Testament*. A form-critical study. 1965. ISBN 90 04 02336 4
14. ORLINSKY, H.M. *Studies on the second part of the Book of Isaiah*. — The so-called 'Ser-vant of the Lord' and 'Suffering Servant' in Second Isaiah. — Snaith, N.H. Isaiah 40-66. A study of the teaching of the Second Isaiah and its consequences. Repr. with additions and corrections. 1977. ISBN 90 04 05437 5
15. *Volume du Congrès* [International pour l'étude de l'Ancien Testament]. Genève 1965. 1966. ISBN 90 04 02337 2
17. *Congress Volume*, Rome 1968. 1969. ISBN 90 04 02339 9
19. THOMPSON, R.J. *Moses and the Law in a century of criticism since Graf*. 1970. ISBN 90 04 02341 0
20. REDFORD, D.B. *A study of the biblical story of Joseph*. 1970. ISBN 90 04 02342 9
21. AHLSTRÖM, G.W. *Joel and the temple cult of Jerusalem*. 1971. ISBN 90 04 02620 7
22. *Congress Volume*, Uppsala 1971. 1972. ISBN 90 04 03521 4
23. *Studies in the religion of ancient Israel*. 1972. ISBN 90 04 03525 7
24. SCHOORS, A. *I am God your Saviour*. A form-critical study of the main genres in Is. xl-lv. 1973. ISBN 90 04 03792 2
25. ALLEN, L.C. *The Greek Chronicles*. The relation of the Septuagint I and II Chroni-cles to the Massoretic text. Part 1. The translator's craft. 1974. ISBN 90 04 03913 9
26. *Studies on prophecy*. A collection of twelve papers. 1974. ISBN 90 04 03877 9
27. ALLEN, L.C. *The Greek Chronicles*. Part 2. Textual criticism. 1974. ISBN 90 04 03933 3
28. *Congress Volume*, Edinburgh 1974. 1975. ISBN 90 04 04321 7
29. *Congress Volume*, Göttingen 1977. 1978. ISBN 90 04 05835 4
30. EMERTON, J.A. (ed.). *Studies in the historical books of the Old Testament*. 1979. ISBN 90 04 06017 0
31. MEREDINO, R.P. *Der Erste und der Letzte*. Eine Untersuchung von Jes 40-48. 1981. ISBN 90 04 06199 1
32. EMERTON, J.A. (ed.). *Congress Vienna 1980*. 1981. ISBN 90 04 06514 8
33. KOENIG, J. *L'herméneutique analogique du Judaïsme antique d'après les témoins textuels d'Isaïe*. 1982. ISBN 90 04 06762 0

34. BARSTAD, H.M. *The religious polemics of Amos*. Studies in the preachings of Amos ii 7B-8, iv 1-13, v 1-27, vi 4-7, viii 14. 1984. ISBN 90 04 07017 6
35. KRAŠOVEC, J. *Antithetic structure in Biblical Hebrew poetry*. 1984. ISBN 90 04 07244 6
36. EMERTON, J.A. (ed.). *Congress Volume*, Salamanca 1983. 1985. ISBN 90 04 07281 0
37. LEMCHE, N.P. *Early Israel*. Anthropological and historical studies on the Israelite society before the monarchy. 1985. ISBN 90 04 07853 3
38. NIELSEN, K. *Incense in Ancient Israel*. 1986. ISBN 90 04 07702 2
39. PARDEE, D. *Ugaritic and Hebrew poetic parallelism*. A trial cut. 1988. ISBN 90 04 08368 5
40. EMERTON, J.A. (ed.). *Congress Volume*, Jerusalem 1986. 1988. ISBN 90 04 08499 1
41. EMERTON, J.A. (ed.). *Studies in the Pentateuch*. 1990. ISBN 90 04 09195 5
42. McKENZIE, S.L. *The trouble with Kings*. The composition of the Book of Kings in the Deuteronomistic History. 1991. ISBN 90 04 09402 4
43. EMERTON, J.A. (ed.). *Congress Volume*, Leuven 1989. 1991. ISBN 90 04 09398 2
44. HAAK, R.D. *Habakkuk*. 1992. ISBN 90 04 09506 3
45. BEYERLIN, W. *Im Licht der Traditionen*. Psalm LXVII und CXV. Ein Entwicklungszusammenhang. 1992. ISBN 90 04 09635 3
46. MEIER, S.A. *Speaking of Speaking*. Marking direct discourse in the Hebrew Bible. 1992. ISBN 90 04 09602 7
47. KESSLER, R. *Staat und Gesellschaft im vorexilischen Juda*. Vom 8. Jahrhundert bis zum Exil. 1992. ISBN 90 04 09646 9
48. AUFFRET, P. *Voyez de vos yeux*. Étude structurelle de vingt psaumes, dont le psaume 119. 1993. ISBN 90 04 09707 4
49. GARCÍA MARTÍNEZ, F., A. HILHORST AND C.J. LABUSCHAGNE (eds.). *The Scriptures and the Scrolls*. Studies in honour of A.S. van der Woude on the occasion of his 65th birthday. 1992. ISBN 90 04 09746 5
50. LEMAIRE, A. AND B. OTZEN (eds.). *History and Traditions of Early Israel*. Studies presented to Eduard Nielsen, May 8th, 1993. 1993. ISBN 90 04 09851 8
51. GORDON, R.P. *Studies in the Targum to the Twelve Prophets*. From Nahum to Malachi. 1994. ISBN 90 04 09987 5
52. HUGENBERGER, G.P. *Marriage as a Covenant*. A Study of Biblical Law and Ethics Governing Marriage Developed from the Perspective of Malachi. 1994. ISBN 90 04 09977 8
53. GARCÍA MARTÍNEZ, F., A. HILHORST, J.T.A.G.M. VAN RUITEN, A.S. VAN DER WOUDE. *Studies in Deuteronomy*. In Honour of C.J. Labuschagne on the Occasion of His 65th Birthday. 1994. ISBN 90 04 10052 0
54. FERNANDÉZ MARCOS, N. *Septuagint and Old Latin in the Book of Kings*. 1994. ISBN 90 04 10043 1
55. SMITH, M.S. *The Ugaritic Baal Cycle. Volume 1*. Introduction with text, translation and commentary of KTU 1.1-1.2. 1994. ISBN 90 04 09995 6
56. DUGUID, I.M. *Ezekiel and the Leaders of Israel*. 1994. ISBN 90 04 10074 1
57. MARX, A. *Les offrandes végétales dans l'Ancien Testament*. Du tribut d'hommage au repas eschatologique. 1994. ISBN 90 04 10136 5
58. SCHÄFER-LICHTENBERGER, C. *Josua und Salomo*. Eine Studie zu Autorität und Legitimität des Nachfolgers im Alten Testament. 1995. ISBN 90 04 10064 4
59. LASSERRE, G. *Synopse des lois du Pentateuque*. 1994. ISBN 90 04 10202 7
60. DOGNIEZ, C. *Bibliography of the Septuagint – Bibliographie de la Septante (1970-1993)*. Avec une préface de Pierre-Maurice Bogaert. 1995. ISBN 90 04 10192 6
61. EMERTON, J.A. (ed.). *Congress Volume*, Paris 1992. 1995. ISBN 90 04 10259 0